Jewell Pfist

Jewell Pfister

Jewell Pfister

LIVING WORLD

LIVING
WORLD

Written by

THERESA GREENAWAY

DR MIRANDA MACQUITTY

STEVE PARKER

SUSANNA VAN ROSE

A Dorling Kindersley Book

LONDON, NEW YORK,
MELBOURNE, MUNICH, AND DELHI

The Eyewitness Guides were conceived by Dorling Kindersley Limited
and Editions Gallimard

Published in the United States by
DK Publishing, Inc.
375 Hudson Street
New York, NY10014

A catalog record for this book is available from the Library of Congress

ISBN 0-7566-0429-X

Reproduced in Singapore by Colourscan
Printed and bound in Hong Kong by Toppan

See our complete product line at
www.dk.com

Contents

SEASHORE

POND & RIVER

JUNGLE

William Smith
(1769-1839)

Monoclinic crystals
of sulfur

Eclogite rock

Granite rock

Goniometer
measuring the
angles on a copper
sulfate crystal

Metallic copper

An orrery showing the Earth's
orbit around the Sun

Malachite in a rock

Laboratory model
simulating formation
of a mountain range

Magnified thin
section of
limestone

EARTH

Snails provided a
clue to the
continental drift
theory

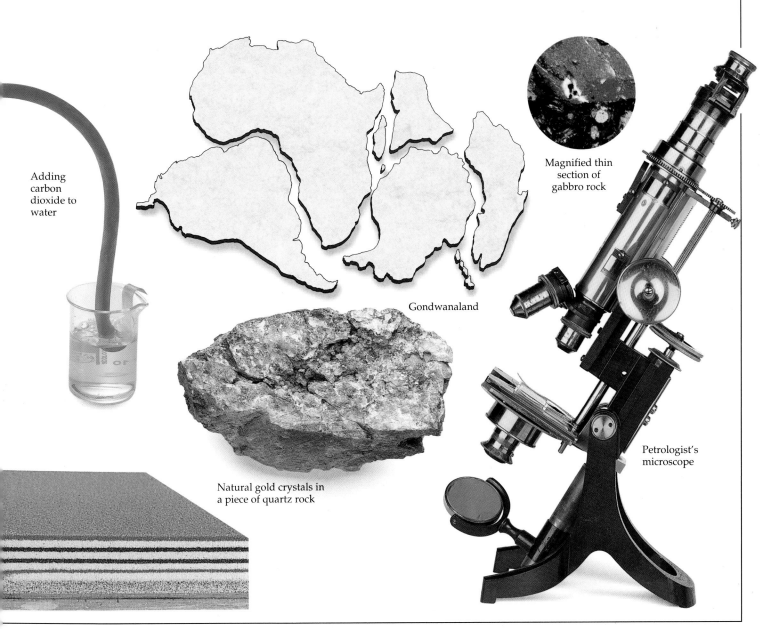

Adding
carbon
dioxide to
water

Magnified thin
section of
gabbro rock

Gondwanaland

Natural gold crystals in
a piece of quartz rock

Petrologist's
microscope

What makes up the Earth?

As A SMALL PLANET in the vast Solar System, the Earth is unique in a number of ways. It has life, it has water, and it has a surface that is continually being renewed. This includes the thin rocky crust beneath our feet. The parts of the Earth that can be seen are just a tiny proportion of the whole planet. Beneath the crust lies the thick, many-layered mantle, which is made of semisolid silicate rock material. At the center is a semisolid nickel iron outer core and a solid nickel iron core. The planet is surrounded by a magnetic field that fluctuates with time and channels the intense radiations from the Sun. The rocky silicate crust is enveloped in a shroud of water and atmospheric gases that have almost entirely come from the eruptions of volcanoes over time. The crust is made up of segments known as plates that move about slowly; over millions of years this movement changes the architecture of the continents as the plates interact.

SATELLITE VIEW OF EARTH
The Earth is not exactly spherical in shape. It is flattened at the poles with a bulge at the equator so that the radius at the poles is 27 miles (43 km) shorter than the equatorial radius. The ancient Greek philosopher Pythagoras (c. 570-500 BC) thought that the Earth might be spherical in shape. This idea came to him as he watched ships approach from over the horizon. First he saw their masts; only as they came closer did the hulls appear.

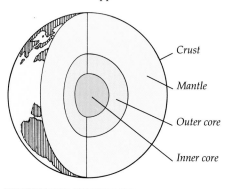

THE INTERIOR OF THE EARTH
The Earth's crust is so thin that the line drawn here is too thick to be in scale. The crust is about 3 miles (5 km) thick under the oceans and 21 miles (35 km) thick under the continents. The underlying mantle is nearly 1,860 miles (3,000 km) thick. The metallic core has a liquid outer portion and a solid inner part. In the core, the pressure is something like a million times that of atmospheric pressure, while the temperature is around 8,000°F (4,500°C). It is impossible to simulate these conditions in a laboratory, so information about the metal that makes up the core is based on informed guesswork.

Crust

Mantle

Outer core

Inner core

EARLY COLLECTORS
Studying rocks in different places gives information about the huge variety of processes involved in the changing surface of the Earth. Mary Anning (b. 1799) was a fossil collector living in the west of England. She found fossils in ancient rock layers that had been exposed at the surface. This sort of information was used by her friend Sir Henry De La Beche (1796-1855), the English geologist who began systematic geological mapping and established the first national Geological Survey in Great Britain in 1835.

THE MAGNETIC FIELD
The liquid metallic outer core of the Earth flows and swirls, thereby generating a magnetic field. From time to time – perhaps in thousands or tens of thousands of years – the direction of the field reverses, though it is not known how this happens. The lines of force of the magnetic field can be imagined as making great loops around the Earth between the North and South Poles, and they act as a shield protecting the Earth from the energetic flood of electrically charged particles coming from the Sun that are known as the solar wind. (This shield creates a magnetic cavity known as the magnetosphere.) When the Earth's magnetic field meets up with the solar wind, the Earth's magnetic field is compressed on the side nearest to the Sun. On the far side it makes a trailing edge. The wire model shows the pattern made by the interaction of the solar wind with the Earth's magnetic field.

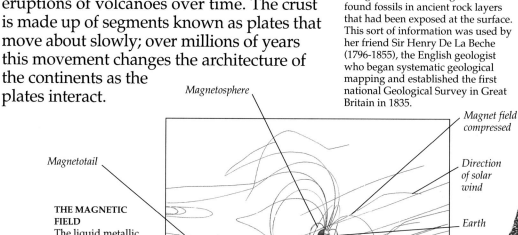

Magnetosphere

Magnetotail

Magnet field compressed

Direction of solar wind

Earth

Wire model of the magnetosphere

Peridotite rock

The Earth's ingredients

Apart from water, air, and rocks, finding out what the rest of the Earth is made up of is not always possible. Some upper mantle rocks are seen at the surface in volcanic eruptions of magma (p. 31). These give clues to the composition of the mantle. It is even more difficult to imagine the conditions of the highly compressed metal at the Earth's solid core. This the densest part of the Earth because it is under great pressure.

ATMOSPHERIC GAS
A very small part of 1 percent of the total mass of the Earth.
• The atmosphere is densest close to the surface of the Earth and becomes progressively less dense farther out. Most of the gas molecules are kept to the surface by the Earth's gravity.

Gas

ICE IN GLACIERS AND SHEETS
• About 0.002 percent of the total volume of the Earth.
• 0.003 percent of the total mass of the Earth.
• The ice sheets of the present day are an inheritance from the Ice Age of the last two million years.

Ice

WATER
• About 0.1 percent of the total volume of the Earth.
• 0.02 percent of the total mass of the Earth.
• Water is a unique substance that covers three-quarters of the Earth's surface.

Water

Oceanic crust (basalt)

THE CRUST
• 0.8 percent of the total volume of the Earth.
• 0.4 percent of the total mass of the Earth.
• Oceanic crust is mostly basalt rock made of silicate rich in iron and magnesium.
• Continental crust is granite-like rock on the surface, and underlying sedimentary rocks or metamorphic rocks.

Continental crust (granite)

TOTAL CORE
• 16 percent of the total volume of the Earth.
• 31 percent of the total mass of the Earth.

THE LIQUID CORE
• Believed to be made of liquid nickel-iron, it is presumed to flow, creating the currents that generate the Earth's magnetic field.

Mercury

Mercury is naturally liquid at the Earth's surface

Solid nickel-iron at the core may look like this

THE SOLID CORE
• The enormous pressure at the center of the Earth means that the molten iron that makes up the outer core is compressed to the point where it becomes a solid in the inner core.

Solid nickel-iron

THE MANTLE
• 83 percent of the total volume of the Earth.
• 68 percent of the total mass of the Earth.
• Composed of dense silicate minerals rich in the heavy element, iron; it is probably made of dense, olivine-rich rocks like peridotite. Over the whole history of the Earth, the mantle must slowly have been changing its composition, because magma has been added to the crust, taking away from the upper mantle the chemical elements that melt most easily.

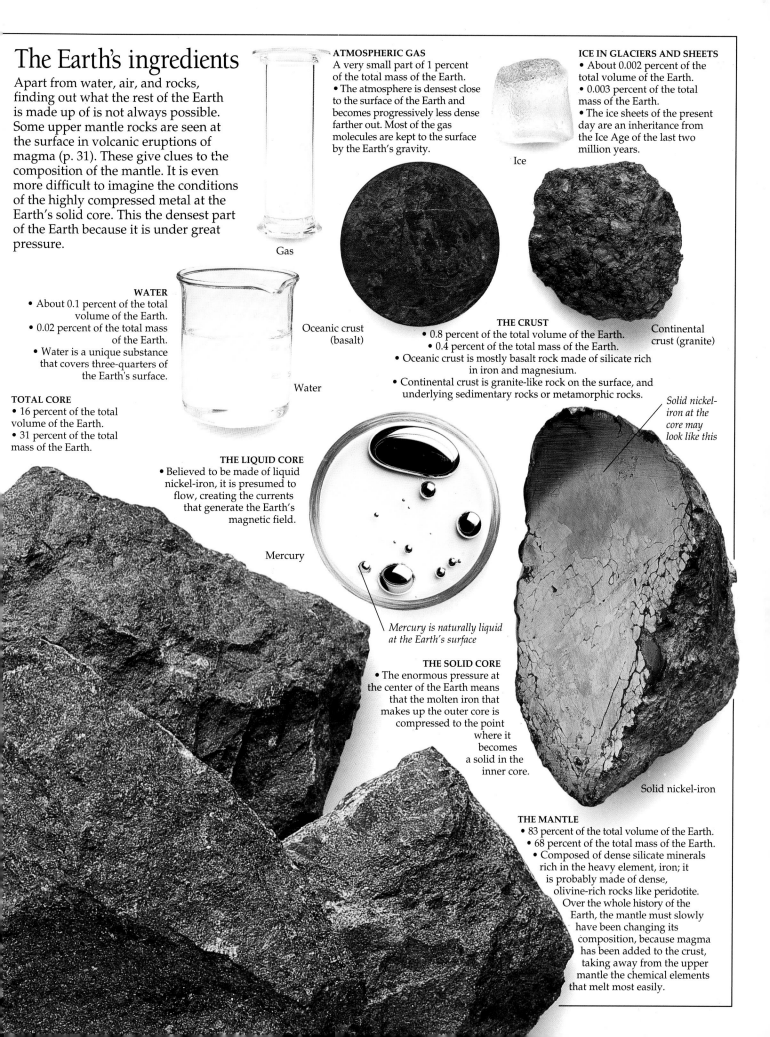

Early ideas about the Earth

MANY EARLY CONCEPTS about the origin and makeup of the Earth were well founded in observation and reason; others were long-held traditions. Sometimes there is a connection between traditional ideas and scientific thought. At other times, it is hard to see any relationship. The development of knowledge and understanding about our surroundings have not always followed a straight line. Although the ancient Greeks and Egyptians established that the Earth is round and calculated its radius with great accuracy, many centuries later some people still believed that the Earth is flat. Early maps were made of local areas and were drawn on flat cloth, so the idea of a flat Earth was a logical extension of the flat-map representation. Early explorers, some of them careful observers, traveled extensively and extended knowledge about coastlines and new lands and oceans. In the 18th century, one of the earliest modern geologists, James Hutton (1726-1797), put forward pioneering ideas about Earth processes. Leaving aside inherited ideas, he worked from observation.

MAP OF THE WORLD
This map of the world (*mappa mundi*) was drawn in the 10th century AD as part of the initial letter on the page of an illuminated manuscript.

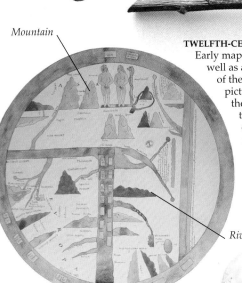

Mountain

River

TWELFTH-CENTURY WORLD MAP
Early maps contained pictures as well as abstract representations of the landscape. These pictures were sometimes of the gods, or drawings of the places to be found on the route. This map features mountains and rivers and covers the area from Babylonia (present-day Iraq) to Caledonia (present-day Scotland).

DIVINING BRANCH
Finding underground water with forked branches is a method that is still used today in places. The diviner's branch is stretched out taut in the diviner's hands. For diviners, it twists violently when it is carried over the underground water.

JAMES HUTTON
Hutton was a Scottish geologist whose interest in agriculture led him to study the fertility of soil. This led him to more wide-ranging observations of the Scottish countryside. His Plutonist ideas about the origins of rocks being related to volcanic activity came from studies of the volcanic rocks in Edinburgh. This contradicted the Neptunists, who held different views about the origin of the rocks (p. 28). It was Hutton's work that gave the first hints of the immensity of geological time.

IN SEARCH OF METALS
Divining the landscape, whether for water, or for minerals, or for favorable sites, is even followed today in some technological societies. In his book, *De Re Metallica*, Georg Bauer, a German doctor, philosopher, and mineralogist known as Agricola (1494-1555), described the physical properties of minerals, where metals are found, and how to extract them. He also illustrated the use of forked branches. He remained skeptical about the usefulness of divination, but admitted that some people were successful with the method.

The diviner

THE STONE AGE

When people first learned to use the materials from which the Earth is made, stone was their first choice. Some rock types were more suitable than others; they could be worked to a sharp edge that lasted, even in heavy use such as felling trees. Not all rocks were suitable for making tools. Some rocks could not be sharpened; other rocks were too weak to retain the sharp edge.

Small hand ax

Flaked cutting edge

Large hand ax

Cutting edge used for cutting plants and wood and skinning animals

DIVINING LANDSCAPE

Feng shui is the ancient Chinese practice of landscape divining. The landscape is believed to contain hidden energy. Feng shui sees rounded hills as having female characteristics (yin) and rugged mountains as having male characteristics (yang). Along with other elements, such as fire and water, these must all be balanced if there is to be harmony and prosperity.

The compass is consulted

Ch'ing dynasty painting showing feng shui compass in use

CHINESE COMPASS

The origins of the feng shui compass are unclear. It may have developed from a simple diviner's board, which was used for direction finding, or its origin may be connected with the chess board, as pieces were thrown on to the board as dice. The name feng shui means wind and water. In Hong Kong, the feng shui diviner is still consulted before any building of significance is built or bought. This ensures that the site, the architectural style, and the purpose of the building are in harmony.

BRINGING HARMONY

Many satisfying buildings throughout the world follow the principles of feng shui. According to feng shui, straight lines are bad because they allow energy to rush too forcefully through the landscape for its beneficial powers to be used. A winding pathway or an undulating wall, as here at Chengde in China, brings better harmony with the universe.

Inner ring with heavenly trigrams

Compass needle

Lacquered wood

The scribe notes the elements in the landscape while measurements are taken

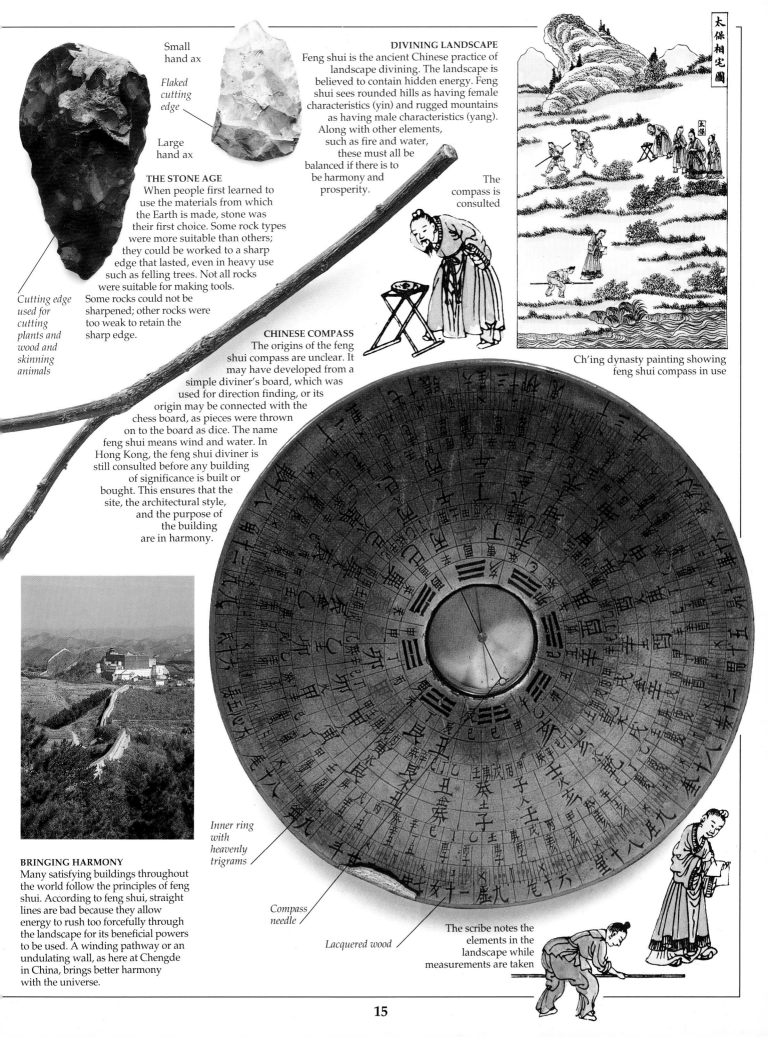

A cocoon of gas

THE OUTERMOST PART OF THE EARTH is its shroud of gas, the atmosphere. It extends out at least 600 miles (1,000 km) above the solid surface of the Earth, but three-quarters of this life-sustaining atmosphere is concentrated in the lowest 6 miles (10 km). The atmosphere is a mixture of different gases that together make up air. The most abundant gas in the lower atmosphere is nitrogen, which makes up 78 percent. Oxygen, so vital in supporting animal life on Earth, makes up about 21 percent. Carbon dioxide, just a small fraction of the total atmosphere, is vital in sustaining plant life; it plays a role in keeping the temperature of the atmosphere steady. Tiny traces of other gases – argon and neon – are clues to the origin of the Earth's atmosphere. The Earth's atmosphere has come mostly from gases spewed out by volcanoes since the Earth began, although some, like oxygen, are a later contribution from plant life. The layer of the atmosphere closest to the land is called the troposphere. Here, temperature and humidity change rapidly, and the air is turbulent, creating our weather patterns.

PERPETUAL BLACK SKY
The Moon has no atmosphere surrounding it. This makes its sky black, because there are no atmospheric gases to trap and scatter sunlight, which would make a blue or white sky. Lack of atmospheric gases also means that the Moon has no weather.

Paralvinella

UNSEEING CREATURES
Some creatures on the Earth exist without atmospheric oxygen. Blind and living in the perpetual darkness of the deep ocean, these sulfide worms have developed an alternative body chemistry to cope with their environment. They get their energy supply from sulfide minerals oozing from hot springs on the ocean floor where temperatures reach 518°F (270°C). Bacterialiving nearby take dissolved carbon dioxide from the ocean water and build organic molecules using the hydrogen sulfide from the mineral springs.

Carbon dioxide
Argon and others
Oxygen
Nitrogen

GASES IN THE ATMOSPHERE
The Earth's atmosphere is unique. If it had formed from gases that are abundant in the Solar System, the Earth would have an atmosphere made up mostly of hydrogen and helium, with some methane and ammonia. Instead, processes such as the evolution of bacterial life forms and plants have created an atmosphere dominated by nitrogen. Another feature of the Earth's atmosphere is that most of its argon is $Ar40$ (argon 40), from radioactive decay of potassium 40, whereas gases in the solar system are dominated by $Ar36$ and $Ar38$.

GREEN SLIME
Oxygen is a relative newcomer in the Earth's atmosphere. It has come from plants which, during photosynthesis, use carbon dioxide to make their food, giving out oxygen. The earliest photosynthesizing plants probably looked like these algae, which today grow in hot volcanic springs. Once the algae had evolved, about 3,600 million years ago, they slowly began to add oxygen to the atmosphere.

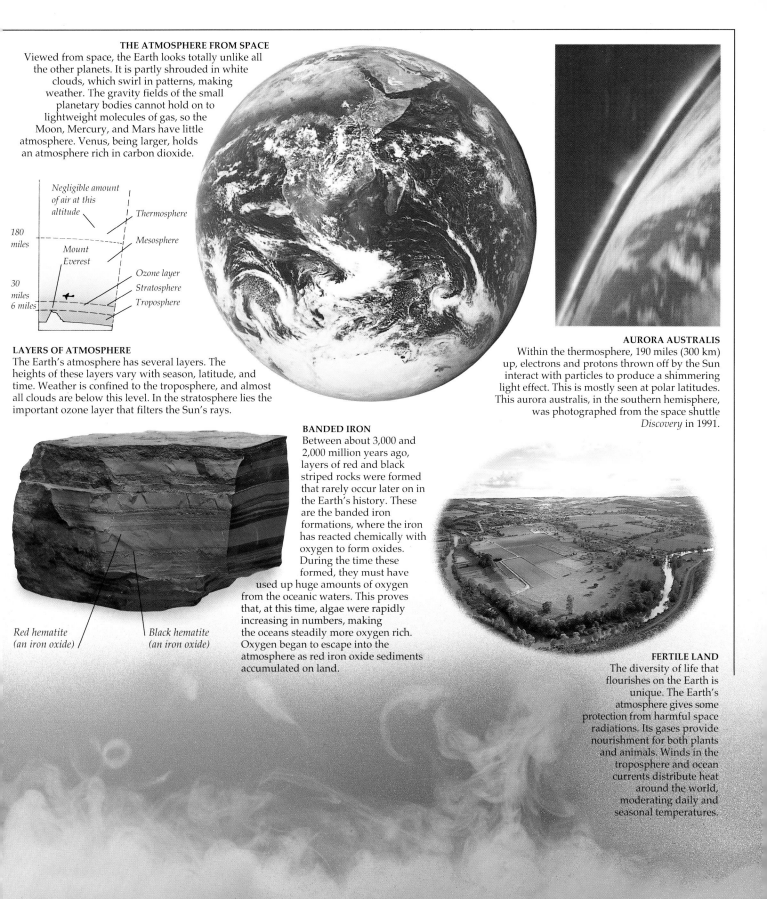

THE ATMOSPHERE FROM SPACE

Viewed from space, the Earth looks totally unlike all the other planets. It is partly shrouded in white clouds, which swirl in patterns, making weather. The gravity fields of the small planetary bodies cannot hold on to lightweight molecules of gas, so the Moon, Mercury, and Mars have little atmosphere. Venus, being larger, holds an atmosphere rich in carbon dioxide.

Negligible amount of air at this altitude

Thermosphere

180 miles

Mesosphere

Mount Everest

Ozone layer

30 miles
6 miles

Stratosphere

Troposphere

LAYERS OF ATMOSPHERE

The Earth's atmosphere has several layers. The heights of these layers vary with season, latitude, and time. Weather is confined to the troposphere, and almost all clouds are below this level. In the stratosphere lies the important ozone layer that filters the Sun's rays.

AURORA AUSTRALIS

Within the thermosphere, 190 miles (300 km) up, electrons and protons thrown off by the Sun interact with particles to produce a shimmering light effect. This is mostly seen at polar latitudes. This aurora australis, in the southern hemisphere, was photographed from the space shuttle *Discovery* in 1991.

BANDED IRON

Between about 3,000 and 2,000 million years ago, layers of red and black striped rocks were formed that rarely occur later on in the Earth's history. These are the banded iron formations, where the iron has reacted chemically with oxygen to form oxides. During the time these formed, they must have used up huge amounts of oxygen from the oceanic waters. This proves that, at this time, algae were rapidly increasing in numbers, making the oceans steadily more oxygen rich. Oxygen began to escape into the atmosphere as red iron oxide sediments accumulated on land.

Red hematite (an iron oxide)

Black hematite (an iron oxide)

FERTILE LAND

The diversity of life that flourishes on the Earth is unique. The Earth's atmosphere gives some protection from harmful space radiations. Its gases provide nourishment for both plants and animals. Winds in the troposphere and ocean currents distribute heat around the world, moderating daily and seasonal temperatures.

Climate in the past

THE ROLE OF THE SUN
In 1941 Croatian meteorologist Milutin Milankovitch suggested that changes in the Earth's orbit around the Sun caused long-term changes in climate. He spent many years working out how much radiation from the Sun had been received at different latitudes over the last 650,000 years to help prove his theories.

THE EARTH'S CLIMATE HAS CHANGED enormously over geological time. The shapes of the continents have altered and they have moved relative to the equator and to the poles. To find out about these changes geologists look into the rocks and read them as a kind of history book, going back 4,000 million years. The rocks show that places that are now far from the equator have had baking deserts at times in the past, and that tropical coral reefs flourished on the shorelines of what is now known as Europe. The positions of the continents have an effect on the movement of air masses and on weather patterns. When all the continents were together as Pangaea, not much rain fell in the interior, which was largely a desert. The rocks also show that in the last 2 million years glaciers covered large areas of the world. Another reason for this climate change is the position of the Earth in its orbit in relation to the Sun.

CHANGING POSITIONS
The Earth's orbit is an ellipse – it is sometimes more circular, and sometimes less circular, so that the distance of the Earth from the Sun varies. The changing positions of the Sun and the Moon give an uneven pull on the Earth's bulging equator. So 11,000 years ago, the northern hemisphere, which then was thick with glacier ice, was nearest the Sun in summer, encouraging the glaciers to melt, helping to bring an end to the Ice Age.

Impression of shell

Earth

Moon

Rock from Mt. Snowdon, Wales

Sun

Distance from the Sun to the Earth varies over 100,000-year cycle

An orrery to show planetary motions

CONTINENTAL HISTORY
Fossils tell us about climate and environment in the past. Sea shells found in rocks of high mountains show that marine sediment deposits have been uplifted to form high plateaux and mountain ranges. The fossil plant *Glossopteris* is found in rocks 350-200 million years old within each of the southern hemisphere continents. This, along with other evidence, indicates that all these landmasses must have been joined together during this time.

Lake Michigan   *Lake Huron*   *Lake Erie*

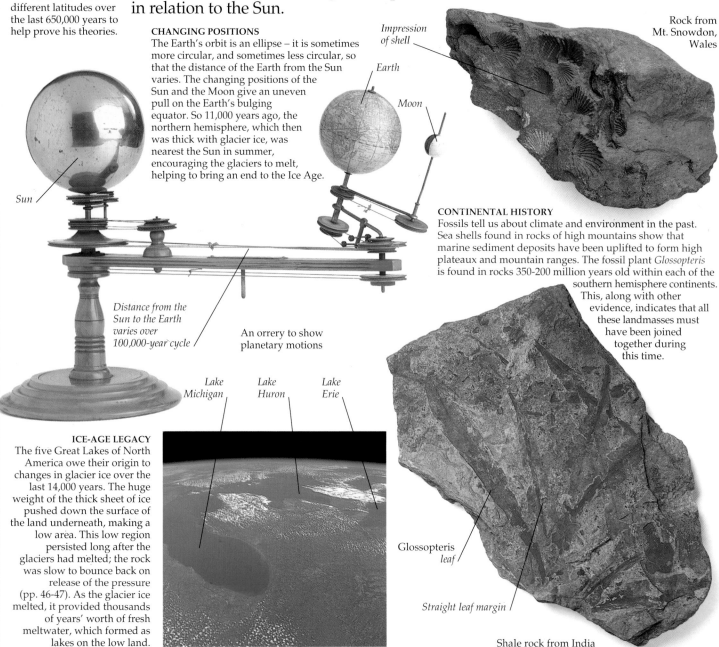

ICE-AGE LEGACY
The five Great Lakes of North America owe their origin to changes in glacier ice over the last 14,000 years. The huge weight of the thick sheet of ice pushed down the surface of the land underneath, making a low area. This low region persisted long after the glaciers had melted; the rock was slow to bounce back on release of the pressure (pp. 46-47). As the glacier ice melted, it provided thousands of years' worth of fresh meltwater, which formed as lakes on the low land.

Glossopteris leaf

Straight leaf margin

Shale rock from India

Investigating a core

One way to find out how climate has changed is to investigate the layers of sediment that have collected on the seafloor. When the climate changed in the past, sea or lake water temperature changed too. Different types of plants and animals flourished in these different conditions. When they died, their remains sank and became part of the sediment. The fossil remains accumulated in the muds and oozes which formed at that time. To investigate the sediment, a special drilling ship makes a borehole down into the seabed (p. 38) and collects the core from the borehole. This core was taken in the Mediterranean Sea and was used to investigate planktonic Foraminifera (forams), tiny marine animals with shells of calcium carbonate.

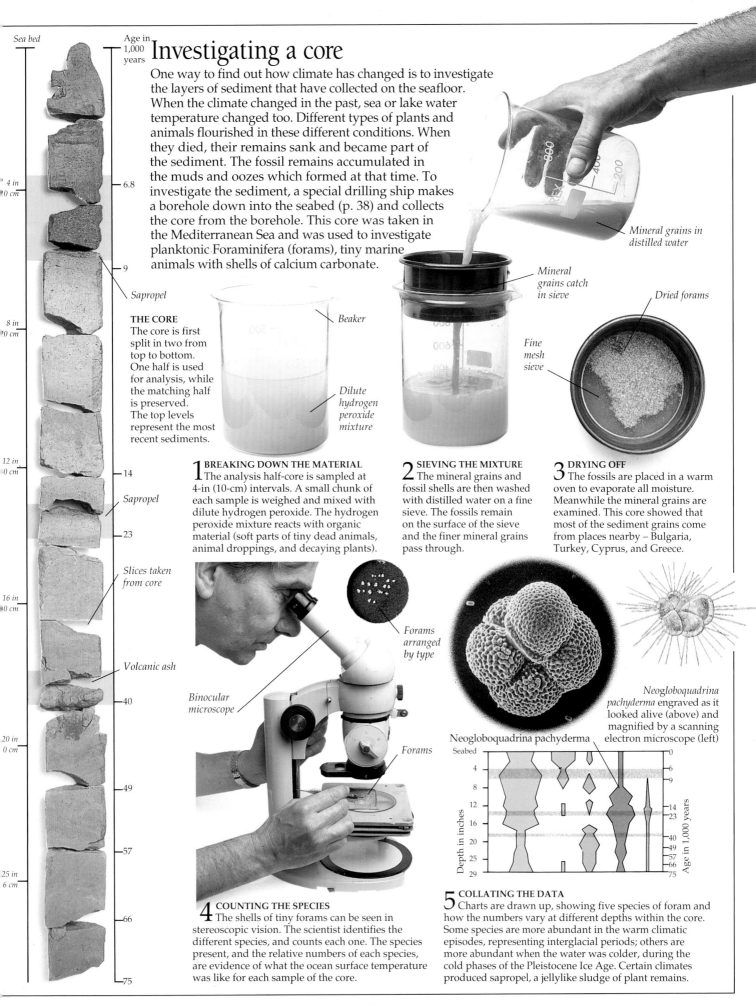

Mineral grains in distilled water

Sapropel

THE CORE
The core is first split in two from top to bottom. One half is used for analysis, while the matching half is preserved. The top levels represent the most recent sediments.

Beaker

Dilute hydrogen peroxide mixture

Mineral grains catch in sieve

Fine mesh sieve

Dried forams

Sapropel

Slices taken from core

Volcanic ash

1 BREAKING DOWN THE MATERIAL
The analysis half-core is sampled at 4-in (10-cm) intervals. A small chunk of each sample is weighed and mixed with dilute hydrogen peroxide. The hydrogen peroxide mixture reacts with organic material (soft parts of tiny dead animals, animal droppings, and decaying plants).

2 SIEVING THE MIXTURE
The mineral grains and fossil shells are then washed with distilled water on a fine sieve. The fossils remain on the surface of the sieve and the finer mineral grains pass through.

3 DRYING OFF
The fossils are placed in a warm oven to evaporate all moisture. Meanwhile the mineral grains are examined. This core showed that most of the sediment grains come from places nearby – Bulgaria, Turkey, Cyprus, and Greece.

Forams arranged by type

Binocular microscope

Forams

Neogloboquadrina pachyderma

Neogloboquadrina pachyderma engraved as it looked alive (above) and magnified by a scanning electron microscope (left)

Seabed

Depth in inches

Age in 1,000 years

4 COUNTING THE SPECIES
The shells of tiny forams can be seen in stereoscopic vision. The scientist identifies the different species, and counts each one. The species present, and the relative numbers of each species, are evidence of what the ocean surface temperature was like for each sample of the core.

5 COLLATING THE DATA
Charts are drawn up, showing five species of foram and how the numbers vary at different depths within the core. Some species are more abundant in the warm climatic episodes, representing interglacial periods; others are more abundant when the water was colder, during the cold phases of the Pleistocene Ice Age. Certain climates produced sapropel, a jellylike sludge of plant remains.

Sea bed

Age in 1,000 years

19

Watery planet

OVER THREE-QUARTERS of the Earth's surface is covered by water – it would be more logical to call the planet "Water" instead of "Earth." Even with the continents scattered around as they are today, one great ocean dominates half the globe. Of the rain that falls on the land, just over one-third runs off into rivers and is quickly returned to the sea. The other two-thirds soaks into the soil and underlying rock and remains for years or even tens of thousands of years as groundwater. It is groundwater that nourishes springs and wells, and keeps rivers flowing in times of drought. All water is involved in a never-ending flow from ocean to atmosphere to rivers to underground rocks, always returning eventually to the ocean. This great journey is called the water cycle. Understanding the way in which water moves from one place to another is the study of hydrology, and someone who looks specifically at the movement of underground water is a hydrogeologist.

Pacific Ocean

BLUE PLANET
Viewed from a satellite above the Pacific Ocean, the Earth appears to be almost completely covered in water. A few chains of islands dot the watery surface. The Pacific is so big that all the land area of the Earth could be fitted into it. The oceans are much deeper on average than the land is high.

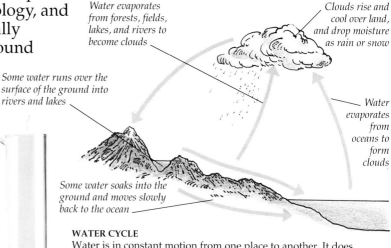

Water evaporates from forests, fields, lakes, and rivers to become clouds

Clouds rise and cool over land, and drop moisture as rain or snow

Some water runs over the surface of the ground into rivers and lakes

Water evaporates from oceans to form clouds

Some water soaks into the ground and moves slowly back to the ocean

WATER CYCLE
Water is in constant motion from one place to another. It does this partly by changing from liquid to vapour and back again. The Sun's heat warms the ocean water near the surface, and some molecules of water are heated enough to evaporate. These energetic molecules escape from the ocean and become water vapor which collects in clouds. When clouds are cooled, they can no longer hold water as vapor, so drops condense and fall as rain and snow. Because of the distribution of land and ocean, most rain falls straight back into the ocean to repeat the cycle. Some rain falls on land and is used by plants and animals. Some gathers in lakes and rivers, only to run downhill into the ocean once more. Some rainfall over land takes longer to return to the ocean; it travels slowly through tiny pores and cracks in underground rocks.

QUANTITIES OF WATER
Most of the world's water is salty. Less than 6 percent accounts for all the fresh water in rivers and lakes, the water underground in rocks, and the moisture in the atmosphere. Some fresh water is temporarily locked up in ice caps and glaciers. The ice has been melting and has raised global sea level by hundreds of feet. If the world climate continues to warm, over the next hundreds or thousands of years the remaining ice could melt and raise global sea level by up to several hundred feet.

Ocean water 94%

Ground water 4.34%

Ice caps and glaciers 1.65%

Rivers and lakes 0.01%

Water vapor

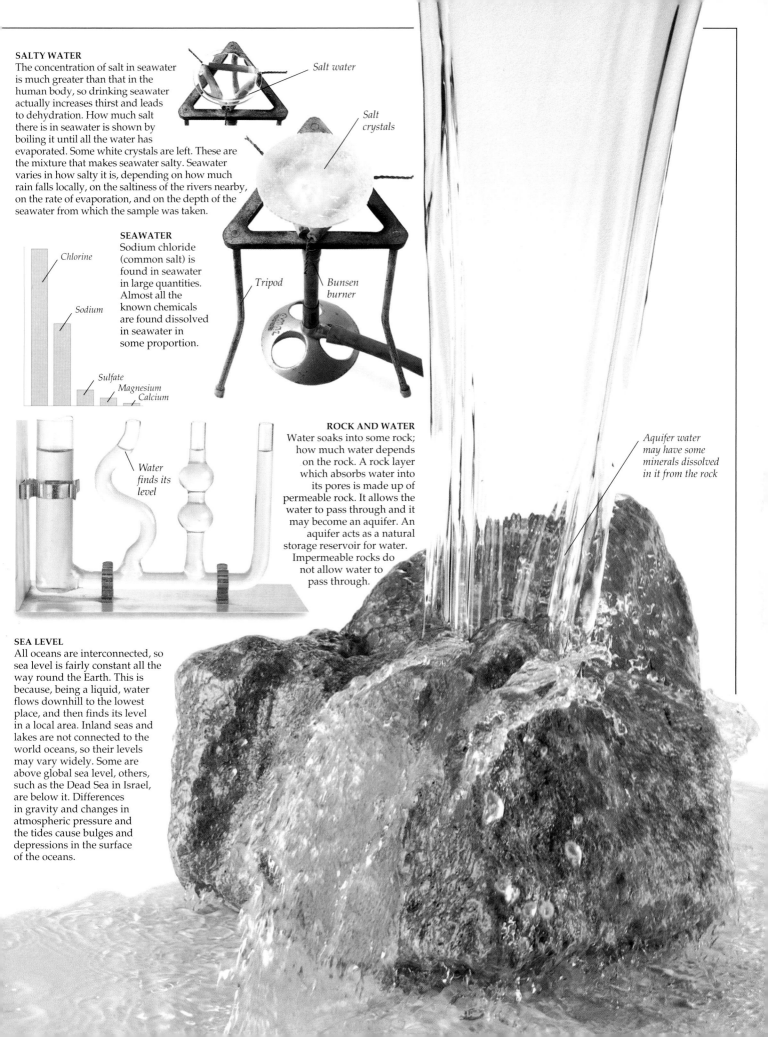

SALTY WATER
The concentration of salt in seawater is much greater than that in the human body, so drinking seawater actually increases thirst and leads to dehydration. How much salt there is in seawater is shown by boiling it until all the water has evaporated. Some white crystals are left. These are the mixture that makes seawater salty. Seawater varies in how salty it is, depending on how much rain falls locally, on the saltiness of the rivers nearby, on the rate of evaporation, and on the depth of the seawater from which the sample was taken.

Salt water

Salt crystals

SEAWATER
Sodium chloride (common salt) is found in seawater in large quantities. Almost all the known chemicals are found dissolved in seawater in some proportion.

Chlorine

Sodium

Sulfate

Magnesium

Calcium

Tripod

Bunsen burner

Water finds its level

ROCK AND WATER
Water soaks into some rock; how much water depends on the rock. A rock layer which absorbs water into its pores is made up of permeable rock. It allows the water to pass through and it may become an aquifer. An aquifer acts as a natural storage reservoir for water. Impermeable rocks do not allow water to pass through.

Aquifer water may have some minerals dissolved in it from the rock

SEA LEVEL
All oceans are interconnected, so sea level is fairly constant all the way round the Earth. This is because, being a liquid, water flows downhill to the lowest place, and then finds its level in a local area. Inland seas and lakes are not connected to the world oceans, so their levels may vary widely. Some are above global sea level, others, such as the Dead Sea in Israel, are below it. Differences in gravity and changes in atmospheric pressure and the tides cause bulges and depressions in the surface of the oceans.

The properties of water

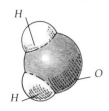

WATER IS AN UNUSUAL LIQUID because of the way its molecules are bonded together. One effect of this bonding is the unusual density of water. Most substances occupy a smaller space – they become more dense – as they are cooled. However, water is most dense at 39.2°F (4°C). Below that temperature, its density becomes less. Ice at 32°F (0°C) is less dense than water at 32°F. This is why ice floats on water. Water takes a huge amount of heat to transform it from its liquid state into a gas, and from its solid state, ice, into a liquid. The relatively uniform temperature on the Earth is largely maintained by these unusual characteristics of water. Water also has high surface tension, which helps in making raindrops in the atmosphere and in the way water is able to travel through rocks and soil. Water is a solvent; it dissolves a great many substances relatively easily. Its ability to do this affects how rocks are weathered, as some of the chemical elements that make up rocks go into solution during weathering.

Solid

Liquid

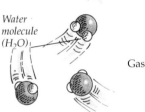

Water molecule (H_2O)

Gas

UNITS OF WATER
Water is made up of two elements – oxygen and hydrogen. Its molecules bind together to form aggregates of water molecules, with a special bond called the hydrogen bond. This causes the molecules to join together, so that at room temperature, water forms droplets, rather than floating around as a gas.

MAKING RAINDROPS
The surface tension of water is the ability of the surface to shrink and "wrap around" the water so that it holds the contents together. The clingy wetness of water is also a result of the surface tension. The force of the surface pulling to hold the water together is enough to allow water to soak up and wet a towel or filter paper when they are dipped into the water.

Water remains in droplets

SOLID, LIQUID, AND GAS
Most molecules pack together into a regular arrangement when they are in a solid state. As a liquid, the ordered arrangement breaks down, and the molecules are more spaced out. With more heat, the spacing gets greater, until eventually molecules are so far apart that the substance becomes a gas. As water is cooled to 39.2°F (4°C), or cold water is heated to 39.2°F, the molecules pack together in a more economical way, so that they occupy less space. This gives water its maximum density at this temperature.

WATER BOATMAN

When a water boatman (*Dolomedes fimbriatus*) lands on a pond, its weight and the way it is distributed over the feet is less than the pulling-together effect of water's surface tension, so the boatman floats. The water surface curves down around its feet. This surface tension effect is how water wets things. As its surface pulls together, it surrounds fibers or grains of rock or soil with which it comes into contact.

Egg sinks in tap water

Egg floats in salty water

Curve on surface of water

Green dye added to water

CAPILLARY ACTION

If a thin tube stands upright in water, the water will rise up inside the tube. There is an upward curve of the water surface where the water touches the tube. The thinner the tube, the higher the water rises, as surface tension pulls the curved surface together. Water soaks into soil and rocks and moves down under the force of gravity. However, water also travels up through rocks by this capillary action. The curved surface always pulls together as the water envelops each tiny grain of rock in turn. Water can therefore be drawn up through soil and rock and evaporated at the surface.

FLOATING EGGS

The density of water changes when it has salt dissolved in it. An egg sinks in fresh water, which means the egg has a density greater than that of the water. Salty water is more dense than fresh water, and when the amount of saltiness – the salinity – is high enough, the egg floats. The varying density of seawater is one of the factors that drives the water currents that circulate water in the oceans.

Weight

MEASURING DENSITY

A hydrometer is an instrument that measures the density of a liquid. It is floated upright in the liquid, sinking more deeply into less dense liquids. Weights are attached to it and the reading taken. This one was used to measure the alcohol content of drinks for assessing the amount of tax payable.

Flotation bulb

Hydrometer

LIMESTONE CAVES

The hydrogen and oxygen that go to make up water are bonded together in such a way that the molecule has a positive charge at one end and a negative charge at the other. This makes it easy for water to attract other charged substances, and it does this by dissolving them. It dissolves the rock limestone to make caves. Later, the dissolved chemicals may become stalagmites and stalactites (p. 57).

Limestone caves at Lascaux in France

Acid

Carbon dioxide gas is given off

ACID RAIN

Pure water is neither acid nor alkaline. Indicator paper held in pure or distilled water shows that it is neutral. Rainwater is always acid, because it contains carbon dioxide. As raindrops fall through the atmosphere, they dissolve some carbon dioxide from the air. This makes the rain a weak acid. In this experiment, carbon dioxide gas is made by adding acid to calcium carbonate chips. The gas is passed into distilled water, which then becomes acid, as shown by the indicator paper. Acid rainwater is a weathering agent; it can dissolve limestone – although slowly.

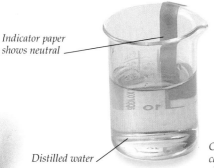

Indicator paper shows neutral

Distilled water

Calcium carbonate chips

Indicator paper shows slight acidity

Carbonic acid

Realms of ice

MANY OF THE WORLD'S HIGH MOUNTAIN RANGES still have glaciers. Both glaciers and ice sheets were much more extensive during the cold glacial phases of the last two million years. Now the Earth is believed to be in an interglacial age with Greenland and Antarctica the only extensively ice-covered lands – leftovers from the last cold phase. The Antarctic ice sheet probably came into existence 35 million years ago when Antarctica broke away from the other land masses. This allowed free circulation of oceanic currents around Antarctica, isolating it from the warmth of the tropical oceanic waters. The water to make ice comes from snow which falls and is compacted. The snow comes from water vapor evaporated from the oceans, so the sea level drops. When glaciers and ice sheets melt, sea level rises again.

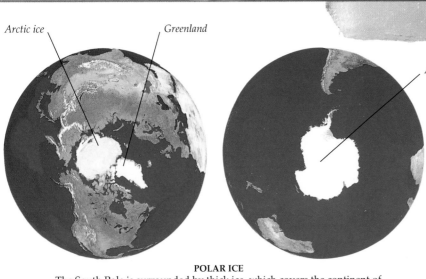

Arctic ice

Greenland

Antarctica

POLAR ICE
The South Pole is surrounded by thick ice, which covers the continent of Antarctica to an average depth of 1½ miles (2.5 km). A small fraction of the Antarctic ice sheet extends beyond the land and floats on the Antarctic Ocean. By contrast, the North Pole has no land. It is a thin floating mass of sea ice – it is possible to travel by submarine to the North Pole under this sea ice.

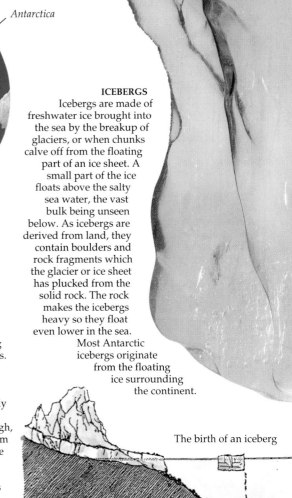

ICEBERGS
Icebergs are made of freshwater ice brought into the sea by the breakup of glaciers, or when chunks calve off from the floating part of an ice sheet. A small part of the ice floats above the salty sea water, the vast bulk being unseen below. As icebergs are derived from land, they contain boulders and rock fragments which the glacier or ice sheet has plucked from the solid rock. The rock makes the icebergs heavy so they float even lower in the sea. Most Antarctic icebergs originate from the floating ice surrounding the continent.

The birth of an iceberg

SEA ICE
Exploring the polar regions means braving the sea ice and icebergs. Polar ships follow the open water "leads" through the icescape. Their hulls are specially strengthened to help batter their way through, and also to protect them from crushing if the ice should freeze around them. The floating ice of both hemispheres is called pack ice. The amount varies from summer to winter.

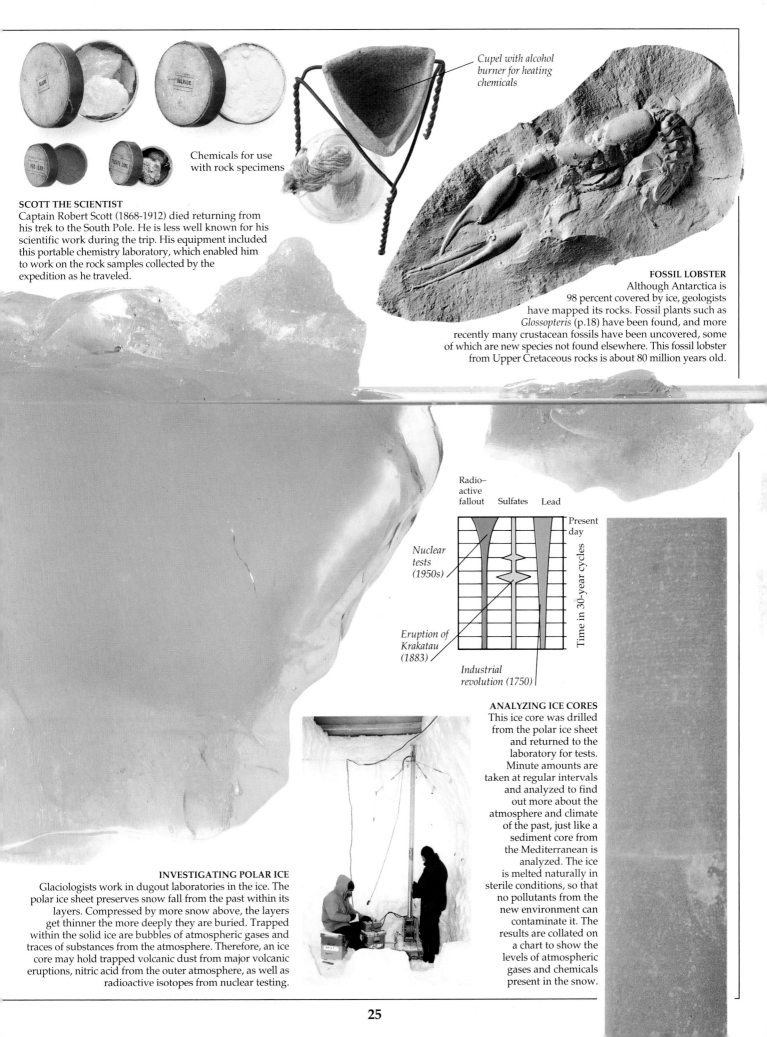

Chemicals for use
with rock specimens

*Cupel with alcohol
burner for heating
chemicals*

SCOTT THE SCIENTIST
Captain Robert Scott (1868-1912) died returning from
his trek to the South Pole. He is less well known for his
scientific work during the trip. His equipment included
this portable chemistry laboratory, which enabled him
to work on the rock samples collected by the
expedition as he traveled.

FOSSIL LOBSTER
Although Antarctica is
98 percent covered by ice, geologists
have mapped its rocks. Fossil plants such as
Glossopteris (p.18) have been found, and more
recently many crustacean fossils have been uncovered, some
of which are new species not found elsewhere. This fossil lobster
from Upper Cretaceous rocks is about 80 million years old.

Radio–
active
fallout   Sulfates   Lead

Present
day

*Nuclear
tests
(1950s)*

Time in 30-year cycles

*Eruption of
Krakatau
(1883)*

*Industrial
revolution (1750)*

ANALYZING ICE CORES
This ice core was drilled
from the polar ice sheet
and returned to the
laboratory for tests.
Minute amounts are
taken at regular intervals
and analyzed to find
out more about the
atmosphere and climate
of the past, just like a
sediment core from
the Mediterranean is
analyzed. The ice
is melted naturally in
sterile conditions, so that
no pollutants from the
new environment can
contaminate it. The
results are collated on
a chart to show the
levels of atmospheric
gases and chemicals
present in the snow.

INVESTIGATING POLAR ICE
Glaciologists work in dugout laboratories in the ice. The
polar ice sheet preserves snow fall from the past within its
layers. Compressed by more snow above, the layers
get thinner the more deeply they are buried. Trapped
within the solid ice are bubbles of atmospheric gases and
traces of substances from the atmosphere. Therefore, an ice
core may hold trapped volcanic dust from major volcanic
eruptions, nitric acid from the outer atmosphere, as well as
radioactive isotopes from nuclear testing.

The building blocks

GOLD IN NATURE
Gold is both an element and a mineral. It is found almost pure in nature where it may be in veins in rocks. The most pure natural gold is 99 percent pure. For commercial purposes, it is often alloyed with silver. Gold forms cubic crystals and has a bright metallic luster. It is very heavy, but not hard; it can easily be cut with a knife.

OVER ONE HUNDRED CHEMICAL ELEMENTS combine to make up all matter. An element contains only one kind of atom, but atoms from different elements can join together to make a variety of substances called compounds. They do this by joining together (bonding) in different ways to make molecules. A few of the elements make up almost all of the types of naturally occurring compounds called minerals. These minerals make up rocks. Most rocks in the Earth's crust are composed of only eight of the chemical elements – oxygen, silicon, aluminum, iron, calcium, magnesium, sodium, and potassium. Two of these elements, silicon and oxygen, combine in silicates, which make up 75 percent of the Earth's rocks. Most minerals are crystalline – the atoms that make up the crystals are arranged in an orderly fashion. It is the job of the mineralogist to understand what minerals are, where they are to be found, and what they can be used for.

SILICON LOCKET
The chemical element silicon does not occur in nature. Silicon is always found as a silicate in combination with oxygen, and it takes a lot of chemical energy to separate out the silicon from the oxygen in a laboratory. When it was first separated, silicon was considered an exotic substance. This piece was mounted in a locket. Nowadays, silicon is made commercially for the electronics industry, where it is the raw material for the microchip.

New Mexico

ELEMENTS IN THE EARTH'S CRUST
The crust is the outermost solid layer on the Earth's surface. Oxygen atoms are so large that almost all of the Earth's crust is made of them with the other elements just filling in the spaces between. Silicon atoms are small and fit happily between four oxygen atoms. Therefore the most abundant elements in the crust are those that readily combine with the relatively lightweight silicon and oxygen to make silicates. These elements fit into the physical spaces in the silicate framework and make up the common rock-forming minerals, such as feldspars, pyroxenes, amphiboles, olivines, and micas.

DIFFERENT SILICATES
Two very different silicates are talc, familiar as the slippery white cosmetic powder, and beryl. Talc is a silicate of magnesium, crystallized with water in its structure. Beryl comes in various colors; the bright green variety in hard, clear crystals is the highly prized gemstone, emerald. Beryl is a silicate with aluminum in combination with the much rarer chemical element, beryllium.

Aluminum

Calcium

Iron

Others

Silicon

Oxygen

Elements in the Earth's crust

WHITE SANDS DESERT
This white sand is made of one mineral, gypsum, which has been weathered by wind. The composition of the mineral is calcium, in combination with sulfur and oxygen, to make the chemical calcium sulfate. The crystals of calcium sulfate in nature contain some water, and this combination goes to make up the mineral gypsum. Crystals of gypsum are soft and can be scratched with a fingernail. Gypsum forms crystals that are uncolored and transparent, and sometimes white.

SILICATES
Silicon and oxygen combine together to form the mineral quartz, and this commonly appears as sand. In silicates, the silicon atoms are each surrounded by four oxygen atoms, but the oxygen may be shared with neighboring silicons. In this way the framework of silicates is made.

Si

O

O

O

O

Beryl

Talc

Telling minerals apart

Calcite, gypsum, and quartz look alike at first glance. All three may come as colorless, transparent crystals. All are used in industry in different ways, so it is important to be able to distinguish one from the other. Minerals are differentiated by their appearance, their color, and whether they are transparent (an image can be read through them), translucent (let light through) or opaque (no light goes into the crystal). Other important properties are the hardness, the luster, the streak (the color of the powder they make), the density, and the crystal form and shape. In a laboratory more sophisticated tests may be done.

Calcite

Gypsum

Quartz

WHICH MINERAL?
To determine the minerals in a piece of rock, a geologist would first look at the rock through a hand lens to check for crystal shape, texture, luster, and color. The next test would probably be the acid test.

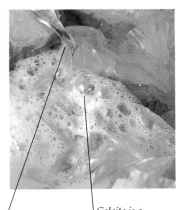

1 ACID TEST
Dilute hydrochloric acid is dropped on to the area being tested. Carbonate rocks effervesce (fizz) to give off carbon dioxide gas when they meet acid. This identifies calcite.

Acid is dropped on to the rock

Calcite is a carbonate rock so it fizzes with acid

Rock containing calcite, gypsum, and quartz

2 HARDNESS TEST
The hardness of minerals is generally measured against a Mohs scale, where talc is 1 (the softest), and diamond is 10, the hardest material known. A steel penknife is used here to do the test. Steel has a hardness of around 6, so quartz at a greater hardness, 7 on the Mohs scale, is not scratched by a knife, but calcite and gypsum are. Gypsum is softer than calcite, so the penknife scratches it easily. Gypsum is so soft it can be scratched with a fingernail (hardness of 2).

3 FINDING QUARTZ
Another useful substance for hardness testing is window glass (5 on the Mohs scale). Calcite is softer than window glass (it has a hardness of only 3), so it will not scratch the glass. Neither will gypsum at 2 on the scale. Quartz is the only one of the three which scratches the glass. So the hardness tests confirm the findings on all three minerals.

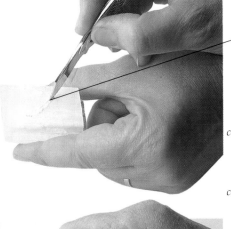

Steel penknife scratches the gypsum

Blue – low copper concentrations

Red – high copper concentrations

Yellow – no suitable data

Quartz scratches the window glass

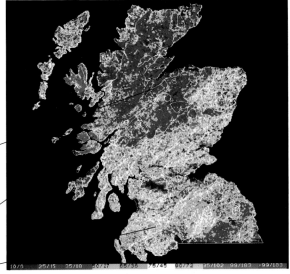

COPPER CONCENTRATIONS IN SCOTLAND
The amount of various minerals in stream sediments is estimated by taking one sample every mile. The results are stored on a computer, and are shown on a map. This map can show concentrations of copper and can be used for mineral exploration and for environmental reasons to check for contamination or pollution. Here high levels of copper are shown in dark red. The 60-million-year-old lavas of the Inner Hebrides Islands are high in copper, and so are granite regions in the Highlands. Copper also shows up high in industrial areas, where there is no relationship to the underlying rocks; the concentration is the direct result of human activity.

Investigating rocks

Neptune – the Roman god of the sea

THE FIRST SYSTEMATIC BOOK ON MINERALOGY was written by Agricola (p.14), in the 16th century. Written in Latin, it was called *De Natura Fossilium*. The word "fossil" then meant "things dug up," and included chiefly minerals and rocks. Agricola based his writings on his own observations, rather than using the speculative or hopeful reasoning that had characterized the writings of the ancient Greeks, and, later, the alchemists. In the 18th century, the Age of Enlightenment encouraged many thinkers to contemplate the origin of the Earth and of rocks. A controversy raged between the Neptunists, led by Abraham Werner, and the Plutonists, who believed the origin of some rocks was undoubtedly volcanic, led by James Hutton (p.14). Europe's scientists were divided into two camps. Toward the end of the 18th century, travel became easier allowing scientists to observe directly many different types of rocks in different places. In 1830, Charles Lyell (p. 68) published his influential work, *Principles of Geology*. This book influenced other geologists, who responded to Lyell's theories about the slow, gradual nature of the Earth's processes.

JAMES DANA
James Dana (1813-1895) was an American geologist best known for his *System of Mineralogy* (1837). He suggested that landscapes were shaped by the ongoing forces of weathering and erosion. His predecessors had imagined that sudden catastrophic events, such as earthquakes, were responsible.

ROCKS FROM WATER
Abraham Werner (1750-1817) was a German geologist who put forward the ideas of Neptunism. The Neptunists opposed the Plutonists. Neptunists believed that the Plutonists. Neptunists believed that dissolved in the ocean waters, and all rocks (including basalt) had come out of this solution. Werner's fame spread from the eloquence of his personal teachings and the dedicated work of his students.

Geologists in the field

Geologists fall into many categories such as paleontologists, petrologists, and geochemists, but they all study the Earth, and the place to start is in the rocks. In the field, geologists record their observations in notebooks, take photographs, and collect specimens. The specimens are labeled and wrapped for transport back to the laboratory.

Geological hammer

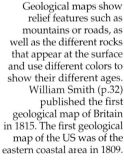
Hand lens

Abraham Werner

TOOLS OF THE TRADE
A geologist uses a hammer to break off rock samples fresh from solid bedrock. This ensures that the samples collected have truly come from the solid rocks of the place being mapped. The small hammer is used for trimming rock samples. A chisel helps in splitting rocks. The hand lens is used to look in detail at the texture of rock, and to see if any fossils are present.

Trimming hammer

Chisel

Chisel

SMITH'S MAP (1819)
Geological maps show relief features such as mountains or roads, as well as the different rocks that appear at the surface and use different colors to show their different ages. William Smith (p.32) published the first geological map of Britain in 1815. The first geological map of the US was of the eastern coastal area in 1809.

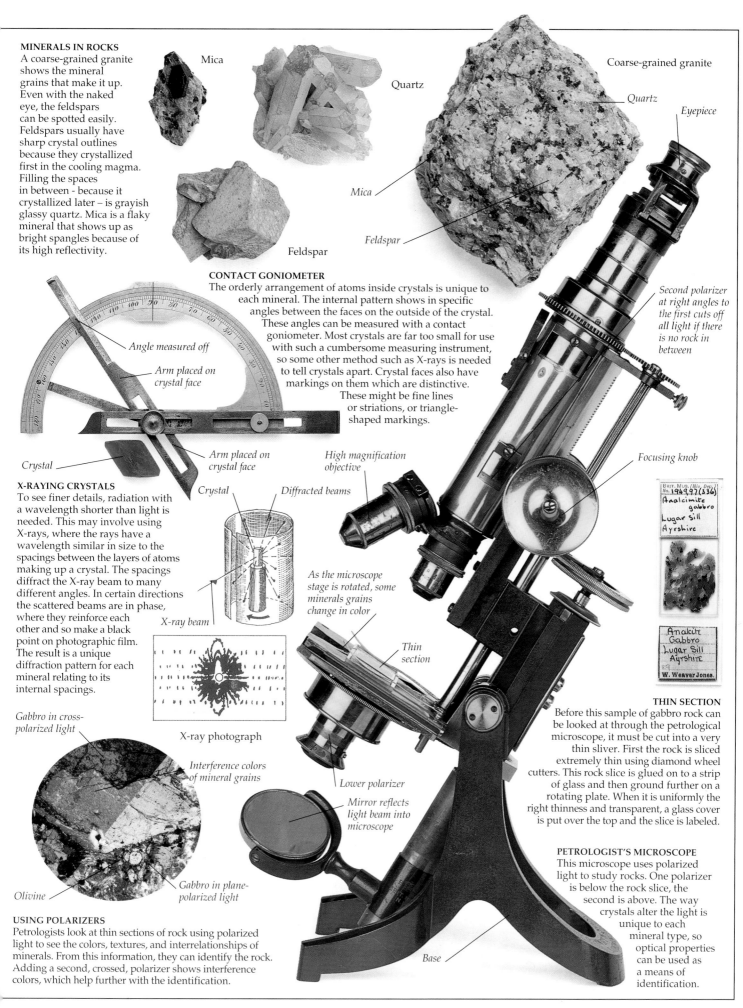

MINERALS IN ROCKS

A coarse-grained granite shows the mineral grains that make it up. Even with the naked eye, the feldspars can be spotted easily. Feldspars usually have sharp crystal outlines because they crystallized first in the cooling magma. Filling the spaces in between - because it crystallized later – is grayish glassy quartz. Mica is a flaky mineral that shows up as bright spangles because of its high reflectivity.

Mica

Quartz

Feldspar

Coarse-grained granite

Quartz

Mica

Feldspar

Eyepiece

Second polarizer at right angles to the first cuts off all light if there is no rock in between

CONTACT GONIOMETER

The orderly arrangement of atoms inside crystals is unique to each mineral. The internal pattern shows in specific angles between the faces on the outside of the crystal. These angles can be measured with a contact goniometer. Most crystals are far too small for use with such a cumbersome measuring instrument, so some other method such as X-rays is needed to tell crystals apart. Crystal faces also have markings on them which are distinctive. These might be fine lines or striations, or triangle-shaped markings.

Angle measured off

Arm placed on crystal face

Crystal

Arm placed on crystal face

Crystal

High magnification objective

Diffracted beams

Focusing knob

X-RAYING CRYSTALS

To see finer details, radiation with a wavelength shorter than light is needed. This may involve using X-rays, where the rays have a wavelength similar in size to the spacings between the layers of atoms making up a crystal. The spacings diffract the X-ray beam to many different angles. In certain directions the scattered beams are in phase, where they reinforce each other and so make a black point on photographic film. The result is a unique diffraction pattern for each mineral relating to its internal spacings.

X-ray beam

As the microscope stage is rotated, some minerals grains change in color

Thin section

BRIT. MUS. (Min. Dep.)
No. 1949,97 (336)
Analcimite gabbro
Lugar Sill
Ayrshire

Analcite
Gabbro
Lugar Sill
Ayrshire
W. Weaver Jones.

X-ray photograph

THIN SECTION

Before this sample of gabbro rock can be looked at through the petrological microscope, it must be cut into a very thin sliver. First the rock is sliced extremely thin using diamond wheel cutters. This rock slice is glued on to a strip of glass and then ground further on a rotating plate. When it is uniformly the right thinness and transparent, a glass cover is put over the top and the slice is labeled.

Gabbro in cross-polarized light

Interference colors of mineral grains

Lower polarizer

Mirror reflects light beam into microscope

Olivine

Gabbro in plane-polarized light

PETROLOGIST'S MICROSCOPE

This microscope uses polarized light to study rocks. One polarizer is below the rock slice, the second is above. The way crystals alter the light is unique to each mineral type, so optical properties can be used as a means of identification.

USING POLARIZERS

Petrologists look at thin sections of rock using polarized light to see the colors, textures, and interrelationships of minerals. From this information, they can identify the rock. Adding a second, crossed, polarizer shows interference colors, which help further with the identification.

Base

Igneous rocks

Guy Tancrède de Dolomieu (1750-1801)

IGNEOUS ROCKS ARE THE PRIMARY original material that makes up the Earth's surface. The first rocks on the Earth were igneous rocks; they formed as the planet started to cool. Magma is the name of the molten material that solidifies and crystallizes in a complex way to make the range of different minerals found in igneous rocks. It is continually being produced deep inside the Earth. This process cannot be observed, so scientists must guess at the mechanism. Because Vesuvius continued to display some volcanic activity throughout the 18th century, French mineralogist Dolomieu was able to watch an active volcano. He became convinced that the origin of the lava was deep inside the Earth. Some magma cools and solidifies inside the Earth's crust in a mass known as an igneous intrusion. At the beginning of the 20th century, Norman Bowen (1887-1956), a Canadian petrologist (a specialist in rocks) studied the way silicate liquids crystallized as they cooled, working with silicate melts which were an approximation to natural magma. Bowen discovered that metal oxide minerals crystallized out first, because they had the highest melting points. The later crystals that formed were a product of interaction between the early crystals and the liquid that remained, which had a different chemical composition.

Erosive agents carry loose grains that collect to make sedimentary rock

If rocks are heated enough, they may melt to become new magma

Sedimentary rocks become buried

Sedimentary rocks may be heated and compressed into metamorphic rocks

WEARING DOWN A MOUNTAIN RANGE
When a mountain range is uplifted, the underlying rocks are elevated. As the mountain range grows higher, so the mountain tops are worn away by erosion over millions of years. This granite on Dartmoor in England crystallized many miles down in the Earth's crust and was part of an igneous intrusion known as a batholith. Erosion has worn away a whole mountain range leaving the hilltop granite tor, the word originally coming from the Celtic name for granite summits in this part of the world.

Eroded granite

THE ROCK CYCLE
The rock cycle continually renews the surface of the Earth. When igneous rocks meet the Earth's atmosphere, they are changed. New minerals are formed, and the crystal grains are separated and carried away by erosive agents to form sediments. They become sedimentary rock and can then be heated or compressed into metamorphic rock, and even melted to make new igneous rock.

Haytor, Dartmoor, southern Britain

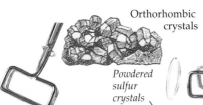

Orthorhombic crystals

Monoclinic crystals

Melted sulfur

Powdered sulfur crystals

LARGE CRYSTALS
Generally, when a liquid cools slowly, it yields large crystals because there is time for the atoms to find their place in the orderly crystal arrangement. The element sulfur makes orthorhombic or monoclinic crystals depending on the temperature at which the crystals grow. The granite of Haytor cooled over perhaps 1 million years, so the crystals are as large as 2 in (5 cm) across.

HEATING CRYSTALS
Powdered crystals of sulfur can be heated until they melt. If the conditions of cooling are faster, needlelike monoclinic crystals form at about 194°F (90°C). These crystals grow in nature in the heat of a volcanic fumarole, or hot spring. They form around the mouth of the fumarole where the cooling occurs.

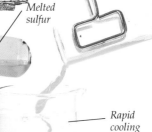

Rapid cooling

Plastic-like sulfur

CHILLED CRYSTALS
A liquid that is chilled suddenly may freeze into a glassy structure that lacks the orderly internal arrangement of crystals. The glassy structure may look quite different from the equivalent crystalline material. Chilled sulfur is stretchy and plastic. A silicate melt or magma that is chilled rapidly makes a natural glass. Over millions of years the glass may begin to crystallize.

THE RECYCLING OF MAGMA

Localized melting in the mantle may form magma which rises through the underlying semisolid or solid rock. Basalt is the igneous rock nearest in composition to its parent material, the mantle. Basalt-like rocks erupt as lava flows (like those on Hawaii, left) to make up the ocean floor. When ocean floor subducts into the mantle, the sinking basaltic rock is melted. This new magma makes its way back toward the Earth's surface, changing in composition as it travels.

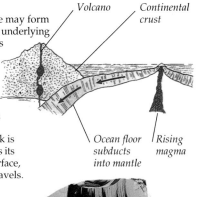

Volcano *Continental crust*
Ocean floor subducts into mantle *Rising magma*

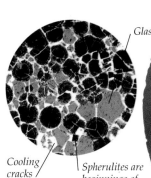

Glass

Cooling cracks *Spherulites are beginnings of crystals*

Thin section of obsidian under cross-polarized light

OBSIDIAN

Obsidian is a natural glass made from magma which was cooled too quickly to crystallize. When it erupts as lava, there is no opportunity for the atoms to arrange themselves in an orderly fashion.

Large crystals in a fine-grained matrix produce a porphyritic texture

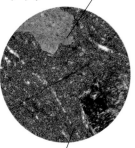

Crystal cooled as lava flows

Thin section of felsite under cross-polarized light

FELSITE

Felsite's larger crystals of quartz and feldspar grew during slow cooling (before eruption), while the small crystals result from rapid cooling at eruption.

Quartz formed later *Mica fits into spaces*

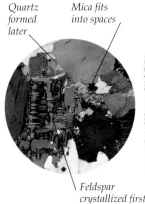

Feldspar crystallized first

Thin section of granite under cross-polarized light

GRANITE

Granite cools most slowly of these three rocks. Obsidian, felsite, and granite are formed from magma of about the same chemical composition – the difference depends on the rate at which they cooled.

Sedimentary rocks

ROCKS THAT COME INTO CONTACT with the atmosphere and with water are gradually weathered, even basalt lavas and granite. Water seeps in between the mineral grains and chemically reacts with the rock to break it down. Particles of the weathered rock are removed by falling rain, or are blown away by the wind and dropped elsewhere. In the new location, layers of sediment are formed, which may become buried by more and more layers. These layers also may contain organic material such as plants and the remains of dead creatures. Eventually the sediments harden and become compacted. Ground water percolates through the sediment, leaving behind minerals which cement the sediment grains together. In this way the sediment is lithified (becomes rock). By understanding how modern sediment forms, it is possible to reconstruct the environment of the past – the paleoenvironment – and to make paleogeographic maps showing the geography of land masses that existed many millions of years ago.

WILLIAM SMITH (1769-1839)
Smith was an English engineer who surveyed routes for canals. He recognized the same types of rock in different places and realized that individual layers of sedimentary rocks were characterized by similar groupings of fossils. As had others before him, he concluded that the oldest rocks were in the lowest layer.

QUARRY OF SAND
The layers of sand in this English quarry are around 100 million years old. They were desposited in a shallow sea. The layers of sandstone are overlaying a layer of gray-colored boulder clay. The sand is quarried as sports turf sand for golf courses, and for filtering drinking water.

SANDSTONE
This sandstone is made from grains of sand, like modern desert sand. The grains are visible even without a magnifying glass. A specimen of sandstone may also show changes of color and banding. The layers of the original sands may be the result of the desert wind sorting the sand grains into different sizes or densities. Some sandstones show mineral grains in typically darker colored bands. These minerals, more dense than ordinary sand grains, are sometimes concentrated in layers.

Grain of quartz

Thin section of sandstone in cross-polarized light

Red sandstone

Even texture

HOW SEDIMENT IS MADE
Fragments of older rocks make up one type of sediment. During a flood, heavy rain loosens the weathered sand and gravel from mountain slopes. Along with the soil, this loosened sediment is carried away in flood waters and is dropped when and where the current slows. A river in flood always has colored turbid water from the sediment it carries which could be a mixture of mud, sand, and pebbles.

Pebble

Fossil shell

Shelly limestone

Origins of oil

Oil is derived from the remains of dead plants. They decay and sink to the seabed, where they become entombed in the thickening sediment. The temperature increases as the sediments are buried ever deeper, and oily liquids are boiled off from the organic remains. The oily material percolates away from the pores of permeable rocks (p. 21) and seeps into sandstone and limestone. Here the oil collects in the pore spaces in the rock.

Sandstone borehole core

Natural oil

LIMESTONE
Plants and animals that live in sea or river water use calcium bicarbonate in solution in the water to make calcium carbonate. Animals may use this to construct shells or skeletons, while plants become surrounded with limy mud. Eventually the mud becomes limestone which often contains the shells of the creatures that made the calcium carbonate.

Fossil shell

Thin section of limestone in plane-polarized light

MUDSTONE
It is impossible to see the grains that make up mudstone without a high-powered microscope. The minute flakes of clay and silt are the smallest particles of sediment to come from the weathering of older rocks. Clay is derived from weathering of feldspars. Grains of silt, which might be quartz or feldspar, are slightly larger in size. Mudstone forms in river estuaries, lakes, and in the sea.

OIL-BEARING ROCK
When sediment becomes rock, there are almost always spaces between the individual grains of sediment, which are not filled with cementing minerals. In the pore spaces of this sandstone rock, 3 pints (1.5 liters) of oil were trapped under pressure. However, it is not possible to extract all oil from rock. Because of the surface tension and the viscosity of oil, some oil remains clinging to the rock grains.

CONGLOMERATE
Sediment that contains many rounded pebbles, usually with some sand filling in the spaces between, is called conglomerate. Originally the sediment may have been gravel in a river bed, the pebbles having been carried along during a flood and dumped along with sand.

Pebbles are made of the hard mineral quartz

DRILLING FOR OIL
If a rock structure is suitable, oil sometimes collects. If it is trapped in the rock layers, it can be collected for commercial use. Potential oil-bearing structures may be detected from the Earth's surface or the seabed. The geologist plays a vital role in predicting where oil traps might exist.

Pipeline

Drilling rig

Impermeable rock

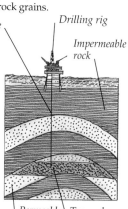

Permeable rock

Trapped oil

Shell

Sand

Metamorphic rocks

STREAKED CIPOLLINO MARBLE
Limestone made of pure calcium carbonate recrystallizes during metamorphism to a pure white marble. Many limestones contain quartz sand, or some clay, or iron. When these are metamorphosed, the result is colored marble, often with folded banding. Many metamorphic rocks show evidence of folding or fracturing, indicating that they reacted as though they were either plastic or brittle during mountain building.

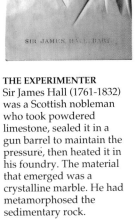

THE EXPERIMENTER
Sir James Hall (1761-1832) was a Scottish nobleman who took powdered limestone, sealed it in a gun barrel to maintain the pressure, then heated it in his foundry. The material that emerged was a crystalline marble. He had metamorphosed the sedimentary rock.

METAMORPHIC ROCKS ARE ROCKS that have been changed. Previously, they were igneous, sedimentary, or other metamorphic rocks. Almost all metamorphism happens deep in young mountain ranges as rocks are folded and compressed beneath other rocks. Although rock never actually melts, the texture and nature of the rock may become "like new", made of different, metamorphic crystals, with no sign of the original minerals or textures. Part of this occurs in response to pressure, and part is the result of the heat. Metamorphism takes a long time, first for the rock to be buried to a depth where metamorphism can begin, and then for the solid recrystallization to take place. Eventually, metamorphic rocks are exposed at the Earth's surface, but only after the mountain chain is uplifted and eroded deeply. This process in which sediment is buried and made into metamorphic rocks may take millions of years.

CONTACT WITH HOT GRANITE
When molten granite intrudes into rocks in mountain ranges, the rocks are metamorphosed around the granite. The halo of changed rock is called a metamorphic aureole. New minerals grow in response to high temperatures, for example, limestone becomes marble.

Sandstone — *Metamorphic aureole* — *Limestone* — *Granite* — *Marble*

SPLITTING SLATE FOR ROOFS
Mica crystals in slate are all parallel to each other. The slate splitter knows the direction, and splits or cleaves the slate along it. This is called the cleavage direction.

INCREASING THE PRESSURE
Metamorphism can transform a featureless mudstone into a sparkling crystalline rock. Muds laid down in shallow seas are carried down during mountain building to deeper levels. The first sign of metamorphism is growth of microscopic crystals of mica. Pressure may cause these to be aligned, which produces slate (1). Phyllite (2) has been recrystallized more intensely, so that the mica crystals are larger and can be seen as a shimmer on the rock surface. Even deeper or longer burial in the mountain range creates a schist, which may have large mica crystals, and grains or crystals of kyanite (3), whose crystallization is also helped by heat.

Increase in pressure 1. Slate

2. Phyllite

Mica — *Quartz* — *Garnet*

MUDSTONE MAKES GARNET
In mudstone, the first metamorphic minerals to grow are mica crystals, orientating themselves in the direction of least pressure. The garnet grew later, pushing mica crystals out of the way.

Blue kyanite

3. Kyanite schist

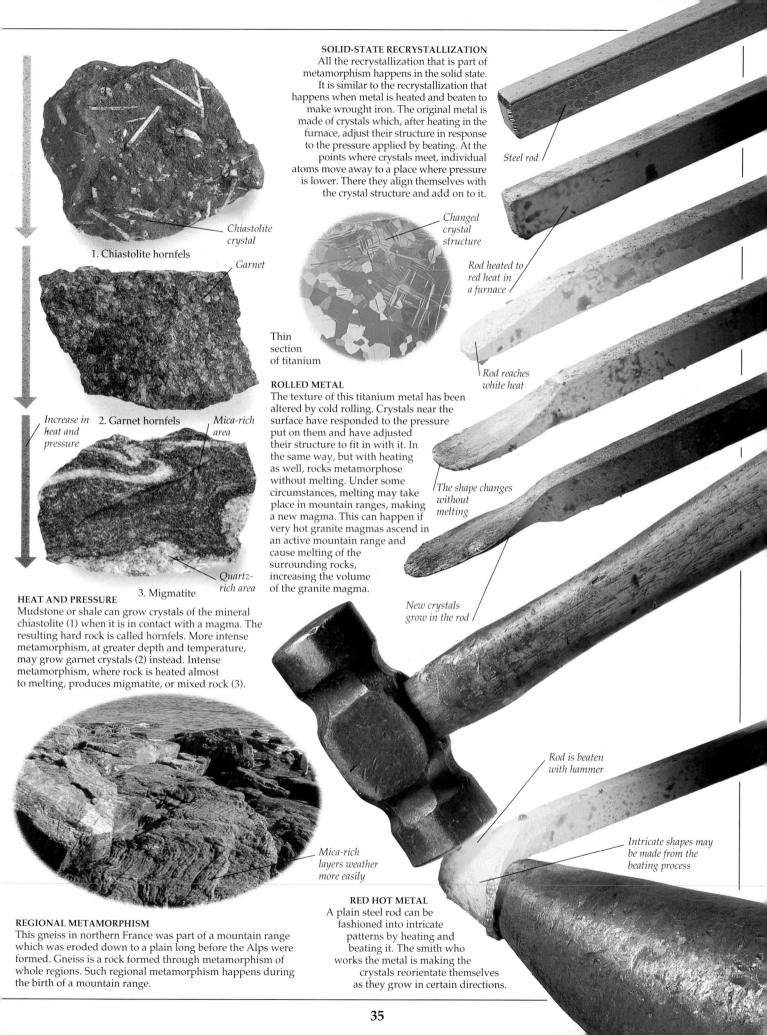

1. Chiastolite hornfels

Chiastolite crystal

2. Garnet hornfels

Garnet

Increase in heat and pressure

3. Migmatite

Mica-rich area

Quartz-rich area

SOLID-STATE RECRYSTALLIZATION

All the recrystallization that is part of metamorphism happens in the solid state. It is similar to the recrystallization that happens when metal is heated and beaten to make wrought iron. The original metal is made of crystals which, after heating in the furnace, adjust their structure in response to the pressure applied by beating. At the points where crystals meet, individual atoms move away to a place where pressure is lower. There they align themselves with the crystal structure and add on to it.

Changed crystal structure

Thin section of titanium

ROLLED METAL

The texture of this titanium metal has been altered by cold rolling. Crystals near the surface have responded to the pressure put on them and have adjusted their structure to fit in with it. In the same way, but with heating as well, rocks metamorphose without melting. Under some circumstances, melting may take place in mountain ranges, making a new magma. This can happen if very hot granite magmas ascend in an active mountain range and cause melting of the surrounding rocks, increasing the volume of the granite magma.

Steel rod

Rod heated to red heat in a furnace

Rod reaches white heat

The shape changes without melting

New crystals grow in the rod

Rod is beaten with hammer

Intricate shapes may be made from the beating process

HEAT AND PRESSURE

Mudstone or shale can grow crystals of the mineral chiastolite (1) when it is in contact with a magma. The resulting hard rock is called hornfels. More intense metamorphism, at greater depth and temperature, may grow garnet crystals (2) instead. Intense metamorphism, where rock is heated almost to melting, produces migmatite, or mixed rock (3).

Mica-rich layers weather more easily

REGIONAL METAMORPHISM

This gneiss in northern France was part of a mountain range which was eroded down to a plain long before the Alps were formed. Gneiss is a rock formed through metamorphism of whole regions. Such regional metamorphism happens during the birth of a mountain range.

RED HOT METAL

A plain steel rod can be fashioned into intricate patterns by heating and beating it. The smith who works the metal is making the crystals reorientate themselves as they grow in certain directions.

The challenge of the ocean

THE BEGINNINGS OF MODERN OCEANOGRAPHY lie at the end of the 19th century with oceanic surveys such as that conducted by the British research vessel *Challenger*. The US was proposing to explore the Atlantic and Pacific oceans, with Alexandre Agassiz (1835–1910) as joint leader, and German and Swedish ships, too, were venturing into the Atlantic. The British government was persuaded to support the *Challenger* expedition to uphold Britain's international prestige. It was hoped that *Challenger*'s exploration would be able to answer pressing questions of the day. Was the deep ocean populated with living creatures? Could ocean currents be measured to confirm theories about how oceanic waters circulated? If sediment lay on the ocean floor, would it be the familiar chalk? *Challenger* was able to answer some of these questions, but the oceanic circulation remained a mystery even at the end of the voyage. It is now known that many variable factors influence the currents. By taking depth soundings, *Challenger* did discover submarine mountains in the middle of the Atlantic Ocean (pp. 44-45), and found the Mariana Trench, 36,000 ft (11,033 m) down in the Pacific Ocean.

IMAGING THE DEEP
In 1869 French writer Jules Verne (1828-1905) wrote the science-fiction novel *Twenty Thousand Leagues under the Sea*. It tells of a submarine whose technology was advanced far beyond its time. In the 20th century the technology of Verne's submarine is commonplace. To appreciate Verne's farsightedness, the reader must realize that he was writing at a time when the undersea world was unexplored.

Reading taken on stem

Glass flask

THE HYDROMETER
Oceanic water was sampled by *Challenger* to discover how salinity and temperature vary with depth and location. This hydrometer measured salinity. The warm surface current in the Atlantic Ocean – the Gulf Stream – was already known, mapped by Benjamin Franklin in the 18th century. *Challenger* showed that there was much colder water at deeper levels which could be the compensating current of cold water.

HISTORIC VOYAGE
The *Challenger*'s epic voyage lasted from 1872 to 1875. The ship sailed 59,900 nautical miles (111,000 km), measuring the ocean characteristics and collecting samples. The expedition did not include a physicist. If it had, maybe the profusion of *Challenger*'s observations could have been used to work out the interrelationships between salinity, temperature and water density, ocean bottom slope, winds, and the effects of evaporation and rainfall, which together affect oceanic circulation.

Engraving showing a hydrometer suspended in liquid

Mercury acts as a weight

END OF THE FLAT EARTH THEORY
In the 16th century an expedition led by the Portuguese Ferdinand Magellan (1480-1521) sailed around the world, finally proving that it was not flat. Magellan tried to calculate the depth of the ocean as he sailed. However, navigators usually kept in sight of land. Here the water is shallower than the great ocean deeps, and the bottom sediments are derived from the land.

ABOARD SHIP
The naturalists on *Challenger* charted ocean-bottom sediments and their relationship to life in the sea. Dredges were used to sample these sediments. The samples showed that the plankton *Globigerina* lived in the surface water of almost all parts of the ocean. Investigations showed that when *Globigerina* dies, the shells sink to the seabed and make the fine carbonate mud known as Globigerina ooze.

Sifting through dredged sediment on *Challenger*

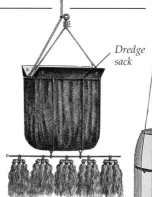

Dredge sack

Corer

Iron sinkers detach before resurfacing

Brass protective container

Flat-headed swabs drag the net along the ocean floor

DREDGING THE DEPTHS
Dredges and cores were used to collect material from all parts of the seabed. Although water samples showed that *Globigerina* lived in the sunlit shallow waters of the Atlantic, the dredges brought up reddish-colored clay from the deep ocean floor instead of the ooze. The deeper the water, the less sign there was of any *Globigerina* shells on the ocean bed. The *Challenger* team supposed, rightly, that at such huge depths *Globigerina* shells had dissolved in seawater; the red clay was dust blown from the land.

Iron sinkers carry line down and force the corer into the sludge

Slides containing samples

Clay from seashore   Globigerina ooze   Shelly sand   Sediment

ASSEMBLING THE EVIDENCE
The task of sending samples to scientists for study and storage, and of writing up and publishing the results of *Challenger*'s work, took 15 years. The material was bottled up with labels that gave latitude and longitude, the depth of water where the sample was collected, and the type of material (ooze or clay, for example).

Mercury and glass thermometer

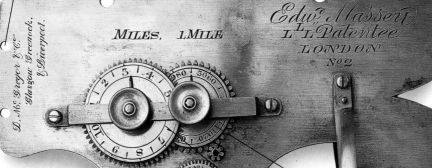

Hemp line attached here

MILES, 1 MILE

Edw. Massey L^L Patentee LONDON Nº2

D. Mc Prayer & Co Glasgow Greenock & Liverpool

SPEED CHECK
To measure ocean currents, the distance the ship traveled had to be known. This device has three dials which turn as the propeller turns to record mileage. At this time, survey ships used hemp lines for all apparatus lowered into the ocean. The lines became enormously heavy when soaked with seawater, so that depth soundings in the ocean deeps took hours because of the time needed to lower and raise the lines.

Dial measures feet   *Propeller*   *Cog wheels on dial show parts of a mile*   *Cog wheels on dial show miles traveled*

TAKING THE TEMPERATURE
At first the *Challenger* team worked with thermometers that recorded only minimum and maximum temperatures. This thermometer registered the temperature of deep water even when it was hauled up to the ship through water that was either cooler or warmer. *Challenger* discovered that off Antarctica surface water was 3°F (-16°C) colder than water at 300 fathoms (550 m).

Weighted line to help container sink

Modern oceanography

TWENTIETH-CENTURY OCEANOGRAPHIC SURVEYS have revolutionized our view of the planet and of how it works, by revealing the surface features – the topography – and nature of the ocean floor. In the early 1960s, there was a plan to drill a borehole to penetrate the mantle. The "Mohole" was to be drilled where the crust was thinnest. This meant drilling in deep water from a floating ship. Seismic investigation had already shown that the ocean floor has a layered structure. The Mohole would sample the ocean floor and reveal the nature of the layers. Mohole never reached the Moho – the boundary where the mantle meets the crust. Instead, in 1964, the US drilling ship *Glomar Challenger* began systematic worldwide drilling of sediment and ocean floor. Detailed mapping is now carried out by remote sensing apparatus towed from floating ships, and in orbiting satellites. Computers are used to visualize oceanic water circulation.

LIFE IN THE OCEAN DEPTHS
The deep ocean is a dark place. Knowing the amount of light in ocean water is vital to our understanding of where and how oceanic plants and animals live. Photosynthesis can take place at light levels as low as 1 percent of sunlight. Creatures like the anglerfish, which emit light to lure their prey, add significantly to light levels in the dark parts of the ocean.

INVESTIGATING THE DEEP
Glomar Challenger's samples led to an understanding of seafloor spreading. They revealed that nearest to the submarine mountains the basalt is young, and farther away it is older. Not only that, but near these ridges the basaltic floor was covered by a thin layer of only present-day sediments. Further from the ridge, these present-day sediments covered the older sediments.

PLANKTON NETS
The food chain in the oceans begins with the inorganic nutrients carried in oceanic currents. The smallest plants and animals are plankton, which float passively. They range from microscopic algae to shrimps. The larger ocean life feeds on these plankton. Oceanographers use special plankton nets to assess the amounts of plankton, and to discover the relative proportions of plant and animal plankton in a given area. Sampling in the seas around Antarctica showed that in oceanic water the animal plankton grazed on the plant plankton, but in coastal waters they fed on bacteria.

PLANKTON FROM SATELLITE
Modern oceanographers and marine geologists use sophisticated technology in their work. Satellites can map the distribution of plankton in surface water – here in the Indian and Pacific oceans. Satellite imagery can also help spot changes in temperature and salinity in oceanic waters which, though small, may have profound effects on oceanic currents.

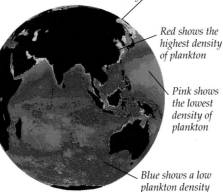

Yellow shows average plankton density

Red shows the highest density of plankton

Pink shows the lowest density of plankton

Blue shows a low plankton density

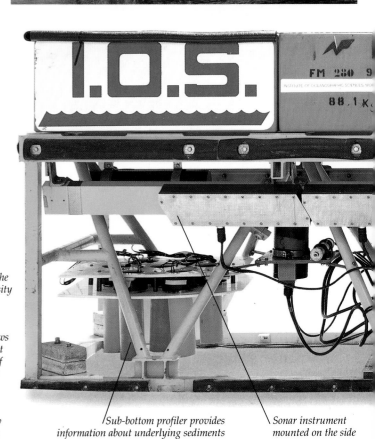

I.O.S.
FM 280 9
88.1 K

Sub-bottom profiler provides information about underlying sediments

Sonar instrument mounted on the side

Sonar imaging

In ocean water, below a few hundred yards, it is too dark for light imaging to tell us anything about the ocean floor. Sound waves, however, can be used instead. Echo sounding was the first such method. Modern sophisticated sound imaging with computer enhancement can now give detailed pictures, and make maps of areas of special interest, such as the economic exclusive zones off coastlines.

Mother ship

Extent of range

Towing cable

Mother ship

Depressor weight

Umbilical cable

Near range

HOW SONAR WORKS

Acoustic images of the ocean floor can be produced by a scanner that transmits regular sound pulses. The echoes show up on a display. The units that make up the image (pixels) cover an area the size of a pool table. Future developments may include a scatterometer to determine the character of the sediment, while fiberoptic towing cables will bring the possibility of remote videoing.

TOWED OCEAN BOTTOM INSTRUMENT (TOBI)

TOBI is a remote-controlled vehicle which is towed behind a ship in water up to 20,000 ft (6,000 m) deep. It acts as a platform for a variety of oceanographic instruments. Its sensors send data through the umbilical cable to the ship where they are stored on an optical disc. The sound pictures, called sonographs, can image by sonar an object as small as 6 ft (2 m) across.

Towing line up to 6 miles (10 km) long

Depressor weight

Signals carried back to ship

TOWING TOBI

TOBI (see below) is towed from a ship using a line and weight that allows it to remain horizontal in the sea. TOBI has a range of 2 miles (3 km) and is towed about 960 ft (300 m) above the seabed at a speed of 3 knots.

COMPUTER MODELING OCEAN CURRENTS

This model simulates ocean currents around the isolated land mass of Antarctica. The currents are strongest where the blue and red colors are closest together. Because the oceans play a major role in controlling our climate, particularly heat circulation, better maps of today's conditions can be used to predict climate change.

Antarctica

Simulated ocean currents

Currents are strongest where blue and red are close together

Submarine river valley off the west coast of the USA

River channel

SUBMARINE RIVER

This TOBI image shows a submarine river valley scoured by sediment-laden currents. The sediment would normally sit on the continental shelf, but it has been disturbed and has flowed down the shelf to the ocean floor.

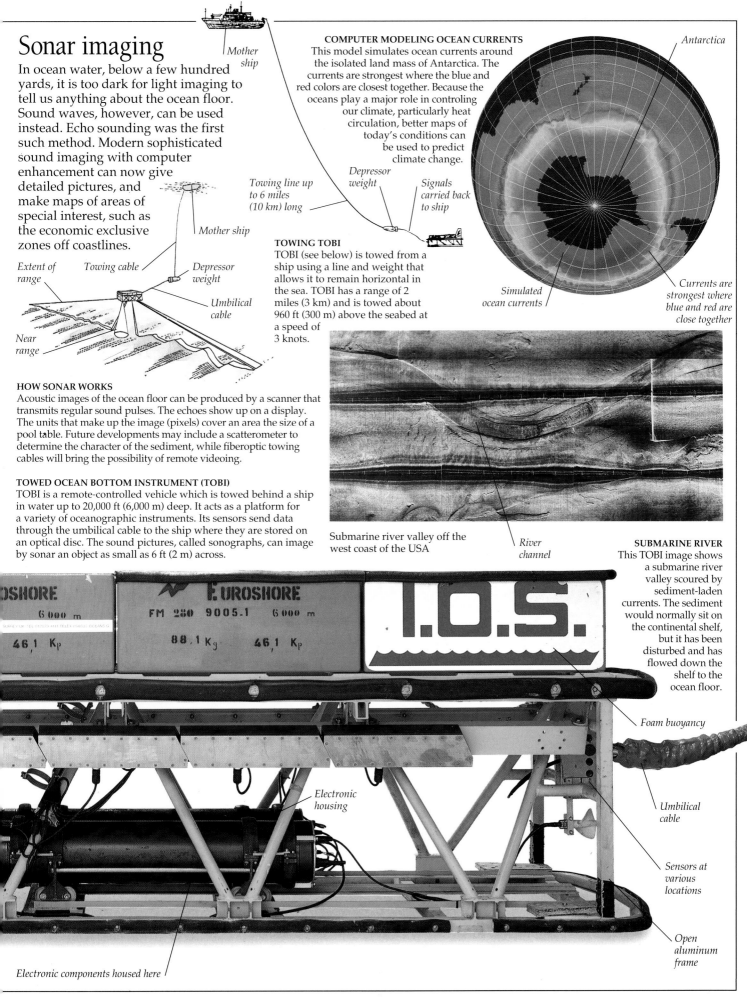

OSHORE
6 000 m
46,1 Kp

EUROSHORE
FM 280 9005.1   6 000 m
88,1 Kg   46,1 Kp

T.O.S.

Foam buoyancy

Umbilical cable

Electronic housing

Sensors at various locations

Open aluminum frame

Electronic components housed here

Continental drift

THE SHAPES AND SIZES of the continents are continually changing, but extremely slowly. The earliest maps of the south Atlantic Ocean showed a remarkable fit between the shapes of the coastlines on either side. It took time to understand what kind of mechanism could move the continents to make this happen. It is now known that the continents are moving, and the rate – only a few inches a year – can be measured. In 1915 Alfred Wegener (1880-1930) published his theory of drifting continents. This told of an ancient "supercontinent" that scientists called Pangaea. When Pangaea started to break up some 300 million years ago (abbreviated to 300 Ma), the Atlantic Ocean began to grow in the place where Africa split away from South America. Eduard Suess (p. 48) proposed that the southern continent be called Gondwanaland, after a region inhabited by a people known as the Gonds in India. Slightly later, the northern continent Laurasia was split apart to separate North America from Europe, isolating Greenland. It seems that the Earth's processes continually either split supercontinents apart or move continents together to make supercontinents, in cyclic events that take hundreds of millions of years to complete.

Atlas holding the world on his shoulders

SIR FRANCIS BACON (1561-1626)
Following the discovery of America, and the mapping of the coastlines of the Atlantic Ocean, the English philosopher Francis Bacon noticed that the coastlines of the two continents seemed to fit each other as though they had been torn apart.

MAPPING THE WORLD
In 1569 Flemish cartographer Gerhardus Mercator (1512-1594) produced a world map based on knowledge brought back by the navigators of the time. Coastlines were becoming better known from exploration of the Americas and the Pacific Ocean. The journeys of Magellan, Vasco de Gama, and Columbus had, in a short period, doubled the known area of the Earth. Mercator's map showed that the land areas are only a small part of the surface of the Earth, with the ocean regions covering three-quarters of the map. Ancient ideas about the ocean, its depth, and its surface extent were previously vague.

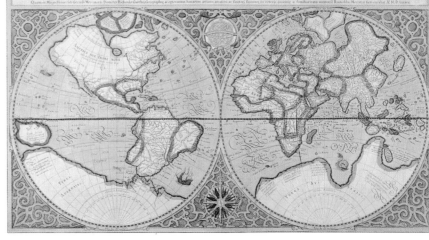

The skull of *Lystrosaurus*

LYSTROSAURUS
Fossil remains of land-living animals such as *Lystrosaurus* show that the southern continents were once linked together. The same types of fossils are found in all the southern continents; the animals must have roamed freely over lands now separated by ocean.

Namibian coastline

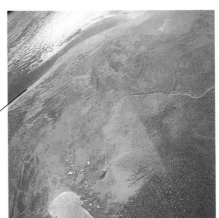

NAMIBIAN DESERT
Rocks found in Namibia in western Africa are similar to those in Brazil in South America. They were formed long before the breakup of the southern continent Gondwanaland.

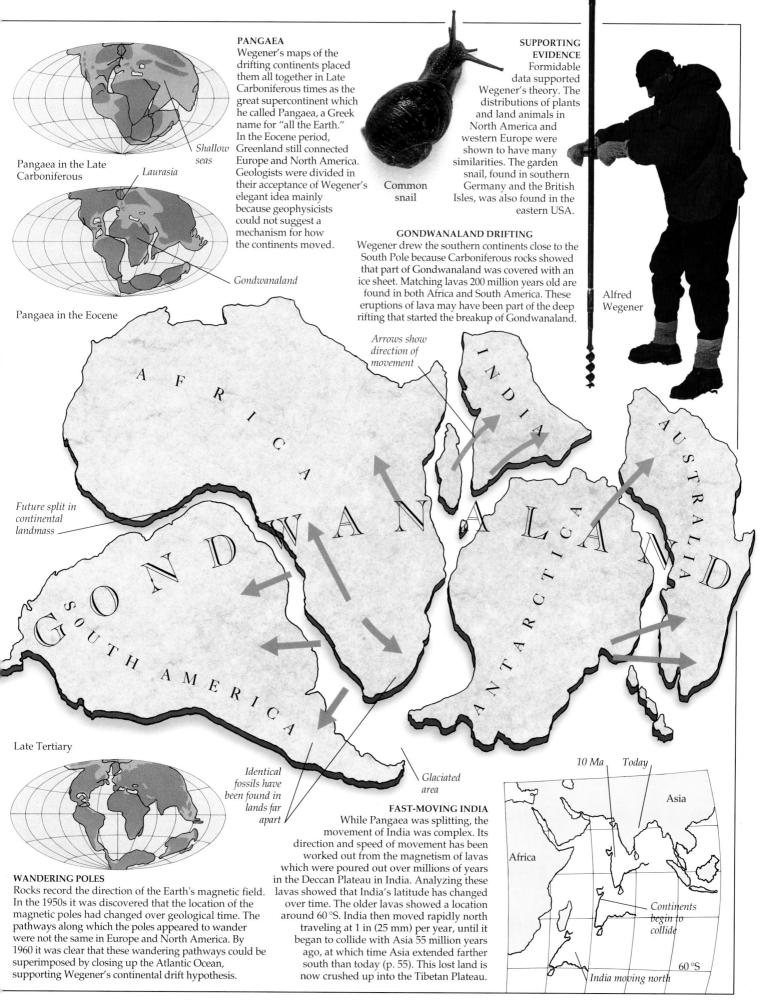

PANGAEA
Wegener's maps of the drifting continents placed them all together in Late Carboniferous times as the great supercontinent which he called Pangaea, a Greek name for "all the Earth." In the Eocene period, Greenland still connected Europe and North America. Geologists were divided in their acceptance of Wegener's elegant idea mainly because geophysicists could not suggest a mechanism for how the continents moved.

Pangaea in the Late Carboniferous

Shallow seas

Laurasia

Gondwanaland

Pangaea in the Eocene

Common snail

SUPPORTING EVIDENCE
Formidable data supported Wegener's theory. The distributions of plants and land animals in North America and western Europe were shown to have many similarities. The garden snail, found in southern Germany and the British Isles, was also found in the eastern USA.

GONDWANALAND DRIFTING
Wegener drew the southern continents close to the South Pole because Carboniferous rocks showed that part of Gondwanaland was covered with an ice sheet. Matching lavas 200 million years old are found in both Africa and South America. These eruptions of lava may have been part of the deep rifting that started the breakup of Gondwanaland.

Alfred Wegener

Arrows show direction of movement

AFRICA

INDIA

AUSTRALIA

Future split in continental landmass

GONDWANALAND

SOUTH AMERICA

ANTARCTICA

Late Tertiary

Identical fossils have been found in lands far apart

Glaciated area

FAST-MOVING INDIA
While Pangaea was splitting, the movement of India was complex. Its direction and speed of movement has been worked out from the magnetism of lavas which were poured out over millions of years in the Deccan Plateau in India. Analyzing these lavas showed that India's latitude has changed over time. The older lavas showed a location around 60 °S. India then moved rapidly north traveling at 1 in (25 mm) per year, until it began to collide with Asia 55 million years ago, at which time Asia extended farther south than today (p. 55). This lost land is now crushed up into the Tibetan Plateau.

WANDERING POLES
Rocks record the direction of the Earth's magnetic field. In the 1950s it was discovered that the location of the magnetic poles had changed over geological time. The pathways along which the poles appeared to wander were not the same in Europe and North America. By 1960 it was clear that these wandering pathways could be superimposed by closing up the Atlantic Ocean, supporting Wegener's continental drift hypothesis.

10 Ma   Today

Asia

Africa

Continents begin to collide

60 °S

India moving north

Plate tectonics

FORTY YEARS AFTER ALFRED WEGENER put forward his controversial continental drift theory, technological advances revealed a great deal of information about the ocean floor. The discovery of magnetic stripes by two British research scientists F. Vine and D. Matthews in 1963 suggested that the ocean floor is made of younger rock than exists on the continents. This led to the all-embracing theory of plate tectonics, which divides the world into plates, made up of parts of continent and parts of ocean. For example, the South American plate includes half the south Atlantic Ocean, as well as the continental mass of South America. New plate is being made all the time at spreading ridges (the submarine mountains found by *Challenger*, p. 36) in the oceans, and old oceanic plate material is being recycled in subduction zones. In the process of subduction (p. 49), some oceanic sediments and even whole islands are plastered on to the continents. Plate tectonics also helps to explain the coincidence between lines of volcanoes, deep ocean trenches, and the location of earthquakes.

Global relief image of the topography of the South Pole and the Pacific, Indian and Antarctic Oceans

AN ALTERNATIVE THEORY
In 1931 British geologist Arthur Holmes (1890-1965) suggested a mechanism that might allow landmasses to move. This theory proposed that the continents moved because of frictional drag from convection currents rising in the mantle. He had no observations at this time to support his theory. Holmes was also a pioneer of radiometric dating (pp. 66-67).

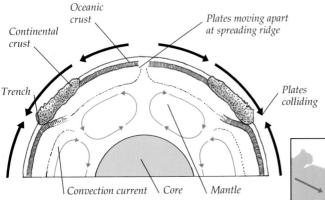

Continental crust

Oceanic crust

Plates moving apart at spreading ridge

Trench

Plates colliding

Convection current \ *Core* \ *Mantle*

PLATE TECTONIC MAP OF THE WORLD
Plate boundaries (or margins) divide up the surface of the Earth. Some pass very close to the junctions between continents and oceans, but the great majority bear no relationship to the edges of the continents. The Australian plate contains Australia and a large part of the Indian Ocean, besides other surrounding oceans. Today, all oceanic crust is less than 200 million years old. It has solidified from magma over this time at the spreading ridges. Any older oceanic crust has been consumed in subduction zones (p. 49). By contrast, the continents are very old.

THE MOVING PLATES
There is still controversy about what moves the plates over the surface of the Earth. Possibly, convection currents in the mantle help to drag them. Heat rises and convection occurs as heat is lost from the core to the mantle. The currents move very slowly, and carry the plates along. As cooled mantle descends, it is replaced by new hot mantle. Scientists believe that the mantle is unresponsive to short-term events, like the sudden shock of earthquake waves passing through, but in response to long-term stress, applied over tens of millions of years, it can move by slow flow. The mantle slowly evolves as it convects, giving up some of its substance to magmas, which make up new edges of plate.

KEY TO MAP

Destructive plate boundary

Constructive plate boundary

Uncertain plate boundary

Direction of plate movement

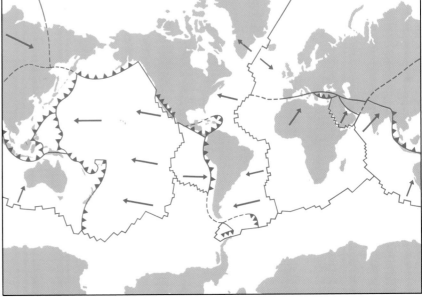

HOT SPOT VOLCANO

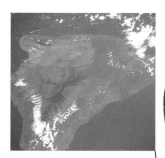

Hawaii, with some of the most active volcanoes in the world, is not at a plate boundary. There are dozens of volcanic areas, not near plate margins, where mantle-generated magma erupts through the thickness of the plate. These are hot spots.

Global relief map of North and South America

SAN ANDREAS REGION

At some plate boundaries, the plates slide past one another, in opposing directions or in the same direction at different speeds. There is no mechanism to produce magma, so there are no volcanoes. This is a boundary where plate is neither made nor destroyed.

ICELAND

At constructive plate boundaries, new oceanic plate is being made as magma emerges from the mantle. It fills a widening rift left as the plates move apart. Iceland is made of oceanic crust material even though it is above sea level (pp. 44-45).

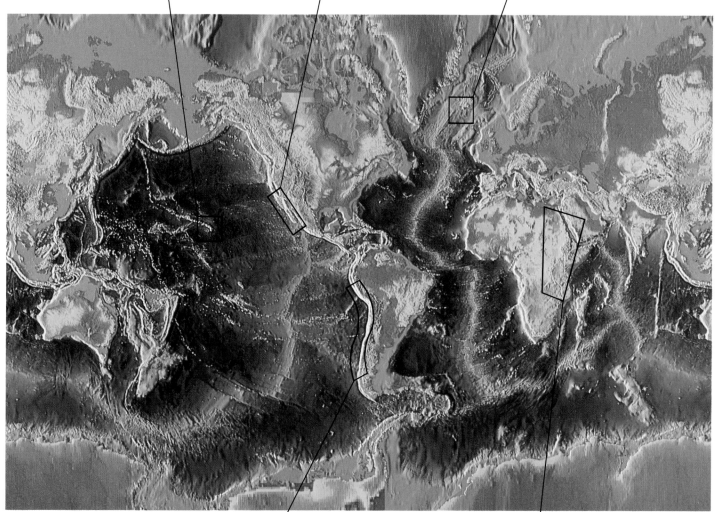

ANDES IN CHILE

Volcanoes, deep ocean trenches, and earthquakes occur at the destructive plate margins called subduction zones. Here, oceanic plate is consumed or destroyed as it goes down into the mantle and is overridden by the neighboring plate.

AFRICAN RIFT VALLEY

Continents begin to split apart along rift valleys. In Africa, a branching rift extends southward from the Red Sea. This area was uplifted some 20 million years ago, and lava erupted. There are still many active volcanoes in this rift valley.

Map of mid-Atlantic Ridge

The formation of the ocean floor

HARRY HESS (1906-1969)
An American geologist, Hess worked in submarines during World War II where he was mapping the topography of the ocean floor. He found that the heat flowing from the ocean floor was much greater than expected. In 1960 he suggested that the ocean floor was young, because of the hot mantle rock continually rising and crystallizing at the ridges. He argued that the ocean floor was moving away from the ridges and was being consumed back into the mantle at the ocean trenches surrounding the Pacific Ocean.

THE SURVEY SHIP *Challenger* discovered that most of the ocean floor lies around 3 miles (5 km) below the level of the sea. This deep ocean floor is all made of relatively young rocks, none older than 200 million years. There was ocean floor in earlier times, but all of that old rock has disappeared, subducted into the Earth's interior at destructive plate boundaries. New ocean floor is being made all the time by sea floor spreading, which takes place at mid-ocean ridges. Here, magma rises from the mantle and fills the crack left as the ocean floor pulls apart. The uppermost layer of the volcanic ocean floor is basalt lava. Beneath this is a layer with vertical structures, and below this a third layer made of coarse-textured gabbro. The Earth's magnetic field reverses its direction from time to time. These reversals are recorded in the new ocean-floor rocks as they crystallize.

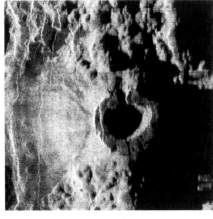

OCEAN-FLOOR VOLCANO
This sonar image shows a volcano on the Mid-Atlantic Ridge. Some ocean-floor volcanoes are active and produce enough lava to make islands. Others, like this one, are well below sea level. A third extinct type have flat tops, and are called guyots. Their tops were once at sea level, where the waves planed them flat. The ocean floor moved away from its spreading ridge, cooling and contracting as it moved, carrying the guyot into deeper water.

BLACK SMOKERS
Hot springs at the spreading ridges emit water heated by the underlying magma. This water is seawater that has seeped into the new hot ocean floor as it cracks during cooling. The water gets hotter as it circulates through the hot rock, enabling it to dissolve more and more minerals from the rock it travels through. When the water is boiled out at the rift in the spreading ridge, it is full of metal sulfides in solution. As these come into contact with cold seawater, they come out of solution as black particles that build up into a smoker, a chimneylike structure that supports specially adapted animals (p. 16).

Kayangel Atoll
in the Pacific Ocean

Manganese nodule

CORAL ATOLLS
Coral atolls are ring-shaped islands constructed by reef-building corals. Charles Darwin (1809-1882) showed them to be reefs around the fringes of extinct volcanic islands that had sunk below wave level. Many of these sunken islands turned out to be guyots – flat-topped mountains in the deep ocean. Harry Hess investigated why some guyots had no coral fringe. Hess realized that they sank beneath the depth of wave erosion as they were transported away from the hot, high ridges, and some had sunk too fast for coral building to keep pace.

MINING THE OCEAN FLOOR
The deep ocean floor is littered with rounded nodules that contain the metal manganese. They are especially common where sediment collects only slowly. They grow gradually by adding another skin of metal around the outside and may join together as here. Measurements of the ages of the rings from radiometric dating (p. 67) show that nodules grow extremely slowly. Their origin is in debate, but the metal content suggests maybe there is a connection with the metal sulfides of black smokers (above).

Mapping the ocean

Following the invention of echo-sounding techniques a ship can chart the water depth as it travels. More sophisticated depth recording in the 1950s mapped the ocean floor and showed the diversity of the topography for the first time. The soundings revealed volcanoes, rivers, trenches and spreading ridges – the longest continuous mountain chain on the Earth, stretching 40,400 miles (65,000 km).

ABOVE SEA LEVEL IN ICELAND
The amount of magma coming from the mantle under Iceland is so great that a huge thickness of lava has built up the Icelandic land mass. Here, the ridge is above sea level. The central feature of the ridge in Iceland is a rift valley where volcanic activity is greatest.

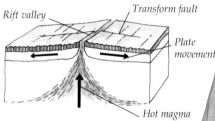

Rift valley   *Transform fault*

Plate movement

Hot magma

HOW OCEAN FLOOR FORMS
Hot magma wells up under a crack – a rift valley – in the ocean. Some of the magma wells right up to the sea bed and crystallizes as basalt lava. Some solidifies in the rift valley itself, making a vertical wall parallel to the length of the rift valley. Some solidifies more slowly below.

Normal polarization

N

Reverse polarization

N

N

Normal polarization

Reverse polarization

MAGNETIC STRIPES
Basalt lava contains minerals that align themselves in the direction of the Earth's magnetic field as they crystallize. The Earth's field reverses its direction from time to time, and the lavas preserve the direction of the field for the time when they crystallized. Over a long period, a whole series of stripes recording normal and reversed polarity events makes up the ocean floor.

The Mid-Atlantic Ridge is above sea level in Iceland

THE MID-ATLANTIC RIDGE
This model of a section of the Mid-Atlantic Ridge was made from sonar images that map the ocean floor precisely. A series of parallel ridges develop as the rift valley cracks and widens, each length of rift wall slumping into the rift. In the center, the rift is shown at its deepest. The red represents hot lava welling up from the underlying mantle. Individual sections of the central rift are offset sideways by transform faults. These transform, or move, the ridge from one place to another.

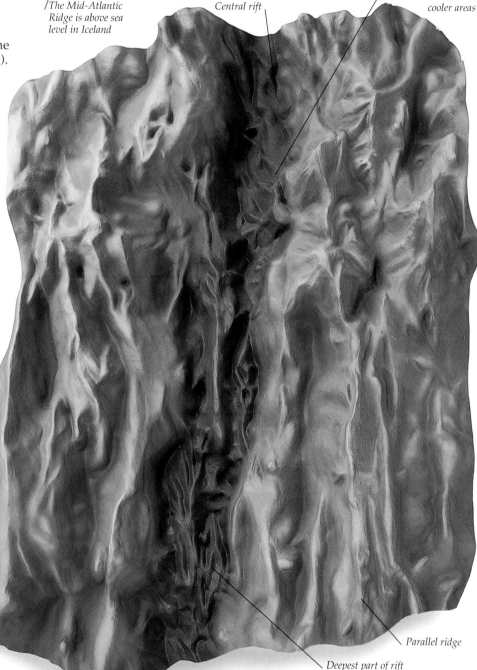

Central rift

Black smokers occur in cooler areas

Parallel ridge

Deepest part of rift

Parallel ridge

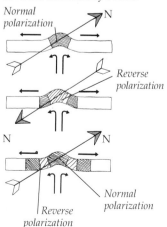

Antarctica

PLOTTING PLATE MOVEMENTS
This satellite image shows the topography, or shapes and structures, over a vast area of the ocean floor between Antarctica and South America. The conspicuous parallel ridges are old parts of the spreading ridge that surrounds the continent of Antarctica. Geologists use these shapes to work out the age and past movements of the plates.

Exploring the interior

THE EARTH'S INTERIOR may remain inaccessible forever, but indirect methods have revealed that it has a layered structure with an inner and outer core, surrounded by a mantle, and a crust around the outside. In 1910, a Croatian scientist, Andrija Mohorovicic (1857-1936) concluded after studying transmission of waves from a local earthquake that there was a boundary about 21 miles (35 km) down. This is now called the Mohorovicic Discontinuity after him – shortened to Moho – and it marks the base of the crust. There are

Subterranean world as imagined in 1665

clues to the nature of the mantle and outer core. Volcanic eruptions bring some samples of mantle silicates to the surface, and the chemistry of the mantle can be guessed at from the chemistry of basalt lavas, which originate by partial melting of the mantle. Other indicators include earthquake waves, which travel at variable speeds through the interior of the Earth, depending on the density of the materials they pass through. Some kinds of waves are cut off altogether in the outer core, indicating that it is liquid as far as wave transmission is concerned, in spite of huge pressure there. By looking at the changes in the orbits of the planets and their moons as well as those of space satellites, it has been shown that the Earth's greatest mass is concentrated in the core.

HEAT FROM BELOW
Temperature increases with depth inside the Earth's crust. Miners have known this for many centuries. In the deepest modern gold mines in South Africa, the geothermal heat is so intense that the mines must be cooled in order to permit any human activity at all. Hot springs, which erupt violently as geysers, are proof that magma chambers also may lie at shallow depths.

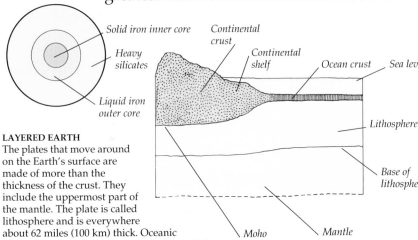

Solid iron inner core

Heavy silicates

Liquid iron outer core

Continental crust

Continental shelf

Ocean crust

Sea level

Lithosphere

Base of lithosphere

Moho

Mantle

LAYERED EARTH
The plates that move around on the Earth's surface are made of more than the thickness of the crust. They include the uppermost part of the mantle. The plate is called lithosphere and is everywhere about 62 miles (100 km) thick. Oceanic lithosphere has oceanic crust at the top, which is only about 3 miles (5 km) thick. Continental lithosphere has continental crust above, which is 21 miles (35 km) thick on average.

Red garnet

GARNET PERIDOTITE
Garnet peridotite, which has approximately the same density as the mantle, is found at the Earth's surface. Volcanic diamond-bearing rocks called kimberlite contain garnet peridotite. To make diamond, high pressure is needed, equivalent to a depth of around 93 miles (150 km) inside the Earth, so maybe the garnet peridotite fragments in the kimberlite are portions of the mantle from the same great depth.

Trucks send out vibrations

USING SEISMIC WAVES
Earthquake waves travel through the Earth, and their travel times can give information about the structure of the material they pass through. Vibrations can also be produced artificially to investigate inaccessible rocks at shallow depths. These special trucks give out a restricted range of vibrations. These are picked up by listening devices called geophones situated various distances away.

Eclogite

Eclogite is found deep in the crust

Granite

Eclogite on scales

Weight in grams

1 WEIGH THE ROCK
The sample of eclogite is first weighed.

2 MEASURE VOLUME
To determine the volume of a rock for density calculation, a Eureka jar is filled with water up to the point where water flows out of the spout. The rock is then put gently inside. The volume of water displaced through the spout is equivalent to the volume of the rock in cubic centimeters.

DENSE ROCKS
We cannot look at or touch the Earth's mantle directly, but some surface rocks have the same density, so maybe they have come from the mantle. The density of a rock gives a guide to what it might be made of. Crustal rocks from the continents on average have a density like that of granite, around 2.8. Mantle rocks are much denser at 3.3. To find the density of a rock, the mass of the rock is compared to an equal volume of water.

Eclogite inside Eureka jar

Displaced water pours out into beaker

Lake Bonneville, Salt Lake City, Utah

BALANCING ACT
The thick, heavy ice sheets of the Pleistocene Ice Age depressed the surface rock layers of the crust beneath, and some of the mantle flowed out of the way. When the ice melted, the crust was unloaded and the mantle slowly flowed back to compensate for the loss of mass. The mantle flowed more slowly than the ice was melting, so Scandinavia is still rising today. This effect of the natural balancing between material of higher and lower density is called isostasy.

FLOATING CITY
Isostasy acts slowly, because the mantle flows slowly. Isostatic readjustment can be seen at the salt flats of Lake Bonneville, where Salt Lake City is built. The salt flats were once occupied by a vast, deep lake, which has been considerably reduced. The area is still rising in isostatic adjustment to the removal of the weight of the water.

The weight causes the wood to float low in the water

The crust is depressed by the ice sheet like the wood with a weight on top

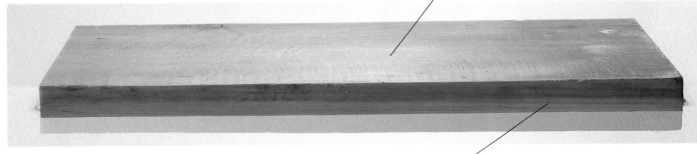

The weight is removed

The wood floats low in the water

The continents float on the mantle like the wood on the water

The wood pops up

Earthquakes and seismology

MOST LARGE EARTHQUAKES HAPPEN at plate boundaries, though a significant number originate in the middle of continental plates. The majority of earthquakes go unnoticed by humans. In the buildup to an earthquake, stress accumulates in a volume of rock. The stress comes about because of the movement of the plates, whether slipping past one another or one plate subducting under the continental crust. At the point and time where stress exceeds the strength of the rock, fracture takes place. The fracture travels out through the region of stressed rock, and energy is released in all directions as seismic waves. Seismographs to measure earthquake shaking are highly sensitive devices, capable of recording earthquake waves from the far side of the globe. The traces recorded on seismographs can be read by seismologists to determine the location of a distant earthquake (its epicenter) and how energetic it was (its Richter magnitude). Intensity, based on the Mercalli scale, is compiled from eyewitness reports and from estimates of the response of buildings.

JAPANESE INSTABILITY
Japan lies over a destructive plate boundary and consequently has many volcanic eruptions and great earthquakes. The land is rapidly being uplifted, making mountains, which themselves are rapidly eroding. Japanese people live with continual upheaval and change of their landscapes.

EDUARD SUESS (1831-1914)
An Austrian geologist, Suess theorized about mountain ranges and their relationships to each other. He did not believe that the Earth had evolved through a series of catastrophes. He saw the continents as stable regions, making exception for the seismic zones where earthquakes occur.

Clock mechanism stops when shaking starts

RECORDING EARTHQUAKES
Early seismographs included a device for picking up the shaking. In addition, it was necessary to keep a written record of the shaking as well as to note the moment of arrival of the first tremor and the duration of shaking. The principle of a seismograph is that the recording part moves with the Earth, but a massive part of the apparatus remains stationary. In early equipment, the heavy, huge mass sometimes weighed many tons. Modern apparatus is small and inconspicuous and uses electronic circuitry.

Tickertape shows reading

GROUND CRACKS
Many people imagine that in an earthquake the ground cracks open and people or animals are swallowed up. This is rare. Sometimes there is cracked ground, and sometimes ground may liquefy during shaking, especially where the underlying rocks are loosely packed sediments and are saturated with water. During liquefaction, heavy buildings may sink into the ground, or buried objects, such as pipelines and even coffins, may rise to the surface. Landslides and avalanches may occur on steep slopes.

The recording apparatus of a seismograph, developed to record earthquakes near Vesuvius in Italy

PRIMARY AND SHEAR WAVES

Earthquake waves travel outward in all directions. Some penetrate into the Earth, and their speed increases as they meet ever denser rocks so that they travel in curved pathways, and are refracted back to the Earth's surface. Those that penetrate to the core are slowed down as they pass into the liquid outer core. Of these, the S waves, which transmit by shearing the rocks they pass through, cannot travel through liquids and are cut off. The primary waves (P waves) have a simpler motion, so they travel faster and are the first to be recorded by a seismograph.

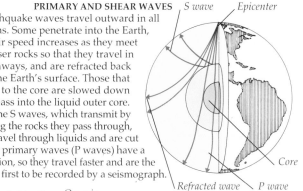

S wave   *Epicenter*

Core

Refracted wave   *P wave*

San Andreas fault

The San Andreas plate boundary is a complex of faults about 62 miles (100 km) wide. Here the Pacific plate is moving northwest in relation to the landmass of continental North America, so that the relative motion along the boundary is sideways. At these plate boundaries, or margins, plate is neither being made, nor consumed.

North America

The San Andreas fault on the west coast of the USA

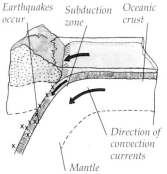

Earthquakes occur   *Subduction zone*   *Oceanic crust*

Direction of convection currents

Mantle

SUBDUCTION ZONES

Earthquakes are concentrated in sloping zones that underlie mountain ranges and island arcs. Plate tectonics explains that these happen where the oceanic crust is carried down (subducted) into the mantle. The greatest depth at which earthquakes originate is 435 miles (700 km). It is assumed that below this depth, the cold descending lithosphere slab has been heated so much in the mantle that it is no longer brittle enough to fracture.

River has been moved sideways by fault

Fault line   *Highway*

FAMOUS FAULT LINE

Earthquake shaking is less intense the farther away it is from the focus, the point where the earthquake originates below the epicentre. Deep earthquakes generally cause less shaking at the Earth's surface above. All the earthquakes on the San Andreas fault are shallow – they originate less than 15 miles (24 km) down.

Transcurrent fault where plates slip past one another

Moving plate   *Sea*   *Land mass*

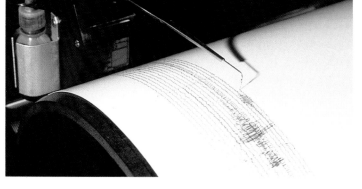

RECORDING EARTHQUAKES

A seismometer records the movement of the ground at strategic points. These readings may be transmitted by radio or telephone line to a recording station. Here a paper record shows one component of the ground motion.

PULLING THE EARTH APART

Some faults occur because rock is under tension. This model (below) shows how faults develop in a series of layered sedimentary rocks. As the layers are stretched, there comes a time when the strength of the rock is no longer able to hold the rock together.

TRANSCURRENT FAULT

Faults that move predominantly sideways are called transcurrent faults. Along some sections of the fault line, movement is almost continuous. In other places, it appears locked, and stress builds up, leading to a large earthquake.

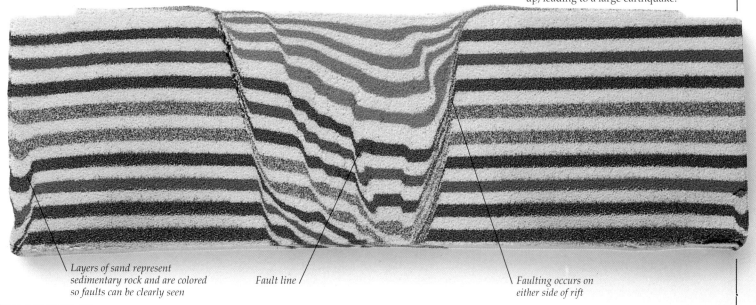

Layers of sand represent sedimentary rock and are colored so faults can be clearly seen

Fault line

Faulting occurs on either side of rift

Volcanology

THE NAME VOLCANO vent applies to the hole in the ground where lava comes out. The mountain built by the eruption of lava from the vent is called a volcanic mountain. Lava erupting from a volcano is a hot silicate liquid containing gas. Its viscosity varies enormously. Some lava is very fluid and flows freely. Other lavas are so viscous that the lava barely flows at all, and instead heaps up around the hole in the ground and builds a dome. If there is a long time interval between eruptions – say hundreds or even thousands of years – the entire top of the volcano may be blown to dust in a major explosion. The formulation of the plate tectonics theory helped to explain the mystery of why volcanoes are not dotted randomly around the globe. Many are to be found around the shores of the Pacific Ocean and in a belt through the Mediterranean to Indonesia. Some volcanoes are at subduction zones (p. 49) where ocean floor moves down into the mantle and is partly melted, making magma. Others occur at the spreading ridges where they make new ocean floor. Other locations are in rift valleys where continents first began to split apart.

Icelandic

Hawaiian

Strombolian

Vulcanian

Pelean

Plinian

THE GRACEFUL MONSTER
Mount Vesuvius in Italy erupted in AD 79. Before the eruption the sides of the volcano were lushly covered in vines. Roman cities on its slopes were engulfed by hot ash. The less-devastating 1872 eruption is shown here.

Long handle allows the volcanologist to stand at a safe distance

The twisted metal hook picks up lava from the flow

COLLECTING LAVA
Many changes take place in lava as it cools and solidifies. Volcanologists (scientists who study volcanoes) watch events during an eruption and collect samples. Sampling helps to understand magma formation and to predict how far flows of lava will travel, and how quickly. This metal rod is used for collecting hot lava.

Twisted shape

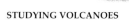

CLASSIFYING ERUPTIONS
Eruptions are described according to the explosiveness of their activity. This ranges from the mildest outpourings of syrupy lava, to vigorous eruptions where magma gases escape in intermittent explosions, or in clouds of hot ash.

STUDYING VOLCANOES
Geologists sometimes risk their lives to observe erupting volcanoes. To get close in to the action, special heat-resistant clothing must be worn. While this protects from heat, gas, and falling lava blobs, it also hinders the volcanologist's freedom of movement. To describe an eruption a volcanologist uses the classifications of eruption type (above right), which are internationally understood. This photograph shows a volcanologist in front of fire fountaining in a Hawaiian-type eruption,

Rough, vesicular surface

Lava bomb

LAVA BOMB
Fragments of lava that are thrown out in fire fountains are still molten as they fly through the air. They cool as they fall, taking on a shape molded by their flight.

Hawaiian volcanoes

The Hawaiian islands are the tops of a chain of volcanic islands situated over a hot spot in the mantle that has been producing magma for the last 6 million years. The site of volcanic activity at the surface appears to have moved, but actually the hot spot in the mantle stays still; it is the Pacific plate that moves, carrying each volcano northwestward.

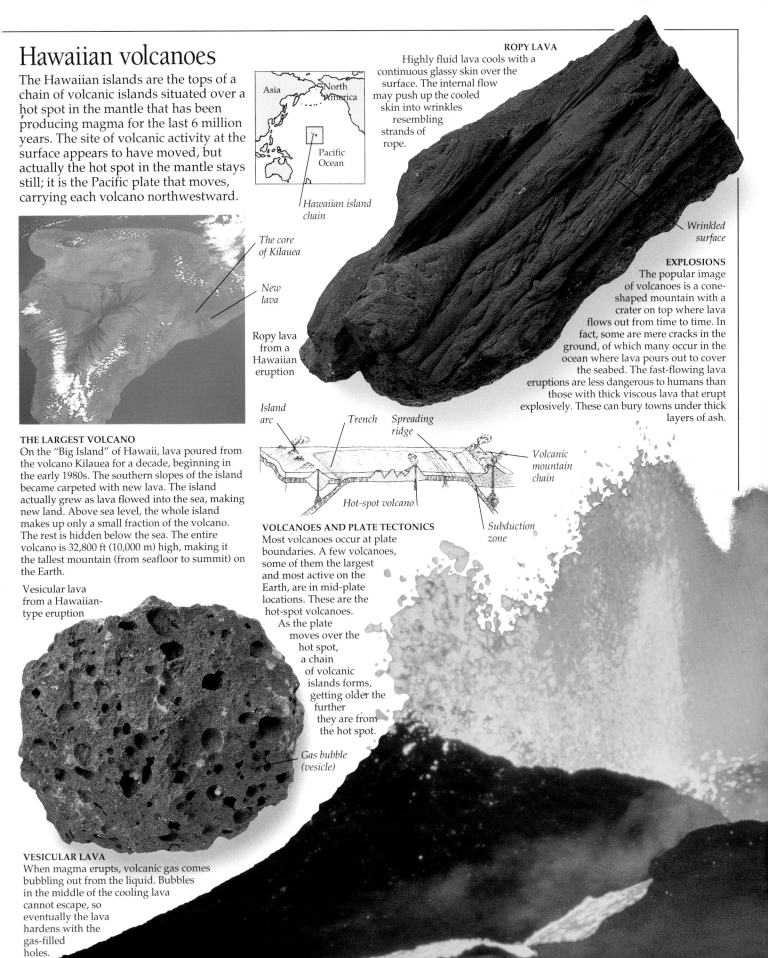

Asia

North America

Pacific Ocean

Hawaiian island chain

The core of Kilauea

New lava

Ropy lava from a Hawaiian eruption

ROPY LAVA
Highly fluid lava cools with a continuous glassy skin over the surface. The internal flow may push up the cooled skin into wrinkles resembling strands of rope.

Wrinkled surface

EXPLOSIONS
The popular image of volcanoes is a cone-shaped mountain with a crater on top where lava flows out from time to time. In fact, some are mere cracks in the ground, of which many occur in the ocean where lava pours out to cover the seabed. The fast-flowing lava eruptions are less dangerous to humans than those with thick viscous lava that erupt explosively. These can bury towns under thick layers of ash.

THE LARGEST VOLCANO
On the "Big Island" of Hawaii, lava poured from the volcano Kilauea for a decade, beginning in the early 1980s. The southern slopes of the island became carpeted with new lava. The island actually grew as lava flowed into the sea, making new land. Above sea level, the whole island makes up only a small fraction of the volcano. The rest is hidden below the sea. The entire volcano is 32,800 ft (10,000 m) high, making it the tallest mountain (from seafloor to summit) on the Earth.

Vesicular lava from a Hawaiian-type eruption

Island arc *Trench* *Spreading ridge* *Volcanic mountain chain*

Hot-spot volcano *Subduction zone*

VOLCANOES AND PLATE TECTONICS
Most volcanoes occur at plate boundaries. A few volcanoes, some of them the largest and most active on the Earth, are in mid-plate locations. These are the hot-spot volcanoes. As the plate moves over the hot spot, a chain of volcanic islands forms, getting older the further they are from the hot spot.

Gas bubble (vesicle)

VESICULAR LAVA
When magma erupts, volcanic gas comes bubbling out from the liquid. Bubbles in the middle of the cooling lava cannot escape, so eventually the lava hardens with the gas-filled holes.

Mountain building

GEOLOGISTS ONCE THOUGHT that the folded structures in mountain ranges showed that the Earth was shrinking, and they likened mountain ranges to wrinkles on a shriveling apple. It is now known that mountain ranges are made up of rocks that have been stacked up and deformed into complicated structures, and that the Earth is not shrinking because new crust is being made in the oceans all the time. Usually there is more than one generation of deformation in the making of a mountain range, so that folds become refolded. Broad common features of mountain ranges are that the foothill rocks are recognizably sedimentary (pp. 32-33), while the middle of the ranges have more complicated rocks and structures – these rocks may be intensely deformed and recrystallized. Young mountain ranges at active plate boundaries may have volcanoes sitting on top of all the deformed structures. There is certainly a great deal of crushing and shortening of the crust in mountain building. However, deformation and uplift in themselves do not create the jagged peaks that are recognizably mountains. Erosion of many miles thickness of rock from the top of the rising landmass exposes the deep core of the mountain range. The entire process that makes mountain ranges is called orogenesis.

CROSSING THE ALPS
The Swiss physicist and explorer Horace Benedict de Saussure (1740-1799) crossed the Alps 17 times in different places to try to understand how mountain ranges are created. In the end, he decided that mountains are a hopeless jumble and that to understand their structures is beyond possibility.

Upper parts of fold have been eroded

Sediment layers used to be horizontal

THE ROCKY MOUNTAINS
In the late 19th century it was assumed that some of the crustal shortening of mountain ranges was brought about by one set of rocks being pushed over another set. This is called thrust faulting. It involves large-scale near-horizontal movements of the upper crustal layers. This seemed a far-fetched idea, but it turned out to be right. The structures in the Rocky Mountains involve multiple thrust faulting, one mass on top of another. It is hard to imagine how these great movements could be accomplished in material as hard and brittle as rock. The upper section of rocks that is pushed in thrust faulting is called a thrust sheet.

The Rocky Mountains on the west coast of North America

FOLD MOUNTAINS
Mountains show layers of sediments that have been folded into complex shapes. These vertical strata in southern England were folded at the same time that the Alps were formed a long way to the south.

Simple deformation of sedimentary rock

Foothills

MODELING MOUNTAINS

It is hard to understand how the complicated structures that geologists map in the field have come into being. Simplified models of mountain ranges forming from continental collisions can be made in a laboratory. A machine spreads colored sand in a tank. A paper sheet is rolled slowly underneath the sand, reducing the length of the layers to imitate subduction.

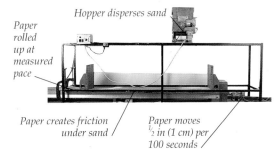

Hopper disperses sand

Paper rolled up at measured pace

Paper creates friction under sand

Paper moves ½ in (1 cm) per 100 seconds

The Andes

There are many signs of continuing uplift and other tectonic activity in the Andes. Many of the world's largest earthquakes originate here. Young marine sediments are found high above sea level, showing that uplift has been rapid. The Andes are distinctive for the large number of active volcanoes that make up many of the highest peaks. These are built above the mountain range itself. The volcanoes have produced great level spreads of ash, making up the elevated plateau of the altiplano.

South America

The Andes mountains

Sediments are laid down

First folds

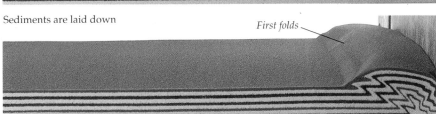

Z-shaped folds develop as the paper is moved at a steady rate

Second Z folds

MOUNTAINS IN CHILE

The jagged nature of mountains comes about from erosion of land that has been raised by thrust faulting and deformation in orogenesis.

Mountain range

Continental crust

Sea

Sediments scraped from ocean floor

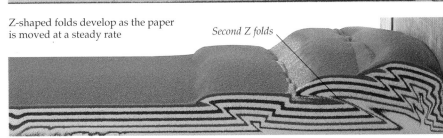

New folds begin to form; the first set are more intensely deformed

DESTRUCTIVE PLATE BOUNDARIES

The destructive plate movement in the Andes occurs when oceanic crust subducts beneath the continental crust. Sediments from the ocean floor are scraped off and added to the continent.

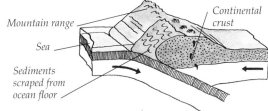

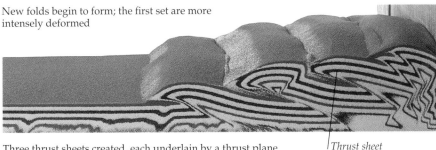

Three thrust sheets created, each underlain by a thrust plane

Thrust sheet

FINAL STAGE

A series of thrusts has placed one nappe on top of another. This model only represents part of what happens in nature. In reality, uplifting, folding, and thrust faulting are accompanied by erosion, intrusions, and volcanoes.

Thrust sheet

Thrust plane

Plateaus and rifts

A TOTALLY NEW PLATE BOUNDARY appears when a continent starts to rift apart. This happened 200 million years ago, when the Atlantic Ocean first began to grow (pp. 44-45). Today, the continent of Africa is splitting apart along the African Rift Valley to make a new plate boundary. Not all rift valleys become oceans. Some remain as rifts to fill up with thick layers of igneous rocks and sediments. Some plateaus form when continents collide with each other. This happens when there is no more oceanic crust between them to be subducted. The rock of continental crust is less dense than ocean crust, and resists being subducted. So if the edges of continents collide, there is major crushing instead of one plate slipping under the other, and this forms a high plateau like the Tibetan Plateau. Other plateaus come about by gentle raising of a whole region.

AUSTRIAN CANYON
A canyon is a deep valley with vertical sides that has been worn away and eroded by river water. The Austrian Alps show many such slotlike canyons in limestone.

JOHN WESLEY POWELL (1834-1902)
Powell was an American who explored the Grand Canyon in 1869. He had lost his right arm in the Civil War, but he managed to climb the canyon walls in places and helped navigate his boats through the fast-flowing waterways.

RIFTING MODEL
The laboratory model below demonstrates the results of rifting. The layers show the fractures that cause rift valleys, sometimes with several more or less parallel faults, each of which allows the rift area to drop further down. The rift section is sometimes known as a graben. In between the dropped blocks are regions that have stayed high. These are called horsts.

THE GRAND CANYON
The great thickness of sediments that make up the Colorado Plateau have been lifted 9,840 ft (3,000 m) over the last 60 million years. Powell's team realized that the Grand Canyon showed no signs of glaciation. The only explanation was that the river had eroded out the huge canyon, cutting first through the softer sediments and – at the bottom of today's canyon – through metamorphic rocks and granites.

Red and white sand shows the sedimentary layers formed at the same time as rifting

Horst

Graben

African Rift Valley

Running through eastern Africa from Mozambique to the Red Sea is a great rifted valley that branches into two parts. Here Africa is splitting apart along faults, where the continental lithosphere (p. 46) has broken right through. Young, active volcanoes and many earthquakes show that the rift is active. At the north, where the Rift Valley joins the Red Sea at the Danakil Depression, the floor of the rift is below sea level and made of oceanic crust, but it is still land. Farther south, none of the rock in the African section has oceanic crust. Some time in the future, a new ocean may separate eastern Africa from the rest of the continent.

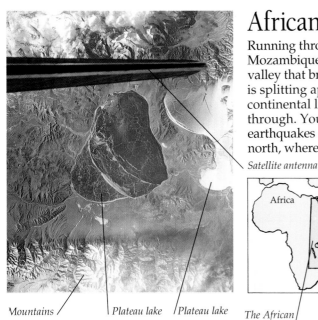

Mountains | Plateau lake | Plateau lake

THE TIBETAN PLATEAU
The highest, level region on Earth is the Tibetan Plateau at 14,760 ft (4,500 m) above sea level. It is surrounded by young mountains to which its origins are linked. Other plateaus, like some in Africa, are not close to young mountain ranges; they seem to have formed from simple uplift.

Satellite antenna

Africa

The African Rift valley

Danakil Depression | Mediterranean Sea

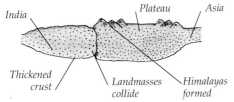

India | Plateau | Asia

Thickened crust | Landmasses collide | Himalayas formed

CRUNCHING LANDMASSES
During the last 10 million years, India has moved northwards into Asia after the total subduction of the Tethys Ocean basin that lay between the two landmasses. As they collided, Asia became compressed, deformed, and fractured, creating the Himalaya mountains. The interior began to compress, making the Tibetan Plateau.

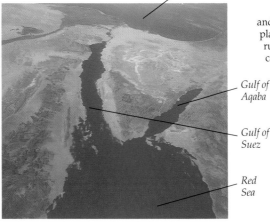

Satellite view of the Gulfs of Suez and Aqaba and the Red Sea

Gulf of Aqaba

Gulf of Suez

Red Sea

KENYAN RIFT SECTION
Rift valleys have volcanoes within the rift, and usually great spreads of basalt lava on the plateaulike areas on either side. The faultlines running along the Great Rift Valley in Kenya can be clearly seen in this aerial photograph.

A MINIATURE OCEAN
Gravity and magnetic surveys of the Red Sea revealed that the submarine sediments were underlaid by oceanic crust. Surveys showed a pattern of magnetic stripes (p. 45) parallel to the length of the Red Sea; from these the spreading rate can be calculated as 1 in (25 mm) per year. As the Red Sea spreads, so Arabia is moving northeastward, away from Africa, and closing up the sea of the Persian Gulf.

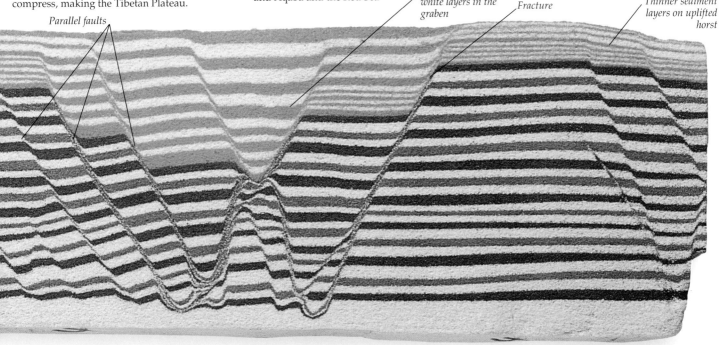

Parallel faults

Thickened red and white layers in the graben

Fracture

Thinner sediment layers on uplifted horst

Weathering processes

Weathering processes leave the landscape with strange shapes

Many of the minerals in rocks are stable at the high temperatures and pressures deep in the crust but are chemically unstable in the oxygen-rich atmosphere of the Earth. Rocks react chemically with the Earth's damp atmosphere in a process called weathering, which takes place right at the Earth's surface. This process contributes to the evolution of landforms. Some weathering is purely chemical – for example, the action of acid rain on limestone. Temperature may also play a role in weathering. During the day, rock may be heated by the Sun. When the temperature drops at night, this change leads to stresses and cracking in the rocks. This will be made more extreme if water freezes in the cracks. Plants and animals, lichens, and fungi also help these processes along. None of these effects, however, happens in isolation. Most landscapes are the result of a combination of many weathering processes. Rock minerals are separated and changed by weathering; this weathered material may be transported and deposited somewhere else.

PLANT ACTION
Plant roots penetrate cracks in rock and take in rock chemicals to use in their metabolism. As roots grow thicker and the plant bigger, the cracks in the rock are widened. Trees help weathering. So do mosses and lichens, which have fungal roots that can penetrate the hardest rocks.

ANIMAL ACTION
Animals such as rabbits and badgers, as well as smaller creatures like beetles, burrow and make channelways in the weathered rock zone where solid rock comes into contact with moist air. This increases the rate of weathering, because it increases the surface area of the rock. This weathered rock is called saprolite.

RUSTING ROCK
Isolated hills, relics of an older, higher surface, stand above a new younger land surface which is almost a level plain. These isolated mountains are known as inselbergs. The red color of Uluru (Ayers Rock) in central Australia is due to iron oxides, the insoluble compound left behind after silicates are broken down by the Australian climate.

CHANGES IN TEMPERATURE
The rocks in these Utah canyons are weathered by temperature, wind, and water. Changes in temperature cause cracking as the rocks expand and shrink. If an area gets very cold and freezing follows rain, the rain water which has percolated into cracks and in between rock grains expands as it freezes, breaking the rock apart.

Haytor on Dartmoor, southern Britain

LIMESTONE WONDER
Limestone is weathered by carbon dioxide in rainwater so that the rock is slowly eaten away. When water carrying the dissolved limestone drips from the roof of a cave, a stalactite forms. If the soil above the cave is an iron-rich clay, the stalactite may be red in color.

Two stalactites have grown into one

Joint planes develop and weathering takes place

Erosion leaves corestones

Granite tor

GRANITE TOR
Cooled granite eventually comes to the surface when a mountain range is being eroded away; the granite cracks apart as the load of rock over the top gets less and less. In places, the cracks, called joints, are widely spaced. In other places, they are close together. Weathering of granite is most intense where the joints are closely spaced. This leaves rounded corestones of unweathered granite, some of which may be several yards or even tens of yards across. The more solid rock stands out as high areas of bare rock known as granite tors.

LIMESTONE LAGOON
The stalactites in this cave on Phra Nang Peninsula, Thailand, were exposed to daylight when the cave collapsed. If the limestone dissolved in water grows up from the floor of the cave, it is known as a stalagmite.

Peeling layers

Cement comes from the weathering of other rocks

Blue resin shows pore spaces

ONION SKINS
Weathering begins on the outside of a rock where it has greatest contact with the atmosphere. Weathering processes penetrate at least ½ in (1 cm) into the rock, even where erosion is rapidly removing the weathered grains. On some rocks, several skins of weathered rock can be seen peeling off from the underlying, more solid rock. This type of weathering is sometimes called onion-skin weathering, or exfoliation.

Thin section of sandstone

Dolerite rock

PORE SPACES
All sedimentary rocks have spaces between the grains of sediment. This may later fill with mineral cement.

Life from rock

Rocks weather at the surface of the Earth, where they come into contact with moist air. As soon as plants take root in the weathered saprolite (rock), the process of making soil begins. Factors which govern how soil is formed include climate, vegetation, topography, and the nature of the rock from which the soil is made. Besides the mineral material from rock, soil also contains organic material, known as humus. This includes plant roots, decaying plant and animal matter, microorganisms, and the organic chemicals that are part of the decomposition of plant and animal matter as fungi and microbes break it down. Animals including snails, and worms are part of the organic matter. Water and air between the particles are a vital part of soil; without them, plants would suffocate or dehydrate. The natural processes that make soil are slow and complex, taking tens of thousands of years. By contrast, soil can be used up rapidly, becoming depleted within as little as a decade.

EARTH MOTHER
In early agricultural civilizations, the fertility of women and the fertility of the soil were seen as two parts of the miraculous continuity of life. In ancient Roman mythology, Proserpina, the daughter of Ceres, the Roman goddess of fruitfulness, was abducted into the underworld where she ate some pomegranate seeds. During the months she was imprisoned, the crops would not grow, animals were no longer fertile and death stalked the land – the months of winter.

TERRACING FOR AGRICULTURE
Artificial terraces, where the hillside is cut into steps, make the slopes easier to farm. They provide land that is level and more convenient to irrigate and plow. Terraces have the added advantage of stabilizing slopes by reducing the rate at which soil is lost from the slope to the valley below. Terracing is commonly found with rice cultivation.

Terraced slopes in Yemen

Terraced slope

SOIL PROFILE
A section dug through soil down to the underlying rock reveals the soil profile. It has a number of distinct layers. The top layer is called the A-horizon. Within this layer, the gardener or farmer digs or plows through the topsoil. Below lies the B-horizon which may contain accumulations of mineral matter precipitated from minerals dissolved in the A-horizon. The B-horizon has more rock fragments from the underlying parent rock. The C-horizon contains a large percentage of broken and weathered rock from which the overlying soil has been derived.

Podzolic soil (found in temperate climates)

A-horizon contains organic matter

B-horizon with little organic matter

C-horizon is the rock layer

Brown earth (high humus content)

A-horizon contains organic matter

Chalk weathered away, leaving flint behind

B-horizon with little organic matter

C-horizon is the rock layer

Chalk

SOIL, AIR, AND WATER

The way soil particles lump together is important to cultivation. So is the size of the mineral grains. Clay soils hold abundant moisture and nutrients, but water passes through slowly. Plants find it difficult to gain root hold and extract nutrients. Sandy soils have large pore spaces and water washes through, so they are relatively poor in nutrients. To investigate the nature of the two soils, the same weight of each soil is placed in a test tube and a measured amount of water is added. The difference in water penetration can be clearly seen. The ideal soil lies somewhere between the two.

Water is quickly absorbed in the air spaces

Water is slow to drain

Sandy soil   Clay soil

Sandy soil   Clay soil

SOIL CREEP

Soil is constantly on the move downhill under the influence of gravity. Animals walking across a slope gently nudge the soil as they go. When it rains, soil is wetted and may move as a mud flow. When it freezes, soil particles move out from the slope. After thawing, these particles settle under gravity lower down the slope. Trees on a hillside often show this movement of the soil. As young saplings, they grow vertically. Gradually the soil creep tips them down the slope, until they stick out at an angle. The tree sometimes grows in a curve as it tries to maintain its vertical growth upward into the light.

A LIVING ORGANISM

Soil is the interface between life and the rocky part of the Earth. Without it, life would be impossible. It is in the soil that chemical exchanges take place that allow plants to grow. When plants die, they give back their chemical content to the soil. Microorganisms in the soil (fungi and bacteria) convert dead plant and animal matter into simpler chemicals that enrich the soil. By harvesting a crop, some of the fertility of the soil is taken away. If the soil is to continue to produce crops, it must regain nutrients from rock weathering, or from added fertilizers.

Wildflowers

Grass

Snail

Decomposing leaf

Dark humus-rich soil

Slug

Pebbles

Roots

Erosion

WEATHERING BREAKS DOWN ROCKS to form loose material or rock minerals in solution. Erosion is all the ways in which the material in solution and the loose rock fragments are removed from the location of the original rock and transported to another place, usually under the influence of gravity. Rock material may be carried by water, it may be transported by glacier ice, or it may be blown by the wind. The amount of rock fragments carried relates to the speed at which water is traveling, so fast-moving rivers in flood can erode huge amounts of landscape. During erosion and transport, the rock fragments are sorted according to their size and density. The chemical elements that went into solution may travel as far as the sea, where they make the sea more salty. In temperate climates where it rains often, clay and sand grains are carried away by rain water washing over slopes, and then by rivers. The heaviest rock fragments are dropped first wherever the speed of the river slackens. At coastlines where cliffs meet the sea, the land is continually being eroded.

WATER FALLING
As rivers cut their pathway from the mountains down to sea level, irregularities in the rocks or any change in the pathway can make rapids, a waterfall, or a lake. Waterfalls mark a place in the river's pathway where active erosion is taking place. Waterfalls are also common in valleys that have been glaciated.

IRREGULAR COASTLINE
Waves beating on a shore hit headlands first. The waves curve around as they meet shallower water and then break against the sides of the headland. If there are joint planes (p. 57) in the rock, or softer rocks, these are eroded away more rapidly than the hard headland rocks. First, an arch forms. Then, if the roof of the arch caves in, an isolated sea stack is left. Waves which hit the coast at an angle move rock fragments along the shore sideways, sometimes for hundreds of miles.

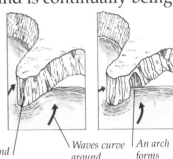

Headland

Waves curve around headland

An arch forms

A sea stack results

CHANGING CLIFF FACE
Waves that meet a steep rocky shore directly break with all their force against the foot of the cliff. Here, solution and weathering happen as salty water continually wets the rock and then dries out at low tide. Salt crystallization occurs and breaks up the grains of the rock. The cliffs are undercut, primarily by wave action, and eventually the upper part falls, breaking along a crack that may be an original joint plane in the rock. The shape of the cliff depends on the resistance of the different rocks to the pounding of the waves.

Man'o War cove, southern Britain

Wave fronts curve

Normandy cliffs, France

Arch

Headland

Sea stack

WAVES AS AGENTS OF EROSION
Waves are formed by winds blowing over water. The wave fronts in deep water are parallel to one another. As they meet shallower water, they bend, hitting the shore in a curve. These curved waves affect the shape of the shoreline. The offshore reef on this coastline breaks up the wave energy. The resulting curved wavelets contribute to the characteristic shape of the cove. Each incoming wave moves pebbles and sand along the beach sideways; the backflowing water moves the material back down the beach.

SALT CRYSTALLIZATION

Pinnacles of rock weathered in a dry climate show hard bands of rock that stand out on the surface. Other layers are more easily weathered and eroded. This uneven sculpting by the weather relates to the changes in grain size and pore size from one rock layer to another. Large pore sizes allow water to penetrate deeply into the rock when it rains. In a dry climate, or where there are high winds, the surface dries before the interior of the rock does. Later, as the pore water dries, salts weathered out from the rock crystallize just under the surface. These push apart the rock grains. The loosened grains are blown away by the wind.

Massive-rock bed has resisted erosion

SANDS OF TIME

Weathering in the desert is a result of fracturing brought about by temperature changes and by salt crystallization. Erosion is mostly brought about by the wind which always blows away the smallest particles and flaky mineral grains, leaving rounded quartz sand. These sand grains are transported a cross the surface of the desert where they form sand dunes. The dunes also move, with sand being blown up the gentle slope and sliding in occasional avalanches down the steep slope.

Sand dune in Morocco

Wadi

Slopes are covered with weathering rock fragments

Natural rock arch

Sand dunes

Rock fragments collect in wadi

MODEL OF A DESERT LANDSCAPE

The notion of deserts as only sandy places is not entirely true. Antarctica is a desert because, like the Sahara, it receives less than 10 in (25 cm) rainfall each year. When torrential rain does come to arid areas, whole mountainsides may be swept clean of boulders, rock fragments, sand, and clay in flash floods which pour down wadis (dry river valleys) to drain into temporary lakes, or playas. The rock fragments building up in gullies at the foot of steep mountainsides may be weathered to make sand. The sand is washed out, or blown away to make dunes.

Area of rock has eroded more easily

HOLES IN THE RIVER BED

Sometimes rivers disappear underground through sinkholes. Some of these are enlarged cracks in limestone, but others are formed by the collapse of the limestone over an underground cave. Limestone weathers and erodes into cave systems if the rock is hard enough to be self-supporting when it is hollowed out. The best limestones for this are fine-grained limy muds that have been cemented together to make a tough rock. More shelly limestones form cave systems less readily.

Deposition

ALL THE ROCK FRAGMENTS broken off from the solid rocky surface of the Earth are deposited somewhere else as sediment. The environment of deposition varies enormously, and this controls the character of the sediment. If the circumstances are just right, the sediments may eventually become new sedimentary rocks. The environments of deposition vary from steep mountain slopes, to flat river valleys, to beaches, to the seabed on the continental shelf, and to the deep ocean floor. Many sediments that are laid down are eroded again fairly soon afterwards. This might happen as pebbles are dropped after a river flood and then picked up and transported further downstream in the next flood. During this time, the pebbles and other grains undergo weathering as well as further transport. The best place for sediments to be made into rock is a location where the land surface is sinking, or where the sea level is rising. Under these circumstances, one sediment layer is rapidly buried by another and is preserved. Once buried, it becomes compressed and hardened to make rock.

Vale of Glamorgan coast, Wales

SHAPING THE BEACH
Coastal beaches are places of continual change. The nature of the waves breaking on this beach causes the banks of pebbles to be scoured and sorted. However, even beaches have definite seasonal cycles. Sand moves on to the beach in summer, while in winter the high waves usually pick the sand up and deposit it offshore.

Terrace gravels   *Flowing river*   *River terrace*

Shotover River, New Zealand   *Erosion on the outside of the curve*

RIVER TERRACES
When a river falls in response to a drop in sea level, the level of the old floodplain is abandoned above the flowing river. These new incised banks are known as terraces. The terraces are made of older sands and gravel that were previously part of the river bed.

MEANDERING RIVER
The flatter parts of river valleys are where the river drops the load of sediment it has collected from the fast-flowing hilly portion of its pathway. Meandering river valleys are flat and wide. The river moves in snakelike fashion, the course changing with every flood to make great loops. If the river cuts through the neck of the loop the abandoned loop is known as an oxbow lake.

Mara River, Tanzania

Deposition of sediment on the inside of the curve   *Neck of loop*

RIVERS OF SAND
Erosion dominates in the steep parts of the river and deposition dominates in the flood plain area. The river erodes its banks on the outside of a bend where the flow is fastest, and the sediment is redeposited on the insides of bends where the flow is slow. In this way, meandering rivers build wide flat valleys, called flood plains, made from their deposited material.

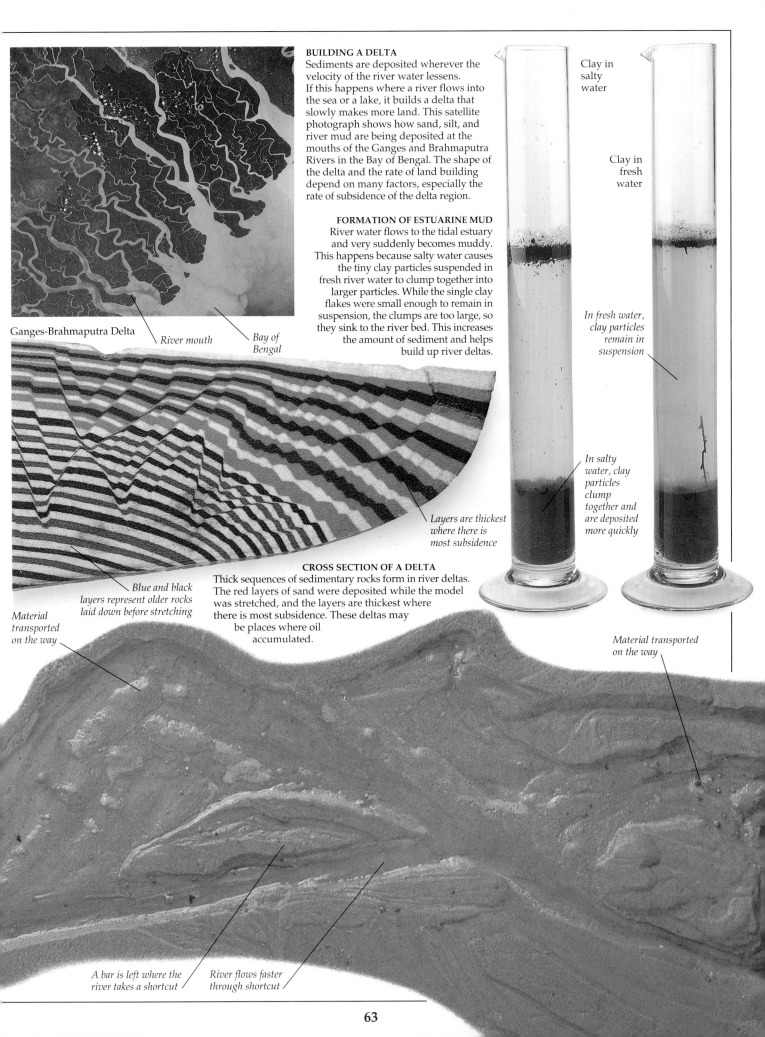

BUILDING A DELTA
Sediments are deposited wherever the velocity of the river water lessens. If this happens where a river flows into the sea or a lake, it builds a delta that slowly makes more land. This satellite photograph shows how sand, silt, and river mud are being deposited at the mouths of the Ganges and Brahmaputra Rivers in the Bay of Bengal. The shape of the delta and the rate of land building depend on many factors, especially the rate of subsidence of the delta region.

Clay in salty water

Clay in fresh water

FORMATION OF ESTUARINE MUD
River water flows to the tidal estuary and very suddenly becomes muddy. This happens because salty water causes the tiny clay particles suspended in fresh river water to clump together into larger particles. While the single clay flakes were small enough to remain in suspension, the clumps are too large, so they sink to the river bed. This increases the amount of sediment and helps build up river deltas.

In fresh water, clay particles remain in suspension

Ganges-Brahmaputra Delta

River mouth

Bay of Bengal

In salty water, clay particles clump together and are deposited more quickly

Layers are thickest where there is most subsidence

Blue and black layers represent older rocks laid down before stretching

CROSS SECTION OF A DELTA
Thick sequences of sedimentary rocks form in river deltas. The red layers of sand were deposited while the model was stretched, and the layers are thickest where there is most subsidence. These deltas may be places where oil accumulated.

Material transported on the way

Material transported on the way

A bar is left where the river takes a shortcut

River flows faster through shortcut

Glaciation

GLACIERS ARE FOUND IN THE HIGH VALLEYS of many mountain ranges today, although most are melting faster than they are replenished by snowfall. This means the valley end of the glacier is continually retreating higher up the mountain. Today's mountain glaciers are but a small leftover from the great glaciers that filled the valleys in the cold stages of the Pleistocene Ice Age. Ten thousand years ago glaciers started to melt faster than they were supplied with snow. Over the last 2 million years, glacier buildup has happened each time a cold, wet, glacial period followed a warmer, interglacial period. The Earth today is thought to be in an interglacial period of glacier melting. As valley glaciers flow, they carve their valleys wider and deeper, eventually making a U-shaped trough. Melting glaciers are hemmed in by great mounds of sediments that were washed out of the ice. These fragments have been scoured or plucked from the surrounding rocks and transported downhill by the glaciers as they move slowly down the valleys. In this way glaciers can transport huge amounts of rock fragments from mountain summits to valley floors.

GLACIER GIANTS
Where a glacier melts at its snout, a tiny water torrent may flow from the bouldery gravel mounds left by the melting ice. The gravel heaps are known as the terminal moraine of the glacier. The great rivers of Europe, such as the Rhine, all have their source in the melting glaciers of the Alps.

CONTINENTAL ICE SHEET
The interiors of Greenland and Antarctica are covered with ice sheets thousands of feet thick. The thickness narrows toward the edge of the land mass. Near the coast of northwest Greenland, valley glaciers are threading their way through mountains that ring the island. Rock fragments are carried along the edges of the glacier (lateral moraines), and also within the ice itself.

Pacific Ocean   *Pack-ice*

SATELLITE SNOWSCAPE
Alaska, Canada, much of the northern USA, and Scandinavia, as well as Antarctica and Greenland, were ice covered at the coldest stages of the Pleistocene Ice Age. Today, some of these regions are still snow covered in winter, while only their mountainous regions have permanent glacier ice. In winter, as shown here in Alaska from satellite, pack-ice builds up around the coast as the sea freezes and the first winter snow falls. In Siberia, Alaska, and northern Canada, great regions still have permanently frozen ground known as permafrost, though this is reducing in area.

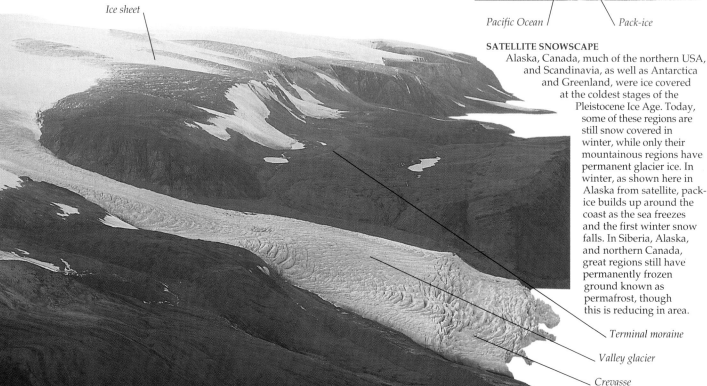

Ice sheet

Terminal moraine

Valley glacier

Crevasse

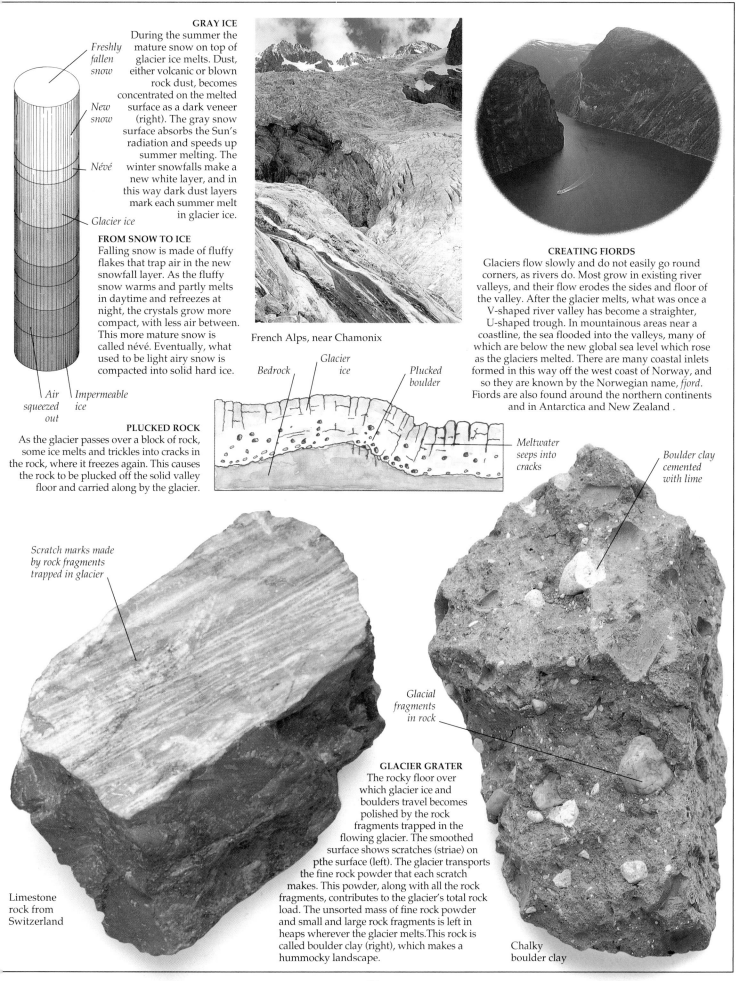

GRAY ICE

During the summer the mature snow on top of glacier ice melts. Dust, either volcanic or blown rock dust, becomes concentrated on the melted surface as a dark veneer (right). The gray snow surface absorbs the Sun's radiation and speeds up summer melting. The winter snowfalls make a new white layer, and in this way dark dust layers mark each summer melt in glacier ice.

Freshly fallen snow

New snow

Névé

Glacier ice

Air squeezed out

Impermeable ice

FROM SNOW TO ICE

Falling snow is made of fluffy flakes that trap air in the new snowfall layer. As the fluffy snow warms and partly melts in daytime and refreezes at night, the crystals grow more compact, with less air between. This more mature snow is called névé. Eventually, what used to be light airy snow is compacted into solid hard ice.

French Alps, near Chamonix

PLUCKED ROCK

As the glacier passes over a block of rock, some ice melts and trickles into cracks in the rock, where it freezes again. This causes the rock to be plucked off the solid valley floor and carried along by the glacier.

Bedrock

Glacier ice

Plucked boulder

Meltwater seeps into cracks

CREATING FIORDS

Glaciers flow slowly and do not easily go round corners, as rivers do. Most grow in existing river valleys, and their flow erodes the sides and floor of the valley. After the glacier melts, what was once a V-shaped river valley has become a straighter, U-shaped trough. In mountainous areas near a coastline, the sea flooded into the valleys, many of which are below the new global sea level which rose as the glaciers melted. There are many coastal inlets formed in this way off the west coast of Norway, and so they are known by the Norwegian name, *fjord*. Fiords are also found around the northern continents and in Antarctica and New Zealand .

Scratch marks made by rock fragments trapped in glacier

Boulder clay cemented with lime

Glacial fragments in rock

GLACIER GRATER

The rocky floor over which glacier ice and boulders travel becomes polished by the rock fragments trapped in the flowing glacier. The smoothed surface shows scratches (striae) on pthe surface (left). The glacier transports the fine rock powder that each scratch makes. This powder, along with all the rock fragments, contributes to the glacier's total rock load. The unsorted mass of fine rock powder and small and large rock fragments is left in heaps wherever the glacier melts.This rock is called boulder clay (right), which makes a hummocky landscape.

Limestone rock from Switzerland

Chalky boulder clay

The age of the Earth

WHEN THINKING ABOUT HOW OLD the Earth might be, James Hutton (p. 14) wrote in 1788 that he could "see no vestige of a beginning, no prospect of an end." Hutton saw geological time as being unimaginably long. It was not until the 20th century, with the understanding of radioactivity, that an accurate method of dating such old materials as Earth rocks was developed. This was radiometric dating, which used a measurable Earth process that happened on a time scale of the right order of magnitude. Another method of dating rocks and therefore the age of the Earth is to study layers in sedimentary rocks, and fossils – dead plants and animals that have become preserved in rocks of the Earth's crust. This record in the rocks also helps reveal past climates, giving information about how the atmosphere used to be on the Earth. The ocean floor preserves the Earth's magnetic field, making a record that goes back 200 million years.

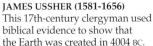

JAMES USSHER (1581-1656)
This 17th-century clergyman used biblical evidence to show that the Earth was created in 4004 BC. He based his calculation on the genealogies in the Bible. Ussher's date was believed by many scientists and the general public for a time. Other religions came up with a date for the beginning of the Earth based on their beliefs.

WILLIAM THOMSON (1824-1907)
This British scientist (later Lord Kelvin) calculated the age of the Earth based on the length of time it had taken to cool to its present temperature. He assumed that the Earth originally had a molten surface. The time he came up with was 40 million years. This was far too short to account for the evolution of life or for the accumulation of sedimentary rock strata.

USING FOSSILS
The British geologist Charles Lyell (p. 68) realized that young rocks contain many fossils that are similar to living life forms, and that progressively older rocks have fewer and fewer species that resemble modern forms. Paleontologists who study fossils and stratigraphers who study rock sequences, have compiled an Earth history that allows rocks to be dated from their fossils. For example, *Acadagnostus* is found in Middle Cambrian rocks, while *Eocyphinium* is found in rocks of Carboniferous age.

Acadagnostus

Eocyphinium

TIME GAPS
The thickness of rock layers might look like a good way to date Earth processes, but the rates of sedimentation are difficult to measure. One problem is that the layers contain many time gaps when no strata were laid down or they were eroded. Some gaps represent a very long time interval. From fossils and radiometric dating, the time interval represented at this rock outcrop in southern Britain is 160 million years: the time between when the lower set of rocks was being laid down as sediments, to when it was submerged and buried by new layers of rocks. Such a time gap between deposition of rock layers is called an unconformity.

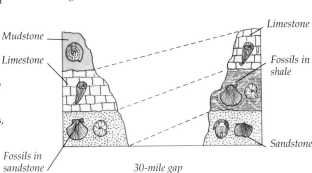

Mudstone
Limestone
Fossils in sandstone
Limestone
Fossils in shale
Sandstone
30-mile gap

CORRELATING WITH FOSSILS
Fossils can be used to match rocks from one place to another. Correlation assumes two things – that evolution of all members of a species took place at the same time worldwide, and that evolution never reproduces a species once it has become extinct. The fossils of creatures that died and were buried at the same time sometimes appear in different rock types. Two rocks, such as sandstone and shale, can be formed at the same time, perhaps where a sandy beach changed along the coastline into a muddy estuary.

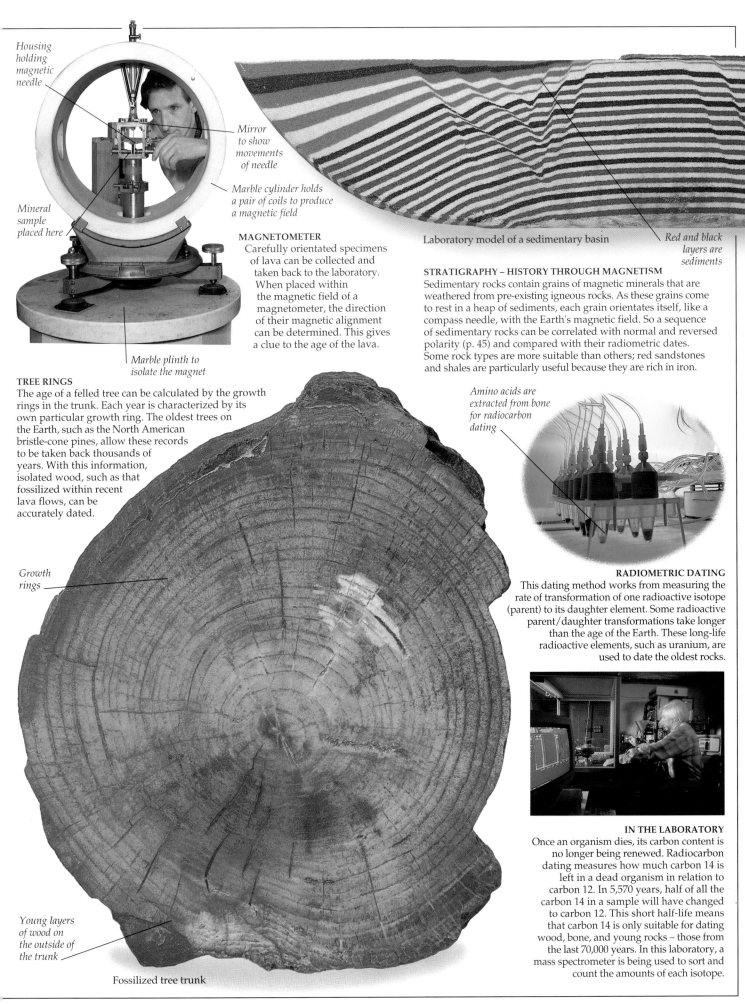

Housing
holding
magnetic
needle

Mirror
to show
movements
of needle

Marble cylinder holds
a pair of coils to produce
a magnetic field

Mineral
sample
placed here

Marble plinth to
isolate the magnet

MAGNETOMETER
Carefully orientated specimens
of lava can be collected and
taken back to the laboratory.
When placed within
the magnetic field of a
magnetometer, the direction
of their magnetic alignment
can be determined. This gives
a clue to the age of the lava.

Laboratory model of a sedimentary basin

Red and black
layers are
sediments

STRATIGRAPHY – HISTORY THROUGH MAGNETISM
Sedimentary rocks contain grains of magnetic minerals that are
weathered from pre-existing igneous rocks. As these grains come
to rest in a heap of sediments, each grain orientates itself, like a
compass needle, with the Earth's magnetic field. So a sequence
of sedimentary rocks can be correlated with normal and reversed
polarity (p. 45) and compared with their radiometric dates.
Some rock types are more suitable than others; red sandstones
and shales are particularly useful because they are rich in iron.

TREE RINGS
The age of a felled tree can be calculated by the growth
rings in the trunk. Each year is characterized by its
own particular growth ring. The oldest trees on
the Earth, such as the North American
bristle-cone pines, allow these records
to be taken back thousands of
years. With this information,
isolated wood, such as that
fossilized within recent
lava flows, can be
accurately dated.

Amino acids are
extracted from bone
for radiocarbon
dating

Growth
rings

RADIOMETRIC DATING
This dating method works from measuring the
rate of transformation of one radioactive isotope
(parent) to its daughter element. Some radioactive
parent/daughter transformations take longer
than the age of the Earth. These long-life
radioactive elements, such as uranium, are
used to date the oldest rocks.

IN THE LABORATORY
Once an organism dies, its carbon content is
no longer being renewed. Radiocarbon
dating measures how much carbon 14 is
left in a dead organism in relation to
carbon 12. In 5,570 years, half of all the
carbon 14 in a sample will have changed
to carbon 12. This short half-life means
that carbon 14 is only suitable for dating
wood, bone, and young rocks – those from
the last 70,000 years. In this laboratory, a
mass spectrometer is being used to sort and
count the amounts of each isotope.

Young layers
of wood on
the outside of
the trunk

Fossilized tree trunk

Naming the Earth

THE MOST RECENT HISTORY of the Earth is the best known, because the younger rocks contain abundant fossils and there is a fairly complete rock record. We know much less about the first 3,000 million years because the rocks contain few and only primitive fossils, and many of the rocks have been metamorphosed several times. Also much of the rock record is either buried by younger rocks or has been eroded to make sedimentary rocks.

CHARLES LYELL (1797-1875)
Lyell's most fundamental contribution to geology was his promotion of Uniformitarianism, that "the present is the key to the past." It is now known that this is a decidedly limited truth, as Precambrian history shows. All Earth processes – plate tectonics, mountain building, weathering, sedimentation – had a beginning, probably early in the Precambrian.

THE AGE OF THE EARTH
The Earth is believed to be about 4,550 million years old. This is supported by the age of the oldest rocks on the Moon, and by dating meteorites, which suggests that our Solar System itself may be about this old. Precambrian time includes major events like the origin of the first life forms, the growth of the continents, the beginnings of plate tectonics, and the buildup of atmospheric oxygen.

Stony meteorite

Paradoxides

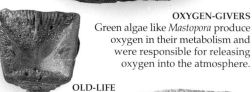

Mastopora

OXYGEN-GIVERS
Green algae like *Mastopora* produce oxygen in their metabolism and were responsible for releasing oxygen into the atmosphere.

SEA SCAVENGERS
The Cambrian marks the time when life became abundant in the oceans and left a clear fossil record of its presence. Trilobites, such as this *Paradoxides*, were bottom dwellers in shallow seas where they scavenged for food.

Goniophyllum

OLD-LIFE CORALS
Corals like *Goniophyllum* are lifeforms that are still familiar.

THE PRECAMBRIAN SHIELD
Sir William Logan (p. 47) realized the Precambrain rocks he mapped in the Canadian Shield were enormously old. He called the peculiar structures in these rocks cryptozooans, meaning hidden animal, because these rocks were thought to predate the existence of life.

Pteraspis

OLD ROCK
Much of the first solid crust on Earth was probably like basalt in composition and similar to today's ocean floor. The first granites that make the continents must have come later. Today, Precambrian granites have been metamorphosed, perhaps many times over.

Granite gneiss

EARLY LIFE
Collenia are stromatolites – blue-green algae that are one of the earliest forms of life. They usually occur in lumpy pillars between high and low tidal water levels.

Collenia

BONY FISH
Some life forms have an external skeleton, such as a shell, while others have an internal skeleton. The earliest fish lived in the sea, had an external skeleton of bony plates, and were jawless like this *Pteraspis*.

ARCHAEAN	PROTEROZOIC		CAMBRIAN	ORDOVICIAN	SILURIAN	DEVONIAN
PRECAMBRIAN			PALEOZOIC			
4,500 Ma	2,500 Ma		590 Ma	500 Ma		400 Ma

EARLY PLANT LIFE

The earliest plant forms are found in Silurian and Devonian rocks. Plants colonized the land in great numbers in the Carboniferous (meaning rich in carbon), making up the swamps which later were buried, compressed and heated, and transformed into coal. Club mosses, like this modern *Lycopodium*, first evolved in the Paleozoic.

Lycopodium

DESERT SANDSTONE

Sandstones of Permian age in Europe show they were formed in a desert climate. The sand grains are well rounded, having been blown around by the wind, and are sometimes in sloping layers.

Shallow seas

CARBONIFEROUS MAP

In his map of Pangaea, Alfred Wegener (p. 41) showed all the continents grouped together at the end of Carboniferous times.

Carboniferous rock

Limy sediment formed in the Jurassic sea

Boreholes made by boring mollusc

BURROWS THROUGH TIME

The gray Carboniferous rock was hardened and eroded. It made a hard rocky seabed in Jurassic times. Shelly molluscs in the Jurassic burrowed into the Carboniferous rock.

ARCHAEOPTERYX

There are so few fossil birds that we know little about their evolution. *Archaeopteryx* was Jurassic in age and was clearly a feathered bird capable of flying, though still possessing teeth.

Finger

Reptilian tail

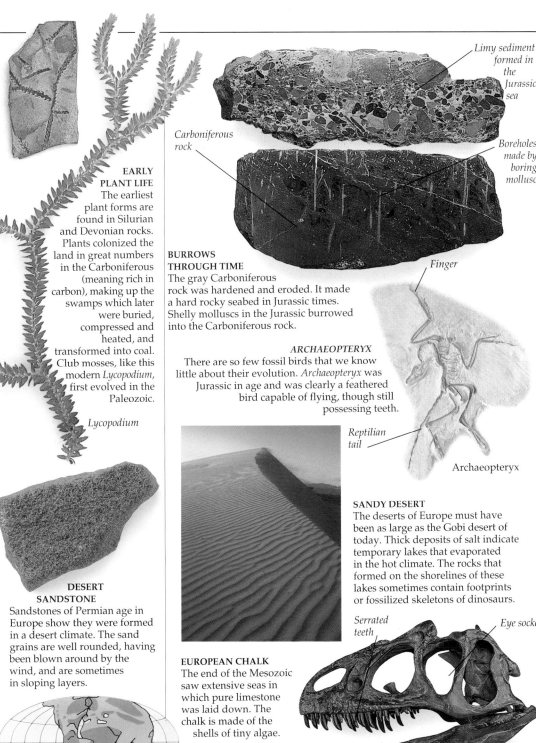

Archaeopteryx

SANDY DESERT

The deserts of Europe must have been as large as the Gobi desert of today. Thick deposits of salt indicate temporary lakes that evaporated in the hot climate. The rocks that formed on the shorelines of these lakes sometimes contain footprints or fossilized skeletons of dinosaurs.

EUROPEAN CHALK

The end of the Mesozoic saw extensive seas in which pure limestone was laid down. The chalk is made of the shells of tiny algae.

Serrated teeth

Eye socket

Land-dwelling Allosaurus

Cavity for jaw muscles

DINOSAUR FOSSILS

Creatures that lived in the water and dropped to the bottom when they died had a better chance of becoming preserved as fossils. The fossil record is dominated by water-dwelling creatures. Land animals like the meat-eating *Allosaurus* were rarely preserved.

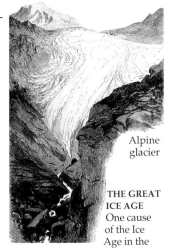

Alpine glacier

THE GREAT ICE AGE

One cause of the Ice Age in the Pleistocene epoch (a subdivision of the Quaternary) may be the high mountains, and their locations, which affected global weather systems by diverting surface winds.

THE ROCKY MOUNTAINS

A high mountain chain was built along the subduction zones on the west of the Americas. Today, global topography is much more varied than is usual in the Earth's history, with many high mountain ranges which are actively being lifted up and eroded.

RECENT LANDSCAPE

Alfred Wegener's map for late Tertiary times showed the world much as it is today, though with a narrower North Atlantic Ocean. During Tertiary times, major mountain ranges were built, such as the modern Alps and Himalayas.

CARBONIFEROUS	PERMIAN	TRIASSIC	JURASSIC	CRETACEOUS	TERTIARY	QUATERNARY
PALEOZOIC		MESOZOIC			CENOZOIC	

300 Ma 200 Ma 100 Ma 65 Ma

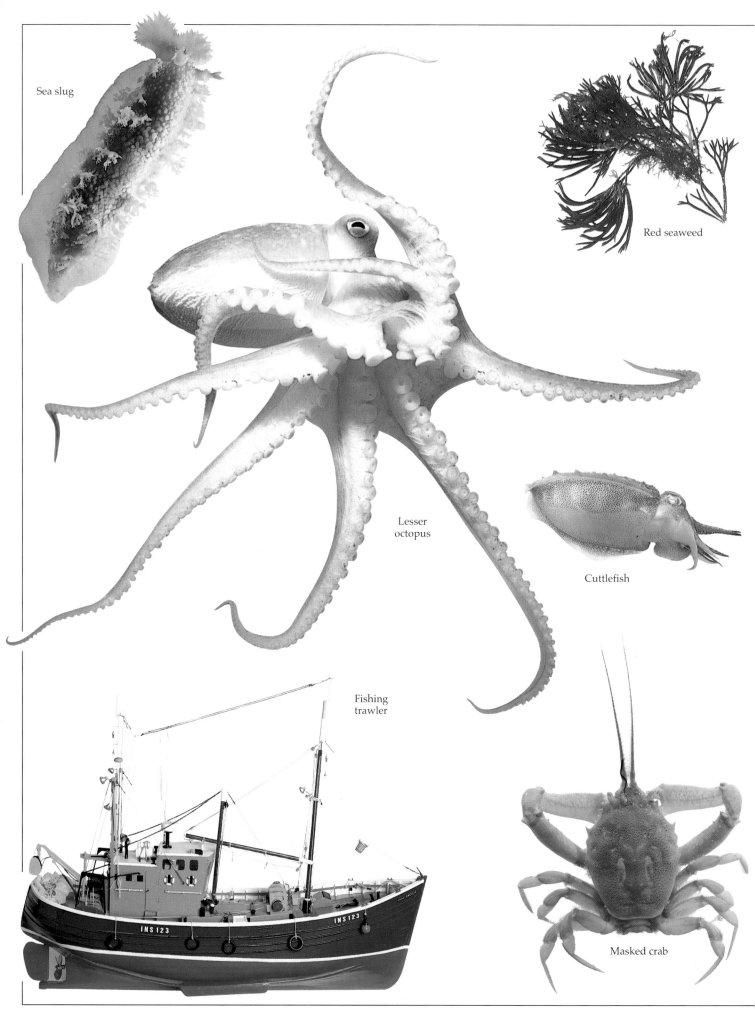

Sea slug

Red seaweed

Lesser
octopus

Cuttlefish

Fishing
trawler

INS 123

Masked crab

Boar fish

OCEAN

European
spiny lobster

Butterfly blenny

Maerl
seaweed

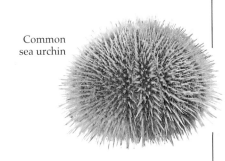
Common
sea urchin

Oceans of the past

THE EARTH, WITH ITS VAST EXPANSES of ocean, has not always looked the way it does today. Water in the form of vapor was present in the atmosphere of the early earth. As the earth cooled, water vapor condensed, making storm clouds. Rain fell from these clouds and filled the first oceans. Over millions of years the land-masses have drifted across the face of the earth as new oceans opened up and old oceans disappeared. Today's oceans took shape only over the last 200 million years of the earth's 4.5-billion-year existence. As the oceans themselves changed, so too did life within the oceans. Simple organisms first appeared 3.3 billion years ago and were followed by more and more complex life forms. Some forms of life became extinct, but others still survive in the ocean today, more or less unchanged.

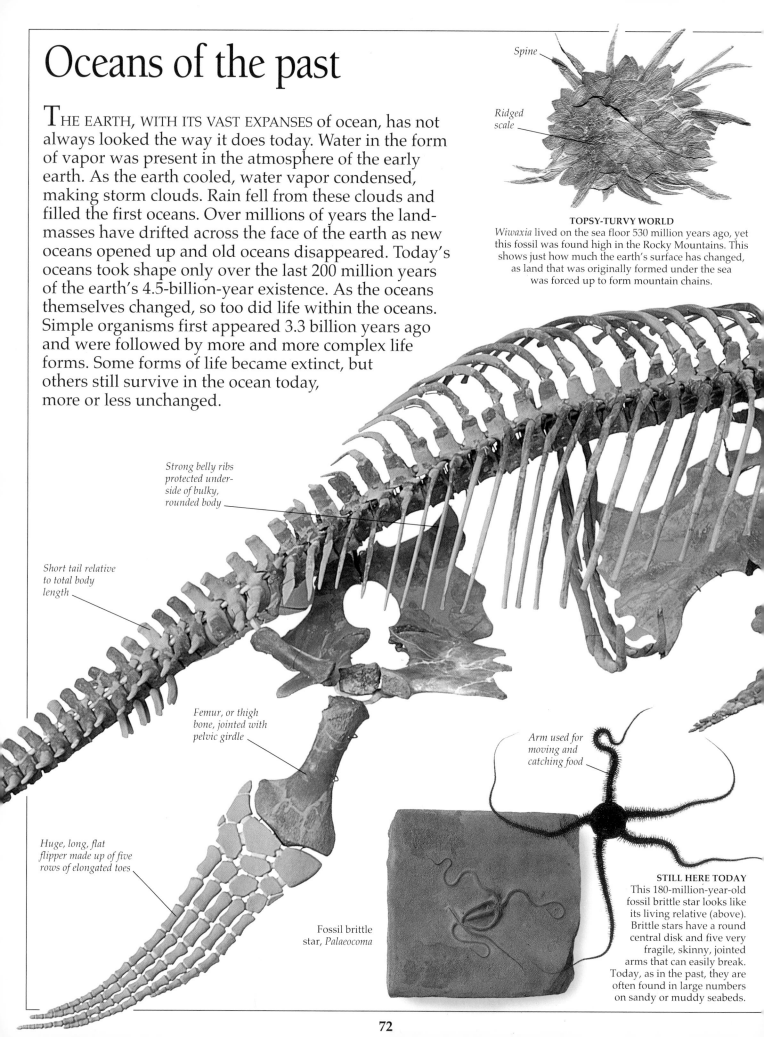

Spine

Ridged scale

TOPSY-TURVY WORLD
Wiwaxia lived on the sea floor 530 million years ago, yet this fossil was found high in the Rocky Mountains. This shows just how much the earth's surface has changed, as land that was originally formed under the sea was forced up to form mountain chains.

Strong belly ribs protected underside of bulky, rounded body

Short tail relative to total body length

Femur, or thigh bone, jointed with pelvic girdle

Huge, long, flat flipper made up of five rows of elongated toes

Arm used for moving and catching food

Fossil brittle star, *Palaeocoma*

STILL HERE TODAY
This 180-million-year-old fossil brittle star looks like its living relative (above). Brittle stars have a round central disk and five very fragile, skinny, jointed arms that can easily break. Today, as in the past, they are often found in large numbers on sandy or muddy seabeds.

ANCIENT CORAL

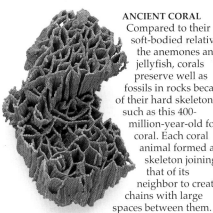

Compared to their soft-bodied relatives, the anemones and jellyfish, corals preserve well as fossils in rocks because of their hard skeletons, such as this 400-million-year-old fossil coral. Each coral animal formed a skeleton joining that of its neighbor to create chains with large spaces between them.

CHANGING OCEANS
One giant ocean, Panthalassa, surrounded the supercontinent Pangaea (1) 290–240 million years ago (mya). At the end of this period, many kinds of marine life became extinct. Pangaea broke up, with part drifting north and part south, with the Tethys Sea between.

CONTINENTAL DRIFT
The northern part split to form the North Atlantic 208–146 mya (2). The South Atlantic and Indian oceans began to form 146–65 mya (3). The continents continued to drift 1.65 mya (4). Today the oceans are still changing shape – the Atlantic ocean gets wider by a few inches each year.

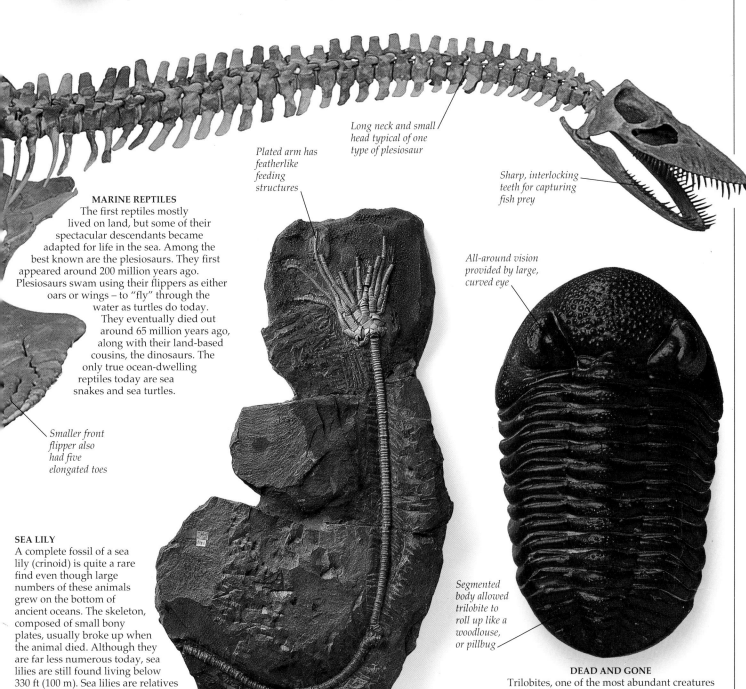

Long neck and small head typical of one type of plesiosaur

Plated arm has featherlike feeding structures

Sharp, interlocking teeth for capturing fish prey

MARINE REPTILES
The first reptiles mostly lived on land, but some of their spectacular descendants became adapted for life in the sea. Among the best known are the plesiosaurs. They first appeared around 200 million years ago. Plesiosaurs swam using their flippers as either oars or wings – to "fly" through the water as turtles do today. They eventually died out around 65 million years ago, along with their land-based cousins, the dinosaurs. The only true ocean-dwelling reptiles today are sea snakes and sea turtles.

Smaller front flipper also had five elongated toes

All-around vision provided by large, curved eye

SEA LILY
A complete fossil of a sea lily (crinoid) is quite a rare find even though large numbers of these animals grew on the bottom of ancient oceans. The skeleton, composed of small bony plates, usually broke up when the animal died. Although they are far less numerous today, sea lilies are still found living below 330 ft (100 m). Sea lilies are relatives of feather stars, but unlike them are usually anchored to the seabed. Their arms surround an upward-facing mouth and are used to trap small particles of food drifting by.

Segmented body allowed trilobite to roll up like a woodlouse, or pillbug

Long, flexible stem anchored crinoid in seabed gardens

DEAD AND GONE
Trilobites, one of the most abundant creatures living in the ancient seas, first flourished over 510 million years ago. They had jointed limbs and an external skeleton like insects or crustaceans, such as crabs and lobsters. They died out some 250 million years ago.

Oceans today

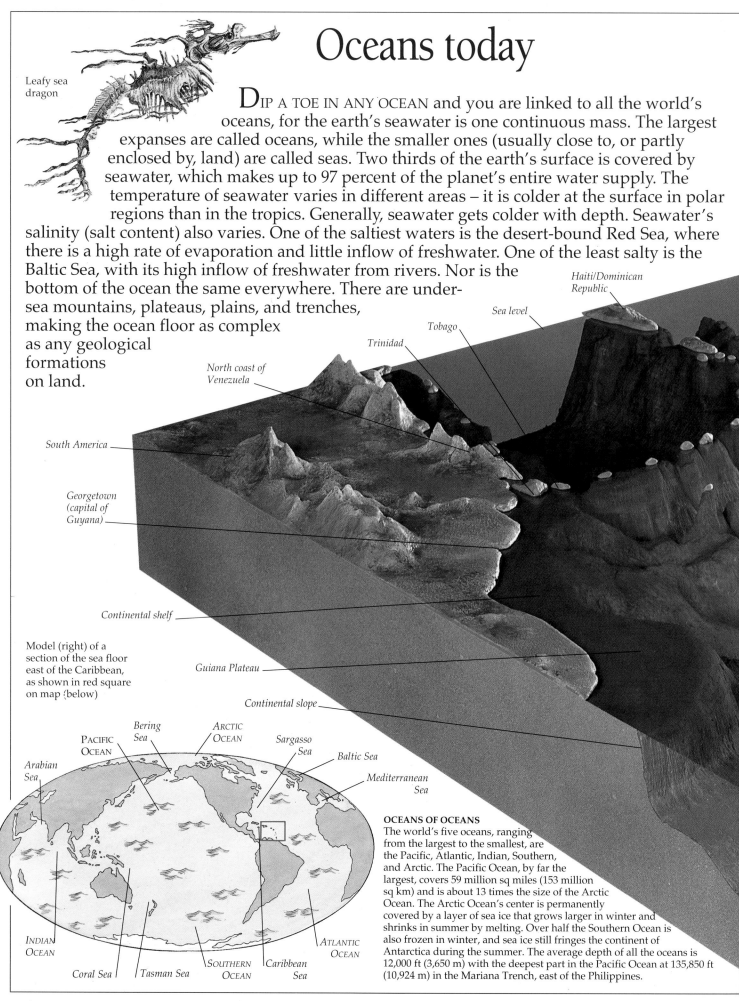

Leafy sea dragon

DIP A TOE IN ANY OCEAN and you are linked to all the world's oceans, for the earth's seawater is one continuous mass. The largest expanses are called oceans, while the smaller ones (usually close to, or partly enclosed by, land) are called seas. Two thirds of the earth's surface is covered by seawater, which makes up to 97 percent of the planet's entire water supply. The temperature of seawater varies in different areas – it is colder at the surface in polar regions than in the tropics. Generally, seawater gets colder with depth. Seawater's salinity (salt content) also varies. One of the saltiest waters is the desert-bound Red Sea, where there is a high rate of evaporation and little inflow of freshwater. One of the least salty is the Baltic Sea, with its high inflow of freshwater from rivers. Nor is the bottom of the ocean the same everywhere. There are under-sea mountains, plateaus, plains, and trenches, making the ocean floor as complex as any geological formations on land.

Haiti/Dominican Republic

Sea level

Tobago

Trinidad

North coast of Venezuela

South America

Georgetown (capital of Guyana)

Continental shelf

Model (right) of a section of the sea floor east of the Caribbean, as shown in red square on map (below)

Guiana Plateau

Continental slope

Bering Sea

ARCTIC OCEAN

PACIFIC OCEAN

Sargasso Sea

Arabian Sea

Baltic Sea

Mediterranean Sea

INDIAN OCEAN

Coral Sea

Tasman Sea

SOUTHERN OCEAN

Caribbean Sea

ATLANTIC OCEAN

OCEANS OF OCEANS
The world's five oceans, ranging from the largest to the smallest, are the Pacific, Atlantic, Indian, Southern, and Arctic. The Pacific Ocean, by far the largest, covers 59 million sq miles (153 million sq km) and is about 13 times the size of the Arctic Ocean. The Arctic Ocean's center is permanently covered by a layer of sea ice that grows larger in winter and shrinks in summer by melting. Over half the Southern Ocean is also frozen in winter, and sea ice still fringes the continent of Antarctica during the summer. The average depth of all the oceans is 12,000 ft (3,650 m) with the deepest part in the Pacific Ocean at 135,850 ft (10,924 m) in the Mariana Trench, east of the Philippines.

SEA OR LAKE?

The water in the Dead Sea is saltier than any ocean because the water that drains into it evaporates in the hot sun, leaving behind the salts. A body is more buoyant in such salty water, making it easier to float. The Dead Sea is a lake, not a sea, because it is completely surrounded by land. True seas are always connected to the ocean by a channel.

Floating on the
Dead Sea

GOD OF THE WATERS

Neptune, the Roman god of the sea, is usually shown riding a dolphin and carrying a trident (pronged spear). It was thought he controlled freshwater supplies, so offerings were made to him at the driest time of the year.

DISAPPEARING ACT

The gigantic plates on the earth's crust move like a conveyor belt. As new areas of ocean floor form at spreading centers, old areas disappear into the molten heart of the planet. This diagram shows one oceanic plate being forced under another (subduction) in the Mariana Trench, creating an island arc.

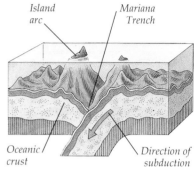

Island arc   *Mariana Trench*

Oceanic crust   *Direction of subduction*

Formation of Mariana Trench

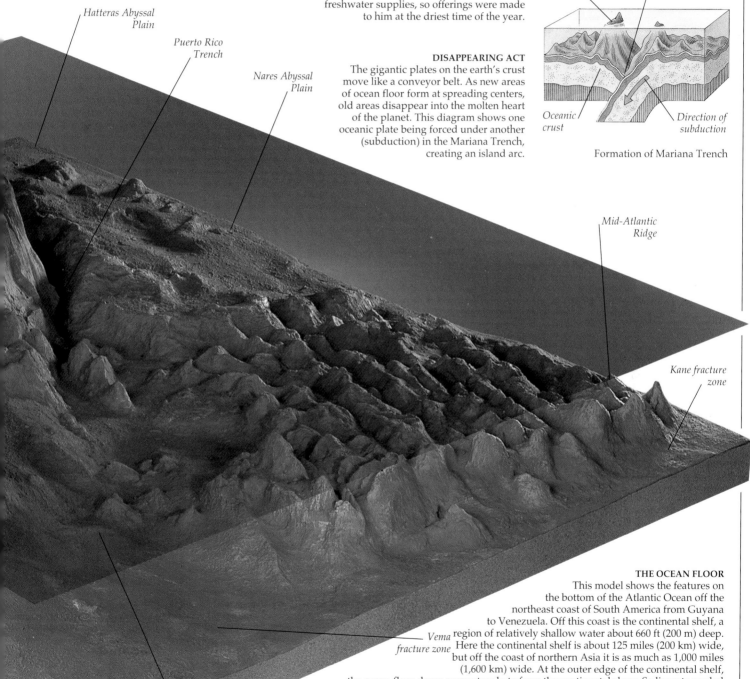

Hatteras Abyssal Plain

Puerto Rico Trench

Nares Abyssal Plain

Mid-Atlantic Ridge

Kane fracture zone

Vema fracture zone

Demerara Abyssal Plain

THE OCEAN FLOOR

This model shows the features on the bottom of the Atlantic Ocean off the northeast coast of South America from Guyana to Venezuela. Off this coast is the continental shelf, a region of relatively shallow water about 660 ft (200 m) deep. Here the continental shelf is about 125 miles (200 km) wide, but off the coast of northern Asia it is as much as 1,000 miles (1,600 km) wide. At the outer edge of the continental shelf, the ocean floor drops away steeply to form the continental slope. Sediments eroded from the land and carried by rivers, such as the Orinoco, accumulate at the bottom of this continental slope. The ocean floor then opens out in virtually flat areas (abyssal plains), which are covered with a deep layer of soft sediments. The Puerto Rican Trench formed where one of the Earth's plates (the North American Plate) is sliding past another (the Caribbean Plate). An arc of volcanic islands have also been created where the North American Plate is forced under the Caribbean Plate. The fracture zones are offsets of the Mid-Atlantic Ridge.

Life in the oceans

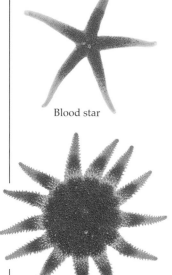

Blood star

Common sun star

SHORE LIFE
Often found on the shore at low tide, starfish also live in deeper water. Sea life on the shore must either be tough enough to withstand drying out, or find shelter in rock pools. The toughest animals and plants live high on the shore. The least able to cope in air are found at the bottom.

FROM THE SEASHORE to the deepest depths, oceans are home to some of the most diverse life on earth. Animals live either on the seabed or in midwater, where they swim or float. Plants are only found in the sunlit zone, where there is enough light for growth. Animals are found at all depths of the oceans, though are most abundant in the sunlit zone, where food is plentiful. Not all free-swimming animals stay in one zone – the sperm whale dives to over 1,640 ft (500 m) to feed on squid, returning to the surface to breathe air. Some animals from cold, deep waters, such as the Greenland shark in the Atlantic, are also found in the cold surface waters of polar regions. Over 90 percent of all species dwell on the bottom. A single rock can be home to over ten major groups, such as corals, mollusks, and sponges. Most ocean animals and plants have their origins in the sea, but some, such as whales and sea grasses, are descended from ancestors that once lived on land.

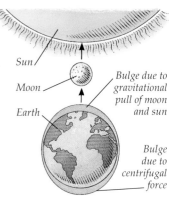

Sun
Moon
Earth

Bulge due to gravitational pull of moon and sun

Bulge due to centrifugal force

TIME AND TIDE
Anyone spending time at the beach or in an estuary will notice the tides. Tides are caused by the gravitational pull of the moon on the earth's mass of seawater. An equal and opposite bulge of water occurs on the side of the earth away from the moon, due to centrifugal force. As the earth spins on its axis, the bulges (high tides) usually occur twice a day in any one place. The highest and lowest tides occur when the moon and sun are in line, causing the greatest gravitational pull. These are the spring tides at new and full moon.

Inside squid's soft body is a horny, penlike shell

SQUISHY SQUID
Squid are among the most common animals living in the ocean. Like fish, they often swim around in schools for protection in numbers. Their torpedo-shaped bodies are streamlined so they can swim fast.

Tentacles reach out to grasp food

Continental shelf

Flying fish
Man-of-war
Shark
Oarweed
Mackerel
Turtle
Brain coral
Continental slope
Sperm whale
Sponges
Octopus
Hatchet fish
Sea pens
Rat-tail fish
Sea spider
Gulper eel
Anglerfish
Sea cucumbers
Abyssal plain
Brittle star
Flower-basket sponge
Tripod fish
Deep-sea anemone

Note: Neither the marine life or zones are drawn to scale

Sunlit zone
0–660 ft
(0–200 m)

Twilight zone
660–3,300 ft
(200–1,000 m)

Dark zone
3,300–13,200 ft
(1,000–4,000 m)

Abyss
13,200–19,800 ft
(4,000–6,000 m)

Trench
Over 19,800 ft
(6,000 m)

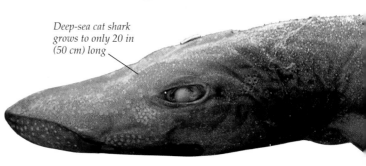

Deep-sea cat shark grows to only 20 in (50 cm) long

THE OCEAN'S ZONES
The ocean is divided into broad zones, according to how far down sunlight penetrates, and water temperature and pressure. In the sunlit zone, there is plenty of light, much water movement, and seasonal changes in temperature. Beneath this is the twilight zone, the maximum depth where light penetrates. Temperatures here decrease rapidly with depth to about 41°F (5°C). Deeper yet is the dark zone, where there is no light and temperatures drop to about 34–36°F (1–2°C). Still in darkness and even deeper is the abyss and then the trenches. There are also zones on the sea bed. The shallowest zone lies on the continental shelf. Below this are the continental slope, the abyssal plains, and the sea-floor trenches.

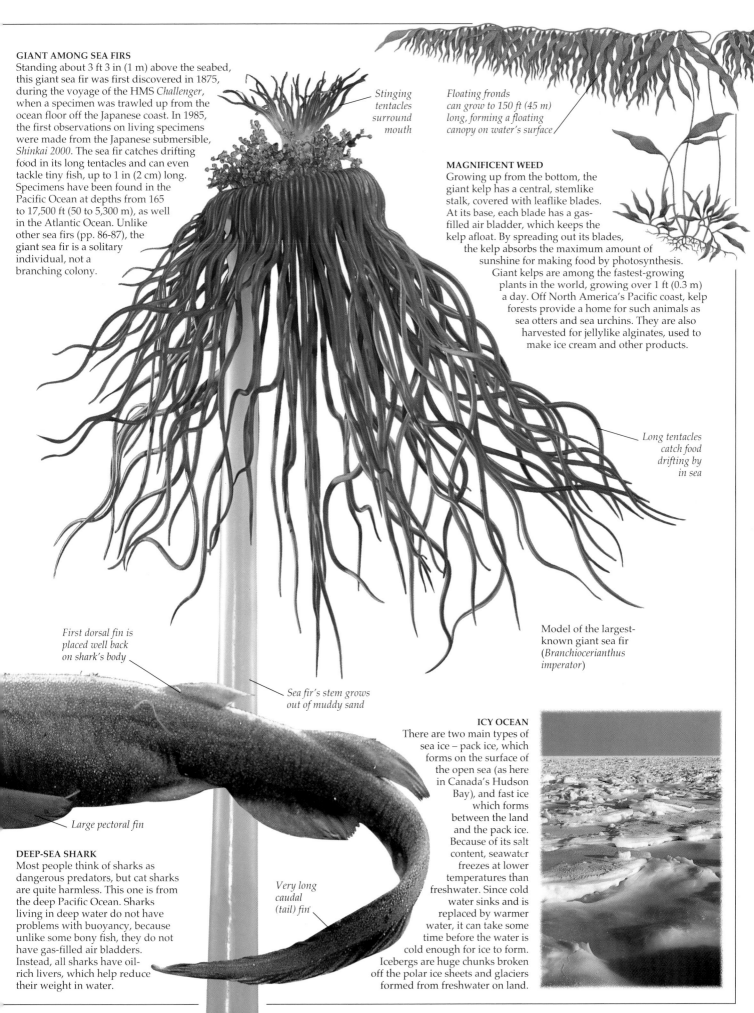

GIANT AMONG SEA FIRS
Standing about 3 ft 3 in (1 m) above the seabed, this giant sea fir was first discovered in 1875, during the voyage of the HMS *Challenger*, when a specimen was trawled up from the ocean floor off the Japanese coast. In 1985, the first observations on living specimens were made from the Japanese submersible, *Shinkai 2000*. The sea fir catches drifting food in its long tentacles and can even tackle tiny fish, up to 1 in (2 cm) long. Specimens have been found in the Pacific Ocean at depths from 165 to 17,500 ft (50 to 5,300 m), as well in the Atlantic Ocean. Unlike other sea firs (pp. 86-87), the giant sea fir is a solitary individual, not a branching colony.

Stinging tentacles surround mouth

Floating fronds can grow to 150 ft (45 m) long, forming a floating canopy on water's surface

MAGNIFICENT WEED
Growing up from the bottom, the giant kelp has a central, stemlike stalk, covered with leaflike blades. At its base, each blade has a gas-filled air bladder, which keeps the kelp afloat. By spreading out its blades, the kelp absorbs the maximum amount of sunshine for making food by photosynthesis. Giant kelps are among the fastest-growing plants in the world, growing over 1 ft (0.3 m) a day. Off North America's Pacific coast, kelp forests provide a home for such animals as sea otters and sea urchins. They are also harvested for jellylike alginates, used to make ice cream and other products.

Long tentacles catch food drifting by in sea

First dorsal fin is placed well back on shark's body

Sea fir's stem grows out of muddy sand

Model of the largest-known giant sea fir (*Branchiocerianthus imperator*)

Large pectoral fin

DEEP-SEA SHARK
Most people think of sharks as dangerous predators, but cat sharks are quite harmless. This one is from the deep Pacific Ocean. Sharks living in deep water do not have problems with buoyancy, because unlike some bony fish, they do not have gas-filled air bladders. Instead, all sharks have oil-rich livers, which help reduce their weight in water.

Very long caudal (tail) fin

ICY OCEAN
There are two main types of sea ice – pack ice, which forms on the surface of the open sea (as here in Canada's Hudson Bay), and fast ice which forms between the land and the pack ice. Because of its salt content, seawater freezes at lower temperatures than freshwater. Since cold water sinks and is replaced by warmer water, it can take some time before the water is cold enough for ice to form. Icebergs are huge chunks broken off the polar ice sheets and glaciers formed from freshwater on land.

Waves and weather

Sᴇᴀ ᴡᴀᴛᴇʀ ɪꜱ ᴄᴏɴꜱᴛᴀɴᴛʟʏ moving. At the surface, wind-driven waves can be 50 ft (15 m) from crest to trough. Major surface currents are driven by the prevailing winds. Both surface and deep-water currents help modify the world's climate by taking cold water from the polar regions toward the tropics, and vice versa. Shifts in this flow affect life in the ocean. In an El Niño climatic event, warm water starts to flow down the west side of South America, which stops nutrient-rich, cold water from rising up, causing plankton growth to slow and fisheries to fail. Heat from oceans creates air movement, from swirling hurricanes to daytime breezes onshore, or nighttime ones offshore. Breezes occur when the ocean heats up more slowly than the land in the day. Cool air above the water blows in, replacing warm air above the land, and the reverse happens at night.

DOWN THE SPOUT
Water spouts (spinning sprays sucked up from the surface) begin when whirling air drops down from a storm cloud to the ocean.

RIVERS OF THE SEA
Currents are huge masses of water moving through the oceans. The course currents follow is not precisely the same as the trade winds and westerlies, because currents are deflected off land and the Coriolis force produced by the earth's rotation. The latter causes currents to shift to the right in the Northern Hemisphere and to the left in the Southern. There are also currents that flow due to differences in density of seawater.

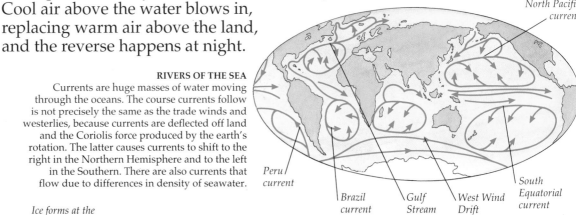

North Pacific current

Peru current

Brazil current

Gulf Stream

West Wind Drift

South Equatorial current

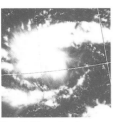

Day 2: Thunderstorms as swirling cloud mass

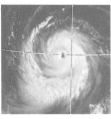

Day 4: Winds have increased in intensity

Day 7: Strong winds

A HURRICANE IS BORN
These satellite photographs show a hurricane developing. On day 2 a swirling cloud mass is formed. By day 4 fierce winds develop at the center. By day 7 winds are the strongest.

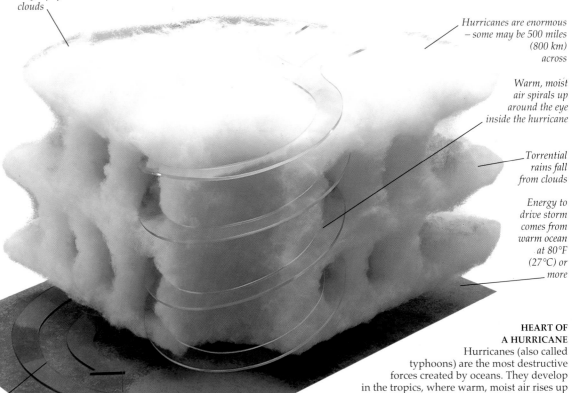

Ice forms at the very top of the clouds

Hurricanes are enormous – some may be 500 miles (800 km) across

Warm, moist air spirals up around the eye inside the hurricane

Torrential rains fall from clouds

Energy to drive storm comes from warm ocean at 80°F (27°C) or more

Strongest winds of up to 220 mph (360 kph) occur just outside the eye

HEART OF A HURRICANE
Hurricanes (also called typhoons) are the most destructive forces created by oceans. They develop in the tropics, where warm, moist air rises up from the ocean's surface and creates storm clouds. As more air spirals upward, energy is released, fueling stronger winds that whirl around the "eye" (a calm area of extreme low pressure). Hurricanes move onto land, causing terrible devastation. Away from the ocean, hurricanes die out.

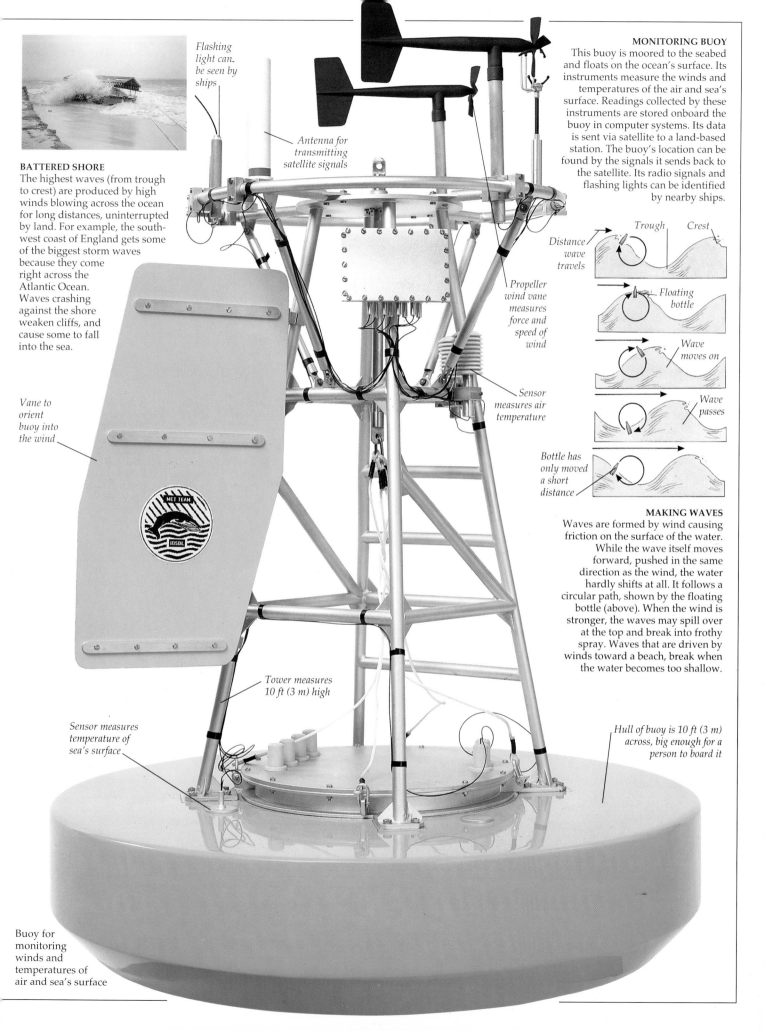

Flashing light can be seen by ships

Antenna for transmitting satellite signals

MONITORING BUOY
This buoy is moored to the seabed and floats on the ocean's surface. Its instruments measure the winds and temperatures of the air and sea's surface. Readings collected by these instruments are stored onboard the buoy in computer systems. Its data is sent via satellite to a land-based station. The buoy's location can be found by the signals it sends back to the satellite. Its radio signals and flashing lights can be identified by nearby ships.

BATTERED SHORE
The highest waves (from trough to crest) are produced by high winds blowing across the ocean for long distances, uninterrupted by land. For example, the south-west coast of England gets some of the biggest storm waves because they come right across the Atlantic Ocean. Waves crashing against the shore weaken cliffs, and cause some to fall into the sea.

Distance wave travels   *Trough*   *Crest*

Floating bottle

Wave moves on

Wave passes

Bottle has only moved a short distance

Vane to orient buoy into the wind

Propeller wind vane measures force and speed of wind

Sensor measures air temperature

MET TEAM
IOSDL

MAKING WAVES
Waves are formed by wind causing friction on the surface of the water. While the wave itself moves forward, pushed in the same direction as the wind, the water hardly shifts at all. It follows a circular path, shown by the floating bottle (above). When the wind is stronger, the waves may spill over at the top and break into frothy spray. Waves that are driven by winds toward a beach, break when the water becomes too shallow.

Tower measures 10 ft (3 m) high

Sensor measures temperature of sea's surface

Hull of buoy is 10 ft (3 m) across, big enough for a person to board it

Buoy for monitoring winds and temperatures of air and sea's surface

Sandy and muddy

In SHALLOW COASTAL WATERS, from the lowest part of the shore to the edge of the continental shelf, sand and mud are washed from the land, creating vast stretches of sea floor that look like underwater deserts. Without rocks, there are no abundant growths of seaweeds to hide among, so animals that move above the sandy floor are exposed to predators. Many creatures protect themselves by burrowing in the soft seabed. Some worms hide inside their own tubes and feed by spreading out a fan of tentacles or by drawing water containing food particles into their tubes. Other worms, such as the sea mouse, move around in search of food. Flatfish (fish with eyes on one side of the head in the adult, like a flounder) are common on the sandy seabed, looking for any readily available food, such as peacock worms. All the animals shown here live in the coastal waters of the Atlantic Ocean.

Tough papery tube protects soft worm inside

Worm can grow up to 16 in (40 cm) long

Bulky body covered by dense mat of fine hairs

Coarse, shiny bristles help it move along seabed

BEAUTIFUL BRISTLE WORM
The sea mouse, or bristle worm, plows its way through muddy sand on the seabed and is often washed up on the beach after storms. The shiny, rainbow-colored spines help propel it along and may make this chunky worm less appetizing to fish. The sea mouse usually keeps its rear end out of the sand to bring in a stream of fresh seawater to help it breathe. Sea mice grow to 4 in (10 cm) long and eat any dead animals they may find in the sand.

Light color helps it merge into sand

Thick trunk looks like peanut when body retracts

Surface of plump, unsegmented body feels rough

Poisonous spines on first dorsal fin

PEANUT WORM
Many different kinds of worms live in the sea. This is one of the sipunculid worms, sometimes called peanut worms. Its stretchy front part can retract into its thicker trunk. Peanut worms usually burrow in sand and mud, but some of the 320 kinds of peanut worm live in empty sea shells and in coral crevices.

Front part can also retract

Poisonous spine on front of gill cover

High-set eye allows all-around vision

Mouth surrounded by tentacles

WARY WEEVER
When a weever fish is buried in sand, its eyes on top of its head help it see what is going on. The weever's strategically placed poisonous spines provide it with extra defense. Its spines can inflict nasty wounds on humans if it is accidentally stepped on in shallow water or caught in fishermen's nets.

FLATFISH
Flounders cruise along the seabed looking for food. They can nibble the tops off peacock worms if they are quick enough to catch them.

Parapodia, or feetlike flaps

Fan-shaped flaps beat to let food pass along worm's body

Feelerlike palps (sense organs)

Mouth

Parchment worm outside its tube

Fan-shaped flap

When buried, the tube is often U-shaped

Parapodia

Red seaweed grows on whitish ends of tube

Tentacle, extended in water, used for feeding and breathing

A LOOK INSIDE
This bizarre looking worm lives in a U-shaped tube with ends that stick out above the mud's surface. The worm feeds by drawing water containing food into its tube. Fan-shaped flaps in the middle of the worm's body create a water current. Food is trapped in a slimy net, which is rolled up and passed toward the mouth. A new net is then made and the process repeated. At night this worm can eject a cloud of glowing material from its burrow, perhaps to ward off predators.

Tentacles disappear fast into tube if danger is present

LIKE A PEACOCK'S FAN
With their crown of tentacles, peacock worms look like plants, not animals. To help them feed and breathe, tiny hairs on the tentacles' fine fingers create a water current, which passes through the crown. Particles in this current are passed down rows of beating hairs into the mouth in the crown's center. Larger particles, such as sand grains, are not eaten but help to make the tube instead.

Peacock worm can be more than 10 in (25 cm) long

Tube made of mud and sand bound together with worm's hardened slime

Soft seabed

SWIMMING OVER a soft seabed, using a mask and snorkel, it is possible to see only a few animals because most of them live buried in the sand. Look closely and you may see signs of buried life – a crab's feathery antennae or a clam's siphon) – which help these animals get a clean supply of water containing oxygen to breathe. Some fish, like the eagle ray, visit the soft seabed to feed on burrowing clams. Other animals are found only where sea grasses grow on sandy bottoms. Sea grasses are not seaweeds but flowering plants. They are food for many animals, including dugongs and manatees – the only plant-eating marine mammals.

Tough skin protects dugong

DOCILE DUGONG
Dugongs live in shallow tropical waters, where they feed on sea grasses growing in the soft seabed. They often dig down into the sand to eat the food-rich roots of sea grasses. These gentle, shy animals are still hunted in some places.

SHELL BOAT
In Botticelli's *The Birth of Venus*, the Roman goddess rises from the water in a scallop shell. In real life, scallop shells found in the soft seabed are too heavy to float.

This sea pen can grow to 8 in (20 cm) in height

ELEGANT PEN
Looking like an old-fashioned quill pen, this relative of the sea anemone (pp. 94-95) lives in the soft seabed. Rows of tiny polyps, or buds, on each side of its body are used to capture small animals drifting by for food. Sea pens glow in the dark if disturbed. Some sea pens grow on the bottom of the deep ocean.

Anemone-like polyp unfurls when feeding

Long dorsal fin runs along almost whole length of body

Long anal fin

Red band fish may grow to 28 in (70 cm) in length

Stem of sea pen anchors in sandy seabed

RED BAND FISH
This fish usually lives in burrows in the soft seabed, down to depths of about 660 ft (200 m). It is also found swimming among sea grasses. Sometimes red band fish are found washed up on the beach after storms. Out of its burrow, the fish swims by passing waves down its body. It feeds on small animals drifting by.

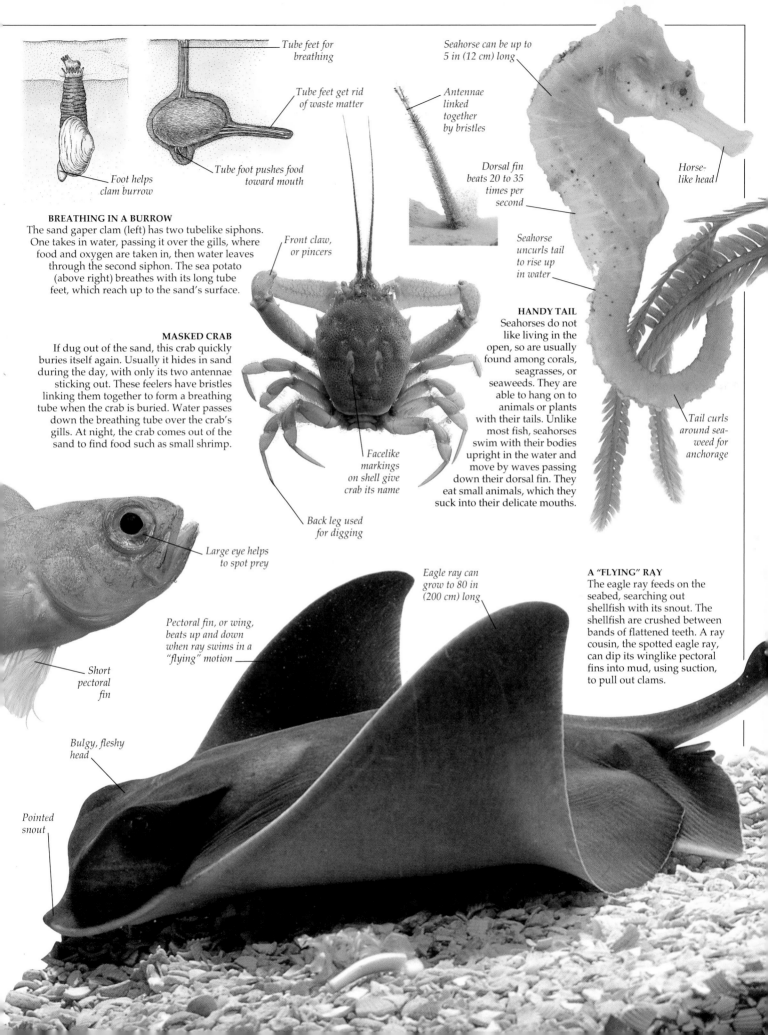

Tube feet for breathing

Foot helps clam burrow

Tube feet get rid of waste matter

Tube foot pushes food toward mouth

BREATHING IN A BURROW
The sand gaper clam (left) has two tubelike siphons. One takes in water, passing it over the gills, where food and oxygen are taken in, then water leaves through the second siphon. The sea potato (above right) breathes with its long tube feet, which reach up to the sand's surface.

Seahorse can be up to 5 in (12 cm) long

Antennae linked together by bristles

Dorsal fin beats 20 to 35 times per second

Horse-like head

Seahorse uncurls tail to rise up in water

Front claw, or pincers

MASKED CRAB
If dug out of the sand, this crab quickly buries itself again. Usually it hides in sand during the day, with only its two antennae sticking out. These feelers have bristles linking them together to form a breathing tube when the crab is buried. Water passes down the breathing tube over the crab's gills. At night, the crab comes out of the sand to find food such as small shrimp.

Facelike markings on shell give crab its name

Back leg used for digging

HANDY TAIL
Seahorses do not like living in the open, so are usually found among corals, seagrasses, or seaweeds. They are able to hang on to animals or plants with their tails. Unlike most fish, seahorses swim with their bodies upright in the water and move by waves passing down their dorsal fin. They eat small animals, which they suck into their delicate mouths.

Tail curls around sea-weed for anchorage

Large eye helps to spot prey

Short pectoral fin

Eagle ray can grow to 80 in (200 cm) long

Pectoral fin, or wing, beats up and down when ray swims in a "flying" motion

A "FLYING" RAY
The eagle ray feeds on the seabed, searching out shellfish with its snout. The shellfish are crushed between bands of flattened teeth. A ray cousin, the spotted eagle ray, can dip its winglike pectoral fins into mud, using suction, to pull out clams.

Bulgy, fleshy head

Pointed snout

Rocks underwater

ROCKY SEABEDS are found in coastal waters where currents sweep away any sand and mud. With the strong water movement, animals have to cling on to the rocks, find crevices to hide in, or take shelter among seaweeds. A few remarkable animals, such as the clamlike piddocks and some sea urchins, can bore into solid rock to make their homes. Sea urchins bore cavities in hard rock, while piddocks drill into softer rocks such as sandstone or chalk. Some creatures hide under smaller stones, but only if they are lodged in the soft seabed. When masses of loose pebbles roll around, animals and seaweeds can be crushed. However, some crustaceans, such as lobsters, can regain a lost limb crushed by a stone, and starfish can even regrow a missing arm. Some animals can survive at the seashore's edge, especially in rock pools, but many need to stay submerged.

Sea urchin boring into rocks

Piddock

ROCK BORERS
Some sea urchins use their spines and teeth beneath their shells to bore spaces in rock, while piddocks drill with the tips of their shells. Using its muscular foot, the piddock twists and turns to drill and hold on to its burrow. Both are found in shallow water and on the lower shore.

BEAUTIFUL BUTTERFLY
Blennies, small fish living in shallow water, often rest on the bottom and hide in crannies. They lay their eggs in sheltered places, such as abandoned bottles, and guard them from predators. Blennies feed on small creatures, such as mites, and live on rocky or stony ground to depths of 66 ft (20 m).

Dorsal fin has eyespot to frighten predators

Spiny shell helps deter predators

SPINY LOBSTER
European spiny lobsters, or crawfish, are reddish brown in life. With their small pincers, spiny lobsters are restricted to eating soft prey, such as worms or dead animals. They live among rocks, hiding in crevices during the day, but venturing out over the seabed at night to find food. Some kinds of spiny lobsters move in long lines, keeping in touch with the lobster in front with their antennae.

Delicate claw on tip of walking leg

European spiny lobster, also known as a crawfish

Leg used for walking

Tail can be flapped so lobster can swim backward

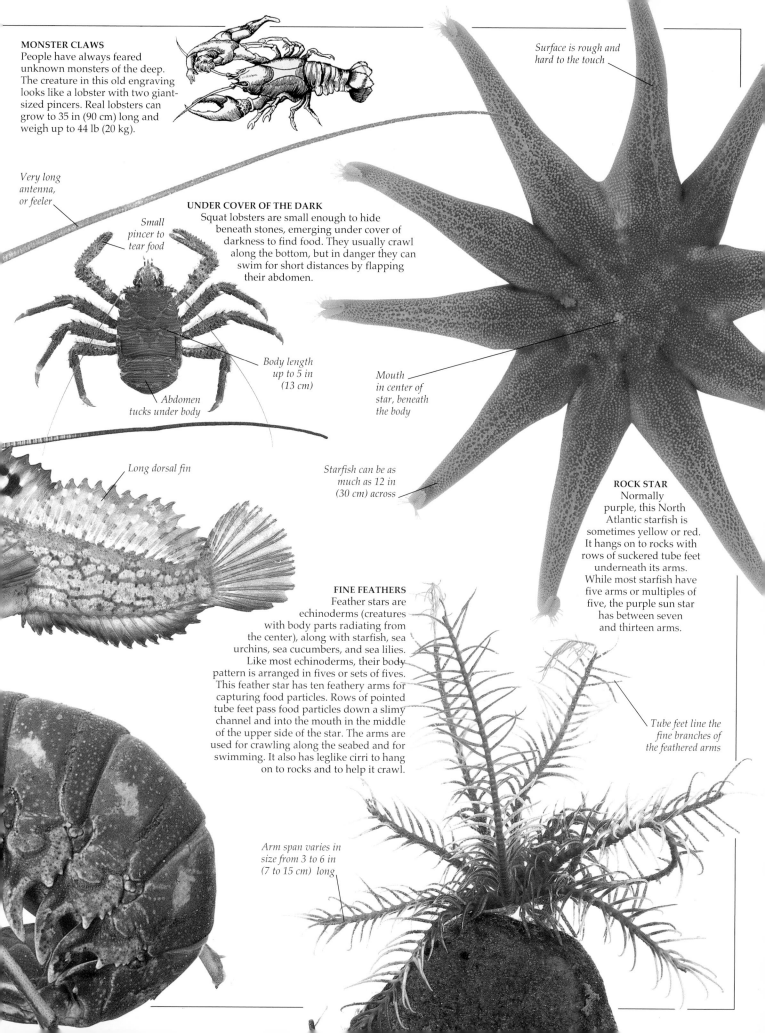

MONSTER CLAWS
People have always feared unknown monsters of the deep. The creature in this old engraving looks like a lobster with two giant-sized pincers. Real lobsters can grow to 35 in (90 cm) long and weigh up to 44 lb (20 kg).

Surface is rough and hard to the touch

Very long antenna, or feeler

Small pincer to tear food

UNDER COVER OF THE DARK
Squat lobsters are small enough to hide beneath stones, emerging under cover of darkness to find food. They usually crawl along the bottom, but in danger they can swim for short distances by flapping their abdomen.

Body length up to 5 in (13 cm)

Abdomen tucks under body

Mouth in center of star, beneath the body

Long dorsal fin

Starfish can be as much as 12 in (30 cm) across

ROCK STAR
Normally purple, this North Atlantic starfish is sometimes yellow or red. It hangs on to rocks with rows of suckered tube feet underneath its arms. While most starfish have five arms or multiples of five, the purple sun star has between seven and thirteen arms.

FINE FEATHERS
Feather stars are echinoderms (creatures with body parts radiating from the center), along with starfish, sea urchins, sea cucumbers, and sea lilies. Like most echinoderms, their body pattern is arranged in fives or sets of fives. This feather star has ten feathery arms for capturing food particles. Rows of pointed tube feet pass food particles down a slimy channel and into the mouth in the middle of the upper side of the star. The arms are used for crawling along the seabed and for swimming. It also has leglike cirri to hang on to rocks and to help it crawl.

Tube feet line the fine branches of the feathered arms

Arm span varies in size from 3 to 6 in (7 to 15 cm) long

On the rocks

IN THE SHALLOW, COOL WATERS above rocky seabeds, forests of large brown seaweeds called kelp provide a home, hunting ground, and resting place for many creatures. Along North America's Pacific coast, sea otters wrap themselves in kelp and snooze on the surface. At the kelp's base, its holdfast, or rootlike anchor, is home for many animals, such as crabs, and other seaweeds. Unlike the roots of land plants, kelp's holdfast is only an anchor – it does not absorb nutrients or water. Other animals live on the kelp's surface or grow directly onto the rocks, capturing food brought to them in the currents. Sea firs look like plants, but are animals belonging to the same group as sea anemones, jellyfish, and corals, and all have stinging tentacles. Mussels anchored to rocks are shelter for animals that live among, or within, their shells.

A type of brown seaweed (kelp) found in the Pacific Ocean

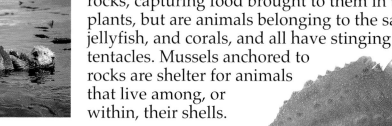

PRETTY BABY
Young lumpsuckers are more beautiful than their dumpy parents, which cling on to rocks with suckerlike fins on their bellies. Adult lumpsuckers move into shallow water to breed, and the father guards the eggs.

DELIGHTFUL MARINE MAMMAL
Sea otters swim and rest among the giant kelp fronds along North America's Pacific coast. They dive down to the seabed to pick up shellfish, smashing them open by banging them against a rock balanced on their chest.

Scaleless body is covered with small warty bumps

Juvenile lumpsucker

Each sturdy, blunt finger measures at least 1.25 in (3 cm) across

ANCHORED ALGAE
Growing in shallow water, kelp is often battered by waves. Holdfasts of the large, tough, brown algae keep it firmly anchored by tightly gripping the rocks.

Fleshy fingers supported by tiny, hard splinters

White, anemone-like polyp captures food from fast-moving currents

Holdfast of oarweed kelp

DEAD MAN'S FINGERS
When this soft coral is washed up on the shore, its rubbery, fleshy form explains its name! Growing on rocks, the colonies consist of many polyps (feeding bodies) within a fleshy, orange, or white base.

Gills

Holdfast must be strong, as some kinds of kelp can grow over 33 ft (10 m) long

SEA MAT
The lacy-looking growth on the surface of this piece of kelp (left) is a bryozoan, or moss animal. These animals live in colonies where many individuals grow next to each other. Each little compartment houses one of these animals, which come out to feed, capturing food in their tiny tentacles. The colony grows, as individuals bud off new individuals. Other kinds of moss animal grow upward and look a little like seaweeds or corals. Between the sea mats, a blue-rayed limpet grazes on the kelp's surface.

SEA SLUG
Many sea slugs are meat eaters. This slug lives on the soft coral known as dead-man's fingers. Some sea slugs are able to eat the stinging tentacles of anemones and keep the stings for their own protection. Sea slug eggs hatch into swimming young, which then settle and turn into adults.

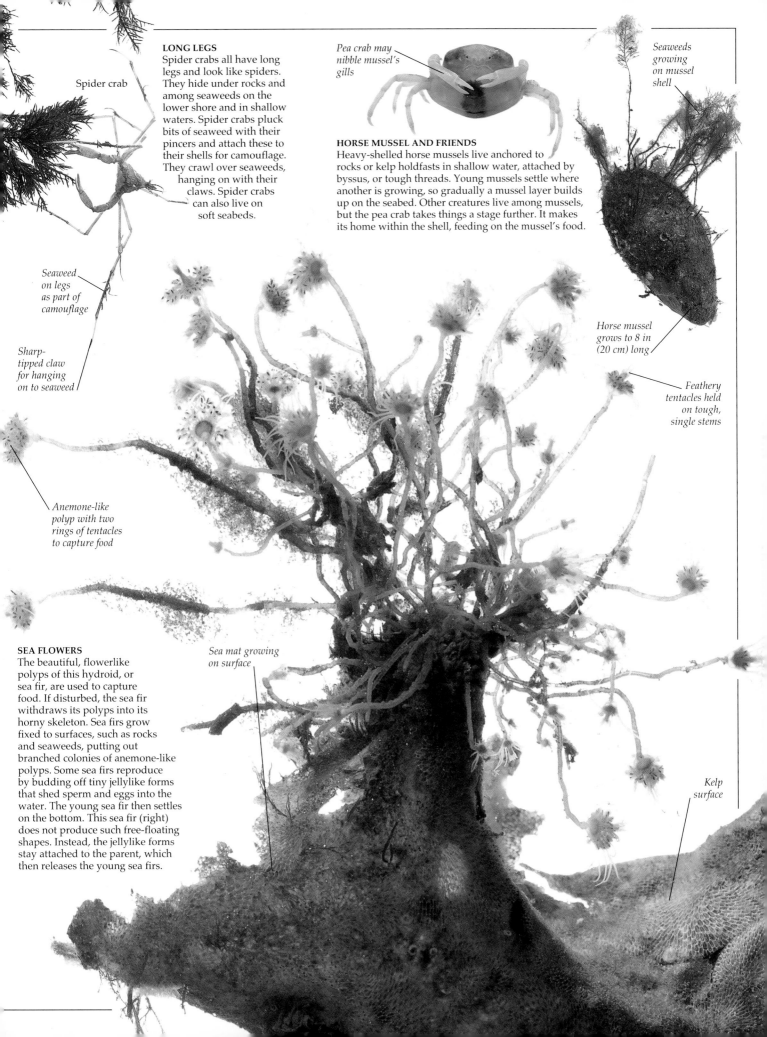

Spider crab

LONG LEGS
Spider crabs all have long
legs and look like spiders.
They hide under rocks and
among seaweeds on the
lower shore and in shallow
waters. Spider crabs pluck
bits of seaweed with their
pincers and attach these to
their shells for camouflage.
They crawl over seaweeds,
hanging on with their
claws. Spider crabs
can also live on
soft seabeds.

*Pea crab may
nibble mussel's
gills*

*Seaweeds
growing
on mussel
shell*

HORSE MUSSEL AND FRIENDS
Heavy-shelled horse mussels live anchored to
rocks or kelp holdfasts in shallow water, attached by
byssus, or tough threads. Young mussels settle where
another is growing, so gradually a mussel layer builds
up on the seabed. Other creatures live among mussels,
but the pea crab takes things a stage further. It makes
its home within the shell, feeding on the mussel's food.

*Seaweed
on legs
as part of
camouflage*

*Sharp-
tipped claw
for hanging
on to seaweed*

*Horse mussel
grows to 8 in
(20 cm) long*

*Feathery
tentacles held
on tough,
single stems*

*Anemone-like
polyp with two
rings of tentacles
to capture food*

SEA FLOWERS
The beautiful, flowerlike
polyps of this hydroid, or
sea fir, are used to capture
food. If disturbed, the sea fir
withdraws its polyps into its
horny skeleton. Sea firs grow
fixed to surfaces, such as rocks
and seaweeds, putting out
branched colonies of anemone-like
polyps. Some sea firs reproduce
by budding off tiny jellylike forms
that shed sperm and eggs into the
water. The young sea fir then settles
on the bottom. This sea fir (right)
does not produce such free-floating
shapes. Instead, the jellylike forms
stay attached to the parent, which
then releases the young sea firs.

*Sea mat growing
on surface*

*Kelp
surface*

The coral kingdom

IN THE WARM, CRYSTAL-CLEAR WATERS of the tropics, coral reefs flourish, covering vast areas. Made of the skeletons of stony corals, coral reefs are cemented together by chalky algae. Most stony corals are colonies of many tiny, anemone-like individuals, called polyps. Each polyp makes its own hard limestone cup (skeleton), which protects its soft body. To make their skeletons, the coral polyps need the help of microscopic, single-celled algae that live inside them. The algae need sunlight to grow, which is why coral reefs are found only in sunny, surface waters. In return for giving the algae a home, corals get some food from them but also capture plankton with their tentacles. Only the upper layer of a reef is made of living corals, which build upon skeletons of dead polyps. Coral reefs are also home to soft corals and sea fans, which do not have stony skeletons. Related to sea anemones and jellyfish, corals grow in an exquisite variety of shapes (mushroom, daisy, staghorn) and some have colorful skeletons.

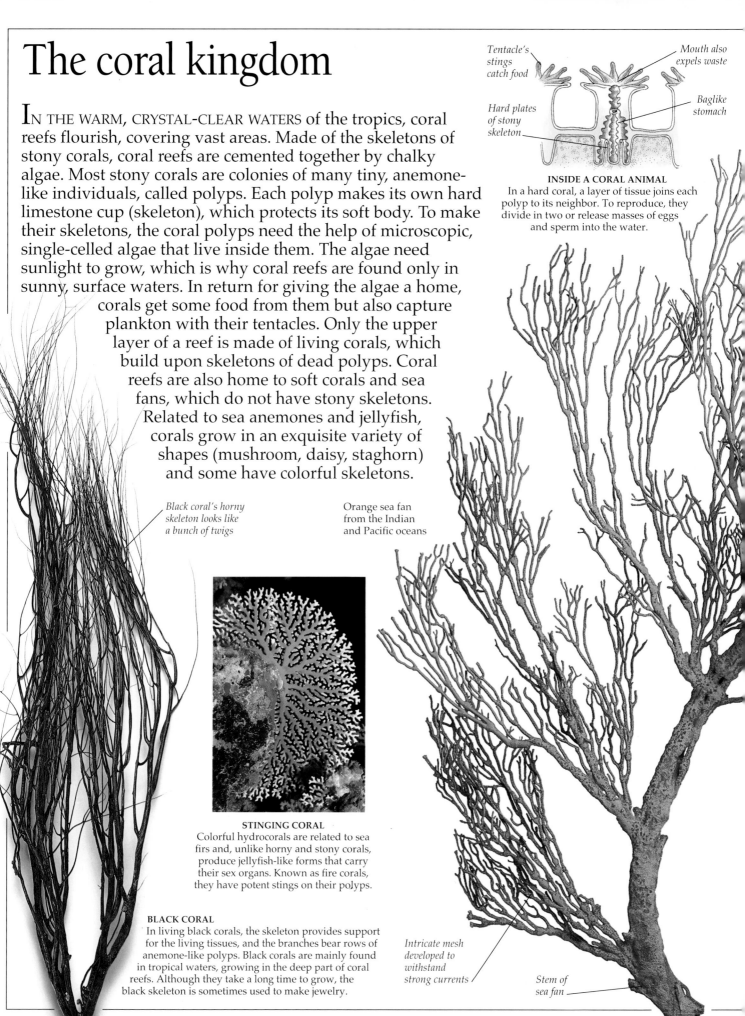

Tentacle's stings catch food

Mouth also expels waste

Hard plates of stony skeleton

Baglike stomach

INSIDE A CORAL ANIMAL
In a hard coral, a layer of tissue joins each polyp to its neighbor. To reproduce, they divide in two or release masses of eggs and sperm into the water.

Black coral's horny skeleton looks like a bunch of twigs

Orange sea fan from the Indian and Pacific oceans

STINGING CORAL
Colorful hydrocorals are related to sea firs and, unlike horny and stony corals, produce jellyfish-like forms that carry their sex organs. Known as fire corals, they have potent stings on their polyps.

BLACK CORAL
In living black corals, the skeleton provides support for the living tissues, and the branches bear rows of anemone-like polyps. Black corals are mainly found in tropical waters, growing in the deep part of coral reefs. Although they take a long time to grow, the black skeleton is sometimes used to make jewelry.

Intricate mesh developed to withstand strong currents

Stem of sea fan

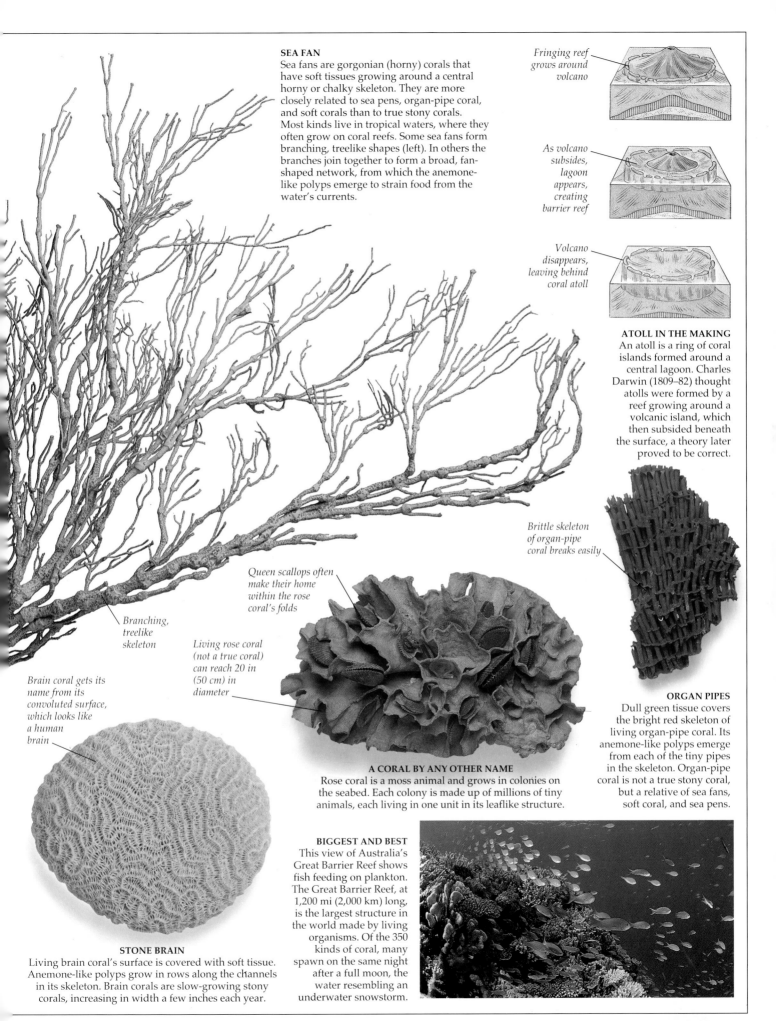

SEA FAN

Sea fans are gorgonian (horny) corals that have soft tissues growing around a central horny or chalky skeleton. They are more closely related to sea pens, organ-pipe coral, and soft corals than to true stony corals. Most kinds live in tropical waters, where they often grow on coral reefs. Some sea fans form branching, treelike shapes (left). In others the branches join together to form a broad, fan-shaped network, from which the anemone-like polyps emerge to strain food from the water's currents.

Fringing reef grows around volcano

As volcano subsides, lagoon appears, creating barrier reef

Volcano disappears, leaving behind coral atoll

ATOLL IN THE MAKING

An atoll is a ring of coral islands formed around a central lagoon. Charles Darwin (1809–82) thought atolls were formed by a reef growing around a volcanic island, which then subsided beneath the surface, a theory later proved to be correct.

Brittle skeleton of organ-pipe coral breaks easily

Branching, treelike skeleton

Queen scallops often make their home within the rose coral's folds

Living rose coral (not a true coral) can reach 20 in (50 cm) in diameter

Brain coral gets its name from its convoluted surface, which looks like a human brain

ORGAN PIPES

Dull green tissue covers the bright red skeleton of living organ-pipe coral. Its anemone-like polyps emerge from each of the tiny pipes in the skeleton. Organ-pipe coral is not a true stony coral, but a relative of sea fans, soft coral, and sea pens.

A CORAL BY ANY OTHER NAME

Rose coral is a moss animal and grows in colonies on the seabed. Each colony is made up of millions of tiny animals, each living in one unit in its leaflike structure.

STONE BRAIN

Living brain coral's surface is covered with soft tissue. Anemone-like polyps grow in rows along the channels in its skeleton. Brain corals are slow-growing stony corals, increasing in width a few inches each year.

BIGGEST AND BEST

This view of Australia's Great Barrier Reef shows fish feeding on plankton. The Great Barrier Reef, at 1,200 mi (2,000 km) long, is the largest structure in the world made by living organisms. Of the 350 kinds of coral, many spawn on the same night after a full moon, the water resembling an underwater snowstorm.

Life on a coral reef

A GIANT CLAM
The giant blue clam grows to about 1 ft (30 cm) long, but the largest giant clams may reach 3 ft 4 in (1 m). The colorful mantle exposed at the edge of their shells contains hordes of single-celled algae that make their own food by using the energy from sunlight. The clam absorbs nutrients from the growing crop of algae.

Mantle

CORAL REEFS HAVE an amazing variety of marine life, from teeming multitudes of brightly colored fish to giant clams wedged into rocks. Every bit of space on the reef provides a hiding place or shelter for some animal or plant. At night, a host of amazing creatures emerge from coral caves and crevices to feed. All the living organisms on the reef depend for their survival on the stony corals, which recycle the scarce nutrients from the clear, blue, tropical waters. People as well as animals rely on coral reefs, for they protect coastlines and attract tourist money. Some island nations even live on coral atolls. Sadly, in spite of being one of the great natural wonders of the world, coral reefs are now under threat. Reefs are being broken up for building materials, damaged by snorkelers and divers touching or stepping on them, dynamited by fishermen, ripped up by curio collectors, covered by soil eroded by the destruction of rain forests, and polluted by sewage and oil spills.

Green color helps camouflage sea slug among seaweeds

Tentacles of sea anemone covered with stings to put off predators

Large eye for keeping a watch for danger

Layer of slimy mucus protects clown fish from anemone's stinging tentacles

Side fin used to steer and change direction

FRILLY LETTUCE
Sea slugs are related to sea snails but do not have shells. Many sea slugs living on coral reefs feed on corals, but the lettuce slug feeds on algae growing on the reef by sucking the sap from individual cells. Chloroplasts, the green part of plant cells, are then stored in the slug's digestive system, where they continue to trap energy from sunlight to make food. Many other reef sea slugs recycle the stings they eat from the coral's tentacles and are brightly colored to warn that they are dangerous.

Stripes break up clown fish's outline, perhaps making it more difficult for predators to see the fish on the reef

LIVING IN HARMONY
Clown fish, which shelter in anemones, live on coral reefs in the Pacific and Indian oceans. Unlike other fish, clown fish are not stung by the anemones. They are protected by a layer of slimy mucus, and the anemone's stinging cells are not even triggered by the fish's presence. Clown fish seldom venture far from their anemone home for fear of attack by other fish. There are many types of clown fish, some living only with certain kinds of anemones.

90

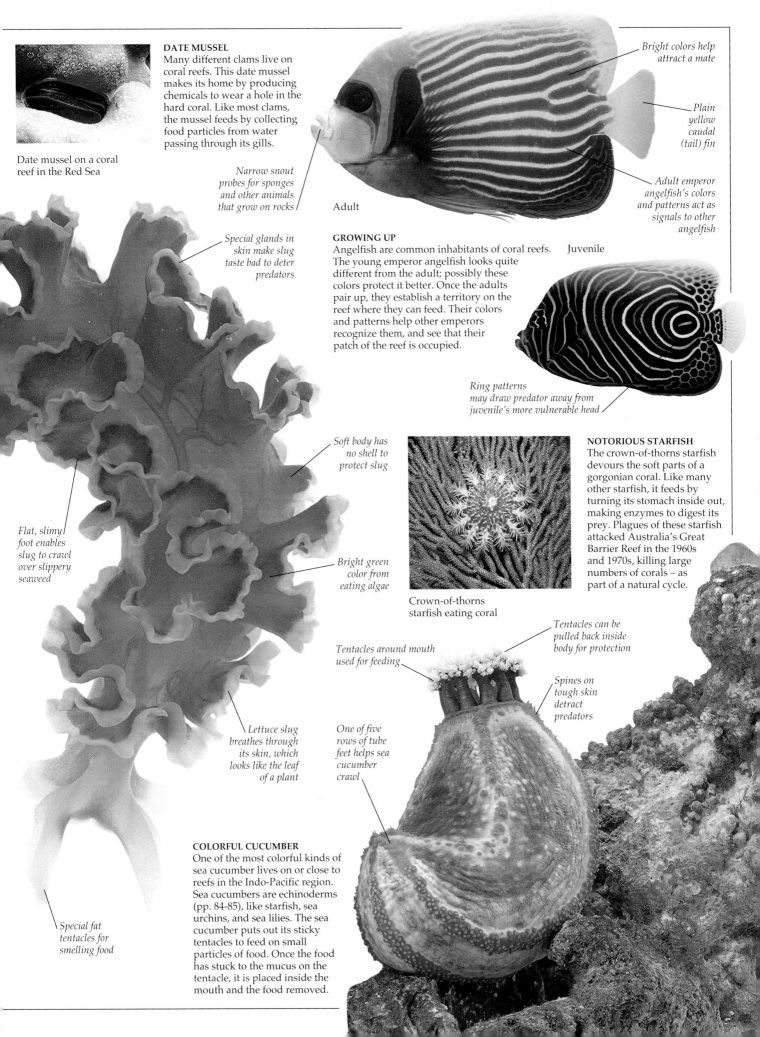

DATE MUSSEL
Many different clams live on coral reefs. This date mussel makes its home by producing chemicals to wear a hole in the hard coral. Like most clams, the mussel feeds by collecting food particles from water passing through its gills.

Date mussel on a coral reef in the Red Sea

Bright colors help attract a mate

Plain yellow caudal (tail) fin

Narrow snout probes for sponges and other animals that grow on rocks

Adult

Adult emperor angelfish's colors and patterns act as signals to other angelfish

Special glands in skin make slug taste bad to deter predators

GROWING UP
Angelfish are common inhabitants of coral reefs. The young emperor angelfish looks quite different from the adult; possibly these colors protect it better. Once the adults pair up, they establish a territory on the reef where they can feed. Their colors and patterns help other emperors recognize them, and see that their patch of the reef is occupied.

Juvenile

Ring patterns may draw predator away from juvenile's more vulnerable head

Soft body has no shell to protect slug

Flat, slimy foot enables slug to crawl over slippery seaweed

Bright green color from eating algae

NOTORIOUS STARFISH
The crown-of-thorns starfish devours the soft parts of a gorgonian coral. Like many other starfish, it feeds by turning its stomach inside out, making enzymes to digest its prey. Plagues of these starfish attacked Australia's Great Barrier Reef in the 1960s and 1970s, killing large numbers of corals – as part of a natural cycle.

Crown-of-thorns starfish eating coral

Lettuce slug breathes through its skin, which looks like the leaf of a plant

Tentacles can be pulled back inside body for protection

Tentacles around mouth used for feeding

Spines on tough skin detract predators

One of five rows of tube feet helps sea cucumber crawl

Special fat tentacles for smelling food

COLORFUL CUCUMBER
One of the most colorful kinds of sea cucumber lives on or close to reefs in the Indo-Pacific region. Sea cucumbers are echinoderms (pp. 84-85), like starfish, sea urchins, and sea lilies. The sea cucumber puts out its sticky tentacles to feed on small particles of food. Once the food has stuck to the mucus on the tentacle, it is placed inside the mouth and the food removed.

Sea meadows

THE MOST ABUNDANT PLANTS IN THE OCEAN are too small to be seen with the naked eye. Often single-celled, these minute, floating plants are called phytoplankton. Like all plants, they need sunlight to grow, so are only found in the ocean's upper zone. With the right conditions, phytoplankton multiplies quickly – within a few days – as each cell divides into two, and so on. To grow, phytoplankton needs nutrients from seawater and lots of sunlight. The most light occurs in the tropics but nutrients, especially nitrogen and phosphorus, are in short supply, restricting phytoplankton's growth. Spectacular phytoplankton blooms are found in cooler waters where nutrients (dead plant and animal waste) are brought up from the bottom during storms, and in both cool and warm waters where there are upwellings of nutrient-rich water. Phytoplankton is eaten by swarms of tiny, drifting animals (zooplankton), which provide a feast for small fish (such as herring), which in turn are eaten by larger fish (such as salmon), which in turn are eaten by still larger fish or other predators (such as dolphins). Some larger ocean animals (whale sharks and blue whales) feed directly on zooplankton.

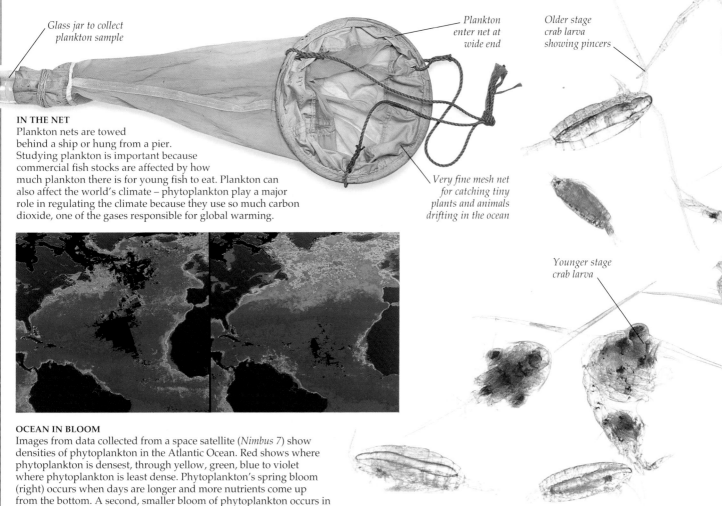

PLANT FOOD
This diatom is one of many phytoplankton that drift in the ocean. Diatoms are the most common kinds of phytoplankton in cooler waters, but single-celled plants called dinoflagellates are common in tropical waters. Many diatoms are single cells, but this one consists of a chain of cells.

Glass jar to collect plankton sample

Plankton enter net at wide end

Older stage crab larva showing pincers

IN THE NET
Plankton nets are towed behind a ship or hung from a pier. Studying plankton is important because commercial fish stocks are affected by how much plankton there is for young fish to eat. Plankton can also affect the world's climate – phytoplankton play a major role in regulating the climate because they use so much carbon dioxide, one of the gases responsible for global warming.

Very fine mesh net for catching tiny plants and animals drifting in the ocean

Younger stage crab larva

OCEAN IN BLOOM
Images from data collected from a space satellite (*Nimbus 7*) show densities of phytoplankton in the Atlantic Ocean. Red shows where phytoplankton is densest, through yellow, green, blue to violet where phytoplankton is least dense. Phytoplankton's spring bloom (right) occurs when days are longer and more nutrients come up from the bottom. A second, smaller bloom of phytoplankton occurs in the autumn. When phytoplankton dies, it sinks to the sea bed with gelatinous zooplankton remains, making sticky clumps called "marine snow."

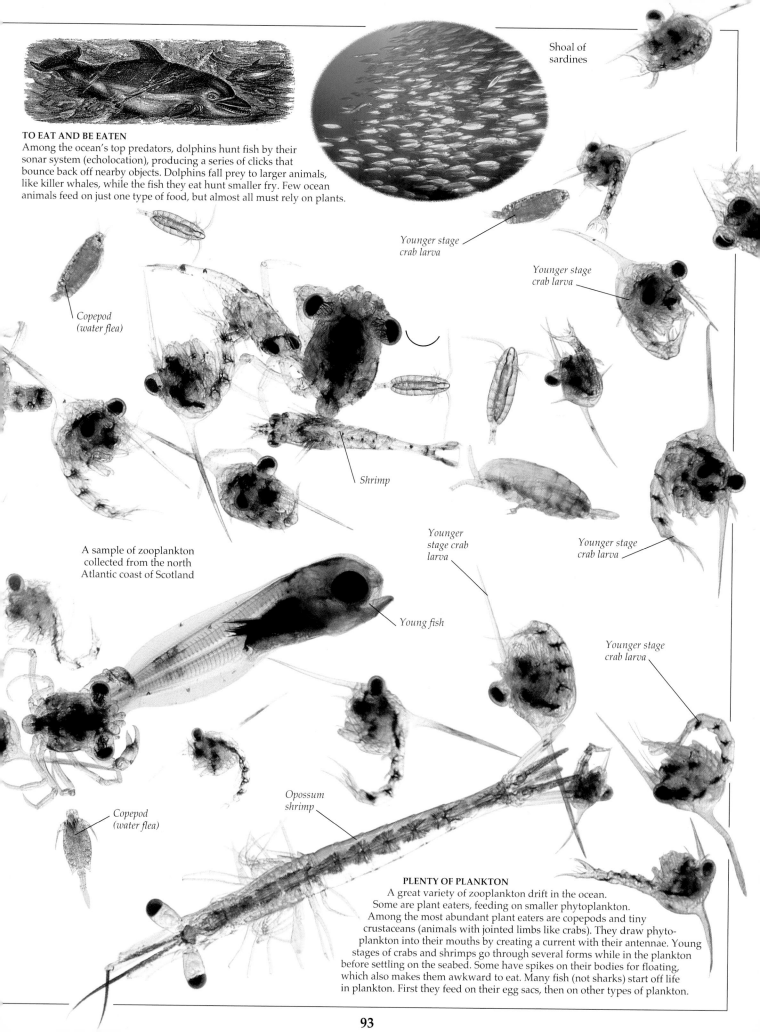

TO EAT AND BE EATEN

Among the ocean's top predators, dolphins hunt fish by their sonar system (echolocation), producing a series of clicks that bounce back off nearby objects. Dolphins fall prey to larger animals, like killer whales, while the fish they eat hunt smaller fry. Few ocean animals feed on just one type of food, but almost all must rely on plants.

Shoal of sardines

Younger stage crab larva

Younger stage crab larva

Copepod (water flea)

Shrimp

A sample of zooplankton collected from the north Atlantic coast of Scotland

Younger stage crab larva

Younger stage crab larva

Young fish

Younger stage crab larva

Opossum shrimp

Copepod (water flea)

PLENTY OF PLANKTON

A great variety of zooplankton drift in the ocean. Some are plant eaters, feeding on smaller phytoplankton. Among the most abundant plant eaters are copepods and tiny crustaceans (animals with jointed limbs like crabs). They draw phytoplankton into their mouths by creating a current with their antennae. Young stages of crabs and shrimps go through several forms while in the plankton before settling on the seabed. Some have spikes on their bodies for floating, which also makes them awkward to eat. Many fish (not sharks) start off life in plankton. First they feed on their egg sacs, then on other types of plankton.

Predators and prey

SOME OCEAN ANIMALS are herbivores (plant eaters), from fish nibbling seaweeds on coral reefs to dugongs chewing sea grasses. There are also many carnivores (meat eaters) in the ocean. Some, such as blue sharks and barracuda, are swift hunters, while others, such as anglerfish and sea anemones, set traps for their prey and wait with snapping jaws or stinging tentacles. Many animals, from the humble sea fan to the giant baleen whale, filter food out of the water. Sea birds find their meals in the ocean by diving for a beakful of prey. Other ocean animals are omnivores – they eat both plants and animals.

COOPERATIVE FEEDING
Humpback whales herd schools of fish by letting out a stream of bubbles as they swim around it. With their mouths open wide to gulp in food and water, whales keep the fish but expel water through sievelike baleen plates in their mouths.

Tiny prey caught in mucus

CAUGHT BY SLIME
Unlike the many jellyfish that trap prey with their stinging tentacles, common jellyfish catch small plankton (drifting animals) in sticky mucus (slime) produced by its bell. The four fleshy arms beneath the bell collect up the food-laden slime, and tiny, hairlike cilia channel it into the mouth.

FANG FACE
The wolffish has strong, fanglike teeth for crunching through the hard shells of crabs, sea urchins, and mussels. As the front set are worn down each year, they are replaced by a new set growing in behind. Wolffish live in cool, deep, northern waters, where they lurk in rocky holes.

Dorsal fin runs along entire length of body

Crooked, yellow, fang-like teeth

Shorter pectoral fin

Tough, wrinkled skin helps protect wolffish living near the seabed

Spines to protect urchin

GRAZING AWAY
The European common sea urchin grazes on seaweeds and animals that grow on the surface of seaweeds, such as sea mats. The urchin uses the set of rasping teeth, called "Aristotle's lantern," on the underside of its shell, which are operated by a complex set of jaws inside. The grazing activities of urchins can control how much seaweed grows in an area. If too many urchins are collected for food or tourist souvenirs, a rocky reef can become overgrown by seaweed.

Pelican diving

Brown pelican catches fish in pouch-like beak

Tube feet used to walk slowly along the seabed

Sea urchin's mouth surrounded by five rasping teeth

Tiny teeth of a basking shark

FISH FEED
Like all pelicans, the brown pelican has a big beak with a large flap of skin, or pouch, to capture a variety of fish. Once they have spotted their prey, they dive into the water, but are too bulky to dive far below the surface. Only brown pelicans dive for their prey. When the pelican surfaces, water is drained from the pouch and the fish swallowed.

TO BITE OR NOT TO BITE
A tiger shark's tooth is like a multipurpose tool, with a sharp point for piercing prey and a serrated bladelike edge for slicing. This shark can eat almost anything, from hard-shelled turtles to soft-bodied seals and sea birds. The rows of a basking shark's tiny teeth are not used, since this shark filters food out of the water with a sieve of gill rakers.

Tiger shark's tooth

TENTACLE TRAPS
The flowerlike dahlia anemones are deadly traps for unwary shrimps and small fish that stray too close to their stinging tentacles. When the prey brush past, hundreds of nematocysts (stinging cells) are triggered and fire their stings. These stings ensnare and weaken prey. The tentacles pass the stricken prey toward the mouth in the center of the anemone – the entrance to the baglike stomach, where the prey is digested.

Stinging tentacle

Any undigested pieces of food are ejected through the mouth

Suckerlike disk lets dahlia anemone attach to any hard surface

Homes and hiding

STAYING HIDDEN is one of the best means of defense –
if a predator cannot see you, it cannot eat you! Many sea
animals shelter among seaweeds, in rocky crevices, or
under the sand. Matching the colors and even the
texture of the background also helps sea
creatures remain undetected. The sargassum
fish even look like bits of seaweed. Hard
shells are useful protection, at least from
weak-jawed predators. Sea snails and clams
make their own shells that cover the body.
Crabs and lobsters have outer shells like suits
of armor, covering the body and each jointed limb.
The hermit crab is unusual because only the front part
of the body and the legs are covered by a hard shell.
Its abdomen is soft, so a hermit crab uses the
empty shell of a sea snail to protect itself.

BLENDING IN
Cuttlefish have different-colored
pigments and rapidly change
color to escape predators.
Their eyes perceive the color
of their surroundings, and
nerve signals are sent by
the brain to tiny bags of
pigment in the skin.
When these pigment
bags contract, the
cuttlefish's color
becomes lighter.

*Cuttlefish
becomes
darker when
pigment bags
expand*

WHAT A WEED!
This fish lives among floating clumps of sargassum
seaweed, where frilly growths on its head, body,
and fins help it avoid being seen by predators,
making a realistic disguise. Many different animals
live in sargassum seaweed, which drifts in large
quantities in the Sargasso Sea of the North Atlantic.

*Hermit crab leaving
old whelk shell*

Anemone

*When out of its shell,
crab is vulnerable
to predators*

*Investigating its new
home by checking size
with its claws*

ALL CHANGE
Like all crustaceans, a hermit crab grows by shedding its
hard, outer skeleton. The hermit crab does this in the safety
of its snail shell home. As it grows, however, it must find a
larger shell to move into. Before leaving its old shell, it will
test the size of a new home. If it is not large enough or is
cracked, the hermit crab looks for another shell. When the
hermit crab has found one that is just right, it carefully pulls its
body out of its old shell, tucking it quickly into the new shell.
As the hermit crab grows larger, it moves into large whelk
shells and lives submerged on the seabed in shallow water.

*Leg with
pointed claws
to get a grip on
seabed when
walking*

Antenna

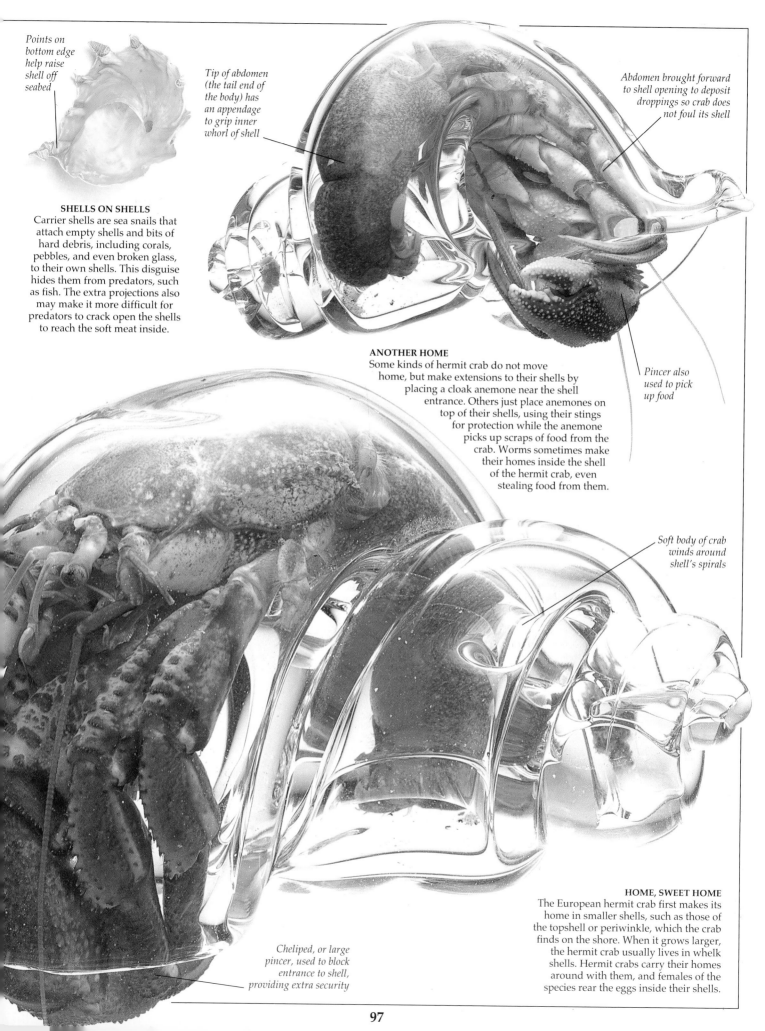

Points on bottom edge help raise shell off seabed

Tip of abdomen (the tail end of the body) has an appendage to grip inner whorl of shell

Abdomen brought forward to shell opening to deposit droppings so crab does not foul its shell

SHELLS ON SHELLS
Carrier shells are sea snails that attach empty shells and bits of hard debris, including corals, pebbles, and even broken glass, to their own shells. This disguise hides them from predators, such as fish. The extra projections also may make it more difficult for predators to crack open the shells to reach the soft meat inside.

Pincer also used to pick up food

ANOTHER HOME
Some kinds of hermit crab do not move home, but make extensions to their shells by placing a cloak anemone near the shell entrance. Others just place anemones on top of their shells, using their stings for protection while the anemone picks up scraps of food from the crab. Worms sometimes make their homes inside the shell of the hermit crab, even stealing food from them.

Soft body of crab winds around shell's spirals

HOME, SWEET HOME
The European hermit crab first makes its home in smaller shells, such as those of the topshell or periwinkle, which the crab finds on the shore. When it grows larger, the hermit crab usually lives in whelk shells. Hermit crabs carry their homes around with them, and females of the species rear the eggs inside their shells.

Cheliped, or large pincer, used to block entrance to shell, providing extra security

Attack and defense

MANY SEA CREATURES HAVE WEAPONS to defend themselves from predators or to attack prey. Some produce venom (poison) for defense and often advertise their danger with distinctive markings. Lionfish's stripes alert their enemies to their venomous spines, but being easy to see, they must try to surprise their prey as they hunt in the open, or ambush them from behind clumps of coral. Stonefish are armed with venomous spines too, blending perfectly with their background when waiting on a reef for prey to swim by. Octopuses change color to match their background. If attacked, the blue-ringed octopus produces blue spots to warn that its bite is poisonous. Disappearing in a cloud of ink is another useful trick used by octopuses, squid, and cuttlefish. Most clams can withdraw their delicate soft parts into their shells, but the gaping file shell's tentacles are a deterrent, producing an irritating sticky fluid. But no defense method is foolproof. Even the most venomous jellyfish can be eaten by carnivorous turtles that are immune to their stings.

DEADLY STONEFISH
The stonefish is one of the deadliest creatures in the ocean. A stonefish's venom, which is projected through the sharp spines on its back, causes such intense pain that a person stepping on one may go into shock and die.

Ink cloud forming around cuttlefish

Long, dorsal spine with venom glands in grooves

INK SCREEN
Cephalopods, which include cuttlefish, squid, and octopi, produce a cloud of ink when threatened, to confuse an enemy and allow time for escape. The ink, produced in a gland linked to the gut, is ejected in a blast of water from a tubelike funnel near its head.

Horny projection above eye

Maerl (a chalky, red seaweed) grows in a thick mass along the stony seabed

Three venomous anal spines

KEEP CLEAR
The striped body of a lionfish warns predators that it is dangerous. A predator trying to bite a lionfish may be impaled by one or more of its poisonous spines. If it survives, the predator will remember the danger and leave the lionfish alone in future. Lionfish can swim openly, looking for smaller prey with little risk of attack. They live in tropical waters from the Indian to the Pacific oceans. In spite of being poisonous, they are popular aquarium fish because of their beauty.

Stripes warn predators that lionfish is dangerous

BLUE FOR DANGER
If this octopus becomes irritated, or when it is feeding, blue-ringed spots appear on its skin, warning of its poisonous bite. This octopus is only about the size of a person's hand, but its bite can be fatal. Blue-ringed octopuses live in shallow waters around Australia and some Pacific Ocean islands.

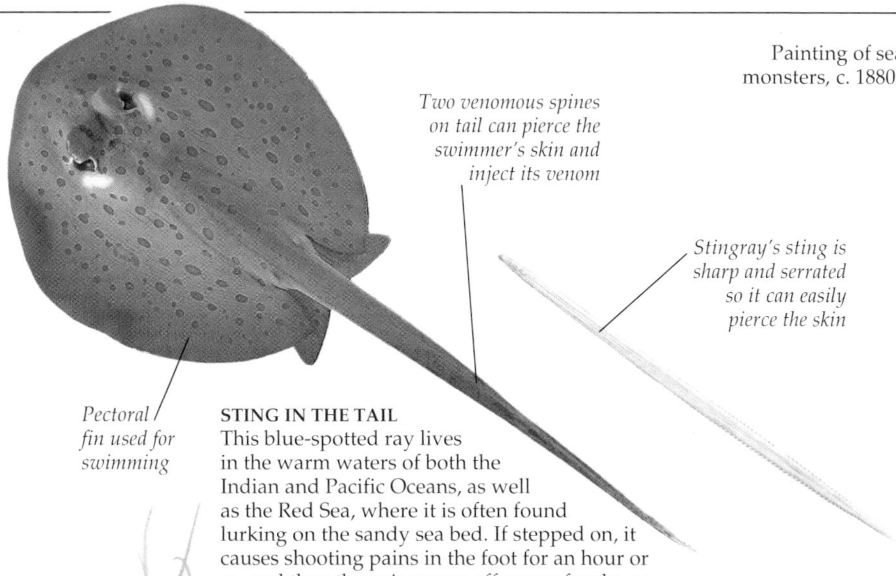

Two venomous spines on tail can pierce the swimmer's skin and inject its venom

Painting of sea monsters, c. 1880s

Stingray's sting is sharp and serrated so it can easily pierce the skin

Pectoral fin used for swimming

STING IN THE TAIL
This blue-spotted ray lives in the warm waters of both the Indian and Pacific Oceans, as well as the Red Sea, where it is often found lurking on the sandy sea bed. If stepped on, it causes shooting pains in the foot for an hour or so, and then the pain wears off over a few hours.

SOMETHING SCARY
Early sailors knew that some creatures living in the sea were dangerous and could kill people. Tales about these sea monsters, though common, often became greatly exaggerated. Monster stories were also invented to account for ships that foundered due to dangerous sea conditions.

When shell is closed, there is still a gap between the shell's two halves

VICIOUS JELLYFISH
Jellyfish are well known for their nasty stings, but none are nastier than those of the box jellyfish, or sea wasp. They often swim near the coasts of northern Australia and southeast Asia. Its stings produce horrible welts on anyone who comes in contact with their trailing tentacles. A badly stung person can die in four minutes.

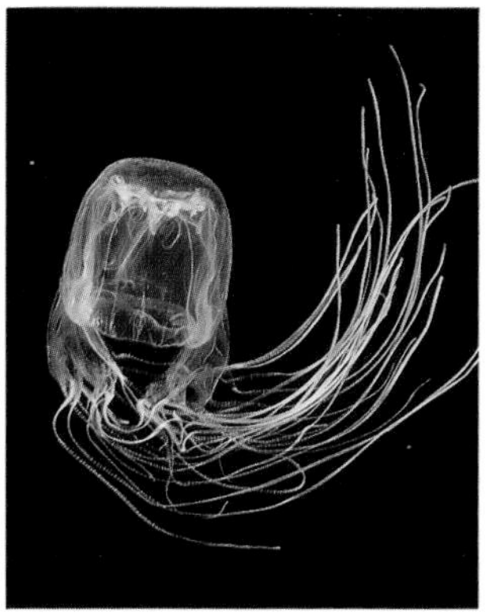

Tentacles stick out when shell "gapes"

SHAGGY SHELLS
These gaping file shells cannot withdraw their masses of orange tentacles inside the two halves of their shell for protection, so the tentacles produce a sour-tasting, sticky substance to deter predators. If tentacles are nibbled off, they can regrow. Gaping file shells make their homes in seaweed, putting out byssus threads for anchorage. They can also make "nests" among horse mussels and oarweeds. If dislodged from their homes, they can move by expelling water from their shell and using their tentacles like oars.

Shell is up to 1 in (2.5 cm) long

The jet set

ONE WAY TO GET AROUND QUICKLY in water is by jet propulsion. Some mollusks, such as clams, squid, and octopuses, do this by squirting water from the body cavity. Jet propulsion can be used both for swimming and to help mollusks escape from predators. Squid are best at jet propulsion – their bodies are permanently streamlined to reduce drag (resistance to water). Some kinds of scallops also use jet propulsion and are among the few clams that can swim. Most clams (bivalves with shells in two halves) can only bury themselves in the sand, or are anchored to the sea bed. The common octopus lives on the rocky sea bed in the coastal waters of the Atlantic Ocean, and the Mediterranean and Caribbean Seas. If attacked, it can jet off.

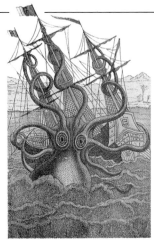

TENTACLE TALES
A Norwegian story tells of the Kraken, a giant sea monster that wrapped its arms around ships before sinking them. The legend may be based on the mysterious giant squid, which live in deep waters. Dead individuals sometimes are washed up on the shore, but no one has ever seen them swimming in the depths.

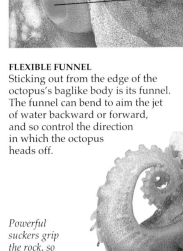

JET PROPULSION
In much the same way as the engines powering jet planes produce jets of air to fly, octopuses, squid, and cuttlefish produce jets of water to propel themselves through the sea.

Funnel

Long arms to grasp prey

1 ON THE BOTTOM
The common octopus hides during the day in its rocky lair, coming out at night to look for such food as crustaceans. The octopus slowly approaches its prey, then pounces, wrapping it between the webbing at the base of its arms.

FLEXIBLE FUNNEL
Sticking out from the edge of the octopus's baglike body is its funnel. The funnel can bend to aim the jet of water backward or forward, and so control the direction in which the octopus heads off.

Powerful suckers grip the rock, so octopus can pull itself along

Sucker is sensitive to touch and taste

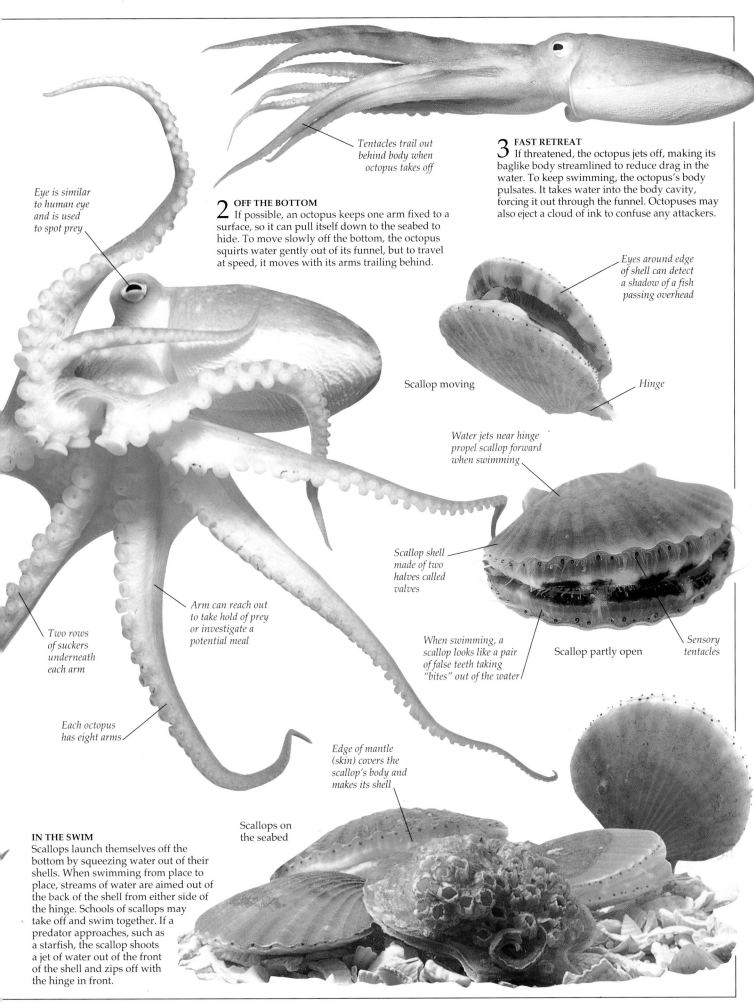

Tentacles trail out behind body when octopus takes off

Eye is similar to human eye and is used to spot prey

2 OFF THE BOTTOM

If possible, an octopus keeps one arm fixed to a surface, so it can pull itself down to the seabed to hide. To move slowly off the bottom, the octopus squirts water gently out of its funnel, but to travel at speed, it moves with its arms trailing behind.

3 FAST RETREAT

If threatened, the octopus jets off, making its baglike body streamlined to reduce drag in the water. To keep swimming, the octopus's body pulsates. It takes water into the body cavity, forcing it out through the funnel. Octopuses may also eject a cloud of ink to confuse any attackers.

Eyes around edge of shell can detect a shadow of a fish passing overhead

Scallop moving

Hinge

Water jets near hinge propel scallop forward when swimming

Scallop shell made of two halves called valves

Arm can reach out to take hold of prey or investigate a potential meal

Two rows of suckers underneath each arm

When swimming, a scallop looks like a pair of false teeth taking "bites" out of the water

Scallop partly open

Sensory tentacles

Each octopus has eight arms

Edge of mantle (skin) covers the scallop's body and makes its shell

IN THE SWIM

Scallops launch themselves off the bottom by squeezing water out of their shells. When swimming from place to place, streams of water are aimed out of the back of the shell from either side of the hinge. Schools of scallops may take off and swim together. If a predator approaches, such as a starfish, the scallop shoots a jet of water out of the front of the shell and zips off with the hinge in front.

Scallops on the seabed

Moving along

EVERY SWIMMER KNOWS that it is harder to move an arm or a leg through seawater than through air. This is because seawater is much denser than air. To be a fast swimmer like a dolphin, tuna, or sailfish, it helps to have a shape that is streamlined like a torpedo to reduce drag (resistance to water). A smooth skin and few projections from the body allow an animal to move through the water more easily. The density of seawater does have an advantage, in that it helps to support the weight of an animal's body. The heaviest animal that has ever lived on Earth is the blue whale, which weighs up to 150 tons. Some heavy-shelled creatures, like the chambered nautilus, have gas-filled floats to stop them from sinking. Some ocean animals, such as dolphins and flying fish, build up enough speed underwater to leap briefly into the air, but not all ocean animals are good swimmers. Many can only swim slowly; others drift along in the currents, crawl along the bottom, burrow in the sand, or stay put, anchored to the sea bed.

FLYING FISH
Gathering speed underwater, flying fish leap clear of the surface to escape predators, then glide for over 30 seconds by spreading out the side fins.

AT SCHOOL
Fish often swim together in a school (like these blue-striped snappers), where a single fish has less chance of being attacked by a predator than when swimming on its own. The moving mass of individuals may confuse a predator; also, there are more pairs of eyes on the lookout for an attacker.

IN THE SWING
During the day, many electric rays prefer to stay hidden on the sandy bottom, relying on their electric organs for defense, but they do swim if disturbed and at night when searching for prey. There are over 30 kinds of electric ray, mostly living in warm waters. Most other rays have spindly tails (unlike the electric ray's broad tail), and move through water using their pectoral fins. Waves pass from the front to the back of the pectoral fins, which, in larger rays like mantas, become so exaggerated that the fins actually beat up and down.

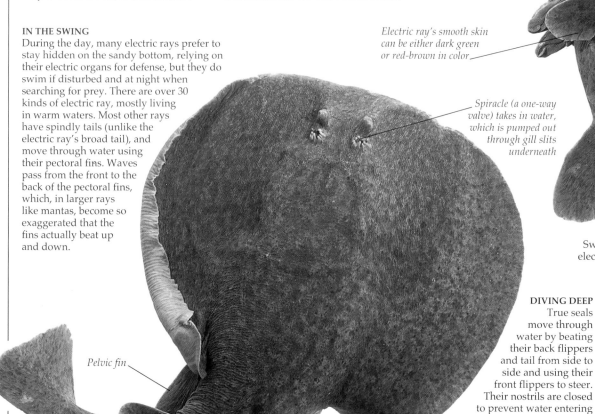

Electric ray's smooth skin can be either dark green or red-brown in color

Spiracle (a one-way valve) takes in water, which is pumped out through gill slits underneath

Electric rays can grow to 6 ft (1.8 m) and weigh as much as 110 lb (50 kg)

Pelvic fin

Swimming sequence of an electric ray, *Torpedo nobiliana*

DIVING DEEP
True seals move through water by beating their back flippers and tail from side to side and using their front flippers to steer. Their nostrils are closed to prevent water entering the airways. Harbor seals (right) can dive to 300 ft (90 m), but the champion seal diver is the Antarctic's Weddell seal, diving to 2,000 ft (600 m). Seals do not get the bends (p. 114), because they breathe out before diving and, unlike humans, do not breathe compressed air. When underwater, seals use oxygen stored in the blood.

Broad tail fin, swinging from side to side, helps propel ray along

Pectoral fin provides extra propulsion as waves pass along flexible edges of its rounded side

Smaller, second dorsal fin

Larger, first dorsal fin

Clasper (male reproductive organ)

Eye

Electric organ, at base of pectoral fin, helps catch fish by stunning them – some species can deliver over 200 volts

Scapula (shoulder blade)

Dolphin's flipper

FLIPPER'S FLIPPER
The ancestors of whales and dolphins once lived on land and had four limbs. As they became adapted for life in the sea, the limbs became modified into flippers and, eventually, the hind limbs were lost. The dolphin's flipper is a version of the standard limb of a mammal. The upper and lower arm bones are short, and the five digits are widely spread to support the broad flipper.

OUT OF THE WATER
Dolphins leap out of water for fun, for signalling to other dolphins, and also when feeding. They can also porpoise (skim over water for short distances) when moving at speed, because it is easier to move in air, which puts less friction on their bodies.

Humerus (upper arm bone)

Ulna (lower arm bone)

Radius

Buoyancy chamber

As nautilus grows, larger and larger chambers form

Bottlenose dolphins can reach speeds of up to 17 mph (27 kph)

Phalange (toe bone)

Metacarpal (short, strong finger bone)

AFLOAT
The sections of a chambered nautilus' shell help keep it afloat, but the nautilus itself lives in the last and biggest chamber, from which its tentacles and body poke out. Nautili are cephalopods (pp. 98-99), like squid and octopi, but are the only ones to have an outer shell. Like other cephalopods, they move by jet propulsion.

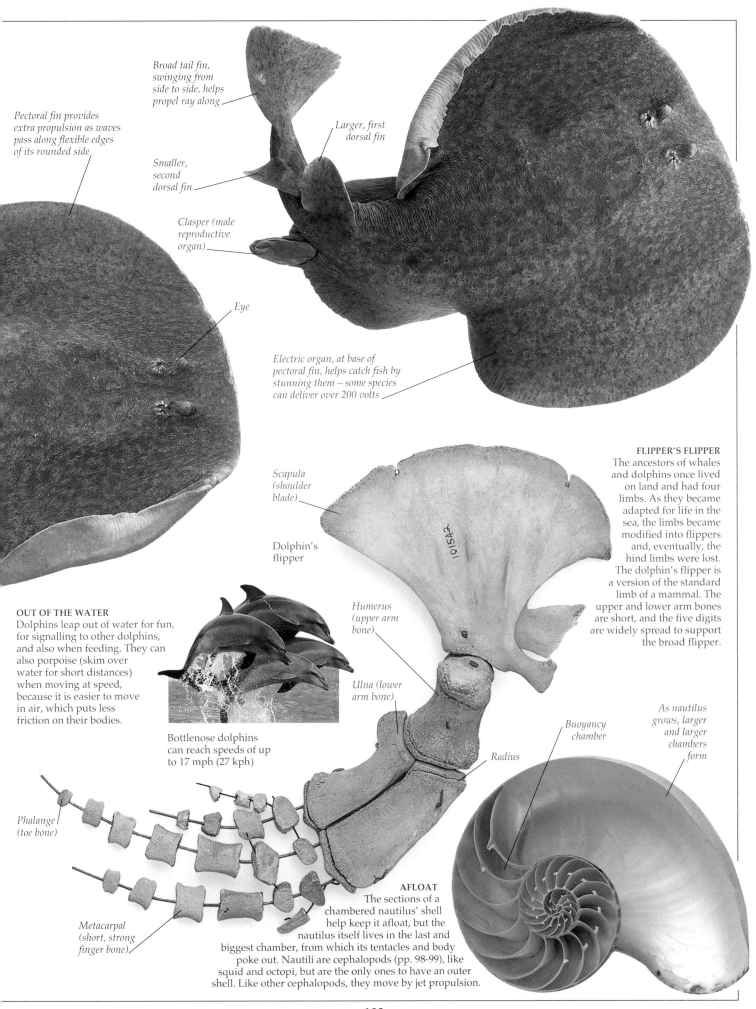

Ocean travelers

To make the most of the vast expanses of water, some sea animals travel great distances, crisscrossing the oceans to find the best places to feed and breed. Whales such as the humpback are well known for feeding in the cold, food-rich waters of the far north or south, traveling to the warm waters of the tropics to breed and give birth. Many long-distance voyagers, such as turtles, seals, and sea birds, feed out at sea, but come ashore to breed. Freshwater eels are unusual because they go to the ocean to breed, then their young travel back to rivers, where they grow to maturity. Salmon do the reverse, growing up in the ocean and returning to rivers to breed (p. 122). Ocean travelers often make use of currents to speed them on their way. Even animals that cannot swim can travel far and wide by hitching a ride on another animal or by drifting along on a piece of wood.

Back pair of flippers used as rudders to steer turtle along

Stalked barnacles on driftwood

Broad surface of front flipper for ease of swimming

BARNACLES ADRIFT
Barnacles grow on surfaces, such as rocks, pieces of wood, hulls of ships – some kinds even grow on turtles and whales. These goose barnacles can drift long distances on pieces of wood. Barnacles are crustaceans (like crabs and lobsters) and have jointed limbs. To protect their bodies and limbs, barnacles have a set of shell-like plates.

Larger eyes form when adult eel migrates to sea

Skin turns silver before eel migrates back to Sargasso Sea

Leaflike larva (young), called leptocephalus

Trailing tentacles armed with vicious stings

Young eels, known as elvers, or glass eels

MYSTERIOUS JOURNEY
For centuries, no one knew where European eels went to breed, only that elvers (young eels) returned in large numbers to the rivers. In the late 1800s, scientists found leaflike larvae in the sea, which developed into elvers. Later they found that the smallest of these larvae came from the Sargasso Sea in the western Atlantic, where the adult eels may breed at depth. The larvae then drift with currents back to the coast of Europe, where they mature.

PORTUGUESE MAN-OF-WAR
Not a true jellyfish but a siphonophore (a relative of the sea fir), the man-of-war has a gas-filled float that keeps it at the surface, where it is blown by the wind and drifts with the currents. Usually found in warm waters, it can be carried to cooler waters and washed ashore after storms.

Swimming sequence
of a green turtle

UNDERWATER FLIER
Green turtles live in the warm waters of the Atlantic, Pacific,
and Indian oceans. Like all turtles, they come ashore to lay
their eggs. First the females mate in shallow water with the
waiting males. Later, under cover of darkness, the females
crawl up the beach to lay their eggs in the sand before
heading back to the water. They may return
several times in one breeding season to lay
further batches of eggs. Some green
turtles are known to travel several
hundred miles or more to reach
their breeding beaches where
they hatched themselves.
Green turtles feed on
sea grasses and
seaweeds.

*Turtle shell is
streamlined for
gliding through
water*

*Front pair of
flippers help
turtle to "fly"
through water*

*Turtles are
air breathers,
so must come
to surface to
breathe
through their
nostrils*

Green turtle
(*Chelonia mydas*)
is on the
endangered
species list

TURTLE TRIP
In the Japanese legend, Urashima Taro rides into the
kingdom of the sea on a turtle. After spending some time in
the depths, he begs the sea goddess to let him go home. She
allows this, but gives him a box that he must never open.
On his return he finds his home has changed and no one
knows him. Hoping for some comfort, he opens the box, but
the spell is broken. He becomes a very old man because
he has spent not three years – but 300 – in the sea.

The twilight zone

BETWEEN THE BRIGHT SUNLIT WATERS of the upper ocean and the pitch-black depths is the half-light of the twilight zone, which ranges from 660 to 3,300 ft (200 to 1,000 m) below the surface. Fish living in the twilight zone often have rows of light organs on their undersides to help camouflage them against the little light filtering down from above. These glowing lights can be produced by chemical reactions or by colonies of bacteria living in the light organs. Many animals, including some lantern fish and a variety of squid, spend only their days in the twilight zone. At night they journey upward to feed in the food-rich surface water. By doing this, they are less at risk from daytime hunters such as seabirds. Others, such as the lancet fish, spend their lives in the twilight zone eating any available food. The skinny lancet fish has a stretchy stomach, so it eats a large meal if it finds one.

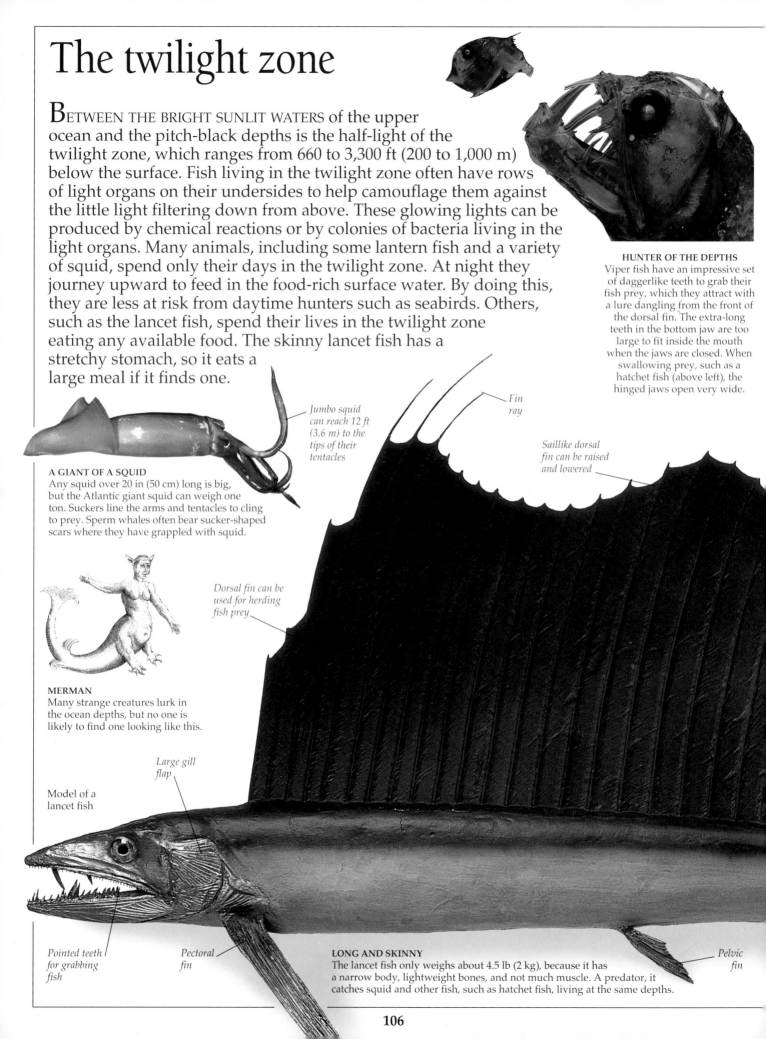

HUNTER OF THE DEPTHS
Viper fish have an impressive set of daggerlike teeth to grab their fish prey, which they attract with a lure dangling from the front of the dorsal fin. The extra-long teeth in the bottom jaw are too large to fit inside the mouth when the jaws are closed. When swallowing prey, such as a hatchet fish (above left), the hinged jaws open very wide.

Jumbo squid can reach 12 ft (3.6 m) to the tips of their tentacles

Fin ray

Saillike dorsal fin can be raised and lowered

A GIANT OF A SQUID
Any squid over 20 in (50 cm) long is big, but the Atlantic giant squid can weigh one ton. Suckers line the arms and tentacles to cling to prey. Sperm whales often bear sucker-shaped scars where they have grappled with squid.

Dorsal fin can be used for herding fish prey

MERMAN
Many strange creatures lurk in the ocean depths, but no one is likely to find one looking like this.

Large gill flap

Model of a lancet fish

Pointed teeth for grabbing fish

Pectoral fin

LONG AND SKINNY
The lancet fish only weighs about 4.5 lb (2 kg), because it has a narrow body, lightweight bones, and not much muscle. A predator, it catches squid and other fish, such as hatchet fish, living at the same depths.

Pelvic fin

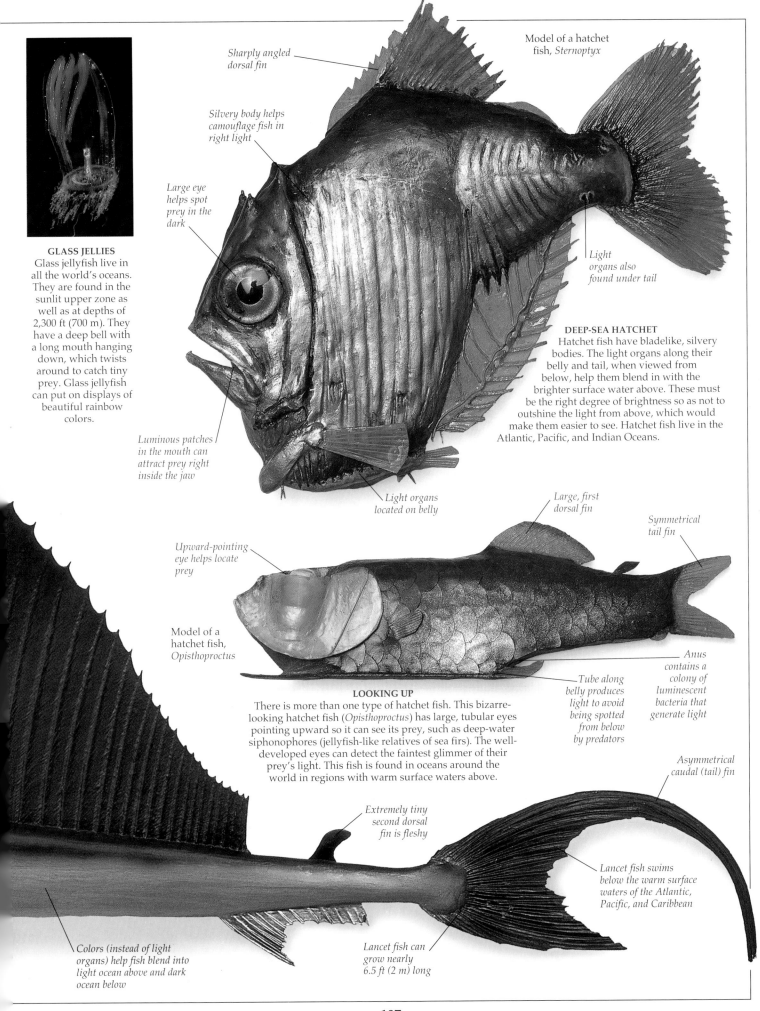

Model of a hatchet fish, *Sternoptyx*

Sharply angled dorsal fin

Silvery body helps camouflage fish in right light

Large eye helps spot prey in the dark

Light organs also found under tail

DEEP-SEA HATCHET
Hatchet fish have bladelike, silvery bodies. The light organs along their belly and tail, when viewed from below, help them blend in with the brighter surface water above. These must be the right degree of brightness so as not to outshine the light from above, which would make them easier to see. Hatchet fish live in the Atlantic, Pacific, and Indian Oceans.

Luminous patches in the mouth can attract prey right inside the jaw

Light organs located on belly

GLASS JELLIES
Glass jellyfish live in all the world's oceans. They are found in the sunlit upper zone as well as at depths of 2,300 ft (700 m). They have a deep bell with a long mouth hanging down, which twists around to catch tiny prey. Glass jellyfish can put on displays of beautiful rainbow colors.

Large, first dorsal fin

Symmetrical tail fin

Upward-pointing eye helps locate prey

Model of a hatchet fish, *Opisthoproctus*

Anus contains a colony of luminescent bacteria that generate light

Tube along belly produces light to avoid being spotted from below by predators

LOOKING UP
There is more than one type of hatchet fish. This bizarre-looking hatchet fish (*Opisthoproctus*) has large, tubular eyes pointing upward so it can see its prey, such as deep-water siphonophores (jellyfish-like relatives of sea firs). The well-developed eyes can detect the faintest glimmer of their prey's light. This fish is found in oceans around the world in regions with warm surface waters above.

Asymmetrical caudal (tail) fin

Extremely tiny second dorsal fin is fleshy

Lancet fish swims below the warm surface waters of the Atlantic, Pacific, and Caribbean

Colors (instead of light organs) help fish blend into light ocean above and dark ocean below

Lancet fish can grow nearly 6.5 ft (2 m) long

The darkest depths

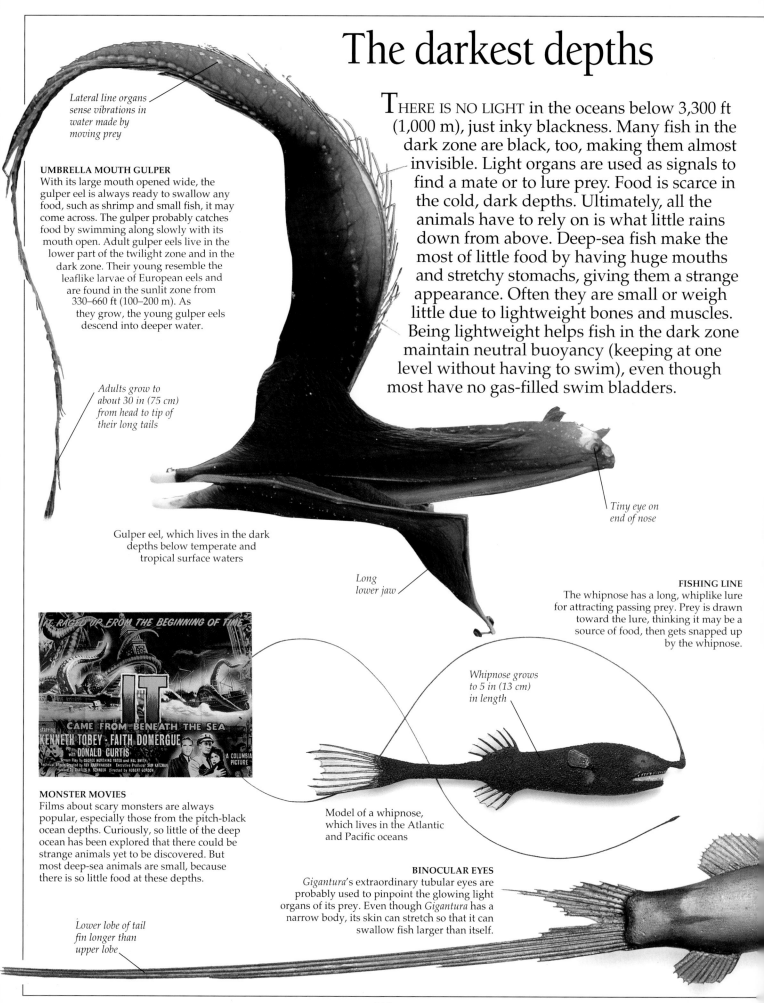

THERE IS NO LIGHT in the oceans below 3,300 ft (1,000 m), just inky blackness. Many fish in the dark zone are black, too, making them almost invisible. Light organs are used as signals to find a mate or to lure prey. Food is scarce in the cold, dark depths. Ultimately, all the animals have to rely on is what little rains down from above. Deep-sea fish make the most of little food by having huge mouths and stretchy stomachs, giving them a strange appearance. Often they are small or weigh little due to lightweight bones and muscles. Being lightweight helps fish in the dark zone maintain neutral buoyancy (keeping at one level without having to swim), even though most have no gas-filled swim bladders.

Lateral line organs sense vibrations in water made by moving prey

UMBRELLA MOUTH GULPER
With its large mouth opened wide, the gulper eel is always ready to swallow any food, such as shrimp and small fish, it may come across. The gulper probably catches food by swimming along slowly with its mouth open. Adult gulper eels live in the lower part of the twilight zone and in the dark zone. Their young resemble the leaflike larvae of European eels and are found in the sunlit zone from 330–660 ft (100–200 m). As they grow, the young gulper eels descend into deeper water.

Adults grow to about 30 in (75 cm) from head to tip of their long tails

Gulper eel, which lives in the dark depths below temperate and tropical surface waters

Tiny eye on end of nose

Long lower jaw

FISHING LINE
The whipnose has a long, whiplike lure for attracting passing prey. Prey is drawn toward the lure, thinking it may be a source of food, then gets snapped up by the whipnose.

Whipnose grows to 5 in (13 cm) in length

MONSTER MOVIES
Films about scary monsters are always popular, especially those from the pitch-black ocean depths. Curiously, so little of the deep ocean has been explored that there could be strange animals yet to be discovered. But most deep-sea animals are small, because there is so little food at these depths.

Model of a whipnose, which lives in the Atlantic and Pacific oceans

BINOCULAR EYES
Gigantura's extraordinary tubular eyes are probably used to pinpoint the glowing light organs of its prey. Even though *Gigantura* has a narrow body, its skin can stretch so that it can swallow fish larger than itself.

Lower lobe of tail fin longer than upper lobe

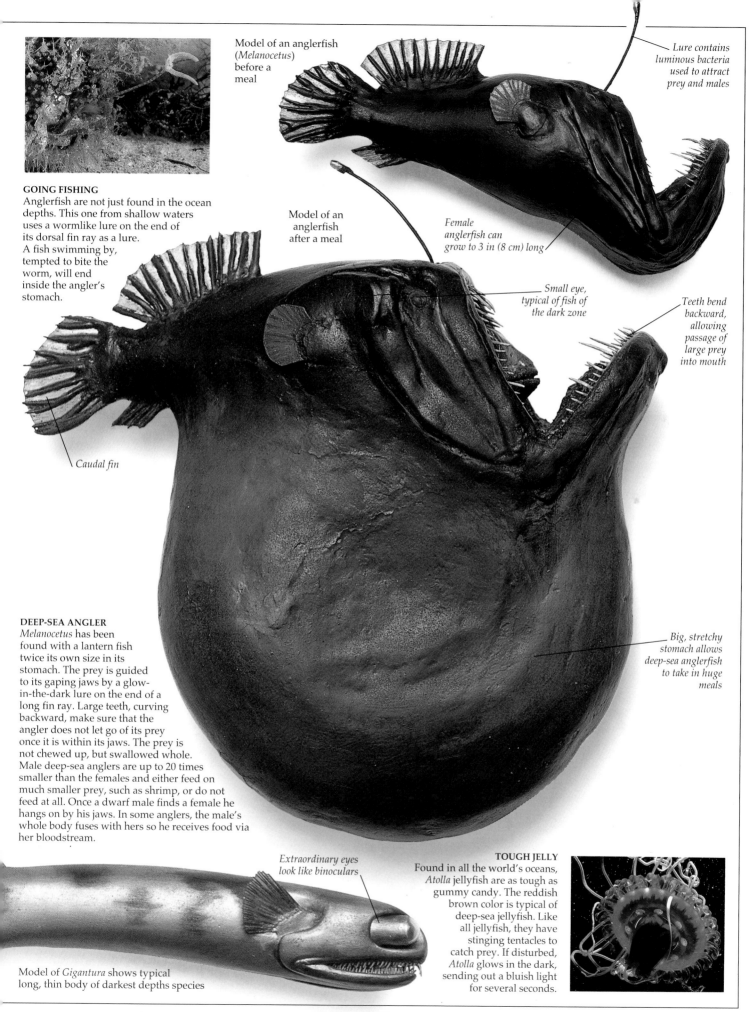

GOING FISHING
Anglerfish are not just found in the ocean depths. This one from shallow waters uses a wormlike lure on the end of its dorsal fin ray as a lure. A fish swimming by, tempted to bite the worm, will end inside the angler's stomach.

Model of an anglerfish (*Melanocetus*) before a meal

Lure contains luminous bacteria used to attract prey and males

Model of an anglerfish after a meal

Female anglerfish can grow to 3 in (8 cm) long

Small eye, typical of fish of the dark zone

Teeth bend backward, allowing passage of large prey into mouth

Caudal fin

DEEP-SEA ANGLER
Melanocetus has been found with a lantern fish twice its own size in its stomach. The prey is guided to its gaping jaws by a glow-in-the-dark lure on the end of a long fin ray. Large teeth, curving backward, make sure that the angler does not let go of its prey once it is within its jaws. The prey is not chewed up, but swallowed whole. Male deep-sea anglers are up to 20 times smaller than the females and either feed on much smaller prey, such as shrimp, or do not feed at all. Once a dwarf male finds a female he hangs on by his jaws. In some anglers, the male's whole body fuses with hers so he receives food via her bloodstream.

Big, stretchy stomach allows deep-sea anglerfish to take in huge meals

Extraordinary eyes look like binoculars

Model of *Gigantura* shows typical long, thin body of darkest depths species

TOUGH JELLY
Found in all the world's oceans, *Atolla* jellyfish are as tough as gummy candy. The reddish brown color is typical of deep-sea jellyfish. Like all jellyfish, they have stinging tentacles to catch prey. If disturbed, *Atolla* glows in the dark, sending out a bluish light for several seconds.

On the bottom

THE BOTTOM OF THE DEEP OCEAN is not an easy place to live. There is little food and it is dark and cold. Much of the seabed is covered with soft clays or mudlike oozes made of skeletons of tiny sea animals and plants. The ooze on the vast open plains of the abyss can reach several hundred yards thick. Animals walking along the bottom have long legs to avoid stirring it up. Some grow anchored to the seabed and have long stems to keep their feeding structures clear of the ooze. Food particles can be filtered out of the water, for example, by the feathery arms of sea lilies or through the many pores in sponges. Some animals, such as sea cucumbers, manage to feed on the seabed by extracting food particles from the ooze. Food particles are the remains of dead animals (and their droppings) and plants that have sunk down from above. Occasionally a larger carcass reaches the bottom uneaten – a real bonanza for any mobile bottom dwellers, which home in on it from all around. Because food is scarce and temperatures so low, most animals living in the deep ocean take a long time to grow.

Underwater cables were laid across the Atlantic Ocean to relay telegraphic messages, c. 1870

GLASSY STRANDS
This sponge grows anchored to the soft seabed by its stem of glass strands. Sea anemones often grow on their stems. When a glass-rope sponge dies, the cup-shaped part disappears and all that is left is the stem stuck in the seabed.

Dried remains of sea anemones

Stem formed by long, glassy, needlelike spikes made of silica

NOT A TRUE SPIDER
Sea spiders look like land spiders, but belong to a separate group called pycnogonids. Some deep-sea spiders have a leg span of 2 ft (60 cm) across, so can stride along without stirring up clouds of particles. They can also swim, launching off the seabed, bringing their legs toward their bodies, then sinking down again.

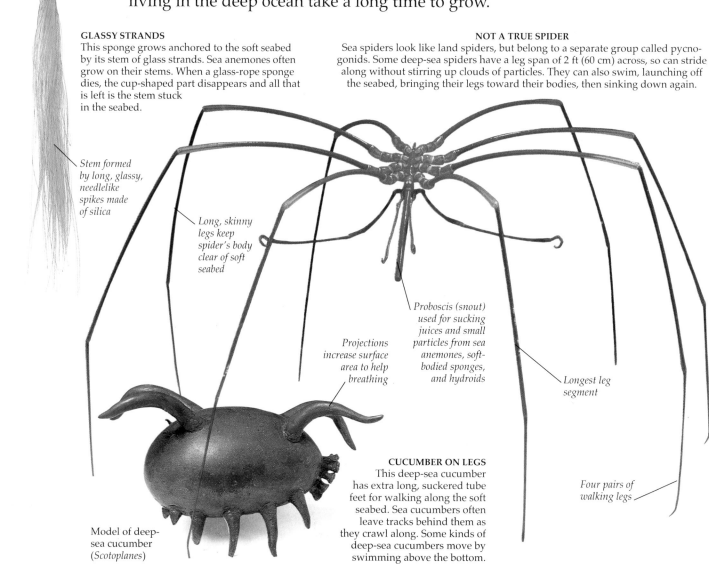

Long, skinny legs keep spider's body clear of soft seabed

Projections increase surface area to help breathing

Proboscis (snout) used for sucking juices and small particles from sea anemones, soft-bodied sponges, and hydroids

Longest leg segment

CUCUMBER ON LEGS
This deep-sea cucumber has extra long, suckered tube feet for walking along the soft seabed. Sea cucumbers often leave tracks behind them as they crawl along. Some kinds of deep-sea cucumbers move by swimming above the bottom.

Model of deep-sea cucumber (Scotoplanes)

Four pairs of walking legs

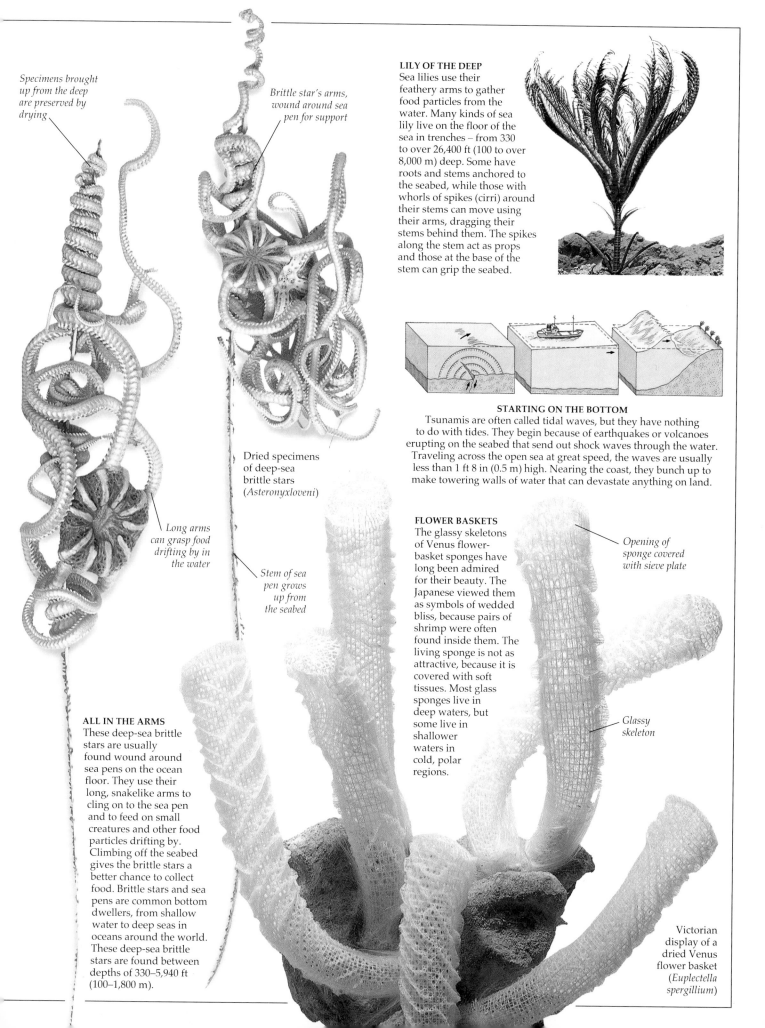

Specimens brought up from the deep are preserved by drying

Brittle star's arms, wound around sea pen for support

LILY OF THE DEEP
Sea lilies use their feathery arms to gather food particles from the water. Many kinds of sea lily live on the floor of the sea in trenches – from 330 to over 26,400 ft (100 to over 8,000 m) deep. Some have roots and stems anchored to the seabed, while those with whorls of spikes (cirri) around their stems can move using their arms, dragging their stems behind them. The spikes along the stem act as props and those at the base of the stem can grip the seabed.

Long arms can grasp food drifting by in the water

Dried specimens of deep-sea brittle stars (*Asteronyxloveni*)

Stem of sea pen grows up from the seabed

STARTING ON THE BOTTOM
Tsunamis are often called tidal waves, but they have nothing to do with tides. They begin because of earthquakes or volcanoes erupting on the seabed that send out shock waves through the water. Traveling across the open sea at great speed, the waves are usually less than 1 ft 8 in (0.5 m) high. Nearing the coast, they bunch up to make towering walls of water that can devastate anything on land.

FLOWER BASKETS
The glassy skeletons of Venus flower-basket sponges have long been admired for their beauty. The Japanese viewed them as symbols of wedded bliss, because pairs of shrimp were often found inside them. The living sponge is not as attractive, because it is covered with soft tissues. Most glass sponges live in deep waters, but some live in shallower waters in cold, polar regions.

Opening of sponge covered with sieve plate

Glassy skeleton

ALL IN THE ARMS
These deep-sea brittle stars are usually found wound around sea pens on the ocean floor. They use their long, snakelike arms to cling on to the sea pen and to feed on small creatures and other food particles drifting by. Climbing off the seabed gives the brittle stars a better chance to collect food. Brittle stars and sea pens are common bottom dwellers, from shallow water to deep seas in oceans around the world. These deep-sea brittle stars are found between depths of 330–5,940 ft (100–1,800 m).

Victorian display of a dried Venus flower basket (*Euplectella spergillium*)

Vents and smokers

IN PARTS OF THE OCEAN FLOOR, there are cracks in the crust from which extremely hot, mineral-rich water gushes. These vents (hot springs) exist at the spreading centers where the gigantic plates that make up the earth's crust are moving apart. Cold seawater sinks deep into cracks, where it heats up and collects quantities of dissolved minerals. At temperatures of up to 750°F (400°C), hot water spews out, depositing some minerals to form black smokers, or chimneys. Hot water produced by vents helps bacterial growth, which creates food from the hydrogen sulfide in the water. Extraordinary animals crowd around the cracks and rely on these microbes for food. Scientists using submersibles in the late 1970s discovered the first vent communities in the Pacific. Since then, vents have been discovered in other spreading centers in the Pacific and the Mid-Atlantic Ridge.

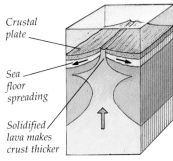

GROWING OCEAN
New areas of ocean floor are continually being created at spreading centers between two crustal plates. When lava (hot, molten rock) emerges from within the crust, it cools and solidifies, adding material to the edge of each adjoining plate. Old areas of ocean floor are destroyed as one plate slides under another. Lava from volcanic eruptions at spreading centers can kill off communities of vent animals.

Crustal plate

Sea floor spreading

Solidified lava makes crust thicker

Animals cook if too close to the hot water in a vent

Plumes of hot water are rich in sulfides, which are poisonous to most animals

Dense numbers of animals crowd around a vent

Fish predators nibble tops off tube worms

BLACK SMOKER
Animal life abounds in an active vent site, such as this one in the Mid-Atlantic Ridge. If the vent stops producing hot, sulfur-rich water, the community is doomed. Animals from dying vents must colonize a new site, which may be several hundred miles away across the cold, almost foodless bottom.

Giant clams in the eastern Pacific can grow to 12 in (30 cm) long

Some animals graze on mats of bacteria covering rocks near a vent

Model of vents found in the eastern Pacific

Chimney made from mineral deposits

Black smoker chimney can reach 33 ft (10 m) high

Alvin by the support ship, *Atlantis II*

Deep-sea fish photographed from Alvin near a vent on the Mid-Atlantic Ridge

CHAMPION SUBMERSIBLE
The U.S. submersible *Alvin* took the first scientists down to observe marine life near the Galápagos vents in the east Pacific in the 1970s. Since then, *Alvin* has completed many dives to vents around the world, to depths of 12,500 ft (3,800 m). Other submersibles that have dived on vent sites include the French *Nautile* (pp. 120-121) and the Russians *Mir I* and *II*.

VENT COMMUNITIES
This model shows the vent communities in the eastern Pacific, where giant clams and tube worms are the most distinctive animals. Vents in other parts of the world have different kinds of animals, such as the hairy snails from the Mariana Trench and eyeless shrimps from vents along the Mid-Atlantic Ridge.

Tube worm can grow to 10 ft (3 m) long

Giant tube worm has bacteria inside its body that provide the worm with food

Diverse divers

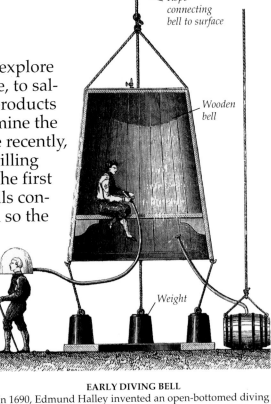

PEOPLE HAVE ALWAYS WANTED to explore the sea, to look for sunken treasure, to salvage wrecks, to bring up marine products like pearls and sponges, or to examine the beautiful underwater world. More recently, underwater oil exploration and drilling have also required divers' skills. The first diving equipment were simple bells containing air and open at the bottom so the diver could work on the seabed. Later, diving suits with helmets were invented for divers to go deeper and stay down longer, with air pumped continually down a line from the surface. In the 1940s, the modern aqualung or scuba (*self-c*ontained *u*nderwater *b*reathing *a*pparatus) was invented. Divers could carry their own supply of compressed air in tanks on their backs.

Umbilical supplies air, as well as electricity for light

Weight belt

Rope connecting bell to surface

Wooden bell

Weight

UNDERWATER WORKER
This diver, wearing a wet suit for warmth, has air pumped into the helmet via a line linked to the surface. A harness around the diver's middle carries tools. Flexible boots help the diver clamber around beneath an oil rig.

EARLY DIVING BELL
In 1690, Edmund Halley invented an open-bottomed diving bell, which could be resupplied with barrels of air lowered from the surface. Heavy weights anchored the bell to the seabed, and a leather tube connected the lead-lined air barrel to the wooden bell. Used at depths of 60 ft (18 m), the bell could house several divers at a time.

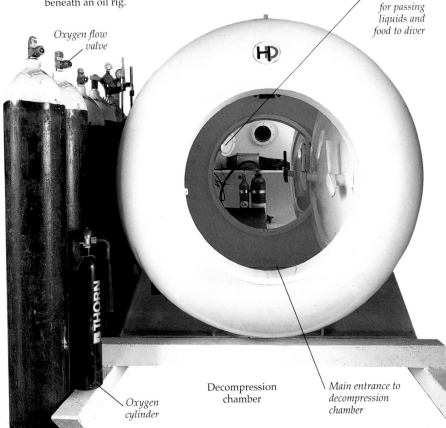

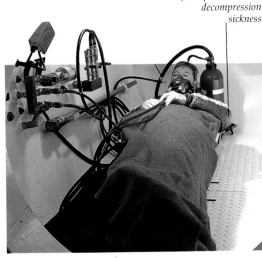

Oxygen flow valve

"Medical lock" for passing liquids and food to diver

Joint pains indicate decompression sickness

Decompression chamber

Main entrance to decompression chamber

Oxygen cylinder

LIFE SAVER
When diving, the pressure on the body increases with the weight of water above. Air is supplied under the same pressure so the diver can breathe. Under more of this increased pressure, the nitrogen in the air supply (air contains 80 percent nitrogen) passes into the blood. If a diver comes up too quickly after a long or deep dive, the sudden release of pressure can cause nitrogen to form bubbles in the blood and tissues. This painful, sometimes fatal condition is called decompression sickness (the bends). The ailing diver is treated in a decompression chamber, its air pressure raised to the same pressure undergone during the dive. Pressure is then slowly reduced to normal pressure at the surface.

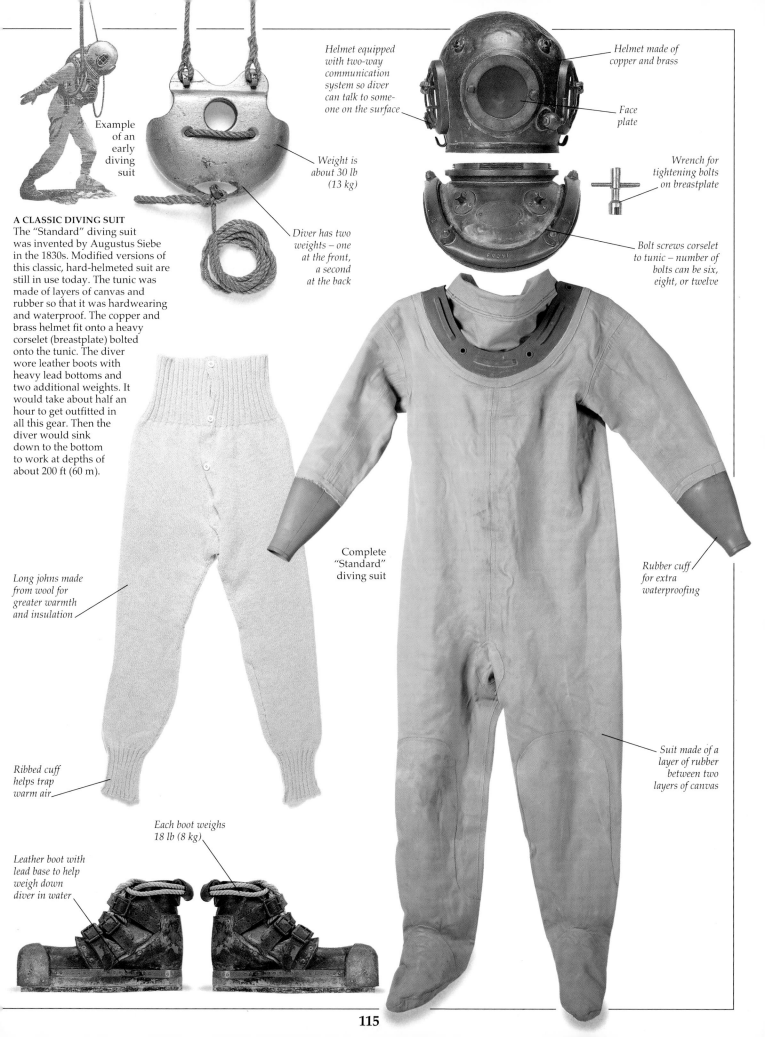

Example of an early diving suit

A CLASSIC DIVING SUIT
The "Standard" diving suit was invented by Augustus Siebe in the 1830s. Modified versions of this classic, hard-helmeted suit are still in use today. The tunic was made of layers of canvas and rubber so that it was hardwearing and waterproof. The copper and brass helmet fit onto a heavy corselet (breastplate) bolted onto the tunic. The diver wore leather boots with heavy lead bottoms and two additional weights. It would take about half an hour to get outfitted in all this gear. Then the diver would sink down to the bottom to work at depths of about 200 ft (60 m).

Helmet equipped with two-way communication system so diver can talk to someone on the surface

Weight is about 30 lb (13 kg)

Diver has two weights – one at the front, a second at the back

Helmet made of copper and brass

Face plate

Wrench for tightening bolts on breastplate

Bolt screws corselet to tunic – number of bolts can be six, eight, or twelve

Complete "Standard" diving suit

Rubber cuff for extra waterproofing

Long johns made from wool for greater warmth and insulation

Ribbed cuff helps trap warm air

Suit made of a layer of rubber between two layers of canvas

Each boot weighs 18 lb (8 kg)

Leather boot with lead base to help weigh down diver in water

Underwater machines

THE FIRST SUBMARINES had simple designs. They allowed travel underwater and were useful in war. More modern submarines were powered by diesel or gasoline on the surface and used batteries underwater. In 1955, the first sub to run on nuclear fuel traversed the oceans. Nuclear power allowed submarines to travel great distances before needing to refuel. Today, submarines have sophisticated sonar systems for navigating underwater and pinpointing other vessels. They can carry high-powered torpedoes to fire at enemy craft or nuclear missiles. Submersibles (miniature submarines), used to explore the deep-sea floor, cannot travel long distances. They need to be lowered from a support vessel on the surface.

Snort mast renews and expels air with help of bellows

Delayed action mine

Augur for drilling into enemy ship to attach mine on rope

Vertical propeller

Side propeller powered by foot pedals

"TURTLE" HERO
A one-man wooden submarine, the *Turtle*, was used during the American Revolution in 1776 to try to attach a delayed-action mine to an English ship blockading New York Harbor. The operator became disoriented by carbon dioxide building up inside the *Turtle*. He jettisoned the mine, which exploded harmlessly. Nevertheless, the explosion was enough to cause the British ship to up anchor and sail away.

External steering bar operated by diver

Internal steering position

Hand pump for pressurizing air reservoir and emptying ballast tanks

Front wheels smaller than back ones for easier turning

UNDERWATER ADVENTURE
Inspired by the recent invention of modern submarines, this 1900 engraving depicted a scene in the year 2000 with people enjoying a journey in a submarine liner. In a way, the prediction has come true, as tourists can now take trips in small submarines to view marine life in places such as the Red Sea. However, most people explore the underwater world by learning to scuba-dive or snorkel.

Torpedo
tube

Torpedo
storage
space

Control
room

Tower with snort
mast, periscope,
and radar aerials

Reactor
compartment

Engine
room

Stabilized
fin

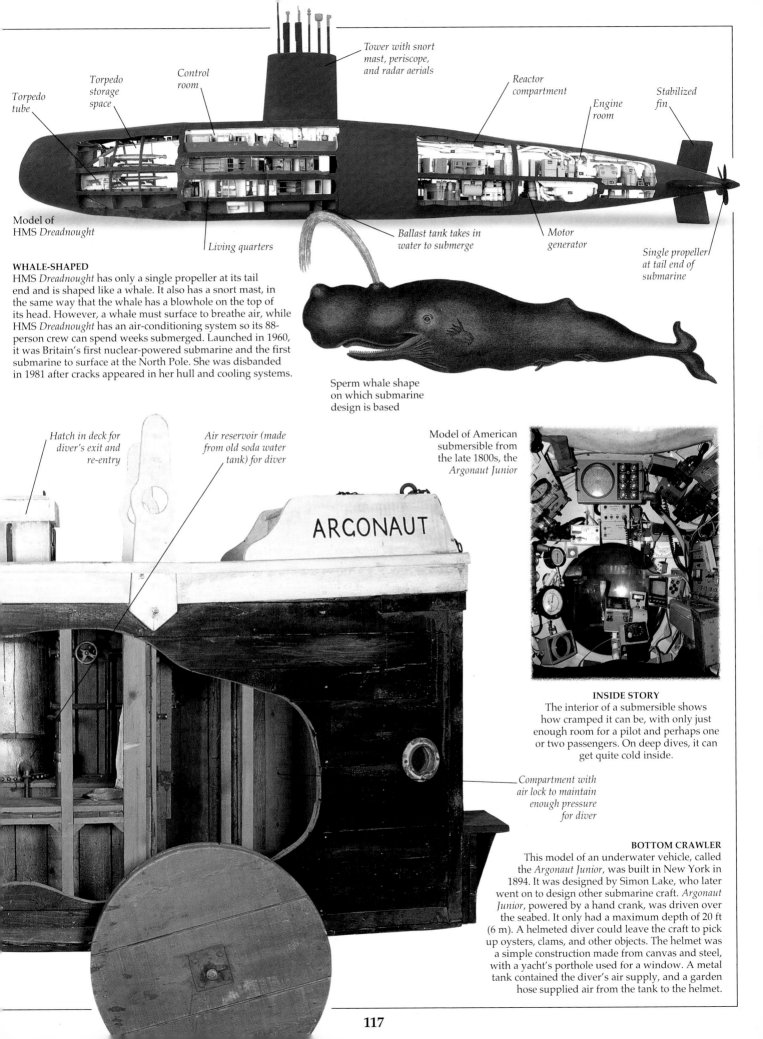

Model of
HMS *Dreadnought*

Living quarters

Ballast tank takes in
water to submerge

Motor
generator

Single propeller
at tail end of
submarine

WHALE-SHAPED
HMS *Dreadnought* has only a single propeller at its tail
end and is shaped like a whale. It also has a snort mast, in
the same way that the whale has a blowhole on the top of
its head. However, a whale must surface to breathe air, while
HMS *Dreadnought* has an air-conditioning system so its 88-
person crew can spend weeks submerged. Launched in 1960,
it was Britain's first nuclear-powered submarine and the first
submarine to surface at the North Pole. She was disbanded
in 1981 after cracks appeared in her hull and cooling systems.

Sperm whale shape
on which submarine
design is based

Hatch in deck for
diver's exit and
re-entry

Air reservoir (made
from old soda water
tank) for diver

Model of American
submersible from
the late 1800s, the
Argonaut Junior

ARGONAUT

INSIDE STORY
The interior of a submersible shows
how cramped it can be, with only just
enough room for a pilot and perhaps one
or two passengers. On deep dives, it can
get quite cold inside.

Compartment with
air lock to maintain
enough pressure
for diver

BOTTOM CRAWLER
This model of an underwater vehicle, called
the *Argonaut Junior*, was built in New York in
1894. It was designed by Simon Lake, who later
went on to design other submarine craft. *Argonaut
Junior*, powered by a hand crank, was driven over
the seabed. It only had a maximum depth of 20 ft
(6 m). A helmeted diver could leave the craft to pick
up oysters, clams, and other objects. The helmet was
a simple construction made from canvas and steel,
with a yacht's porthole used for a window. A metal
tank contained the diver's air supply, and a garden
hose supplied air from the tank to the helmet.

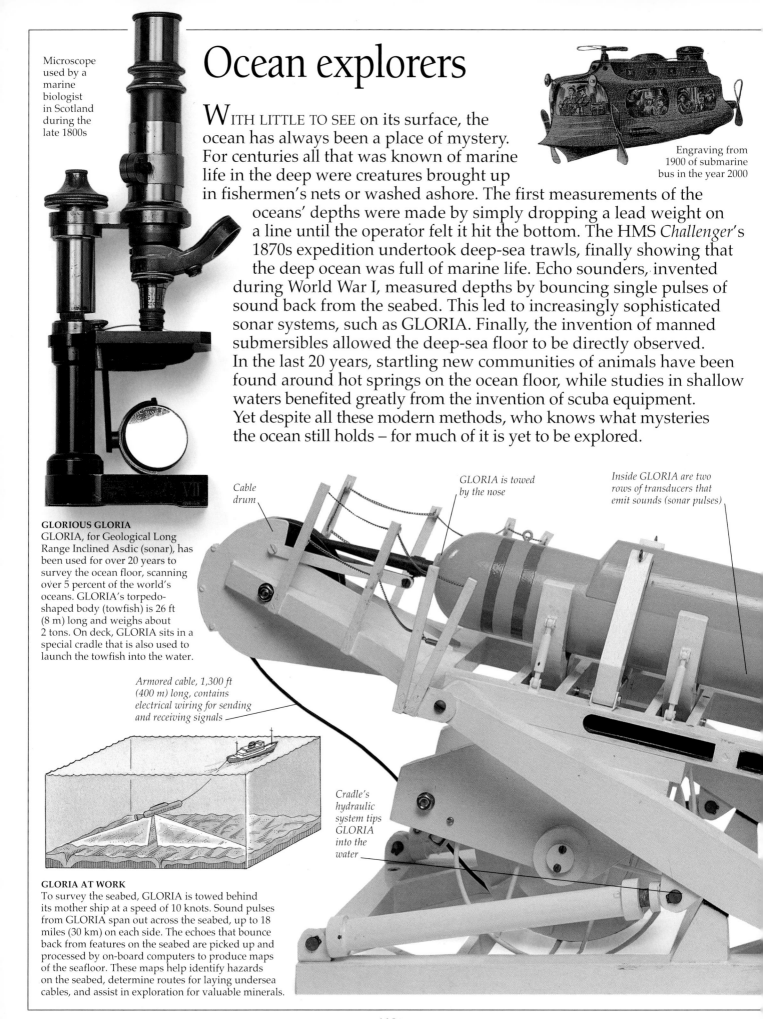

Ocean explorers

Microscope used by a marine biologist in Scotland during the late 1800s

W ITH LITTLE TO SEE on its surface, the ocean has always been a place of mystery. For centuries all that was known of marine life in the deep were creatures brought up in fishermen's nets or washed ashore. The first measurements of the oceans' depths were made by simply dropping a lead weight on a line until the operator felt it hit the bottom. The HMS *Challenger*'s 1870s expedition undertook deep-sea trawls, finally showing that the deep ocean was full of marine life. Echo sounders, invented during World War I, measured depths by bouncing single pulses of sound back from the seabed. This led to increasingly sophisticated sonar systems, such as GLORIA. Finally, the invention of manned submersibles allowed the deep-sea floor to be directly observed. In the last 20 years, startling new communities of animals have been found around hot springs on the ocean floor, while studies in shallow waters benefited greatly from the invention of scuba equipment. Yet despite all these modern methods, who knows what mysteries the ocean still holds – for much of it is yet to be explored.

Engraving from 1900 of submarine bus in the year 2000

GLORIOUS GLORIA
GLORIA, for Geological Long Range Inclined Asdic (sonar), has been used for over 20 years to survey the ocean floor, scanning over 5 percent of the world's oceans. GLORIA's torpedo-shaped body (towfish) is 26 ft (8 m) long and weighs about 2 tons. On deck, GLORIA sits in a special cradle that is also used to launch the towfish into the water.

Cable drum

GLORIA is towed by the nose

Inside GLORIA are two rows of transducers that emit sounds (sonar pulses)

Armored cable, 1,300 ft (400 m) long, contains electrical wiring for sending and receiving signals

Cradle's hydraulic system tips GLORIA into the water

GLORIA AT WORK
To survey the seabed, GLORIA is towed behind its mother ship at a speed of 10 knots. Sound pulses from GLORIA span out across the seabed, up to 18 miles (30 km) on each side. The echoes that bounce back from features on the seabed are picked up and processed by on-board computers to produce maps of the seafloor. These maps help identify hazards on the seabed, determine routes for laying undersea cables, and assist in exploration for valuable minerals.

SNORKELING
A simple way to observe life underwater is to snorkel. The snorkel goes under the strap of the face mask and sticks out above the water. By breathing in through the mouthpiece, air is drawn down the snorkel, and air is expelled through the snorkel by breathing out.

Air expelled through end of snorkel

Fins propel swimmer along, but arms should be kept near the body for streamlining

Face mask traps air to let swimmer view life in the water

Diver looking at grouper fish in the Red Sea

Swimmer breathes in air and expels it through mouthpiece

Snorkel tube

SCUBA DIVING
Use of scuba equipment has proved invaluable in the study of marine life in shallow waters. Instead of bringing animals into an aquarium, marine biologists can observe them in the wild. However, some animals, such as hammerhead sharks, are sensitive to the noises made by air bubbles and may be scared away.

Fins used in snorkeling and scuba diving

Rope guide, used during recovery of GLORIA

Deep Star can reach depths of 4,000 ft (1,200 m)

DEEP STARS
Many different submersibles have been used for underwater exploration (left). The deepest dive ever was to 35,800 ft (10,912 m) in the Mariana Trench by Swiss engineer Jacques Piccard and US Navy Lieutenant Don Walsh in their bathyscaphe in 1960.

GLORIA covers 7,700 sq mi (20,000 sq km) in a day

Launching cradle weighs about 13 tons

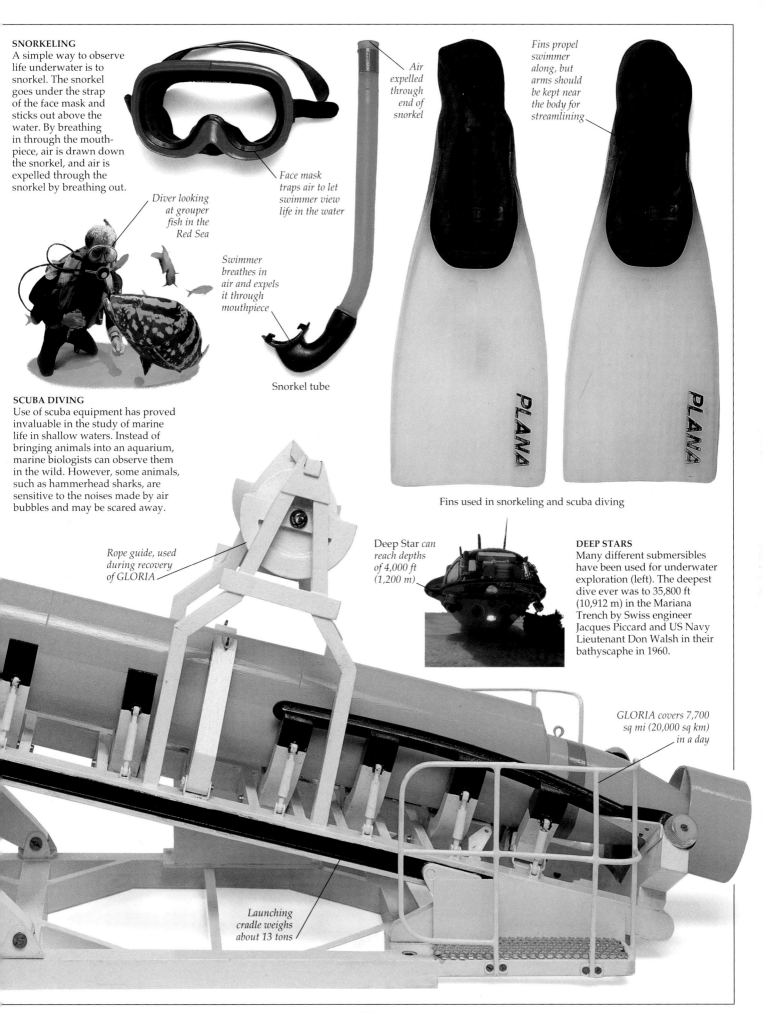

Wrecks on the seabed

Ever since people took to the sea in boats, there have been wrecks on the seabed. Drifts of mud and sand cover them, preserving wooden boats for centuries. This sediment protects the timbers from wood-boring animals by keeping out the oxygen they need. Seawater, however, badly corrodes metal-hulled ships. The *Titanic*'s steel hull could disintegrate within a hundred years. Wrecks in shallow water get covered by plant and animal life and turn into living reefs. Animals such as corals and sponges grow on the outside of the ship, while fish use the inside as an underwater cave to shelter in. Wrecks and their contents tell much about life in the past, but first archeologists must survey them carefully. Objects brought up must be washed clean of salt or preserved with chemicals. Treasure seekers, unfortunately, can do much damage.

GLITTERING GOLD
Gold is among the most sought-after treasure. These Spanish coins, much in demand by pirates, sometimes ended up on the seabed when a ship sunk.

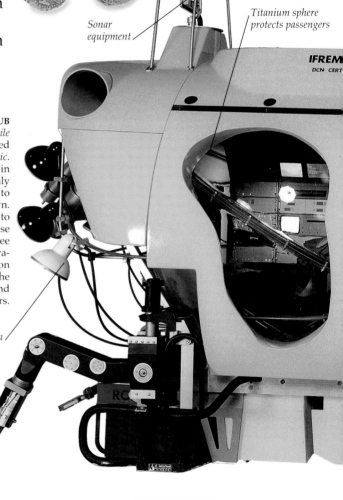

Sonar equipment

Titanium sphere protects passengers

IFREM
DCN CERT

SUPER SUB
The French submersible *Nautile* recovered objects from the seabed surrounding the wreck of the *Titanic*. When the ship went down, it broke in two, scattering objects far and wide. Only a submersible could dive deep enough to reach the *Titanic*, 2.3 mi (3,780 m) down. A sphere made of titanium metal to withstand the immense pressure at these depths, the *Nautile* has space for only three – a pilot, a co-pilot, and an observer. Extra-thick, curved Plexiglas portholes flatten on the dive due to pressure. The journey to the wreck takes about an hour and a half, and *Nautile* can stay down for eight hours.

Lights for video camera

Manipulator arm for picking objects off seabed

VALUABLE PROPERTY
In 1892, divers worked on the wreck of the tug *L'Abeille*, which sank off Le Havre, France. For centuries, people have salvaged wrecks to bring up items of value.

SAD REMINDERS
Many items recovered from the *Titanic* wreck were not valuable but everyday items used by those aboard. Personal effects, such as buttons or just cutlery, remind us of those who died.

THE UNSINKABLE SHIP
In 1912, the *Titanic* sailed from England to New York on her maiden voyage. Because of her hull's water-tight compartments, she was thought unsinkable, but hit an iceberg four days into the voyage. She took two hours and forty minutes to sink, with only 705 people saved of 2,228. She was discovered in 1985 by a French-U.S. team using remote-controlled video equipment. Submersibles *Alvin* (United States) and *Mir* (Russia) have also dived to the wreck since then.

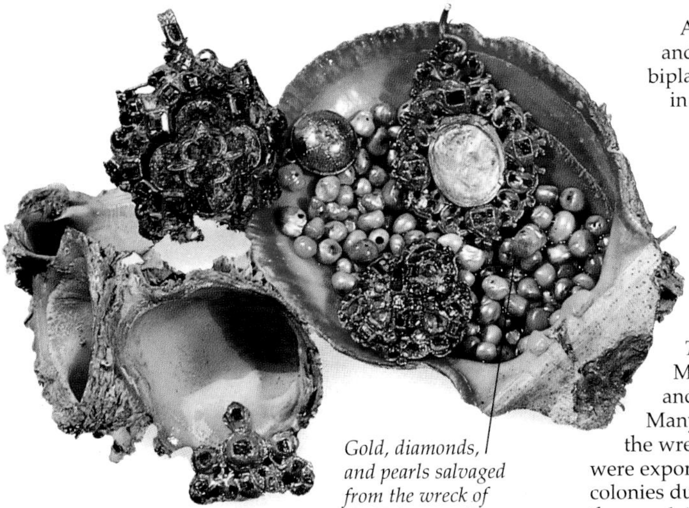

PLANE WRECK
Airplanes sometimes crash into the sea and sink to the bottom, like this Japanese biplane discovered off Papua New Guinea in the Pacific. The Bermuda Triangle, an area in the Atlantic, is famous for the many planes and ships that mysteriously disappeared there.

SUNKEN TREASURE
These precious jewels are among many valuable items salvaged from the wreck of a Spanish galleon, the *Tolossa*, in the 1970s. Bound for Mexico in 1724, a hurricane blew up and it foundered on a massive coral reef. Many luxury goods were recovered from the wreck, which show that the Spanish were exporting fine things to their New World colonies during the 1700s. Other items from the wreck include brass guns, iron grenades, and hundreds of pearls.

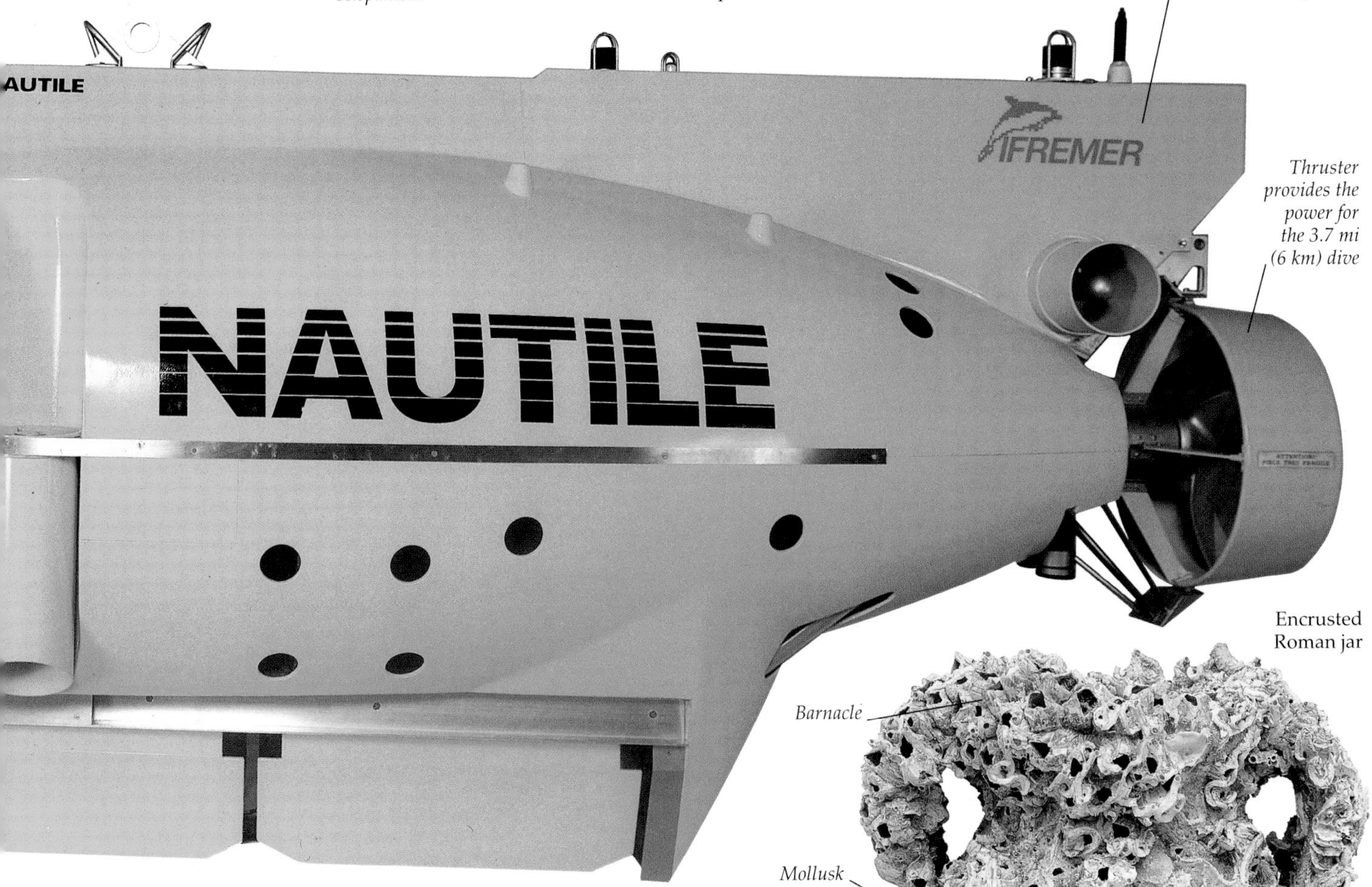

Gold, diamonds, and pearls salvaged from the wreck of the Tolossa off Hispaniola

Nautile measures 26 ft 3 in (8 m) in length

Thruster provides the power for the 3.7 mi (6 km) dive

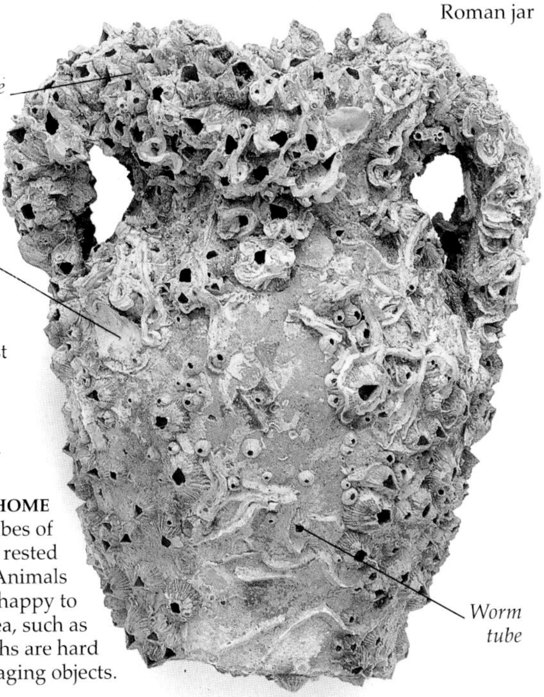

NAUTILE

IFREMER

Encrusted Roman jar

Barnacle

Mollusk

MISSING LAND
This poster advertises a film about the lost continent of Atlantis, which supposedly sank beneath the sea. This myth may be true, since a Greek island sank beneath the waves after an earthquake in 1450 B.C.

HOME, SWEET HOME
Hard barnacle shells and tubes of worms grew on this Roman jar while it rested for hundreds of years on the seabed. Animals that normally live on rocks are just as happy to settle on any hard objects left in the sea, such as shipwrecks, but some animal growths are hard to remove without damaging objects.

Worm tube

Harvesting fish

F ISH ARE THE MOST popular kind of seafood, with some 70 million ton caught around the world each year. Some fish are caught by hand-thrown nets and traps in local waters, but far more are caught at sea by modern fishing vessels using the latest technology. Some fish are caught on long lines with many hooks, or ensnared when they swim into long walls of drift nets. Bottom-dwelling fish are trawled or whole shoals are gathered up in huge nets set in mid-water. Using sonar to detect shoals means there are few places where fish can escape notice. Even fish living in deep waters, such as orange roughy at depths of 3,300 ft (1,000 m), are brought up in large numbers. Many people are concerned that too many fish are being caught, because numbers take a long time to recover. Competition for fish stocks is fierce, and it is difficult for fishermen to make a living. But some fish, such as salmon, are farmed to help meet demand.

2 YOUNG SALMON
At a few weeks old, the egg sac disappears, so young salmon must feed on tiny insects in the river. Soon dark spots appear on the parr (young salmon). The parr stay in the river for a year or more before turning into silvery smolt that head for the sea.

3 AT SEA
Atlantic salmon spend up to four years at sea, feeding on other fish. They grow rapidly, putting on several pounds (or kilos) annually. Then the mature salmon return to their home rivers and streams, where they hatch. They recognize their home stream by a number of clues, including its "smell" – combinations of tiny quantities of substances in the water.

Fin rays are well developed

Large, first dorsal fin

Pelvic fin

Pectoral fin

Operculum (flap covering gills)

Mouth for feeding and taking in water to "breathe".

FISH FARMING
Salmon are among the few kinds of sea fish to be farmed successfully. Young salmon are reared in fresh water, then, when large enough, released into floating pens in calm sea waters, such as sea lochs. To help them grow quickly, the salmon are fed with dried fish pellets. Environmentalists are concerned that fish parasites, called sea lice, common among farmed salmon, are infecting and killing wild salmon. Biologists are investigating ways to combat this problem.

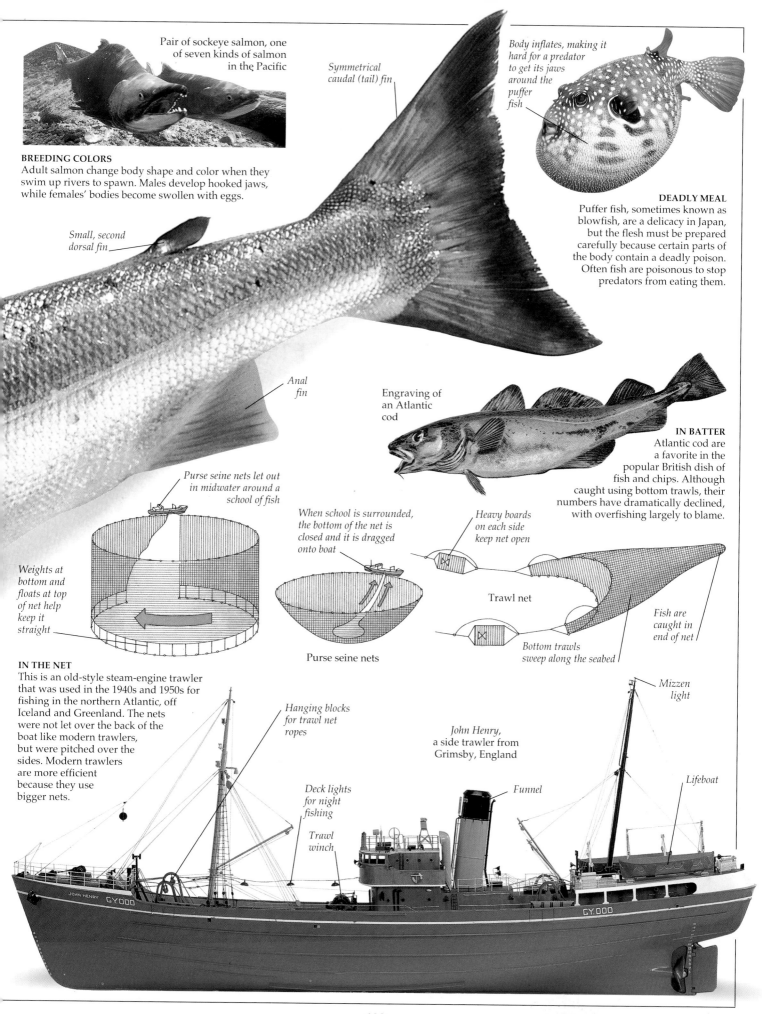

Pair of sockeye salmon, one of seven kinds of salmon in the Pacific

Symmetrical caudal (tail) fin

Body inflates, making it hard for a predator to get its jaws around the puffer fish

BREEDING COLORS
Adult salmon change body shape and color when they swim up rivers to spawn. Males develop hooked jaws, while females' bodies become swollen with eggs.

Small, second dorsal fin

DEADLY MEAL
Puffer fish, sometimes known as blowfish, are a delicacy in Japan, but the flesh must be prepared carefully because certain parts of the body contain a deadly poison. Often fish are poisonous to stop predators from eating them.

Anal fin

Engraving of an Atlantic cod

IN BATTER
Atlantic cod are a favorite in the popular British dish of fish and chips. Although caught using bottom trawls, their numbers have dramatically declined, with overfishing largely to blame.

Purse seine nets let out in midwater around a school of fish

When school is surrounded, the bottom of the net is closed and it is dragged onto boat

Heavy boards on each side keep net open

Weights at bottom and floats at top of net help keep it straight

Trawl net

Fish are caught in end of net

Purse seine nets

Bottom trawls sweep along the seabed

IN THE NET
This is an old-style steam-engine trawler that was used in the 1940s and 1950s for fishing in the northern Atlantic, off Iceland and Greenland. The nets were not let over the back of the boat like modern trawlers, but were pitched over the sides. Modern trawlers are more efficient because they use bigger nets.

Hanging blocks for trawl net ropes

John Henry, a side trawler from Grimsby, England

Mizzen light

Deck lights for night fishing

Funnel

Lifeboat

Trawl winch

JOHN HENRY GY.000

GY.000

Ocean products

PEOPLE HAVE ALWAYS HARVESTED plants and animals from the ocean. Many different kinds are collected for food, from fish, crustaceans (shrimp, lobsters), mollusks (clams, squid) to more unusual foods such as sea cucumbers, barnacles, and jellyfish. Seaweeds also are eaten, either in a recognizable state or as an ingredient of ice cream and other processed foods. The products made from sea creatures are amazing, although many (such as mother-of-pearl buttons and sponges) are now made with synthetic materials. Yet the appeal of natural ocean products is so great that some animals and seaweeds are grown in farms. Among the sea creatures cultivated today are sponges, giant clams (for their pretty shells), mussels (for food), and pearl oysters. Farming is one way to meet product demand, and to avoid over-harvesting the ocean's wildlife.

Yarn dyed purple from pigment of sea snails

ROYAL PURPLE
Sea snails were used to make purple dye for clothes worn by kings in ancient times. Making dye was a smelly business, as huge quantities of salted snails were left in vats gouged out of rocks. The purple liquid was collected and heated to concentrate the dye. These sea snails (from Florida and the Caribbean) are used to make purple dye.

Slate-pencil sea urchin from tropical coral reefs in the Indo-Pacific

Short, blunt spines surround mouth

Long, very strong spines help protect urchin from predators

Five strong white teeth protrude from urchin's mouth (viewed from underneath)

Soft skeleton is all that is left after processing living sponge

USEFUL SPINES
The spines of this urchin were once used as pencils to write on slate boards. Slate-pencil urchins are still collected, their spines used for wind chimes. The spines, hung from threads, clink together when the wind blows through them. Urchins use their big spines to help them walk across the seabed when they emerge from crevices to feed at night.

Spines help urchin move and stay in place

SOFT SKELETON
Bath sponges grow among sea grasses in reef lagoons. When harvested from the bottom, the sponges are covered with slimy, living tissues. Collected from the Mediterranean, Caribbean, and Pacific, natural sponges are prone to diseases and over-collecting.

SEAWEED FARM
In Japan, seaweeds are used in crackers or to wrap up bites of raw fish. Nori, a red seaweed, is grown in the sea on bamboo poles, collected, and dried. Laver, another red seaweed, is eaten in Wales, in the U.K. Agar, a jelly-like substance, is made from red seaweeds and used in foods and in medical research. Seaweeds are also used in fertilizers.

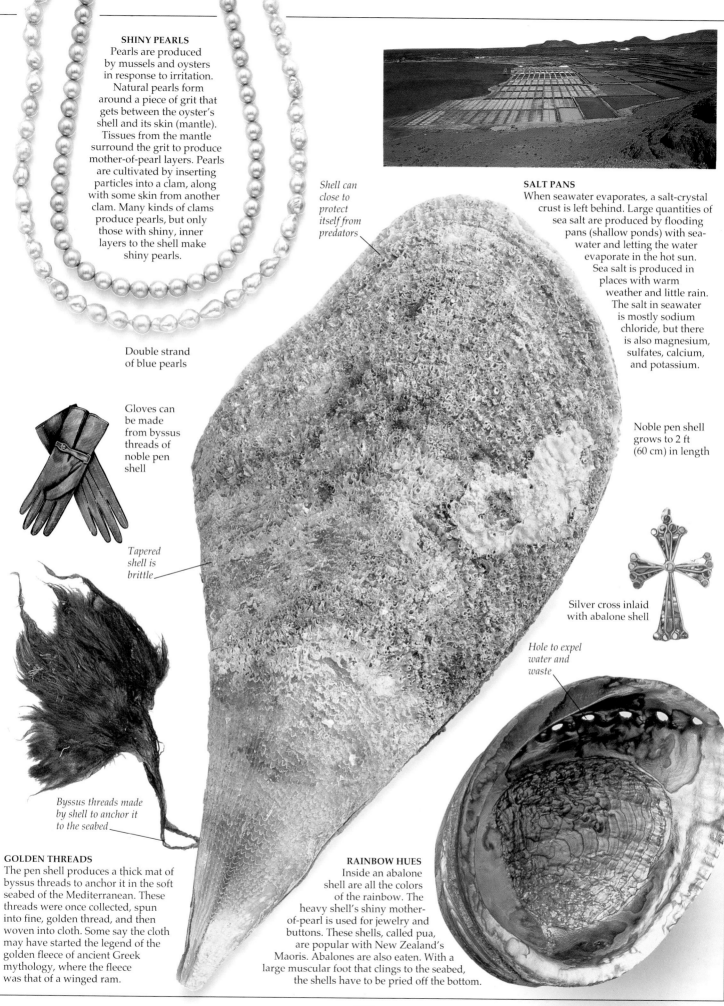

SHINY PEARLS
Pearls are produced by mussels and oysters in response to irritation. Natural pearls form around a piece of grit that gets between the oyster's shell and its skin (mantle). Tissues from the mantle surround the grit to produce mother-of-pearl layers. Pearls are cultivated by inserting particles into a clam, along with some skin from another clam. Many kinds of clams produce pearls, but only those with shiny, inner layers to the shell make shiny pearls.

Double strand of blue pearls

Shell can close to protect itself from predators

SALT PANS
When seawater evaporates, a salt-crystal crust is left behind. Large quantities of sea salt are produced by flooding pans (shallow ponds) with seawater and letting the water evaporate in the hot sun. Sea salt is produced in places with warm weather and little rain. The salt in seawater is mostly sodium chloride, but there is also magnesium, sulfates, calcium, and potassium.

Gloves can be made from byssus threads of noble pen shell

Noble pen shell grows to 2 ft (60 cm) in length

Tapered shell is brittle

Silver cross inlaid with abalone shell

Hole to expel water and waste

Byssus threads made by shell to anchor it to the seabed

GOLDEN THREADS
The pen shell produces a thick mat of byssus threads to anchor it in the soft seabed of the Mediterranean. These threads were once collected, spun into fine, golden thread, and then woven into cloth. Some say the cloth may have started the legend of the golden fleece of ancient Greek mythology, where the fleece was that of a winged ram.

RAINBOW HUES
Inside an abalone shell are all the colors of the rainbow. The heavy shell's shiny mother-of-pearl is used for jewelry and buttons. These shells, called pua, are popular with New Zealand's Maoris. Abalones are also eaten. With a large muscular foot that clings to the seabed, the shells have to be pried off the bottom.

Oil and gas exploration

VALUABLE RESERVOIRS OF OIL AND GAS lie hidden in rocks on the seabed. They are tapped by drilling into the rock, but first geologists must know where to drill. Only certain kinds of rocks hold oil and gas, and must be in shallow enough water to be reached by drilling. Geologists use underwater air guns and explosions on the surface to send shock waves through the seabed and distinguish between rock layers by returning signals. After a source is pinpointed, temporary rigs are set up to see if the oil is the right quality and quantity. If it is, a more permanent oil platform is built and firmly anchored to the seabed. As the oil or gas is extracted, it is off-loaded from the platform's storage tanks into larger tankers or sent ashore via pipelines. There is a great demand for oil and gas, but the earth's supplies are limited. As reservoirs dry up, new sources have to be found. Today's main offshore oil fields are in the North Sea, Gulf of Mexico, Persian Gulf, and the coasts of South America and Asia.

ON FIRE
Oil and gas are highly flammable. Despite precautions, accidents do happen, like the North Sea's Piper Alpha disaster in 1988 when 167 people died. Since then safety measures have been improved.

MILK ROUND
Helicopters deliver supplies to oil platforms far out at sea. Up to 400 people can live and work on an oil platform, but fly by helicopter for breaks onshore every few weeks.

OIL PLATFORM
One of the smaller oil platforms in the North Sea has concrete legs. Platforms are built in sections on shore. The largest section is towed out to sea and tipped upright onto the seabed, then living quarters are added. A tall derrick holds drilling equipment – several pipes tipped with strong drill bits for grinding the rocks. Special mud is sent down the pipes to cool the drill bit, wash out ground-up rock, and keep oil from gushing out. Oil platforms extract oil or gas, but rigs drill wells during exploration.

Tallest structure on this platform is flare stack, for safety reasons

Flare stack for burning off any gas that rises with the oil and cannot be used

Fireproof lifeboat gives better chance of survival

Derrick (a steel tower) holds drilling equipment

Crane hoists supplies up to platform from ship

Hand rail to protect personnel

Helicopter brings fresh food and milk to the platform

Helicopter pad

Living quarters

DEATH AND DECAY
Plant and bacteria remains from ancient seas fell to the seafloor and were covered by mud layers. Heat and pressure turned them into oil, then gas, which moved up through porous rocks, to be trapped by impermeable rocks.

Impermeable rock prevents oil from traveling farther

Oil is trapped in porous reservoir rock

Porous rock that oil can pass through

Formation of fossil fuels

AT WORK
On an oil platform, some people work on deck operating the drill, while others work inside with computers. Geologists examine rock, oil, and gas samples. Mechanics keep the machinery going. There are also cooks and cleaners to look after the crew.

ON THE BOTTOM
Divers (minus Newt suits) doing repairs underwater work longer if they return to a pressurized chamber, then back into the sea, without having to decompress after each dive.

Strong structure to withstand buffeting by wind and waves

Oxygen carried in cylinders on the back

NEWT SUIT
Thick-walled suits, like the one above, resist pressure. When underwater, the diver breathes air at normal pressure, as if inside a submersible. This means a diver can go deeper without having to undergo decompression. Newt suits (above) are used in oil exploration to depths of 1,200 ft (365 m). Joints in the arms and legs allow the diver to move.

Oceans in peril

Jewelry made of teeth of great white shark, now protected in some areas

THE OCEANS AND THE LIFE THEY SUPPORT are under threat. Sewage and industrial waste are dumped and poured from pipelines into the oceans. Carrying chemicals and metals, waste creates a dangerous buildup in the food chain. Oil spills, which smother marine life, do obvious damage. Garbage dumped at sea also kills. Turtles mistake plastic bags for jellyfish, and abandoned fishing nets entangle both seabirds and sea mammals. Over-harvesting has depleted many ocean animals, from whales to fishes. Even the souvenir trade threatens coral reefs. The situation is improving, however. New laws stop ocean pollution, regulations protect marine life, and in underwater parks people can look at ocean life without disturbing it.

Opening carved like a helmet

HAVE A HEART
Many people collect sea shells because of their beauty, but most shells sold in shops have been taken as living animals. If too many shelled creatures are collected from one place, such as a coral reef, the pattern of life can be disrupted. Shells should only be bought if the harvest is properly managed. It is better to go beachcombing and collect shells of already dead creatures. Always check before taking even empty shells, as some nature reserves do not permit this.

Heart cockle shells

OIL SPILL
Oil is needed for industry and motor vehicles. Huge quantities are transported at sea in tankers, sent along pipelines, and brought up from the seabed. Accidents happen and massive amounts of oil are spilled. Sea birds and sea mammals die of the cold, because their feathers or fur no longer contain pockets of air to keep them warm. Trying to clean themselves, animals die from consuming the oil, which also blocks their airways. Some are rescued, cleaned, and released back into the wild.

SAVING BEAUTY
No one can help but admire this beautiful 17th-century chambered nautilus shell. There are six kinds of nautilus living in the Pacific and Indian oceans, where they are all at risk from over-collecting. Live nautili are easily hunted at night when they rise to the surface, though dead shells can also be collected because they too float at the surface. Chambered nautili grow slowly, reaching maturity in six or more years. If too many are collected, the populations can take a long time to recover.

WORSE FOR WHALES

For centuries, whales have been hunted for their meat, oil, and bones. Whale oil was used in foods, as lubricants, and in soap and candles, and the broad baleen plates were made into household items such as brushes. The wholesale slaughter by commercial whalers drastically reduced the number of whales. Now most whales are protected, but scientists doubt whether some populations will ever recover their former numbers. Some kinds of whales are still caught for food, mainly by local people.

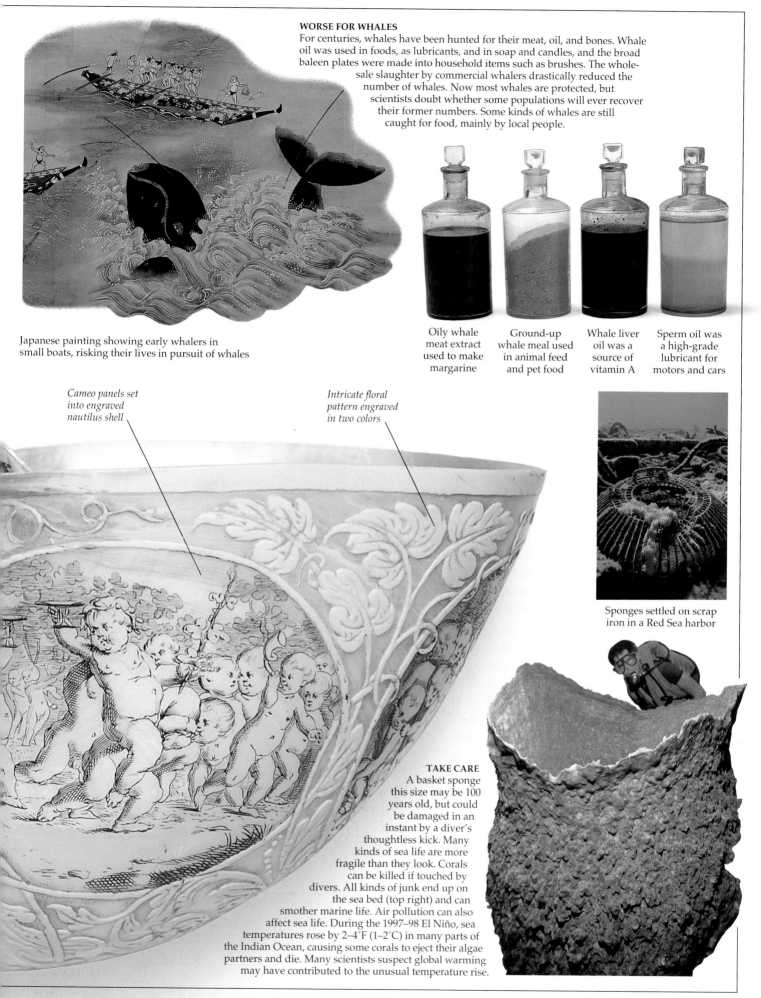

Japanese painting showing early whalers in small boats, risking their lives in pursuit of whales

Oily whale meat extract used to make margarine

Ground-up whale meal used in animal feed and pet food

Whale liver oil was a source of vitamin A

Sperm oil was a high-grade lubricant for motors and cars

Cameo panels set into engraved nautilus shell

Intricate floral pattern engraved in two colors

Sponges settled on scrap iron in a Red Sea harbor

TAKE CARE

A basket sponge this size may be 100 years old, but could be damaged in an instant by a diver's thoughtless kick. Many kinds of sea life are more fragile than they look. Corals can be killed if touched by divers. All kinds of junk end up on the sea bed (top right) and can smother marine life. Air pollution can also affect sea life. During the 1997–98 El Niño, sea temperatures rose by 2–4°F (1–2°C) in many parts of the Indian Ocean, causing some corals to eject their algae partners and die. Many scientists suspect global warming may have contributed to the unusual temperature rise.

Sugar kelp

Bladder wrack

Dog whelk

Dogfish eggcases
containing embryos

Carrageen

Hebrew cone shells

Dulse

Common cormorant

Rock oyster

SEASHORE

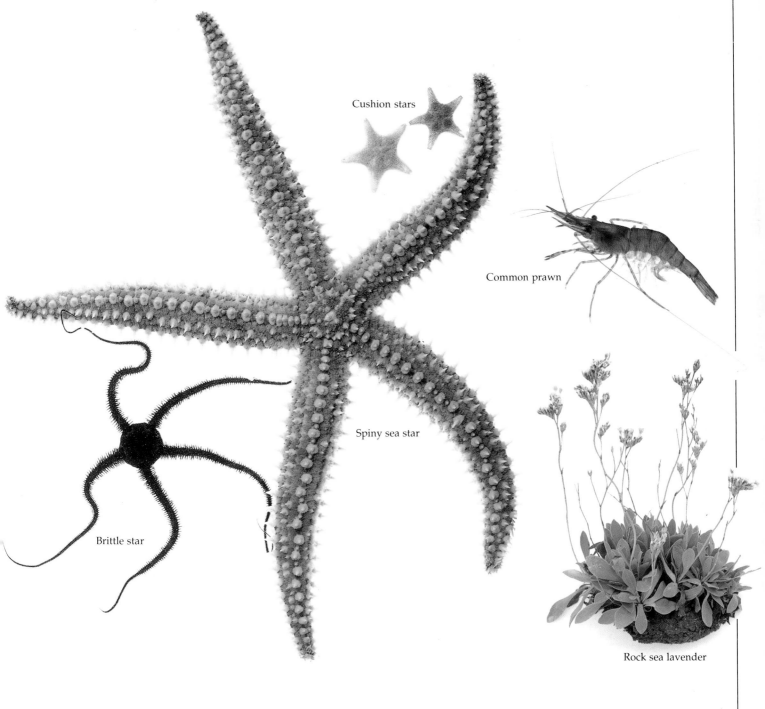

Cushion stars

Common prawn

Spiny sea star

Brittle star

Rock sea lavender

The world of the seashore

Two thirds of our planet is covered with water. Every fragment of land, from the great continent of Eurasia to the tiniest Pacific island, has a shore. The total length of shorelines is huge. Yet the width is hardly measurable in comparison - it is often just a few yards. Shores are strange places, being the edge of the land as well as the edge of the sea. The sea level rises and falls with the tides, making the shore sometimes wet and sometimes dry. Winds drive unchecked across the open ocean and hit the coast with great force. As they blow, they whip up waves that endlessly crash into the land. No two stretches of shore are the same. Each is shaped by many variable factors - the tides, winds, waves, water currents, temperature, and climate, and the types of rock from which the land is made. Along each shore a group of highly adapted plants and animals - many of them strange to our land-orientated eyes - make their homes. This book explores the world of the seashore and describes how its inhabitants adapt to their constantly changing surroundings.

Shaping the shoreline

FOR MILLIONS OF YEARS, every few seconds of each day, waves have hit the seashore. Generated and driven by wind, in calm weather they may be slight ripples, but in a fresh breeze they tumble in foaming heaps onto rocks or sandy beach. In a storm, huge breakers pound the shore like massive hammer blows. Waves erode the shore in three different ways. One is by the hydraulic (water) pressure they exert as they move up the shore and then crash down upon it as they break. A second is by the pneumatic (air) pressure created as water is hurled against rock.

It traps pockets of air that are forced into every tiny crack and fissure, like a compressed-air gun. In this way small crevices are widened. Tunnels may be forced along joints in the rock of a low cliff and out at the top, forming blowholes through which each wave shoots spray-filled air. The third way in which waves wear away the land is by corrasion. This is the grinding action of the rocks of all sizes - from giant boulders to tiny sand grains - that are picked up by the waves and flung against the shore. Under this constant barrage, no coastline can remain unchanged.

WHO'S WINNING?
The sea is gradually wearing away the land on some stretches of coast. But the land may be slowly rising, too - making the struggle more even. Plants such as marram grass help to reduce erosion on sand dunes by binding the grains with their roots and creating sheltered pockets where other plants can grow.

ON THE WAY TO SAND
The sea gradually wears down large blocks of stone into boulders, then into pebbles, like these, then into sand grains, and finally to tiny particles of silt.

POUNDING SURF
Waves exert tremendous force as they crash onto the coast. The weight of the sea slapping the shore every few seconds can create pressures of more than 25 tons per square yard - 30 times the pressure under your foot as you stand.

RISING TIDE
Time and tide wait for no one, especially picnickers at the seashore who have failed to keep an eye on the water level.

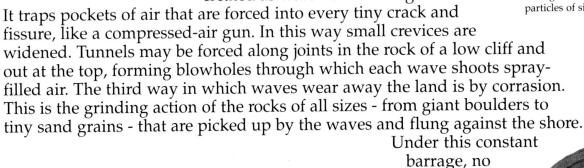

Sun   Moon   Bulge of water   Earth

FORCES FROM SPACE
Twice each day the sea rises up the shore and then goes back out. These movements of water are called tides and are caused by the moon and to a lesser extent, the sun, pulling the earth's water toward them, creating a bulge. When the sun and moon are in line, as shown above, the bulge is most pronounced and the tides are at their highest and lowest.

As hard as rock?

The type of rock of which the shore is made is one of the chief factors determining the nature of a coastline. Hard rocks such as granites, basalts, and some sandstones are resistant to erosion and often form high headlands and tall, stable cliffs on which plants can gain a footing.

Granite colored pink by the mineral orthoclase

COARSE OF GRAIN
Granite is an igneous rock; that is, it is formed as molten (liquid) rock cools and the different minerals in it crystallize. Its crystals are relatively large; granite is said to be coarse-grained.

Granite tinted white by the mineral plagioclase

VARIABLE IN COLOR
As granite is worn by the sea and the weather, its less-resistant mineral parts, such as feldspar, change to softer claylike substances. The quartz and mica mineral particles are much harder: they become separated from the soft clay and may eventually become sand on a beach.

VOLCANIC ISLANDS
This lava, from the island of Madeira off northwest Africa, is full of holes created by bubbles of gas trapped as the rock hardened.

LAVA COAST
Some parts of the coast are formed of dark lava flows such as these on the island of Hawaii.

Hexagonal columns created by cooling pattern in basalt

Mainland sandstone cliff

NATURAL COLUMNS
Basalt is another hard igneous rock. It is sometimes worn into startling geometric columns, such as this 230 ft (70 m) deep cave on the west coast of Scotland, known as Fingal's Cave, and the huge "stepping stones" of the Giant's Causeway in Ireland.

Isolated stack of sandstone formed by the collapse of a bridge joining it to the mainland

ONCE A BEACH
The grains show clearly in this sample of sandstone. Perhaps on an ancient beach they settled, were cemented together, were then lifted by huge movements of the Earth's crust, and now lie exposed again on a coastal cliff.

Rocks from ancient seas

Many softer rocks, such as chalk and limestone, are sedimentary in origin. They were formed when small particles of calcite (calcium carbonate), which were largely the remains of plants and animals, settled out as sediment on the bottom of an ancient sea. More particles settled on top, and those underneath were gradually squeezed and cemented into solid rock. Sometimes whole plants and animals were trapped in the sediments, and these were gradually turned into rock to become fossils.

DISAPPEARING CLIFF
Shores made of soft material such as sand, clay, and other loose particles may be quickly worn down by waves, and the material carried away by currents. On some stretches of shore, wooden barriers called groynes are built to reduce the amount of sediment removed by currents.

WORK OF THE WAVES
As waves approach a headland, they are bent so that they crash into its sides. Headlands made of rocks such as sandstones and limestones may have their lower sides eroded completely, causing an arch to form. In time this becomes a "tower" of rock called a stack.

THE END OF THE ROAD
Where the coastal rock is soft and crumbly, whole seaside communities have been swallowed by the sea. This road led originally to some houses, whose ruins are now under the waves.

Stalks of sea lilies

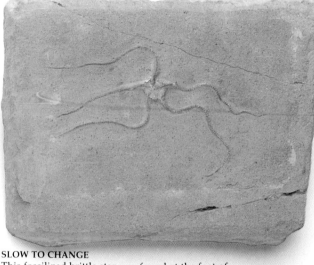

SLOW TO CHANGE
This fossilized brittle star was found at the foot of a cliff. It lived some 200 million years ago, but is very similar to those living today.

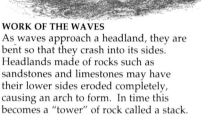

GROOVED "PEBBLES"
Hard shells make good fossils. These "pebbles" are brachiopods, or lampshells, which are similar to shellfish like cockles. They are common in many sedimentary rocks and help to date the rocks.

STONE BULLETS
These are the fossilized internal shells of belemnites, prehistoric squidlike mollusks.

LACY STALKS
This is a bed of fossilized crinoids or sea lilies, which lived 200 million years ago. Crinoids are animals related to sea stars.

WHITE CLIFFS

Chalk is a type of limestone, often dazzling white in color, which may form tall cliffs. Here the various strata (layers) laid down at different times can be seen. At the foot of the cliff, lumps eroded from above are found with pebbles brought by currents from other parts of the coast.

Strata (layers) of chalk laid down at the bottom of an ancient sea

ANCIENT SEA LIFE

Chalk is made of fragments of fossilized microscopic sea plants and animals. Large fossils such as mollusk shells are sometimes embedded in it.

SOLID MUD

Shale is a soft rock which splits easily along its layers and is quickly eroded where it is exposed at the coast. Types that contain the decomposed remains of sea plants and animals are known as oil shale. When heated, oil shale releases a type of crude oil. It may become an important natural resource in the future.

Fossilized shells in limestone

ONCE A SEABED

Limestone sometimes forms breathtaking cliffs, arches, and stacks. This is the 650 ft (200 m) high plateau of the Nullarbor Plain, in southern Australia, which itself was once a seabed. Limestone is a sedimentary rock, often rich in fossils. Lumps may fall from the cliff and split open to reveal remains of prehistoric animals and plants.

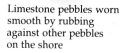

Limestone pebbles worn smooth by rubbing against other pebbles on the shore

Profile of the shore

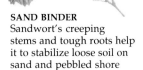

SAND BINDER
Sandwort's creeping stems and tough roots help it to stabilize loose soil on sand and pebbled shore

No TWO COASTS are quite the same. But a naturalist can look at an un-familiar shore (especially a rocky one) and tell at a glance how high the tide rises, how low it falls, whether the area is exposed to wind and waves, or whether it is sheltered. The journey from the edge of the land to the beginning of the sea passes through a series of bands or zones, each with characteristic animals and plants that need to be covered by the sea for different lengths of time. The highest band is the splash or spray zone, which is above the high-water level of the highest tides and is occasionally drenched by spray. Land plants and animals that are adapted to salty conditions live here. Lichens, which are fungi and algae growing in partnership, are found here, as well as a few straying sea-snails. The lower limit of the splash zone is generally marked by barnacles, the first truly marine creatures. The next band is the intertidal ("between the tides") zone, which is regularly covered and uncovered by water. It extends from the barnacles down through the wrack seaweeds to the low-tide area, where larger kelp seaweeds begin to take over.

The third broad band is the subtidal ("below the tides") zone, stretching from the kelp fringe into the permanent shallows.

SALT'S INCREASING INFLUENCE
The influence of salt water increases from the cliff top, occasionally splashed by storm spray, down through layers that are regularly splashed or sometimes covered by water , to the permanently submerged subtidal zone. Different plants and animals are found in each zone.

High-water mark of spring tides

THE HIGHEST HIGH TIDE
Every two weeks, the moon and sun are in line with the earth. At this time their gravity pulls with the greatest strength on the sea, and so causes the greatest "bulge" of water. This produces the highest high tides and the lowest low tides. They are called spring tides.

High-water mark of average tides

AVERAGE HIGH TIDE
The upper shore lies around and just below the average high-tide mark, at the upper fringe of the inter-tidal zone. The high-tide mark itself moves up the beach during the course of a week, finally reaching the spring-tide level. Then it moves gradually back down over the next week. On the upper shore, animals and plants are usually covered by water for one to two hours in each tidal cycle; at a spring high tide they may be covered longer.

BARNACLED BOTTOMS
Feathery-limbed barnacles (right) will settle on any stable surface, including the hulls of ships. Their crusty growths are a problem, as they slow a ship's speed. Special paints have been developed for hulls containing chemicals that stop young barnacles from settling.

A barnacle extends its feathery limbs to grasp and draw food into its mouth, inside the shell plates

FIGHTING IN SLOW MOTION
Limpets are found throughout the intertidal zone. Some species guard territories to protect their food – a green "garden" of algae. Here a light-colored limpet strays onto a neighbor's territory; the occupant crawls over and wedges its shell under the intruder, who then slides away defeated.

Barnacles

The middle and lower shore is on pages 140-141

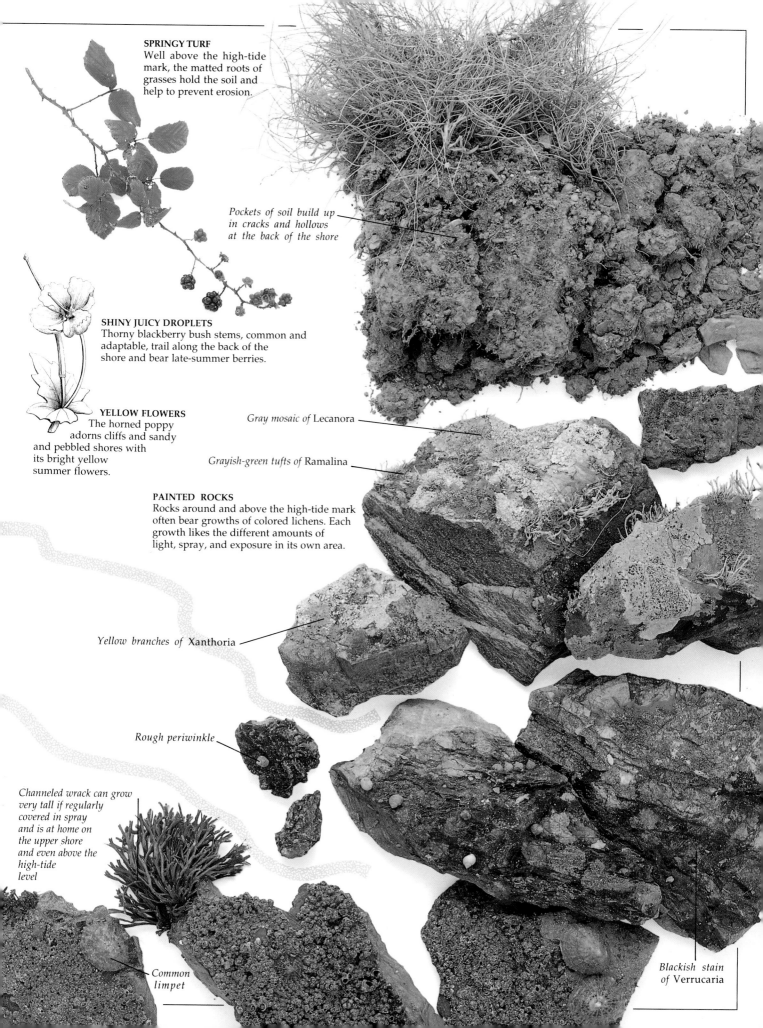

SPRINGY TURF
Well above the high-tide mark, the matted roots of grasses hold the soil and help to prevent erosion.

Pockets of soil build up in cracks and hollows at the back of the shore

SHINY JUICY DROPLETS
Thorny blackberry bush stems, common and adaptable, trail along the back of the shore and bear late-summer berries.

YELLOW FLOWERS
The horned poppy adorns cliffs and sandy and pebbled shores with its bright yellow summer flowers.

Gray mosaic of Lecanora

Grayish-green tufts of Ramalina

PAINTED ROCKS
Rocks around and above the high-tide mark often bear growths of colored lichens. Each growth likes the different amounts of light, spray, and exposure in its own area.

Yellow branches of Xanthoria

Rough periwinkle

Channeled wrack can grow very tall if regularly covered in spray and is at home on the upper shore and even above the high-tide level

Common limpet

Blackish stain of Verrucaria

THE LOWEST HIGH TIDE
Alternating with the spring tides
every two weeks are the neap tides. When the moon
and sun are at right angles, their gravitational
pulls cancel each other out, so there is no very
high or very low tide. Any stationary (nonmoving)
plant or animal that must be underwater for
at least a few minutes on each tide cannot
live above the neap high-tide level.

High-water
mark of neap tides

The limpet Patella aspera
*is found on the middle and
lower shore*

HARSH LICKERS
Purple top shells
crawl among the
wrack sea-
weeds on
the middle
shore,
scraping off
tiny algal growths
with their filelike tongues.

ROVER ON THE SHORE
The predatory dog whelk roves over most of
the shore, feeding on mussels and barnacles.

KELP FANCIERS
These painted top shells graze on the
kelp seaweeds of the lower shore.

NO WET FEET
Mussels live in estuaries (places where a river meets the
sea) and on more exposed rocky shores, generally on the lower
shore below the barnacle belt. Collecting them during
spring low tides prevents getting the feet wet.

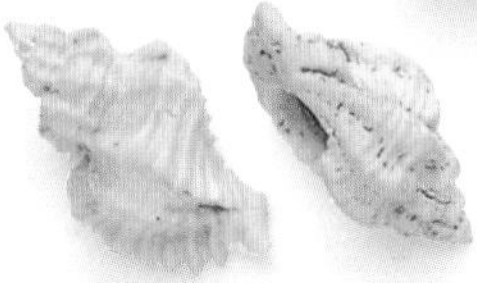

OYSTER BORE
The whelk tingle feeds by boring
through oyster, mussel, and barnacle
shells to reach the flesh.

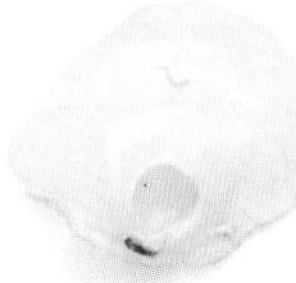

FIXED ATTACHMENT
The saddle oyster attaches
itself to lower-shore and
offshore rocks.

THE HIGHEST LOW TIDE
Just as neap high tides do not reach
very far up the shore, so neap low
tides do not run very far
down. The tidal range
at neaps may be less
than half of the
range at springs.

Low-water
mark of neap tides

AVERAGE LOW TIDE
The lower shore lies around and just
above the average low-tide mark, at the
lower fringe of the intertidal zone. Here,
life can be sure of always being
covered during
the neap-tide
period.

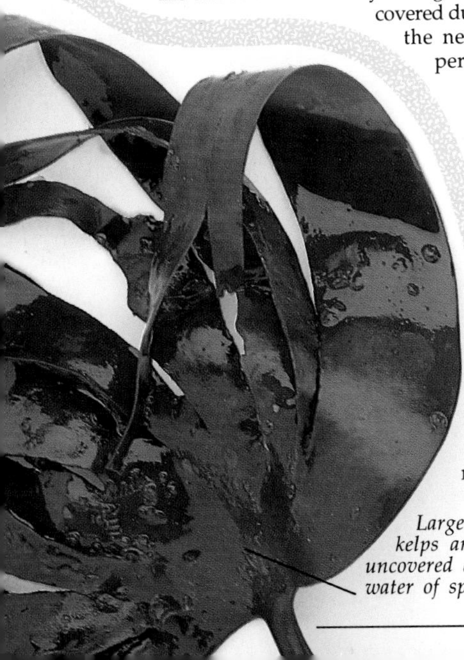

Low-water
mark of average tides

*Large brown
kelps are only
uncovered at the low
water of spring tides*

THE BARNACLE BELT

Away from shelter, as exposure to wind and waves increases, the wrack seaweeds have trouble surviving. Their place on the upper and middle rocky shore is taken by the barnacles, which form a distinct belt along many coasts. On some Australian shores, there are more than 120,000 barnacles to the square yard.

Barnacles

SEABORNE FOOD

Many fixed creatures, such as these horse mussels, rely on the sea to bring them food in the form of tiny floating particles.

Mussels encrusted with barnacles and bryozoans

TIDE RIGHT OUT

The best time to study the rocky shore is at low spring tide.

Living on the edge of land

APPROACHING THE COAST from inland, we notice how conditions change. There is usually more wind - the sea breeze blows unrestricted across the open ocean. There is also a salty tang to the air, as tiny droplets of seawater are blown off the waves by the wind. Plants growing near the shore must be able to withstand strong winds and, if they are in the splash zone, salt spray. They tend to grow low to the ground to avoid the wind. Another problem plants face, especially on pebbled shores and stony cliff tops, is a shortage of water. Rain soon dries in the breeze or trickles away between the rocks. Some species, such as rock samphire, have thick, fleshy, tough-skinned leaves that store plenty of reserve water. A number of plants that are found on the coast are well adapted to dry habitats and may also grow under similar conditions inland.

THE EDGE OF LAND
Many of the world's people live on or near coasts. The higher and rockier a shoreline, the harder it is for people to visit it, so a greater variety of wildlife is found there.

ROCK-DWELLING LAVENDER
Rock sea lavender is a close relative of the sea lavender of salt marshes, but it is unrelated to the herb lavender.

EVERLASTING THRIFT
Sea pink is another name for wild thrift, which grows in a cushion as protection against the wind. It retains its color when dried and is a favorite with flower arrangers.

Fleshy leaves

Fruit

AT HOME ON STONE
Stonecrops really do grow in dense mats (crops) among stones. After they have flowered, reddish-brown fruits are left on the flowering stems.

SEASIDE MAYWEED
The sea mayweed has daisy-like flowers and fleshy leaves. It flowers in late summer (not May), and grows under cliffs, in barren, rocky ground, and on pebbled shores.

FROM FLOWER TO FRUIT
The tiny, fluffy-looking, yellow-green midsummer flowers of rock samphire have faded and are now developing into brown, "corky" fruits. The juicy leaves of this coastal plant were eaten in the past, either pickled or lightly cooked and served with butter.

Fruit

Fleshy leaves covered by tough skin

Each flower has five tiny petals

RED OR WHITE
Red valerian sometimes has white or pink flowers. It is found in rocky places: by the coast on cliffs and pebbled shores and inland on stone walls.

Tiny oil glands on undersurfaces of leaves

CUSHION OF THYME
Wild thyme is not confined to the coast - it also grows in other dry habitats, such as sand dunes, barren plains, and cliff tops. It has low, creeping stems and it flowers throughout the summer. Like its cultivated relative, wild thyme has a sweet, pungent scent which comes from thymol, its natural aromatic oil.

A collection of scurvy grasses

ANTLER LEAVES
Plantains are tough, stringy, and grow low to the ground, as gardeners well know. The buck's horn plantain is named after its branched antler-like leaves and is common in many coastal areas.

FULL OF VITAMINS
Scurvy grass leaves are rich in vitamin C and were eaten by sailors to ward off the disease scurvy. It is not a grass but a member of the cabbage family.

WITHERED BY WIND
Most trees struggle to grow in the windy and salty conditions on cliff tops over the ocean. This oak has been bent and withered by the wind.

Plants of the sea

ALONG THE SHORE - and in the sea itself - are plants quite unlike the familiar trees and flowers that grow on land. Seaweed is their common name, and indeed these plants grow like weeds along many coasts. They are also known as algae. Unlike garden weeds, the algae do not flower and then scatter seeds. They reproduce in a variety of ways, some by means of swollen stem tips which release male and female cells into the water. The algae do not have true roots, stems, or leaves like land plants. But the larger types do have stipes (stems) and fronds (leaves), and sometimes rootlike anchoring holdfasts (pp. 148-149). Most algae also lack a network of tube-like "plumbing" to transport water and dissolved nutrients throughout the plant. Instead they absorb nutrients directly from seawater. The three groups found on rocky shores are green, brown, and red seaweeds.

FEATHERY FRONDS
The delicate structure of many red seaweeds, such as this cockscomb, is best seen when under water. Red seaweeds add splashes of color to the lower shore and the shallows.

SEAWEEDS AT HOME
Seaweeds are difficult to keep in aquariums. Marine salts can help to make "imitation" seawater, but most seaweeds also need constant water movement bringing fresh nutrients and oxygen, and regular tidal cycles that submerge and expose them.

GREEN RIBBONS
Several similar species of *Enteromorpha* thrive on rocky shores. They also grow in estuaries or where a freshwater stream runs over the rocks making the water less salty.

Enteromorpha

INVADER ON THE SHORE
Japanese sargassum has found its way to the United States and elsewhere. It was probably introduced with oyster spat (eggs) imported from Japan. Closely related to this plant are the dense masses of floating seaweed that form in the Sargasso Sea and are occasionally washed on to our shores.

Japanese sargassum

RICH PICKINGS
Shore birds will eat seaweeds, such as *Enteromorpha* and *Ulva*, and will also snap up the small animals sheltering under them. Several species of birds make a living by searching through seaweed beds during low tide.

RED-FEATHERED ROCK DWELLER
Featherweed is a crimson-red seaweed found anchored to rocks in shaded places on the middle and lower shore. Its body branches out into feathery clusters.

SIGN OF SUMMER
In spring and summer this branching brown seaweed, *Bifurcaria*, bears spotty, swollen tips that contain its reproductive structures. The species is found in pools on the middle and lower shore, where it is always covered by water.

Bifurcaria

CRUMB OF BREAD SPONGE
Attached to the rock near the hairlike *Spongomorpha* weed is a deep-green sponge. This is the common crumb of bread sponge found in shady gullies and under boulders on the lower shore. Sponges are primitive animals that draw in seawater from which they take out oxygen and floating particles of food.

Red seaweed growing on Bifurcaria

Spongomorpha (left)

Water passes into the sponge through tiny holes and passes out through the larger, visible holes

Developing swollen tips contain reproductive structures

Channeled wrack

MARKING HIGH WATER
Dry-looking bunches of channeled wrack hang from rocks along the upper shore, often marking the high-water line. This plant gets its name from the channels or grooves along its fronds.

Reproductive structures in swollen tips

COLORFUL CORAL WEED
There are many types of coralline weed or coral weed along the shore. These red seaweeds lay down a chalky deposit. They grow in tide pools and shady places from the middle shore downward.

Coral weed

HAIR WEED
This is one type of *Cladophora*, a common hairlike green seaweed with a branching structure. It is found up and down the shore.

Featherweed

Cladophora

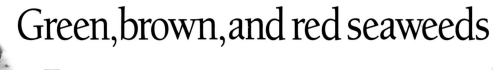
Green, brown, and red seaweeds

THE MOST NOTICEABLE seaweeds on the shore are the large brown seaweeds known as wracks and kelps. Wracks are leathery, straplike seaweeds that grow in bands between the high- and low-tide marks. Some species have air bladders that keep the thallus (the main body) of the plant afloat as the waves come and go. The kelps have much broader bladelike fronds and tend to live around the low-water mark and below. Red seaweeds are generally smaller and prefer shady tide pools and deeper water beyond the kelp zone. They contain phycoerythrin, a red pigment that masks out the green pigment chlorophyll, which is present in all plants. Phycoerythrin is better at using the dim light filtering through seawater than the fucoxanthin pigment of the brown seaweeds. This means that the reds are able to grow at greater depths than other seaweeds.

FROM HIGH TO LOW
On rocky shores seaweeds are found in horizontal bands or zones. These bands of bright-green seaweeds, greenish-brown wracks, red seaweeds, and brown kelps at the low-tide mark form a basic pattern which is repeated, with variations in the species, all over the world.

Air pocket

SWOLLEN TIPS
A mature bladder wrack has swollen tips containing reproductive organs.

POCKETS OF AIR
Some specimens of bladder wrack develop large air pockets in pairs along the center of the frond. Other specimens, especially from exposed coasts, have few or even no bladders. No one knows why this is so.

Serrated
wrack

Sea lettuce

SEAWEED SALAD
left and above
Sea lettuce, which looks a lot like the plant we eat in salads, can grow in many different habitats - in the slightly salty water of estuaries, in seawater, and even in mildly polluted waters. This green seaweed is very common. It can be found attached to rocks, floating freely, or washed up on shore.

SEAWEED WITH TEETH
Serrated or toothed wrack is named after the sawlike teeth along the edges of its fronds. It is a member of the Fucus group, but unlike its close relatives it has no air bladders.

SUGAR AMONG THE SALT
The sugar kelp is a big brown seaweed of the low-water level and below. Its crinkly frond and wavy edges are distinctive, as is the sweet taste of the white powder that forms on its drying surface. It is eaten as a delicacy in the Far East.

LONG THONGS
Sea thong is a leathery, straplike, brown seaweed found near the low-water level. Its narrow fronds may grow more than 10 ft (3 m) long. Like many seaweeds, it has a tough, rubbery texture to protect it as the waves pound it against the rocks.

Sugar kelp

Sea thong

BUTTON-SHAPED BASE
The button- or mushroom-shaped base is one stage in the life cycle of the sea thong. In the plant's second year of growth, the thongs develop from this base and contain the reproductive structures.

Bladder wrack

TWO RED WEEDS
Carrageen (left) and dulse (below) are both red seaweeds that are harvested commercially. Carrageen provides a gel for jellies; dulse can be eaten raw, cooked as a vegetable, or added to stews and soups.

Carrageen

Dulse

The holdfast habitat

SEAWEEDS do not have true roots. The gnarled, rootlike structures of large brown seaweeds are called, appropriately, holdfasts. They hold tight to the rock and provide anchorage, like a tree's roots in the soil. Unlike true roots, the rootlets of a holdfast do not take up water or nutrients; instead these are absorbed through the whole surface of the seaweed. However, holdfasts do provide shelter on the shore. Just as trees protect a woodland's interior from wind, driving rain, and hot sun, leathery fronds and tough holdfasts shield the low-shore kelp forests from the sun and the force of the waves and wind. Many smaller plants and numerous shore animals, such as crabs, fish, prawns, and mollusks, take advantage of the calmer conditions within the forests of brown seaweeds. During storms, weaker seaweeds are torn from the rocks. In the storm's aftermath, huge mounds of kelp are found on the shore, often with their inhabitants still clinging to the fronds. The Californian sea otter is a well-known inhabitant of the kelp beds of the Pacific coast. When it rests on the surface, it secures itself by wrapping kelp fronds around its body.

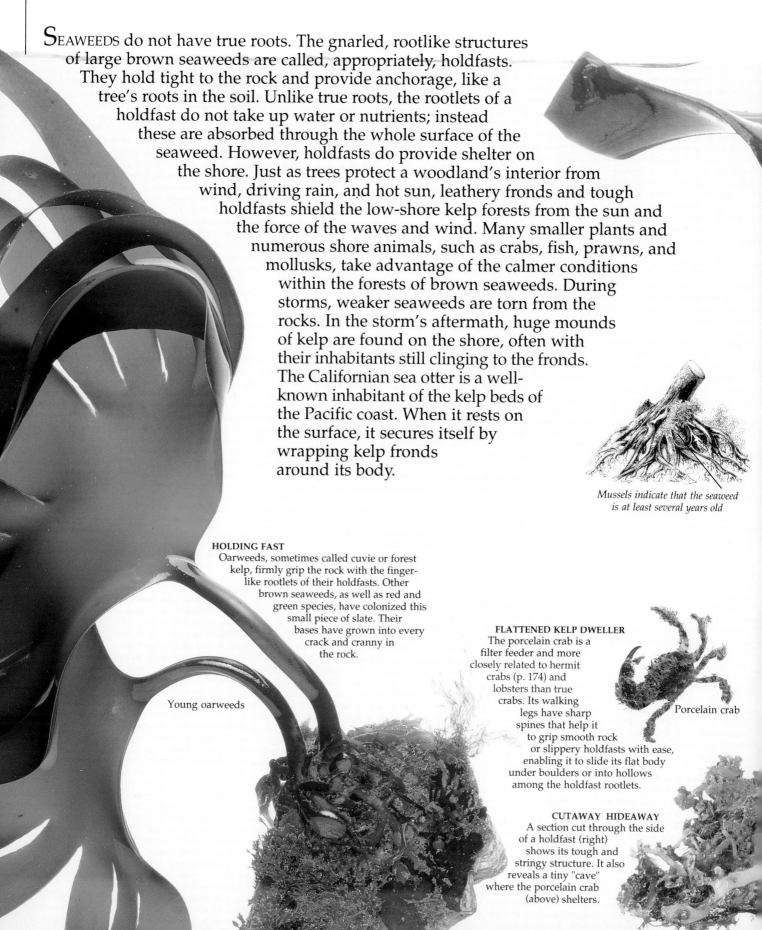

Mussels indicate that the seaweed is at least several years old

HOLDING FAST
Oarweeds, sometimes called cuvie or forest kelp, firmly grip the rock with the finger-like rootlets of their holdfasts. Other brown seaweeds, as well as red and green species, have colonized this small piece of slate. Their bases have grown into every crack and cranny in the rock.

Young oarweeds

FLATTENED KELP DWELLER
The porcelain crab is a filter feeder and more closely related to hermit crabs (p. 174) and lobsters than true crabs. Its walking legs have sharp spines that help it to grip smooth rock or slippery holdfasts with ease, enabling it to slide its flat body under boulders or into hollows among the holdfast rootlets.

Porcelain crab

CUTAWAY HIDEAWAY
A section cut through the side of a holdfast (right) shows its tough and stringy structure. It also reveals a tiny "cave" where the porcelain crab (above) shelters.

FRILLS AND FURBELOWS
One of the most distinctive brown seaweeds is furbelows. Its stipe (stem) has wavy edges and divides into long fanlike fronds that may grow to 6 ft (2 m) or more.

Furbelows

Hollow underside

Rootlets of holdfast

PLANT OR PLASTIC?
Like other large kelps, furbelows grows at the low-tide level and below. Its holdfast is covered in growths that look like bubble-filled plastic packaging. The holdfast grows in one year, which means this plant is an annual.

DRYING THE SHORE'S HARVEST
Seaweeds are nutritious plants, especially rich in some vitamins and minerals such as iodine. In many regions they are eaten regularly as a side dish or chopped and grated as garnish. In Japan kelp and laver (a red seaweed) are cultivated and sold as kombu and nori respectively.

TUG-OF-WAR WITH THE WAVES
Similar species of coastal kelps are found around the world. This holdfast anchors a *Macrocystis* (a type of giant kelp) from New Zealand. The entire plant is tens of yards long. Waves and water currents pull on the enormous fronds with great force, so the holdfast must be equal to the challenge. More than 600 species of seaweeds have been recorded in New Zealand waters.

The rest of the kelp is shown on the next page

A SHARP TONGUE
Blue-rayed limpets commonly graze on kelps, scraping away at the seaweed and any plants and animals crusted on it. Sometimes this mollusk erodes a "home base" (p. 155) in the holdfast.

Red seaweeds growing on kelp

Porcelain crab in hollow of holdfast

CLEANING THE KELP

The common sea urchin is one of many shore creatures that graze the rocks and seaweeds. Using its powerful jaws, the urchin scrapes the rocks and kelp stipes clean, eating small algal growths and tiny settled animals. Sometimes too many urchins occur and strip away all new growth from the rocks, leaving them bare and lifeless.

Blade base splits into fronds

Stipe of kelp

GIANT SEAWEEDS

The *Macrocystis*, or giant kelp, makes up the California kelp forests, home of the sea otter. Some types of giant kelp may grow 3 ft (1 m) in a day under good conditions and reach lengths of 325 ft (100 m).

Ends of fronds are
decaying

*Scar tissue formed over wounds
caused by feeding animals*

Coastal rowers may get their oars
tangled in the oarweed
forests

LACY MATS
The lacy
patterns seen on
some kelps are called bryozoans. They are made up of
many tiny compartments with
an individual animal
in each.

Dogfish lay their eggs
among seaweed

Shells of the shore

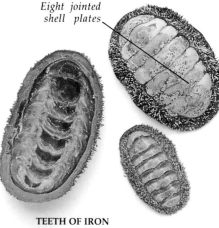

Eight jointed shell plates

ON THE SEASHORE many of the animals that live inside shells are mollusks. They are commonly known as shellfish. Mollusks are an enormous and varied animal group, with over 120,000 species worldwide. The typical mollusk has a soft body, a muscular foot on which it moves, and a hard shell made of calcium carbonate and other minerals taken from seawater; but there are many variations. On the shore the group includes gastropods (snail-like mollusks) such as limpets, abalones, top shells, nerites, periwinkles, conches, whelks, cowries, and cone shells.

Most of the edible mollusks are bivalves, which have two parts, or valves, to the shell. These include cockles, mussels, scallops, clams, oysters, razor clams, and ship worms. Tusk shells, chitons, sea slugs, squid, and octopuses also belong to the mollusk group.

SHE SELLS SEASHELLS
The beauty and hardness of seashells has made them favorites for jewelery and for gifts such as the decorative shell boxes sold by the little girl in the picture. In some coastal areas certain shells were used as currency, such as the "money cowries" of tropical islands.

TEETH OF IRON
Chitons, are common mollusks on many rocky shores, but are difficult to spot because they blend in with the rocks. This species is a mid-shore seaweed grazer from the Indian Ocean. Its tiny teeth are capped with a hard substance that contains iron and keeps them from wearing down.

STRIPES AND SPOTS
Top shells, with their striped and spotted cone-shaped shells, are bright and familiar inhabitants of tide pools (p. 156). This species lives in the Red Sea, and grazes on algae on the lower shore.

PEARLY INSIDE
Abalones are known for the beautiful, rainbow-sheen mother-of-pearl on the inside of their shells. These relatives of top shells and limpets graze on algae and are them-selves eaten as a seafood delicacy, especially in western North America (where this species comes from) and the South Pacific.

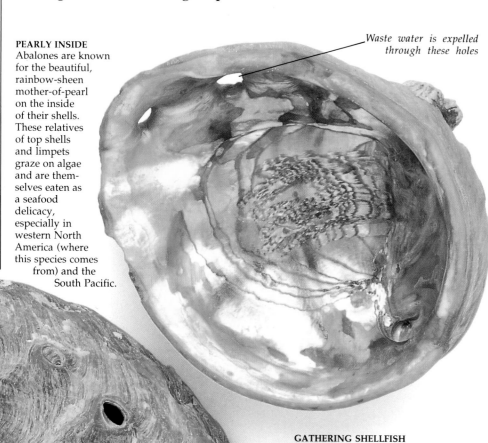

Waste water is expelled through these holes

DEEP-DOWN SHINE
The serpent's-head cowrie is common around many shores of the Indian and Pacific Oceans, including all but the south coast of Australia. It crops small algae from the rocks and the outer edges of coral reefs, where the surf breaks. The animal withdraws into the slit on the shell's underside when in danger.

GATHERING SHELLFISH
Oysters have been gathered and eaten for many years. This Japanese woodcut print shows oyster fishermen at work near the sacred twin rocks in Ise Bay.

LIKE A PATTERNED TOY TOP
Monodonta is another boldly patterned top shell from the Indian Ocean. Top shells belong to the gastropod group of mollusks. Gastropod means "stomach-foot" and these animals, like their snail cousins, appear to slide along on their bellies.

RAW IN ITS JUICE
The oyster's two shells are held firmly together by a strong muscle. To get at the flesh, the shells must be pried open with a knife. Oysters are often eaten raw in their natural juices, straight from the shell.

SHORE HERBIVORE
Nerites are found on many tropical coasts - these are from the Caribbean, where they live on the middle shore. These gastropods are herbivores (plant eaters); they scrape tiny algae from rocks, roots, and large seaweeds.

Spine for prying apart the plates of a barnacle

THE PREDATORY WHELK
Unlike many dog whelks, the Chilean dog whelk is not snail-shaped but more limpet-like and has a very large foot. It patrols the middle and lower shore of South America's Pacific coast, preying on barnacles and mussels.

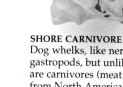

FILTERING THE SEA
There are many species of oysters from different regions. This one, the rock oyster, cements itself to the rock, usually by its right-hand shell. Like many of its bivalve relatives, the oyster is a filter feeder. It draws in a current of seawater, filters out tiny floating food particles, and passes these into its digestive system, using tiny beating hairs called cilia.

SHORE CARNIVORE
Dog whelks, like nerites (above), are gastropods, but unlike the nerites they are carnivores (meat eaters). This species, from North America's west coast, uses its spine to pry apart the plates of a barnacle and reach the flesh within.

MOLLUSK WITH DART
The Hebrew cone from the Indian and Pacific oceans is an intertidal species belonging to the cone shells, a large group of gastropods. Cone shells have tiny poison "darts," harpoon-like structures that are fired into worms and other prey to paralyze them.

WORM-HUNTING WHELK
The red-mouthed drupe is another type of dog whelk, named for its reddish "mouth" or shell opening. This species comes from the Indo-Pacific region, where it feeds on worms on the lower shore.

European cowries, smaller than their tropical counterparts, feed on seasquirts on the lower shore

MUSSEL PROTECTION
Like its common relative the blue mussel, the green mussel attaches itself to rocks and pilings by tough threads called byssus. This species is found in Southeast Asia. Mussels are collected for food and bait.

SEA FOOD
In a clambake, depicted here by the 19th-century American artist Winslow Homer, the clams are cooked in a steaming bed of seaweed over hot stones.

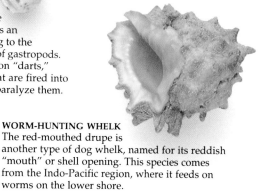

Gripping the rock

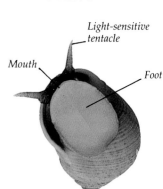

Foot

Mouth

Girdle

Chitons from above and below

ROCKY SEASHORES can be
very harsh habitats as waves
pound unyielding stone. Many
intertidal creatures have responded
by evolving hard outer shells,
which also protect them from predators and the sun's drying heat.
Mollusks such as limpets have low,
volcano-shaped shells that present
little resistance to waves. The peri-
winkle's shell is thick, tough, and rounded; if it is
detached it soon rolls to rest in a gully. Another
aid to survival is a good grip. Sea stars and sea urchins have
hundreds of tiny tube feet; limpets and sea
snails have a single
large suction
foot.

HELD BY SUCTION
The broad foot of the chiton
anchors it to the shore. This mollusk
can also clamp down its fleshy girdle
(shell edge) to make a good seal
and then raise its body inside to
suction itself to the rock. If
dislodged, it flexes its body
and rolls its jointed
shell plates into
a ball.

GRIPPING BY A STALK
Goose barnacles, which are often
washed up on the shore, have tough
stalks to grip any floating debris
such as wood or pumice stone.
These crustaceans live at sea,
filtering tiny food particles from
the water like their rock-bound
shore relatives. Once people
believed that these barnacles
hatched into geese - perhaps
because their frilly limbs looked
like feathers, or maybe to explain
the mysterious disappearance of
the geese in winter.

ANCHORED BY FEET
The five-rayed symmetry (evenness) of the common sea urchin
shows that it is a cousin of the sea star. It is protected by
sharp spines that can be tilted on ball-and-socket
joints at their bases. It uses its long tube feet to anchor
itself to the rock, drag itself along, seize bits
of food, and get rid
of debris.

Light-sensitive
tentacle

Mouth

Foot

SEALING UP THE CRACKS
Edible or common periwinkles have long
been gathered from the lower shore for
food. Like its land relation, the snail,
the periwinkle moves on a muscular,
fleshy foot lubricated by a film of mucus.
When not walking, it often nestles in a
crack or gully and seals the gap between
its shell and the
rock with mucus.

Sea urchin's test

*Holes where
tube feet
passed
through*

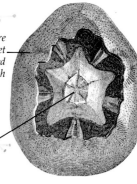

*Mouth
(Aristotle's lantern)*

Anchoring tube feet

Underside of common
sea urchin

*Tube feet
searching water*

THE INNER URCHIN
When the spines and skin are
removed, the beautifully patterned
test (internal shell) of the sea urchin
is revealed. The system of five lever-
operated teeth with which the
urchin grazes on seaweeds is
called Aristotle's lantern.

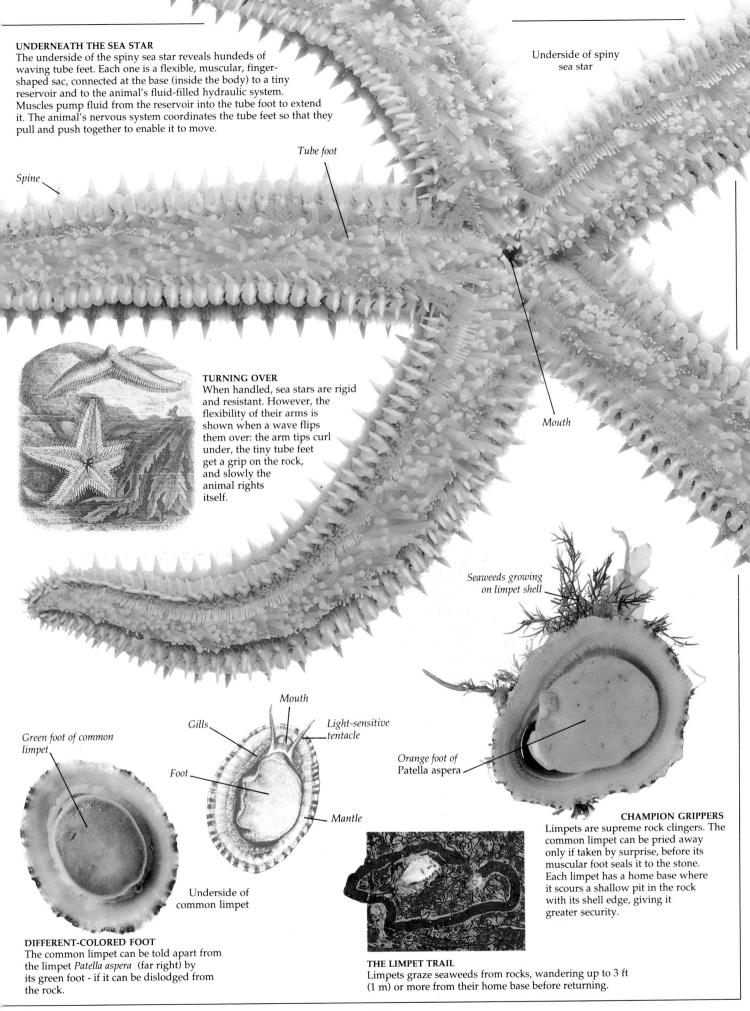

UNDERNEATH THE SEA STAR
The underside of the spiny sea star reveals hundeds of waving tube feet. Each one is a flexible, muscular, finger-shaped sac, connected at the base (inside the body) to a tiny reservoir and to the animal's fluid-filled hydraulic system. Muscles pump fluid from the reservoir into the tube foot to extend it. The animal's nervous system coordinates the tube feet so that they pull and push together to enable it to move.

Underside of spiny sea star

Spine

Tube foot

Mouth

TURNING OVER
When handled, sea stars are rigid and resistant. However, the flexibility of their arms is shown when a wave flips them over: the arm tips curl under, the tiny tube feet get a grip on the rock, and slowly the animal rights itself.

Seaweeds growing on limpet shell

Green foot of common limpet

Mouth

Gills

Light-sensitive tentacle

Foot

Orange foot of Patella aspera

Mantle

Underside of common limpet

CHAMPION GRIPPERS
Limpets are supreme rock clingers. The common limpet can be pried away only if taken by surprise, before its muscular foot seals it to the stone. Each limpet has a home base where it scours a shallow pit in the rock with its shell edge, giving it greater security.

DIFFERENT-COLORED FOOT
The common limpet can be told apart from the limpet *Patella aspera* (far right) by its green foot - if it can be dislodged from the rock.

THE LIMPET TRAIL
Limpets graze seaweeds from rocks, wandering up to 3 ft (1 m) or more from their home base before returning.

Inside a tide pool

A TIDE POOL is a natural world in miniature - a specialized habitat in which plants and animals live together. A wide range of plants is found here, from the film of microscopic algae coating almost any bare surface, to wracks and other large seaweeds. These plants capture light energy from the sun and obtain nutrients from seawater. They provide food for periwinkles, limpets, and other plant eaters. Flesh-eating animals such as sea stars, small fish, whelks, and other creatures eat the plant eaters. And then there are crabs, prawns, and other scavengers that eat both plant and animal material. Filter feeders such as barnacles and mussels consume tiny particles of floating food, which may be miniature animals and plants, or bits of long-dead larger organisms.

NATURE STUDY
Naturalists have always been fascinated by tide pools. The great 19th-century English naturalist Philip Gosse studied shore life in Devon, in southwest England. His son Edmund described how his father would "wade breast-high into one of the huge pools and examine the worm-eaten surface of the rock. . .there used often to lurk a marvellous profusion of animal and vegetable forms."

STRINGS OF EGGS
Sea hares come to the shore in spring and summer to browse on the seaweeds and lay their pinkish purple, stringlike spawn.

SLUGS OF THE SEA
Tide pools occasionally trap sluglike creatures, such as this *Hypselodoris* from Guam, in the Pacific. They are called sea slugs or nudibranchs, a name that means "naked gills," after the feathery tufts on their backs which absorb oxygen from seawater. Sea slugs (like land slugs) are mollusks without shells.

TENTACLES LIKE A HARE'S EARS?
The sea hare is not considered a true sea slug, since it has a thin, flexible shell under the folds on its back.

RECYCLED STINGS
Some sea slugs are equipped with stinging cells absorbed from anemones that they eat.

SPONGE EATER
The sea lemon has a mottled yellowish body. It feeds on crumb of bread sponges.

NOT RECOMMENDED
The bright colors of many sea slugs warn potential predators that they taste horrible.

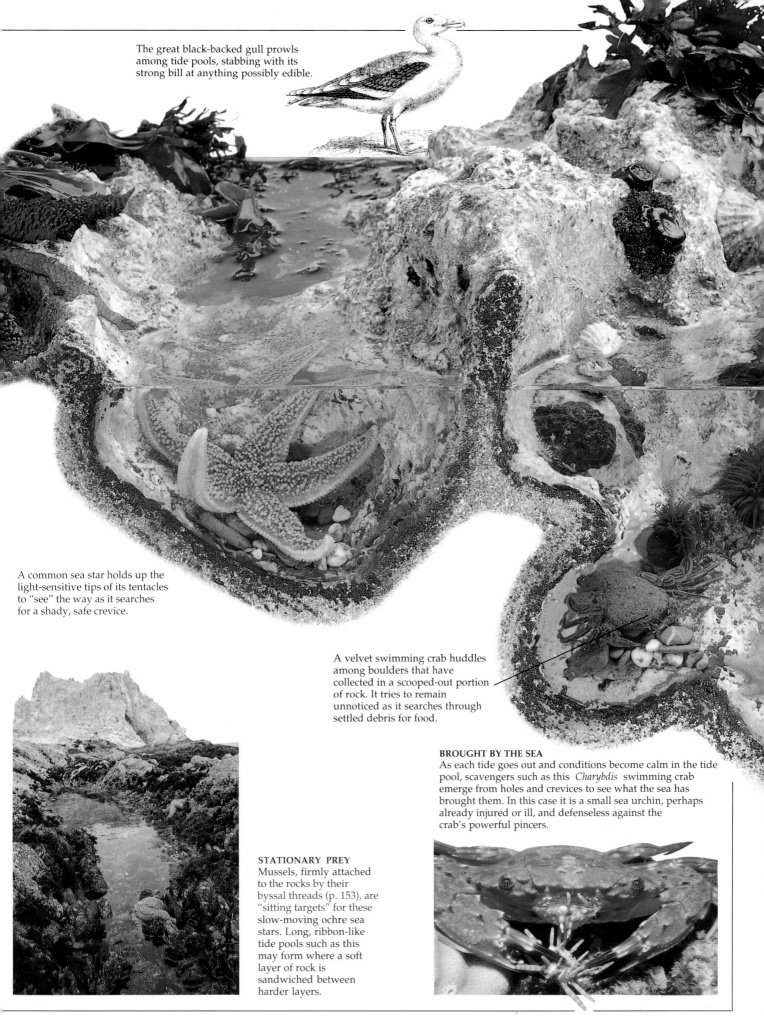

The great black-backed gull prowls among tide pools, stabbing with its strong bill at anything possibly edible.

A common sea star holds up the light-sensitive tips of its tentacles to "see" the way as it searches for a shady, safe crevice.

A velvet swimming crab huddles among boulders that have collected in a scooped-out portion of rock. It tries to remain unnoticed as it searches through settled debris for food.

BROUGHT BY THE SEA
As each tide goes out and conditions become calm in the tide pool, scavengers such as this *Charybdis* swimming crab emerge from holes and crevices to see what the sea has brought them. In this case it is a small sea urchin, perhaps already injured or ill, and defenseless against the crab's powerful pincers.

STATIONARY PREY
Mussels, firmly attached to the rocks by their byssal threads (p. 153), are "sitting targets" for these slow-moving ochre sea stars. Long, ribbon-like tide pools such as this may form where a soft layer of rock is sandwiched between harder layers.

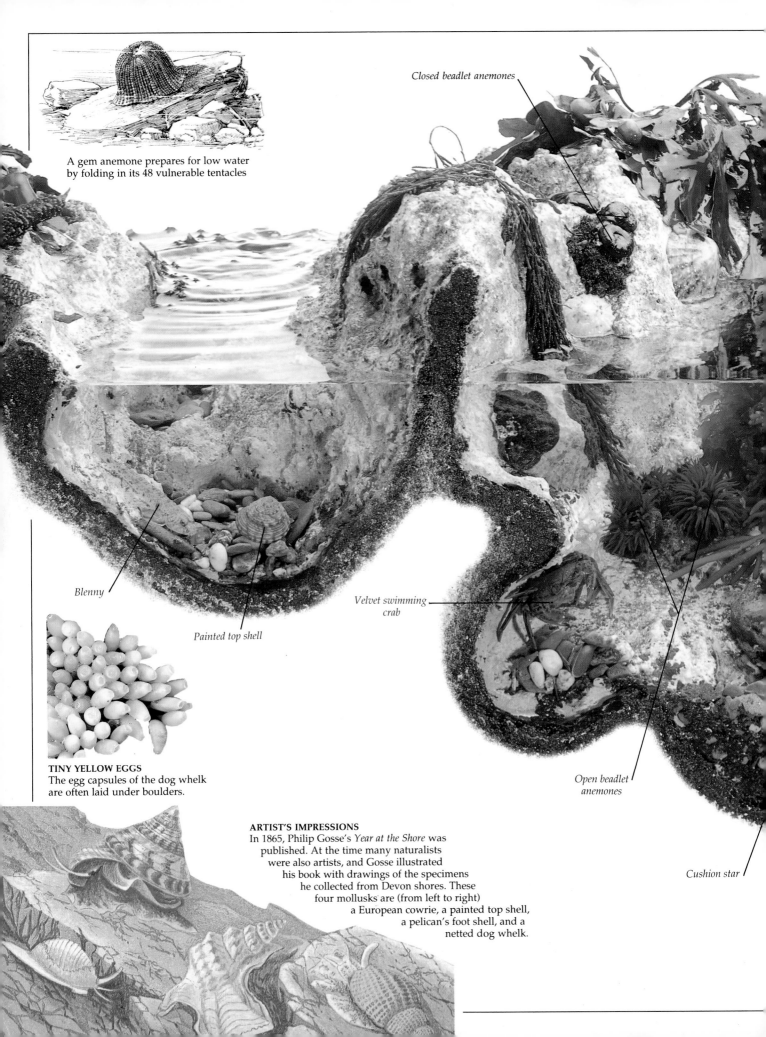

A gem anemone prepares for low water by folding in its 48 vulnerable tentacles

Closed beadlet anemones

Blenny

Painted top shell

TINY YELLOW EGGS
The egg capsules of the dog whelk are often laid under boulders.

Velvet swimming crab

Open beadlet anemones

Cushion star

ARTIST'S IMPRESSIONS
In 1865, Philip Gosse's *Year at the Shore* was published. At the time many naturalists were also artists, and Gosse illustrated his book with drawings of the specimens he collected from Devon shores. These four mollusks are (from left to right) a European cowrie, a painted top shell, a pelican's foot shell, and a netted dog whelk.

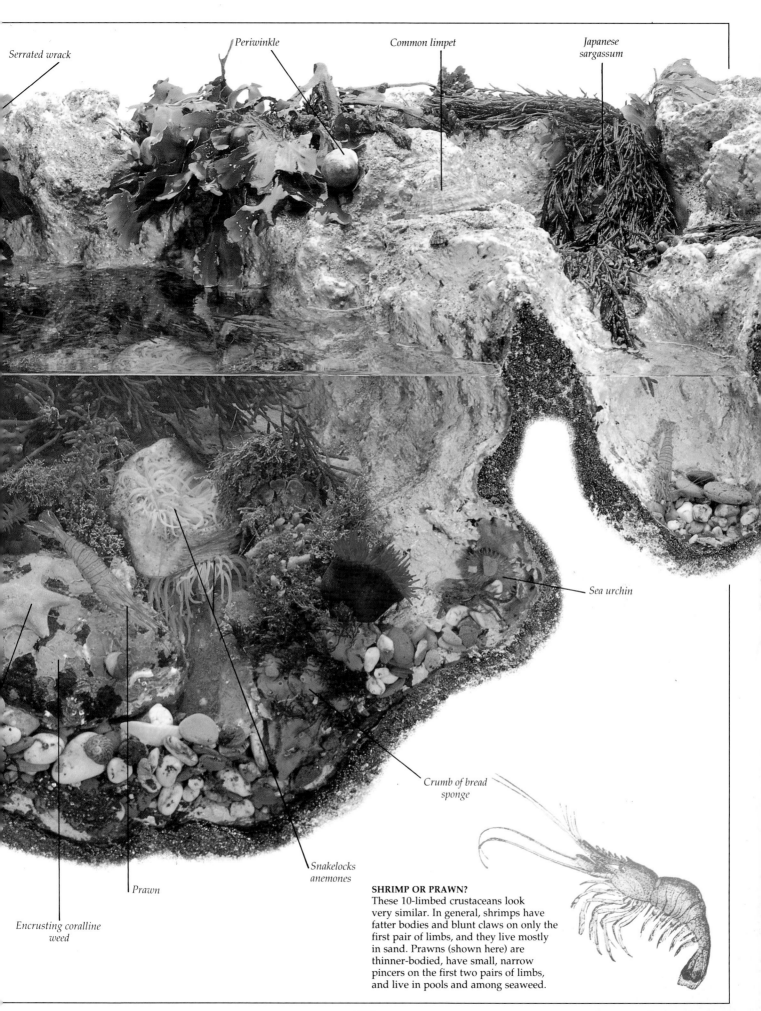

Serrated wrack

Periwinkle

Common limpet

Japanese sargassum

Sea urchin

Crumb of bread sponge

Snakelocks anemones

Prawn

Encrusting coralline weed

SHRIMP OR PRAWN?
These 10-limbed crustaceans look very similar. In general, shrimps have fatter bodies and blunt claws on only the first pair of limbs, and they live mostly in sand. Prawns (shown here) are thinner-bodied, have small, narrow pincers on the first two pairs of limbs, and live in pools and among seaweed.

Tide-pool fish

LIFE FOR SMALL ANIMALS such as the tiny fish that live in tide pools is full of danger. If it rains heavily, the seawater in a small pool is greatly diluted, so that for a few hours the fish (and other inhabitants) must adjust their body chemistry to cope with the lower concentration of salt. The falling tide may maroon them in a shallow puddle, so that they have to wriggle across bare rock to the safety of a deeper pool. In an hour, the sun can turn a cool pool into a warm bath, causing animals to leave the water and find refuge under a cool, moist rock rather than suffer a form of heatstroke. At low tide, gulls feed on tide-pool inhabitants; on the returning tide, small creatures can be crushed by rolling boulders. Fish predators are a constant threat: conger eels lurk in crevices, and hungry bass follow the tide in, snapping up any stragglers. The fish shown here have to be hardy creatures to survive the constantly changing conditions and physical threats in the miniature habitat of the tide pool.

DANGER AFOOT
Many shore creatures are so well camouflaged that they are unseen by walkers on the shore, and must dart away from a descending foot.

A FLICK OF THE FINS
There are about 1,500 species in the goby family, most of them small, flat, tough-looking shore dwellers. These are sand gobies, which can cover themselves in sand with a flick of their fins.

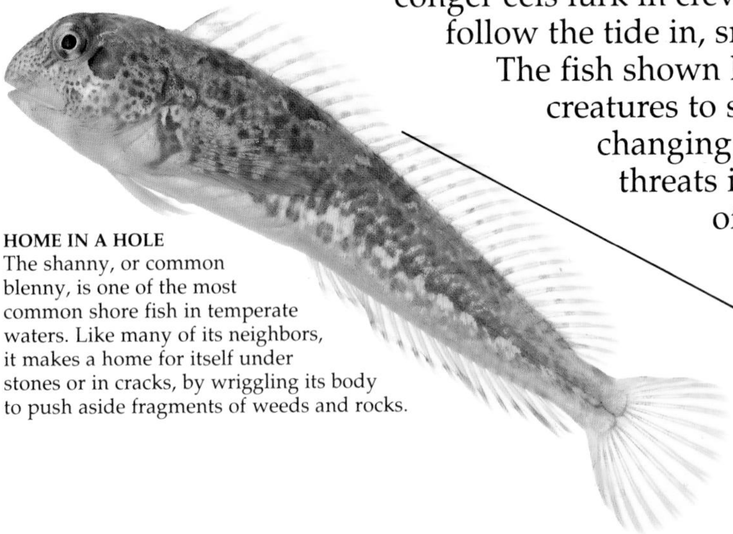

HOME IN A HOLE
The shanny, or common blenny, is one of the most common shore fish in temperate waters. Like many of its neighbors, it makes a home for itself under stones or in cracks, by wriggling its body to push aside fragments of weeds and rocks.

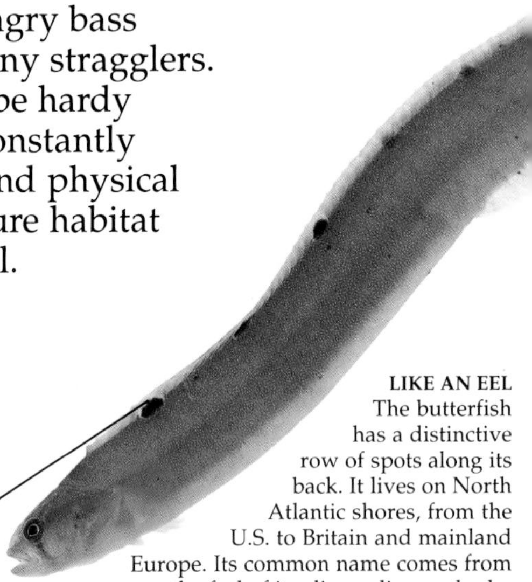

Distinctive dip in the middle of the dorsal (back) fin

Dark spots along the base of the dorsal fin

LIKE AN EEL
The butterfish has a distinctive row of spots along its back. It lives on North Atlantic shores, from the U.S. to Britain and mainland Europe. Its common name comes from the feel of its slimy, slippery body.

LOOKING UPWARD
Shore fish have eyes which are closer to the tops of their heads than many other fish. This enables them to watch for predators from above, such as sea birds.

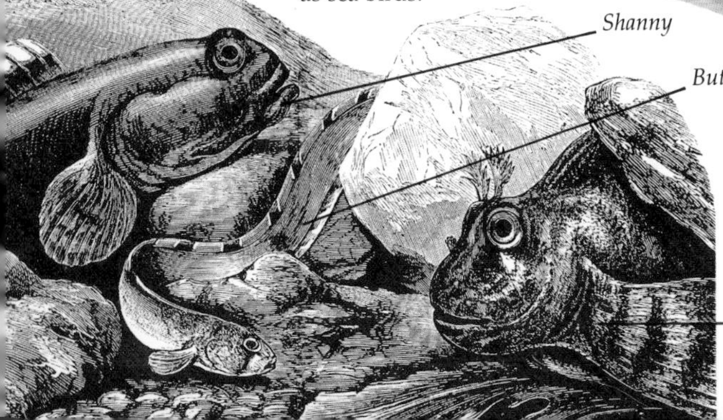

Shanny

Butterfish

Blenny

SPOTTED GOLD
The dark spots on the front of the dorsal fin and upper tail identify the goldsinny, a member of the numerous and varied wrasse group. Large individuals reach about 8 in (20 cm) in length.

EQUIPPED WITH A SUCKER
The clingfish uses its belly-sucker to hang on to rocks. Like many shore fish, it has rubbery, scaleless skin. This enables it to squeeze with ease past stones and seaweed.

Two blue spots on the back

The blurry brownish markings on the fins help to camouflage the goby

THE GOBY IN THE TANK
It is very difficult to study shore fish. At low tide their natural behavior is to retreat into cracks and holes. At high tide they come out to feed, but they are extremely wary.

PROTECTIVE COLORING
Tide-pool fish, like this goby, tend to have mottled and spotted patterning to help conceal them among the patchy rocks, shells, seaweed growths, and rippling shadows of the pool.

WELL DISGUISED
Pipefish, which are related to sea horses, can be almost invisible as they hide among the eelgrass and seaweed fronds, watching for small fish and shellfish.

The eyes are placed high on the sides of the goby's head so that it can see upward and identify predators

Line of brownish spots on the middle of each flank

The worm pipefish swims in an upright position and is well disguised among the swaying stems of seaweed in a tide pool

The sea scorpion can change its coloring to match that of its surroundings

WITH AND WITHOUT FINS
As the worm pipefish evolved, it lost almost all its fins - even the tail fin has gone. The sea scorpion, in contrast, has frilly fins. If startled, it raises its spiked gill covers to frighten away enemies.

Flower-like animals

Scallop shell

ANEMONES are the surprising "flowers" of the shore - surprising because they are not flowers at all. They are hollow, jelly-like animals belonging to a group called the coelenterates or cnidarians, which also includes jellyfish and corals. Their "petals" are actually tentacles with special stinging cells that poison their prey. The prey is then pulled toward the mouth (p. 165). Like flowers, anemones have evolved in many colors, from salmon pink to emerald green and jet black. In many there is great color variation even within the same species. Another remarkable feature is that many can move, if only slowly, sliding their muscular bases along the rock surface. Certain species burrow in sand and gravel; others slide their bodies into crevices in the rocks so that only their tentacles show. As the tide ebbs most anemones on the shore pull in their tentacles and become jelly-like blobs to avoid drying out.

OPEN FOR DINNER
Beautiful but deadly: the waving tentacles of an anemone colony are a forest of danger for small sea creatures.

Mouth in center of body

TRAFFIC-LIGHT ANEMONES
Beadlet anemones come in various colors, including red, amber, and green. When the tide recedes, they fold in their tentacles, looking like overgrown gumdrops scattered on the rocks. When fully grown they have about 200 tentacles.

SWEEPING THE SEA
Fan worms are sometimes mistaken for anemones, but they belong to a different group of animals - the annelids (which include earthworms). The tentacles of the "fan" filter tiny food particles from the water but withdraw into the tube in a flash if danger threatens.

BLEMISH OR BEAUTY?
The wartlike knobs on this creature's body have led to one of its common names - wartlet anemone. The warts can be seen on the closed wartlet anemone on the opposite. page

Calcareous (chalky) algae encrusting rock

"FLOWER" ON A "STALK"
This side view of a grayish beadlet anemone shows its stubby "stalk" (body) with a rainbow-like sheen around the base. Beadlets can survive being out of water for some time and can live very high on the shore.

FEATHERY PLUMES
The plumose or frilled anemone is brown, reddish, or white and may grow up to 1 ft (30 cm) tall. Its feathery tentacles catch very small bits of food and waft them down to the mouth by the beating action of tiny hairs called cilia.

Snow-white tentacles and brown body of a beadlet anemone

PINK-TIPPED TENTACLES
Snakelocks anemones range in color from gray with delicate sheens of pink or green to all-over deep green. The pink-tipped tentacles do not withdraw in this species even when it is out of water.

Living cup coral with tentacles extended

Chalky skeleton of dead cup coral

LIVING CORAL
Corals are similar to anemones and are members of the same overall group, the coelenterates. This cup coral lives alone, unlike its (mostly) tropical reef-building cousins.

Side view of dead cup coral

The body "warts" of this wartlet anemone are visible in this closed-up individual

GIANT OF ITS KIND
The giant green anemone of tropical waters is one of the largest anemones in the world. It may grow to more than 3 ft (1 m) across.

Strings (acontia) of stinging cells

TINY GHOSTS
There are many different species of these tiny, ghost-white encrusting anemones covering some areas of rocky shore.

STINGING STRINGS
The colorful sagartia anemone is one of several species that feeds and defends itself by shooting pale strings of stinging cells through its mouth or through slits in its body. The "strings" are in fact parts of the animal's guts!

MINIATURE FANS
Fan worms (see opposite page) live inside protective, chalky tubes. Some species live buried in the mud; others attach themselves to rocks, like this one. Look to the left - can you spot another small fan worm on the opposite corner of this stone?

Encrusted remains of barnacle shells

Coiled, chalky remains of tube worm

Tentacles and stings

Gray snakelocks anemone

KRAKEN AHOY
The kraken, a sea monster of Norse legend, made short work of ships and their crews. As is often the case, the fable has some basis in fact. The kraken looks suspiciously like the squid, a member of the mollusk group. Atlantic giant squid have been recorded up to 50 ft (15 m) long, including tentacles, and weighing two tons. Their remains are sometimes found washed up on the shore (p. 182).

THE COELENTERATE (CNIDARIAN) ANIMALS (jellyfish, anemones, and corals) are the stingers of the shore. These creatures do not not have brains or complex sense organs such as eyes and ears. Unable to move quickly, they cannot escape from predators or pursue prey. Instead, they protect themselves and capture food with tiny stinging cells in their tentacles. Inside each cell is a capsule called a nematocyst, which contains a long, coiled thread. In some species these are barbed, in others they contain venom. Triggered by touch or by certain chemicals, the threads flick out and then either the barbs hold on to the prey, or venom is injected into it. Then the animal drags its victim into the digestive cavity within the body. Some jellyfish have extremely powerful venom that can cause great pain to swimmers who brush against them. Their nematocysts remain active for a while even after the animal is washed up and dies on the shore. The best known jellyfish is the Portuguese man-of-war. This is not a true jellyfish, but a colony of small animals from the same group. A swimmer may be stung without ever seeing the creature responsible, since the tentacles trail in the current several yards behind the floating body. The box jellyfish, or sea wasp, of tropical waters has tentacles up to 33 ft (10 m) long and its sting is lethal to humans.

Common prawn

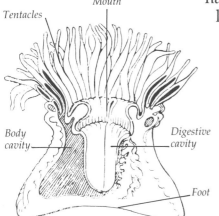

Mouth

Tentacles

Body cavity

Digestive cavity

Foot

INSIDE AN ANEMONE
Anemones, and their coelenterate (cnidarian) relatives, are simply constructed creatures. The ring of tentacles surrounds a mouth that leads to the digestive cavity inside the body. Prey is pushed into the cavity, digested, and absorbed, and any remains excreted through the mouth.

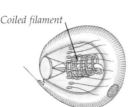

Coiled filament

Discharged filament

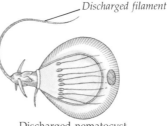

Undischarged nematocyst

Discharged nematocyst

THE STINGING THREAD
Under the microscope it is possible to see tiny sting-containing cells on the tentacles of coelenterate (cnidarian) animals. When the cell is triggered by touch or certain chemicals, its internal fluid pressure quickly increases. This forces the thread-like filament to shoot out. Some filaments are barbed; others contain venom.

PRAWN SNACK
This snakelocks anemone is in the process of capturing a common prawn and pulling it toward its mouth. The barbed stinging cells in the tentacles help to paralyze the prey. When the prawn is drawn into the anemone's stomach, more stings will finish it off.

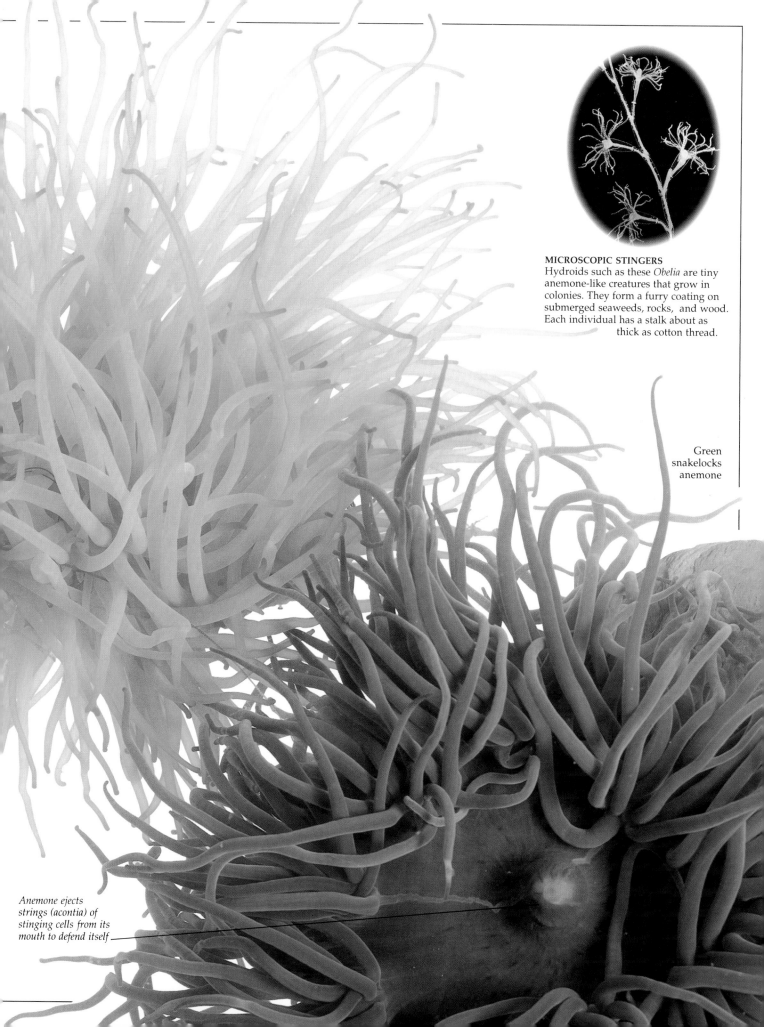

MICROSCOPIC STINGERS
Hydroids such as these *Obelia* are tiny anemone-like creatures that grow in colonies. They form a furry coating on submerged seaweeds, rocks, and wood. Each individual has a stalk about as thick as cotton thread.

Green snakelocks anemone

Anemone ejects strings (acontia) of stinging cells from its mouth to defend itself

Stars of the sea

On almost any seashore, somewhere, there will be sea stars - and probably a few of their relatives such as brittle stars, sea urchins, and sea cucumbers. These creatures belong to a group called the echinoderms (meaning "spiny skinned") and they have been around for perhaps 500 million years. Sea stars that are not spiny are protected by an exoskeleton (outer skeleton) of hard, chalky plates embedded just under the tough skin. Although there are more than 6,000 species of echinoderms - 2,000 more species than there are within the mammal group - these creatures are sea dwellers, so they are unfamiliar to most people. They also seem strange because their body plan consists of "arms" arranged like rays coming from a central point. There is no front end: when a sea star goes for a walk to follow the retreating tide or find a cool spot out of the sun, any arm can take the lead.

Light-sensitive tips of arms often turn up to "see" the way

Spiny sea star

IN THE LIMELIGHT
Sunbeams shining through the surface of a tide pool spotlight shore sea stars. The "sausage with a frill" (upper right) is a sea cucumber. In this relative of the sea star, the arms are tentacles around the mouth end.

A THORNY PROBLEM
The crown-of-thorns sea star feeds on coral. From time to time its numbers increase dramatically, causing much damage in places like Australia's Great Barrier Reef. Whether this is a natural cycle or the result of pollution is not clear.

NEWLY ARMED
Sea stars can grow new arms. If an arm is crushed by a boulder or torn by a predator, it can be cast off and a new one grows. In fact, as long as most of the central disk is intact, one remaining arm can grow four new ones.

SNAKING MOVEMENT
The brittle star throws its fragile arms into serpent-like shapes as it glides swiftly through a tide pool. The arms really are brittle and easily broken, but the brittle star is able to grow new ones.

Brittle star

Blood star

SEEING RED
The blood star, seen occasionally on rocky shores, lives up to its other name of "bloody Henry" with its vivid red body marks.

MUSSEL POWER
This common sea star preys on mussels and other mollusks. It wraps itself around the victim, grips with its tube feet, gradually pulls open the two shells, and sticks out its stomach to digest the prey's soft parts.

COVERED IN SPINES
Stiff and muscular, the spiny sea star is one of the larger sea-shore species. Each calcareous (chalky) spine is surrounded by tiny pincer-like organs (pedicellariae). It uses these to rid itself of parasites, small hitchhikers, and other debris. This sea star feeds on bivalve mollusks.

Spiny
sea star

LEFT STRANDED
Most sea stars live low on the shore or in deeper
water. Those washed up by stormy seas and
stranded out of the water may not survive until
the tide returns.

HUNGRY STARLETS
Small cushion stars, or "starlets," are as
carnivorous (meat-eating) as their larger
cousins, devouring little mollusks,
brittle stars, and
shore worms.

COMMONLY ORANGE
Many common sea stars are
orange, but some are brown,
red, or even purple.
Color variation is
frequent among
these creatures.

Goosefoot sea star
(right)

Spiny
sun star
(below)

WEBBED ARMS
Although the goosefoot sea star
(far right) looks like a five-sided
bandage, it is an active predator
and feeds on crustaceans, mollusks,
and other sea stars.

TWELVE-RAYED SUN
This spiny sun star (right) has
12 arms, but individuals with as
few as 8 or as many as 13 are not
unusual. Like the goosefoot
sea star, it will eat other
echinoderms such as
the common sea star.

Borers and builders

Date mussels in limestone

ON THE COAST OF CALIFORNIA in the late 1920s, steel girders and piles were installed for a seaside pier. About 20 years later, the .4 in (1 cm) thick steel was honeycombed with holes. The culprit was the purple sea urchin. This animal, like many others on the shore, takes refuge from waves, predators, sunshine, and cold by boring into the shore itself. Sand and mud, softer than solid rock, contain many burrowers, such as razor clams, cockles, clams, and tellins. (A razor clam is said to burrow as fast as a human can dig down after it.) Yet even on a rocky shore there are burrowers, boring, scraping, and dissolving their way into the rock. They include the piddock which, as it wears away the surface layer of its shell by drilling, moves its body over the worn area and lays down a fresh layer of hard, chalky shell. Pieces of wood riddled with long holes some .8 in (2 cm) across are often cast up on the beach. These are the work of shipworms, which despite their appearance are not worms but bivalve mollusks like piddocks.

HIDEY-HOLES IN THE ROCK
Rock-boring sea urchins have made many holes in this section of limestone coast at The Burren, in southwest Ireland. Unoccupied holes collect pebbles that are swirled around by the sea, scouring the rock still more. In these ways, rock-boring urchins and mollusks contribute to the erosion of the shore.

DISSOLVING STONE
The date mussel of the Mediterranean is one of several mollusks that can insert themselves into solid rock. Here two small specimens have bored into limestone. Instead of physically drilling into the rock like the piddock, these mussels secrete chemicals which dissolve the chalky stone. Their scientific name is *Lithophaga*, which means "eating rock." The growth rings typical of many bivalve mollusks are visible on the larger individual.

Growth ring

BUILDING A HOME
Several kinds of marine worms make tubes around themselves, chiefly to protect their soft bodies. *Terebella* (left) moves tiny particles with its tentacles and glues them together with a sticky body secretion. *Serpula* (center) makes a chalky, trumpet-shaped tube. Fan worms (right) make tubes that protrude above lower-shore sand.

Feathery tentacles collecting food

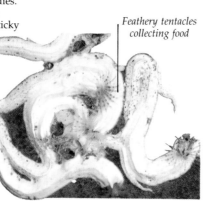

TRIANGLE TUBES
Keelworms are another type of tube-building marine worm. Their chalky tubes have a "keel" or edge, so that they appear triangular in cross section. Their feathery tentacles collect tiny bits of food from seawater.

Piddock in mudstone

PRISONER IN SOLID ROCK
The piddock's ridged shell resembles the sharply ribbed drilling bit of an oil rig, and not without reason. This mollusk twists and rocks the two parts (valves) of its shell in order to drill itself a hole in solid rock. Two long, fleshy tubes called siphons reach up through the hole. Seawater is drawn in through one tube to supply the animal with oxygen and food; waste and rock debris are passed out through the other.

GROW IN A BURROW
Several species of sea urchin are able to make shallow depressions in the rock, and some can burrow almost out of sight. The rock–boring or burrowing purple sea urchin moves its strong, stout spines back and forth and gradually rasps its way into the rock. It also grinds away the rock with its gnawing mouth–parts. As it grows and burrows, it may be unable to escape from its tunnel and becomes dependent on capturing food with its tube feet.

Skeleton (test)

Urchins shelter in shallow "caves" excavated in rock

Spines are purple in life

ROCK RESIDENT
The purple sea urchin lives on the lower shore and in the shallows. Above the low-tide mark, it scrapes a shallow "home" in the rock.

Holes where sponge's breathing and feeding pores are exposed

Borings of yellow sponge

Shell of flat oyster

A BORING ANIMAL
The yellow boring sponge makes branching tunnels in limestone or in a thick, chalky seashell by dissolving the minerals with an acidic secretion. Small parts of the sponge project above each tunnel. They have either one large hole (pore) through which waste water passes out, or several smaller sieve-covered holes through which water is drawn in.

Hard cases

SOME OF THE MOST CURIOUS LOOKING creatures of the shore are crabs, prawns, and lobsters. They are members of a large and varied group of animals called the crustaceans. In the same way that insects swarm on land, so crustaceans teem in the sea. Both groups are arthropods, or joint-legged animals. Crustaceans usually have jointed limbs (up to 17 pairs in some species), two pairs of antennae, and a hard shell, or carapace, that encloses and protects much of the body. However, the animals themselves vary enormously. They range from microscopic creatures that make up a large part of the floating plankton (the "soup" that nourishes so many filter-feeding sea animals), to the giant spider crabs of Japan, which measure more than 12 ft (3.5 m) across the claw tips. Some of the most surprising members of the crustacean group are the barnacles (cirripeds). These animals begin life as tiny, free-swimming larvae. Some species then settle on the shore, cement their "heads" to the rock, grow hard plates around their bodies, and use their six pairs of feathery, jointed "legs" to kick food into their mouths! The crustaceans most familiar to us are the decapods, which include shore creatures such as crabs, lobsters, crayfish, hermit crabs, prawns, and shrimps. Decapod means "10-legged," and most of these creatures have 10 main limbs. Four pairs are for walking or swimming, and there is one pair of handlike pincers.

POTTED CRAB
Crabs have long been caught, cooked, and eaten by people. Crab pots are filled with rotting fish flesh as bait; once the crab has entered, it is unable to climb out. Crabs are also eaten by shore birds and mammals, by fish such as bass, and by octopuses.

The combative shore crab, pincers held up in self-defense, is known in France as *le crabe enragé*

THE RED CARPET
In some areas of the Galápagos Islands off the coast of Ecuador, Sally Lightfoot crabs cover surf-splashed rocks like a moving red carpet. This brilliantly colored species has bright red limbs and a sky-blue underside.

BATTLE-SCARRED SCUTTLER
This shore crab has lost one of its limbs. A herring gull's powerful bill, or perhaps a small rock rolled by a wave, has removed its right first walking leg. Accidents like this often happen to crabs on rocky shores. However, this individual is not disabled by the loss and displays a variety of postures: caution (below), a mock attack, a crouching defense, and finally a retreat.

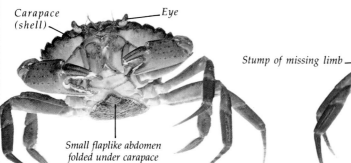

Carapace (shell)

Eye

Stump of missing limb

Four pairs of walking limbs

Pincers poised in mock attack

Small flaplike abdomen folded under carapace

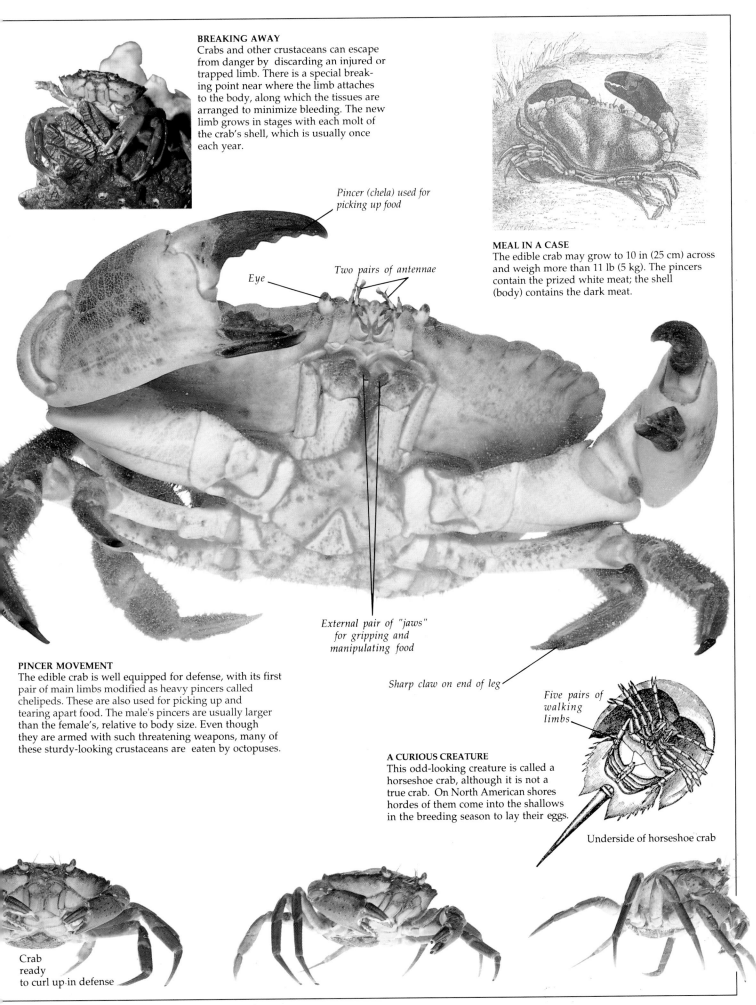

BREAKING AWAY
Crabs and other crustaceans can escape from danger by discarding an injured or trapped limb. There is a special breaking point near where the limb attaches to the body, along which the tissues are arranged to minimize bleeding. The new limb grows in stages with each molt of the crab's shell, which is usually once each year.

Pincer (chela) used for picking up food

Eye

Two pairs of antennae

MEAL IN A CASE
The edible crab may grow to 10 in (25 cm) across and weigh more than 11 lb (5 kg). The pincers contain the prized white meat; the shell (body) contains the dark meat.

External pair of "jaws" for gripping and manipulating food

PINCER MOVEMENT
The edible crab is well equipped for defense, with its first pair of main limbs modified as heavy pincers called chelipeds. These are also used for picking up and tearing apart food. The male's pincers are usually larger than the female's, relative to body size. Even though they are armed with such threatening weapons, many of these sturdy-looking crustaceans are eaten by octopuses.

Sharp claw on end of leg

Five pairs of walking limbs

A CURIOUS CREATURE
This odd-looking creature is called a horseshoe crab, although it is not a true crab. On North American shores hordes of them come into the shallows in the breeding season to lay their eggs.

Underside of horseshoe crab

Crab ready to curl up in defense

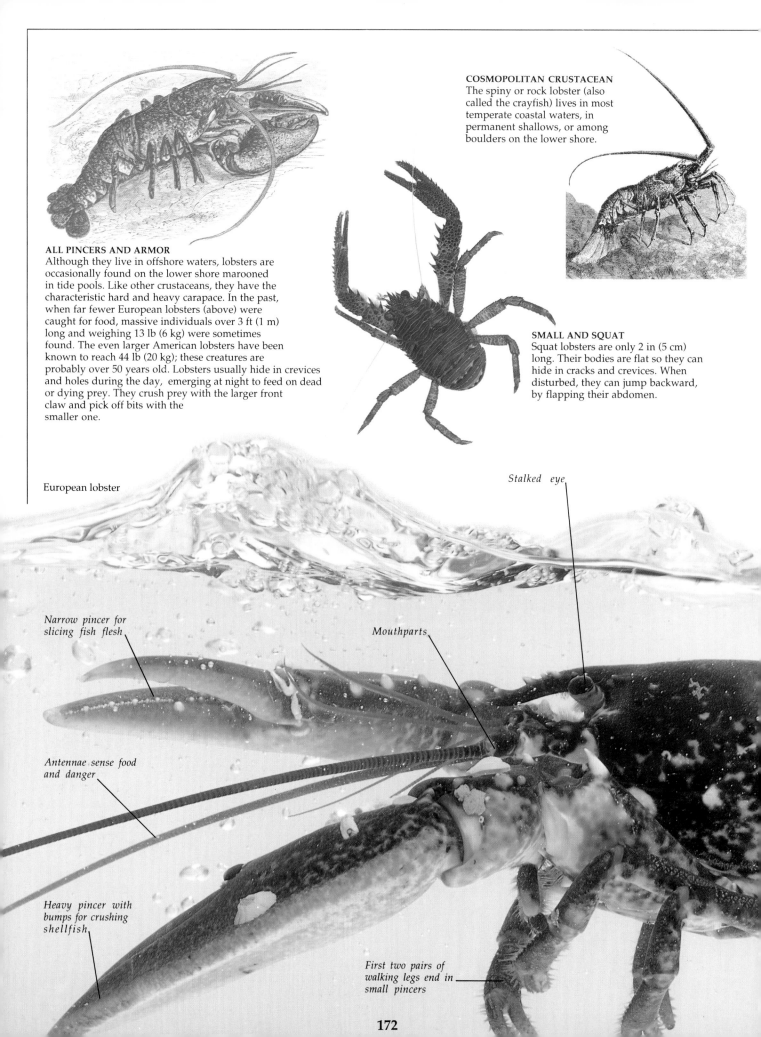

COSMOPOLITAN CRUSTACEAN
The spiny or rock lobster (also called the crayfish) lives in most temperate coastal waters, in permanent shallows, or among boulders on the lower shore.

ALL PINCERS AND ARMOR
Although they live in offshore waters, lobsters are occasionally found on the lower shore marooned in tide pools. Like other crustaceans, they have the characteristic hard and heavy carapace. In the past, when far fewer European lobsters (above) were caught for food, massive individuals over 3 ft (1 m) long and weighing 13 lb (6 kg) were sometimes found. The even larger American lobsters have been known to reach 44 lb (20 kg); these creatures are probably over 50 years old. Lobsters usually hide in crevices and holes during the day, emerging at night to feed on dead or dying prey. They crush prey with the larger front claw and pick off bits with the smaller one.

SMALL AND SQUAT
Squat lobsters are only 2 in (5 cm) long. Their bodies are flat so they can hide in cracks and crevices. When disturbed, they can jump backward, by flapping their abdomen.

European lobster

Stalked eye

Narrow pincer for slicing fish flesh

Mouthparts

Antennae sense food and danger

Heavy pincer with bumps for crushing shellfish

First two pairs of walking legs end in small pincers

172

NOT ONLY ROCK-BOTTOM
The coral crab lives in various habitats, frequenting rocky-bottomed shores, sandy areas, and sponges on coral reefs. It is found along the east coast of North America.

CRAB IN THE SKY
Early astronomers saw a crablike pattern of stars in the northern night sky and named it Cancer after the Latin word for a crab. Cancer is also the fourth sign of the zodiac, with the sun passing through from about June 21 to July 22.

A CLEANER COAST
Most crabs are adept scavengers, and the furrowed crab is no exception, picking up almost anything edible from the seabed. It lives around European coasts.

Barnacle cemented to lobster's body

Growth of bryozoans, a colony of tiny anemone-like animals

Tail fan helps to propel lobster backward when the tail is straightened and then suddenly flexed

Tail (abdomen)

Second two pairs of walking legs end in claws

Curly, protective tube of small marine worm

Swimmerets under tail enable lobster to bounce and swim as it moves along the bottom

173

Unusual partnerships

THERE ARE MANY TYPES of relationships in the animal world. A very familiar example is when one animal hunts and eats another. This is the predator-prey relationship. Yet nature is not always so cut and dried. On the seashore, as in other habitats, different kinds of animals are regularly seen together. This does not happen by chance - there is a reason. Scientists have different names for these relationships. In the relationship that is called parasitism, one partner, the parasite, benefits, but the other, the host, loses. Some shore crabs are host to *Sacculina*, a strange creature related to the barnacles. *Sacculina* attaches itself to a young crab and then grows "tentacles" that eat into the crab's body. This parasite gets food while disabling the crab. Another type of relationship, in which both partners benefit, is called symbiosis. The hermit crab and the calliactis anemone live in this way. The calliactis is sometimes called the parasitic anemone, but it does not harm its hermit host. It feeds on particles of food that the crab drops, and the crab is protected by the stinging tentacles.

HERMITS AT HOME
Hermit crabs do not have shells of their own, so they hide their soft bodies in the shells of dead animals. Sometimes an anemone is attached to the shell. As the crab grows and moves to a larger shell, it often takes the anemone along with it. There are also land hermit crabs in the tropics. Some species live in hollow mangrove roots or bamboo stems.

THREE-IN-ONE
Each of the three animals in this "partnership" comes from a different major animal group. The hermit crab is a crustacean (p. 170). The anemone is a coelenterate (p. 162). The shell once belonged to a whelk, which is a sea snail and member of the mollusk group (p. 152).

STING IN THE PINCER
The boxer crab carries small anemones in its pincers. They act as "stinging clubs" and are waved at any creature posing a threat.

Keelworm tubes inside shell

CLAW IN THE DOOR
In its defensive position, the hermit crab pulls itself deep inside the shell. The right front claw (cheliped), which bears the large pincer, is usually bigger than the left one, and the crab holds it across the shell's entrance to make an effective door. (In this example the pincer is missing; it may have been bitten off by a predator or squashed by a boulder.)

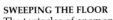

SWEEPING THE FLOOR
The tentacles of anemones reach upward for floating or swimming victims. However, a calliactis anemone on a hermit crab's shell tends to hang down and sweep the rocks for bits of food "spilled" by the hermit crab.

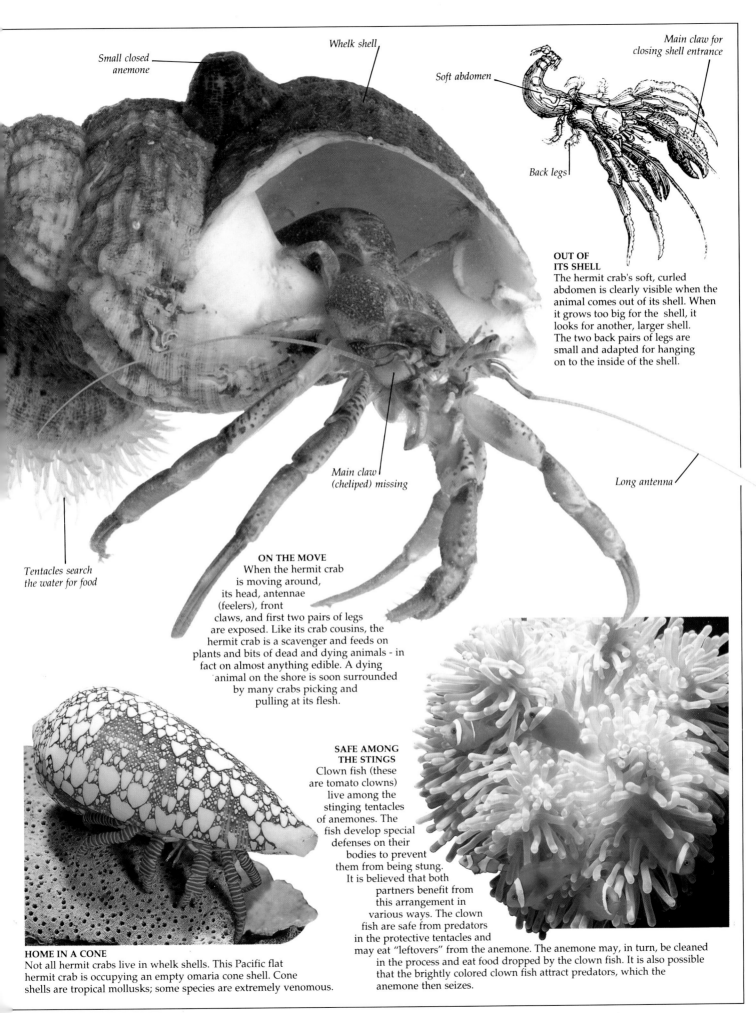

Small closed anemone

Whelk shell

Main claw for closing shell entrance

Soft abdomen

Back legs

OUT OF ITS SHELL
The hermit crab's soft, curled abdomen is clearly visible when the animal comes out of its shell. When it grows too big for the shell, it looks for another, larger shell. The two back pairs of legs are small and adapted for hanging on to the inside of the shell.

Main claw (cheliped) missing

Long antenna

Tentacles search the water for food

ON THE MOVE
When the hermit crab is moving around, its head, antennae (feelers), front claws, and first two pairs of legs are exposed. Like its crab cousins, the hermit crab is a scavenger and feeds on plants and bits of dead and dying animals - in fact on almost anything edible. A dying animal on the shore is soon surrounded by many crabs picking and pulling at its flesh.

SAFE AMONG THE STINGS
Clown fish (these are tomato clowns) live among the stinging tentacles of anemones. The fish develop special defenses on their bodies to prevent them from being stung. It is believed that both partners benefit from this arrangement in various ways. The clown fish are safe from predators in the protective tentacles and may eat "leftovers" from the anemone. The anemone may, in turn, be cleaned in the process and eat food dropped by the clown fish. It is also possible that the brightly colored clown fish attract predators, which the anemone then seizes.

HOME IN A CONE
Not all hermit crabs live in whelk shells. This Pacific flat hermit crab is occupying an empty omaria cone shell. Cone shells are tropical mollusks; some species are extremely venomous.

175

Disguises

A CASUAL GLANCE into a tide pool may reveal only a few strands of seaweed and some dead-looking shells. But wait patiently, sitting low and still to avoid being seen, and watch carefully. A dark patch of rock may suddenly glide forward: it is a blenny, on the look-out for food. A slightly hazy-looking area of sand walks away: it is a prawn adjusting the spots and lines on its body to blend perfectly with the background. A small pebble slides off: it is a periwinkle grazing on algae. A patch of gravelly bottom ripples and two eyes appear: a flatfish has tossed small pebbles and shell fragments over its body to break up its outline. All these creatures use camouflage to help conceal themselves. Looks are not everything, though – behavior is important too. The eel-like pipefish tends to swim in an upright position to blend in with the ribbons of seaweed and eelgrass in which it hides.

PALE UNDERSIDE
Flatfish are usually well camouflaged when viewed from the surface of the water. The underside, flat against the seabed, has no need of special coloring, so in many species it is white or pale.

LOOKING LIKE A WEED
The leafy sea dragon, from the coastal waters of southern Australia, is a type of sea horse. Its loose lobes of skin resemble the seaweed fronds in which it hides.

URCHIN COVER-UP
Several species of sea urchins grasp pebbles, shells, and pieces of seaweed with their long tube feet and hold them over their bodies. A well-draped urchin can be difficult to spot. These are green sea urchins, which are found on the lower shore and inshore waters.

DAB HAND AT CHANGE
Many flatfish can change their coloring to match the bottom on which they are resting. Some minutes earlier, this young dab was a light sandy color. It soon became several shades darker when placed on selected dark pebbles. The marks on its upper side became almost black. The largest dabs reach about 16 in (40 cm) long.

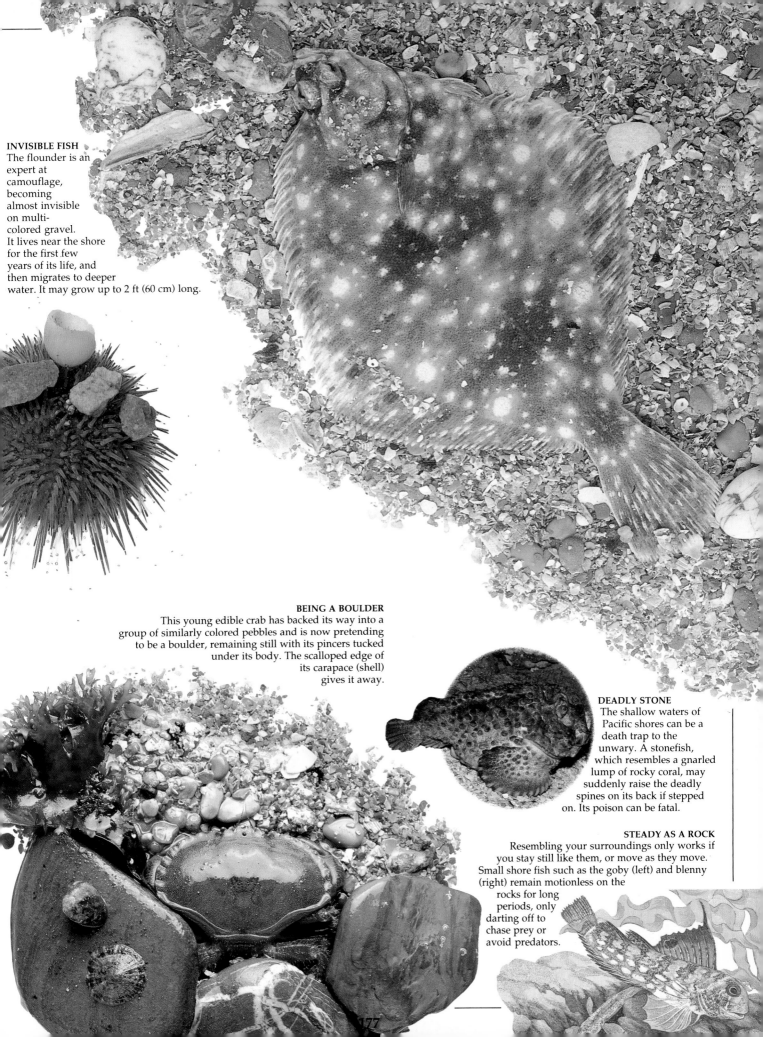

INVISIBLE FISH
The flounder is an expert at camouflage, becoming almost invisible on multi-colored gravel. It lives near the shore for the first few years of its life, and then migrates to deeper water. It may grow up to 2 ft (60 cm) long.

BEING A BOULDER
This young edible crab has backed its way into a group of similarly colored pebbles and is now pretending to be a boulder, remaining still with its pincers tucked under its body. The scalloped edge of its carapace (shell) gives it away.

DEADLY STONE
The shallow waters of Pacific shores can be a death trap to the unwary. A stonefish, which resembles a gnarled lump of rocky coral, may suddenly raise the deadly spines on its back if stepped on. Its poison can be fatal.

STEADY AS A ROCK
Resembling your surroundings only works if you stay still like them, or move as they move. Small shore fish such as the goby (left) and blenny (right) remain motionless on the rocks for long periods, only darting off to chase prey or avoid predators.

Life on a ledge

A SEABIRD BREEDING COLONY is one of the most spectacular sights on a rocky coastline. Coastal cliffs, rocky islets, and isolated islands can be reached only by flight and so make safe nesting places for birds. Here they are out of reach of all but the most agile ground-based predators, such as snakes and rats, and just beneath the waves there is a rich source of food. The sight of more than 50,000 gannets nesting on an offshore island is breathtaking. The impression is of a blizzard of large white birds coming and going, wheeling on their 6 ft (1.8 m) wings in currents of air, rising up the sheer cliff, regurgitating fish for their chicks, and screeching and pecking at any intruder - gannet or otherwise - that comes within reach of their spearlike bills.

EGG ON A ROCK
The razorbills of the Northern Hemisphere resemble their southern relatives, the penguins, although unlike penguins they are good fliers. On cliffs they form breeding colonies which may number tens of thousands of birds. Each female lays a single egg.

WARNING
All the eggs shown here come from a museum collection. (The colors have faded slightly.) Collecting or handling wild birds' eggs is now illegal.

EGGS DOWN A HOLE
Puffins nest in burrows. They dig their own holes in soft soil or take over an old shearwater or rabbit tunnel. Puffin eggs are white because, since they are hidden, they have no need of camouflage.

A puffin near a cliff-top burrow by the British bird artist Archibald Thorburn

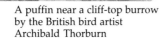

SUITABLY SHAPED
The blotchy patterned egg of the guillemot is suitably shaped for life on a ledge, as it tapers narrowly to a point at one end. If it is blown around by the wind or kicked by the bird on the bare rock (the guillemot does not make a nest), it rolls around in a tight circle until it comes to rest.

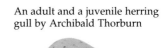
An adult and a juvenile herring gull by Archibald Thorburn

FIERCE FEEDER
Herring gulls are noisy and aggressive. The squawks and screams coming from their nesting colonies are deafening. The average clutch consists of three eggs.

Common or great cormorant

Sharp, hooked bill for
holding on to slippery
prey

A NATURAL FERTILIZER
Guano, the accumulated droppings from a sea bird (or
bat) colony, is rich in nitrogen, potassium, and
phosphorus. Mining guano was a world trade in the last
century; most of it came from South American and African
coasts and islands, and was shipped to Europe
and North America for use as a fertilizer.

DRYING AFTER A DIP
Common or great cormorants are the largest of
the 29 species in the cormorant group and are
found almost worldwide. They swim and dive
after crabs, fish, and other aquatic prey.
Afterward they stand in a typical pose with
wings outstretched to dry them. Why cormorants
have not evolved water-repellent oils, like
many other sea birds, is a mystery.

Long flexible neck for
darting at victims

SHIFT WORK
Many cormorants nest by the sea on cliffs, rocky
ledges, and sloping stone slabs. Both cormorant
parents build their nest from sticks, seaweed, and
other locally gathered plant material. The parents
take turns incubating their three to five eggs
for about one month
until the chicks
hatch.

All four toes are webbed,
enabling the cormorant
to swim well

Feeding by the sea

FISH are wriggly, slippery creatures. Many animals that catch them have specially adapted mouths that can hang on to their awkward prey. Fish-eating mammals such as seals have many small, pointed teeth for this purpose. Fish-eating birds are generally equipped with long, sharp, dagger-like bills (beaks), and the bills of cormorants and many of the gulls also have a down-curved tip that prevents fish from slipping out of the end. Gulls are a familiar sight along the coasts of the Northern Hemisphere. They hunt along the shore, catching tide-pool fish, pecking at crabs, and hammering open shellfish. Like many other sea birds, they tend to feed near land during the breeding season, but then wander off to lead a mostly pelagic (open-ocean) life for the rest of the year.

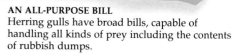

AN ALL-PURPOSE BILL
Herring gulls have broad bills, capable of handling all kinds of prey including the contents of rubbish dumps.

SHAPED LIKE A CHISEL
Oystercatchers use their chisel-like bills to pry open or hammer through the shells of mussels, cockles, oysters, and other shellfish.

SPEARED FROM ABOVE
The gannet dives from as high as 100 ft (30 m) to catch herring, sardines, mackerel, and other fish. This bird also uses its bill to fight enemies and to stab at those who intrude into its nesting space.

A HOOKED BILL
Fulmars nest in groups on rocky islands and cliffs. They feed on surface-dwelling fish and their beaks are hooked at the end. They have prominent tubelike nostrils lying along the top or sides of the bill.

Tubelike nostrils

Small wings are used as paddles in the water, and flap rapidly in flight

DANGEROUS WORK
Sea birds and their eggs are still caught and eaten along some remote shores. On the island of St. Kilda, off the northwest coast of Scotland, this practice continued until the 1940s. Birds flying past an outcrop were caught in a net; eggs and nestlings were collected by hand. Gannets, fulmars (right), and various auks were the main victims.

FISHERMAN'S FRIEND
For centuries, coastal people in eastern Asia have fished with trained cormorants. A collar and lead is put on the bird so that it can catch fish but not swallow them. The bird is then pulled back to the boat by the lead. Today this "fishing" has become a tourist attraction.

A BILL FULL OF EELS
After a diving session, a catch of up to 10 small fish (such as these sand eels) is not unusual for the stripe-billed puffin. This bird lives throughout the North Atlantic.

GOOD FOR SWIMMING
The guillemot or murre has relatively large, powerful feet with strong webs. Its legs are positioned far back along its body so that it swims efficiently, but on land it waddles rather than walks, with an upright, penguin-like stance.

Guillemot often rests on "heels" (shanks) on a ledge, rather than standing

SWOOPING ON THE SHORE
It is thought that the gull's pale underside matches the sky or clouds, making this bird less visible to fish, crabs, and other prey as they look up, on the watch for danger. This is a young herring gull with mottled plumage. Adult birds have white bellies.

Claw-tipped toes

UNDERWATER PROPELLERS
The gannet's great webbed feet can propel the bird at remarkable speed under the water as it chases after fish. It also uses its feet to cover and help incubate the egg.

During the breeding season, the egg is balanced on the large, webbed feet

Visitors to the shore

NOW AND AGAIN, we may be lucky enough to see some of the larger visitors to the shore. Marine turtles crawl onto land under cover of darkness to lay their eggs in the warm sand. Seals sunbathe, and sometimes the bulls (males) fight each other for the right to mate with a harem of females. In the Arctic, white-tusked walruses lie in steaming heaps on the icy rock; near the Equator, marine iguana lizards crop seaweeds from the rocky shores of the Galápagos Islands. In Antarctica, penguins gather by the millions to rest and breed. However, some visitors to the shore come by accident. The strandings of schools of live whales have long puzzled scientists.

SUN, SEA, AND SAND
During the last century the seaside became popular with one mammal in particular. As is usual with this species, it has greatly changed the habitat. Nowadays, beaches are crowded with its family groups, while the inshore waters are congested with its brightly colored toys, such as yachts and windsurfing boards.

LARDER WITH FLIPPERS
The green turtle, the only plant eater among the six species of sea turtles, travels across the world's tropical oceans. Females come ashore to lay eggs in shallow holes in the sand. They tend to use the same breeding places, or rookeries, year after year - making it easy for hunters to capture them and steal their eggs. This species grows to 3 ft (1 m) long and 400 lb (180 kg) in weight. It is sometimes called the edible turtle, and in former times it was hunted mercilessly for its flesh, oil, skin, and shell. Today it is officially listed as an endangered species.

STRANDED SQUID
Giant squid, voracious deep-sea predators, are occasionally washed up on the shore. Such stranded individuals are probably injured, ill, or already dead when swept in by shore-bound currents. Giant squid are the largest of all invertebrate animals (those without backbones). They grow to more than 50 ft (15 m) in total length and weigh up to 2 tons.

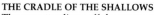

THE CRADLE OF THE SHALLOWS
The sea otter lives off the coasts of the Pacific Ocean but rarely comes ashore, preferring to lie in the calm of a kelp bed. It feeds on sea urchins, crustaceans, and shellfish, and will use a stone as a tool to crush the hard shells of its prey. This is the heaviest of the 12 otter species, sometimes weighing as much as 100 lb (45 kg). The sea otter became extremely rare, as it was hunted for its fur, but in 1911 an international agreement (one of the first of its kind) rescued it from extinction.

LIFE ON THE OCEAN WAVE
Harbor seal pups (these are about three months old) are born on land, but they can swim and dive almost immediately after birth. Seals haul themselves out of the water to bask on rocks and sand-banks, or to give birth. Harbor seals live in coastal waters in the North Pacific and North Atlantic. Recently a viral illness has killed many thousands of those living in the North Sea.

Beachcombing

TWICE EACH DAY the sea rises up the shore and then retreats, depositing debris along the high-tide mark. This is the strandline, a ribbon of objects left stranded high and dry. It is a treasure trove for the nature detective. Shells, bits of seaweed, feathers, and driftwood lie jumbled together, each with a story to tell. Stones, shells, and wood have often been smoothed and sculpted by the sea, rolled back and forth in the sand or crashed against the rocks and split open. Seaweeds torn from rocks are carried along in currents and washed up farther along the coast. Large-scale ocean currents such as the Gulf Stream can transport floating objects thousands of miles and dump them on some distant shore.

Certain plants use the sea to spread their seeds; the coconut is a famous example. The familiar nut itself ripens inside an even larger husk of stringy gray fibers (the coir, which is woven into rough mats and ropes) encased in a brownish leathery skin. This makes a fine "float" and, when a coastal coconut palm drops a husk almost straight into the ocean, it is carried by currents and deposited on a distant shore, where it may grow. In this way coconut palms have spread to fringe tropical shores around the world.

A PEACEFUL PASTIME
Beachcombing is rewarding, as almost anything may be washed up on the shore. In the past people made a living by collecting and selling curios, food, and other objects found on the shore. Today not all shores are suitable for beachcombing, as many are strewn with man-made litter, and inshore waters are often polluted.

FOOD FOR FREE
Many seaweeds are gathered as food, both for humans and animals (p. 149), and for use as fertilizers. Algae such as carrageen are rich in nutrients. For some coastal peoples they are a good source of trace elements - minerals that the human body needs in small quantities. Seaweed also has medical applications: recently a jelly-like seaweed extract used as a lining for bandages for burns has been found to be very effective.

DRIED FLOAT
Rockweed, which grows in large quantities on sheltered rocky shores, becomes green-black when dry. It has large air bladders which enable the weed to float at high tide.

Air bladder

DEAD HANDS
Dead-man's fingers is a common name given to a variety of sponges, soft corals, and bryozoans. These primitive animals tend to live off-shore and only the spongy, rubbery skeletons are cast up on the beach. Small animals and fish often find hiding places in the tunnel-ridden remains.

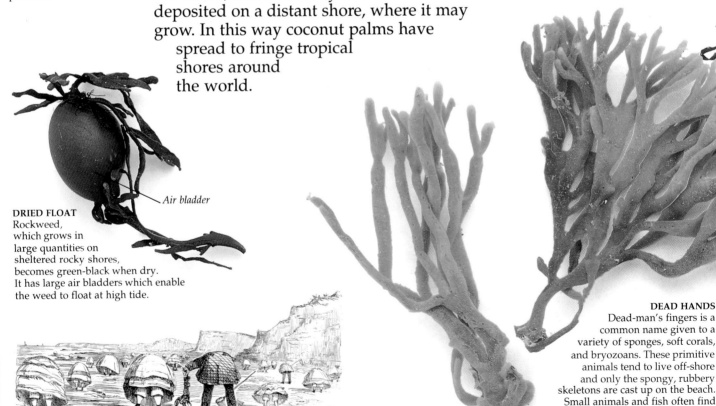

A 19th-century engraving entitled *Common objects at the sea-side...*

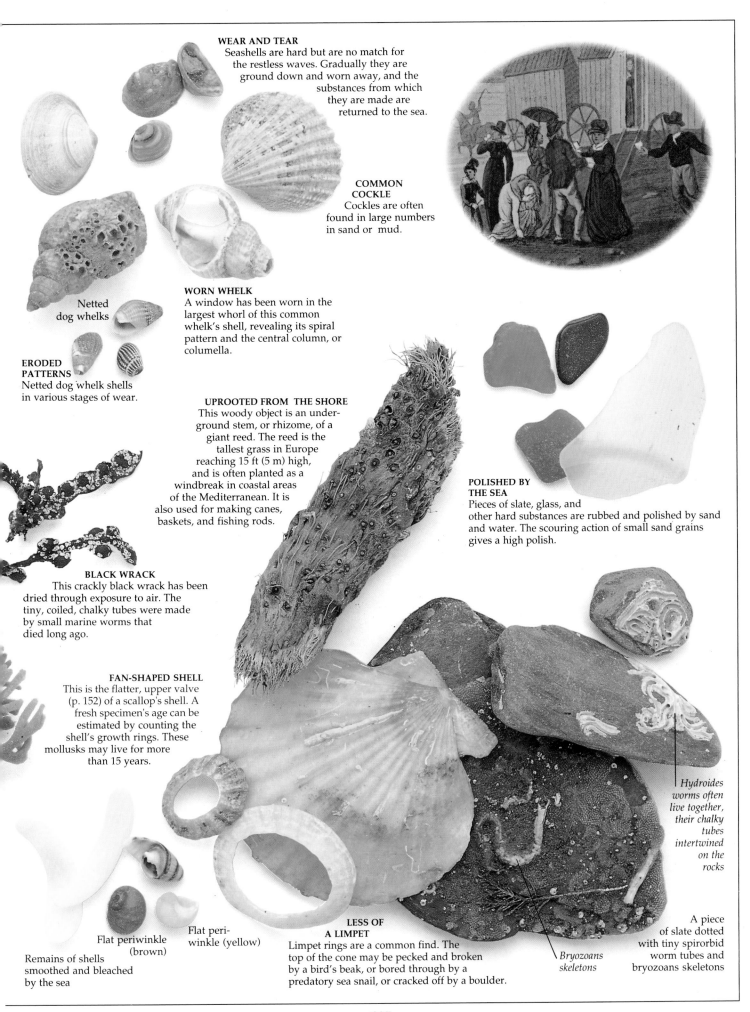

WEAR AND TEAR
Seashells are hard but are no match for the restless waves. Gradually they are ground down and worn away, and the substances from which they are made are returned to the sea.

COMMON COCKLE
Cockles are often found in large numbers in sand or mud.

Netted dog whelks

ERODED PATTERNS
Netted dog whelk shells in various stages of wear.

WORN WHELK
A window has been worn in the largest whorl of this common whelk's shell, revealing its spiral pattern and the central column, or columella.

UPROOTED FROM THE SHORE
This woody object is an underground stem, or rhizome, of a giant reed. The reed is the tallest grass in Europe reaching 15 ft (5 m) high, and is often planted as a windbreak in coastal areas of the Mediterranean. It is also used for making canes, baskets, and fishing rods.

POLISHED BY THE SEA
Pieces of slate, glass, and other hard substances are rubbed and polished by sand and water. The scouring action of small sand grains gives a high polish.

BLACK WRACK
This crackly black wrack has been dried through exposure to air. The tiny, coiled, chalky tubes were made by small marine worms that died long ago.

FAN-SHAPED SHELL
This is the flatter, upper valve (p. 152) of a scallop's shell. A fresh specimen's age can be estimated by counting the shell's growth rings. These mollusks may live for more than 15 years.

Hydroides worms often live together, their chalky tubes intertwined on the rocks

A piece of slate dotted with tiny spirorbid worm tubes and bryozoans skeletons

Bryozoans skeletons

LESS OF A LIMPET
Limpet rings are a common find. The top of the cone may be pecked and broken by a bird's beak, or bored through by a predatory sea snail, or cracked off by a boulder.

Flat periwinkle (brown)

Flat periwinkle (yellow)

Remains of shells smoothed and bleached by the sea

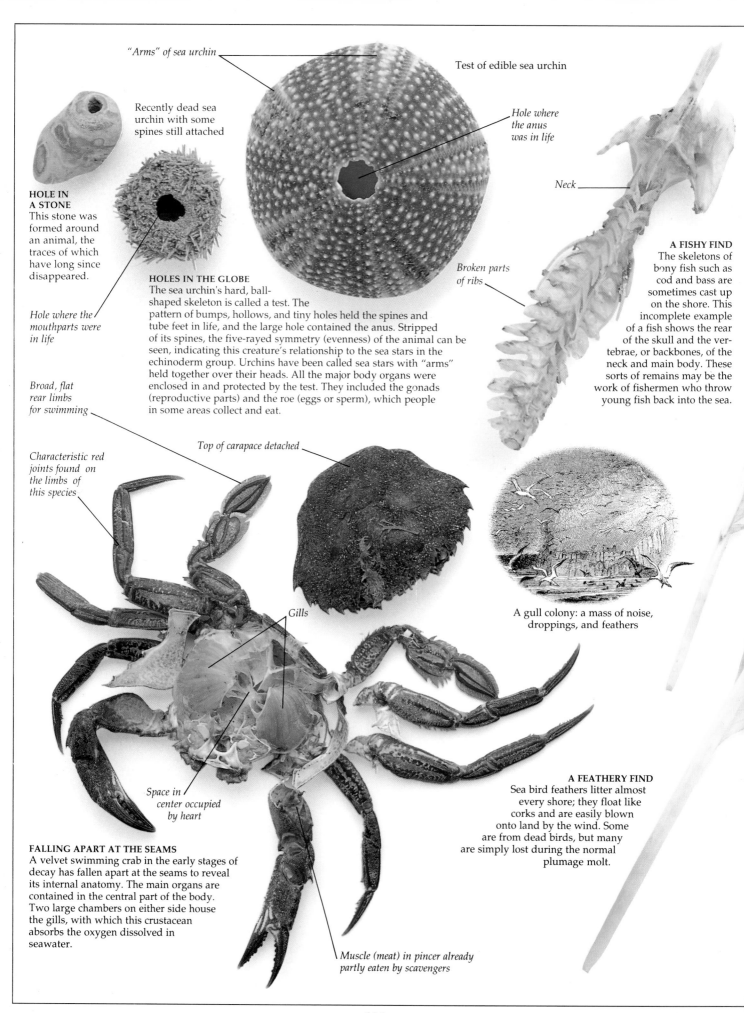

"Arms" of sea urchin

Test of edible sea urchin

Recently dead sea urchin with some spines still attached

Hole where the anus was in life

Neck

HOLE IN A STONE
This stone was formed around an animal, the traces of which have long since disappeared.

A FISHY FIND
The skeletons of bony fish such as cod and bass are sometimes cast up on the shore. This incomplete example of a fish shows the rear of the skull and the vertebrae, or backbones, of the neck and main body. These sorts of remains may be the work of fishermen who throw young fish back into the sea.

Hole where the mouthparts were in life

HOLES IN THE GLOBE
The sea urchin's hard, ball-shaped skeleton is called a test. The pattern of bumps, hollows, and tiny holes held the spines and tube feet in life, and the large hole contained the anus. Stripped of its spines, the five-rayed symmetry (evenness) of the animal can be seen, indicating this creature's relationship to the sea stars in the echinoderm group. Urchins have been called sea stars with "arms" held together over their heads. All the major body organs were enclosed in and protected by the test. They included the gonads (reproductive parts) and the roe (eggs or sperm), which people in some areas collect and eat.

Broken parts of ribs

Broad, flat rear limbs for swimming

Characteristic red joints found on the limbs of this species

Top of carapace detached

Gills

A gull colony: a mass of noise, droppings, and feathers

Space in center occupied by heart

FALLING APART AT THE SEAMS
A velvet swimming crab in the early stages of decay has fallen apart at the seams to reveal its internal anatomy. The main organs are contained in the central part of the body. Two large chambers on either side house the gills, with which this crustacean absorbs the oxygen dissolved in seawater.

A FEATHERY FIND
Sea bird feathers litter almost every shore; they float like corks and are easily blown onto land by the wind. Some are from dead birds, but many are simply lost during the normal plumage molt.

Muscle (meat) in pincer already partly eaten by scavengers

ALL WASHED UP
Pine cones and other light, woody objects may wash up on the seashore after floating down a small stream into a river and then into the sea.

Barred feather typical of young gull

Mature gull's wing feather

WIND POWER
An onshore wind tends to blow floating items toward the land, improving the beachcomber's chances of finding unusual things.

Cast-up and dried-out young dogfish

Shark in the shallows

The lesser-spotted dogfish, often simply called the dogfish, is a type of shark. It is harmless and grows to about 3 ft (1 m) in length. Dogfish spend most of their lives offshore, in water around 100-325 ft (30-100 m) deep. However, in late autumn, winter, and spring, females swim into shallow water near the shore to lay their eggs among seaweed.

OUT OF THE CASE
A newly hatched dogfish is about 4 in (10 cm) long. It usually still has part of the yolk sac attached, but this shrivels as the youngster begins to feed for itself. As an adult, it will hunt bottom-dwelling creatures such as shellfish.

WATER BABIES
The baby dogfish develop inside their egg cases, each nourished by its yolk sac. They continue to grow for up to 10 months before hatching.

BUNDLE OF EGGS
Empty egg cases of the whelk are another common beachcombing find. They are fixed to stones when laid, and tiny but fully formed young whelks crawl out of the cases.

THE MAGIC PURSE
The dogfish egg case is tied to anchoring weed by long tendrils at each corner. Empty cases are often washed up on the shore and are called mermaid's purses.

Studying our shores

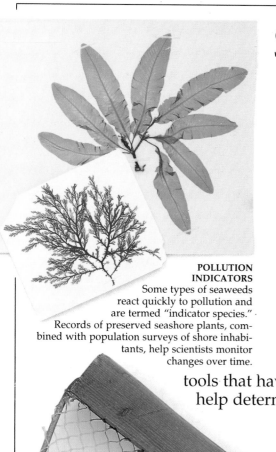

W E ENJOY OUR SEASHORES in many different ways. Children paddle in the ripples, surfers ride the waves, naturalists study plants and animals, local people collect seaweed and shellfish for food, and anyone may appreciate the beauty of unspoiled stretches of shore. However, our seashores are being damaged by the increasing pollution of the sea. Throughout history, scientists and researchers have studied our shorelines to understand the way nature works and the way nature is changing. Here we look at some of the tools that have been used in the past and today to help determine the health of our coastlines.

POLLUTION INDICATORS
Some types of seaweeds react quickly to pollution and are termed "indicator species." Records of preserved seashore plants, combined with population surveys of shore inhabitants, help scientists monitor changes over time.

DIVING IN A GARBAGE CAN
In the 1930s the first scientific surveys of life in the permanent shallows were made. The scientists wore primitive diving hoods. Air was provided by two car pumps operated from the shore, and each hood contained a radio telephone.

SHELL SHOCK
Shell surveys show how the numbers of some species have been reduced by pollution or overfishing.

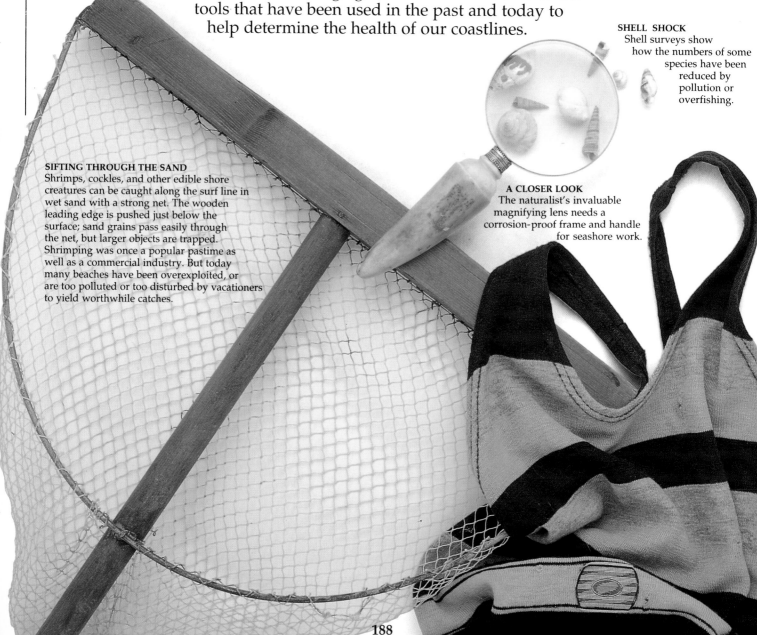

SIFTING THROUGH THE SAND
Shrimps, cockles, and other edible shore creatures can be caught along the surf line in wet sand with a strong net. The wooden leading edge is pushed just below the surface; sand grains pass easily through the net, but larger objects are trapped. Shrimping was once a popular pastime as well as a commercial industry. But today many beaches have been overexploited, or are too polluted or too disturbed by vacationers to yield worthwhile catches.

A CLOSER LOOK
The naturalist's invaluable magnifying lens needs a corrosion-proof frame and handle for seashore work.

TIDE GUIDE
Tide tables are essential for anyone who leaves the main beach to study rocks or flats. The tables give relative water heights as well as dates and times of low and high water. Most of the shore is exposed at the lowest spring tide.

ROCK RECORD
For scientific studies of the shoreline, a geological map is very important. Different types of rocks are color-coded, and height contours are given as on ordinary maps. Granite, sandstone, and similar hard rocks tend to form stable rocky shores; soft rocks like chalk and limestone are eroded more quickly.

ARTIST'S INSPIRATION
Many people are fascinated by the sea. They are in awe of its destructive power and attracted by its constant motion and sudden changes of mood. Artists have been inspired to sketch and paint hundreds of beach scenes, from tranquil summer afternoons to ferocious winter storms.

FASHION OF THE TIME
Fashionable bathing suits of the 19th century may seem rather quaint today. But how will today's suits be regarded a century from now?

Waterproof flashlight

WATERPROOF EQUIPMENT
Modern waterproof cameras allow us to record nature without harming it. An underwater flashlight is another useful piece of equipment. Many larger animals, such as lobsters and crabs, hide themselves in caves and crevices on the cool, shadowy side of rocks. It is always a good idea to shine a light before putting in a hand, just in case!

STUDYING SHORE LIFE
One way of studying the zonation of life on the shore is to stretch a piece of string down to the sea's edge, if possible from the high-tide strandline to the low-tide mark. Begin at low tide, and move up the string, recording the commonest types of seaweeds and creatures at each stage. Don't forget: after an hour or so, the tide will start to return.

OUT OF THEIR ELEMENT
Keep shore creatures only for essential study. They are out of their element: would you like to be dragged into the sea for an hour?

LIFE IN THE BALANCE
We cannot see any of the dissolved chemicals in seawater, but their levels mean life or death for all sea creatures. Testing kits reveal amounts of substances, such as nitrites and nitrates, that indicate the degree of pollution present in the seawater. Large amounts of fertilizers, which contain nitrogen, are washed into the sea by rivers carrying soil eroded from the land. The hydrometer measures the density or "heaviness" of the seawater, which reveals the concentration of dissolved salts.

LIMPET LEVER
When examining snails and limpets, a knife helps to pry them gently from the rock. Always put them back in the same place.

NEVER USE A JACKNIFE WITHOUT AN ADULT TO HELP YOU

Swan mussel shell

Common reed

Common reed
fruiting head

Water snail shell

Otter skull

Kingfisher skull

Mayfly

Reed-mace
fruit

Mallard egg

Reed bunting nest
and eggs

Great diving beetle

Kingfisher wing

Bittern egg

Snipe egg

Banded demoiselle damselfly

Great ram's-horn shell

POND & RIVER

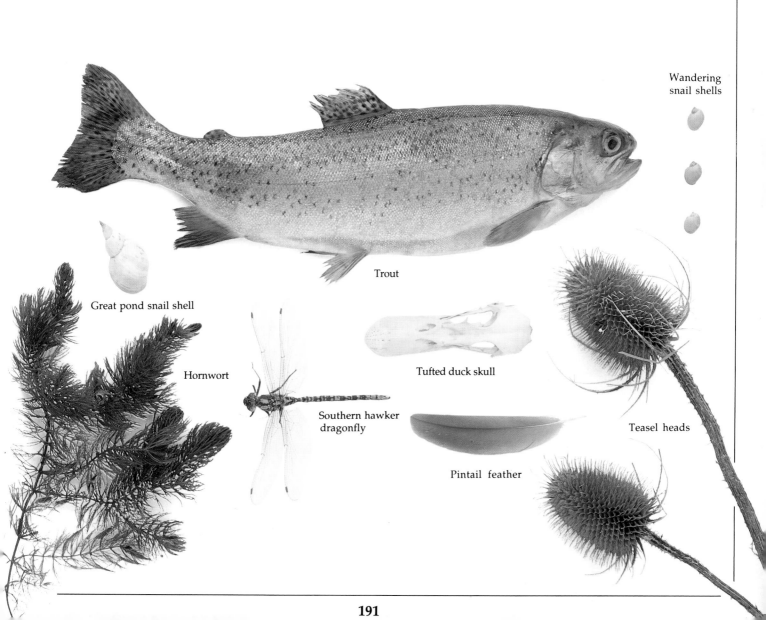

Wandering snail shells

Great pond snail shell

Trout

Hornwort

Southern hawker dragonfly

Tufted duck skull

Pintail feather

Teasel heads

Spring plants

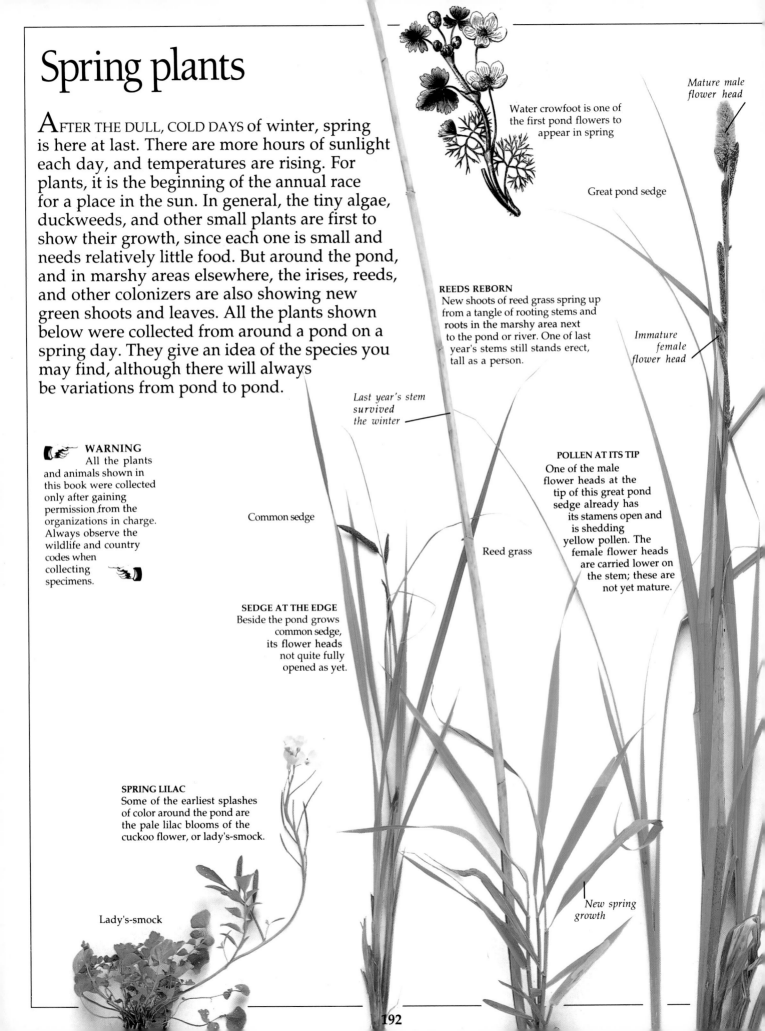

AFTER THE DULL, COLD DAYS of winter, spring is here at last. There are more hours of sunlight each day, and temperatures are rising. For plants, it is the beginning of the annual race for a place in the sun. In general, the tiny algae, duckweeds, and other small plants are first to show their growth, since each one is small and needs relatively little food. But around the pond, and in marshy areas elsewhere, the irises, reeds, and other colonizers are also showing new green shoots and leaves. All the plants shown below were collected from around a pond on a spring day. They give an idea of the species you may find, although there will always be variations from pond to pond.

Water crowfoot is one of the first pond flowers to appear in spring

Mature male flower head

Great pond sedge

REEDS REBORN
New shoots of reed grass spring up from a tangle of rooting stems and roots in the marshy area next to the pond or river. One of last year's stems still stands erect, tall as a person.

Immature female flower head

Last year's stem survived the winter

POLLEN AT ITS TIP
One of the male flower heads at the tip of this great pond sedge already has its stamens open and is shedding yellow pollen. The female flower heads are carried lower on the stem; these are not yet mature.

WARNING
All the plants and animals shown in this book were collected only after gaining permission from the organizations in charge. Always observe the wildlife and country codes when collecting specimens.

Common sedge

Reed grass

SEDGE AT THE EDGE
Beside the pond grows common sedge, its flower heads not quite fully opened as yet.

SPRING LILAC
Some of the earliest splashes of color around the pond are the pale lilac blooms of the cuckoo flower, or lady's-smock.

New spring growth

Lady's-smock

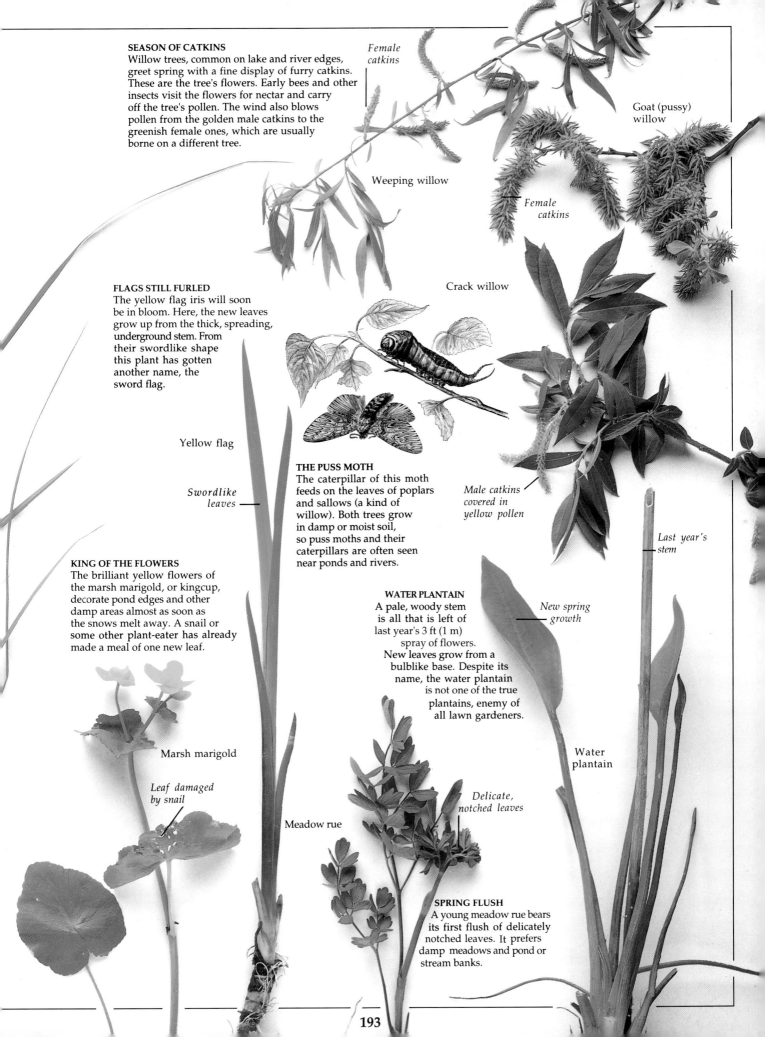

SEASON OF CATKINS
Willow trees, common on lake and river edges, greet spring with a fine display of furry catkins. These are the tree's flowers. Early bees and other insects visit the flowers for nectar and carry off the tree's pollen. The wind also blows pollen from the golden male catkins to the greenish female ones, which are usually borne on a different tree.

Female catkins

Goat (pussy) willow

Weeping willow

Female catkins

Crack willow

FLAGS STILL FURLED
The yellow flag iris will soon be in bloom. Here, the new leaves grow up from the thick, spreading, underground stem. From their swordlike shape this plant has gotten another name, the sword flag.

Yellow flag

Swordlike leaves

THE PUSS MOTH
The caterpillar of this moth feeds on the leaves of poplars and sallows (a kind of willow). Both trees grow in damp or moist soil, so puss moths and their caterpillars are often seen near ponds and rivers.

Male catkins covered in yellow pollen

Last year's stem

KING OF THE FLOWERS
The brilliant yellow flowers of the marsh marigold, or kingcup, decorate pond edges and other damp areas almost as soon as the snows melt away. A snail or some other plant-eater has already made a meal of one new leaf.

WATER PLANTAIN
A pale, woody stem is all that is left of last year's 3 ft (1 m) spray of flowers. New leaves grow from a bulblike base. Despite its name, the water plantain is not one of the true plantains, enemy of all lawn gardeners.

New spring growth

Marsh marigold

Water plantain

Leaf damaged by snail

Meadow rue

Delicate, notched leaves

SPRING FLUSH
A young meadow rue bears its first flush of delicately notched leaves. It prefers damp meadows and pond or stream banks.

Spring animals

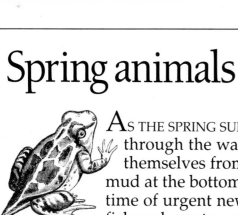

As THE SPRING SUN'S WARMTH spreads through the water, animals begin to stir themselves from among the weeds and mud at the bottom of the pond. It is a time of urgent new life. Frogs and toads, fish and newts, are courting, mating, and laying eggs. Their offspring soon hatch in the warming water, eager to cash in on the spring burst of life that provides food for all. "Cold-blooded" aquatic creatures become more active with the rising water temperature, and in a mild spring the smaller ponds, which warm up faster than large ones, are soon seething with newborn snails, insects, amphibians, and many other creatures.

Frog spawn

Protective jelly surrounding egg

Black egg

THE SPAWN IS BORN
As early as January, adult frogs gather in ponds to mate and spawn, or lay eggs. Around March, the female lays up to 3,000 eggs, fertilized by the male, who clings to her back. The water-absorbing jelly around each egg swells, and soon the whole mass is many times her body size.

BIG BROTHERS AND SISTERS
Tadpoles hatch from spawn some two to three weeks after laying. The warmer the water, the faster they develop. Here, common frog tadpoles from a large, cool pond, only two weeks out of their eggs, mingle with four-weekers from a small pond that warmed up more quickly.

Tiny tadpoles from a cool pond

Tadpoles from a warm pond

This engraving of a water flea shows its complex anatomy

BORN ONTO THEIR FOOD
Each adult pond snail lays up to 400 eggs, buried in a jelly-like "rope" attached to the underside of a submerged leaf on which the young snails will feed.

Common toad

Dry, warty skin

A NEW LEAF
In spring, water snails lay their eggs under leaves like these water lily leaves.

Water lily leaves

Protective jelly

Snail eggs

Pond snails

Water fleas

SPRING BLOOM
Water fleas and other tiny animals and plants bring a pea-soup look to many ponds in spring. This is the early "bloom" of microorganisms that provides food for larger creatures.

TWO SEXES IN ONE
Many adult pond snails are hermaphrodites, having both male and female reproductive organs.

Damage to leaf edge caused by natural splitting

SECOND SPRING
This young water beetle, common in small ponds and ditches, may well be celebrating its second birthday. Two years ago it was an egg, in that autumn a larva, last spring a pupa, and last summer a newly emerged adult.

FIRST SPRING
A water beetle larva has large jaws ready to tackle and eat any small creature the spring pond has to offer. Some species stay as larvae for two years or more before changing into adults.

KING OF THE BEETLES
The great diving beetle is the king of the carnivores in many small ponds, feeding on tadpoles, small fish, and almost anything else it can catch. In fact the dull, furrowed "back" (hard wing covers) on this one indicates it is not a king but a queen - a female. The male's wing cases are smooth and shiny.

SOME WEEKS TO TAKEOFF
A mayfly larva displays its characteristic three tails. Despite its name, this larva might become adult and fly off in April or June.

Female beetles have furrowed wing covers

Pale-green fronds

Water beetle

Water beetle larva

Erpobdella leech

Mayfly larva

Water slater

Duckweed

Crest along male's back

Male newt

Female newt

LOOKING FOR A WORM
The erpobdella leech loops through the water in search of a meal. This leech does not suck blood, but attacks worms and other soft-bodied small creatures and swallows them whole.

FINDING A MATE
The female water slater piggybacks the male as he fertilizes the eggs, which she keeps in a pouch under her body.

BREEDING NEWTS
In spring the male newt develops a crest along his back and black spots over his skin. The female's skin remains olive-brown.

GREEN CEILING
In the spring sunshine, duckweed soon spreads across the pond (p. 230). The tiny fronds provide food for snails and insect larvae.

Common frog

Smooth, shiny skin

ONE-YEAR-OLDS
In addition to breeding adults, spawn, and tadpoles, you may also find last year's babies around the pond in spring.

EARLY FLOWERS
The water crowfoot is an aquatic type of buttercup. The broad, flat leaves that float on the surface shade the water beneath, providing a good hiding place for fish.

Leaves that float on the surface are flat and broad

READY TO MATE
In spring, the male stickleback's throat and underside turn bright red (a red tinge can even be seen from above, as on the male shown here). In this breeding coloration, he entices the female to lay eggs in the nest he has built on the pond bed.

Frogs lose their tail soon after emerging

Leaves that grow under water are finely divided

Male stickleback

Female stickleback

Early summer plants

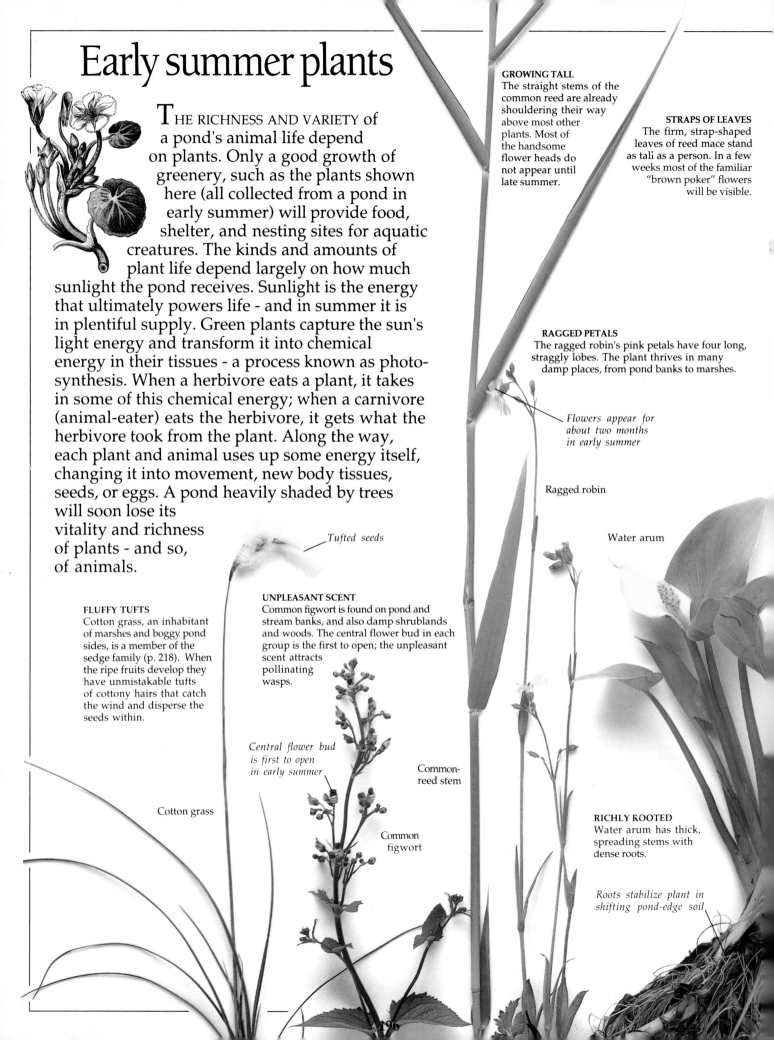

THE RICHNESS AND VARIETY of a pond's animal life depend on plants. Only a good growth of greenery, such as the plants shown here (all collected from a pond in early summer) will provide food, shelter, and nesting sites for aquatic creatures. The kinds and amounts of plant life depend largely on how much sunlight the pond receives. Sunlight is the energy that ultimately powers life - and in summer it is in plentiful supply. Green plants capture the sun's light energy and transform it into chemical energy in their tissues - a process known as photosynthesis. When a herbivore eats a plant, it takes in some of this chemical energy; when a carnivore (animal-eater) eats the herbivore, it gets what the herbivore took from the plant. Along the way, each plant and animal uses up some energy itself, changing it into movement, new body tissues, seeds, or eggs. A pond heavily shaded by trees will soon lose its vitality and richness of plants - and so, of animals.

GROWING TALL
The straight stems of the common reed are already shouldering their way above most other plants. Most of the handsome flower heads do not appear until late summer.

STRAPS OF LEAVES
The firm, strap-shaped leaves of reed mace stand as tall as a person. In a few weeks most of the familiar "brown poker" flowers will be visible.

RAGGED PETALS
The ragged robin's pink petals have four long, straggly lobes. The plant thrives in many damp places, from pond banks to marshes.

Flowers appear for about two months in early summer

Ragged robin

Water arum

Tufted seeds

FLUFFY TUFTS
Cotton grass, an inhabitant of marshes and boggy pond sides, is a member of the sedge family (p. 218). When the ripe fruits develop they have unmistakable tufts of cottony hairs that catch the wind and disperse the seeds within.

UNPLEASANT SCENT
Common figwort is found on pond and stream banks, and also damp shrublands and woods. The central flower bud in each group is the first to open; the unpleasant scent attracts pollinating wasps.

Central flower bud is first to open in early summer

Cotton grass

Common-reed stem

Common figwort

RICHLY ROOTED
Water arum has thick, spreading stems with dense roots.

Roots stabilize plant in shifting pond-edge soil

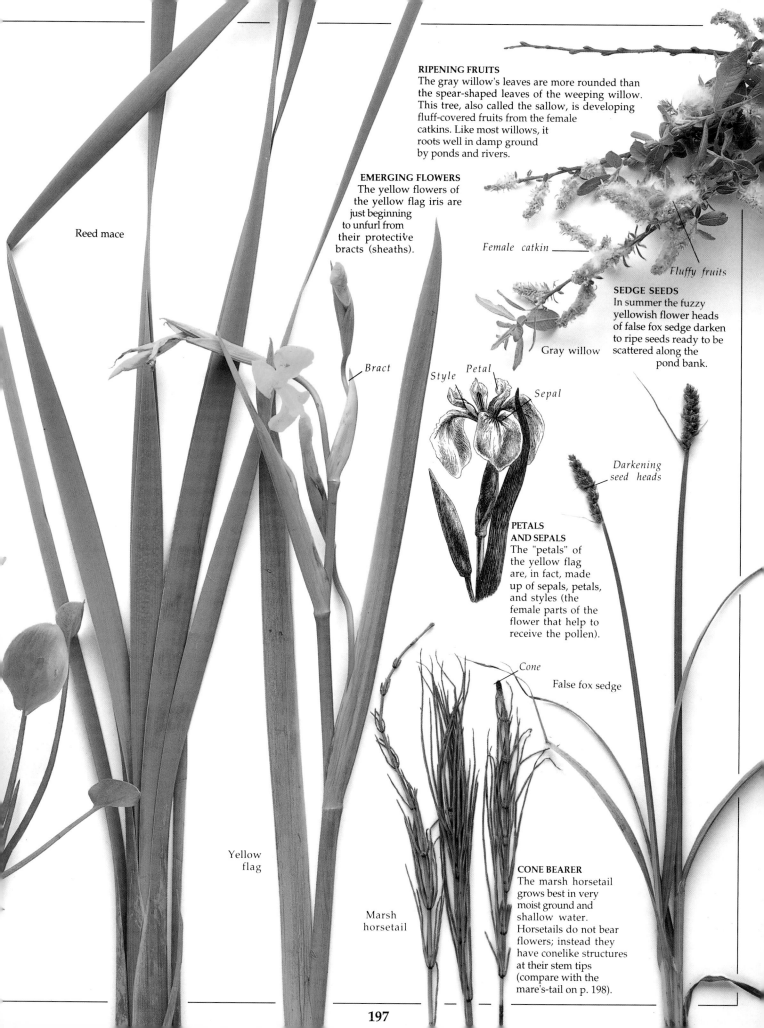

RIPENING FRUITS
The gray willow's leaves are more rounded than the spear-shaped leaves of the weeping willow. This tree, also called the sallow, is developing fluff-covered fruits from the female catkins. Like most willows, it roots well in damp ground by ponds and rivers.

EMERGING FLOWERS
The yellow flowers of the yellow flag iris are just beginning to unfurl from their protective bracts (sheaths).

Reed mace

Female catkin

Fluffy fruits

Gray willow

SEDGE SEEDS
In summer the fuzzy yellowish flower heads of false fox sedge darken to ripe seeds ready to be scattered along the pond bank.

Bract

Style *Petal*

Sepal

Darkening seed heads

PETALS AND SEPALS
The "petals" of the yellow flag are, in fact, made up of sepals, petals, and styles (the female parts of the flower that help to receive the pollen).

Cone

False fox sedge

Yellow flag

Marsh horsetail

CONE BEARER
The marsh horsetail grows best in very moist ground and shallow water. Horsetails do not bear flowers; instead they have conelike structures at their stem tips (compare with the mare's-tail on p. 198).

197

Early summer animals

ᴇᴀʀʟʏ ꜱᴜᴍᴍᴇʀ is a time of thinning out and fattening up for pond animals. The swarms of young tadpoles, insect larvae, and water snails feed greedily on the abundant plant growth of this season. But they are gradually thinned out by larger predatory creatures, such as beetle larvae and dragonfly nymphs (p. 234), newts, and small fish. These grow fat and in their turn may be eaten by larger creatures, from frogs to fish, by visiting birds like herons, and perhaps by water shrew, mink, and other mammals. And so the food chain of the pond builds up: plants first, then herbivores (plant-eaters), to carnivores (meat-eaters). But this is not the end. Death comes to all and, when it does, creatures such as water slaters move in to consume plant and animal remains. Droppings of all creatures enrich the water, providing minerals and other raw materials for fresh plant growth. So the nutrients go around and around, being recycled in the miniature ecosystem that is the pond.

Silver water beetle, wing cases lifted to show wings

Common toad

GOOD-BYE FOR THIS YEAR
A few of the dozens of breeding toads may still be hanging around near the pond. But most have now gone to their favorite damp corners, in hedges, under logs, and among the undergrowth. They will not return to the pond until next spring.

PETAL-LESS FLOWERS
Mare's-tail is a shallow-water plant of ponds and streams. The numerous tiny pond creatures of this season squirm and swim around its stems. Where the leaves join the stem, it bears tiny flowers without petals.

Tadpoles with developing back legs

BACK LEGS FIRST
Frog tadpoles are now fewer in number; many of their siblings have been eaten by fish, newts, diving beetles, and dragonfly nymphs. They have their back legs, which appear after about seven weeks. This change in body shape, from tadpole to adult frog, is called "metamorphosis."

Great pond snail

GROWN UP
This great pond snail is nearing full size, about 2 in (5 cm) long. It slides slowly over the bottom of the pond, eating decaying plant remains.

Mare's-tail

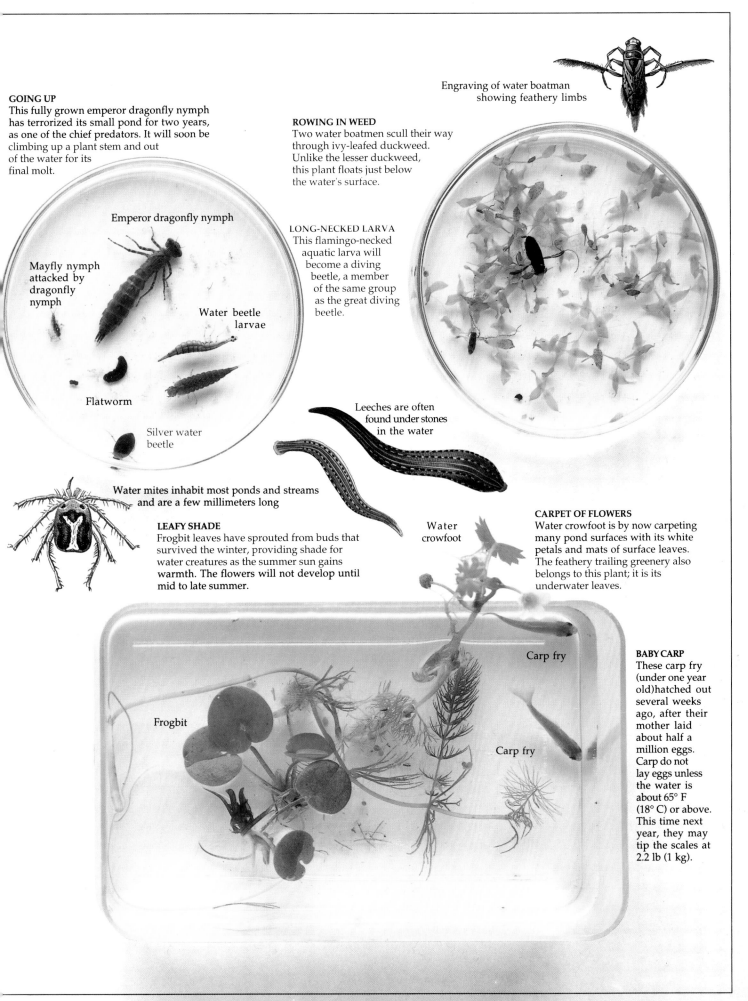

GOING UP
This fully grown emperor dragonfly nymph has terrorized its small pond for two years, as one of the chief predators. It will soon be climbing up a plant stem and out of the water for its final molt.

Engraving of water boatman showing feathery limbs

ROWING IN WEED
Two water boatmen scull their way through ivy-leafed duckweed. Unlike the lesser duckweed, this plant floats just below the water's surface.

Emperor dragonfly nymph

Mayfly nymph attacked by dragonfly nymph

LONG-NECKED LARVA
This flamingo-necked aquatic larva will become a diving beetle, a member of the same group as the great diving beetle.

Water beetle larvae

Flatworm

Silver water beetle

Leeches are often found under stones in the water

Water mites inhabit most ponds and streams and are a few millimeters long

LEAFY SHADE
Frogbit leaves have sprouted from buds that survived the winter, providing shade for water creatures as the summer sun gains warmth. The flowers will not develop until mid to late summer.

Water crowfoot

CARPET OF FLOWERS
Water crowfoot is by now carpeting many pond surfaces with its white petals and mats of surface leaves. The feathery trailing greenery also belongs to this plant; it is its underwater leaves.

Carp fry

BABY CARP
These carp fry (under one year old) hatched out several weeks ago, after their mother laid about half a million eggs. Carp do not lay eggs unless the water is about 65° F (18° C) or above. This time next year, they may tip the scales at 2.2 lb (1 kg).

Frogbit

Carp fry

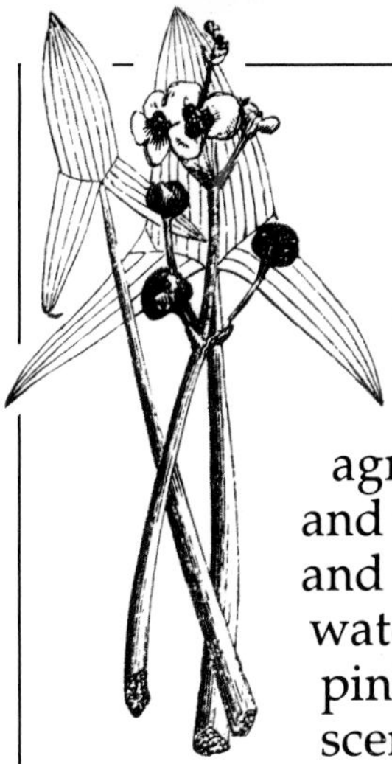

Midsummer plants

Arrowhead

Flowering rush

Pink flowers on stalks

Developing fruits

T HE MIDSUMMER POND is fringed with blooms
of all colors, from the dusky pink of hemp
agrimony to the many yellows of St.-John's-wort
and the buttercups, and the tall purple loosestrife
and rosy-red great willow herb. Out on the
water, lilies of various colors and the bright
pink blooms of water bistort enhance the
scene. Early-flowering species are by now
fading as their petals fall and their fruits form
from the swelling lower part of the flower head.

RUSH IN BLOOM
The dark pink blooms of
flowering rush are carried on
stems up to 5 ft (1.5 m) tall.
The flowering rush is not
a true rush, though its
leaves are rushlike and
grow in a rosette from the
stem base. It is often
planted to decorate
ornamental ponds.

Common figwort

FROTHY FLOWER
Meadowsweet's tiny, creamy
flowers combine to form a
foamy mass carried on a firm
stem, often more than 3 ft
(1 m) tall. This relative of the
rose likes pond sides, boggy
areas, and wet meadows.

GROWN UP
The figwort shown on
page 10 has now grown
to its full height of almost
3 ft (1 m). The flowers
are spaced at regular
intervals on the upper
section of stem.

FRUITS FORMING
The water arum's fruits are
ripening as the specialized
cup-shaped leaves around
them, called spathes,
begin to yellow and wither
(see also p. 196).

Mass of tiny flowers

Spathe

Developing fruits

Meadowsweet

Water arum

*Dark-green leaves
have notched edges*

*Figwort's stem has
a distinctive square
cross section*

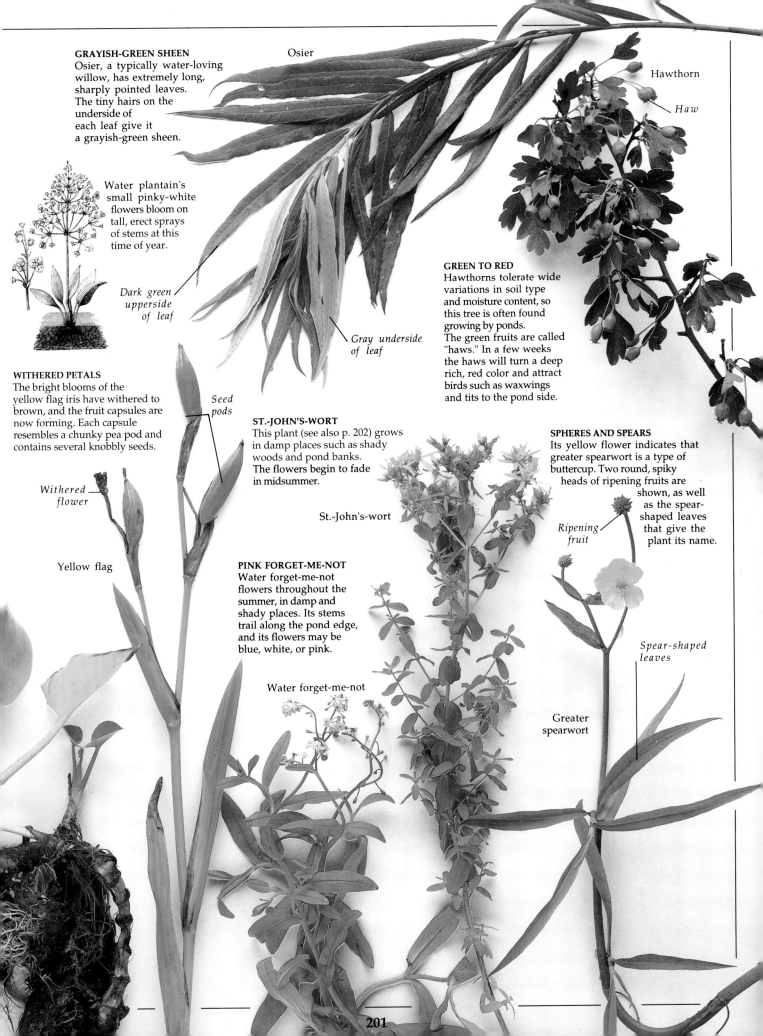

GRAYISH-GREEN SHEEN
Osier, a typically water-loving willow, has extremely long, sharply pointed leaves. The tiny hairs on the underside of each leaf give it a grayish-green sheen.

Osier

Hawthorn

Haw

Water plantain's small pinky-white flowers bloom on tall, erect sprays of stems at this time of year.

Dark green upperside of leaf

Gray underside of leaf

GREEN TO RED
Hawthorns tolerate wide variations in soil type and moisture content, so this tree is often found growing by ponds. The green fruits are called "haws." In a few weeks the haws will turn a deep rich, red color and attract birds such as waxwings and tits to the pond side.

WITHERED PETALS
The bright blooms of the yellow flag iris have withered to brown, and the fruit capsules are now forming. Each capsule resembles a chunky pea pod and contains several knobbly seeds.

Seed pods

ST.-JOHN'S-WORT
This plant (see also p. 202) grows in damp places such as shady woods and pond banks. The flowers begin to fade in midsummer.

SPHERES AND SPEARS
Its yellow flower indicates that greater spearwort is a type of buttercup. Two round, spiky heads of ripening fruits are shown, as well as the spear-shaped leaves that give the plant its name.

St.-John's-wort

Withered flower

Ripening fruit

Yellow flag

PINK FORGET-ME-NOT
Water forget-me-not flowers throughout the summer, in damp and shady places. Its stems trail along the pond edge, and its flowers may be blue, white, or pink.

Spear-shaped leaves

Water forget-me-not

Greater spearwort

Midsummer animals

MIDSUMMER IS A TIME OF GROWTH and departure in the pond. The frantic spring and early-summer rush of new life is slowing down. The surviving youngsters of this year's eggs, now fewer in number, settle down to the serious business of growing, building up stores of fat in their bodies, and preparing for the shorter, colder days ahead. Frog and toad tadpoles have changed into air-breathing mini-adults, ready to leave the water and take their first hops on land. A few young newts may stay as tadpoles with gills through the coming autumn and winter, but others, now adult in shape, are also moving away. The departure from the pond continues as aquatic insect larvae of many kinds develop into adults, from tiny gnats, midges, and mosquitoes to the mighty dragonflies that prey on them.

Tiny gnats (male and female) dance above the pond's surface during long summer evenings

Not rowing but flying, this water boatman shows its strong wings.

Water snail

Growth rings

Toadlet

Newtlets

Gills

Toadlet

NEWTLETS
These young newts still have their gills to help absorb oxygen from the warm summer pond water. They hide among weeds, eating water fleas and other tiny creatures.

TOADLETS
By now, toad tadpoles have grown their front legs and lost their tails, to resemble their parents. In midsummer they leave the pond for life on land.

RINGS AND BANDS
Periods of slow growth are visible on this water snail's shell. They are the thin rings toward the opening which cross the spiral banding pattern.

HAPPY WANDERER
The wandering snail is more tolerant of water with fewer minerals than, for example, the great pond snail is - and so is more widespread in ponds and slow rivers.

SQUARE STEM
There are several species of St.-John's-wort. This one is square-stemmed, and lines watersides, marshes, and damp shrubland.

BABY BIVALVES
In about 10 years, these young freshwater mollusks will be many times this size. In their early years they are busy feeding and absorbing calcium from the water to build their shell.

Young freshwater mollusks

Wandering snails

Snail emerging from shell

Square-stemmed St.-John's-wort

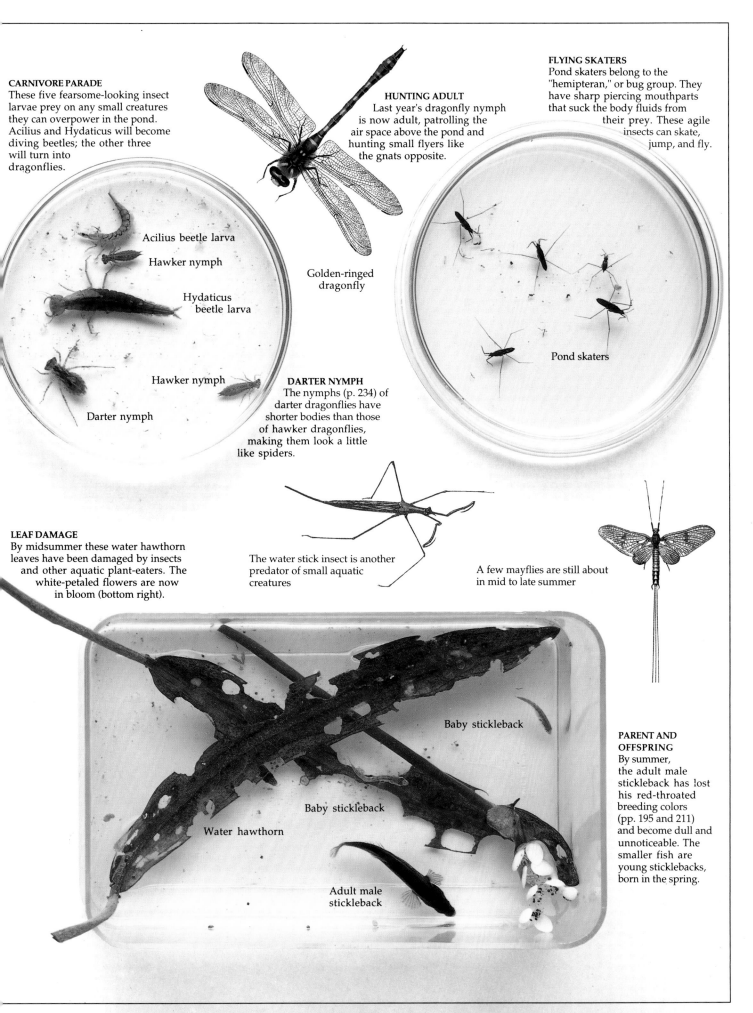

CARNIVORE PARADE
These five fearsome-looking insect larvae prey on any small creatures they can overpower in the pond. Acilius and Hydaticus will become diving beetles; the other three will turn into dragonflies.

HUNTING ADULT
Last year's dragonfly nymph is now adult, patrolling the air space above the pond and hunting small flyers like the gnats opposite.

FLYING SKATERS
Pond skaters belong to the "hemipteran," or bug group. They have sharp piercing mouthparts that suck the body fluids from their prey. These agile insects can skate, jump, and fly.

Acilius beetle larva

Hawker nymph

Hydaticus beetle larva

Golden-ringed dragonfly

Hawker nymph

Darter nymph

DARTER NYMPH
The nymphs (p. 234) of darter dragonflies have shorter bodies than those of hawker dragonflies, making them look a little like spiders.

Pond skaters

LEAF DAMAGE
By midsummer these water hawthorn leaves have been damaged by insects and other aquatic plant-eaters. The white-petaled flowers are now in bloom (bottom right).

The water stick insect is another predator of small aquatic creatures

A few mayflies are still about in mid to late summer

Baby stickleback

PARENT AND OFFSPRING
By summer, the adult male stickleback has lost his red-throated breeding colors (pp. 195 and 211) and become dull and unnoticeable. The smaller fish are young sticklebacks, born in the spring.

Baby stickleback

Water hawthorn

Adult male stickleback

The pond in autumn

GRADUALLY THE SUMMER ENDS and the hours of daylight shorten. Although the sun's rays may still be warm in midafternoon, the nights are increasingly chilly. Autumn has arrived and pond wildlife is slowing down and preparing for winter. Summer-visiting birds have departed, but their place is taken by waterfowl such as the brent goose, Bewick swan, and pintail duck, which fly in from their far-north breeding grounds to enliven larger ponds, lakes, and marshes. Mammals and resident birds feed greedily on the ripe fruits, building up their fat stores for the winter. However, their shelters and hiding places are gradually being whittled away as the cold wind rattles crackly brown leaves from their stems, making the pond's banks look bare and untidy.

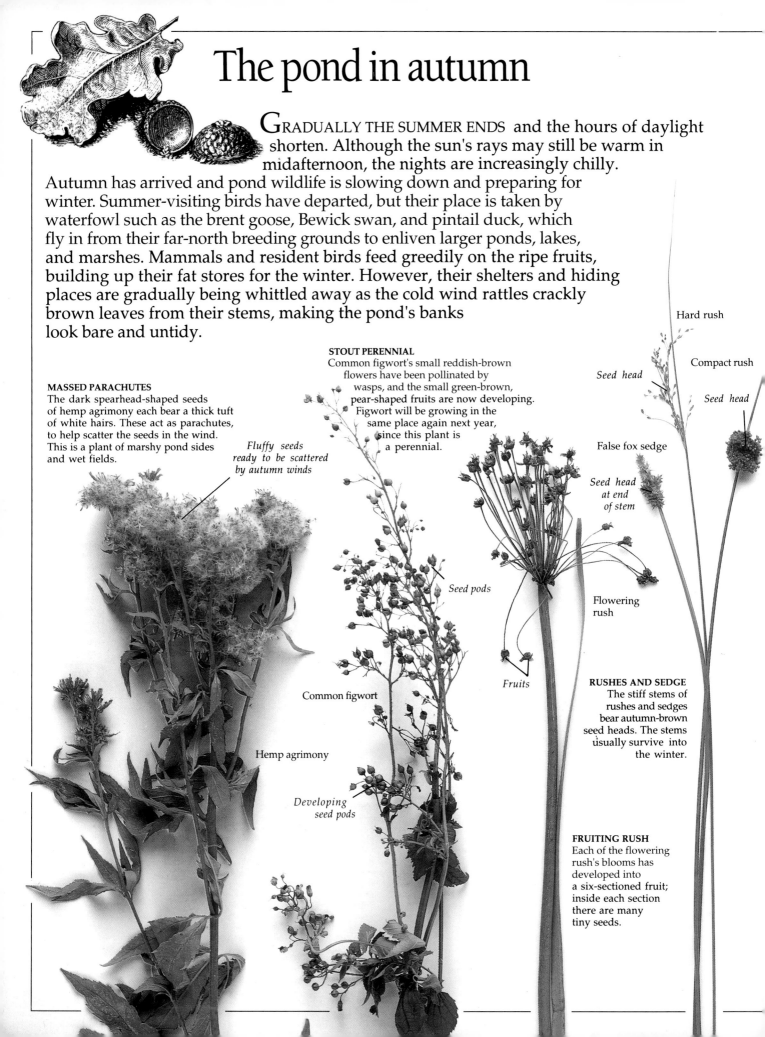

MASSED PARACHUTES
The dark spearhead-shaped seeds of hemp agrimony each bear a thick tuft of white hairs. These act as parachutes, to help scatter the seeds in the wind. This is a plant of marshy pond sides and wet fields.

Fluffy seeds ready to be scattered by autumn winds

Hemp agrimony

STOUT PERENNIAL
Common figwort's small reddish-brown flowers have been pollinated by wasps, and the small green-brown, pear-shaped fruits are now developing. Figwort will be growing in the same place again next year, since this plant is a perennial.

Seed pods

Common figwort

Developing seed pods

Hard rush

Compact rush

Seed head

Seed head

Seed head

False fox sedge

Seed head at end of stem

Fruits

Flowering rush

RUSHES AND SEDGE
The stiff stems of rushes and sedges bear autumn-brown seed heads. The stems usually survive into the winter.

FRUITING RUSH
Each of the flowering rush's blooms has developed into a six-sectioned fruit; inside each section there are many tiny seeds.

WINTER POKER
Reed mace's familiar brown "poker" of seeds stands guard over marshes and ponds, usually throughout the winter. In spring the poker bursts to scatter the fluffy-haired seeds.

Brown "poker" full of seeds

SNAILS SLOWING DOWN
Falling water temperatures mean that even pond snails begin to move around more slowly, tending to stay in deeper water.

Pond snails

Caddis fly cases

Alder cones

Alder

ALDER "CONES"
In autumn the alder's green fruits ripen to a brown-black color and stay on the tree during winter. They are sometimes mistaken for small pine cones, but the alder is not a conifer. It prefers pond banks and the sides of streams, and its light seeds drop onto the water and float to new ground.

Reed mace

Newtlet

Dragonfly nymph

HOME IN A TUBE
Rectangular leaf fragments stuck into a spiral pattern and curled into a tube signal the larval case of the great red sedge, a type of caddis fly. These larvae will emerge as adult flies next year.

Seed pods

NEXT YEAR'S ADULT
Dragonfly nymphs found in the pond at this time of year will survive the winter and emerge next year.

AUTUMN JUVENILE
A young common newt, still equipped with gills, will spend the winter as a "juvenile" and finish its change into an adult next year.

RECYCLING FUNGI
Animal and plant corpses are digested by fungi, and their nutrients are recycled. Here, an old pond-side tree was attacked and weakened by bracket fungi.

Yellow flag

Bracket fungi grow on the outside of the trunk

ON THE BOTTOM
Leaves, twigs, and other debris blow into the pond or are washed in by heavy autumn rains. This heap of debris, lying over the mud of the pond bed, will shelter all kinds of small water creatures during the winter months.

SOON TO SET SEED
The seed capsules of the yellow flag iris are now thick with ripening brown seeds (compare the same "pods" on p. 201). Eventually the fleshy capsule walls dry out and split into three boat-shaped segments; these peel back to release the seeds.

Oak leaf

Willow leaf

Birch leaf

Willow twigs

The pond in winter

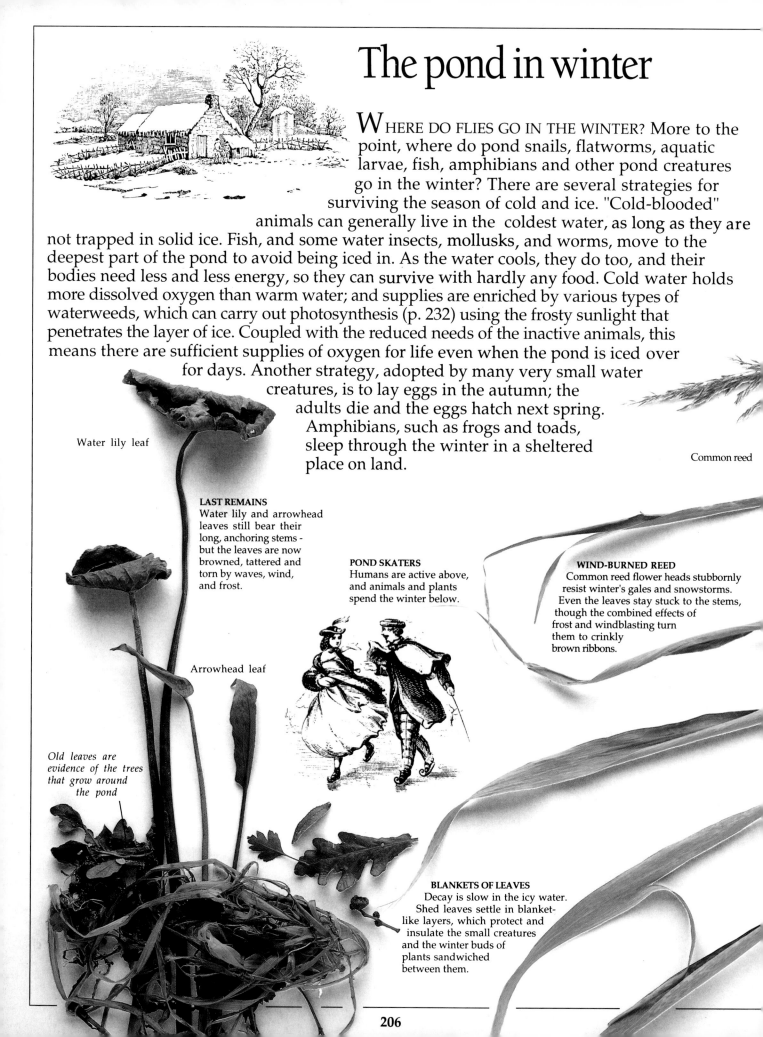

WHERE DO FLIES GO IN THE WINTER? More to the point, where do pond snails, flatworms, aquatic larvae, fish, amphibians and other pond creatures go in the winter? There are several strategies for surviving the season of cold and ice. "Cold-blooded" animals can generally live in the coldest water, as long as they are not trapped in solid ice. Fish, and some water insects, mollusks, and worms, move to the deepest part of the pond to avoid being iced in. As the water cools, they do too, and their bodies need less and less energy, so they can survive with hardly any food. Cold water holds more dissolved oxygen than warm water; and supplies are enriched by various types of waterweeds, which can carry out photosynthesis (p. 232) using the frosty sunlight that penetrates the layer of ice. Coupled with the reduced needs of the inactive animals, this means there are sufficient supplies of oxygen for life even when the pond is iced over for days. Another strategy, adopted by many very small water creatures, is to lay eggs in the autumn; the adults die and the eggs hatch next spring. Amphibians, such as frogs and toads, sleep through the winter in a sheltered place on land.

Common reed

Water lily leaf

LAST REMAINS
Water lily and arrowhead leaves still bear their long, anchoring stems - but the leaves are now browned, tattered and torn by waves, wind, and frost.

POND SKATERS
Humans are active above, and animals and plants spend the winter below.

WIND-BURNED REED
Common reed flower heads stubbornly resist winter's gales and snowstorms. Even the leaves stay stuck to the stems, though the combined effects of frost and windblasting turn them to crinkly brown ribbons.

Arrowhead leaf

Old leaves are evidence of the trees that grow around the pond

BLANKETS OF LEAVES
Decay is slow in the icy water. Shed leaves settle in blanket-like layers, which protect and insulate the small creatures and the winter buds of plants sandwiched between them.

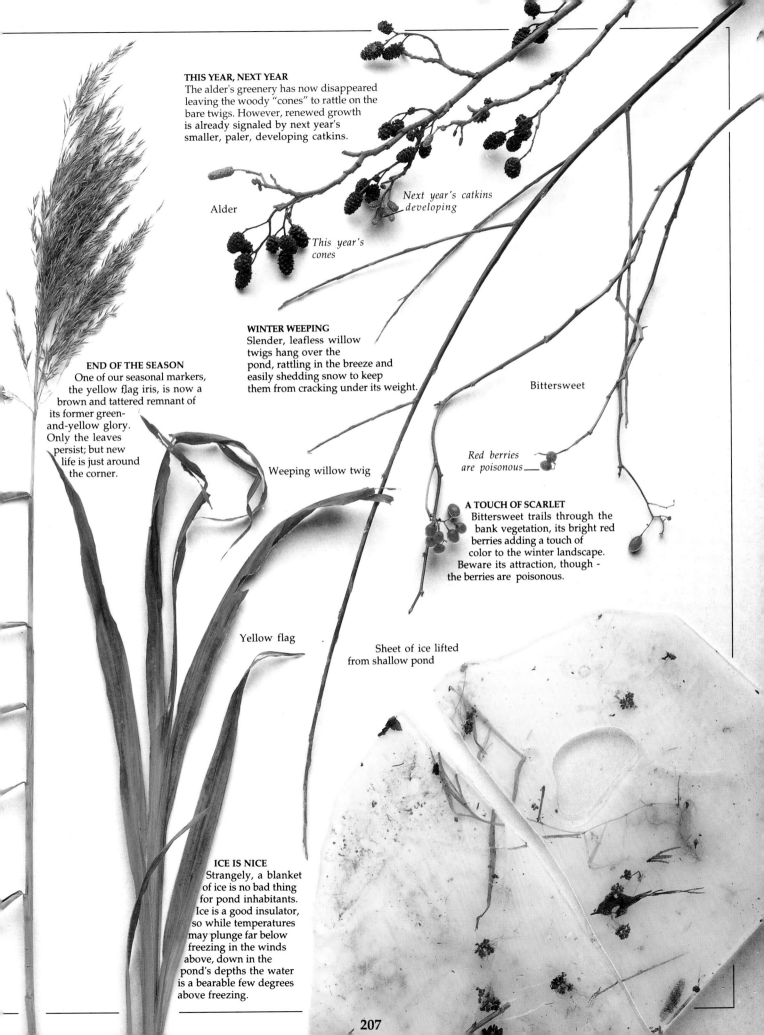

THIS YEAR, NEXT YEAR
The alder's greenery has now disappeared leaving the woody "cones" to rattle on the bare twigs. However, renewed growth is already signaled by next year's smaller, paler, developing catkins.

Alder

Next year's catkins developing

This year's cones

WINTER WEEPING
Slender, leafless willow twigs hang over the pond, rattling in the breeze and easily shedding snow to keep them from cracking under its weight.

Bittersweet

END OF THE SEASON
One of our seasonal markers, the yellow flag iris, is now a brown and tattered remnant of its former green-and-yellow glory. Only the leaves persist; but new life is just around the corner.

Weeping willow twig

Red berries are poisonous

A TOUCH OF SCARLET
Bittersweet trails through the bank vegetation, its bright red berries adding a touch of color to the winter landscape. Beware its attraction, though - the berries are poisonous.

Yellow flag

Sheet of ice lifted from shallow pond

ICE IS NICE
Strangely, a blanket of ice is no bad thing for pond inhabitants. Ice is a good insulator, so while temperatures may plunge far below freezing in the winds above, down in the pond's depths the water is a bearable few degrees above freezing.

207

Freshwater fish

Eels are snakelike fish that live in rivers and estuaries

Most people have seen pond and river fish as dark torpedo shapes cruising silently below the surface, or perhaps a flash of silver as a drowning fly is gobbled up. On the next six pages, a variety of life-sized freshwater fish reveal their full splendor. Supremely suited to underwater life, fish swim with powerful muscles that flex the body back and forth, producing a thrashing motion of the tail that moves the animal along. The fins are used chiefly for stabilizing, steering, and braking. The fish shown here demonstrate what is known as countershading. The back is dark and dull, so that when viewed from above, it blends in with the murky water and the pond or river bed. The belly is shiny and silvery, so that when seen from below, the fish blends in with the ripples and flashes at the under side of the water's surface and is not seen by its enemies.

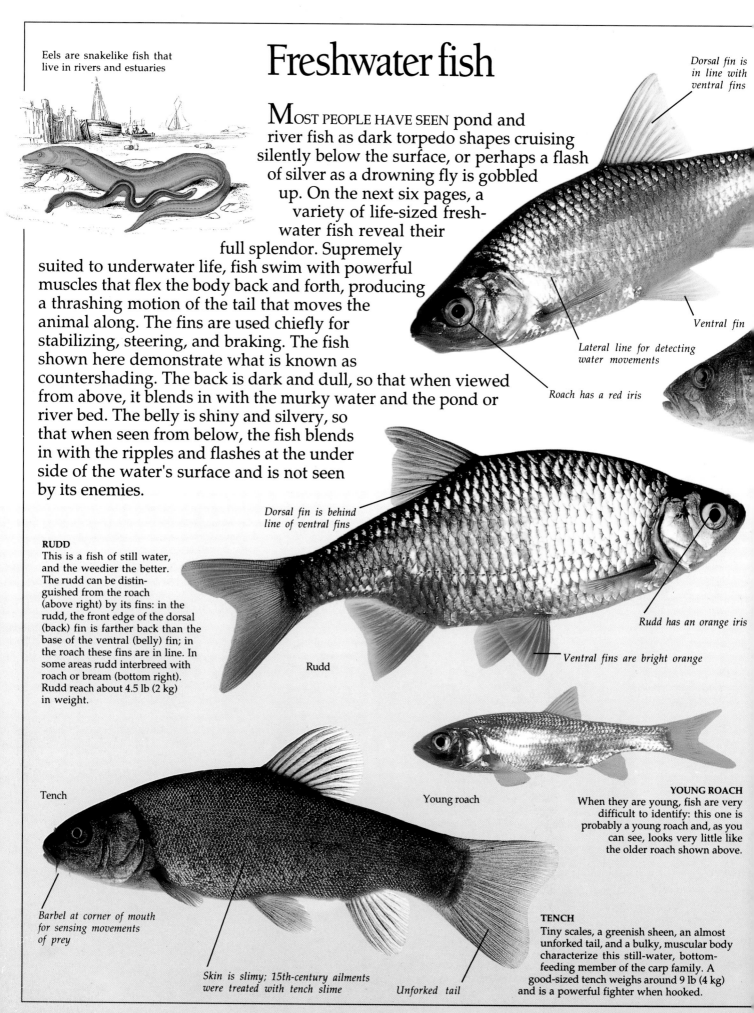

Dorsal fin is in line with ventral fins

Ventral fin

Lateral line for detecting water movements

Roach has a red iris

Dorsal fin is behind line of ventral fins

Rudd has an orange iris

Ventral fins are bright orange

Rudd

RUDD
This is a fish of still water, and the weedier the better. The rudd can be distinguished from the roach (above right) by its fins: in the rudd, the front edge of the dorsal (back) fin is farther back than the base of the ventral (belly) fin; in the roach these fins are in line. In some areas rudd interbreed with roach or bream (bottom right). Rudd reach about 4.5 lb (2 kg) in weight.

Tench

Young roach

YOUNG ROACH
When they are young, fish are very difficult to identify: this one is probably a young roach and, as you can see, looks very little like the older roach shown above.

Barbel at corner of mouth for sensing movements of prey

Skin is slimy; 15th-century ailments were treated with tench slime

Unforked tail

TENCH
Tiny scales, a greenish sheen, an almost unforked tail, and a bulky, muscular body characterize this still-water, bottom-feeding member of the carp family. A good-sized tench weighs around 9 lb (4 kg) and is a powerful fighter when hooked.

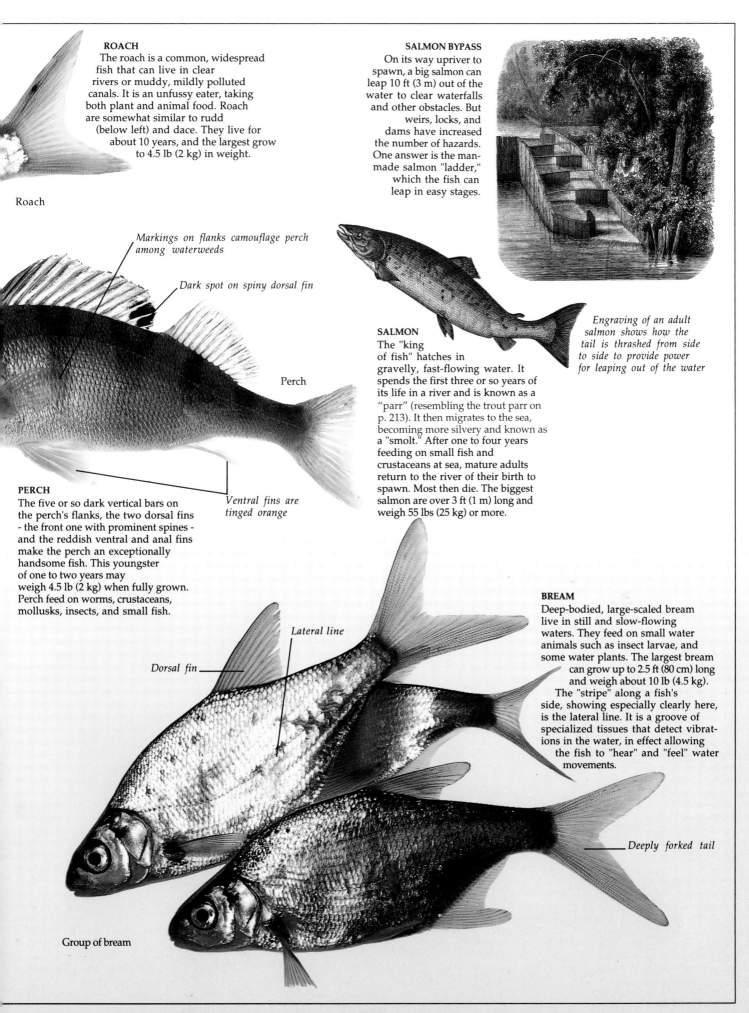

ROACH

The roach is a common, widespread fish that can live in clear rivers or muddy, mildly polluted canals. It is an unfussy eater, taking both plant and animal food. Roach are somewhat similar to rudd (below left) and dace. They live for about 10 years, and the largest grow to 4.5 lb (2 kg) in weight.

Roach

SALMON BYPASS

On its way upriver to spawn, a big salmon can leap 10 ft (3 m) out of the water to clear waterfalls and other obstacles. But weirs, locks, and dams have increased the number of hazards. One answer is the man-made salmon "ladder," which the fish can leap in easy stages.

Markings on flanks camouflage perch among waterweeds

Dark spot on spiny dorsal fin

Perch

SALMON

The "king of fish" hatches in gravelly, fast-flowing water. It spends the first three or so years of its life in a river and is known as a "parr" (resembling the trout parr on p. 213). It then migrates to the sea, becoming more silvery and known as a "smolt." After one to four years feeding on small fish and crustaceans at sea, mature adults return to the river of their birth to spawn. Most then die. The biggest salmon are over 3 ft (1 m) long and weigh 55 lbs (25 kg) or more.

Engraving of an adult salmon shows how the tail is thrashed from side to side to provide power for leaping out of the water

PERCH

The five or so dark vertical bars on the perch's flanks, the two dorsal fins - the front one with prominent spines - and the reddish ventral and anal fins make the perch an exceptionally handsome fish. This youngster of one to two years may weigh 4.5 lb (2 kg) when fully grown. Perch feed on worms, crustaceans, mollusks, insects, and small fish.

Ventral fins are tinged orange

Lateral line

Dorsal fin

BREAM

Deep-bodied, large-scaled bream live in still and slow-flowing waters. They feed on small water animals such as insect larvae, and some water plants. The largest bream can grow up to 2.5 ft (80 cm) long and weigh about 10 lb (4.5 kg). The "stripe" along a fish's side, showing especially clearly here, is the lateral line. It is a groove of specialized tissues that detect vibrations in the water, in effect allowing the fish to "hear" and "feel" water movements.

Deeply forked tail

Group of bream

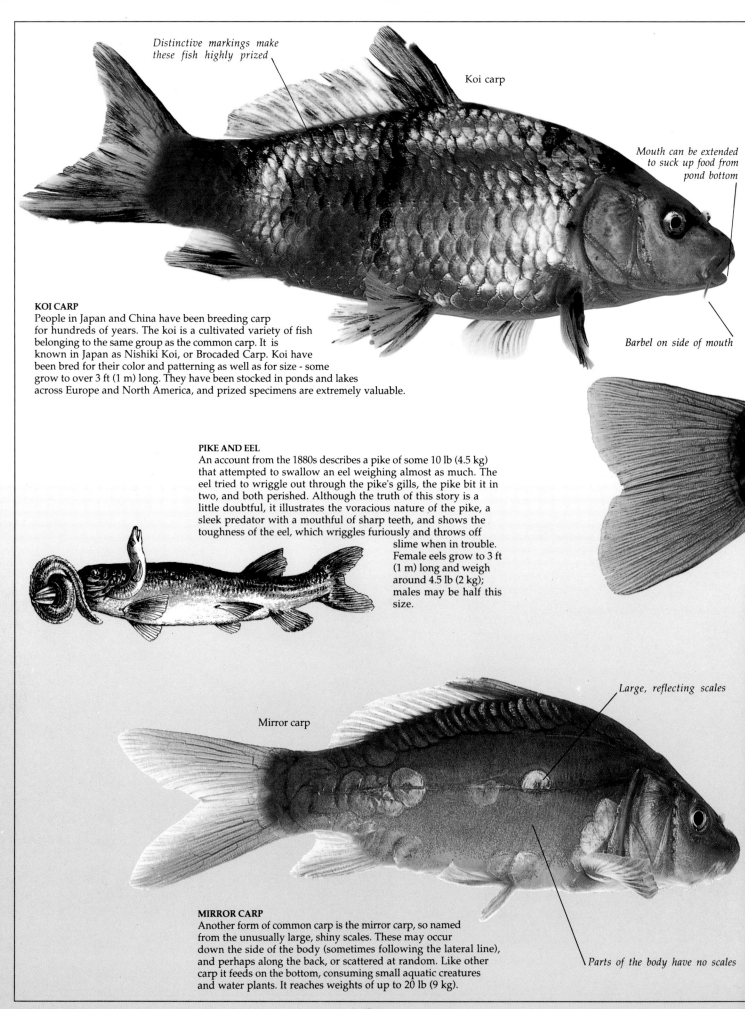

Distinctive markings make these fish highly prized

Koi carp

Mouth can be extended to suck up food from pond bottom

Barbel on side of mouth

KOI CARP
People in Japan and China have been breeding carp
for hundreds of years. The koi is a cultivated variety of fish
belonging to the same group as the common carp. It is
known in Japan as Nishiki Koi, or Brocaded Carp. Koi have
been bred for their color and patterning as well as for size - some
grow to over 3 ft (1 m) long. They have been stocked in ponds and lakes
across Europe and North America, and prized specimens are extremely valuable.

PIKE AND EEL
An account from the 1880s describes a pike of some 10 lb (4.5 kg)
that attempted to swallow an eel weighing almost as much. The
eel tried to wriggle out through the pike's gills, the pike bit it in
two, and both perished. Although the truth of this story is a
little doubtful, it illustrates the voracious nature of the pike, a
sleek predator with a mouthful of sharp teeth, and shows the
toughness of the eel, which wriggles furiously and throws off
slime when in trouble.
Female eels grow to 3 ft
(1 m) long and weigh
around 4.5 lb (2 kg);
males may be half this
size.

Large, reflecting scales

Mirror carp

MIRROR CARP
Another form of common carp is the mirror carp, so named
from the unusually large, shiny scales. These may occur
down the side of the body (sometimes following the lateral line),
and perhaps along the back, or scattered at random. Like other
carp it feeds on the bottom, consuming small aquatic creatures
and water plants. It reaches weights of up to 20 lb (9 kg).

Parts of the body have no scales

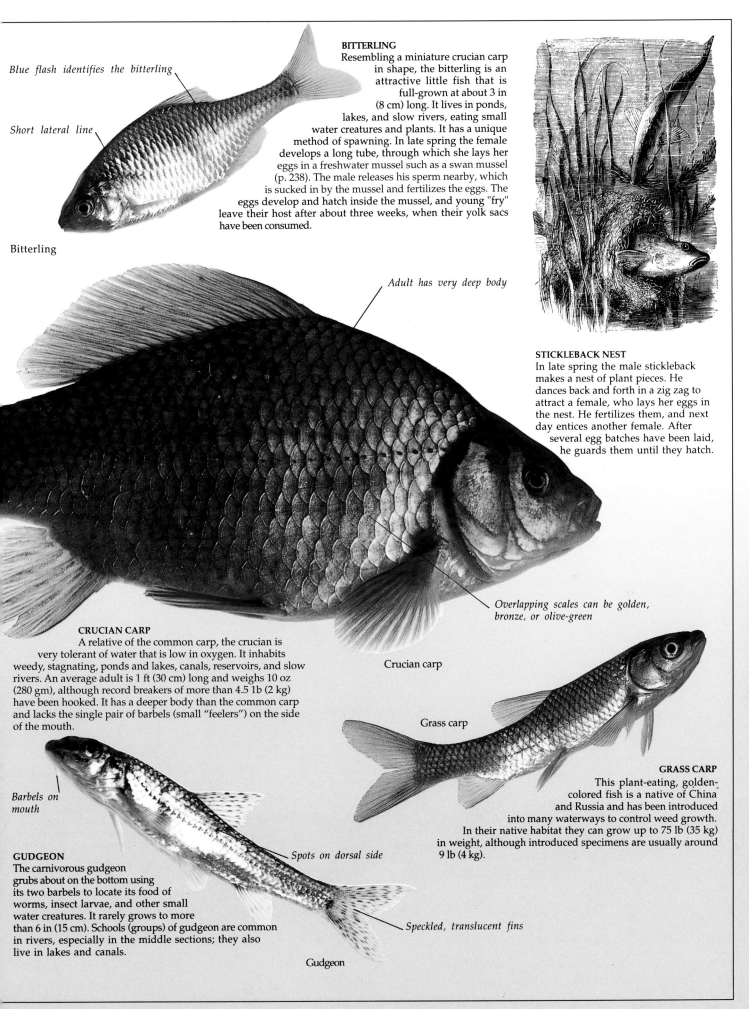

Blue flash identifies the bitterling

Short lateral line

Bitterling

BITTERLING
Resembling a miniature crucian carp in shape, the bitterling is an attractive little fish that is full-grown at about 3 in (8 cm) long. It lives in ponds, lakes, and slow rivers, eating small water creatures and plants. It has a unique method of spawning. In late spring the female develops a long tube, through which she lays her eggs in a freshwater mussel such as a swan mussel (p. 238). The male releases his sperm nearby, which is sucked in by the mussel and fertilizes the eggs. The eggs develop and hatch inside the mussel, and young "fry" leave their host after about three weeks, when their yolk sacs have been consumed.

Adult has very deep body

STICKLEBACK NEST
In late spring the male stickleback makes a nest of plant pieces. He dances back and forth in a zig zag to attract a female, who lays her eggs in the nest. He fertilizes them, and next day entices another female. After several egg batches have been laid, he guards them until they hatch.

Overlapping scales can be golden, bronze, or olive-green

Crucian carp

Grass carp

CRUCIAN CARP
A relative of the common carp, the crucian is very tolerant of water that is low in oxygen. It inhabits weedy, stagnating, ponds and lakes, canals, reservoirs, and slow rivers. An average adult is 1 ft (30 cm) long and weighs 10 oz (280 gm), although record breakers of more than 4.5 lb (2 kg) have been hooked. It has a deeper body than the common carp and lacks the single pair of barbels (small "feelers") on the side of the mouth.

Barbels on mouth

Spots on dorsal side

GUDGEON
The carnivorous gudgeon grubs about on the bottom using its two barbels to locate its food of worms, insect larvae, and other small water creatures. It rarely grows to more than 6 in (15 cm). Schools (groups) of gudgeon are common in rivers, especially in the middle sections; they also live in lakes and canals.

GRASS CARP
This plant-eating, golden-colored fish is a native of China and Russia and has been introduced into many waterways to control weed growth. In their native habitat they can grow up to 75 lb (35 kg) in weight, although introduced specimens are usually around 9 lb (4 kg).

Speckled, translucent fins

Gudgeon

The trout

FEW FRESHWATER FISH match the trout for natural beauty and grace, for fighting power when hooked - and for taste when cooked! Trout belong to the salmon family. The brown trout and the sea trout are, in fact, different forms of the same species. The brown trout lives all its life in fresh water; the sea trout feeds in the sea and enters its home stream in summer, to breed in autumn. Adult brown trout may reach 3 ft (1 m) in length; sea trout can be half as long again. There are many variations between these two forms, telling them apart is difficult, because sea trout darken when they have been in fresh water for a few weeks and look like brown trout. In any case, trout differ greatly in appearance, depending on where they live, the nature of the water, the type of stream or lake bed, and the food they eat. Rainbow trout are another trout species altogether.

TYPICAL TROUT COUNTRY
An ideal trout stream - clear and cool running water, high in dissolved oxygen, with a gravelly bed for spawning. Trout are also found in clean lakes, usually in the shallows near their food.

Lateral line

Movements of the very mobile pectoral fins enable the fish to swim upward or downward

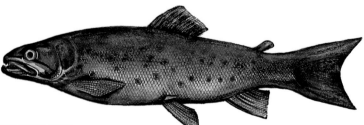

Brown trout

STREAMLINED PREDATOR
Brown trout, like other trout, are carnivorous. Food varies from tiny water fleas, flies, aquatic insect larvae (such as caddis larvae) and freshwater shrimps, to shellfish and other mollusks. The big brown trout, from large, deep lakes, prey on other fish such as char or whitefish.

COLORS OF THE RAINBOW
Rainbow trout were originally found in western North America (especially California). Like the brown trout, there are sea, lake, and river forms. Their eggs were brought to Europe in the 1900s, and these fish have since been introduced into many rivers, reservoirs, and lakes to provide sport and food. Rainbow trout breed in some large reservoirs, but rivers have to be regularly stocked with young produced in hatcheries (trout farms). The rainbow trout can live in warmer, less oxygenated water than the brown trout, so they are stocked in small lakes and large ponds where the brown trout would probably not survive.

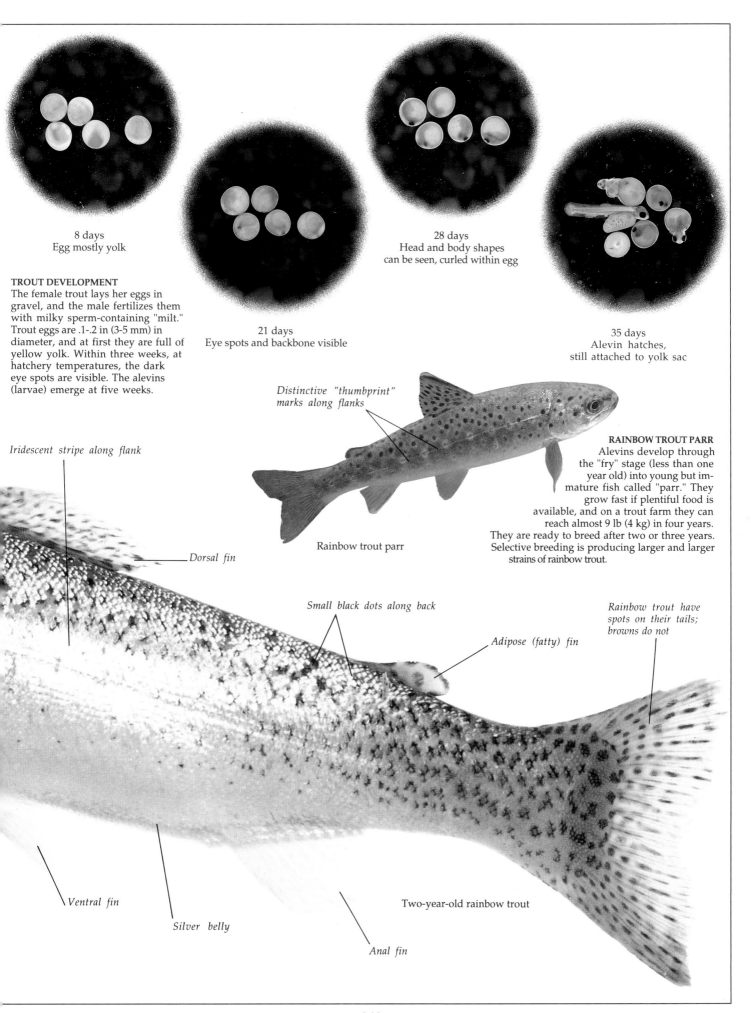

8 days
Egg mostly yolk

21 days
Eye spots and backbone visible

28 days
Head and body shapes
can be seen, curled within egg

35 days
Alevin hatches,
still attached to yolk sac

TROUT DEVELOPMENT
The female trout lays her eggs in gravel, and the male fertilizes them with milky sperm-containing "milt." Trout eggs are .1-.2 in (3-5 mm) in diameter, and at first they are full of yellow yolk. Within three weeks, at hatchery temperatures, the dark eye spots are visible. The alevins (larvae) emerge at five weeks.

Distinctive "thumbprint" marks along flanks

RAINBOW TROUT PARR
Alevins develop through the "fry" stage (less than one year old) into young but immature fish called "parr." They grow fast if plentiful food is available, and on a trout farm they can reach almost 9 lb (4 kg) in four years. They are ready to breed after two or three years. Selective breeding is producing larger and larger strains of rainbow trout.

Rainbow trout parr

Iridescent stripe along flank

Dorsal fin

Small black dots along back

Adipose (fatty) fin

Rainbow trout have spots on their tails; browns do not

Ventral fin

Silver belly

Anal fin

Two-year-old rainbow trout

Waterfowl

WATER AND ITS RESIDENT WILDLIFE attract
an amazing variety of birds. Quite at home
on ponds, lakes, and rivers (as well as
seashores) across the world are about 150
species of wildfowl, including swans, geese,
and ducks. These generally heavy-bodied
birds have webbed feet for swimming and
long, flexible necks for dabbling in the water
and rummaging in the muddy bed for food.
During spring, dense plant growth on the bank
provides many species with safe and sheltered
nesting sites. In summer, the proud parents can
be seen leading their fluffy chicks across the
water. Aquatic plants and animals are a ready
source of food for most of the year. In winter,
when ponds freeze over, many wildfowl retreat
to parks and gardens where they feast on scraps
donated by well-wishing humans. Others fly south,
often covering vast distances to find a more favorable
climate in which to spend the winter.

Eider duck nest
and eggs

Soft down feathers insulate
the eggs in the nest

Teal nest and eggs

SPECIALLY GROWN DOWN
Ultra-soft eiderdown feathers
grow on the female eider duck's
breast. She plucks them
to cocoon her eggs as she
nests on seashore, lake shore
or riverbank.

TEAL NEST
The teal makes its nest
in dense undergrowth.
The female is very
careful when visiting
her chicks, so as not
to attract predators.

TUFTED DUCK EGG
The six to 14 eggs are laid in a nest
close to the water's edge. The chick
hatches after 25 days in the egg,
and within a day it is
swimming.

Teal, one of the
smallest ducks

*Nest would be
lined with down
when being used*

ECLIPSE
Out of the breeding season,
the pintail drake molts to
his unnoticeable "eclipse"
plumage, which looks like the
female's coloring.

Pintail
wing

MALE AND FEMALE
In the breeding
season, most male
ducks, like the pintail
(far right), have bright
plumage to catch the
female's eye. The
female (right) is duller,
for camouflage on the nest.

Tufted duck

PARTIAL TO MUSSELS
The tufted duck feeds on freshwater
mussels, as well as small fish, frogs,
and insects.

Tufted duck
skull

ON THE WING
All wildfowl are strong
flyers, many covering
vast distances during
their annual migration.

MUSCOVY DUCK
This native of Central and South
American ponds and marshes has
a broad bill that scoops up aquatic
plants and animals alike.

Muscovy duck

Muscovy duck
skull

Vane

Swan

BEWARE THE ORANGE BILL
The mute swan's bill is usually covered by an
orange sheath. Male swans can be extremely
vicious, particularly in the breeding season when
defending their territory.

*The broad bill shape is
suitable for dabbling
for plants in the water*

Quill

FROM THE MOLT
Water-dwelling birds depend on
their feathers to keep them dry,
and much time is spent
preening to keep the feathers
in good condition.

Mute swan skull

Flight feathers

Water birds

Kingfisher

A STRETCH OF WATER acts as a magnet for all types of bird life. Many species, from sparrows to pheasants, come to drink. Others come to feed, from the tall, elegant heron that stands motionless as it watches for prey, to the flash of shimmering blue that signifies a kingfisher diving for its dinner. Bank plants, floating and submerged waterweeds, fish, frogs, insect larvae, shellfish, and other aquatic life provide food for many birds. Some species, like reed buntings and warblers, find security in the dense reed beds and waterside vegetation. Here they nest and raise their chicks, safe from predators such as foxes and hawks.

Kingfisher wing

Tail and wing markings vary from species to species

Short wings beat rapidly when flying

Sharp bill for stabbing fish

THE EXPERT FISHER
The brilliantly colored kingfisher dives from its favorite perch for fish, tadpoles, and shellfish. The sword-shaped bill is ideal for stabbing or spearing fish, then holding the slippery prey until it can be beaten into stillness on a branch and swallowed headfirst.

The white eggs have a glossy surface

Kingfisher eggs

KINGFISHER WING AND TAIL
The electric colors act as a warning to predatory birds, advertising that the flesh is foul-tasting.

Kingfisher tail

Kingfisher skull

WHITE EGGS
Kingfishers nest in a streambank burrow up to 3 ft (1 m) long, so their eggs are white - there is no need for camouflaging colors.

Long, sharp bill for spearing fish

Heron skull

Heron

LONG AND LANKY
Herons inhabit ponds, marshes, and rivers, stalking fish and frogs in the shallows.

HERON'S HARPOON
The heron's fearsome bill makes an excellent fish-stabbing spear. This bird stands patiently until prey comes within reach, then darts out its long neck, stabs the victim, tosses it around, and swallows it whole.

Bittern skull

BITTERN
This bird points its bill skyward and sways with the reeds to avoid detection. It can also climb up reed stems. The bittern builds a shallow platform of reed leaves and stalks hidden deep in the reed beds. The five to six eggs take four weeks to hatch.

STEALTHY STALKER
The bittern is a solitary, daytime feeder, using its pointed beak to catch frogs, small fish, and insects.

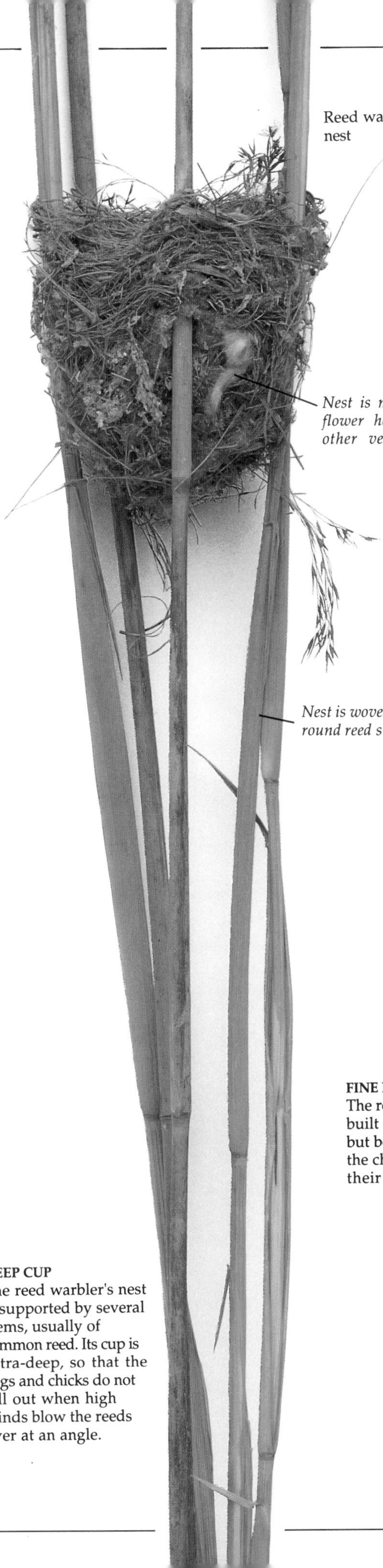
Reed warbler nest
Nest is made from reed flower heads and other vegetation
Nest is woven round reed stalks

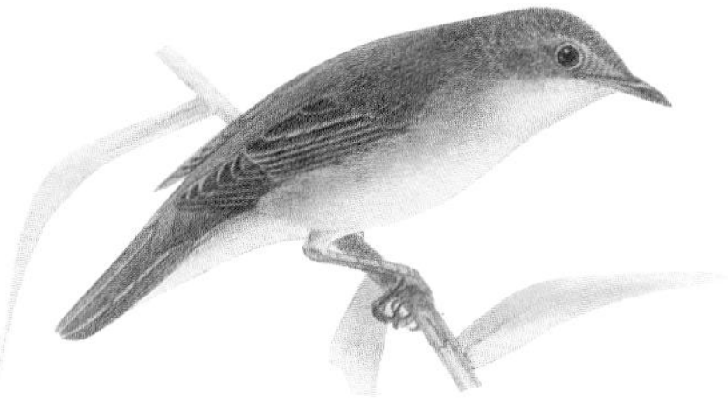

Reed warbler

WARNING All the eggs shown here come from established museum collections. Collecting or handling wild birds' eggs is now illegal.

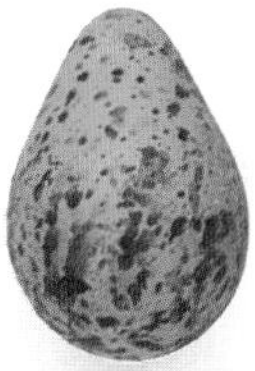

SNIPE EGG
The coloring camouflages the eggs in the nest of this small wading bird.

LITTLE GREBE EGG
White when laid, eggs get discolored by plants and mud. The little grebe is also known as the "dabchick."

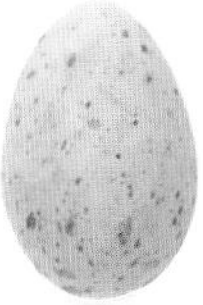

WATER RAIL EGG
Water rails are shy birds of waterside undergrowth. There can be as many as 15 eggs in a clutch.

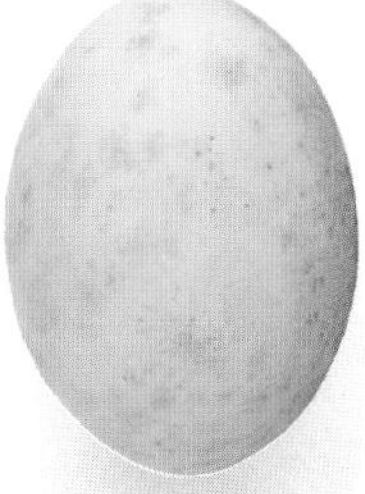

HERON EGG
The blue eggs are laid in well-defended nests built of sticks and twigs.

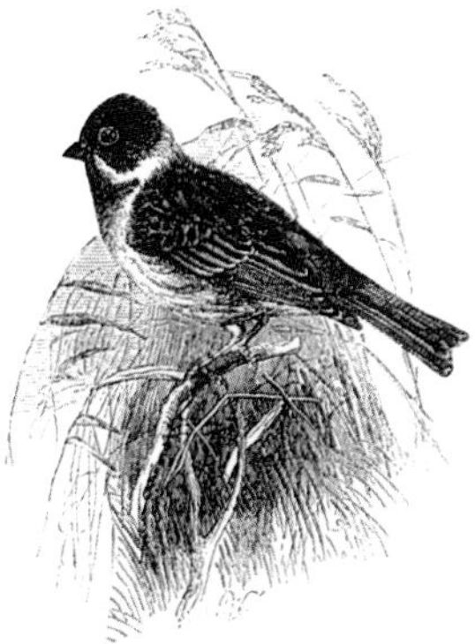

Reed bunting

FINE RUSHWORK
The reed bunting's nest is built by the female alone, but both parents feed the chicks on insects and their larvae.

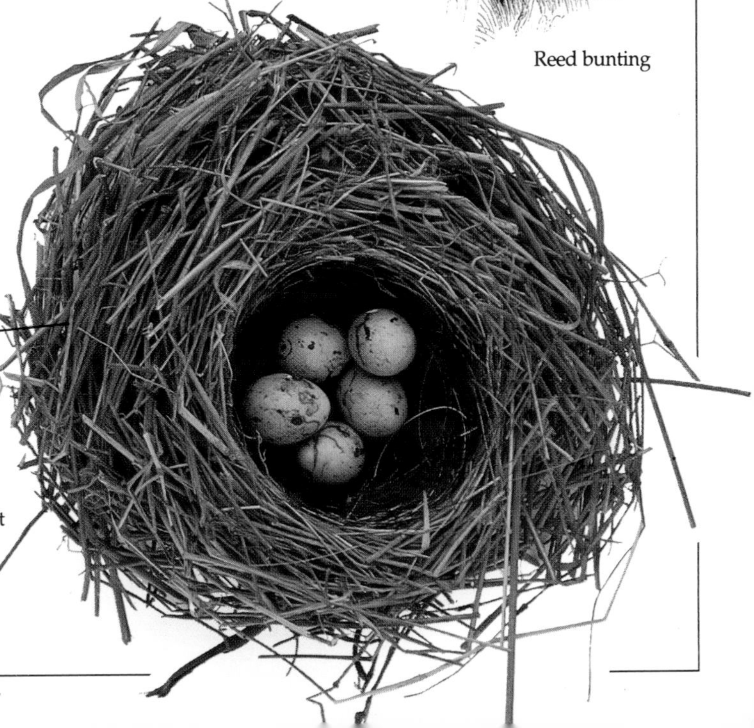
The nest is made of grasses and moss

Reed bunting nest

DEEP CUP
The reed warbler's nest is supported by several stems, usually of common reed. Its cup is extra-deep, so that the eggs and chicks do not fall out when high winds blow the reeds over at an angle.

Rushes and reeds

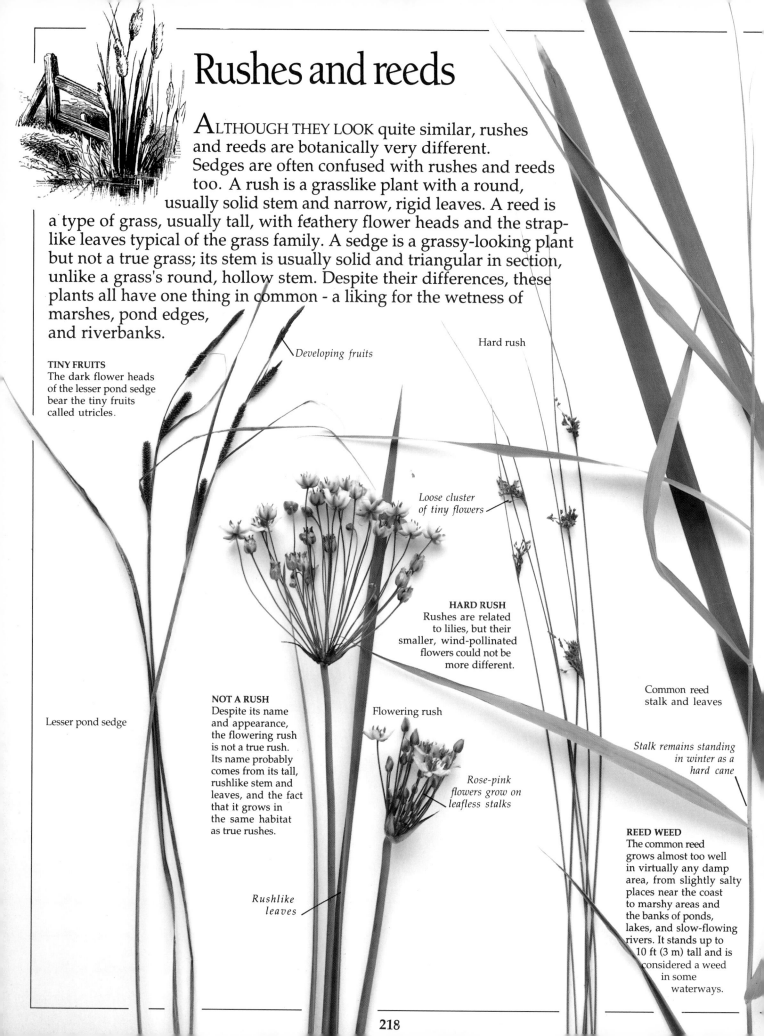

ALTHOUGH THEY LOOK quite similar, rushes and reeds are botanically very different. Sedges are often confused with rushes and reeds too. A rush is a grasslike plant with a round, usually solid stem and narrow, rigid leaves. A reed is a type of grass, usually tall, with feathery flower heads and the strap-like leaves typical of the grass family. A sedge is a grassy-looking plant but not a true grass; its stem is usually solid and triangular in section, unlike a grass's round, hollow stem. Despite their differences, these plants all have one thing in common - a liking for the wetness of marshes, pond edges, and riverbanks.

TINY FRUITS
The dark flower heads of the lesser pond sedge bear the tiny fruits called utricles.

Developing fruits

Hard rush

*Loose cluster
of tiny flowers*

HARD RUSH
Rushes are related to lilies, but their smaller, wind-pollinated flowers could not be more different.

Common reed
stalk and leaves

Lesser pond sedge

NOT A RUSH
Despite its name and appearance, the flowering rush is not a true rush. Its name probably comes from its tall, rushlike stem and leaves, and the fact that it grows in the same habitat as true rushes.

Flowering rush

*Rose-pink
flowers grow on
leafless stalks*

*Stalk remains standing
in winter as a
hard cane*

REED WEED
The common reed grows almost too well in virtually any damp area, from slightly salty places near the coast to marshy areas and the banks of ponds, lakes, and slow-flowing rivers. It stands up to 10 ft (3 m) tall and is considered a weed in some waterways.

*Rushlike
leaves*

Male flowers release clouds of pollen

Female flowers are fertilized by wind-carried pollen from male flowers, and fluffy seeds are released when the flower head splits open

Ten to 20 male flower heads

Branched bur reed

Two to four female flower heads

Male and female flowers in the same flower head

Great reed mace

False fox sedge

BRANCHING OUT
Each stem of branched bur reed bears both male and female flowers. The smaller, ball-shaped ones toward the tip are male; the female ones are larger and spiky, like a rolled-up hedgehog.

Triangular stem has sharp edges if rubbed downward

FALSE FOX SEDGE
On top of sharp-edged stems sit the tufty, yellow-green flower heads containing both male and female flowers.

TWO HEADS IN ONE
The great reed mace's poker-shaped flower head is in two parts. Above are hundreds of golden pollen-bearing male organs, and below are thousands of tiny female flowers packed into the brown cigar shape. The whole resembles the mace, a weapon of 15th-century knights, hence the name. The plant is commonly, but wrongly, called the bulrush, after the paintings of *Moses in the Bulrushes* (p. 221).

Branched bur reed

Flower stalk

Bract at base of each branch of flower stalk

219

The reed bed

THE REED BED IS THE SILENT INVADER OF OPEN WATER. Dense growths of tall, marsh-ground plants, such as reed mace and common reed, spread around the pond's edge by thick underground rhizomes (stems). These grow sideways through the mud toward the water and send up fresh shoots at intervals. They spread into the shallows, pushing aside water lilies and mare's-tails. The reed stems slow the movement of water and trap particles carried by the current. At the end of each season the old leaves, stems, and fruits add to the growing tangle. In a few years, previously open water can be turned into thickly vegetated marsh. Some years later the reed bed has moved on, still swallowing up the shallows, and drier-ground plants such as osiers and sallows (types of willow) have moved in at the back of the bed. This conversion of water to land by characteristic stages is an example of "ecological succession."

Fool's watercress

WATER TO DRY LAND
Shown below are characteristic plants of pond and lake edge, with sallows and sedges higher up the shore, reed beds toward the middle, and mare's-tails and long-stemmed lilies in deeper water. As the reeds spread and invade the water, this becomes clogged and marshy and, over the years, the whole pattern of plant growth moves toward the center of the pond. Of course, this does not happen in all bodies of water. People clear or harvest the reeds, and storms, flood currents, plant diseases, and hungry animals keep a natural balance.

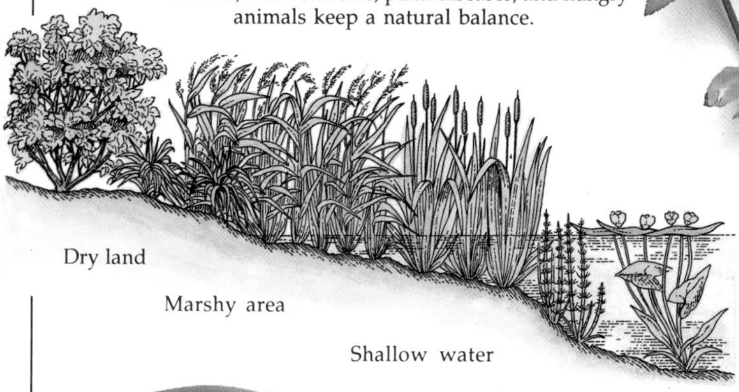

Dry land

Marshy area

Shallow water

Open water

A REED ROOF OVER THEIR HEADS
The strong, long-wearing reeds are used as roofing material in many regions, from huts in Egypt and Sudan, to houses on stilts in Indonesia and wooden cabins in southern North America. The English thatch style (above) repels rain and insulates at the same time. A skilled thatcher working with quality reeds can make a roof that remains weatherproof for 40 years or more.

CREEPING CRESS
The fool's watercress gets its name because its leaves resemble true watercress. It is found in large quantities at the back of many reed beds, and its horizontal, straggling stems add to the general tangle of vegetation.

READY FOR RECYCLING
The thick, black mud of reed-bed areas is rich in decaying plant and animal remains. Its nutrients are soon recycled by the rushes, reeds, and other plants.

Reed-bed mud

Underground rhizome

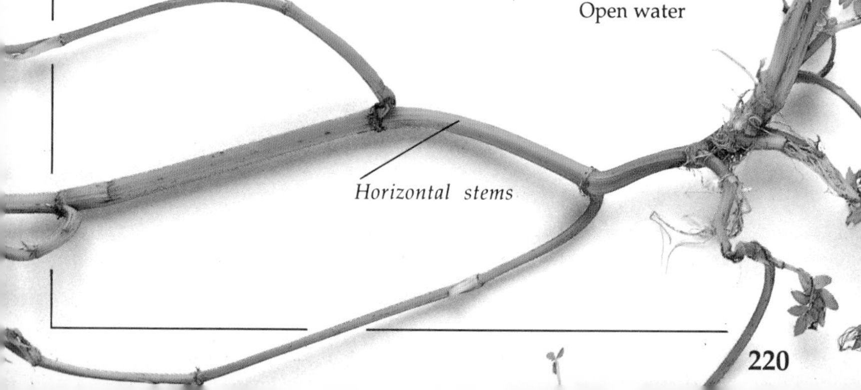

Horizontal stems

Sweet flag · Long straight stalks

Flower head may be 8 ft (2.5 m) above the roots

Dark-greeen leaves have pale undersides

EARLY HARVEST
The reed cutter's season is usually the tail end of winter and early spring. Last year's stems are cut near the base before this year's shoots emerge, which ensures a future harvest.

THICK AND FLESHY
The juicy, strap-shaped leaves of sweet flag sprout from a thick horizontal stem. The stem has many small roots that hold the marshy mud together.

Osier shoot

Top of common reed stem

The thin leaves dry very quickly when picked

MOSES IN THE . . . ?
As a baby, Moses was supposedly hidden in a basket in a reed bed on the bank of the Nile River in Egypt. Illustrations showing this are titled *Moses in the Bulrushes* although most versions portray the baby in a clump of reed mace. This confusion has led to the name "bulrush" being given to reed mace (p. 219); the true bulrush is somewhat similar to the spike rush.

WILLOWS FOR WEAVING
Osiers are found at the back of reed beds, on less marshy ground. They have long, straight shoots and a shrubby shape. They are often coppiced (cut at ground level) to provide flexible stems ("withes") for woven chairs and baskets.

THE STRAIGHT AND NARROW
The straight, narrow stems of common reed are ideal thatching material. They are also used to make paper and other pulp-based products. Plant growth in reed beds is often very fast because there is plenty of water and nutrients, and the slender stems and leaves allow light to reach the lower levels.

Base of common reed stem

Waterside mammals

FRESHWATER HABITATS, from rivers and streams to the marshy edges of lakes and ponds, provide a home and food for a number of mammals. All the "aquatic" mammals shown here have fur coats adapted to their watery habitat. The fur of a mink, for example, is of two main types. Long, thick, flattened "guard hairs" provide physical protection and camouflaging coloration. For each guard hair there are 20 or more softer hairs of the underfur, only half as long, which trap air to keep water out and body heat in. The owners sensibly spend much time combing and cleaning their fur, keeping it in tip-top condition. Another adaptation for watery life is webs between the toes, for more efficient swimming.

FURRY FORAGER
The water shrew's dark-furred body is only about 3 in (8 cm) long. This bustling insect-eater often lives in a bankside system of narrow tunnels that press water from its coat as it squeezes through. It eats small fish, water insects, and even frogs, and hunts on dry land for worms and other small creatures.

Mink

ADAPTABLE CARNIVORE
Minks are less specialized hunters than otters and, besides fish, will eat birds, aquatic insects, and land animals such as rabbits. The broad, webbed back feet provide the main swimming power.

American mink skull

- Canine teeth

Molar teeth

TOOTHLESS "BEAK"
When a baby platypus hatches it has teeth, but these are soon lost. Adults grind up the food of shellfish, water insects, and worms using horny plates along their jaws.

TEARERS AND CUTTERS
The mink's four long canine teeth, toward the front of its mouth, are built for catching prey and tearing flesh. The molars, at the back, are ridged for cutting.

Platypus

Platypus skull

Long bill for grinding food

DUCK'S BILL, MAMMAL'S FUR
The Australian platypus, a monotreme (egg-laying mammal), has a "bill" covered with leathery, sensitive skin. The bill is its only means of finding food - by touch - as it forages in muddy creek beds. It closes its eyes and ears when diving.

LODGE IN THE RIVER
A beaver family lives in a semi-submerged mud-and-stick house called a "lodge." The beavers build a dam of branches, twigs, stones, and mud across the stream, which raises the local water level and isolates the lodge for safety. During winter they swim under the ice to a "deep freezer" food store of woody stems and twigs.

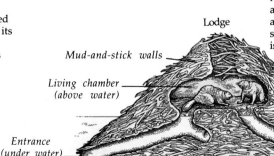

Lodge

Mud-and-stick walls

Living chamber (above water)

Food store

Raised water level

Dam

Entrance (under water)

*Long canine teeth
for grasping fish*

Otter skull

WATCHFUL SWIMMER
Nostrils, eyes, and ears are
placed high on the head
so that the otter can
swim almost
submerged yet still
breathe, look,
and listen.

HUNTING THE OTTER
Otter hunting was once considered a sport and still occurs in
some places, although in many countries this animal is now
protected by law. Today these creatures are also at risk from
pollution and from development of waterways for fishing
and boating.

THE GAME OF LIFE
Otters spend much
time at play, either
on their own or with
one another. Such "games"
may help to sharpen hunting
skills.

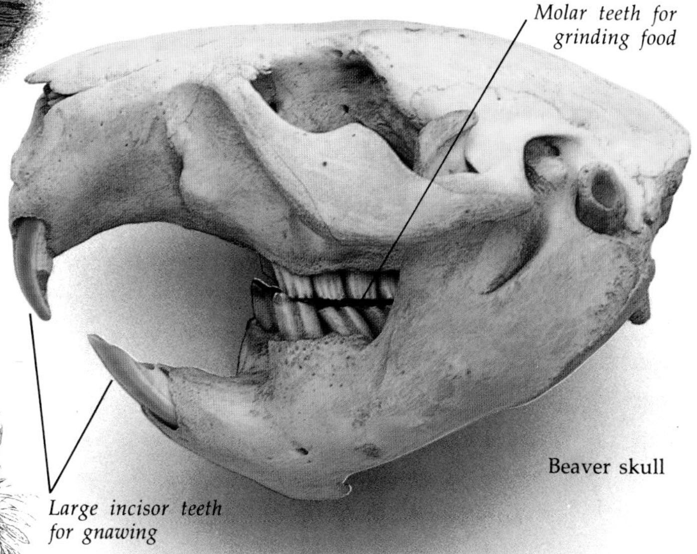

*Molar teeth for
grinding food*

ENORMOUS GNAWERS
The beaver's large
chisel-like front teeth
(typical of rodents) can
gnaw through tree trunks
with ease.

NATURE'S LOGGERS
Beavers cut down trees for food
and also to build homes in lakes
they create for themselves
(below left). They eat
waterweeds, leaves,
and other plant
matter.

*Large incisor teeth
for gnawing*

Beaver skull

Beaver

FLAT SLAP
The beaver's tail is flattened and scaly. Besides its use
as a rudder and paddle, it can be slapped on the
water's surface to warn other beavers of danger.

Beaver tail

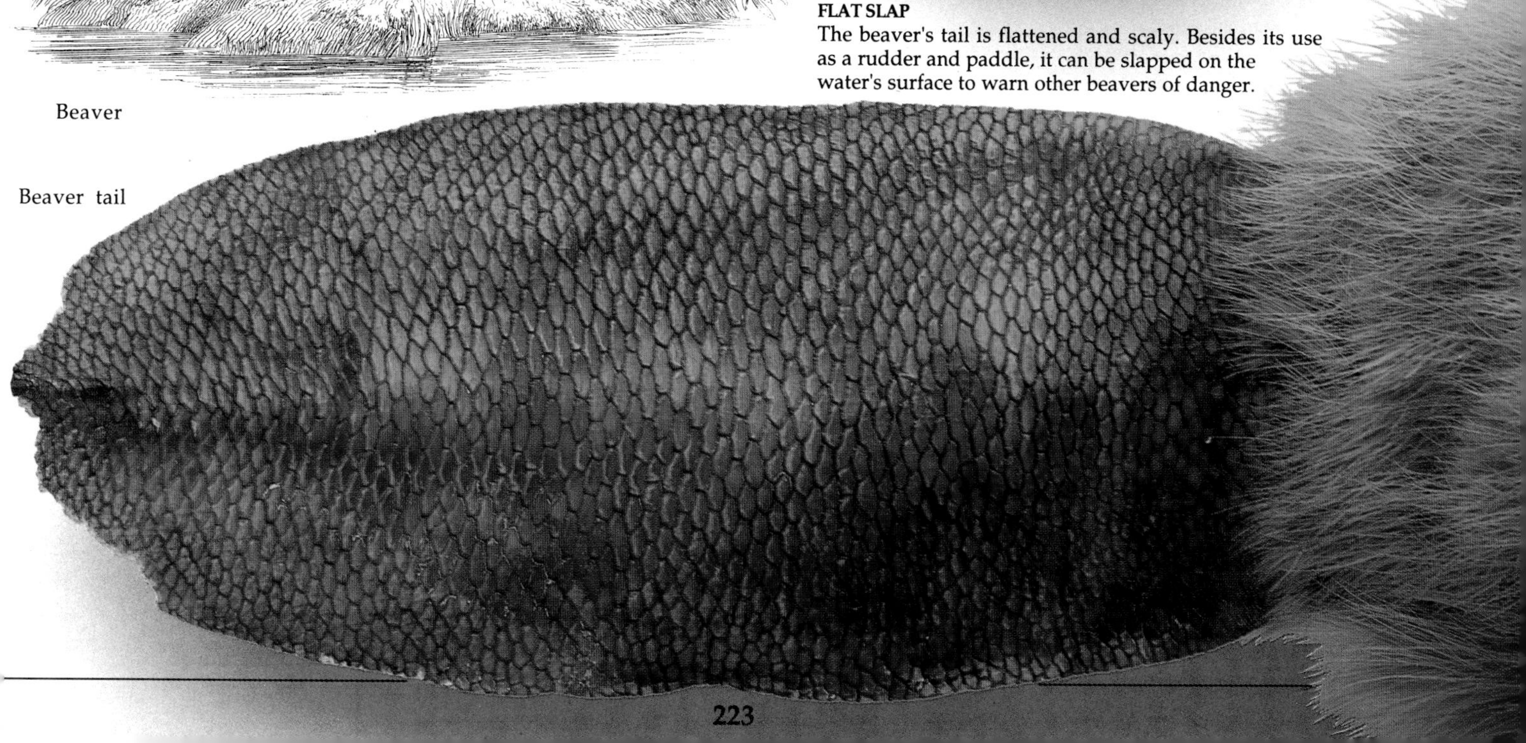

Frogs, toads, and newts

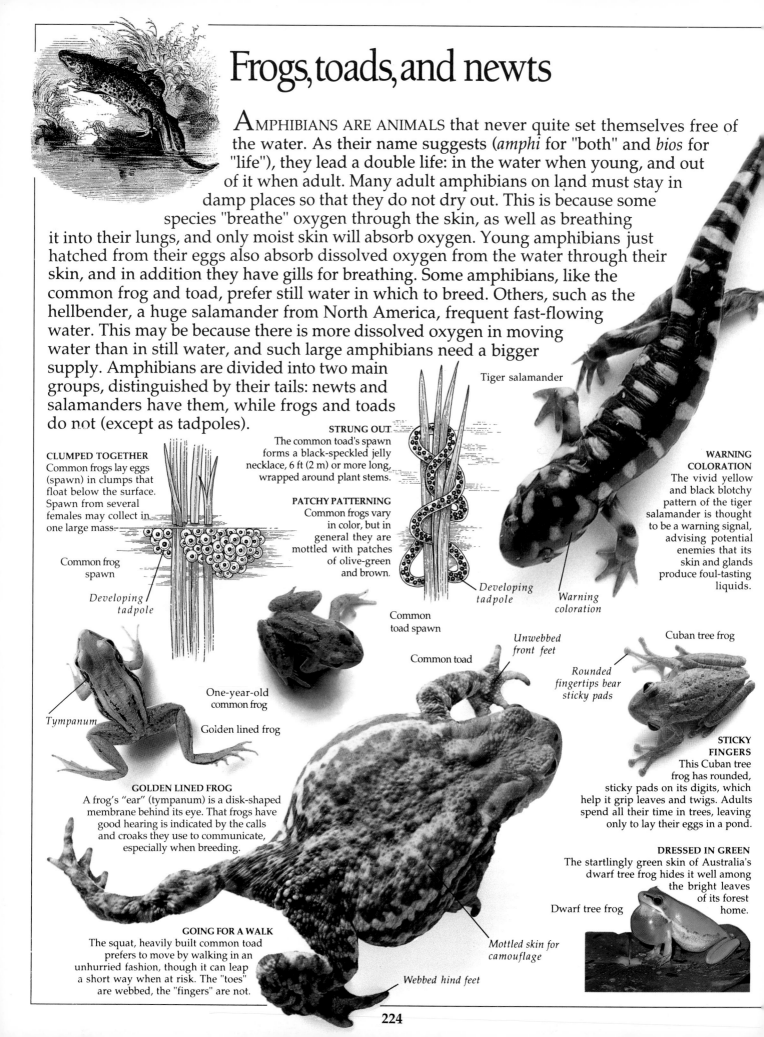

AMPHIBIANS ARE ANIMALS that never quite set themselves free of the water. As their name suggests (*amphi* for "both" and *bios* for "life"), they lead a double life: in the water when young, and out of it when adult. Many adult amphibians on land must stay in damp places so that they do not dry out. This is because some species "breathe" oxygen through the skin, as well as breathing it into their lungs, and only moist skin will absorb oxygen. Young amphibians just hatched from their eggs also absorb dissolved oxygen from the water through their skin, and in addition they have gills for breathing. Some amphibians, like the common frog and toad, prefer still water in which to breed. Others, such as the hellbender, a huge salamander from North America, frequent fast-flowing water. This may be because there is more dissolved oxygen in moving water than in still water, and such large amphibians need a bigger supply. Amphibians are divided into two main groups, distinguished by their tails: newts and salamanders have them, while frogs and toads do not (except as tadpoles).

CLUMPED TOGETHER
Common frogs lay eggs (spawn) in clumps that float below the surface. Spawn from several females may collect in one large mass.

Common frog spawn

Developing tadpole

STRUNG OUT
The common toad's spawn forms a black-speckled jelly necklace, 6 ft (2 m) or more long, wrapped around plant stems.

PATCHY PATTERNING
Common frogs vary in color, but in general they are mottled with patches of olive-green and brown.

Developing tadpole

Common toad spawn

Tiger salamander

WARNING COLORATION
The vivid yellow and black blotchy pattern of the tiger salamander is thought to be a warning signal, advising potential enemies that its skin and glands produce foul-tasting liquids.

Warning coloration

One-year-old common frog

Tympanum

Golden lined frog

GOLDEN LINED FROG
A frog's "ear" (tympanum) is a disk-shaped membrane behind its eye. That frogs have good hearing is indicated by the calls and croaks they use to communicate, especially when breeding.

Common toad

Unwebbed front feet

Cuban tree frog

Rounded fingertips bear sticky pads

STICKY FINGERS
This Cuban tree frog has rounded, sticky pads on its digits, which help it grip leaves and twigs. Adults spend all their time in trees, leaving only to lay their eggs in a pond.

DRESSED IN GREEN
The startlingly green skin of Australia's dwarf tree frog hides it well among the bright leaves of its forest home.

Dwarf tree frog

GOING FOR A WALK
The squat, heavily built common toad prefers to move by walking in an unhurried fashion, though it can leap a short way when at risk. The "toes" are webbed, the "fingers" are not.

Mottled skin for camouflage

Webbed hind feet

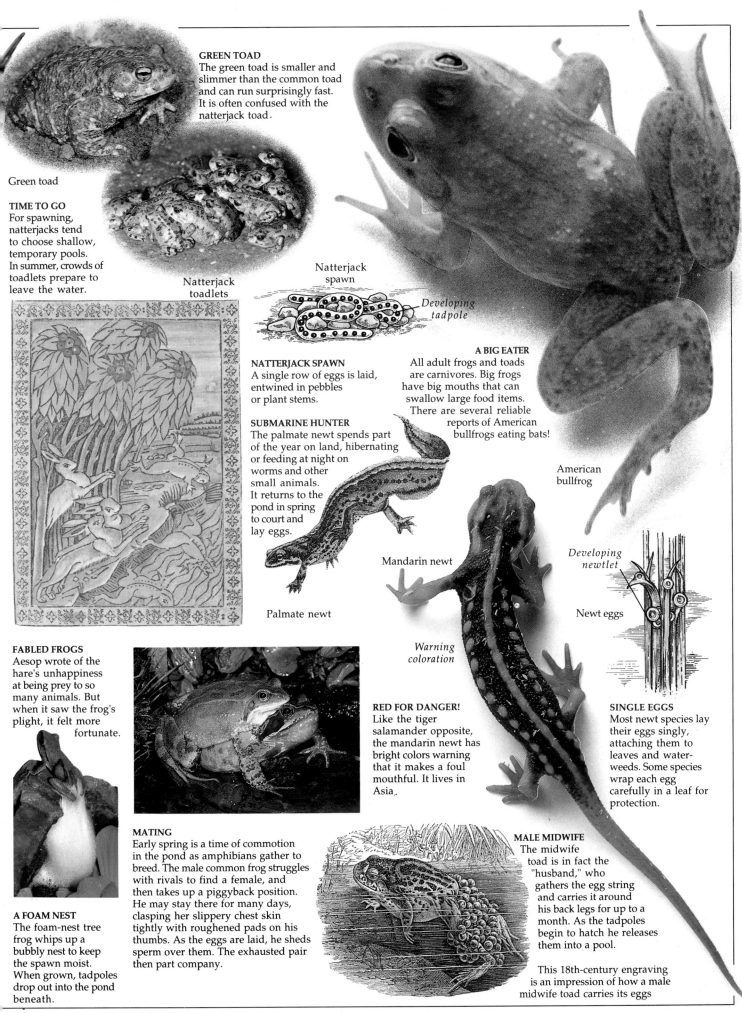

GREEN TOAD
The green toad is smaller and slimmer than the common toad and can run surprisingly fast. It is often confused with the natterjack toad.

Green toad

TIME TO GO
For spawning, natterjacks tend to choose shallow, temporary pools. In summer, crowds of toadlets prepare to leave the water.

Natterjack toadlets

Natterjack spawn

Developing tadpole

NATTERJACK SPAWN
A single row of eggs is laid, entwined in pebbles or plant stems.

SUBMARINE HUNTER
The palmate newt spends part of the year on land, hibernating or feeding at night on worms and other small animals. It returns to the pond in spring to court and lay eggs.

Palmate newt

A BIG EATER
All adult frogs and toads are carnivores. Big frogs have big mouths that can swallow large food items. There are several reliable reports of American bullfrogs eating bats!

American bullfrog

Mandarin newt

Developing newtlet

Newt eggs

Warning coloration

FABLED FROGS
Aesop wrote of the hare's unhappiness at being prey to so many animals. But when it saw the frog's plight, it felt more fortunate.

RED FOR DANGER!
Like the tiger salamander opposite, the mandarin newt has bright colors warning that it makes a foul mouthful. It lives in Asia.

SINGLE EGGS
Most newt species lay their eggs singly, attaching them to leaves and water-weeds. Some species wrap each egg carefully in a leaf for protection.

A FOAM NEST
The foam-nest tree frog whips up a bubbly nest to keep the spawn moist. When grown, tadpoles drop out into the pond beneath.

MATING
Early spring is a time of commotion in the pond as amphibians gather to breed. The male common frog struggles with rivals to find a female, and then takes up a piggyback position. He may stay there for many days, clasping her slippery chest skin tightly with roughened pads on his thumbs. As the eggs are laid, he sheds sperm over them. The exhausted pair then part company.

MALE MIDWIFE
The midwife toad is in fact the "husband," who gathers the egg string and carries it around his back legs for up to a month. As the tadpoles begin to hatch he releases them into a pool.

This 18th-century engraving is an impression of how a male midwife toad carries its eggs

Hunters in the water

MORE THAN 300 MILLION YEARS AGO, the reptiles appeared on Earth, They probably evolved from amphibians. Their big advantage was that they had made a complete break from life in water. Unlike amphibians, which needed water in which to lay their jelly-covered eggs, reptiles had hard-shelled eggs that could be laid on land. Soon, as dinosaurs, they would come to dominate life on land. Since that time, however, some groups of reptiles have made an "evolutionary U-turn" and gone back to life in the water. Many snakes readily take to water, swim well, and hunt fish, frogs, aquatic insects, and land creatures that come to the pond or riverbank for a drink. Indeed, certain groups of reptiles, such as crocodiles and turtles, have never really left their watery environment, though they come on to land to lay their eggs.

GIANT IN THE WATER
One of the longest, and certainly the heaviest, of snakes is the water boa, or anaconda, of northern South America. Lengths of 30 ft (9 m) and weights of over 440 lb (200 kg) have been recorded. It can consume creatures as large as a pig.

Water moccasin

DOWN IN THE SWAMPS
This old engraving shows the water moccasin, a venomous swamp dweller of the southeastern U.S. When this snake is threatened it opens its mouth wide to reveal the white inside lining, hence its other name of "cottonmouth."

Viperine water snake

Zig zag markings on the snake's back are similar to those of a common viper, or adder

Snake swims by wave-like motions of its body

Turtle... or terrapin?

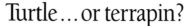

There is little biological difference between a turtle and a terrapin. Most experts call the entire group (chelonians) turtles. Small freshwater species may be named terrapins, from a North American Indian word that referred originally to the diamondback terrapin. But the numerous exceptions confuse the issue. Whatever our labels, however, many turtles are well equipped for an aquatic life, either in fresh water or in the sea. Some have webbed or flipperlike feet and leathery skin covering the shell on their underside, through which oxygen can be absorbed. They tend to eat anything, from aquatic animals to the fruit of bankside trees to the remains of dead creatures.

SCARCELY A RIPPLE
The viperine water snake of Europe is quite at home in the water, swimming easily across its surface. It will strike at just about any suitably sized prey, from fish to frogs and even small mammals. Adults grow to 2.5 ft (80 cm) or more (this one is about life-sized, but young). Despite its name and its zig zag markings like the adder's, it is a relative of the grass snake and is not poisonous.

Yellow-bellied terrapin

Distinctive brown and yellow markings

OPPOSITE FEET FORWARD
The yellow-bellied terrapin may walk along the bed of a river or lake, or swim by paddling alternately with two limbs - the front foot on one side and the back foot on the other.

Left-hand foreleg is forward when right-hand foreleg is back

Smooth plates on shell

Shell lacks bony plates

Ridged bony plates on shell

Strong horny jaws in mouth

Soft-shelled turtle

Webbed feet for swimming

THE SOFT SHELL
Soft-shelled turtles lack the hard, bony plates carried by the hard-shelled types. This life-size youngster will grow to about 1 ft (30 cm) long.

SNAPPY CUSTOMER
This young common snapper will reach almost 20 in (50 cm) when adult. Its strong, sharp-ridged jaws will be able to crack the shells of other turtles, which form part of its diet.

Common snapper

Water snakes will eat all kinds of freshwater life, including this unfortunate frog

Eastern water dragon

DIVING DRAGON
Eastern water dragons live in watercourses in eastern Australia. This lizard is a powerful swimmer, using its vertically flattened tail and long legs. It has a body length of nearly 3 ft (1 m), a tail more than double this, and it eats all kinds of water and shore life, from worms and frogs to shellfish, small mammals, and fruit.

Floating flowers

IN ANCIENT TIMES people were amazed to see that, when a previously dry watercourse filled with recent rains, the splendid blooms of water lilies would soon appear.

These aquatic plants gained a reputation as a symbol of immortality; the ancient Egyptians even worshipped one type of water lily, the sacred lotus. Water lily flowers are made more mysterious by their daily routine: they remain closed during the morning, open to reveal their beauty at around noon, and towards evening close again and sink slightly into the water. This may be an adaptation to aid pollination by flying insects, which are more likely to be active in the afternoon's warmth. On overcast days they might not open fully at all. During gray weather, signaling wind and rain, the closed flowers are less likely to be swamped. The flowers and leaves grow on tough, rubbery stems - 10 ft (3 m) long in some species - anchored in the mud on the beds of ponds, lakes, and slow rivers.

Flower bud

THE "BEAUTIFUL NUISANCE"
The water hyacinth is a free-floating flowering plant that spreads rapidly, often clogging rivers, canals, and ditches.

Red hybrid - "Escarboucle"

Leaves may be heart shaped, oval, or round

Yellow water lily leaves are patterned with a red tinge.

White water lily flower

Leathery leaves repel water droplets

Pink hybrid

Noticeable yellow stamens

LILIES AND THEIR HYBRIDS
There are some 60 species of water lily around
the world (in some areas they are known as lotuses).
Their beautiful waxy-looking flowers and bold
circular leaves have made them favorites in ponds,
ornamental water gardens, and landscaped lakes.
Plant growers have bred many differently
colored flowers.

Yellow hybrid -
"Chromatella"

Waxy petals

Pink hybrid

FLOATING SAUCERS
Some of the largest leaves of any plant
belong to the Amazonian water lily.
A single leaf may be more than 5 ft (1.5 m)
across, with an upturned rim and stiff
reinforcing ribs beneath.

LILY LEAF CASE
The china mark moth's caterpillar cuts out
an oval of leaf and fastens it to the underside
with silk thread
to form a
protective
case.

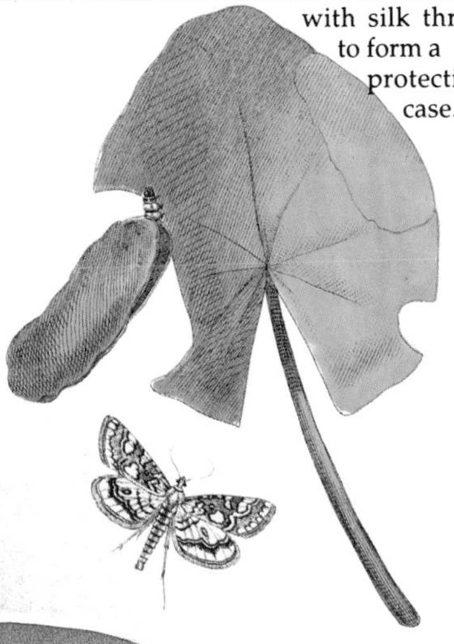

Water lily
leaf

WELL-USED LEAVES
The leaves (lily "pads") are used by many water creatures.
Pond snails browse on them and lay their speckled, jelly-sausage
egg masses on their undersides. Frogs rest on or under them,
waiting to snap up unwary insects. In some places the pads grow so
densely that certain creatures can walk on them. The African jaçana
bird has long, widespread toes and is known as the "lily trotter,"
as it steps delicately on the leaves in search of insects and seeds.

Plants at the pond's surface

MANY WATER PLANTS are not rooted in the mud at the bottom of the pond but are free to float over the surface of the water. Most have trailing roots that balance the plant and absorb minerals, and some have no roots at all. At first sight, these plants seem to have few problems. Unlike some land plants, they are well supported and, out in the middle of the pond, they cannot be shaded by trees or taller plants. But there are disadvantages: the water's surface can be whipped by the wind into waves that drag and tear at them, rain might collect on a leaf and sink it, or the leaf may be frozen under water!

SMALLEST PLANTS
The duckweeds are among the smallest and simplest flowering plants in the world. Flowers are produced only in shallow water that receives plenty of sunlight. The "leaves" contain air-filled spaces called lacunae that keep them afloat.

Tiny roots absorb minerals from the water

Blanket weed

Duckweed

Surface view

Side view

Three of the many species of duckweed are shown here

Pale-green mass is made up of hundreds of threadlike plants

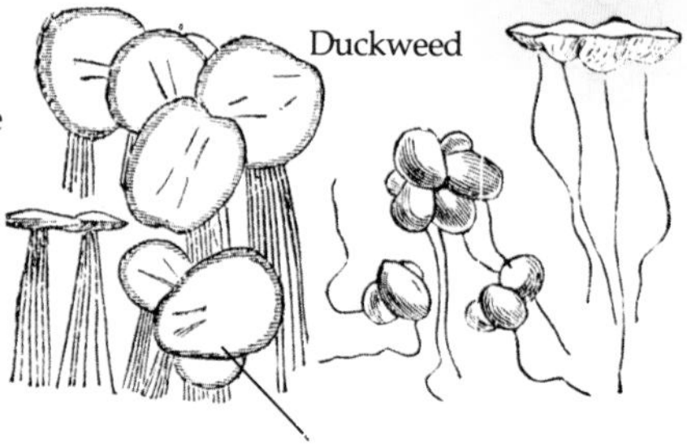

New plants produced by side shoots that break off and float away

A GREEN BLANKET
"Blanket weed" is a popular name for the green hairlike masses of algae that burst into growth in the spring. These plants can spread so quickly that they cover the surface like a blanket of green wool, blocking out light to the plants below.

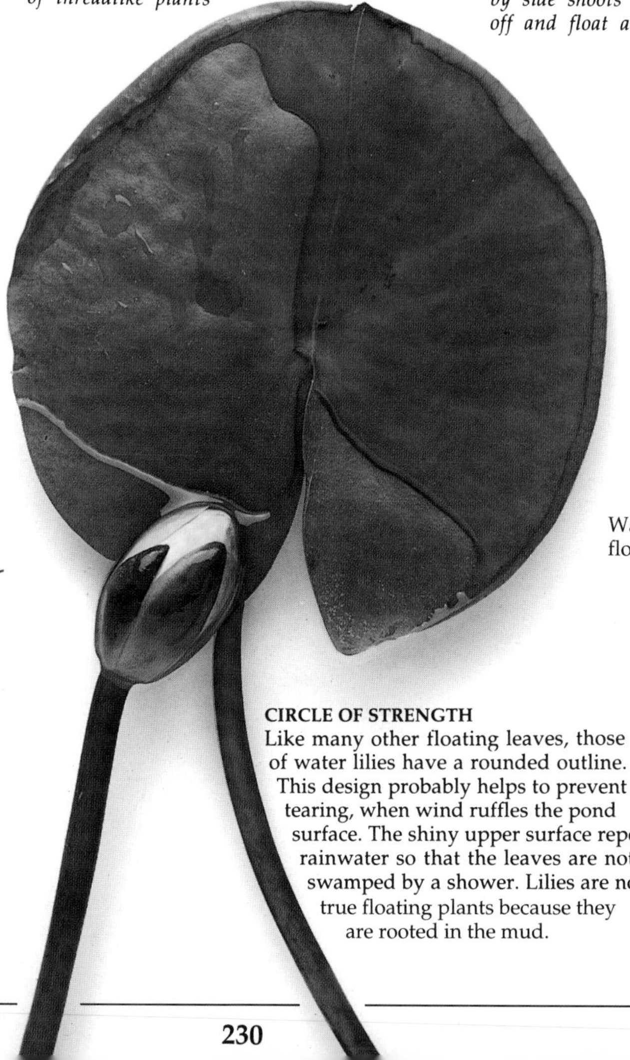

Two new leaves developing from old leaf

Ivy-leaved duckweed

Water lily leaf and flower bud

FLOWERING FLOATER
This engraving shows another species of duckweed that floats on the water surface only when it is flowering; otherwise it floats just under the water surface. The ivy-leaf shape is formed when two new leaves develop, one on each side of the original leaf.

CIRCLE OF STRENGTH
Like many other floating leaves, those of water lilies have a rounded outline. This design probably helps to prevent tearing, when wind ruffles the pond surface. The shiny upper surface repels rainwater so that the leaves are not swamped by a shower. Lilies are not true floating plants because they are rooted in the mud.

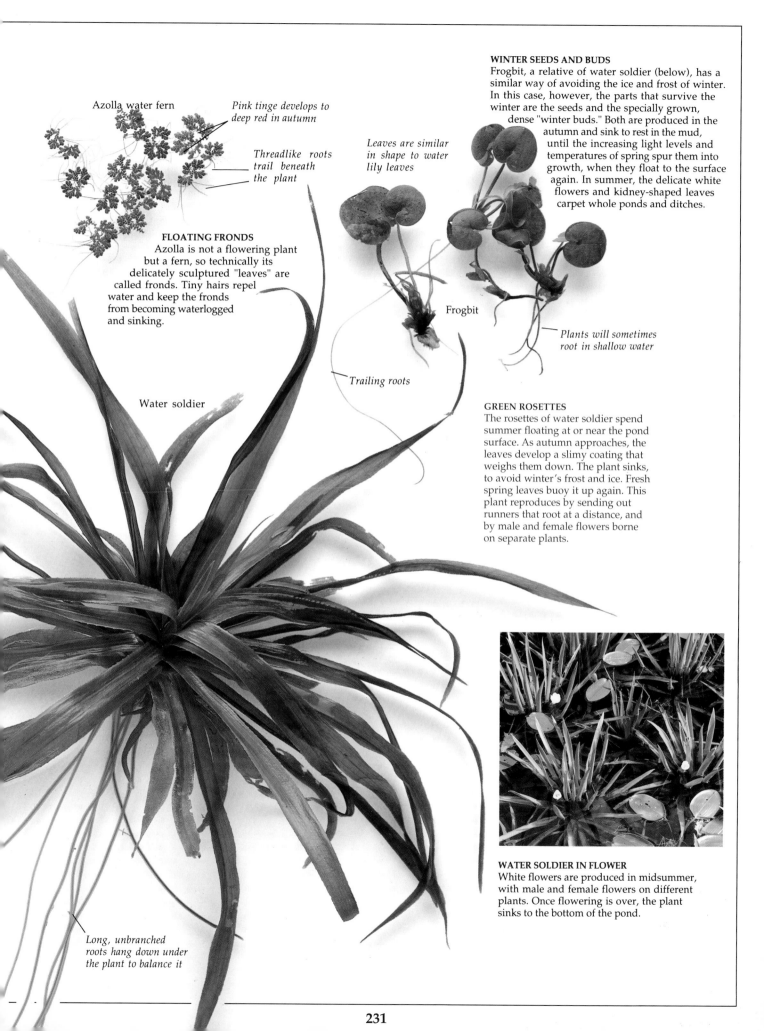

Azolla water fern

Pink tinge develops to deep red in autumn

Threadlike roots trail beneath the plant

FLOATING FRONDS

Azolla is not a flowering plant but a fern, so technically its delicately sculptured "leaves" are called fronds. Tiny hairs repel water and keep the fronds from becoming waterlogged and sinking.

Water soldier

Long, unbranched roots hang down under the plant to balance it

WINTER SEEDS AND BUDS

Frogbit, a relative of water soldier (below), has a similar way of avoiding the ice and frost of winter. In this case, however, the parts that survive the winter are the seeds and the specially grown, dense "winter buds." Both are produced in the autumn and sink to rest in the mud, until the increasing light levels and temperatures of spring spur them into growth, when they float to the surface again. In summer, the delicate white flowers and kidney-shaped leaves carpet whole ponds and ditches.

Leaves are similar in shape to water lily leaves

Frogbit

Trailing roots

Plants will sometimes root in shallow water

GREEN ROSETTES

The rosettes of water soldier spend summer floating at or near the pond surface. As autumn approaches, the leaves develop a slimy coating that weighs them down. The plant sinks, to avoid winter's frost and ice. Fresh spring leaves buoy it up again. This plant reproduces by sending out runners that root at a distance, and by male and female flowers borne on separate plants.

WATER SOLDIER IN FLOWER

White flowers are produced in midsummer, with male and female flowers on different plants. Once flowering is over, the plant sinks to the bottom of the pond.

231

Underwater weeds

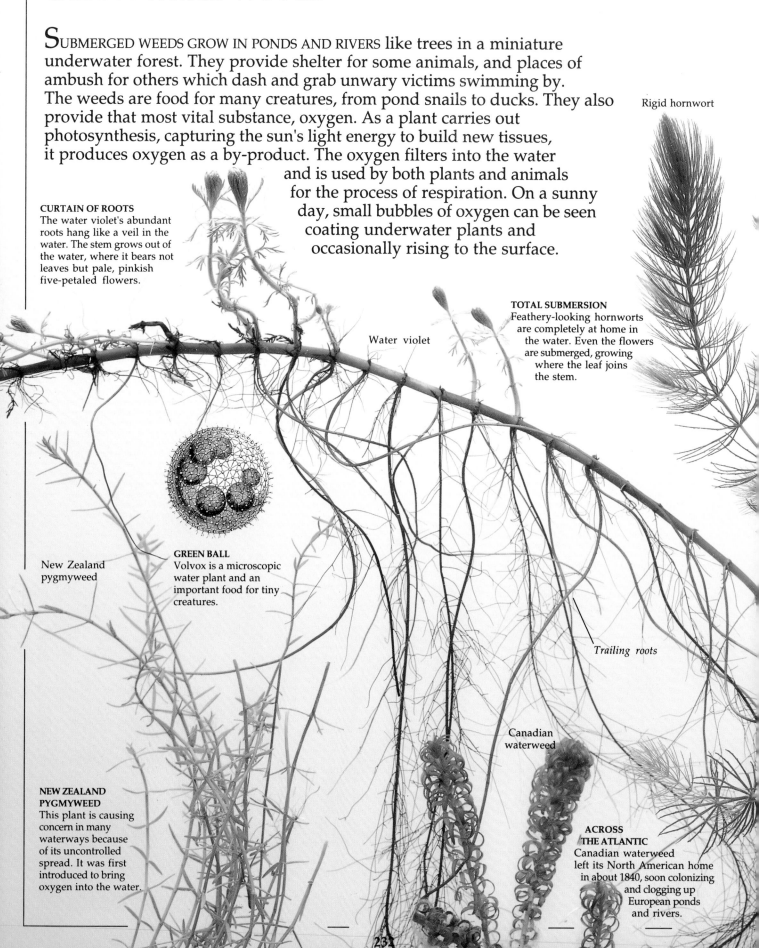

SUBMERGED WEEDS GROW IN PONDS AND RIVERS like trees in a miniature underwater forest. They provide shelter for some animals, and places of ambush for others which dash and grab unwary victims swimming by. The weeds are food for many creatures, from pond snails to ducks. They also provide that most vital substance, oxygen. As a plant carries out photosynthesis, capturing the sun's light energy to build new tissues, it produces oxygen as a by-product. The oxygen filters into the water and is used by both plants and animals for the process of respiration. On a sunny day, small bubbles of oxygen can be seen coating underwater plants and occasionally rising to the surface.

Rigid hornwort

CURTAIN OF ROOTS
The water violet's abundant roots hang like a veil in the water. The stem grows out of the water, where it bears not leaves but pale, pinkish five-petaled flowers.

Water violet

TOTAL SUBMERSION
Feathery-looking hornworts are completely at home in the water. Even the flowers are submerged, growing where the leaf joins the stem.

New Zealand pygmyweed

GREEN BALL
Volvox is a microscopic water plant and an important food for tiny creatures.

Trailing roots

Canadian waterweed

NEW ZEALAND PYGMYWEED
This plant is causing concern in many waterways because of its uncontrolled spread. It was first introduced to bring oxygen into the water.

ACROSS THE ATLANTIC
Canadian waterweed left its North American home in about 1840, soon colonizing and clogging up European ponds and rivers.

POND "PLANKTON"
At 25X magnification, the microscopic world of underwater plants is revealed.

PERCH IN THE GRASS
Tape grass is one of the popularly named "river" grasses. It offers a hideout for fish, particularly the perch, which is camouflaged by its vertical stripes.

Tape grass

Narrow leaves resemble the needles of a fir tree

Bulbous rush

SLENDER WATERWEED
The pale-green water starwort sways in clumps in the water.

FLUSHED RUSH
The bulbous rush is usually rooted on the pond's side, but sometimes it grows underwater, and becomes very long.

Water starwort

Dragonflies and damselflies

THESE LARGE, POWERFUL FLYERS speed back and forth along the bank and over the water's surface, using their enormous eyes to search out small creatures. Like those of other insects, the dragonfly's eyes are made up of many separate lenses that probably give a mosaic-like picture of the world. As the adults dart about above, the water-dwelling nymphs (babies) crawl on the pond bottom. Like their parents, they seize and eat any small creature they can catch, from other water insects to tadpoles and fish.

Damselflies

These are smaller and more slender relatives of dragonflies. Although at first glance they appear very similar in shape and way of life, there are several important differences that set them apart from the dragonflies - most obviously the fact that the damselfly holds its two pairs of wings together over its back when resting, while the dragonfly holds them out flat at the sides of its body.

SIMILAR WINGS
A damselfly's wings are roughly equal in size, with rounded ends, unlike the dragonfly's wings.

Blue-tailed damselfly

Emerald damselfly

Eyes protrude from side of head

Rounded wing tips

MALE AND FEMALE
In most damselflies, the female has a slightly wider and less colorful abdomen than the male.

Azure damselfly

Large red damselfly

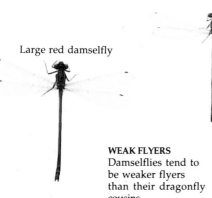

SMALLER EYES
The small eyes of the damselfly are set on the sides of the head; the dragonfly's eyes meet at the top of the head.

WEAK FLYERS
Damselflies tend to be weaker flyers than their dragonfly cousins.

Cast-off nymphal skin

Broad-bodied libellula nymph

Mask — Hooks on mask spear prey

Young southern hawker nymph

— Mask

THE DEADLY MASK
Dragonfly nymphs are the scourge of the pond, eating anything they can catch with their "mask." This is a horny flap, like the lower lip, which has two vicious hooks at the end (above). Normally the mask is folded under the head, but it is hinged so that it can suddenly shoot out to spear prey, which is then pulled back to the mouth.

CAST-OFF CLOTHING
This perfectly detailed empty skin is from a brown hawker dragonfly's final molt. New adults usually emerge at night or early in the morning, to avoid enemies.

THE MATING GAME
The male dragonfly clasps the female and she bends to pick up the sperm from a special organ at the front of his abdomen.

THE LIFE OF THE DRAGONFLY
A dragonfly begins life as an egg laid in water. It hatches into a larva that grows by splitting its skin and forming a new, larger skin. There are between eight and 15 molts over two years or more, depending on the species. A gradual change to adult form like this (compared with a sudden change; for example, caterpillar to butterfly) is called "incomplete metamorphosis." During the in-between stages the insect is referred to as a nymph. Finally the nymph climbs up a stem into the air, splits its skin a final time, and the adult emerges.

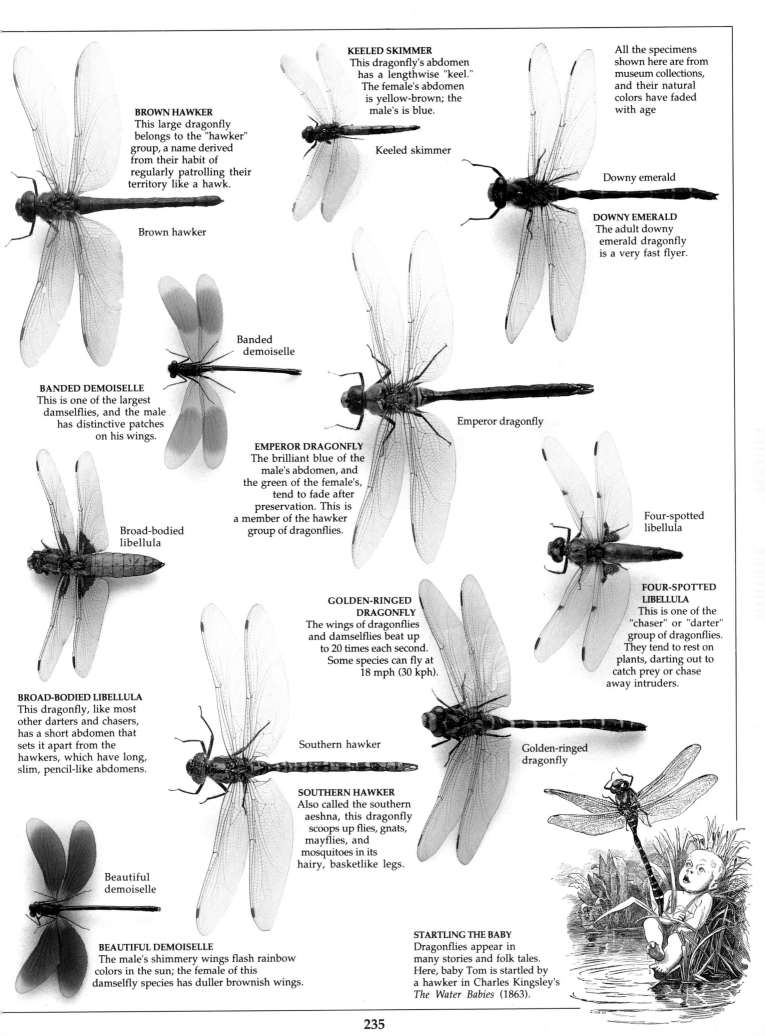

BROWN HAWKER
This large dragonfly belongs to the "hawker" group, a name derived from their habit of regularly patrolling their territory like a hawk.

Brown hawker

KEELED SKIMMER
This dragonfly's abdomen has a lengthwise "keel." The female's abdomen is yellow-brown; the male's is blue.

Keeled skimmer

All the specimens shown here are from museum collections, and their natural colors have faded with age

Downy emerald

DOWNY EMERALD
The adult downy emerald dragonfly is a very fast flyer.

Banded demoiselle

BANDED DEMOISELLE
This is one of the largest damselflies, and the male has distinctive patches on his wings.

Emperor dragonfly

EMPEROR DRAGONFLY
The brilliant blue of the male's abdomen, and the green of the female's, tend to fade after preservation. This is a member of the hawker group of dragonflies.

Broad-bodied libellula

Four-spotted libellula

FOUR-SPOTTED LIBELLULA
This is one of the "chaser" or "darter" group of dragonflies. They tend to rest on plants, darting out to catch prey or chase away intruders.

GOLDEN-RINGED DRAGONFLY
The wings of dragonflies and damselflies beat up to 20 times each second. Some species can fly at 18 mph (30 kph).

BROAD-BODIED LIBELLULA
This dragonfly, like most other darters and chasers, has a short abdomen that sets it apart from the hawkers, which have long, slim, pencil-like abdomens.

Southern hawker

Golden-ringed dragonfly

SOUTHERN HAWKER
Also called the southern aeshna, this dragonfly scoops up flies, gnats, mayflies, and mosquitoes in its hairy, basketlike legs.

Beautiful demoiselle

BEAUTIFUL DEMOISELLE
The male's shimmery wings flash rainbow colors in the sun; the female of this damselfly species has duller brownish wings.

STARTLING THE BABY
Dragonflies appear in many stories and folk tales. Here, baby Tom is startled by a hawker in Charles Kingsley's *The Water Babies* (1863).

235

Insects in the water

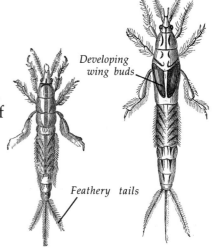

INSECTS, the most adaptable creatures on earth, can live in places ranging from glaciers to hot springs, from deserts to tropical forests. About half of the 25 major groups of insects live in fresh water. Some, such as water beetles and bugs, spend nearly all their lives in water. Others, like mayflies and caddis flies, have a watery "childhood" and emerge into the air when adult. Certain aquatic insects, including the water beetles, are air-breathing and visit the surface regularly to obtain supplies, which they store by various clever means. Others have specialized "gills" to take oxygen from the water, and still others can absorb dissolved oxygen through their skin.

Developing wing buds

Feathery tails

Like dragonfly larvae, mayfly larvae are called nymphs

As the nymph matures, small "wing buds" grow with each molt

Rat-tailed maggots (drone fly larvae)

Breathing tube

Adult drone fly

MAGGOT'S PARENT
The rat-tailed maggot is the larva of the drone fly, a type of hover fly, named because it looks like the drones of the honey bee.

Adult mayfly

Long "tails" identify this insect

MAGGOT WITH SNORKEL *above*
The rat-tailed maggot has a long breathing tube of three sections that telescope into one another. It lives in the mud of shallow ponds, sucking up decaying food.

THREE-TAILED FLY
Like its larvae, the adult mayfly has three very distinctive trailing "tails." Mayflies are known as "spinners" by people who fish.

GROWN-UP CADDIS
Adult caddis flies are less well-known than their water-dwelling youngsters. The adults are drab gray or brown, come out at dusk or night, and are easily confused with small moths. They flit about near water, rarely feed, and seldom live more than a few days.

Larval cases may be attached to water plants or lie on the pond bottom

STICKS AND STONES
Many species of caddis fly have aquatic larvae that build protective cases around themselves. The construction material is characteristic of each species. As the larva grows, it adds more material to the front of the case.

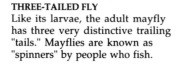

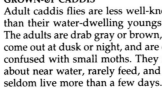

Case is extended by adding material to the front end

Head of larva emerges from case to feed

Every species makes a distinctive case

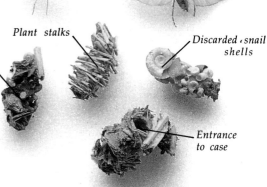

SPRING FEAST
Mayfly adults emerge in huge swarms in spring. They fly weakly, have no mouths and so cannot feed, and spend their few days of adult life mating and laying eggs by dipping their abdomens in water. The "dance of the mayflies" attracts hungry fish - and anglers (people who fish) who use mayfly lures to catch trout.

Adult caddis flies

Wings covered with fine hairs

Antennae often as long as the body

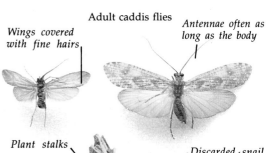

Plant stalks

Discarded snail shells

Small stones

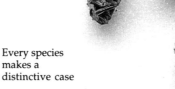

Entrance to case

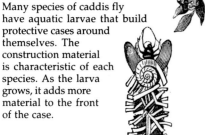

Cases built by caddisfly larvae

Front legs seize prey

Water stick insect

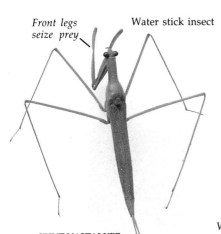

Front legs catch tadpoles and other prey

Water scorpion

Water scorpion

Pond skater

Rowing legs

Steering legs

DEAD LEAF?
When disturbed, the water scorpion sinks to the bottom and stays still, looking like a dead leaf.

WATER WALKER
The back four feet of the pond skater have thick pads of hair that repel water, and keep this bug from sinking as it rows across the surface of the pond.

SPINDLY STALKER
The water stick insect grabs any small underwater creature with its mantis-like front legs and then sucks the juices from inside, using its needle-shaped mouthparts. A short trip to the surface allows fresh supplies of air to be sucked through the long tail, the two parts of which are usually held together by bristles to form a tube.

Parts of breathing tube

Breathing tube

Wing covers

Back swimmer

Water boatman

Hair-covered legs for swimming

STING IN THE TAIL?
No, the "tail" of the water scorpion is a harmless breathing tube, unlike the poisonous version of its dry-land namesake. The dangerous parts are the powerful clawlike front legs and stinging beak-shaped mouth.

BACK SWIMMER . . .
The back swimmer is a bug, not a beetle. This unusual top view shows its hard wing cases that cover strong flying wings. Most of its time, however, is spent hanging upside down below the water surface.

WATER BOATMAN
This insect's name refers to the oarlike rowing motions of its legs as it moves itself through the water. It eats any plant debris or algae it can grub up or catch in its sieve-like front legs.

Air bubble

THE BUBBLE CHAMBER
The air-breathing water spider (not actually an insect but an arachnid) makes a "diving bell" to live in. It weaves a web among water plants and stocks it with air from the surface (below). The air being transported in its body hairs gives the spider's abdomen a silvery sheen (left).

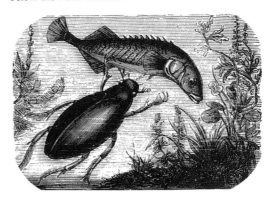

BEETLE POWER
In a small pond, the great diving beetle has few predators but many prey - insects, tadpoles, and small fish such as this unlucky stickleback.

SPARE AIR
Water beetles are air-breathing insects and have devised clever methods for collecting air from the surface. Many aquatic beetles trap air on the hairs under their bodies. Others trap air under their wing cases, making them buoyant and always struggling to swim downward. Some, like the silver water beetle shown here, use both methods.

Silver water beetle

Freshwater shells

ALL THE LIFE-SIZED SHELLS shown here have two features in common: their builder-owners live in fresh water, and they belong to the mollusk group. The mollusk's shell is made chiefly of calcium-containing minerals such as calcium carbonate (lime). To make its shell, the animal must absorb minerals from the water. In general, aquatic mollusks are more common in "hard-water" areas, where water is naturally richer in dissolved minerals. The mussels and cockles (bivalves) feed by sucking in a stream of water and filtering out tiny food particles. Most snails and limpets (gastropods) "graze", on water plants and the algal "scum" on submerged stones, but some species can filter-feed.

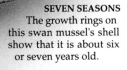

SEVEN SEASONS
The growth rings on this swan mussel's shell show that it is about six or seven years old.

How do mollusks breathe?

Water snails are divided into two groups, depending on how they breathe. The great pond snail, ram's-horn snail, and bladder snail are known as pulmonates - they breathe air, like land snails. They float up to the surface, open a breathing aperture (hole) and take a gulp of air into a lung-like cavity. The other group, including valve, river, and spire snails, are called prosobranchs. They breathe by absorbing oxygen from the water through gills.

DUCK MUSSEL
This bivalve's shell is more swollen than that of the swan mussel.

RIGHT-HANDERS
Usually great pond snail shells curl to the right, but "left-handers" are known.

WANDERING SNAIL
The whorls of this wandering snail are squashed up at its tip.

SEE-THROUGH SNAIL
The nautilus ram's-horn is so small that its shell is semi-transparent.

BIVALVE PANTRY
Pea mussels are the staple food of many fish and water birds.

CURLY WHORLY
The tightly coiled white ram's-horn is from ponds and streams.

MARBLED SNAIL
The nerite snail has an attractively speckled and whorled shell.

JOINTED SHELL
The horny pea cockle is a bivalve mollusk as it has two shells.

River shellfish

The mollusks below and left (swan and duck mussels) tend to live in flowing water, rather than the still waters of ponds and lakes. The growth rings of the mussels indicate their age, which might be up to a dozen years for a large individual. Growth rings can be seen on snails, too, but they are less clearly divided into a year-by-year pattern.

Snails grow by adding new material at the open end of the shell

TWISTING TUBE
Snail shells are coiled, gradually widening tubes, clearly seen on this Lister's river snail.

MINERAL COLLECTOR
River snail's shells may be over 2 in (5 cm) long - a lot of calcium to collect.

LISTENING SNAIL
The ear pond snail's flared opening resembles a human ear.

SWOLLEN JOINT
This tumid unio mussel has an inflated "umbo" near its hinge line.

ZEBRA MUSSEL
This bivalve is anchored to rocks by sticky threads.

WATERWEED EATER
The great ram's-horn water snail browses on underwater plants.

DISTINCTIVE SHELL
The last whorl on the bladder snail's shell is large compared to the other whorls.

STUBBY AND SHINY
These shiny, compact shells belong to the common bithynia.

BITHYNIA LEACHI
These bithynias have no common name; only a scientific name.

STRAIGHT SNAIL
The river limpet is a true snail, but its shell is not coiled.

OPEN AND SHUT
The "valve" of the valve snail is the door or operculum, of its shell.

SLOW WATER
The lake limpet can often be found in slow-flowing rivers.

OPENING THE DOOR
The operculum, or door, to the shell allows the snail to emerge to feed.

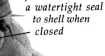

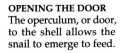

Operculum makes a watertight seal to shell when closed

TWO TINY SHELLS
Pea shell cockles are tiny, filter-feeding bivalve mollusks.

SALTY AND FRESH
Jenkin's spire shells are found in estuaries as well as in ponds and rivers.

The head of the river

MANY RIVERS begin life as fast-flowing upland streams, cascading across open areas or through craggy woodlands. The deep, rocky gulleys, the overhanging trees, and the splashing waters create contrasting worlds: damp, shady banks with lush green vegetation, and stream beds where rushing water washes away nearly all plant life and any but the most stubbornly clinging animals. In a flood, entire plant and animal communities may be swept away. Yet somehow new seeds and spores soon spring up, and creatures creep out from under rocks to fight their way back upstream.

Dipper

UNDERWATER WALKER
The dipper bobs its head as it stands on midstream rocks, watching for small animal prey. It can also walk along the river-bed, head facing upstream and tail acting as a rudder in the current, to keep its feet firmly on the bottom.

ARMORED CRAYFISH
Hard (mineral-rich) water is favored by the freshwater crayfish, a relative of the marine lobster. It needs plenty of calcium minerals to build its shell.

Hard outer shell made up from minerals in the water

Freshwater crayfish

BANKSIDE MOISTURE LOVERS
Succulent growths of mosses, liverworts, ferns, and other damp-loving plants colonize the banks and splash-zone rocks. The larger heart-shaped leaves are marsh violet.

Polytrichum moss

Fern

Puffball

Liverwort

YOUNG BALL
Fungi, such as this young member of the puffball group, prefer shady stream-side conditions.

LICHEN BRANCH
Shady, damp conditions are ideal for certain lichens, which are co-operative combinations of fungi and algae. Two different kinds of leafy lichen are growing on this branch.

Great wood rush

Liverwort

Marsh violet

Bullhead

UPSTREAM FISH
Despite the fast current fish, such as the bullhead, are found at the head of the river. The bullhead's flattened shape allows it to hide under stones.

Oak leaves

FOOD FROM ABOVE
Trees such as the oak hang
over the water, and if their
fruits and leaves fall into the
water they provide food for
river-dwellers.

Fontinalis
moss

Acorns

*Galls (swellings) caused
by insects*

*Deeply divided
fronds*

Great wood rush

BETWEEN THE BOULDERS
Groups of midstream boulders
often support a thriving
island of life; here, great
wood rush sprouts from soil
collected by the current.

UNDERWATER MOSS
Fontinalis or "willow moss," anchored to a
stone or fallen log, moves back and forth with
the current in slower streams and rivers.

*Shiny,
undivided
fronds*

*Rows of
spores*

*Layer of moss
growing on
boulders*

Male fern

FEATHERY FRONDS
Many types of ferns thrive in the
shaded, humid conditions along
riverbanks. The hart's-tongue
fern (far right) has riblike
rows of brown spore cases
on the undersides of its fronds.
It is unusual among ferns
in having solid,
unbranched fronds.

*Feathery,
pale-green
fronds*

*Shiny,
dark-green
fronds*

Hard-
fern

Lady fern

Hart's-tongue
fern

Brown spore cases

Life along the riverbank

As STREAMS BECOME MORE SEDATE and their courses join up and widen, the river comes into being. But when does a stream become a river? One definition is that streams are less than 15 ft (5 m) wide, while rivers are more. Larger rivers usually have a slower current, allowing rooted plants to grow well at the water's edge. Whatever the distinction, riverbank life suits many kinds of plants and animals. On a high-banked river, the soil at the water's edge is nearly always saturated, but it becomes drier higher up the bank. So plant life often grows in zones, with mud-rooted irises and water plantains lower down, and the damp-ground hemp agrimony, balsam, and similar flowers slightly higher.

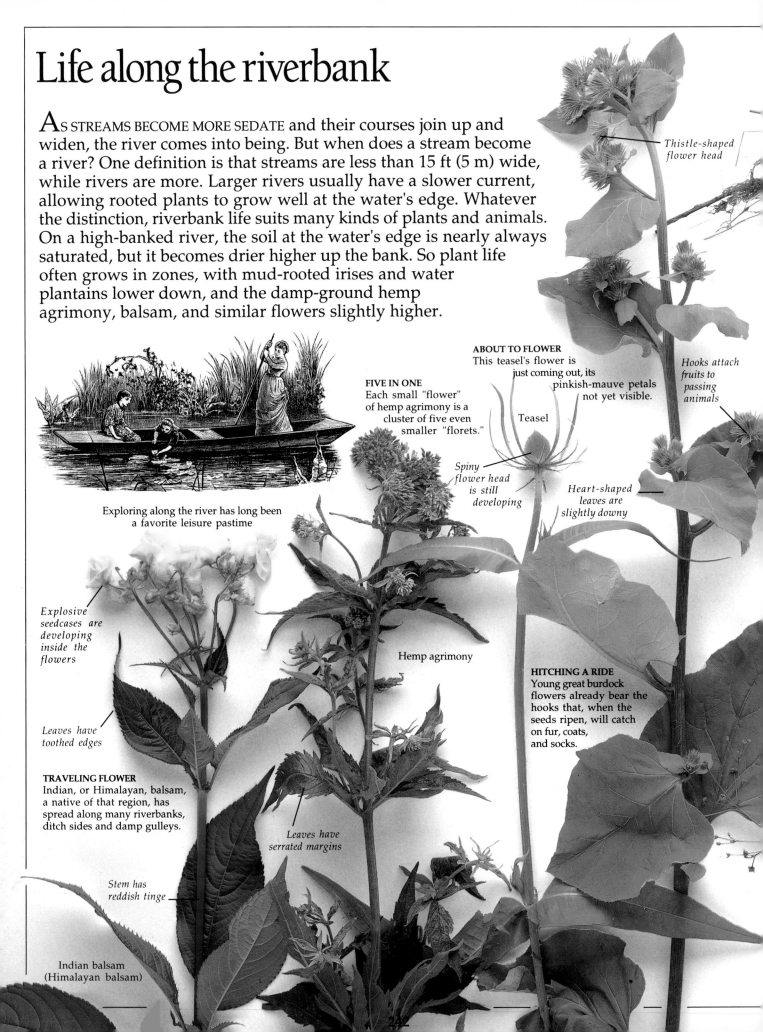

Thistle-shaped flower head

Hooks attach fruits to passing animals

ABOUT TO FLOWER
This teasel's flower is just coming out, its pinkish-mauve petals not yet visible.

FIVE IN ONE
Each small "flower" of hemp agrimony is a cluster of five even smaller "florets."

Teasel

Spiny flower head is still developing

Heart-shaped leaves are slightly downy

Exploring along the river has long been a favorite leisure pastime

Explosive seedcases are developing inside the flowers

Hemp agrimony

HITCHING A RIDE
Young great burdock flowers already bear the hooks that, when the seeds ripen, will catch on fur, coats, and socks.

Leaves have toothed edges

TRAVELING FLOWER
Indian, or Himalayan, balsam, a native of that region, has spread along many riverbanks, ditch sides and damp gulleys.

Leaves have serrated margins

Stem has reddish tinge

Indian balsam (Himalayan balsam)

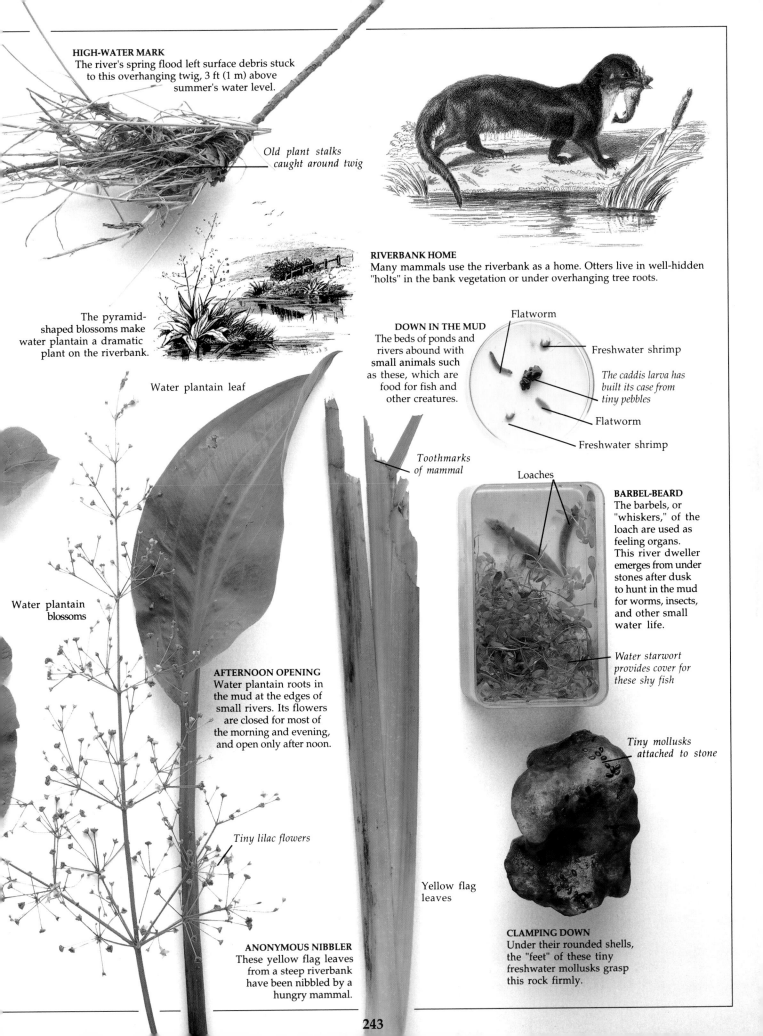

HIGH-WATER MARK
The river's spring flood left surface debris stuck to this overhanging twig, 3 ft (1 m) above summer's water level.

Old plant stalks caught around twig

The pyramid-shaped blossoms make water plantain a dramatic plant on the riverbank.

Water plantain leaf

Water plantain blossoms

RIVERBANK HOME
Many mammals use the riverbank as a home. Otters live in well-hidden "holts" in the bank vegetation or under overhanging tree roots.

Flatworm

DOWN IN THE MUD
The beds of ponds and rivers abound with small animals such as these, which are food for fish and other creatures.

Freshwater shrimp

The caddis larva has built its case from tiny pebbles

Flatworm

Freshwater shrimp

Toothmarks of mammal

Loaches

BARBEL-BEARD
The barbels, or "whiskers," of the loach are used as feeling organs. This river dweller emerges from under stones after dusk to hunt in the mud for worms, insects, and other small water life.

Water starwort provides cover for these shy fish

AFTERNOON OPENING
Water plantain roots in the mud at the edges of small rivers. Its flowers are closed for most of the morning and evening, and open only after noon.

Tiny lilac flowers

Yellow flag leaves

Tiny mollusks attached to stone

ANONYMOUS NIBBLER
These yellow flag leaves from a steep riverbank have been nibbled by a hungry mammal.

CLAMPING DOWN
Under their rounded shells, the "feet" of these tiny freshwater mollusks grasp this rock firmly.

The river's mouth

T HE RIVER'S COURSE is ended. Its banks curl out to become the seashore, and the tide brings in salt water that begins to impose itself on the plant and animal life. The last stretch of a river is known as the estuary, and it is here that the river's currents slow down to a crawl and the smallest mud and silt particles slowly settle on the bed and banks. The water, mixed by waves and tides, is often cloudy so submerged plants are rare, since they do not receive enough light for photosynthesis (p. 196). Relatively few plants and animals are adapted to the enormous variations in salt concentration, but those that are face little competition and so are often found in huge numbers. The specimens shown below were all collected from an estuary, to give some idea of the range of animals and plants that can be found at the mouth of the river.

MOLTED FEATHERS
Discarded feathers are a common find on the estuary and are evidence of the species that live there.

Molted feathers

Washed-up bone

Gull

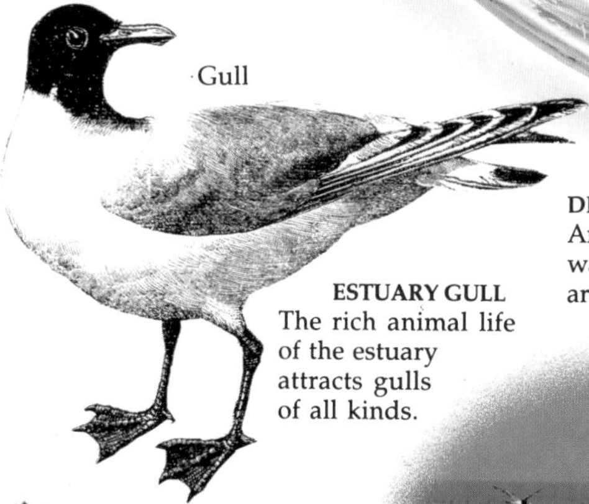

ESTUARY GULL
The rich animal life of the estuary attracts gulls of all kinds.

DISCARDED SKELETONS
Among the treasures you can find washed up on the edge of the estuary are various bones.

Glasswort

Sea spurge

GLASS FROM PLANTS
The glassworts are so named because in former times their ashes (being high in sodium carbonate) were used to make glass. They are common on estuaries and salt marshes and have thick, juicy leaves.

CREEPING ABOUT
The sea spurge's creeping stem spreads through the sand dunes at the river's mouth. Like glasswort, it has thick, fleshy leaves.

DINNERTIME AT LOW TIDE
Flocks of oystercatchers and other waders crowd on to the estuary mud at low tide, pecking and probing for worms, shrimps, shellfish, and crabs.

Fleshy leaves store water

Glasswort

Sea sandwort

Eel grass

Feathers

Roots begin to stabilize estuary mud

ESTUARY DUMP
The calmer waters of the estuary's tidal inlets are nature's dumping ground for all kinds of seaside debris, from dried-out seaweeds and eel grass to feathers, bits of weeds, and dead crabs.

A LOT TO LEARN
Oystercatcher chicks hatch from eggs laid in open or short vegetation around the estuary. The chicks can take up to 26 weeks to learn the specialized feeding techniques from their parents.

Tellina

Winkles

Cockle

Periwinkle

Mussel

Oyster shell

Tellina shell

Young crab

Cockleshell

Hole pecked by bird

HOLE IN ONE
These mollusk shells have been pecked through by estuary birds and the animal inside has been eaten.

Oystercatcher and chick

Cockleshell

Tellina shell

UNDER THE BREAKWATER
Any "obstruction" on the flat estuary, such as a breakwater or pier, soon becomes colonized by a variety of life that can tolerate the different salt levels. The sea slater is a crustacean, cousin of the wood louse, and also a relative of the crab.

Sea slater

Lugworm

Oyster shell

SHORE WORM
Squiggly marks on the estuary mud mark the position of a lugworm's U-shaped burrow.

Sheldrake and chick

Slipper limpet

Cockle-shell

Barnacles

SHELDRAKE DUCKLING
Young sheldrakes look like most other ducklings, but the adults look more like geese. This waterfowl eats not only shellfish but also fish, worms, and other small animals.

Razor shell

IN FROM THE SEA
The shells of true seashore mollusks are often washed up on the estuary shore, as was this small barnacle-encrusted stone, loosened by a storm.

Crab

PIPEFISH
This relative of the seahorse has hardened outer skin and moves using its dorsal (back) fin. It copes well in the changing salt levels of estuary water.

Pipefish

Spiral wrack

SHORE WEED
In the more sheltered and seaward sites, shore algae can gain a foothold. This spiral wrack is characteristic of the upper shore zone.

The salt marsh

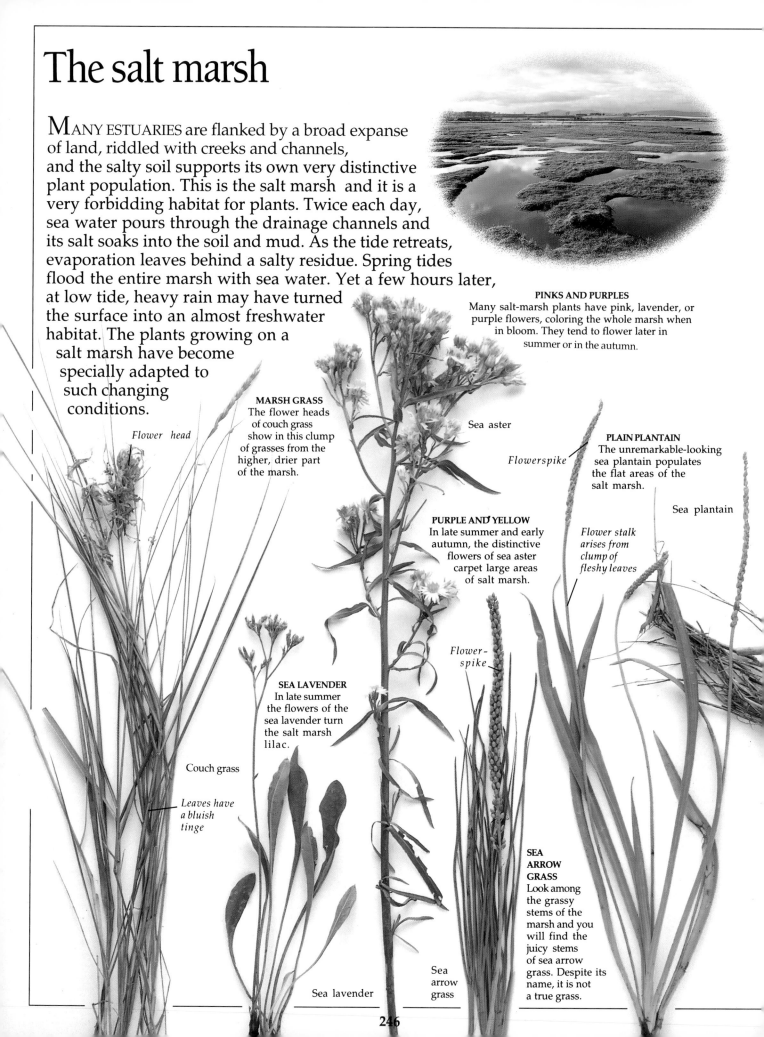

MANY ESTUARIES are flanked by a broad expanse
of land, riddled with creeks and channels,
and the salty soil supports its own very distinctive
plant population. This is the salt marsh and it is a
very forbidding habitat for plants. Twice each day,
sea water pours through the drainage channels and
its salt soaks into the soil and mud. As the tide retreats,
evaporation leaves behind a salty residue. Spring tides
flood the entire marsh with sea water. Yet a few hours later,
at low tide, heavy rain may have turned
the surface into an almost freshwater
habitat. The plants growing on a
salt marsh have become
specially adapted to
such changing
conditions.

Flower head

MARSH GRASS
The flower heads
of couch grass
show in this clump
of grasses from the
higher, drier part
of the marsh.

Sea aster

PINKS AND PURPLES
Many salt-marsh plants have pink, lavender, or
purple flowers, coloring the whole marsh when
in bloom. They tend to flower later in
summer or in the autumn.

PLAIN PLANTAIN
The unremarkable-looking
sea plantain populates
the flat areas of the
salt marsh.

Flowerspike

Sea plantain

PURPLE AND YELLOW
In late summer and early
autumn, the distinctive
flowers of sea aster
carpet large areas
of salt marsh.

*Flower stalk
arises from
clump of
fleshy leaves*

*Flower-
spike*

SEA LAVENDER
In late summer
the flowers of the
sea lavender turn
the salt marsh
lilac.

Couch grass

*Leaves have
a bluish
tinge*

SEA
ARROW
GRASS
Look among
the grassy
stems of the
marsh and you
will find the
juicy stems
of sea arrow
grass. Despite its
name, it is not
a true grass.

Sea lavender

Sea
arrow
grass

246

SILVER-GREEN LEAVES
The silvery leaves are covered with tiny air-filled protective scales. Sea purslane grows along the edges of the channels and creeks within the salt marsh.

Ripening seed heads

Sea purslane

Leaves take up or lose water as the salt level changes

FLESHY LEAVES
The thick, fleshy leaves of salt-marsh dwellers are well represented by this annual seablite.

Juicy leaves store water

BINDING IN THE MARSH
Cord grass, an early colonizer of the bare mud, is often planted on the lower parts of marshes and estuaries to stabilize them with its underground stems and thick root system.

Cord grass

RICH PICKINGS
Knots and other wading birds probe the mud of salt-marsh channels for food.

Glasswort

Swollen, jointed stems store water

Annual seablite

The leaves produce salt crystals to rid the plant of excess salt

Thick roots

SALT-MARSH STABILIZER
Glasswort is one of the first plants to colonize the estuary mud, its delicate roots beginning the stabilizing process.

TIDAL DEBRIS
Each tide sweeps old stems, bits of crabs, and other debris along the channels that riddle the marsh.

CAST-UP REMAINS
Young shore crabs, young cockles, and a whelk's spongy, empty egg case are some of the items found when "marsh-combing" along the channel edges.

Crabs

SQUELCHING OOZE
This is the stuff of life in the salt marsh and estuary - thick, shiny mud, rich in organic matter.

Empty shells

Salt-marsh mud

Roots bind the slippery mud

Whelk egg case

Study and conservation

THE FASCINATING WILDLIFE OF PONDS AND RIVERS is suffering in our modern world. Pollution, demand for housing or farming land, and more people using the water for relaxation and recreation are all taking their toll. Conserving and preserving our natural freshwater habitats is increasingly important. It begins with study and understanding. Students of nature are interested in what lives where, and why – and they find out through observation rather than interference. When out on a field trip, they show respect for nature and obey wildlife laws. If you wish to more about ponds and rivers, use the internet or a local directory to find wildlife organizations and fisheries in your area.

THE MICROSCOPIC WORLD
A drop of pond water may look clear, but under a microscope such as this, it will be teeming with tiny water plants and animals. Magnification of about 20X to 200X is most useful.

Magnifying glasses

LOOKING THROUGH LENSES
Magnifiers enable you to identify small water creatures or examine a flower's structure. A 10X lens is about right.

Field guide

Note pad

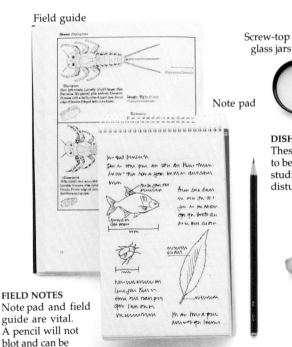

Screw-top glass jars

SHORT-STAY HOMES
Screw-top glass jars are useful for temporary storage and examination. Do not leave animals and plants in them for long.

DISHES AND DROPPERS
These allow small items to be moved gently and studied without too much disturbance.

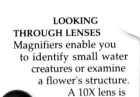

Glass dish

Dropper

SPOON AND BRUSH
These pieces of equipment enable small, delicate plants and animals to be moved for study and then replaced without harm.

Plastic spoons

FIELD NOTES
Note pad and field guide are vital. A pencil will not blot and can be sharpened carefully with a pocket knife.

FARM WASTE
Accidental spillage of farm wastes into this river killed chub, dace, roach - and thousands of smaller animals.

Waterproof camera

DAMP-PROOF SNAPS
Modern waterproof cameras allow photographs to be taken in the wettest places, even in the spray of a fast stream. Photos record nature without disturbing it.

The dangers of pollution

Ponds, rivers, and other freshwater habitats are under constant threat of pollution. Fertilizers, pesticides, and other farming chemicals are washed through the soil by rain and into watercourses, where they may badly affect the balance of nature. Industrial wastes that may enter rivers can damage water life for long stretches downstream. Most authorities have clean-water laws, but these are not always observed; "accidents" happen, and inspectors cannot monitor every backwater. We can all contribute, by reporting suspicions to the authorities, or by volunteering to help clean out and restock a weed-choked pond, or by clearing a stream used as a rubbish tip.

Folding
pocket
knife

Plant cutter

Plastic bags
and ties

Fine-mesh sieve

WATERPROOFING
Aquatic plants dry out
quickly in air. Keep them
wet by carrying them in
plastic bags.

A CLEAN CUT
Take plant samples only with permission,
and with a sharp blade for minimum damage.

Fork

Trowel

SIEVE FOR SORTING
A fine-mesh sieve can
be rocked gently in
water to sort small
animals from mud
and silt.

TAKING A SAMPLE
A bucket on a string
can be tossed from a
bridge, bank, or boat
to sample the water.

Sealable plastic containers

SPLASH-PROOF CONTAINERS
Pack animals carefully in
sealable containers, using
waterweed as "padding"
to minimize splashing.

SMALL DIGGERS
If you are permitted to dig up plants
or search for muddy-bottom
creatures, use a clean, sharp
fork or trowel and take
great care.

Water-sampling
bucket

Large-mesh net

Fine-mesh net

NET RESULTS
Nets have different mesh
(sizes) for large or small specimens.
Be careful not to uproot plants.
After sorting, replace the net's contents in the water
as quickly as possible.

Black-and-
white colobus
Colobus guereza

Kapok pod
and seeds
Ceiba pentandra

Abarema idiopoda

Blue–and–
yellow macaw
Ara ararauna

Rainforest house
(South America)

250

White-lipped
tree frog
Litoria infrafronata

JUNGLE

*Clerodendrum
splendens*

Climbing fern
Leptochilus decurrens

Medicinal
Heckel
chewstick
Garcinia kola

Stone axe
(Guyana)

What is a rain forest?

TROPICAL RAIN FORESTS are perhaps the least understood and most valuable of the world's ecosystems. They are structurally complex, ages old, and have a climate that allows year-round growth. They contain a larger diversity of plants and animals than anywhere else on Earth – for example, there are 20–100 different kinds of trees in one acre of rain forest alone. These jungles have three layers – an evergreen canopy in the middle, a layer of smaller plants on the forest floor, and towering above the canopy, scattered taller trees known as emergents. The speed at which the vegetation grows and fills any gap or forest clearing impresses modern visitors as much as it did the early explorers. Rain forests all around the world are amazingly uniform in many respects. Similar niches on different continents have been filled by species that look alike but are unrelated.

COLOR IN THE CANOPY
Splashes of color in the canopy may indicate that a tree has burst into flower. It is just as likely that a flush of red, orange, pink, or white new leaves has unfurled.

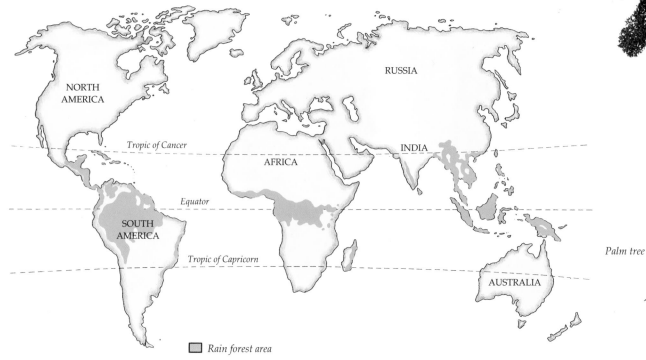

NORTH AMERICA

RUSSIA

Tropic of Cancer

INDIA

AFRICA

Equator

SOUTH AMERICA

Tropic of Capricorn

AUSTRALIA

☐ *Rain forest area*

WARM AND VERY WET
Tropical rain forests are found in permanently wet, warm areas near the equator. There are at least 60 in (1,500 mm) of rain a year, with little or no dry season. The rain falls almost every day, in torrential downpours of huge raindrops. The average temperature is around 77°F (25°C), and there is little seasonal variation.

THE FOREST FLOOR
Swamp forest soils are regularly enriched by silt-laden floodwaters. Away from flooded areas, much of the lowland forest has surprisingly poor, infertile soils called oxisols. Nutrients are locked up in living plants and animals until released by organisms such as termites and fungi.

Palm tree

Undergrowth

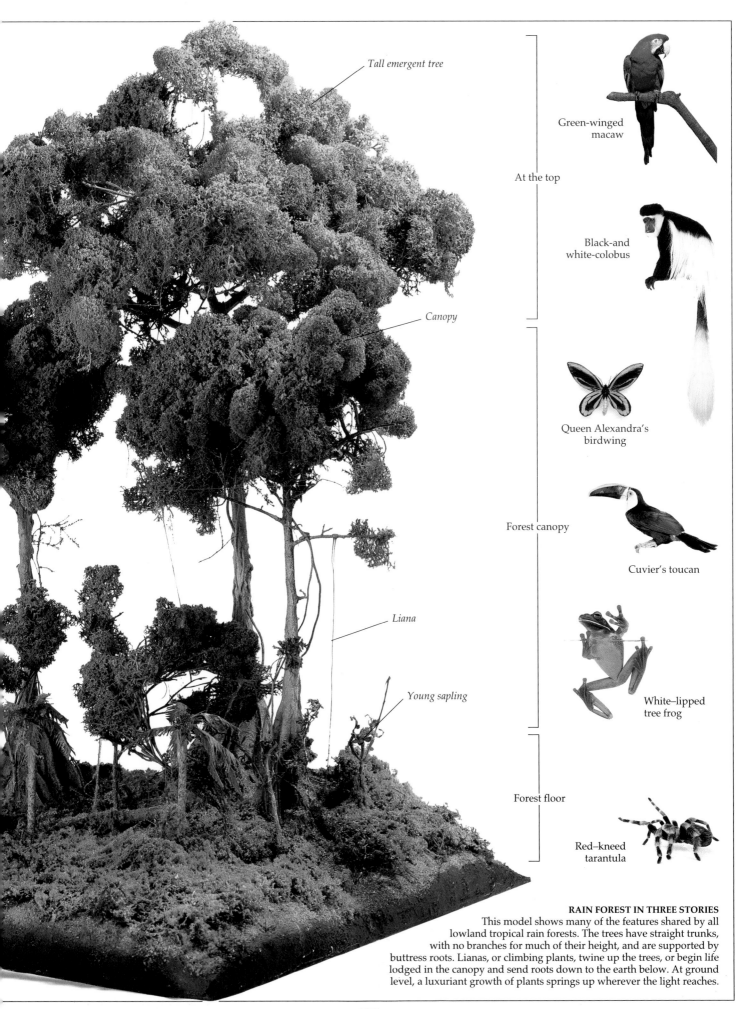

Tall emergent tree

Green-winged
macaw

At the top

Black-and
white-colobus

Canopy

Queen Alexandra's
birdwing

Forest canopy

Cuvier's toucan

Liana

Young sapling

White–lipped
tree frog

Forest floor

Red–kneed
tarantula

RAIN FOREST IN THREE STORIES
This model shows many of the features shared by all
lowland tropical rain forests. The trees have straight trunks,
with no branches for much of their height, and are supported by
buttress roots. Lianas, or climbing plants, twine up the trees, or begin life
lodged in the canopy and send roots down to the earth below. At ground
level, a luxuriant growth of plants springs up wherever the light reaches.

Tropical forests

THERE ARE SEVERAL different types of tropical forest. Lowland rain forest covers the greatest area and is found in the warm, wet lowlands where there is little or no dry season. Tropical mountainsides are thickly forested. At altitudes over 3,000 feet (900 m), lowland rain forest changes to montane or high-altitude forest, which is divided into lower montane, upper montane, and cloud forest. Cloud forest begins at heights above 10,500 feet (3,200 m). At this altitude the stunted, gnarled trees are shrouded in mist and covered with mosses and liverworts. Sometimes the division between rain forest types is clear, but often two rain forest types merge so there is no clear boundary. Seasonal or monsoon forest – not technically rain forest – also has heavy rainfall, but there is a dry season of three months or longer, during which the trees shed their leaves. Lianas and epiphytes cannot survive these dry conditions.

MONTANE FOREST
In Malaysia, lowland rain forest gives way to lower montane forest at altitudes of about 3,000 ft (900 m). The climate is cooler but still moist. There is dense tree cover, but the height of the canopy gets lower and lower. The trees have smaller leaves, and tree ferns are abundant, as are magnolias, rhododendrons, myrtles, and laurels.

CLOUD FOREST
At higher altitudes, a permanent heavy mist envelops the forest. The climate of cloud forests, such as this reserve in Ecuador, is cool and very damp. Moisture in the mists condenses on the surface of the leaves and constantly drips from them. Mosses and liverworts cover everything with a spongy blanket. Because of the lower temperatures, the leaf litter decomposes very slowly. A thick layer builds up on the ground, eventually turning into peat.

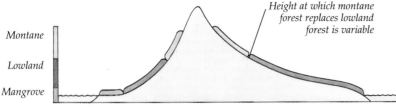

Height at which montane forest replaces lowland forest is variable

Montane

Lowland

Mangrove

RAIN FOREST LEVELS
Lowland rain forest can extend down to the coast. Wherever conditions allow (p. 9), mangrove forest grows along the coast and in river estuaries. With every 330 ft (100 m) increase in altitude, there is a drop in temperature of about 1.1°F (0.6°C).

LOWLAND RAIN FOREST
The structure of this lowland rain forest in Peru is clearly visible from the Rio de Los Amigos. In the foreground, young climbers, ferns, and saplings flourish in the higher light levels beside the river. A cycad, a remnant of a truly ancient group of plants, also grows in this clearing. Tall palms make up a large proportion of the canopy. The umbrella-shaped crowns of the huge emergent trees tower above the canopy.

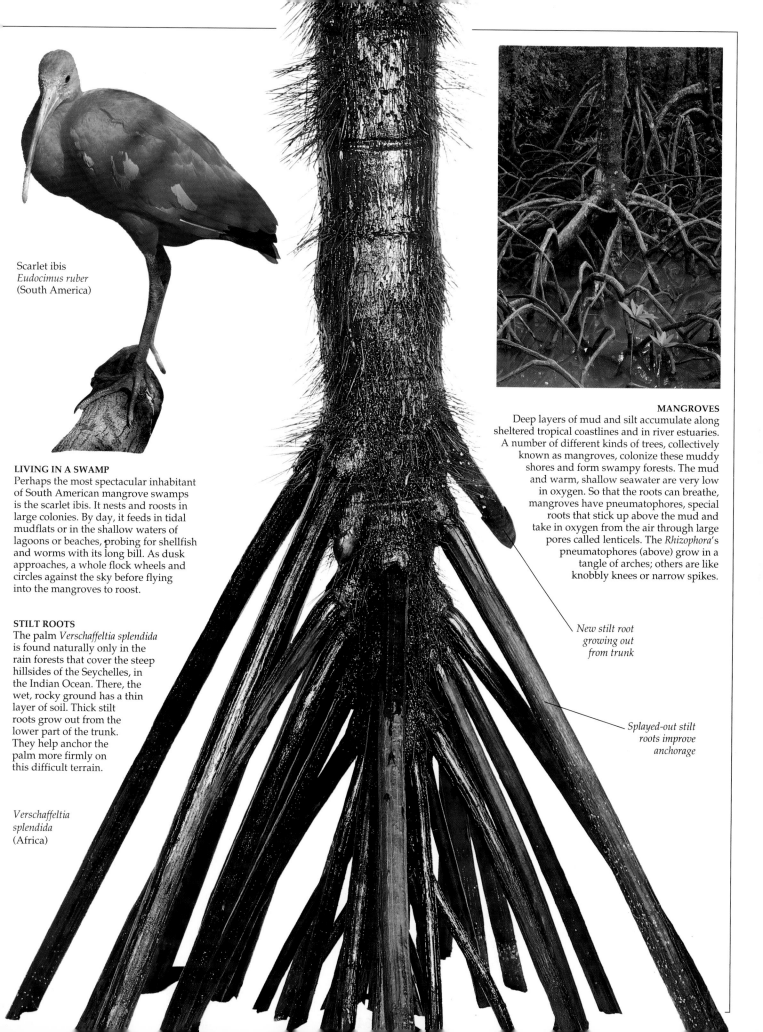

Scarlet ibis
Eudocimus ruber
(South America)

LIVING IN A SWAMP
Perhaps the most spectacular inhabitant of South American mangrove swamps is the scarlet ibis. It nests and roosts in large colonies. By day, it feeds in tidal mudflats or in the shallow waters of lagoons or beaches, probing for shellfish and worms with its long bill. As dusk approaches, a whole flock wheels and circles against the sky before flying into the mangroves to roost.

STILT ROOTS
The palm *Verschaffeltia splendida* is found naturally only in the rain forests that cover the steep hillsides of the Seychelles, in the Indian Ocean. There, the wet, rocky ground has a thin layer of soil. Thick stilt roots grow out from the lower part of the trunk. They help anchor the palm more firmly on this difficult terrain.

Verschaffeltia
splendida
(Africa)

MANGROVES
Deep layers of mud and silt accumulate along sheltered tropical coastlines and in river estuaries. A number of different kinds of trees, collectively known as mangroves, colonize these muddy shores and form swampy forests. The mud and warm, shallow seawater are very low in oxygen. So that the roots can breathe, mangroves have pneumatophores, special roots that stick up above the mud and take in oxygen from the air through large pores called lenticels. The *Rhizophora's* pneumatophores (above) grow in a tangle of arches; others are like knobbly knees or narrow spikes.

New stilt root
growing out
from trunk

Splayed-out stilt
roots improve
anchorage

At the top

TALL EMERGENT TREES tower above the rest of the jungle canopy, a few reaching heights of 200-230 ft (60-70 m). These scattered trees have straight trunks, often buttressed at the base, and a cauliflower-shaped crown. It is hotter and drier at the top of the canopy, and the temperature and humidity vary greatly. The trees are also much more windblown, and the fruit or seeds of some species are dispersed by the moving air. Many emergent trees are leafless for short periods of time, but seldom shed alltheir leaves at once. The epiphytes that live on the boughs of these trees include drought-resistant species of bromeliads, lichens, and cacti.

MONKEY BUSINESS
The striking black-and-white colobus monkey lives at the top of the jungle, feeding on leaves.

PENANG FOREST
Tualang trees (*Koompassia excelsa*) often reach 230 ft (70 m) – but a 285 ft (87 m) tualang holds the record for the tallest broad-leaved rain forest tree. Malaysians believe that spirits live in these trees.

Sun conure
Aratinga solstitialis
(South America)

FLYING FORAGER
Conures live in noisy flocks high up in the treetops. They fly restlessly from tree to tree, feeding on flower buds, fruits, seeds, and insects.

Leaves have a waxy surface

GREEN SHADES
The tall canopy tree *Carapa guianensis* belongs to the mahogany family and is found predominantly in swampy or seasonally flooded parts of the forest. Mature trees may produce 300 or more large corky fruits that split into four segments, each containing two or three large seeds— most of which are eaten by animals.

Carapa guianensis
(Central and South America)

EAGLE-EYED

The harpy, one of the world's largest eagles, leaves its post in a tall emergent tree to swoop with speed and agility through the canopy. With its strong legs and immense talons (its feet are the size of a man's hands), it snatches howler monkeys or sloths, wrenching them free from a tightly grasped branch. Harpy eagles use the same nest site every year. They build a bulky nest of sticks lined with leaves and fur in the boughs of an emergent kapok tree, 165 ft (50 m) or so above the ground.

Harpy eagle
Harpia harpyja
(Central and South America)

Rhipsalis baccifera
(South America)

*Small
white fruit*

CACTUS AT THE TOP

Its fleshy, leafless stems mean that this epiphytic cactus can survive the long, hot dry spells between downpours. The small white fruits have a sticky pulp that helps them adhere to the bark.

*Young
developing leaf*

Abarema idiopoda
(Central America)

Bi-pinnate leaf

LEAF DIVISION

Rain forest trees have large leaves. These leaves are either simple, with a smooth outline and a waxy surface, or compound, when the leaf is divided into separate leaflets. *Abarema* is bi-pinnate – its leaves are twice divided and have small leaflets. *Carapa and Abarema* are leafless for brief periods, when there is a dry spell, or the tree is flowering.

Forest canopy

LIFE IN THE CANOPY
This male tawny rajah (*Charaxes bernardus*) is one of many kinds of butterfly that may spend their entire life cycle up in the forest canopy.

IN THE CANOPY of a rainforest, 80-150 ft (25-45 m) above the ground, it is always green and leafy. The crown of each tree is taller than it is broad, making a sun-speckled layer 20-23 ft (6-7 m) thick. This leafy roof shields the ground and absorbs most of the sunlight. It also lessens the impact of heavy rainfall and high winds. The teeming life of a jungle canopy is only glimpsed from below. Some creatures are so adapted to their treetop existence that they seldom, if ever, descend to the forest floor. It is difficult even to match up fallen fruits or flowers with the surrounding tree trunks. Many species were totally unknown – or their numbers grossly underestimated – before walkways strung up in the canopy allowed biologists to find out what life was really like in the treetops.

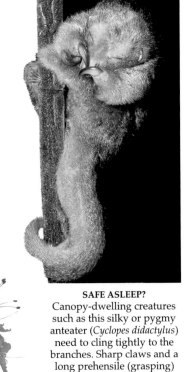

SAFE ASLEEP?
Canopy-dwelling creatures such as this silky or pygmy anteater (*Cyclopes didactylus*) need to cling tightly to the branches. Sharp claws and a long prehensile (grasping) tail are adaptations shared by unrelated canopy animals.

REACHING THE HEIGHTS
Lianas are plants that need a lot of light, which they have to compete for against tall rainforest trees. By using these trees for support, the lianas do not invest energy and materials in a thick trunk of their own. Instead, their slender climbing stems reach the canopy, and the light, very quickly. Once up among the branches, they loop through the tree tops, growing leaves, flowers, and fruit.

Liana
Clerodendrum splendens
(Africa)

White-lipped tree frog
Litoria infrafrenata
(Australasia)

STICKY-TOED TREE TRAVELER
To avoid the hottest part of the day, thin-skinned tree frogs hide in damp leafy crevices among canopy epiphytes. The smaller tree frogs may spend their entire lives in the canopy, even breeding in the reservoirs of water trapped by bromeliad leaves. Others, such as this white-lipped tree frog, laboriously make their way down to forest pools to mate and spawn. Long legs and sticky toe pads enable them to climb with complete ease.

Cecropia glaziovii
(Central and South
America)

CANOPY FOLIAGE
The large leaves of lowland rainforest trees may
be simple in shape, or divided into leaflets or
lobed. The canopy remains leafy all year, but
within it, some trees shed their foliage
for short intervals – sometimes
as little as a few days.
Leaf-fall usually coincides
with the driest time
of the year, but it
is not always
synchronized,
even in trees
of the same
species.

Large lobed leaf

Ficus religiosa
(Southeast Asia)

DRIP-TIPS
This typical rain forest leaf has
a shiny, waxy surface, and it
is drawn out into a narrow
point, or drip-tip. Both these
features are designed to
encourage rainwater to run
off quickly. This prevents
the growth of tiny algae
and liverworts.

FLEETING BEAUTY
Completely invisible from the ground,
epiphyte-laden boughs are like treetop
gardens. Of all the different plants
perched on these branches,
orchids are among the
most fascinating. The
perfect white orchids
(right) last just
one day.

One-day orchid
Sobralia sp.
(Central America)

INSECT LIFE
Only some canopy insects have been
classified and named, like this click
beetle (*Chalculepidium* sp.). Even
then, little is known about them.

259

The forest floor

THE AIR NEAR the shady forest floor is still, hot, and humid. Only about two percent of the light reaching the canopy penetrates the thick blanket of foliage. This dim light inhibits the growth of tree seedlings and other light-demanding plants. In the deepest jungle, the ground is a maze of roots littered with fallen leaves, twigs, and branches. When a tree crashes down, the scene is very different – the extra light allows an upsurge of saplings, herbaceous plants, and lianas. Rates of growth are impressive; giant bamboo grows 9 in (23 cm) a day.

FOREST FUNGI
Bacteria, molds, and fungi such as this *Marasmius* grow quickly in the humid conditions of the forest floor. A mass of fungal threads called a mycelium takes nutrients from the litter of dead leaves, and the brightly colored toadstools produce spores.

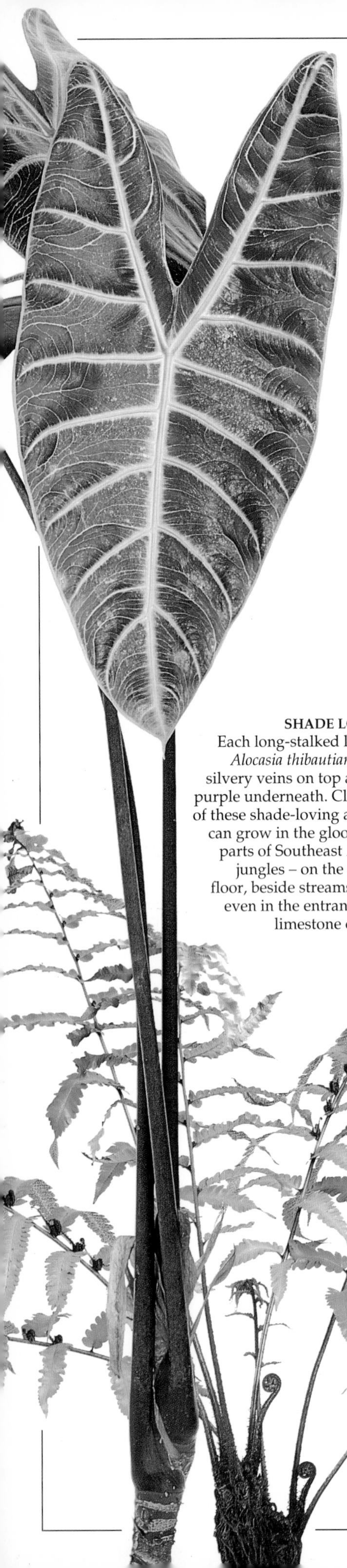

SHADE LOVER
Each long-stalked leaf of *Alocasia thibautiana* has silvery veins on top and is purple underneath. Clumps of these shade-loving aroids can grow in the gloomiest parts of Southeast Asian jungles – on the forest floor, beside streams, and even in the entrances of limestone caves.

A SPLASH OF COLOR
A luxuriant growth springs up wherever there is enough light. Heliconias, with their bright red flowerheads, are widespread in Central American jungles.

TRAPPING LIGHT
The leaves of *Fittonia* contain red pigments that trap the dim light that reaches the forest floor. Amerindian tribes use the plant to treat a variety of ailments.

Diplazium proliferum
(Southeast Asia)

Fittonia albivenis
(South America)

FLOURISHING
Ferns thrive best where it is warm and damp. Many tolerate low light levels, so they are abundant on the jungle floor. This fern produces bulbils on its fronds that will sprout and take root, either when they are knocked off or when the frond dies.

BURROWING WORM
The black-and-white amphisbaenid (*Amphisbaena fuliginosa*) is neither a lizard or a snake. It is a wormlike reptile that lives in burrows in the damp soil and leaf litter of the forest floor. It feeds on worms and other invertebrates, detecting prey by touch.

Banded pitta
Pitta guajana
(Malaysia)

BROWSING BIRD
Using its good eyesight and sense of smell, the pitta forages for snails, ants, and other insects in the leaf litter.

BUTTRESS ROOTS
These enormous roots are characteristic of lowland tropical rain forest, where soil is thin or subject to flooding. The curving shapes rise from lateral roots. Buttress roots may spread up the trunk to 30 ft (9 m), forming supporting wings of particularly hard wood.

In the water

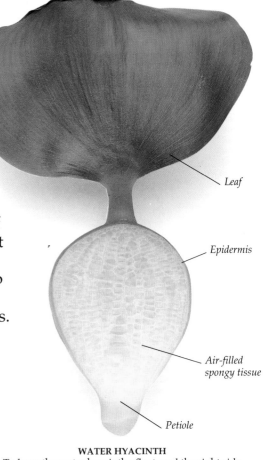

THE RAIN FOREST is awash with water. It drips from the leaves, collects in puddles, runs down mountainsides, and eventually drains into huge, meandering rivers. The Amazon is the largest river of all – together with its tributaries, which number 1,000 or more, it holds two-thirds of the world's fresh water. This vast water system supports an incredible diversity of life. It contains around 5,000 species of freshwater fish, and there may be another 2,000 that have yet to be discovered. Where rain forest rivers flood, they spread nutrient-rich silts over the surrounding land, creating swamp forests. When they join the sea, more silt is deposited in estuaries and deltas, contributing towards mangrove swamps.

Leaf

Epidermis

Air-filled spongy tissue

Petiole

WELL CAMOUFLAGED
Lurking immobile in shallow water, the craggy carapace of the matamata (*Chelus fimbriatus*) looks like a rock. This Amazonian turtle has nostrils at the tip of its long, uptilted snout which is used like a snorkel as it lies in wait for prey.

RUNNING ON WATER
The Jesus Christ lizard, or basilisk, runs using its tail to balance itself. It has scales and a flap of skin on its hind toes to increase surface area, so it can run on *water* to chase prey or escape danger.

WATER HYACINTH
To keep the water hyacinth afloat, and the right side up, the petiole (base) of each leaf stalk is swollen into an air-filled float. Cutting this in half reveals that each float is made up of a mass of air-filled spongy tissue. The leaf and stem are encased in a smooth, tough skin, called the epidermis.

Long tail used as extra leg on land

Large back feet stop lizard sinking on water

Jesus Christ lizard
Basiliscus basiliscus
(Central America)

Pacu
Colossoma oculus
(South America)

FRUIT-EATING FISH
The varzea and the igapo are two areas of swamp forest flooded every year by the Amazon. Fruits falling from palms and other trees attract fish such as the pacu.

Water hyacinth
Eichhornia crassipes

DANGER IN THE WATER
Armed with fearsome rows of sharp, triangular teeth, the predatory piranha is dangerous only in the dry season, when water levels are low and the fish gather in schools of 20 or more. By feeding collectively, the fish are able to tackle large animals, although their usual prey is other fish, mollusks, fruits, or seeds.

Piranha
Serrasalmus niger
(South America)

FLOATING PLANT
The water hyacinth (above) floats with its feathery roots dangling down into the water. The plants grow very quickly, forming large rafts on the surfaces of lakes and slow streams. Smaller clumps are dispersed by the wind, blown along like small, unsinkable sailboats.

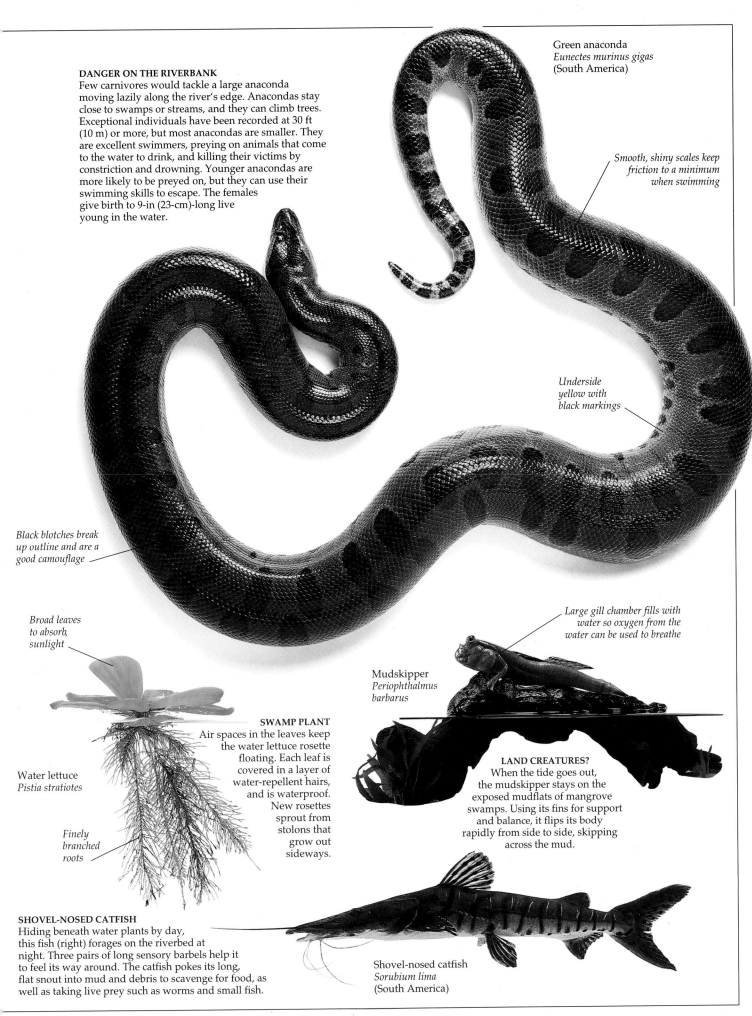

DANGER ON THE RIVERBANK
Few carnivores would tackle a large anaconda
moving lazily along the river's edge. Anacondas stay
close to swamps or streams, and they can climb trees.
Exceptional individuals have been recorded at 30 ft
(10 m) or more, but most anacondas are smaller. They
are excellent swimmers, preying on animals that come
to the water to drink, and killing their victims by
constriction and drowning. Younger anacondas are
more likely to be preyed on, but they can use their
swimming skills to escape. The females
give birth to 9-in (23-cm)-long live
young in the water.

Green anaconda
Eunectes murinus gigas
(South America)

*Smooth, shiny scales keep
friction to a minimum
when swimming*

*Underside
yellow with
black markings*

*Black blotches break
up outline and are a
good camouflage*

*Broad leaves
to absorb
sunlight*

*Large gill chamber fills with
water so oxygen from the
water can be used to breathe*

Mudskipper
*Periophthalmus
barbarus*

SWAMP PLANT
Air spaces in the leaves keep
the water lettuce rosette
floating. Each leaf is
covered in a layer of
water-repellent hairs,
and is waterproof.
New rosettes
sprout from
stolons that
grow out
sideways.

Water lettuce
Pistia stratiotes

*Finely
branched
roots*

LAND CREATURES?
When the tide goes out,
the mudskipper stays on the
exposed mudflats of mangrove
swamps. Using its fins for support
and balance, it flips its body
rapidly from side to side, skipping
across the mud.

SHOVEL-NOSED CATFISH
Hiding beneath water plants by day,
this fish (right) forages on the riverbed at
night. Three pairs of long sensory barbels help it
to feel its way around. The catfish pokes its long,
flat snout into mud and debris to scavenge for food, as
well as taking live prey such as worms and small fish.

Shovel-nosed catfish
Sorubium lima
(South America)

Epiphytes

Up in the rain forest treetops, a special group of plants clothe the branches so thickly that the bark is hidden. These are called epiphytes—plants that live on other plants. They anchor themselves to the stems, trunks, branches, or even leaves of other plants. They do not take either water or food from their hosts. Instead, they use them as a means of reaching the light. After heavy rain, the combined weight of epiphytes and the water they have trapped can be enough to bring down whole branches. In the wettest forests, up to 25 percent of flowering plants and ferns are epiphytes, and there are many more kinds of mosses, liverworts, and lichens. The highest number of epiphytic species are found in Central and South American forests.

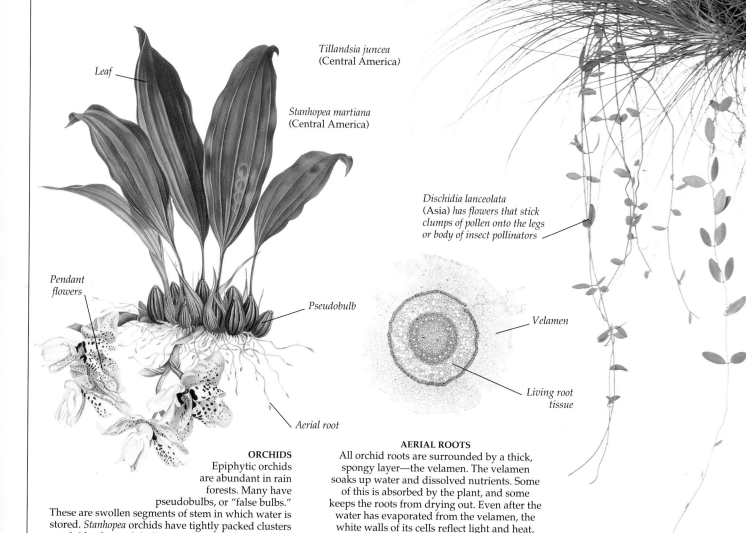

PLATYCERIUM
The bracket fronds of this large epiphytic fern loosely clasp the tree trunk, so that a litter of plant debris collects behind it. This compost is moistened by rainwater trickling down the trunk, and a rich humus develops into which the fern grows roots. Hanging clear of the trunk are the fertile, spore-bearing fronds.

Leaf

Tillandsia juncea
(Central America)

Stanhopea martiana
(Central America)

Pendant flowers

Pseudobulb

Dischidia lanceolata (Asia) has flowers that stick clumps of pollen onto the legs or body of insect pollinators

Velamen

Living root tissue

Aerial root

ORCHIDS
Epiphytic orchids are abundant in rain forests. Many have pseudobulbs, or "false bulbs." These are swollen segments of stem in which water is stored. *Stanhopea* orchids have tightly packed clusters of ridged pseudobulbs, each one with a single leaf.

AERIAL ROOTS
All orchid roots are surrounded by a thick, spongy layer—the velamen. The velamen soaks up water and dissolved nutrients. Some of this is absorbed by the plant, and some keeps the roots from drying out. Even after the water has evaporated from the velamen, the white walls of its cells reflect light and heat, protecting the living root tissues.

Anthurium salviniae
(Central America)

*This plant has leaves
that channel rain, dew, and
debris down to a mat of roots*

*This plant absorbs water
from the air through
scales on the leaves*

*This plant has silver-
veined leaves that have
a velvety upper surface*

WATER TANKS
Epiphytic bromeliads, or urn plants, are found in New World rain forests. Each plant has a rosette of stiff leaves around a short stalk. The tightly overlapping leaf bases form a series of cups that collect rainwater. Plant fragments also become trapped, releasing nutrients into the water as they rot. Both water and dissolved minerals are absorbed by the bromeliad through specialized hairs on the leaf surface. These pools support an incredible number of aquatic insects and other creatures. Some frogs even breed in them.

Aechmea fasciata
(South America)

Anthurium crystallinum
(South America)

Oncidium excavatum
(South America)

Tillandsia usneoides
(Central America)

*Young seedlings
like this have
anchoring roots;
the mature air
plants are a tangle
of stems and
narrow leaves*

Branching out
Heavy rain soon drains through the canopy, and the sunshine, though patchy, is very hot. This means that water and dissolved nutrients can be in short supply. Because of this, epiphytes share many of the characteristics of plants that grow in arid (hot and dry) conditions. The leaves have a thick, waxy, waterproof outer layer to reduce evaporation and grow so that rainwater funnels to the roots. The decomposing organic matter caught in water traps provides a source of fertilizer.

Guzmania lingulata
(Central America) *is a
bromeliad that prefers shade*

*Aechmea
purpurea-rosea*
(Brazil)

Climbers

ONE OF THE MOST impressive features of a tropical forest is the abundance of lianas, or climbing plants. Some lianas grow to a huge size, with long stems that climb to the forest canopy in search of light, looping from branch to branch and linking the crowns of trees. Once up in the canopy, they develop branches that bear leaves and flowers. Lianas send feeding roots—also called aerial roots because they dangle in midair—toward ground. When they reach soil, they bury themselves and branch rapidly. These long roots in turn act as supports for other climbing plants.

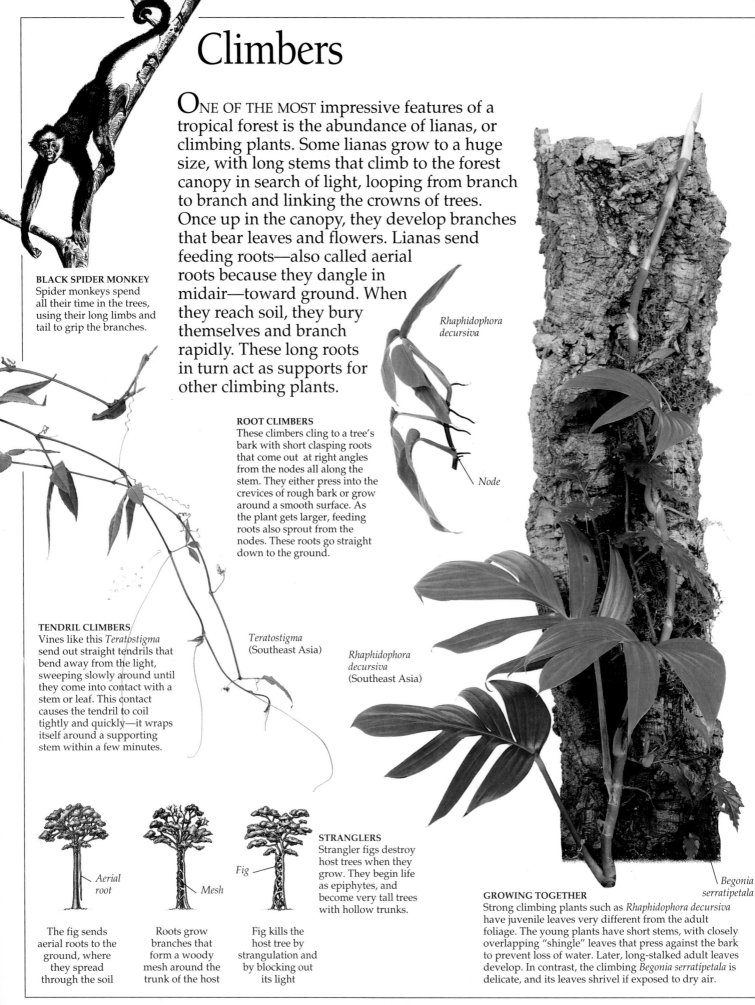

BLACK SPIDER MONKEY
Spider monkeys spend all their time in the trees, using their long limbs and tail to grip the branches.

ROOT CLIMBERS
These climbers cling to a tree's bark with short clasping roots that come out at right angles from the nodes all along the stem. They either press into the crevices of rough bark or grow around a smooth surface. As the plant gets larger, feeding roots also sprout from the nodes. These roots go straight down to the ground.

Rhaphidophora decursiva

Node

TENDRIL CLIMBERS
Vines like this *Teratostigma* send out straight tendrils that bend away from the light, sweeping slowly around until they come into contact with a stem or leaf. This contact causes the tendril to coil tightly and quickly—it wraps itself around a supporting stem within a few minutes.

Teratostigma (Southeast Asia)

Rhaphidophora decursiva (Southeast Asia)

Aerial root

Mesh

Fig

STRANGLERS
Strangler figs destroy host trees when they grow. They begin life as epiphytes, and become very tall trees with hollow trunks.

The fig sends aerial roots to the ground, where they spread through the soil

Roots grow branches that form a woody mesh around the trunk of the host

Fig kills the host tree by strangulation and by blocking out its light

Begonia serratipetala

GROWING TOGETHER
Strong climbing plants such as *Rhaphidophora decursiva* have juvenile leaves very different from the adult foliage. The young plants have short stems, with closely overlapping "shingle" leaves that press against the bark to prevent loss of water. Later, long-stalked adult leaves develop. In contrast, the climbing *Begonia serratipetala* is delicate, and its leaves shrivel if exposed to dry air.

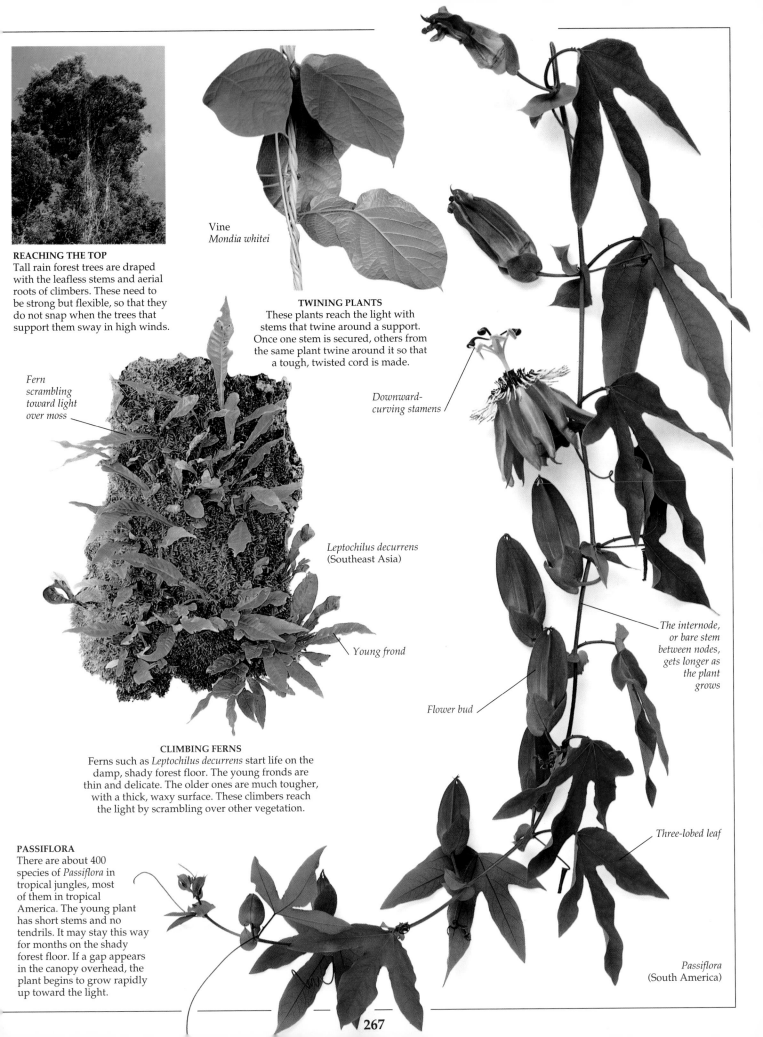

REACHING THE TOP
Tall rain forest trees are draped with the leafless stems and aerial roots of climbers. These need to be strong but flexible, so that they do not snap when the trees that support them sway in high winds.

Vine
Mondia whitei

TWINING PLANTS
These plants reach the light with stems that twine around a support. Once one stem is secured, others from the same plant twine around it so that a tough, twisted cord is made.

Fern scrambling toward light over moss

Downward-curving stamens

Leptochilus decurrens (Southeast Asia)

The internode, or bare stem between nodes, gets longer as the plant grows

Flower bud

Young frond

Three-lobed leaf

CLIMBING FERNS
Ferns such as *Leptochilus decurrens* start life on the damp, shady forest floor. The young fronds are thin and delicate. The older ones are much tougher, with a thick, waxy surface. These climbers reach the light by scrambling over other vegetation.

PASSIFLORA
There are about 400 species of *Passiflora* in tropical jungles, most of them in tropical America. The young plant has short stems and no tendrils. It may stay this way for months on the shady forest floor. If a gap appears in the canopy overhead, the plant begins to grow rapidly up toward the light.

Passiflora (South America)

Central American jungles

ONCE THE CENTERS of the great Maya and Aztec civilizations, the small countries bridging North and South America contain an incredible diversity of plant and animal life. A large number of plants native to the region are found nowhere else, and it is home to many important tropical crops, including pawpaws, allspice, and vanilla. Central America and the Caribbean islands are particularly rich in bird life. The small country of Panama has more bird species than are found in the whole of North America, including migratory species that overwinter in the warm rain forests, before returning to North America to breed.

ANCIENT CULTURE
The Maya civilization flourished in Belize and Guatemala until A.D. 800. Mayans left many examples of intricately decorated pottery showing how they admired animals, such as this jaguar.

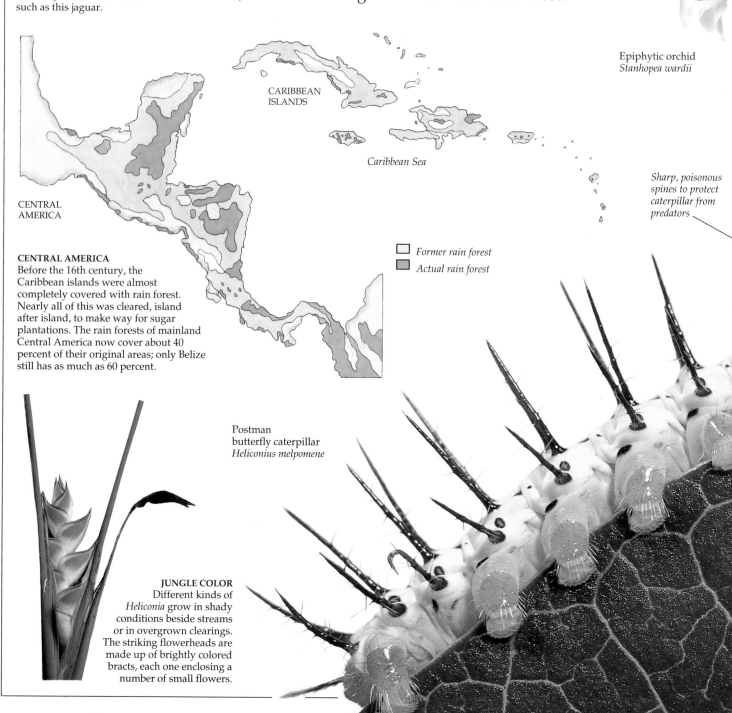

CARIBBEAN
ISLANDS

Caribbean Sea

CENTRAL
AMERICA

Epiphytic orchid
Stanhopea wardii

Sharp, poisonous spines to protect caterpillar from predators

☐ *Former rain forest*
▨ *Actual rain forest*

CENTRAL AMERICA
Before the 16th century, the Caribbean islands were almost completely covered with rain forest. Nearly all of this was cleared, island after island, to make way for sugar plantations. The rain forests of mainland Central America now cover about 40 percent of their original areas; only Belize still has as much as 60 percent.

Postman
butterfly caterpillar
Heliconius melpomene

JUNGLE COLOR
Different kinds of *Heliconia* grow in shady conditions beside streams or in overgrown clearings. The striking flowerheads are made up of brightly colored bracts, each one enclosing a number of small flowers.

WELL NOURISHED
These butterflies are able to live for six to nine months because they feed on protein-rich pollen as well as nectar. They squirt enzymes onto the pollen, which turns it into a "soup" that can be sucked up. Their longer lifespan means that they can lay more eggs.

*Winged central
column*

Postman butterfly
Heliconius melpomene

BRIEF BEAUTY
Hanging in fragrant sprays, the large waxy flowers of this lowland epiphytic orchid are short-lived, withering after pollination. Each flower has a winged central column with fleshy lips, designed to attach the clumps of pollen firmly to its pollinator, the euglossine bee.

Scarlet macaw
Ara macao

WINGS IN THE TREETOPS
Raucous calls reveal the presence of these macaws in the treetops. These brightly colored, social birds squabble over nesting sites – tree holes at least 100 ft (30 m) above the ground. Their diet consists mostly of seeds, many of which are protected by a hard shell. The macaw uses its tongue to position a seed in the upper part of its beak, then cracks it with the lower part – just like a pair of pincers.

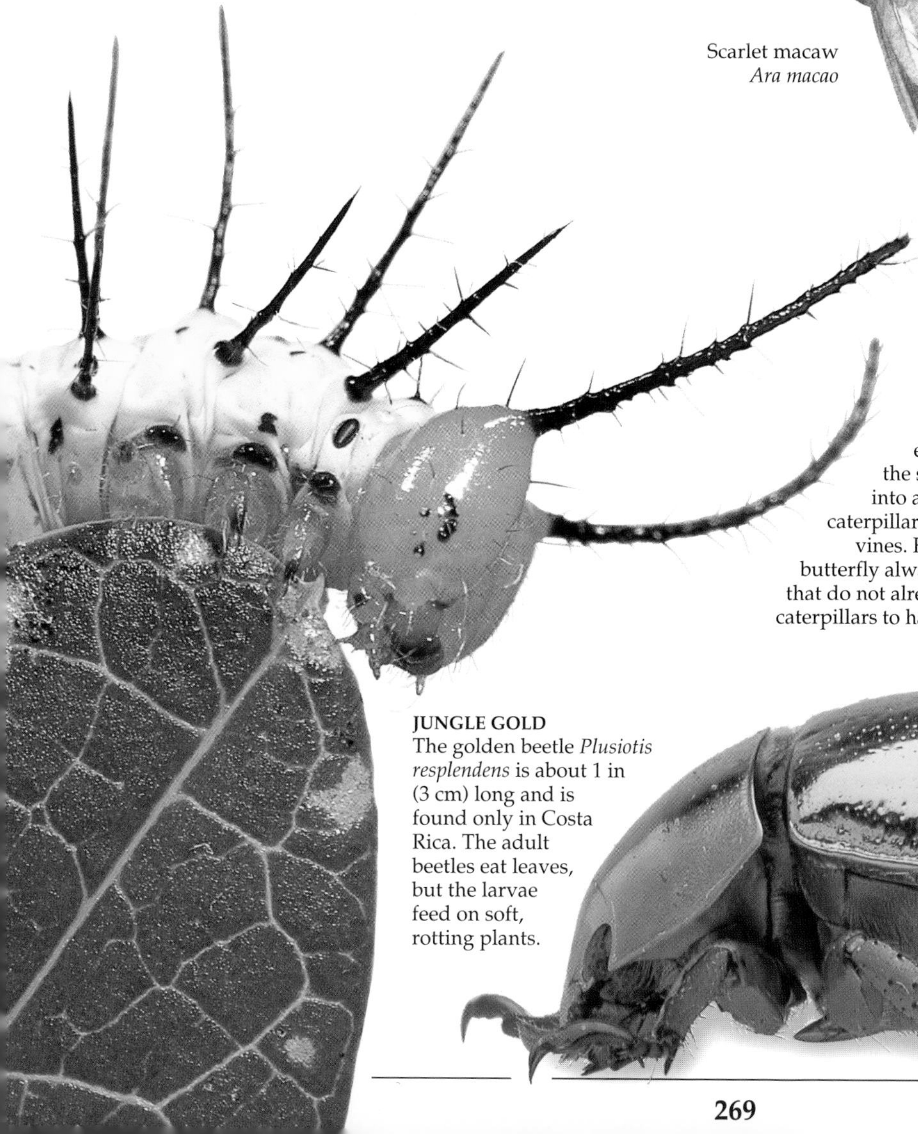

PROGRAMMED TO EAT
The postman butterfly caterpillar eats enormous numbers of leaves in the short time before it metamorphoses into a butterfly. Many postman butterfly caterpillars feed on *Passiflora* (passion flower) vines. For egg-laying purposes, the female butterfly always selects young shoots or tendrils that do not already have eggs on them, as the first caterpillars to hatch will devour any younger ones.

JUNGLE GOLD
The golden beetle *Plusiotis resplendens* is about 1 in (3 cm) long and is found only in Costa Rica. The adult beetles eat leaves, but the larvae feed on soft, rotting plants.

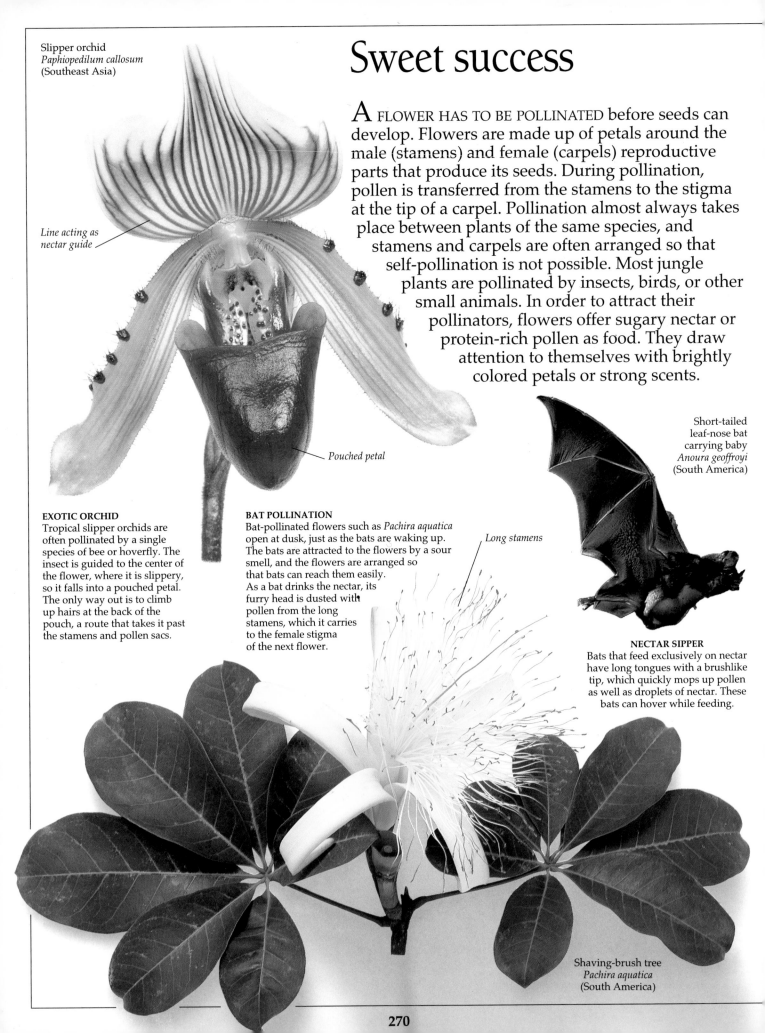

Slipper orchid
Paphiopedilum callosum
(Southeast Asia)

Sweet success

A FLOWER HAS TO BE POLLINATED before seeds can develop. Flowers are made up of petals around the male (stamens) and female (carpels) reproductive parts that produce its seeds. During pollination, pollen is transferred from the stamens to the stigma at the tip of a carpel. Pollination almost always takes place between plants of the same species, and stamens and carpels are often arranged so that self-pollination is not possible. Most jungle plants are pollinated by insects, birds, or other small animals. In order to attract their pollinators, flowers offer sugary nectar or protein-rich pollen as food. They draw attention to themselves with brightly colored petals or strong scents.

Line acting as nectar guide

Pouched petal

EXOTIC ORCHID
Tropical slipper orchids are often pollinated by a single species of bee or hoverfly. The insect is guided to the center of the flower, where it is slippery, so it falls into a pouched petal. The only way out is to climb up hairs at the back of the pouch, a route that takes it past the stamens and pollen sacs.

BAT POLLINATION
Bat-pollinated flowers such as *Pachira aquatica* open at dusk, just as the bats are waking up. The bats are attracted to the flowers by a sour smell, and the flowers are arranged so that bats can reach them easily. As a bat drinks the nectar, its furry head is dusted with pollen from the long stamens, which it carries to the female stigma of the next flower.

Long stamens

Short-tailed leaf-nose bat carrying baby
Anoura geoffroyi
(South America)

NECTAR SIPPER
Bats that feed exclusively on nectar have long tongues with a brushlike tip, which quickly mops up pollen as well as droplets of nectar. These bats can hover while feeding.

Shaving-brush tree
Pachira aquatica
(South America)

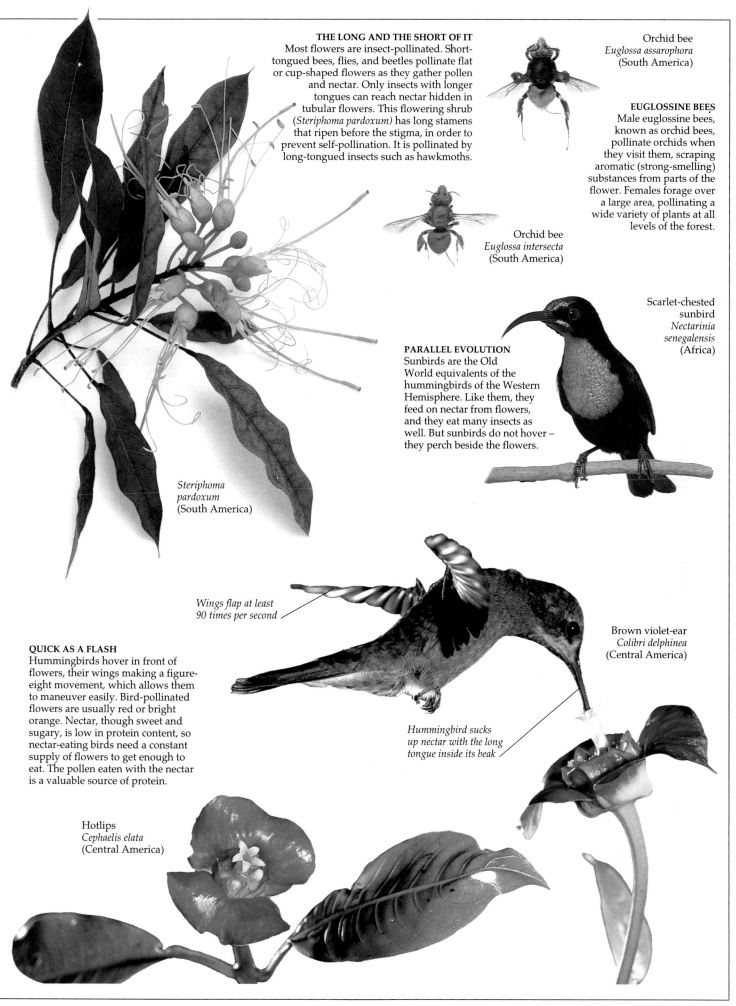

THE LONG AND THE SHORT OF IT

Most flowers are insect-pollinated. Short-tongued bees, flies, and beetles pollinate flat or cup-shaped flowers as they gather pollen and nectar. Only insects with longer tongues can reach nectar hidden in tubular flowers. This flowering shrub (*Steriphoma pardoxum*) has long stamens that ripen before the stigma, in order to prevent self-pollination. It is pollinated by long-tongued insects such as hawkmoths.

Orchid bee
Euglossa assarophora
(South America)

EUGLOSSINE BEES

Male euglossine bees, known as orchid bees, pollinate orchids when they visit them, scraping aromatic (strong-smelling) substances from parts of the flower. Females forage over a large area, pollinating a wide variety of plants at all levels of the forest.

Orchid bee
Euglossa intersecta
(South America)

PARALLEL EVOLUTION

Sunbirds are the Old World equivalents of the hummingbirds of the Western Hemisphere. Like them, they feed on nectar from flowers, and they eat many insects as well. But sunbirds do not hover – they perch beside the flowers.

Scarlet-chested sunbird
Nectarinia senegalensis
(Africa)

Steriphoma pardoxum
(South America)

Wings flap at least
90 times per second

QUICK AS A FLASH

Hummingbirds hover in front of flowers, their wings making a figure-eight movement, which allows them to maneuver easily. Bird-pollinated flowers are usually red or bright orange. Nectar, though sweet and sugary, is low in protein content, so nectar-eating birds need a constant supply of flowers to get enough to eat. The pollen eaten with the nectar is a valuable source of protein.

Brown violet-ear
Colibri delphinea
(Central America)

Hummingbird sucks
up nectar with the long
tongue inside its beak

Hotlips
Cephaelis elata
(Central America)

271

Seed dispersal

PLANTS NEED to spread their seeds so that they have room to grow. Because they cannot move around, they rely on wind, animals, water, or explosive pods to scatter their seeds. The fruit wall is part of this scattering mechanism. Some fruits are winged or cottony to help the seeds become airborne. Some are air-filled and float on water. More familiar are the juicy, brightly colored fruits that spread their seeds by enticing animals, including people, to eat their succulent flesh. These seeds are spread when animals spit them out, let them fall, or pass them out in droppings deposited some distance away.

HEALTHY APPETITE
The great Indian hornbill (*Buceros bicornis*) is an avid fruit eater. Seeds germinate from its droppings.

Hard seed case

ATTRACTIVE MORSEL
This *Elaeocarpus angustifolia* seed was enclosed in a purple fruit with oily flesh. The fruit is swallowed whole by birds, such as hornbills.

BURIED AND FORGOTTEN
Inside the fibrous case of *Loxococcus rupicola* is a hard nutty seed that is dispersed by rodents. These gnawing animals bury seeds for future feasts. Forgotten caches germinate and grow.

RATTAN PALMS
Rattan palms produce clusters of fruits. These usually contain a single seed enveloped in a fleshy layer that is eaten by birds and animals. As hard-shelled seeds pass through the digestive tract of an animal, their outer wall is eaten away by digestive juices. This makes water absorption and germination easier.

Fruit is in clusters at base of frond

Rattan seeds
Calamus paspalanthus
(Southeast Asia)

Red lemur palm fruit
Lemurophoenix halleuxii
(Madagascar)

A CASE THAT IS HARD TO CRACK?
Larger animals and fruit-eating bats often carry fruit to a safe place before eating it. Some seeds are then spat out or discarded, especially if they are too hard to crack.

Pigafetta filaris
(Australasia)

Hard, nutty seed

FRUIT EATER
This lemur lives in tall trees beside rivers in southern Madagascar. Fruit is the most important part of its diet, although it also eats insects and leaves.

Ring-tailed lemur
Lemur catta
(Madagascar)

Sago palm
Metroxylon sagu
(Australasia)

SCALY FRUIT
Pigafetta, sago, and rattan palms are closely related species with fruits enclosed in shiny, overlapping scales. Beneath a sago palm's scales is a corky layer that enables the fruit to float, thus dispersing its single seed. A sago palm dies after it has fruited.

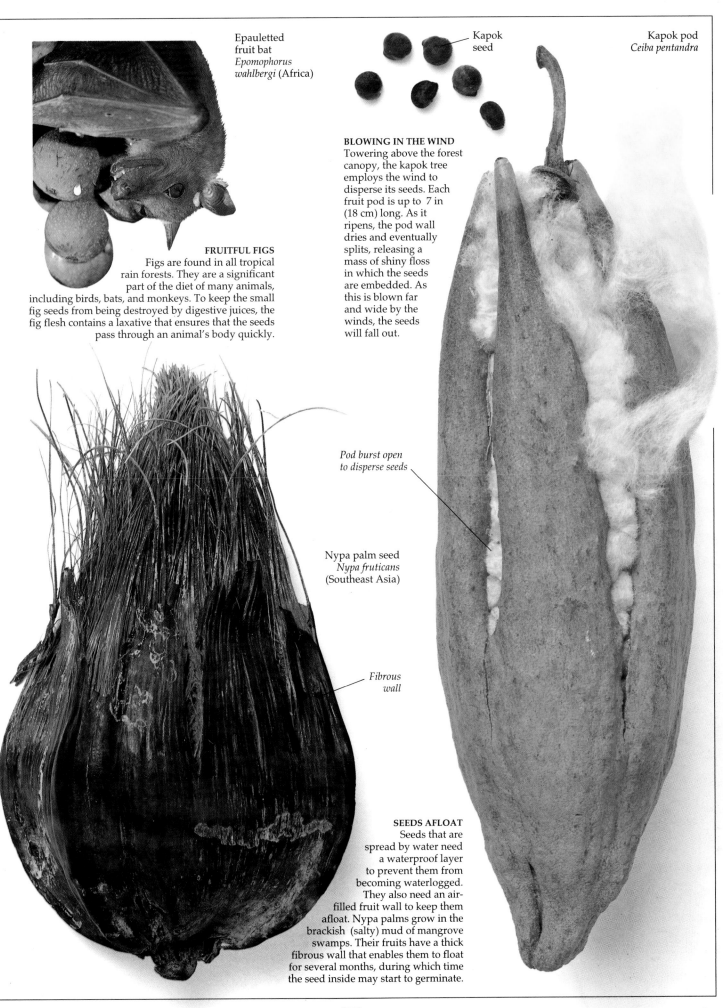

Epauletted
fruit bat
*Epomophorus
wahlbergi* (Africa)

Kapok
seed

Kapok pod
Ceiba pentandra

BLOWING IN THE WIND
Towering above the forest
canopy, the kapok tree
employs the wind to
disperse its seeds. Each
fruit pod is up to 7 in
(18 cm) long. As it
ripens, the pod wall
dries and eventually
splits, releasing a
mass of shiny floss
in which the seeds
are embedded. As
this is blown far
and wide by the
winds, the seeds
will fall out.

FRUITFUL FIGS
Figs are found in all tropical
rain forests. They are a significant
part of the diet of many animals,
including birds, bats, and monkeys. To keep the small
fig seeds from being destroyed by digestive juices, the
fig flesh contains a laxative that ensures that the seeds
pass through an animal's body quickly.

*Pod burst open
to disperse seeds*

Nypa palm seed
Nypa fruticans
(Southeast Asia)

*Fibrous
wall*

SEEDS AFLOAT
Seeds that are
spread by water need
a waterproof layer
to prevent them from
becoming waterlogged.
They also need an air-
filled fruit wall to keep them
afloat. Nypa palms grow in the
brackish (salty) mud of mangrove
swamps. Their fruits have a thick
fibrous wall that enables them to float
for several months, during which time
the seed inside may start to germinate.

Dusk to dawn

NIGHT COMES SWIFTLY in the tropics, where there are no lingering hours of twilight. As the sun sinks toward the horizon, daytime creatures return to their roosts or nests, and a new group of animals awakens. Because some animals are active by day and others by night, different species of animals that would otherwise compete for food and space are separated. The cooler night air brings out insects and amphibians with thin, moist skins, and small mammals that hunt on the forest floor. Nocturnal (nighttime) animals are specially adapted—many have huge eyes or acutely sensitive ears and noses. Yet the jungle is never completely dark. The moon shines on clear nights. Fireflies flash through the trees, and phosphorescent fungi glow eerily on the forest floor, until they are devoured by beetles.

NIGHT FEEDER
By day, Franquet's epauleted bats roost in small groups, hanging from thin branches usually 13-20 ft (4-6 m) above the ground. As night falls, they fly off to feed on fruit, large numbers often gathering in a heavily laden tree. Fruit bats have large eyes with good vision, but they locate ripe fruit with their keen sense of smell.

Franquet's epauleted bat
Epomops franqueti
(Africa)

Wings folded when roosting

FLYING HOME TO ROOST
Just before darkness falls, parties of toucans fly off to roost in selected trees. They look ungainly in flight, but although large, their colorful bills are very light in weight. As dawn breaks, the flock once more takes to the air in search of ripe fruit.

Large curved beak for picking and eating fruit

Cuvier's toucan
Rhamphastos cuvieri
(South America)

NIGHT-LIGHTS
Fireflies are not the only insects that glow. Males of this species of click beetle, *Pyrophorus*, from tropical America, fly among the trees flashing in special sequences that are answered only by females of the same species.

NECTAR-SIPPERS

Night-flying moths feed on the nectar of sweetly scented, pale-colored flowers, many of which are open only for a single night. This African moon moth is one of the largest species, with a wingspan of 5 in (12 cm). The feathery antennae of the male are so sensitive that they can pick up the slightest trace of pheromones (sex hormones) wafting from a female moth.

African moon moth
Argema mimosae
(Africa)

BIG EYES

The vertical pupils of the red-eyed tree frog *Agalychnis callidryas* open up at night to help it see in the very low light levels. By day, the pupils become slits. These frogs live and feed up in the canopy. Only the female comes down to absorb water from a stream before she lays her eggs.

DAWN CHORUS

Just before dawn breaks, howler monkeys set up a noisy chorus. The deafening howls can be heard up to 2 miles (3 km) away, and are produced by air passing over the hyoid bone in the large larynx. Mature males, such as this one, make the loudest howl. The howl can be amplified by their body position. This early morning symphony is a warning to other groups of howlers not to come too close to them and their food supply.

Large eyes for night vision

Red howler monkey
Alouatta seniculus
(South America)

NIGHT MONKEY

The douroucouli, or night monkey, is the only nocturnal monkey in the world. As night falls, douroucoulis emerge from tree holes to feed on fruit, leaves, insects, and other small animals. Their large, forward-pointing eyes are typical of nocturnal primates, and help them to see in the near-darkness as they climb and leap from branch to branch.

Douroucouli
Aotus trivirgatus
(South America)

DIGGING DOWN

The scaly Indian pangolin, *Manis crassicaudata*, digs a burrow in which it spends the day, emerging at night to forage on the forest floor. Though its sight is weak, it has an acute sense of smell, which it uses to locate ant and termite mounds. Breaking in with the long powerful claws on its forelimbs, the pangolin flicks its very long sticky tongue into chambers full of insects, eggs, and pupae. It is toothless, so the swallowed insects are ground up in the lower part of its stomach.

South American jungles

THE AMAZON BASIN covers a vast area, nearly 2.5 million sq miles (6 million sq km), and is covered by the world's largest expanse of tropical rainforest. This jungle supports more species of plants and animals than anywhere else – about one-fifth of the world's bird and flowering plant species, and about one-tenth of all mammal species. No definite figure can be put on the number of different insects, because many have yet to be identified – or even discovered – by scientists. Amerindian tribes have lived in these forests for about 12,000 years, during which time they have built up a detailed and valuable knowledge of the jungle plants, many of which they use in their everyday lives.

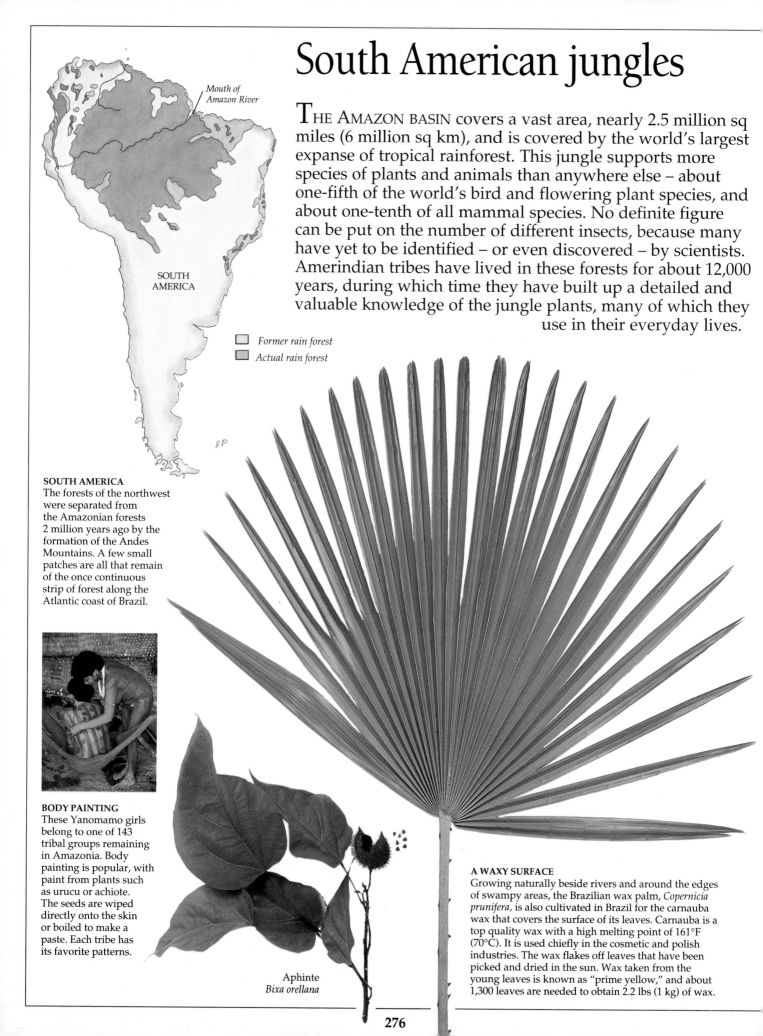

Mouth of Amazon River

SOUTH AMERICA

☐ *Former rain forest*
☐ *Actual rain forest*

SOUTH AMERICA
The forests of the northwest were separated from the Amazonian forests 2 million years ago by the formation of the Andes Mountains. A few small patches are all that remain of the once continuous strip of forest along the Atlantic coast of Brazil.

BODY PAINTING
These Yanomamo girls belong to one of 143 tribal groups remaining in Amazonia. Body painting is popular, with paint from plants such as urucu or achiote. The seeds are wiped directly onto the skin or boiled to make a paste. Each tribe has its favorite patterns.

Aphinte
Bixa orellana

A WAXY SURFACE
Growing naturally beside rivers and around the edges of swampy areas, the Brazilian wax palm, *Copernicia prunifera*, is also cultivated in Brazil for the carnauba wax that covers the surface of its leaves. Carnauba is a top quality wax with a high melting point of 161°F (70°C). It is used chiefly in the cosmetic and polish industries. The wax flakes off leaves that have been picked and dried in the sun. Wax taken from the young leaves is known as "prime yellow," and about 1,300 leaves are needed to obtain 2.2 lbs (1 kg) of wax.

ONE OF MANY
The malachite butterfly is just one of more than 2,000 species of butterfly in the Amazonian jungles. They fly during the day, pausing to feed on over-ripe fruit fermenting on the forest floor.

Malachite butterfly
Metamorpha stelenes

GOLD IN THE FOREST
This beautiful golden monkey is found only in Atlantic coastal rain forests. Golden lion tamarins live in mature forest, where they forage for invertebrates, small animals, and fruit 10-30 ft (3-10 m) up in the liana-covered trees. They came near to extinction in the 1960s, because their habitat was being destroyed and hundreds were being exported as pets every year. Since then, captive breeding programs established in the United States and Europe have resulted in the release of golden lion tamarins back into the wild.

Long tail for balancing

Golden lion tamarin
Leontopithecus rosalia

Buriti palm
Mauritia flexuosa

THE TREE OF LIFE
Nothing of this tall palm goes to waste. The Amerindians use it as a source of food, fibers, wood, cork, and thatching. Wine made from its vitamin C-rich fruits is given to the elderly and sick.

NOT SO LAZY
Despite its name, the three-toed sloth *Bradypus tridactylus* is not a lazy animal. It is perfectly adapted to its life up in the canopy. There is little protein in its diet, and to conserve energy it hangs upside down and its strong claws lock so tightly onto branches that it does not fall off even when asleep – or dead!

Amazon lily
Eucharis amazonica

MYSTERIOUS POWERS
The Amazon lily grows on the lower slopes of the Andes. The Kofan tribes of western Colombia and northern Ecuador boil the whole plant, including its bulb, to make a tea. This is drunk by men before they hunt monkeys, in the belief that it will make them more accurate with the blowpipe.

Beside the water

THE RIVERBANK IS THE DOMAIN of animals that live both on land and in water. The vegetation here is particularly dense, since the open expanse of water allows extra light to reach the ground. This mosaic of water, overhanging branches, and tangles of waterside ferns, sedges, and saplings provides an ideal environment for animals that live and breed on land but enter the water to hunt and feed. However, heavy rains sometimes cause a river to overflow its banks, and this puts animals nesting close to the water's edge at risk.

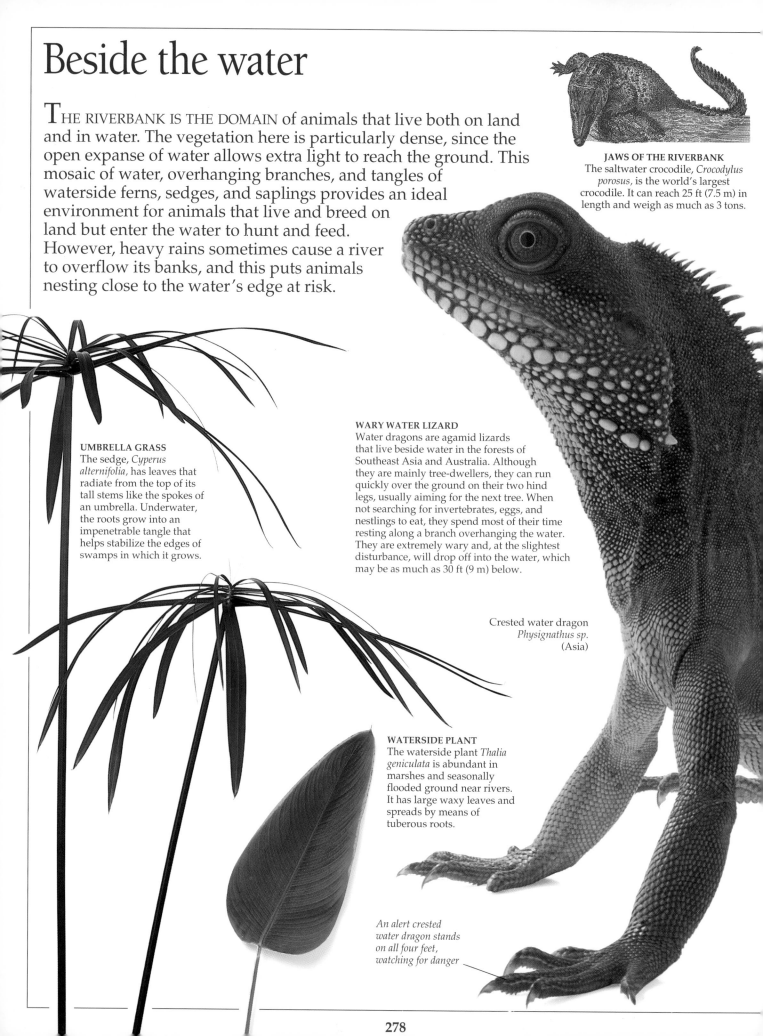

JAWS OF THE RIVERBANK
The saltwater crocodile, *Crocodylus porosus*, is the world's largest crocodile. It can reach 25 ft (7.5 m) in length and weigh as much as 3 tons.

UMBRELLA GRASS
The sedge, *Cyperus alternifolia*, has leaves that radiate from the top of its tall stems like the spokes of an umbrella. Underwater, the roots grow into an impenetrable tangle that helps stabilize the edges of swamps in which it grows.

WARY WATER LIZARD
Water dragons are agamid lizards that live beside water in the forests of Southeast Asia and Australia. Although they are mainly tree-dwellers, they can run quickly over the ground on their two hind legs, usually aiming for the next tree. When not searching for invertebrates, eggs, and nestlings to eat, they spend most of their time resting along a branch overhanging the water. They are extremely wary and, at the slightest disturbance, will drop off into the water, which may be as much as 30 ft (9 m) below.

Crested water dragon
Physignathus sp.
(Asia)

WATERSIDE PLANT
The waterside plant *Thalia geniculata* is abundant in marshes and seasonally flooded ground near rivers. It has large waxy leaves and spreads by means of tuberous roots.

An alert crested water dragon stands on all four feet, watching for danger

278

GIANT OTTER
Each family group of giant otters has its own territory. Ungainly on land, these creatures are excellent swimmers—they use their large, webbed feet as paddles and their muscular tail as a rudder. When they catch a fish, they carry it to the surface to eat.

Eyes on long stalks watch for danger; rest of body is camouflaged

Fiddler crab
Uca vocans

FROGS IN DANGER
Originally inhabitants of Madagascan rain forests, these endangered tomato frogs, *Dyscophus autongili*, are now adapting to other habitats, as the forests dwindle in size.

SWAMP DWELLER
The fiddler crab makes its burrow in the thick mud of mangrove swamps, emerging when the tide goes out. Only the males have a single, much enlarged front pincer. Useless for gathering food, it is used to signal alluringly to female crabs, and also to wrestle with rival males.

Bat has a wingspan of 24 in (60 cm)

FISHING FOR FOOD
The bulldog, or fisherman, bat, *Noctilio leporinus*, skims low over still water, using echolocation to detect ripples. It uses its sharply hooked claws to gaff fish out of the water. Its prey is either eaten on the wing or carried to a nearby roost.

Long tail for balance and to use as a rudder in water

Dry, scaly skin that is regularly shed, or sloughed off, to reveal a new layer

Powerful sharp-clawed feet for climbing

Hidden dangers

CURARE
The rough bark or roots of some *Strychnos* vines are ingredients of curare, used as an arrow poison by some tribes. In the past, each tribe had its own closely guarded secret recipe for making the poison.

Solid lump of prepared curare

L**URKING IN THE DEPTHS** of the jungle are animals and plants equipped with a lethal battery of foul-tasting poisons. They either manufacture the poisons themselves, or use those that were in their food, advertising their hidden armory with their bright colors. Venomous creatures such as snakes and spiders need powerful toxins to subdue prey that might inflict injury during a struggle. Plants contain poisons to prevent herbivores from eating all their foliage. The only indications that their green leaves are unpleasant are the smell and taste. They can afford to lose a few leaves, and animals soon learn to avoid them.

TAKING AIM
This Penan hunter in Borneo uses darts tipped with poisons. The poisons kill the catch quickly, so that it falls close to the hunter.

POTTED POISON
After the ingredients for curare are pounded together, the mixture is boiled or mixed with cold water. The thick liquid is strained off and kept in hollow gourds.

Arrow tipped with coating of curare

Living with poisons
The poisonous nature of animals and plants are understood by the peoples who live in the jungle. Many highly toxic plants are used in everyday life, both for hunting and, in far smaller doses, as medicines. Arrows are tipped with concoctions of plant or animal poisons. Poisonous leaves or sap are used to contaminate stretches of water so that many fish die at the same time. The poisons are mostly inactive if taken by mouth, so the meat is safe to eat.

Arrows used to hunt monkeys and other mammals

SAFETY TIPS
South American hunters tie their arrows together with cord and keep them securely in a bamboo quiver for safety. They have to be careful that they do not accidentally prick themselves with a poisoned tip.

Bamboo quiver

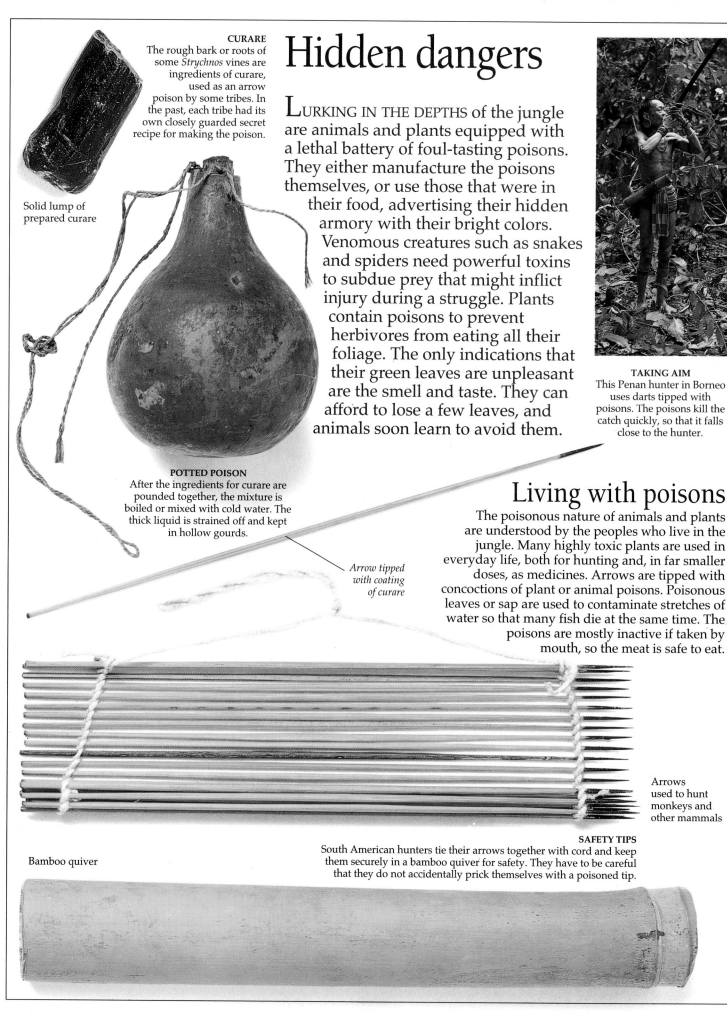

IMMUNE TO DANGER

A female postman butterfly lays her eggs on the youngest *Passiflora* leaves, because they contain the least poison. The larvae absorb the poisons into their bodies.

Small postman butterfly
Heliconius erato
(South America)

Blue poison dart frog
Dendrobates azureus
(South America)

POISON DART FROG

This forest-floor frog exudes powerful poisons from all over its skin if anything bothers it. Amerindian hunters use the poison to coat their blowpipe darts.

POISONOUS PLANT

If a plant loses most or all of its leaves, its ability to take in carbon dioxide and manufacture sugars is greatly reduced. The foliage of this large *Passiflora* climber contains a complex cocktail of chemicals, including bitter-tasting alkaloids and compounds that contain cyanide. Mammals will not eat it, and only a few leaf-eating insects such as postman butterflies and some species of beetle have evolved ways of overcoming its toxicity.

Thai monocled cobra
Naja kaouthia
(South-Eastasia)

Eyes set at side of head

Characteristic hood

Giant tiger centipede
Scolopendra gigantea
(Africa)

FATAL FEET

Dramatic orange and black stripes warn of this centipede's toxicity. It injects its prey with poisonous venom, using the first pair of its many legs, which have sharply tipped claws.

SUDDEN DEATH

This cobra is greatly feared. It inhabits buildings and scrubland as well as dense jungle, hunting at dusk and in the early morning. It takes prey, such as other reptiles and small mammals, by striking and gripping with front fangs that inject a highly toxic venom. The poison is also fatal to people, acting quickly on the nerves of the human respiratory system and the heart. When threatened, cobras rear up, hiss, and expand their "hood" by raising the elongated ribs of the neck region.

Nature's architects

THE RAIN FOREST PROVIDES tree holes, tangles of lianas, and plenty of other hideaways. In spite of this, numerous creatures build custom-made homes from forest materials. Social insects such as bees, wasps, ants, and termites construct elaborate nests inside of which a teeming mass of insects live and tend their larvae. These large colonies need well-protected structures to keep predators out. Some structures last for years. Birds are master weavers, but their nests are used only to rear young. Even less permanent are the beds made by gorillas. Every night, they prepare a mattress of leaves on the ground or among low branches.

THE CUTTING EDGE
Leafcutter ants (*Atta* sp.) live in underground nests in colonies of up to five million. "Media" workers only 10 mm long travel up into the canopy, where they snip out neat pieces of leaves with their jaws. A continuous trail of ants carries these like flags back to the nest. There, 2-mm-long "minima" workers chew the leaves to a paste, mixing it with feces. This concoction is used to grow a fungus on which the ants feed.

Ant domatia
Myrmecodia tuberosa

Scar left by fallen leaf

Stem is not lived in by ants

Thick fibrous stem

CLOSE PARTNERSHIP
The relationship between *Iridomyrmex* ants and the epiphyte *Myrmecodia tuberosa* is just one of many fascinating jungle partnerships. The ants enter air spaces inside the plant through tiny holes in the plant wall. They establish their colony, rearing young and setting up fungus gardens. Fragments of dead plants and animals are brought in to nourish the fungus. The decaying matter then provides valuable internal compost for the host plant.

Airholes where ants enter

BAT CAMP
A few species of New World spear-nosed bats make their own daytime shelters from large leaves such as palm fronds and *Heliconia* foliage. They either bite a neat line across the veins of fan-shaped leaves, or along the midrib of long leaves, so that part of the leaf blade flops down. During the day, the bats roost in their green tents. Males are usually solitary, but females, such as these Honduran white bats (*Ectophylla alba*), cluster in small groups, especially while rearing their young.

Swollen base of plant

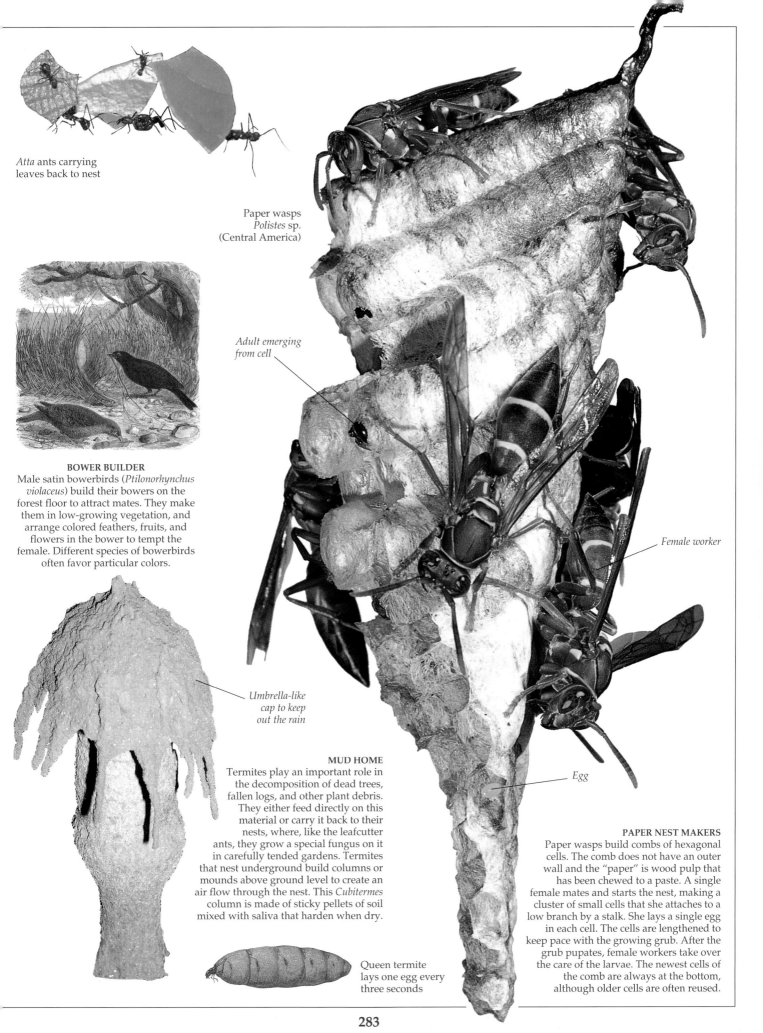

Atta ants carrying
leaves back to nest

Paper wasps
Polistes sp.
(Central America)

*Adult emerging
from cell*

Female worker

BOWER BUILDER
Male satin bowerbirds (*Ptilonorhynchus
violaceus*) build their bowers on the
forest floor to attract mates. They make
them in low-growing vegetation, and
arrange colored feathers, fruits, and
flowers in the bower to tempt the
female. Different species of bowerbirds
often favor particular colors.

*Umbrella-like
cap to keep
out the rain*

MUD HOME
Termites play an important role in
the decomposition of dead trees,
fallen logs, and other plant debris.
They either feed directly on this
material or carry it back to their
nests, where, like the leafcutter
ants, they grow a special fungus on it
in carefully tended gardens. Termites
that nest underground build columns or
mounds above ground level to create an
air flow through the nest. This *Cubitermes*
column is made of sticky pellets of soil
mixed with saliva that harden when dry.

Egg

PAPER NEST MAKERS
Paper wasps build combs of hexagonal
cells. The comb does not have an outer
wall and the "paper" is wood pulp that
has been chewed to a paste. A single
female mates and starts the nest, making a
cluster of small cells that she attaches to a
low branch by a stalk. She lays a single egg
in each cell. The cells are lengthened to
keep pace with the growing grub. After the
grub pupates, female workers take over
the care of the larvae. The newest cells of
the comb are always at the bottom,
although older cells are often reused.

Queen termite
lays one egg every
three seconds

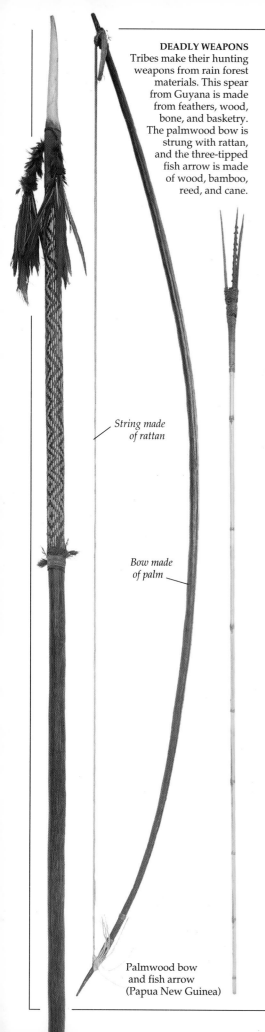

DEADLY WEAPONS
Tribes make their hunting weapons from rain forest materials. This spear from Guyana is made from feathers, wood, bone, and basketry. The palmwood bow is strung with rattan, and the three-tipped fish arrow is made of wood, bamboo, reed, and cane.

String made of rattan

Bow made of palm

Palmwood bow and fish arrow (Papua New Guinea)

House and home

WHEN PEOPLE NEED shelter, there is no shortage of building materials in the jungle. Slender tree trunks are felled for use as walls; palm fronds are cut for thatching; and tough cording is prepared from lianas. Some tribes build separate family homes grouped together in a forest clearing. Others favor one enormous structure that houses the whole community, and inside of which each family has its own hearth. Styles vary, but the houses share some features, such as an overhanging thatched roof to keep out the rain. Inside, each dwelling contains everyday utensils and weapons, skillfully made from natural materials such as bamboo and cane.

POTTER'S ART
The neolithic Kintampo culture brought pottery to the African rain forests. Containers such as this partly glazed pot from lower Zaire are still made today.

Model of a rain forest house without walls (South America)

Sturdy tree trunks form basic structure

WELL SHIELDED
Warring tribespeople held shields to ward off blows from spears or arrows. Today, they are more often used for ceremonial purposes. This colorful shield from Borneo is decorated on the front with human hair. The reverse depicts tigers and dragons, symbols of strength and invincibility.

Human hairs

Dyak shield (Borneo)

HIGH AND DRY
This hill tribe house in northern Thailand has central living quarters. It is well screened from the rain by thatching that sweeps down on all sides. The house is set on poles above the ground to keep the floor dry. Outside, there is plenty of shelter beneath the roof for outdoor tasks.

NATIVE HOUSE AT DORERI
Traveling by water is the easiest way to get around much of New Guinea because of the dense jungle vegetation. Many settlements are therefore built on the riverside or by the coast. This large house has been built on stilts over the water, probably in order to escape destructive insects such as termites.

LIVING IN THE RAIN FOREST
This model gives some idea of the the furniture and utensils found in a native rain forest house in South America. The occupants sleep in hammocks, knotted from cords. They weave lightweight vessels from cane or palm leaves, but heavy duty containers are made with strips of wood. Canoe paddles and weapons are also shaped from wood, and all of these items are stored by hanging them on the walls of the house. Clay pots are not made by all tribes, but are often acquired by trading.

Hammock

Fishing basket

CHIEF'S YAM HOUSE
Yams are an important staple food. On the Trobriand Islands, off the coast of New Guinea, yams are also a central part of complicated rituals that maintain goodwill and kinship between clans related by marriage. After the yam harvest, the chief's yam house is filled first. This brightly decorated house is thatched and has well-ventilated walls. This allows air to circulate so that the yams do not get moldy.

African jungles

OIL PALM
This 33-65 ft (10-20 m) palm (*Elaeis guineensis*) yields two valuable oils – palm oil from the red fibrous fruit pulp and palm kernel oil from the seeds.

ALTHOUGH THEY CONTAIN an impressive 17,000 species of flowering plants, African rain forests have fewer species than those of either America or Asia. There are also fewer kinds of ferns. This is because the climate of Africa became much drier during the last ice age, which ended about 12,000 years ago. Many animals, insects, and plants died out during this period. Those that survived lived in three well-separated pockets of forest that remained moist. As the ice retreated from the lands farther north, the climate became wetter, and the surviving rain forest species spread out from their isolated refuges.

STICKY FEET
The Madagascan day gecko (*Phelsuma madagascariensis*) has Velcro-like toe pads so it can cling to branches – and even run along their undersides.

☐ *Former rain forest*
☐ *Actual rain forest*

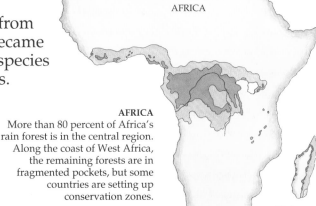

AFRICA

Madagascar

AFRICA
More than 80 percent of Africa's rain forest is in the central region. Along the coast of West Africa, the remaining forests are in fragmented pockets, but some countries are setting up conservation zones.

FLOWERS IN THE CANOPY
Of all the epiphytic flowering plants and ferns that grow in African jungles, over 60% are different kinds of orchids, and little is known about their life histories. *Polystachya galeata* comes from Sierra Leone, where new reserves will help to safeguard its future and that of other vulnerable species.

FAST GROWTH
Hibiscus shrubs grow quickly, up to 7 ft (2 m) tall. They flourish along the edges of the forest, where there is the most light. Their large flowers attract pollinators such as bees and butterflies.

Hibiscus
Hibiscus calyphyllus

GOOD APPETITES
African elephants prefer to browse the dense vegetation of clearings and forest margins. Over half of their diet is foliage from trees and large climbers, but they will travel far into the depths of the jungle to find their favorite tree fruits.

Black-and-white colobus
Colobus guereza
(Africa)

FLASH OF COLOR
The green and gold Senegal
parrots migrate across savanna
grassland into the forest to
take advantage of ripening
crops of fruits and seeds. They
nest in unlined tree holes.

FAMILY GROUP
The guereza is one of four
kinds of black-and-white
colobus monkey that live
in family groups in the
treetops. It is found in
central and eastern
Africa. Because these
monkeys eat a wide
range of readily
available leaves,
they do not need
a very large
home range.

*Only males have
a silver back*

*Large,
powerful
hands*

HEAD OF THE TRIBE
This silverback lowland gorilla *(Gorilla gorilla gorilla)*
is a mature male. He is the dominant head of a social
group that also contains mature females and young gorillas.
Silverbacks are gentle with their young, but as the males
reach maturity, they have to leave the troop and form their
own social group. Gorillas travel slowly through the forest,
resting, playing, and eating leaves, stems, and shoots.

Wing-stalked yam powder

Medicines

MOST OF THESE PLANTS are very poisonous. Yet, if taken at the right dosage, they help save lives or alleviate suffering. A rain forest can be compared to a giant pharmacy where tribespeople find remedies for all their ills. Only some of the medicinal plants have been screened scientifically. It is important to do this either before the plants become extinct, or the tribes, with their accumulated knowledge, disappear. Many plants are known to contain beneficial compounds. Others have a more spiritual importance. Some tribespeople think if a plant looks like a bodily organ, it will cure that organ of all ailments.

Wing-stalked yam
Dioscorea alata
(Southeast Asia)

INDIAN YAM
Yams are a good source of diosgenin, a compound used in oral contraceptives. It is also used in treatments for rheumatoid arthritis and rheumatic fever.

SKIN MEDICINE
Chaulmoogra ointment is an Indian preparation rubbed onto the skin to treat leprosy and skin infections.

Seed oil used in chaulmoogra ointment

Hydnocarpus fruit and seeds
Hydnocarpus kurzii
(Southeast Asia)

Red cinchona bark
Cinchona succirubra
(South America)

Dried tongue of pirarucu fish
(South America)

Guarana bark
Paullinia cupana
(South America)

Quinine stored in the bark

HARD MEDICINE
This hard fruit comes from the *Hydnocarpus* tree, grown in Burma, Thailand, and India for its medicinal properties.

PRECIOUS PLANT
The red cinchona tree is one of four commercial kinds of *Cinchona*. The quinine extracted from the bark and roots is an important part of the treatment of malaria, although synthetic drugs are also available today.

Heckel chew stick
Garcinia kola
(Africa)

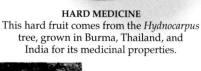

STIMULATING DRINKS
Guarana plants contain caffeine and are made into tonic drinks all over South America. Tribes grate the seeds (above) or bark into water with the rough, dried tongue of the pirarucu fish. Strong bitter doses are used to get rid of intestinal worms. The seeds are used commercially in carbonated drinks.

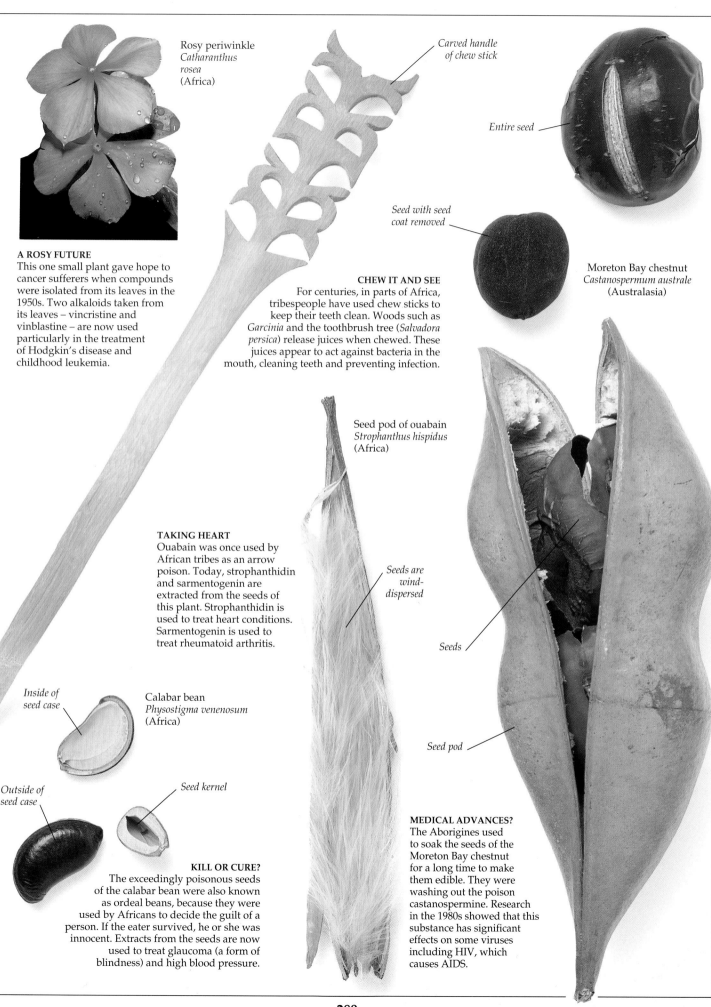

Rosy periwinkle
Catharanthus rosea
(Africa)

Carved handle
of chew stick

Entire seed

A ROSY FUTURE
This one small plant gave hope to cancer sufferers when compounds were isolated from its leaves in the 1950s. Two alkaloids taken from its leaves – vincristine and vinblastine – are now used particularly in the treatment of Hodgkin's disease and childhood leukemia.

Seed with seed
coat removed

CHEW IT AND SEE
For centuries, in parts of Africa, tribespeople have used chew sticks to keep their teeth clean. Woods such as *Garcinia* and the toothbrush tree (*Salvadora persica*) release juices when chewed. These juices appear to act against bacteria in the mouth, cleaning teeth and preventing infection.

Moreton Bay chestnut
Castanospermum australe
(Australasia)

Seed pod of ouabain
Strophanthus hispidus
(Africa)

TAKING HEART
Ouabain was once used by African tribes as an arrow poison. Today, strophanthidin and sarmentogenin are extracted from the seeds of this plant. Strophanthidin is used to treat heart conditions. Sarmentogenin is used to treat rheumatoid arthritis.

Seeds are
wind-
dispersed

Inside of
seed case

Calabar bean
Physostigma venenosum
(Africa)

Seeds

Outside of
seed case

Seed kernel

Seed pod

KILL OR CURE?
The exceedingly poisonous seeds of the calabar bean were also known as ordeal beans, because they were used by Africans to decide the guilt of a person. If the eater survived, he or she was innocent. Extracts from the seeds are now used to treat glaucoma (a form of blindness) and high blood pressure.

MEDICAL ADVANCES?
The Aborigines used to soak the seeds of the Moreton Bay chestnut for a long time to make them edible. They were washing out the poison castanospermine. Research in the 1980s showed that this substance has significant effects on some viruses including HIV, which causes AIDS.

Forest apes

THE TROPICAL RAIN FORESTS are home to all
of the world's apes, and most of its monkeys,
although there are no primates in New Guinea
and Australia. Many species are able to live close
together because they inhabit different levels in the
forest canopy, or eat different food. Even
so, some groups are highly territorial: one of the
lasting impressions of the jungle is the hollering
and screeching of monkeys and apes defending
their feeding area.

Very long arms

Jungle swinger

Gibbons like this siamang use their arms
to swing from branch to branch. This
process, called brachiation, is an
effective way of moving very quickly
through the forest canopy and is their
usual means of locomotion. They do fall
sometimes, with fatal results, but it is
the most efficient way of finding the
trees that have ripe fruit to eat.
Although gibbons use brachiation most,
chimpanzees and some monkeys
also use this method.

Siamang
Hylobates syndactylus
(Southeast Asia)

*Opposable
big toe*

GOING FOR A WALK
A gorilla moves around the forest floor
on the flat of its feet and its knuckles
in quest of the vast quantities of
vegetation that it needs to eat
every day. Although usually
slow-moving, it is capable
of bursts of speed when
necessary, for example
when chasing off a rival.

Gorilla
Gorilla gorilla
(Africa)

Gorillas have broad feet; the
big toes are opposable so
they can curl around to grip

Chimpanzees walk and
climb in lower canopy,
using both hands and feet

Gibbons spend all
their time up in trees;
they have narrow feet

JUNGLE CHORUS
The siamang is the largest of the gibbons. Each pair lives in the treetops with their offspring. They guard their territory and its vital food supply from neighboring siamangs with a morning and afternoon duet of ear-splitting shrieks and barks. The calls, which can be heard up to 0.6 miles (1 km) away, are given extra resonance by their inflated throat sacs.

Long, narrow hands with thumb cleft almost to the wrist

Forearm that can rotate 180°

Shoulder joint will rotate 360°

Powerful shoulder muscles

Leg outstretched to maximize forward movement

Broad chest

Legs curled up to increase upward stroke of swing

Legs shorter than arms

Long and opposable big toe

CLEVER CHIMP
This primate is very good with its hands. Most chimpanzees use twigs to get tasty morsels from difficult places, but some crack open nuts with stones or branches. They carry their "hammers" for long distances.

Chimpanzee
Pan troglodytes
(Africa)

Mandrill
Mandrillus sphinx
(Africa)

Humboldt's monkey
Lagothrix lagotricha
(South America)

MONKEY ON THE MARCH
Male mandrills live mostly on the forest floor. Females and their young climb up into low undergrowth.

TAIL GRIP
Tree-dwelling woolly monkeys use their prehensile (grasping) tails to grip slippery branches in the canopy.

Hunters and killers

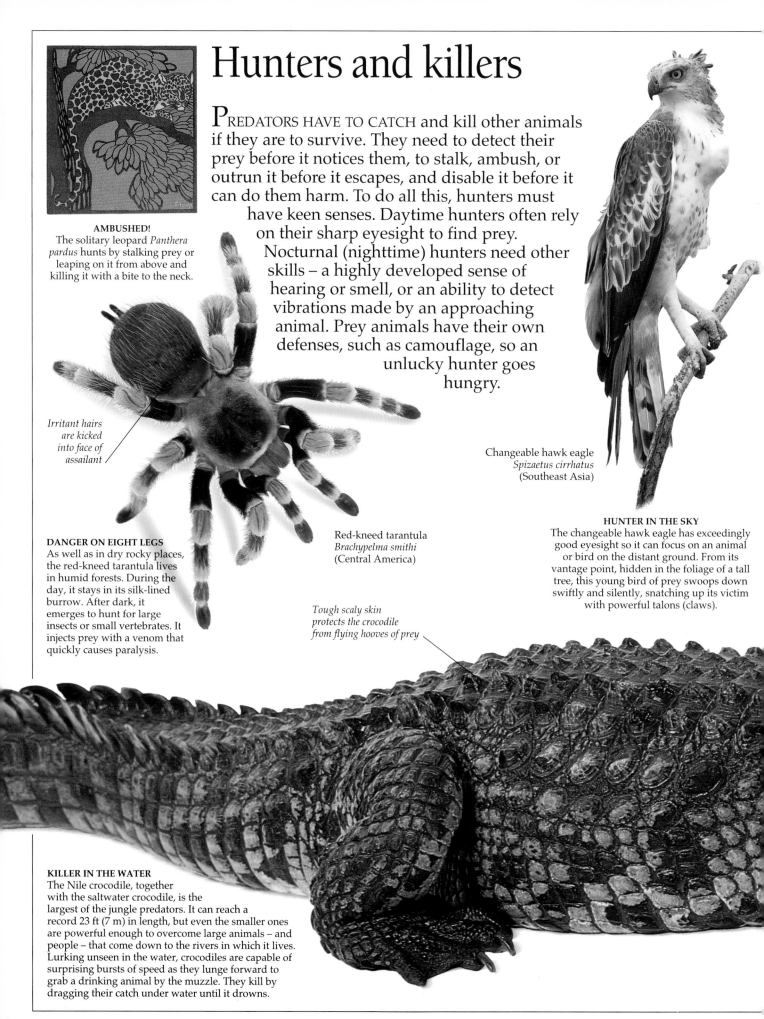

PREDATORS HAVE TO CATCH and kill other animals if they are to survive. They need to detect their prey before it notices them, to stalk, ambush, or outrun it before it escapes, and disable it before it can do them harm. To do all this, hunters must have keen senses. Daytime hunters often rely on their sharp eyesight to find prey. Nocturnal (nighttime) hunters need other skills – a highly developed sense of hearing or smell, or an ability to detect vibrations made by an approaching animal. Prey animals have their own defenses, such as camouflage, so an unlucky hunter goes hungry.

AMBUSHED!
The solitary leopard *Panthera pardus* hunts by stalking prey or leaping on it from above and killing it with a bite to the neck.

Irritant hairs are kicked into face of assailant

DANGER ON EIGHT LEGS
As well as in dry rocky places, the red-kneed tarantula lives in humid forests. During the day, it stays in its silk-lined burrow. After dark, it emerges to hunt for large insects or small vertebrates. It injects prey with a venom that quickly causes paralysis.

Red-kneed tarantula
Brachypelma smithi
(Central America)

Changeable hawk eagle
Spizaetus cirrhatus
(Southeast Asia)

HUNTER IN THE SKY
The changeable hawk eagle has exceedingly good eyesight so it can focus on an animal or bird on the distant ground. From its vantage point, hidden in the foliage of a tall tree, this young bird of prey swoops down swiftly and silently, snatching up its victim with powerful talons (claws).

Tough scaly skin protects the crocodile from flying hooves of prey

KILLER IN THE WATER
The Nile crocodile, together with the saltwater crocodile, is the largest of the jungle predators. It can reach a record 23 ft (7 m) in length, but even the smaller ones are powerful enough to overcome large animals – and people – that come down to the rivers in which it lives. Lurking unseen in the water, crocodiles are capable of surprising bursts of speed as they lunge forward to grab a drinking animal by the muzzle. They kill by dragging their catch under water until it drowns.

Juvenile lures prey with yellow tail

SMALL BUT DEADLY
The Southern fer-de-lance is nocturnal and
locates warm-blooded prey with heat-
sensitive pits between its eyes and
nostrils. When a victim is in range, this
viper gapes open its mouth, and two
long front fangs swing forward. As the
snake strikes, these fangs stab, injecting
a lethal venom. Most human deaths
from snake bites in South America are
due to this species.

Southern fer-de-lance
Bothrops atrox
(South America)

SQUEEZED TO DEATH
The boa constrictor waits motionless
until its prey comes close. The animal's air-
borne scent is picked up by the snake's tongue and transferred to
the sensitive Jacobson's organs on the roof of its mouth. The snake
strikes open-mouthed, gripping its catch with its fangs and coiling
around the animal's body. Each time the animal breathes out, the
snake tightens its coils a little more, until the prey is suffocated.

Boa constrictor
Boa constrictor
(Central and South
America)

*Formidable array of sharp teeth
that are replaced continuously
throughout the crocodile's life*

*Powerful jaws
to swallow
large prey*

Nile crocodile
Crocodylus niloticus
(Africa)

*Strong claws to
climb quickly up
slippery riverbanks*

TOOTH AND CLAW
The tiger *Panthera tigris* is a
solitary animal that hunts by
day or night. The tiger stalks a
victim, pouncing on it with
formidably clawed forepaws
and killing it with a bite to the
neck. A tiger's usual diet is deer,
goats, and sometimes large
cattle. Some tigers, particularly
old or injured animals, will go
after anything, including people.

Tropical Asia

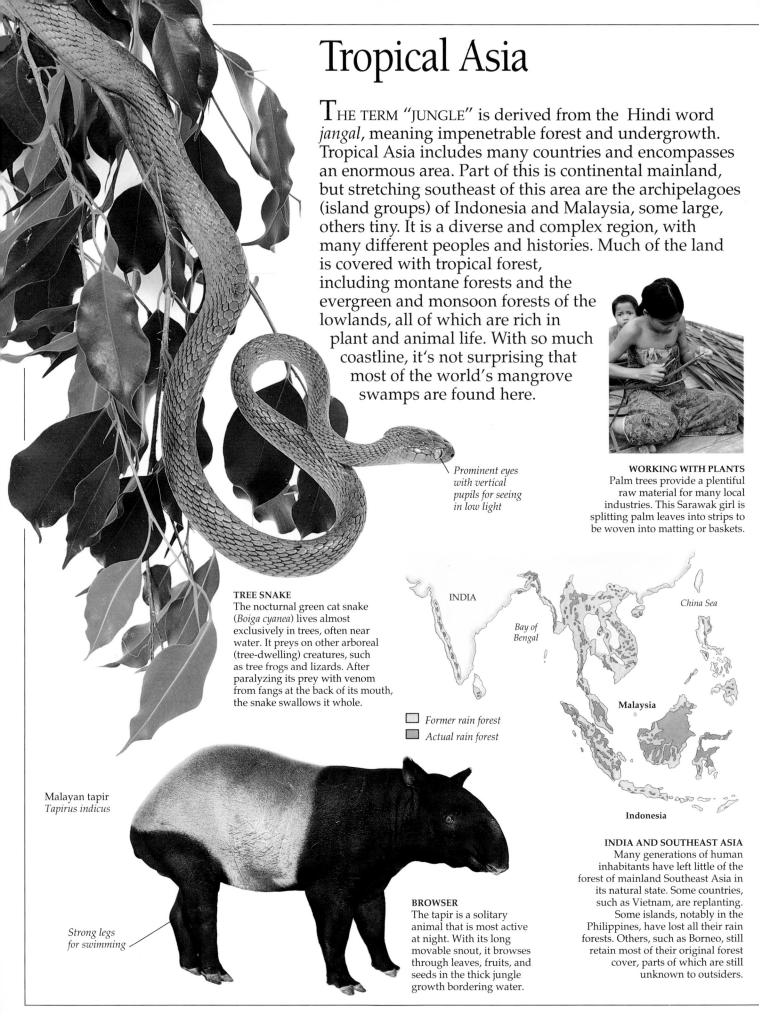

THE TERM "JUNGLE" is derived from the Hindi word *jangal*, meaning impenetrable forest and undergrowth. Tropical Asia includes many countries and encompasses an enormous area. Part of this is continental mainland, but stretching southeast of this area are the archipelagoes (island groups) of Indonesia and Malaysia, some large, others tiny. It is a diverse and complex region, with many different peoples and histories. Much of the land is covered with tropical forest, including montane forests and the evergreen and monsoon forests of the lowlands, all of which are rich in plant and animal life. With so much coastline, it's not surprising that most of the world's mangrove swamps are found here.

Prominent eyes with vertical pupils for seeing in low light

WORKING WITH PLANTS
Palm trees provide a plentiful raw material for many local industries. This Sarawak girl is splitting palm leaves into strips to be woven into matting or baskets.

TREE SNAKE
The nocturnal green cat snake (*Boiga cyanea*) lives almost exclusively in trees, often near water. It preys on other arboreal (tree-dwelling) creatures, such as tree frogs and lizards. After paralyzing its prey with venom from fangs at the back of its mouth, the snake swallows it whole.

INDIA

Bay of Bengal

China Sea

Malaysia

☐ *Former rain forest*
☐ *Actual rain forest*

Indonesia

Malayan tapir
Tapirus indicus

Strong legs for swimming

BROWSER
The tapir is a solitary animal that is most active at night. With its long movable snout, it browses through leaves, fruits, and seeds in the thick jungle growth bordering water.

INDIA AND SOUTHEAST ASIA
Many generations of human inhabitants have left little of the forest of mainland Southeast Asia in its natural state. Some countries, such as Vietnam, are replanting. Some islands, notably in the Philippines, have lost all their rain forests. Others, such as Borneo, still retain most of their original forest cover, parts of which are still unknown to outsiders.

Rattan palm
Calamus caesius

RATTAN PALMS
There are about 600 species of rattans. These are climbing palms that reach the canopy by means of whips on the tips of the fronds; these whips are covered with hooked spikes. Rattan canes are commercially important for making furniture that is exported all around the world.

Stem can reach over 660 ft (200 m) in length

Shape of petals attracts insects

ONE OF THE FEW
There are about 70 species of tropical slipper orchid, all of which are found in Southeast Asia. Most of them grow on the ground, but a few grow on trees or rocks. Many slipper orchids are naturally rare because they have specific habitat requirements. Since 1964, 20 new species have been described, and *Paphiopedilum primulinum* itself was only discovered in 1972.

Flower bud

Slipper orchid
Paphiopedilum primulinum

Leaf sheath covered in hooked spines

THE GINGER LILY
Many ginger lilies (*Hedychium* spp.) have fragrant, attractive flowers, and their thick underground stems often contain aromatic (nice-smelling) oils. After the tubular flower wilts, a fruit capsule develops. When this is ripe, it splits to reveal three rows of seeds.

Disguise and warning

ANIMALS AND INSECTS use camouflage in an effort to avoid being eaten. Color and shape either make an animal indistinguishable from its background, or trick a predator into thinking that it is dealing with something bigger or more dangerous. Animals with cryptic coloration have colors or patterns that closely match their background. Some patterns seem bold and conspicuous, but they actually make it impossible to see the animal against a mosaic of leaves, twigs, sunshine, and shadow by breaking up the animal's outline. Mimicry takes this kind of camouflage a stage further, in insects that look like leaves, bark, or twigs. The disguise of many insects is so good that, rather than waste time looking for them, flocks of several species of birds will move noisily through the forest like a wave. What small creatures one bird dislodges or disturbs, the bird behind snaps up.

MIMICKING A SNAKE
When disturbed, the caterpillar of the hawkmoth *Leucorhampha ornatus* mimics a small venomous pit viper. It does this by swinging the front part of its body upside down, inflating its thorax to look like a snake's head.

False leaf katydid
Ommatopia pictifolia
(Central America)

STARTLE DISPLAY
The forewings of the false leaf katydid are near-perfect replicas of dead leaves. When motionless, it blends in well with low-growing vegetation. However, if it is discovered, this katydid has a second line of defense. In one quick movement, the forewings part to reveal a startling display of eyespots. This display should scare a predator long enough for the katydid to escape.

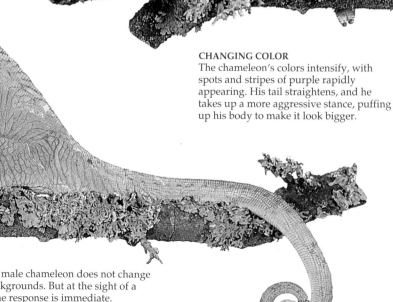

Parson's chameleon
Chamaeleo parsonii
(Africa)

CHANGING COLOR
The chameleon's colors intensify, with spots and stripes of purple rapidly appearing. His tail straightens, and he takes up a more aggressive stance, puffing up his body to make it look bigger.

REACTION TIME
Contrary to popular belief, a male chameleon does not change colour to match different backgrounds. But at the sight of a rival entering his territory, the response is immediate.

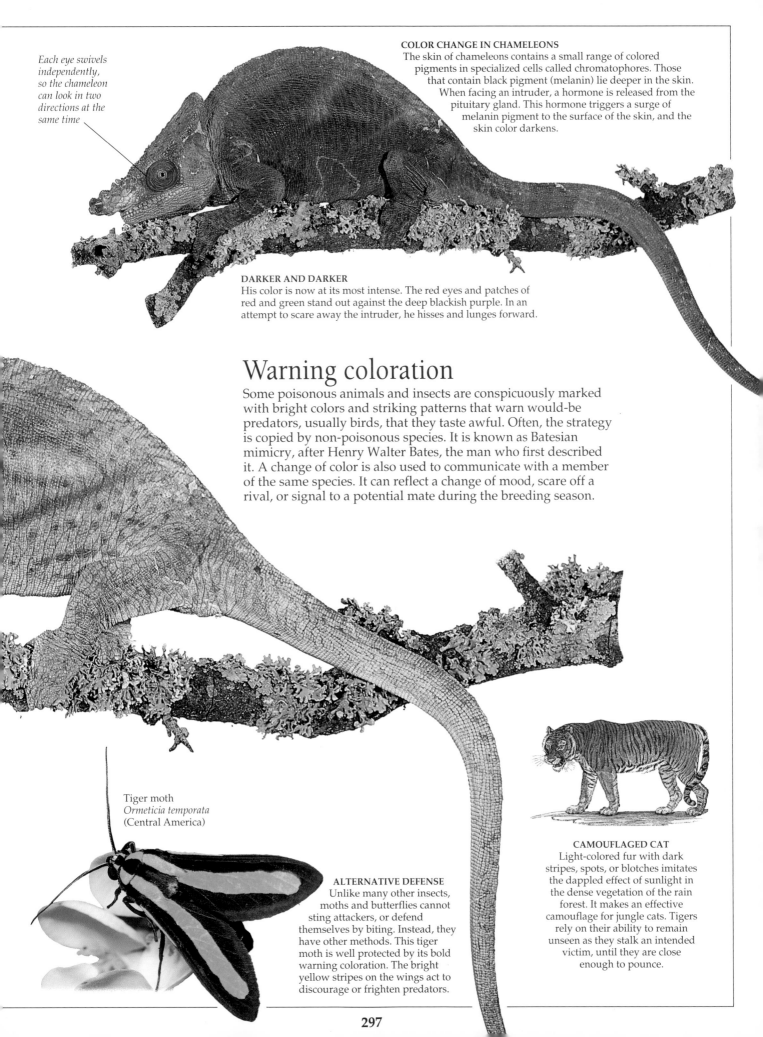

Each eye swivels independently, so the chameleon can look in two directions at the same time

COLOR CHANGE IN CHAMELEONS
The skin of chameleons contains a small range of colored pigments in specialized cells called chromatophores. Those that contain black pigment (melanin) lie deeper in the skin. When facing an intruder, a hormone is released from the pituitary gland. This hormone triggers a surge of melanin pigment to the surface of the skin, and the skin color darkens.

DARKER AND DARKER
His color is now at its most intense. The red eyes and patches of red and green stand out against the deep blackish purple. In an attempt to scare away the intruder, he hisses and lunges forward.

Warning coloration

Some poisonous animals and insects are conspicuously marked with bright colors and striking patterns that warn would-be predators, usually birds, that they taste awful. Often, the strategy is copied by non-poisonous species. It is known as Batesian mimicry, after Henry Walter Bates, the man who first described it. A change of color is also used to communicate with a member of the same species. It can reflect a change of mood, scare off a rival, or signal to a potential mate during the breeding season.

Tiger moth
Ormeticia temporata
(Central America)

ALTERNATIVE DEFENSE
Unlike many other insects, moths and butterflies cannot sting attackers, or defend themselves by biting. Instead, they have other methods. This tiger moth is well protected by its bold warning coloration. The bright yellow stripes on the wings act to discourage or frighten predators.

CAMOUFLAGED CAT
Light-colored fur with dark stripes, spots, or blotches imitates the dappled effect of sunlight in the dense vegetation of the rain forest. It makes an effective camouflage for jungle cats. Tigers rely on their ability to remain unseen as they stalk an intended victim, until they are close enough to pounce.

Tricks and traps

At ALL LEVELS of the rain forest, there is a host of alert, wary creatures with a strong instinct for survival. A predator always has to outsmart its prey if it is to catch enough to eat. Some hunters combine trickery and deception with patience and the ability to move at lightning speed. Plants have a few tricks of their own. Sap-sucking insects may have their mouthparts gummed up by an unexpected flow of sticky latex. Plants that grow on poor or peaty soils cannot get enough nutrients. In order to survive, some of these plants have turned into carnivores.

Nectar-secreting gland

Leaf blade

Monkey cup
Nepenthes mirabilis

SLIPPERY SLOPE
The rim of the pitcher plant is very slippery. Small vertebrates and insects lose their footing and fall into the trap.

Partly digested insects

Digestive gland

NETTED
Instead of waiting for an insect to fly into its web, the net-casting spider (*Dinopus* spp.) nets its prey. Suspended from lines of silk attached to a twig, it spins a small web. Holding the web with its four front legs, the spider hangs upside down and waits. When an unsuspecting insect comes close, the spider drops the net and captures its prey.

Pitcher develops at tip of leaf

HUNGRY PLANT
Insects are attracted by the color of the pitcher plants and by nectar secreted around the rim. Once the insect falls in, it can't get out. It is digested by enzymes in the water half-filling each pitcher and is absorbed into the plant. The largest pitcher plants have pitchers 30 cm (12 in) long that hold 4 pints (2 liters) of water.

DEADLY LEAVES
The gaboon viper (*Bitis gabonica*) is patterned just like the sun-flecked leaves on the forest floor. It remains motionless and invisible until a small mammal or bird strays too close. Its 2-in-long (5 cm-) fangs inject a venom that is almost instantly fatal.

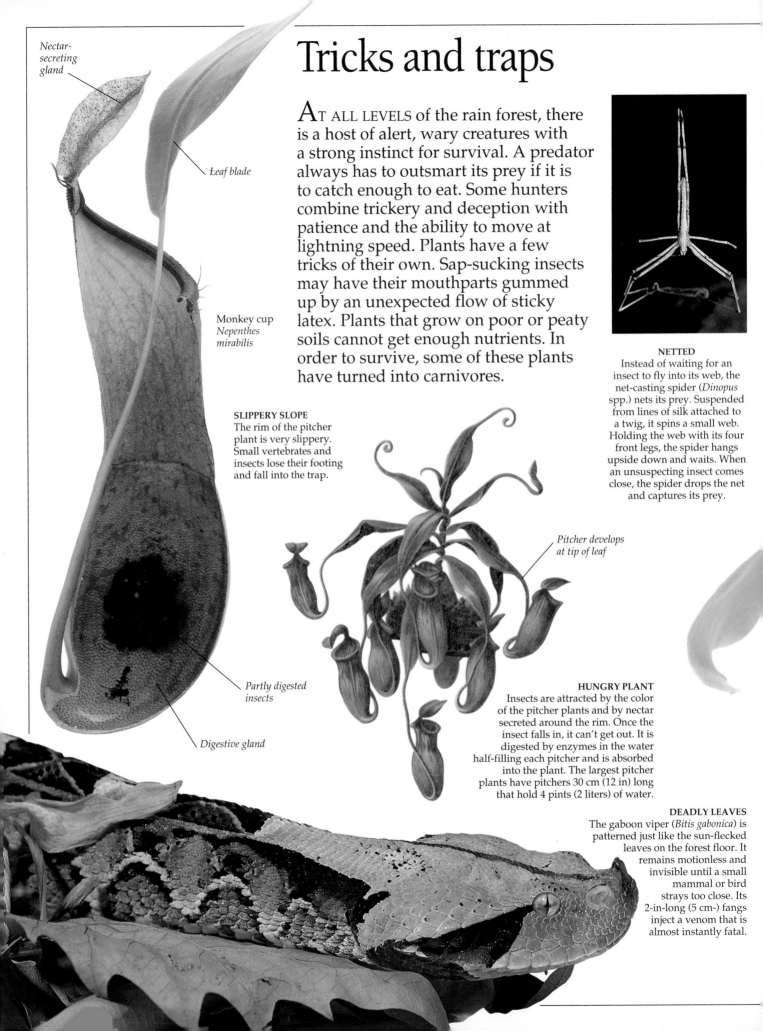

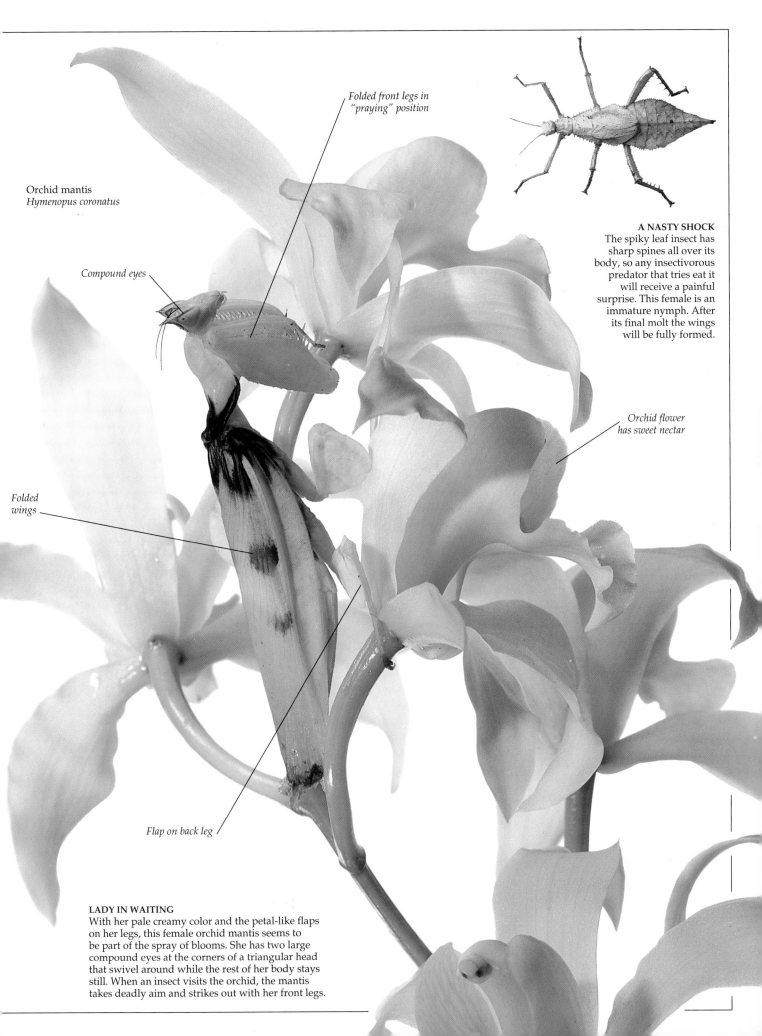

Orchid mantis
Hymenopus coronatus

*Folded front legs in
"praying" position*

Compound eyes

*Folded
wings*

Flap on back leg

A NASTY SHOCK
The spiky leaf insect has
sharp spines all over its
body, so any insectivorous
predator that tries eat it
will receive a painful
surprise. This female is an
immature nymph. After
its final molt the wings
will be fully formed.

*Orchid flower
has sweet nectar*

LADY IN WAITING
With her pale creamy color and the petal-like flaps
on her legs, this female orchid mantis seems to
be part of the spray of blooms. She has two large
compound eyes at the corners of a triangular head
that swivel around while the rest of her body stays
still. When an insect visits the orchid, the mantis
takes deadly aim and strikes out with her front legs.

Flying high

LIVING IN THE CANOPY many yards above the ground is fine until an animal needs to travel from one treetop to the next in search of food or to escape a predator. Running down one tree trunk, along the ground, and up the next is hazardous and a waste of energy. Traveling through the air overcomes this, but only birds, bats, and insects have the wings and muscles that permit controlled flight. However, an assortment of other creatures have evolved ways of gliding through the air by increasing their body area, often with flaps of skin. When airborne, these flaps spread out like parachutes, increasing their wind resistance and slowing down the rate of descent. This prevents a damaging collision with the ground below. Many of these gliders can alter direction in midair by moving their legs, tail, or body, and some travel remarkable distances in this way.

FROG BEETLE
This Malayan frog beetle (*Sagra buqueti*) has its wings folded under wing cases called elytra.

BEETLING ABOUT
Before flying, this leaf beetle (*Doryphorella langsdorfii*) opens its elytra and spreads its wings.

BIRDS OF PARADISE
The splendid plumage of male birds of paradise is used simply to attract a mate. Males gather in groups called leks in order to display. Some choose a high treetop and, as day breaks, give a colorful display, flashing their bright, iridescent plumage, while making loud calls.

FLYING GECKO
This nocturnal gecko (*Ptychozoon kuhli*) lives in trees and relies on camouflage to hide it from predators. If it is spotted, it escapes by launching itself into the air and gliding to safety. Loose flaps of skin along each side of its body, and smaller flaps on its legs, spread out and fill with air.

Wide scales along tail

Flaps make lizard wider and flatter for gliding

Long legs for running

FLYING FROG
The Malaysian flying frog (*Rhacophorus reinwardii*) is one of a small number of rain forest tree frogs that leap out of a tree to escape from a pursuer. The digits of their very large hands and feet are connected by webs of skin. During long gliding leaps, these webs of skin serve as parachutes.

HUNTING WASP
The electric blue female hunting wasp (*Chlorion lobatum*) cruises low over the forest floor, hunting for crickets. It grips its prey with powerful jaws and paralyzes it with venom injected by its stinger. It drags the insect into a burrow and lays a single egg in it so that, on hatching, the larva has food until it pupates.

Webbing between toes

Blue-and-yellow macaw
Ara ararauna
(South America)

EXPERT PILOTS
Macaws have short, broad wings
so that they can skillfully maneuver
between the leafy branches of the forest canopy.
They fly considerable distances in search of trees
bearing ripe fruits. By changing the position of their
wings and tail feathers, they can glide and brake
before landing on a branch or at a tree-hole nesting site.

FLYING SNAKE
The flying tree snake (*Chrysopelea
pelias*) is one of five species from
Southeast Asia that can glide through
the air. By raising its ribs upward and
outward, the snake flattens its body and
manages to travel distances of up to 165
ft (50 m) from one tree to another.

Flying
dragon
Draco spp.

FLYING LIZARD
Flying dragons have six or
seven pairs of elongated ribs
covered with a membrane of
skin. These "wings" fold up
against the lizard's body,
but open out so it can glide
long distances.

*Wing
pattern and
colors help
males and
females find
each other*

GIANT MOTH
The Atlas moth (*Attacus atlas*) is
one of the largest moths, with a
wingspan of 10-12 in (25-30 cm).
Unlike those of other insects, the wings
of moths and butterflies are covered
with minute, overlapping scales. These
are richly colored, some because they
contain colored pigments, others
because of the way that they reflect
the light that falls on them.

Australasian rain forests

ONE HUNDRED MILLION years ago, Australia was part of Antarctica, and rain forest covered the moist coastal regions of this vast southern continent. As Australia separated and drifted north, it became drier, and Antarctica colder. Australia's rain forests are all that is left of this ancient jungle, and contain some primitive flowering plants and conifers. Apart from the bats, all the native animals are pouch-bearing marsupials. New Guinea is to the north, a heavily forested island with a mixture of Asian and Australian plants and animals.

DANGER UNDERFOOT
The marbled scorpion (*Lychas marmoreus*) is found under bark and among leaf litter, where it hunts for small invertebrates. It usually overpowers its victims with its front claws and jaws. The venomous sting in the tail is used primarily for defense.

RARE AND BEAUTIFUL
Living only in a small area of the extreme southeast of Papua New Guinea, this is one of the world's rarest butterflies. It is also the largest—the female has a wingspan of up to 11 in (28 cm). These butterflies are found in the forest margins, but little is known about them.

The male is smaller than the female

Queen Alexandra's birdwing
Ornithoptera alexandrae

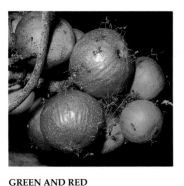

GREEN AND RED
The tiny flowers of this fig (*Ficus racemosus*) are contained in the fleshy green swellings that will eventually become sweet fruits. When the figs ripen, they turn red.

IN THE SHADE
This fleshy-stemmed fern lives beside water in shady forests. There is little strengthening tissue in the leaf stalks, and they soon wilt in dry conditions. *Angiopteris* ferns are very similar to the primitive ferns and tree ferns that were alive 325 to 280 million years ago, in the Upper Carboniferous period.

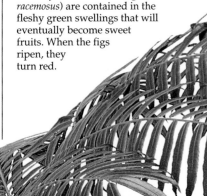

Long, arching leaf stalk

Marattia fern
Angiopteris lygodiifolia

SOGERI SING-SING
In Papua New Guinea elaborate rituals and ceremonies such as the sing-sings have always been an important part of tribal life. New Guinea men adorn themselves with brightly colored body paints, feathers, shells, and beads. Head-dresses made with bird of paradise feathers are especially prestigious.

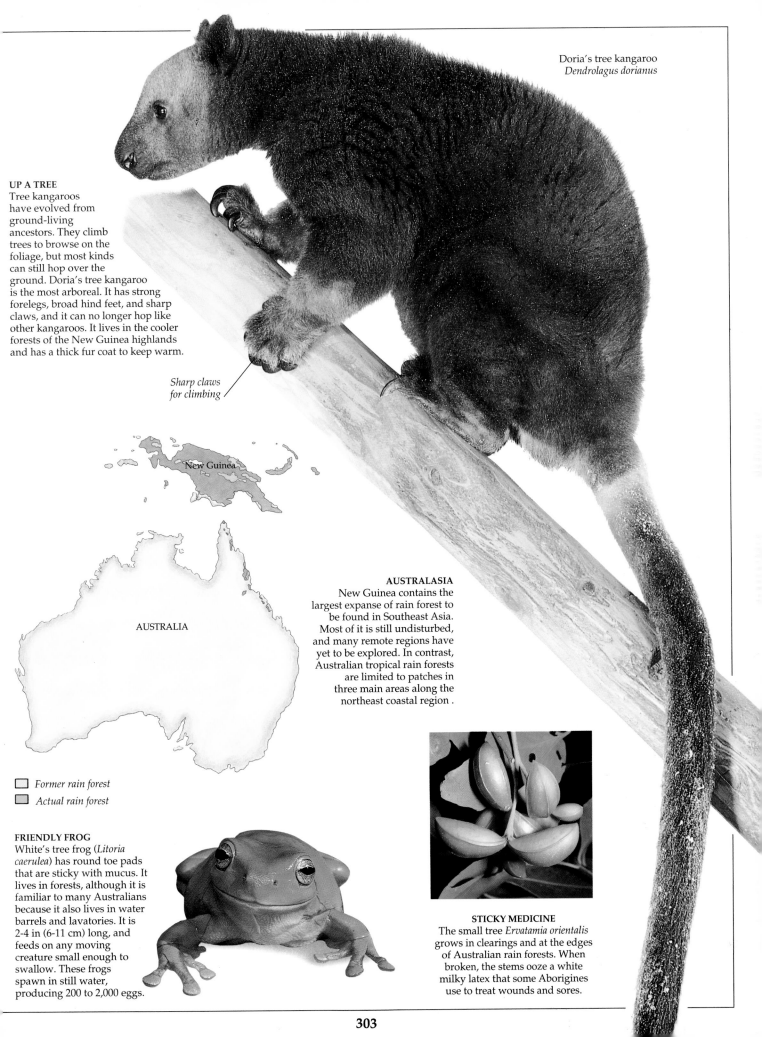

Doria's tree kangaroo
Dendrolagus dorianus

UP A TREE
Tree kangaroos
have evolved from
ground-living
ancestors. They climb
trees to browse on the
foliage, but most kinds
can still hop over the
ground. Doria's tree kangaroo
is the most arboreal. It has strong
forelegs, broad hind feet, and sharp
claws, and it can no longer hop like
other kangaroos. It lives in the cooler
forests of the New Guinea highlands
and has a thick fur coat to keep warm.

*Sharp claws
for climbing*

New Guinea

AUSTRALIA

☐ *Former rain forest*
☐ *Actual rain forest*

AUSTRALASIA
New Guinea contains the
largest expanse of rain forest to
be found in Southeast Asia.
Most of it is still undisturbed,
and many remote regions have
yet to be explored. In contrast,
Australian tropical rain forests
are limited to patches in
three main areas along the
northeast coastal region .

FRIENDLY FROG
White's tree frog (*Litoria
caerulea*) has round toe pads
that are sticky with mucus. It
lives in forests, although it is
familiar to many Australians
because it also lives in water
barrels and lavatories. It is
2-4 in (6-11 cm) long, and
feeds on any moving
creature small enough to
swallow. These frogs
spawn in still water,
producing 200 to 2,000 eggs.

STICKY MEDICINE
The small tree *Ervatamia orientalis*
grows in clearings and at the edges
of Australian rain forests. When
broken, the stems ooze a white
milky latex that some Aborigines
use to treat wounds and sores.

Jungle produce

FOR MANY CENTURIES, jungle products have been carried all around the world. A few, such as rubber, sugar, and chocolate, are now so much a part of everyday life it is easy to forget their rain forest origins. Products sold all over the world are grown mostly in plantations. However, some, such as Brazil nuts, are still gathered from the forest. Many of the fruits and seeds that the native peoples have enjoyed for a long time are only now beginning to find new markets in North America and Europe. In the future, we may be enjoying ice creams and using cosmetics that contain ever more exotic ingredients from the jungle.

NUTMEG PLANT
The red aril around the nutmeg seed is also used as a spice called mace.

VAN HOUTEN'S
ROVA COCOA
PURE SOLUBLE

A POPULAR FLAVOR
Over 1,227,000 tons of cocoa beans are produced every year to manufacture chocolate, cocoa, and cocoa butter.

SPICING IT UP
Strongly flavored spices such as pepper, ginger, cloves, and nutmeg were highly prized and very expensive in Europe in the Middle Ages. They were used to hide the tainted flavor of bad meat. Today, they are used to enhance the flavor of food, and to make medicines and toothpastes taste better. Spices are prepared from different parts of plants. For example, nutmeg is a seed, cloves are unopened flower buds, cinnamon comes from bark, and ginger is a root. Spices are dried and can be ground into a powder.

Ginger
Zingiber officinale

Cloves
Syzygium aromaticum

Nutmeg
Myristica fragrans

Cinnamon
Cinnamomum zeylanicum

COCOA BEANS
Cocoa trees have been cultivated for over 2,000 years in Central America. The Aztecs called the pods "cacahual," and believed that Quetzalcoatl, the plumed serpent god, dined on them. When ripe, cocoa pods are cut and split open by hand. The wet, pulpy mass of seeds is piled into baskets and allowed to ferment to lose unwanted pulp and develop the flavor. Then the seeds – the cocoa beans – are dried, cleaned, and polished, ready for export.

Cocoa pod
Theobroma cacao

Pulp

Rows of 20-60 oval seeds are embedded in a sweet pulp

304

Starfruit
Averrhoa carambola

Pineapple
Ananas comosus

STARFRUIT
Starfruits grow wild in Indonesian forests, but are planted widely in tropical Asia. They are an attractive garnish on food, as well as a source of vitamin C and iron.

SWEET POTATO
This starchy root (*Ipomoea batatas*) originated in tropical America and contains sugars, so it is pleasantly sweet. Sweet potatoes are boiled, roasted, or dried and ground into flour.

BREADFRUIT
The mass of flowers on this plant develop into the breadfruit, which is 8-12 in (20-30 cm) across and can weigh as much as 4 lb 4 oz (2 kg). Its moist, starchy flesh is cooked as a vegetable.

RUBBER
Over 1,000 kinds of plants produce the white, sticky latex that can be made into rubber. The para rubber tree (*Hevea brasiliensis*) is by far the most commonly used.

Pineapple cloth, or piña

Breadfruit
Artocarpus altilis

PINEAPPLE
Originating in South America, pineapples are now grown in many tropical countries. Both fresh and canned pineapples are popular foods, but the leaves have a different use. In the Philippines, thin fibers are extracted, prepared, spun, and woven by hand to make a fine sheer cloth called piña. Piña shirts are part of the national costume.

Explorers

Large, sturdy prehensile tail

THE PROFITABLE spice market drew Portuguese, English, and Dutch explorers to the forested islands of Southeast Asia in the 15th, 16th, and 17th centuries. At the same time, Spanish conquistadors were exploring Central America and Peru, interested more in ransacking Aztec and Inca gold than in the jungles. From the 16th century onward, rival European nations fought to extend their empires in tropical regions. The 18th and 19th centuries saw a steady rise in scientific curiosity about these areas, with explorers such as Darwin and Wallace evolving the theories that have shaped modern thinking.

WILLIAM BLIGH (1754-1817)
For explorers who sailed the seas in bygone days, conditions were harsh. In 1789, Captain Bligh was skipper of the *Bounty*, commissioned to transport young breadfruit trees from the islands of Tahiti to the West Indies. His crew, who wanted to stay on Tahiti, rebelled, and the famous mutiny took place. A second attempt to deliver the trees succeeded and one, planted by Bligh on St. Vincent, is still standing.

AIMÉ BONPLAND (1773-1858)
With von Humboldt, the Frenchman Aimé Bonpland explored both montane and lowland rain forests. Bonpland was a gifted artist and botanist, and recorded over 3,000 new species of plant, such as this *Melastoma coccinea*, in a splendid series of paintings.

Simia ursina painted by Alexander von Humboldt

ALEXANDER VON HUMBOLDT (1769-1859)
This German naturalist landed in Venezuela in 1799, with Bonpland. Von Humboldt had a keen scientific interest in the animals, plants, and places he discovered.

IT'S ALL IN THE NAME
This woolly monkey, *Lagothrix lagotricha* (left), comes from the Orinoco and Upper Amazon basins. It is often called Humboldt's monkey to commemorate the intrepid explorer, who had to put up with swarms of biting insects and fevers in this very humid region.

Livingstone's compass

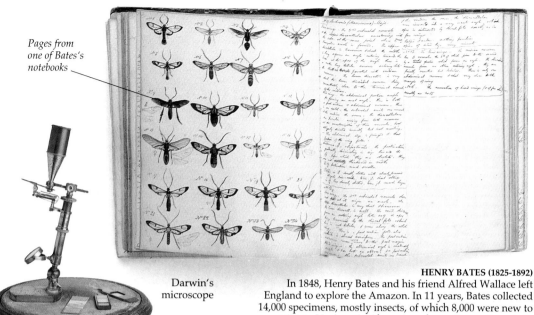

Pages from one of Bates's notebooks

Darwin's microscope

DAVID LIVINGSTONE (1813-1873)
Livingstone, a Scotsman, traveled to Africa to combine his missionary calling with exploration of "the interior". He made three expeditions, traveling by river and mapping the Zambesi River and parts of the Nile.

CHARLES DARWIN (1809-1882)
Abandoning medicine and the priesthood, Darwin joined the crew of the *Beagle* in 1831. He was hired to record wildlife found during the ship's mission to chart the South American coastline. The observations he made formed the basis for his theory of evolution.

HENRY BATES (1825-1892)
In 1848, Henry Bates and his friend Alfred Wallace left England to explore the Amazon. In 11 years, Bates collected 14,000 specimens, mostly insects, of which 8,000 were new to science. He described how some harmless species mimic poisonous ones; this is now known as Batesian mimicry.

Glass roof like greenhouse

BRINGING IT HOME
Transporting specimens back from the rainforests has always been difficult. This early 20th-century Wardian case (left) is a portable greenhouse used to carry plants safely back to the Royal Botanic Gardens in Kew, England. Plant specimens were also preserved by being pressed flat between sheets of absorbent paper. Succulent plants and fruits were preserved in spirits to stop them from getting moldy.

YOUNG VENTURER
Since the 1970s, Colonel John Blashford-Snell has probably done most to enable biologists and young people called Venturers to investigate the canopy. In Operations Drake and Raleigh, the biologists and Venturers studied plants and animals from lightweight aluminium walkways many feet above the ground.

Under threat

EVERY YEAR BETWEEN ONE AND TWO PERCENT of the world's rainforest is cleared. The trees may be felled, often illegally, for logs and to clear land for farming. Some areas of rainforest have been polluted by mining activities. New roads have opened up once inaccessible regions, and people settling alongside them clear more land to grow crops. Conserving rainforests is one of the biggest challenges for environmentalists. At the current rate of deforestation, some scientists estimate that 17,000 species of rainforest plants and animals become extinct every year.

CLEARANCE FOR CATTLE RANCHING
In South and Central America, cleared tropical rainforest provides pasture for beef cattle. When ranchers move into the forest, they burn trees to clear the land for farming. After five years, each animal needs 12.5 acres (5 hectares) to graze. After 10 years the land is useless. Overgrazing, the impact of the animals' hooves, and the loss of the trees lead to soil erosion.

ENVIRONMENTAL INFLUENCES
Rainforests influence the carbon cycle and have a profound effect on rainfall. The uneven surface of treetops causes air turbulence that increases the amount of water evaporating from the forest. This forms clouds that fall as rain. If the forests disappear, less rain will fall, it will drain more quickly, and air and soil temperatures will rise.

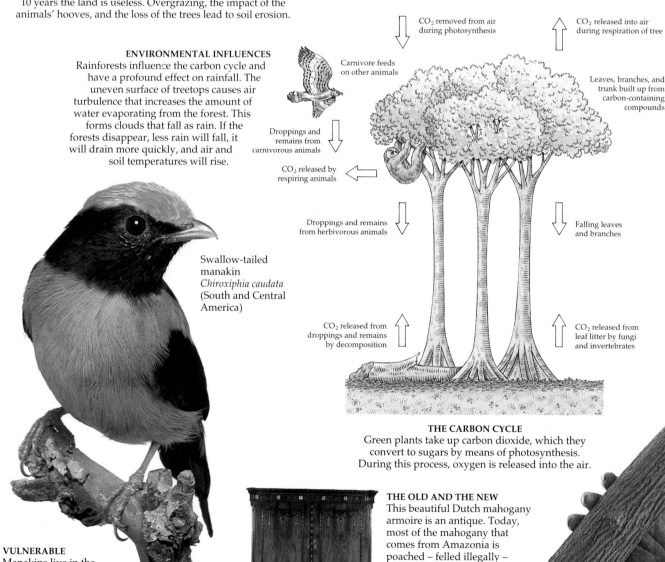

CO_2 removed from air during photosynthesis

CO_2 released into air during respiration of tree

Carnivore feeds on other animals

Leaves, branches, and trunk built up from carbon-containing compounds

Droppings and remains from carnivorous animals

CO_2 released by respiring animals

Droppings and remains from herbivorous animals

Falling leaves and branches

CO_2 released from droppings and remains by decomposition

CO_2 released from leaf litter by fungi and invertebrates

THE CARBON CYCLE
Green plants take up carbon dioxide, which they convert to sugars by means of photosynthesis. During this process, oxygen is released into the air.

Swallow-tailed manakin
Chiroxiphia caudata
(South and Central America)

VULNERABLE
Manakins live in the thickest forests and are not endangered at present. But their lifestyle and specialized diet of small soft fruits makes them vulnerable to forest disturbance.

THE OLD AND THE NEW
This beautiful Dutch mahogany armoire is an antique. Today, most of the mahogany that comes from Amazonia is poached – felled illegally – at the expense of the lives and livelihood of the Amerindian tribespeople.

EMBROIDERED CLOTH, NILGIRI HILLS
In the Nilgiri Hills, in India, a large area of forest has been made into a Biosphere Reserve. Tribal groups are encouraged to live there in a traditional way, and they supplement their livelihood by making items for export.

Maxillaria fulgens (Central America)

WIGMAN OF THE HULI TRIBE
Papua New Guinea has some of the least disturbed areas of rain forest. Many tribes live there, but the harmony with their surroundings is easily disrupted.

OBSESSIVE COLLECTION
Many of the estimated 18,000 species of orchid are found in rain forests. Their exotic blooms attract collectors, and the trade in these flowers, although frequently illegal, is worth a lot of money. Orchids are highly susceptible to over-collection, and some face extinction in the wild.

Orangutan
Pongo pygmaeus
(Southeast Asia)

Arms are much longer than legs

Short fifth toe to help grip branches when swinging

NOWHERE TO LIVE
Selective logging removes target trees but leaves the rest. The increased light stimulates new growth, which benefits some animals, such as leaf-eating primates that prefer young foliage. Others are not so adaptable. The adult orangutan forages over a wide area on its own and is highly sensitive to disturbance. Like all other jungle creatures, this "man of the forest" has a right to survive.

Desert rose

Tuareg cross

Uzbeki children's mobile

Uzbeki camel drape

Lanner falcon

Tewa Indian boy's rattle decorated with hummingbird tracks

Jordanian Bedouin coffee pots

Tadpole
shrimp

Tadpole
shrimp

DESERT

Tuareg
dagger

Tuareg
dagger

What is a desert?

WITH LITTLE RAIN and extreme temperatures, deserts are some of the harshest places on Earth. A desert is strictly defined as a place with 10 in (25 cm) of rain or less a year. Hot deserts are found around the tropics, where the Earth's wind system brings cloudless days. This means that there are no clouds to shield the ground, which in the summer becomes baking hot during the day, then cold at night as the heat is lost back to the atmosphere. Deserts at higher latitudes are cold deserts. Land formations also affect rainfall: some deserts occur within large land masses, such as Australia, where winds from the coast have lost all their moisture by the time they get there; others occur on the lee (far) side of mountains, where there is no rain left in the wind which has blown over the mountains.

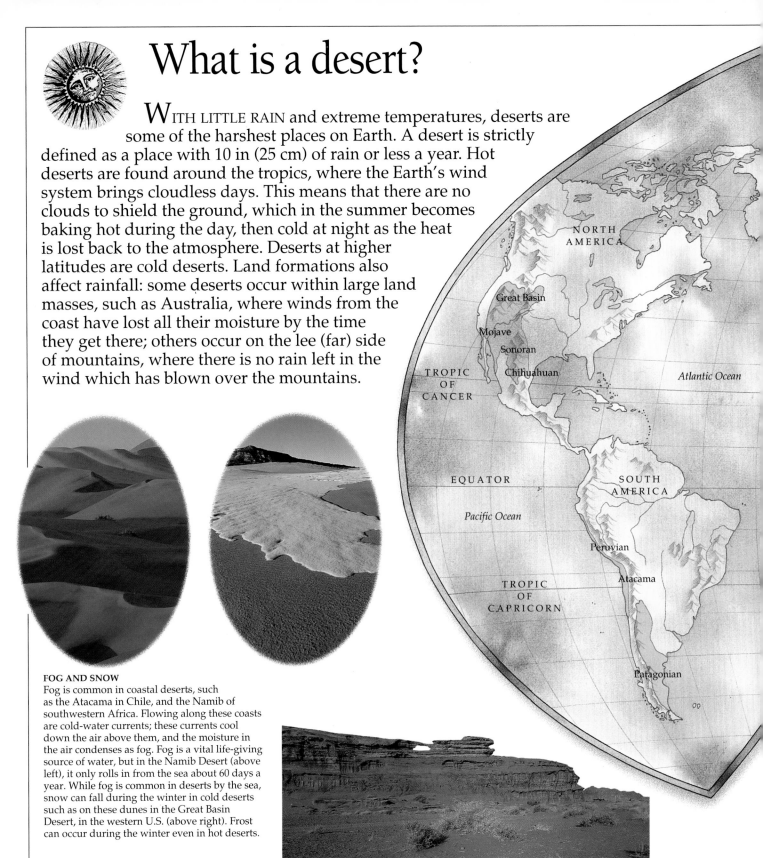

FOG AND SNOW
Fog is common in coastal deserts, such as the Atacama in Chile, and the Namib of southwestern Africa. Flowing along these coasts are cold-water currents; these currents cool down the air above them, and the moisture in the air condenses as fog. Fog is a vital life-giving source of water, but in the Namib Desert (above left), it only rolls in from the sea about 60 days a year. While fog is common in deserts by the sea, snow can fall during the winter in cold deserts such as on these dunes in the Great Basin Desert, in the western U.S. (above right). Frost can occur during the winter even in hot deserts.

PAST CLIMATES
Fossil remains of a small kind of hippopotamus have been found in the Arabian Desert, showing that 6 million years ago the climate was much wetter: hippopotamuses need lush and humid conditions. Remains from the Stone-Age show that hippos also lurked in marshes once found in the Sahara, which has gone through several wet and dry climate cycles.

WEATHERED ROCKS *above*
Rocks in the desert are weathered or worn away by wind, extreme temperatures, and rare but torrential rains. Strong winds pick up sand, which then scours away at the rock, much like the sandblasting process used to clean dirt off old stone buildings. These sandstone cliffs are in the Jordanian desert. At the top of the cliff is a natural bridge.

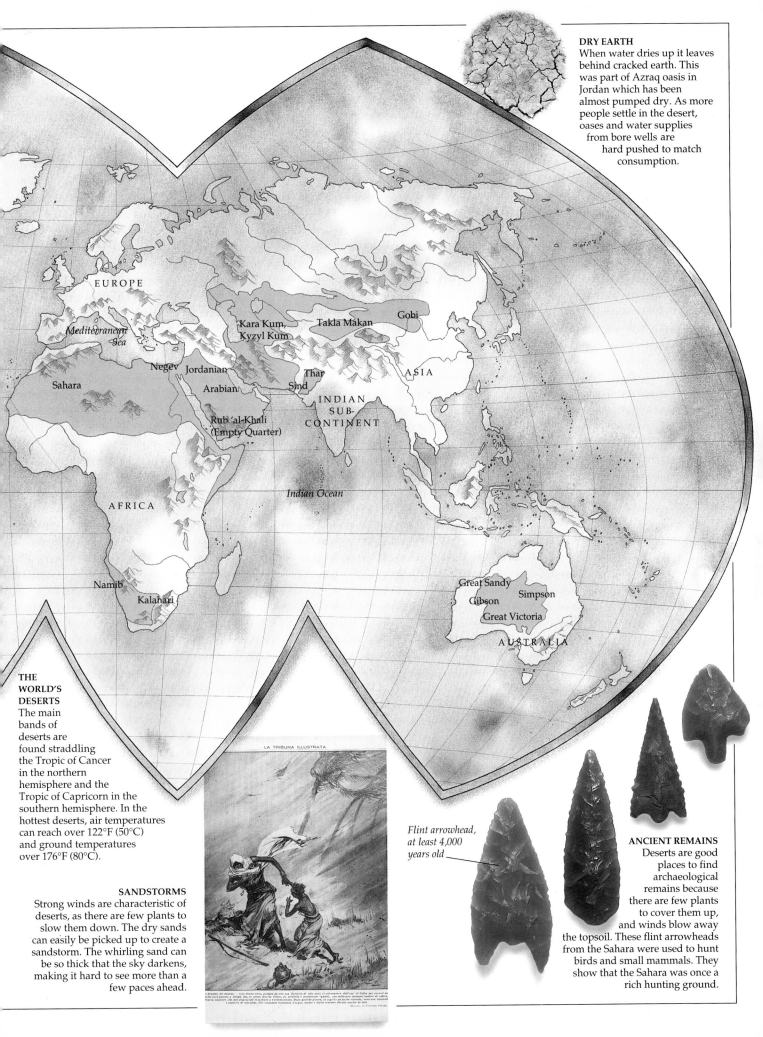

DRY EARTH
When water dries up it leaves behind cracked earth. This was part of Azraq oasis in Jordan which has been almost pumped dry. As more people settle in the desert, oases and water supplies from bore wells are hard pushed to match consumption.

EUROPE

Mediterranean Sea

Kara Kum, Kyzyl Kum

Takla Makan

Gobi

Negev

Jordanian

Thar

ASIA

Sahara

Arabian

Sind

INDIAN SUB-CONTINENT

Rub 'al-Khali (Empty Quarter)

AFRICA

Indian Ocean

Namib

Kalahari

Great Sandy

Gibson

Simpson

Great Victoria

AUSTRALIA

THE WORLD'S DESERTS
The main bands of deserts are found straddling the Tropic of Cancer in the northern hemisphere and the Tropic of Capricorn in the southern hemisphere. In the hottest deserts, air temperatures can reach over 122°F (50°C) and ground temperatures over 176°F (80°C).

SANDSTORMS
Strong winds are characteristic of deserts, as there are few plants to slow them down. The dry sands can easily be picked up to create a sandstorm. The whirling sand can be so thick that the sky darkens, making it hard to see more than a few paces ahead.

LA TRIBUNA ILLUSTRATA

Flint arrowhead, at least 4,000 years old

ANCIENT REMAINS
Deserts are good places to find archaeological remains because there are few plants to cover them up, and winds blow away the topsoil. These flint arrowheads from the Sahara were used to hunt birds and small mammals. They show that the Sahara was once a rich hunting ground.

What is a desert made of?

MOST PEOPLE THINK OF DESERTS as vast expanses of sand dunes, but deserts of rocks and stone are in fact far more common. Desert sand started out as rock, which over the ages was weathered (worn down) to form particles. The finer the particle, the farther it can be blown by wind or carried by floodwater from the rare rains. Both wind and water sort the particles according to size. In some deserts, only the rocks are left behind after wind has carried the sand away. Water dissolves minerals, such as salt, out of rocks, and these then recrystallize elsewhere. Desert soils are composed mostly of minerals from rocks; there is little plant or animal material such as dead leaves and dung, mostly because the weather is too dry for these to be broken down to enrich the soil. Some minerals, such as oil, are hidden deep within rocks below the desert surface.

DEVIL'S GOLF COURSE
This bed of rock-hard salt crystals lies in Death Valley, California, which is one of the hottest places in the world. Water draining from the surrounding mountains carries down dissolved salts, which then recrystallize and form a salt bed as the water evaporates.

WADI
After rare rains, water rushes along the wadi (dry river bed) in the desert in Jordan. The cliffs on either side of the wadi are sandstone, which is gradually worn away by the heat, wind, and rain.

Sandstone cliffs

Pink sand on the desert floor

Drought-resistant plants

BLACK DESERT
Black basalt, once spewed out as volcanic lava flows, now forms a vast rocky desert in Jordan.

FINE SAND
This sample of red sand comes from Wadi Rum in Jordan, where it looks much lighter under the full glare of the sun. The sand is partly sorted into particles of a similar size by the wind. Bits of windblown plant material litter the surface.

COARSE SAND
Most of the sand particles in this sample from the Jordanian desert are of similar size. The sand comes from the bottom of a wadi, where any fine material is washed away when the wadi fills with rainwater. Like most sand, it is made of the mineral quartz.

DUST TO DUST
This soil from the Jordanian desert contains a range of particles, from dust to pebbles. When dust is picked up by whirlwinds, dust 'devils form: these are columns of dust that whirl along the desert floor. Once picked up by wind, desert dust may be carried far beyond the desert before it lands.

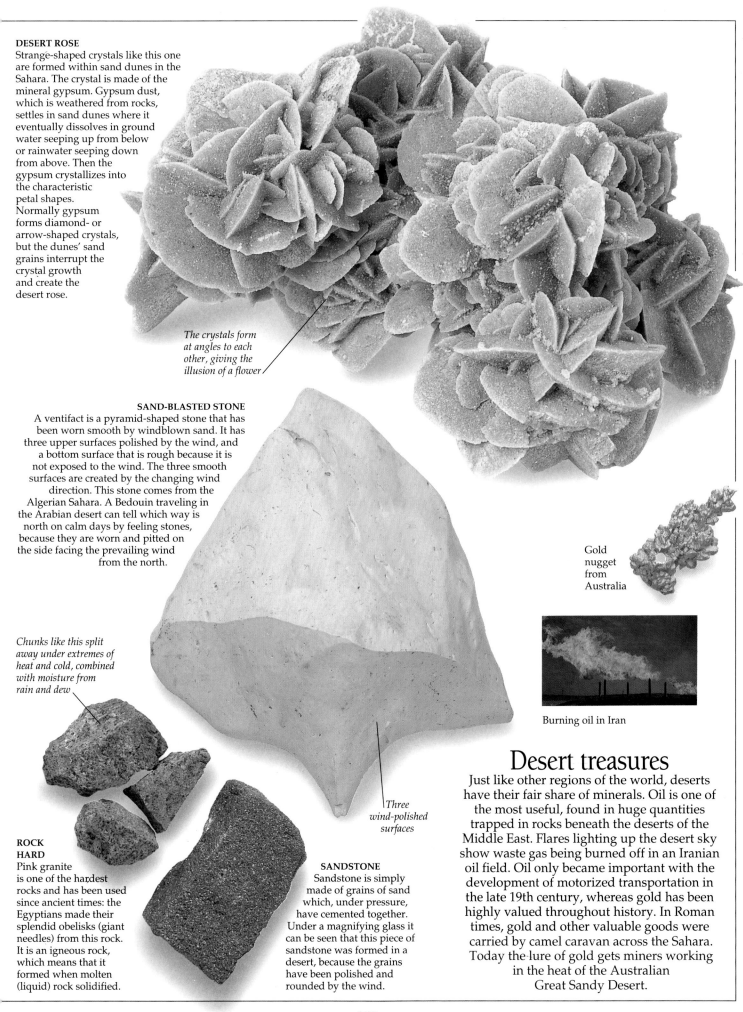

DESERT ROSE
Strange-shaped crystals like this one are formed within sand dunes in the Sahara. The crystal is made of the mineral gypsum. Gypsum dust, which is weathered from rocks, settles in sand dunes where it eventually dissolves in ground water seeping up from below or rainwater seeping down from above. Then the gypsum crystallizes into the characteristic petal shapes. Normally gypsum forms diamond- or arrow-shaped crystals, but the dunes' sand grains interrupt the crystal growth and create the desert rose.

The crystals form at angles to each other, giving the illusion of a flower

SAND-BLASTED STONE
A ventifact is a pyramid-shaped stone that has been worn smooth by windblown sand. It has three upper surfaces polished by the wind, and a bottom surface that is rough because it is not exposed to the wind. The three smooth surfaces are created by the changing wind direction. This stone comes from the Algerian Sahara. A Bedouin traveling in the Arabian desert can tell which way is north on calm days by feeling stones, because they are worn and pitted on the side facing the prevailing wind from the north.

Chunks like this split away under extremes of heat and cold, combined with moisture from rain and dew

ROCK HARD
Pink granite is one of the hardest rocks and has been used since ancient times: the Egyptians made their splendid obelisks (giant needles) from this rock. It is an igneous rock, which means that it formed when molten (liquid) rock solidified.

Three wind-polished surfaces

SANDSTONE
Sandstone is simply made of grains of sand which, under pressure, have cemented together. Under a magnifying glass it can be seen that this piece of sandstone was formed in a desert, because the grains have been polished and rounded by the wind.

Gold nugget from Australia

Burning oil in Iran

Desert treasures
Just like other regions of the world, deserts have their fair share of minerals. Oil is one of the most useful, found in huge quantities trapped in rocks beneath the deserts of the Middle East. Flares lighting up the desert sky show waste gas being burned off in an Iranian oil field. Oil only became important with the development of motorized transportation in the late 19th century, whereas gold has been highly valued throughout history. In Roman times, gold and other valuable goods were carried by camel caravan across the Sahara. Today the lure of gold gets miners working in the heat of the Australian Great Sandy Desert.

Rocky deserts

ROCKS IN THE SAHARA
Only one-fifth of the Sahara is covered with sand. The rest is made up of rocky desert, and gravelly or rocky plains.

As ELSEWHERE, LANDFORMS in the desert begin when rocks are thrust upward, such as during mountain building. Over millions of years, the rocks are gradually weathered by heat, cold, wind, rain, and chemical processes. In deserts, the scarce rainfall means that there are few plants to protective the soil from erosion, so the landscape is angular. When it does rain, it pours, and the torrents and floods are important in shaping the landscape: boulders and stones are carried down temporary rivers, gouging out the bedrock. Wind-borne sand scours away at the rocks, sculpting strange-looking formations. Rocks crack due to the extreme variation in daily temperatures: they expand when heated up under the hot sun, only to contract during the cold nights. As they cool, the rocks sometimes split with a loud bang. All these processes result in some of the most spectacular rock formations on Earth.

Birds nest in crevices in the rock

BRIDGING THE GAP
A man is standing on a natural sandstone bridge in the desert in Jordan. Bridges and arches are made when rainwater seeps into the rock, loosening particles that are then blasted away by wind-borne sand. Once a hole forms it is made bigger by rock falls and further erosion (weathering).

MUSHROOM ROCK
Mushroom rocks come in a variety of shapes and sizes but all have a cap-like top on a narrower base. In a sandstorm, the wind can only bounce along the ground to a height of about 3 ft (1 m). This scours away the base of the rock but not the top. This sandstone mushroom rock in the Jordanian desert is about 26 ft (8 m) high.

Dry cliffs under attack from wind, water, and extreme temperatures

Wind blows the sand into ripples

Plants in the desert grow far enough away from each other so that each gets sufficient water

ROCK PANORAMA
Over millions of years, these rock cliffs in the Jordanian desert will be worn down to make a flat sandy plain. Because of the dry climate, the weathering process takes much longer than in more humid areas. Heaped along the bottom of the cliffs is a skirt of eroded rock which has fallen down from the upper layers.

IN A WADI

The line of plants shows that there is some moisture along the floor of this wadi (dried-up river bed) in Jordan. Wadis are called arroyos in North America. They become very dangerous when they fill with torrents of rainwater which sweep away boulders, pebbles, and sand in a churning mass. The walls of the wadi are steep-sided, and are cut back farther with each flood.

Glasswort

Asphodel

PLANTS OF SAND AND ROCK

Some plants survive all year in the desert, such as the spiky, dry-looking bush which is seen below growing on the sandy Jordanian desert floor. This bush is a kind of glasswort which is a succulent (a plant that can store water) with scale-like leaves. Asphodel, in the lily family, grows among rocks and compacted soils. It has an tuber (swollen root) for food storage.

GRAND CANYON

One of the natural wonders of the world, the Grand Canyon is 277 mi (446 km) long and cuts through 1.2 mi (1.9 km) of rock in northwest Arizona. At the bottom is the Colorado River, which began to erode the plateau over a million years ago, and continues to erode materials from the riverbed. The walls of the canyon show several geological ages, with the oldest rocks at the bottom dating back over 1.6 billion years.

PINNACLES

These 6.5-ft (2-m) limestone pinnacles are found in the desert of Western Australia. They were first formed at the roots of plants growing on dunes over 20,000 years ago. Over thousands of years, the limestone dissolved and reformed to create these rock formations, which were revealed when the surrounding soil blew away.

The desert floor is gravelly sand

Layers of rock are easy to see without plant cover

Windblown sand collects around the base of plants

Seas of sand

Nowhere captures the romance of the desert more than the great sand seas with their endless stretches of beautiful dunes. The largest continuous expanse of sand is the Empty Quarter, part of the Arabian Desert, which covers 250,000 sq mi (647,500 sq km). The huge quantities of sand that make sandy deserts were originally eroded from mountains and highlands. The sand was carried by rivers or floods to the lowlands where it was picked up by the winds and dropped in the desert. Some desert sand also comes from the shores of lakes and seas. Winds blow dunes into a variety of shapes; some shapes, such as the star dune, are quite stable, while others, such as the barchan (crescent-shaped) dune, shift as much as 66 ft (20 m) a year.

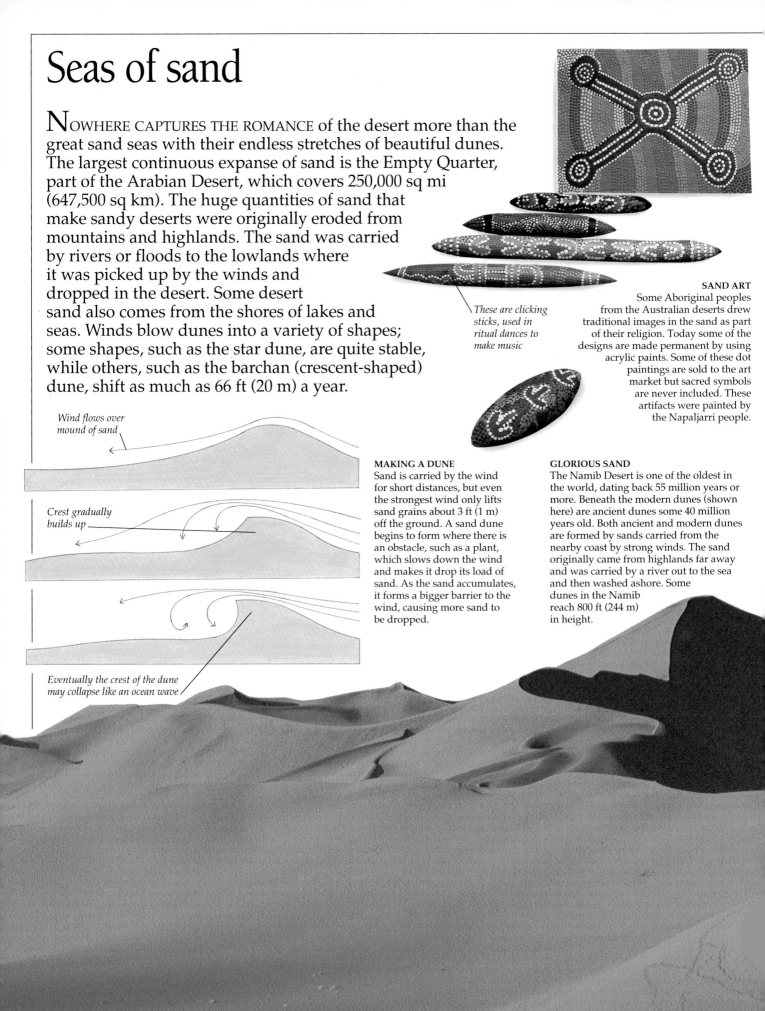

These are clicking sticks, used in ritual dances to make music

SAND ART
Some Aboriginal peoples from the Australian deserts drew traditional images in the sand as part of their religion. Today some of the designs are made permanent by using acrylic paints. Some of these dot paintings are sold to the art market but sacred symbols are never included. These artifacts were painted by the Napaljarri people.

Wind flows over mound of sand

Crest gradually builds up

Eventually the crest of the dune may collapse like an ocean wave

MAKING A DUNE
Sand is carried by the wind for short distances, but even the strongest wind only lifts sand grains about 3 ft (1 m) off the ground. A sand dune begins to form where there is an obstacle, such as a plant, which slows down the wind and makes it drop its load of sand. As the sand accumulates, it forms a bigger barrier to the wind, causing more sand to be dropped.

GLORIOUS SAND
The Namib Desert is one of the oldest in the world, dating back 55 million years or more. Beneath the modern dunes (shown here) are ancient dunes some 40 million years old. Both ancient and modern dunes are formed by sands carried from the nearby coast by strong winds. The sand originally came from highlands far away and was carried by a river out to the sea and then washed ashore. Some dunes in the Namib reach 800 ft (244 m) in height.

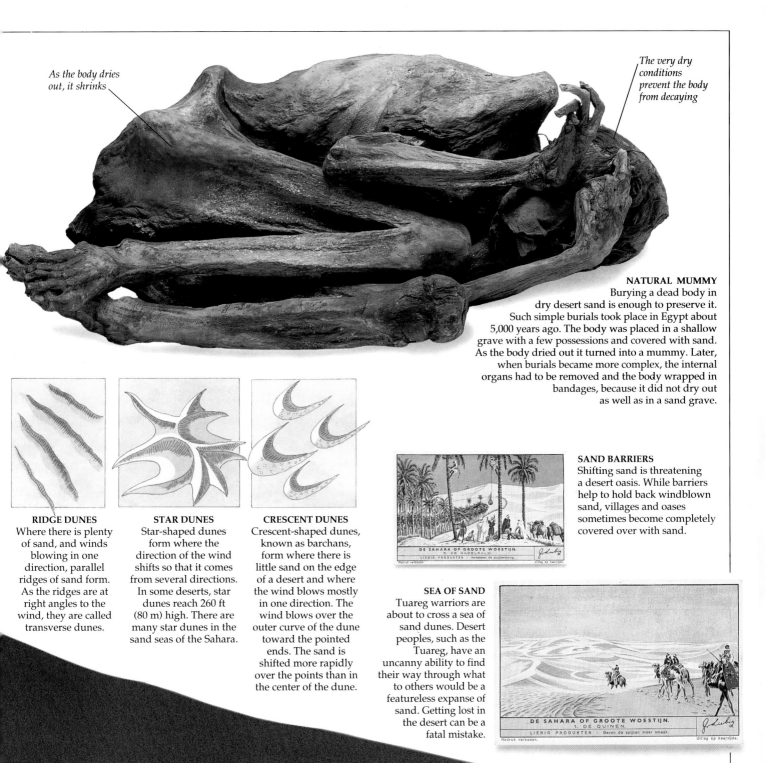

As the body dries out, it shrinks

The very dry conditions prevent the body from decaying

NATURAL MUMMY
Burying a dead body in dry desert sand is enough to preserve it. Such simple burials took place in Egypt about 5,000 years ago. The body was placed in a shallow grave with a few possessions and covered with sand. As the body dried out it turned into a mummy. Later, when burials became more complex, the internal organs had to be removed and the body wrapped in bandages, because it did not dry out as well as in a sand grave.

RIDGE DUNES
Where there is plenty of sand, and winds blowing in one direction, parallel ridges of sand form. As the ridges are at right angles to the wind, they are called transverse dunes.

STAR DUNES
Star-shaped dunes form where the direction of the wind shifts so that it comes from several directions. In some deserts, star dunes reach 260 ft (80 m) high. There are many star dunes in the sand seas of the Sahara.

CRESCENT DUNES
Crescent-shaped dunes, known as barchans, form where there is little sand on the edge of a desert and where the wind blows mostly in one direction. The wind blows over the outer curve of the dune toward the pointed ends. The sand is shifted more rapidly over the points than in the center of the dune.

SAND BARRIERS
Shifting sand is threatening a desert oasis. While barriers help to hold back windblown sand, villages and oases sometimes become completely covered over with sand.

SEA OF SAND
Tuareg warriors are about to cross a sea of sand dunes. Desert peoples, such as the Tuareg, have an uncanny ability to find their way through what to others would be a featureless expanse of sand. Getting lost in the desert can be a fatal mistake.

DE SAHARA OF GROOTE WOESTIJN.
5. DE DADELPALM.
LIEBIG PRODUKTEN : Verbeteren de spijsvertering.

DE SAHARA OF GROOTE WOESTIJN.
1. DE DUINEN.
LIEBIG PRODUKTEN : Geven de spijzen meer smaak.

Water in the desert

SOME PARTS OF THE DESERT are not dry and barren: occasional rainfall turns pockets of the desert green and fills dry riverbeds with floods of water. Some of this water is trapped behind small dams or, after it has seeped underground, is tapped by means of wells dug into the riverbed. Water from deep layers of rock comes to the surface at oases, where crops such as date palms are cultivated. With the help of various irrigation methods, more of the desert can be cultivated. Today vast areas of the desert are green as a result of pumping water from deep bore wells. But there is a danger that underground water may run dry, especially when more people settle in the desert and when crops needing a large amount of water are grown.

Azraq oasis in Jordan is shrinking because of the amount of water pumped out

BUCKET AND POLE
Water is taken from a well using a shaduf. The bucket on the long pole is lowered into a well to fill it, then swung up with the help of the counterweight on the end of the long pole.

RAIN NECKLACE
The figure on this Native American Zuni necklace represents a shalako, a messenger of the rainmakers. People dressed as shalakos take part in a special ceremony.

WATER WHEEL
Water is drawn up by a water wheel at an Egyptian oasis. The cow is blindfolded so that it will walk around in a circle turning the big spoked wheel. As this wheel turns it drives the water wheel around, filling the metal buckets. The water pours out of the buckets into an irrigation channel to water the crops. In the past, clay pots would have been used instead of metal buckets.

Water in aquifer (porous rock)

Impermeable rock

Oasis

Water flows up fault to oasis

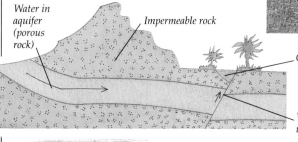

WATER FROM FAR AWAY
Rain seeps into the ground and filters through porous rocks to low places in the desert. The water comes to the surface at an oasis where a split in the rock blocks its passage. Rocks that hold water are called aquifers. Wells are often drilled through the rocks to reach aquifer water. The water contained in an aquifer may be rain which fell thousands of years ago on distant mountains.

BABY DAM
To capture the water that drains from these Jordanian cliffs during rain, the Bedouin have built a small dam. The water is for their own use as well as for their livestock. In places where there are water supplies, the Bedouin may live a more settled existence.

Tail

View from below of tadpole shrimp

A series of limbs are used to push food into their mouths

Tadpole shrimps are 1.5 in (3 cm) long

Shield covering head and front of trunk

Eyes

Top view of a tadpole shrimp

THIRSTY SHRIMPS
The eggs of these tadpole shrimp survive in dry sands for ten years or more before rain comes to bring them to life. The shrimp must grow quickly to reach maturity and produce eggs before the desert pool in which they live dries up and they die.

The cobra only sees movements, not shapes

Windpipe enables the cobra to breathe while swallowing its prey

SPITTING COBRA
The red spitting cobra lurks in palm groves at oases in eastern Africa. If disturbed, it usually tries to escape, but if it is provoked any further, it rears up and spits toxic venom, and can hit a target 6.5 ft (2 m) away. If the venom hits an animal or a person in the eye it is extremely painful, and if untreated can cause blindness. The venom is ejected from tiny holes in the fangs at the front of the mouth. This cobra eats lizards, toads, birds, and small mammals.

WATER ON THE WAY
Water from an oasis is sent on its way to water the palms through a series of channels. Some channels are permanent, like this one in Oman; others are confined in mud banks and are broken down and rebuilt to send the water in different directions. Palms do not need to be irrigated if there is enough ground water close to the surface. They provide dates to eat, wood for building, leaves for thatching and fencing, and fibers to make rope.

Enlarged glands secrete a strong poison to deter predators

GREEN TOAD
Green toads live at oases where there are permanent water supplies in which to lay their eggs. During the day they hide under rocks; at night they come out to hunt insects near water holes and around palm trees.

GREENING THE DESERT
An aerial view shows giant green crop circles on the fringes of the Sahara desert in Morocco. The circles are made by sprinkler systems which rotate like the hands of a watch. Huge quantities of water pumped up from underground are used to keep crops, such as wheat, growing in the desert. While these crops provide much-needed food, there is a danger that the water from aquifers is used up much faster than it is replaced.

After the rains

SOME PLANTS AND ANIMALS SURVIVE in the desert by avoiding the driest times, only growing or becoming active after occasional rains. Plants exist in the dry soil for years as seeds. When the rains come, it may take several good soakings before the seeds germinate. This prevents seeds from germinating unless there is enough water for them to flower and produce seeds. The eggs of desert crustaceans, such as brine and tadpole shrimp, also need water to bring them to life. Not all the eggs hatch the first time around. Some eggs are left for the next rains, in case the pools dry out, and the first batch of shrimp die before they reproduce. Spadefoot toads face a similar problem, so not all breed after the first rains. In the dry season, the toads remain inactive, buried in the soil. They come out as soon as they hear the drumming of rain on the surface.

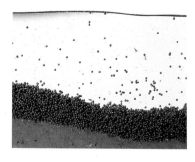

BRINE SHRIMP
Brine shrimp live in salt lakes and pools around the world. During dry periods these lakes evaporate, and the brine shrimp die, leaving eggs behind. Some of the eggs are drought resistant – they can withstand high temperatures and live for decades.

JUST ADD WATER
Within 48 hours of a rainfall, the dormant eggs of the brine shrimp hatch into larvae (young forms). The larvae feed on small food particles in the water and grow, like all crustaceans, by shedding their outer skeletons.

ADD LEGS
The young shrimp go through several molts, adding more pairs of legs. The length of the life cycle depends on the temperature of the water and the amount of food available; brine shrimp can reach maturity about three weeks after hatching.

ADD EGGS
Adult shrimp are quick to mate and produce eggs before the lake dries up. A female can produce 140 eggs in a single batch, and she can live for four months laying eggs every four days.

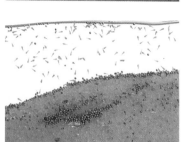
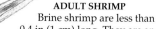

ADULT SHRIMP
Brine shrimp are less than 0.4 in (1 cm) long. They are an important food for birds visiting salt lakes. Brine shrimp are tolerant of a wide range of salt concentrations, from nearly fresh water to water five times as salty as seawater.

BLOOMS IN THE NEGEV
This member of the daisy family only grows in good years when there is enough rain in the Negev Desert in Israel. Plants grow along the edges of gulleys where rain collects but cannot survive in the gulleys where they would be washed away. The leaves have a strong smell because they contain oils that deter grazing animals.

DESERT PEA
The bold flowers of Sturt's desert pea add to the blooms which carpet parts of the central deserts of Australia after good rains. Sturt's desert pea rambles along the ground for several yards. By the time the ground dries up again the pea has already produced seeds which will spring to life with the next rains.

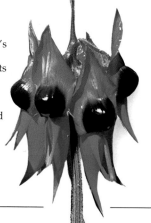

DESERT LILY
This desert lily (above) blooms in the deserts of the Southwest from March to May. The lily shoots up each year after the rains from a bulb underground. It can grow up to 6 ft (1.8 m) tall. The bulbs were once used by the Native Americans for food.

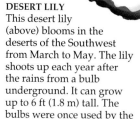

LITTLE SNAPDRAGON VINE
Seeds of the snapdragon vine from the Chihuahuan and Sonoran Deserts germinate after the rains. The long vines curl around other desert plants. In the colder winter months the vine dies back into the sand or gravelly soil. Snapdragon vines also grow in juniper forests.

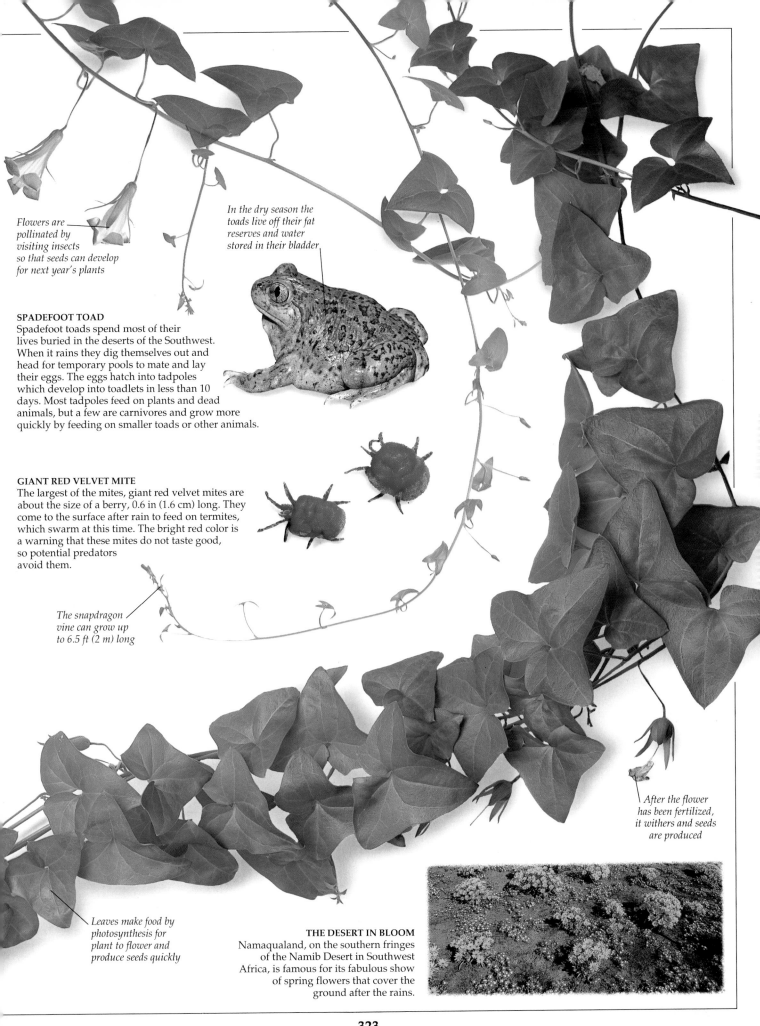

Flowers are pollinated by visiting insects so that seeds can develop for next year's plants

In the dry season the toads live off their fat reserves and water stored in their bladder

SPADEFOOT TOAD
Spadefoot toads spend most of their lives buried in the deserts of the Southwest. When it rains they dig themselves out and head for temporary pools to mate and lay their eggs. The eggs hatch into tadpoles which develop into toadlets in less than 10 days. Most tadpoles feed on plants and dead animals, but a few are carnivores and grow more quickly by feeding on smaller toads or other animals.

GIANT RED VELVET MITE
The largest of the mites, giant red velvet mites are about the size of a berry, 0.6 in (1.6 cm) long. They come to the surface after rain to feed on termites, which swarm at this time. The bright red color is a warning that these mites do not taste good, so potential predators avoid them.

The snapdragon vine can grow up to 6.5 ft (2 m) long

After the flower has been fertilized, it withers and seeds are produced

Leaves make food by photosynthesis for plant to flower and produce seeds quickly

THE DESERT IN BLOOM
Namaqualand, on the southern fringes of the Namib Desert in Southwest Africa, is famous for its fabulous show of spring flowers that cover the ground after the rains.

How plants survive in the desert

PLANTS THAT LIVE IN DESERTS either spring up from dormant seeds after a rain (p. 322), or stay alive all year adapting to the meager supply of water. The more permanent plants have a variety of ways to get water. Some have long roots to reach water deep in the soil, some spread their roots to collect water over a wide area, and some can absorb dew through their leaves. Many desert plants, including cacti, are succulents that are able to store water. A thick waxy layer on the stems and leaves helps retain this water and protects tissues from the intense sun. Reducing leaf size, shedding leaves in times of drought, or even having no leaves at all, also help to reduce water loss by keeping the surface area of the plant to a minimum.

DATE PALMS
A grove of date palms cultivated at an oasis in Oman. Only female trees produce dates, so just a few male trees are grown to produce pollen. Palm trees can live for up to 200 years.

Very long roots to seek out water

FLESHY LEAF
Haworthias grow in places with some shade, next to rocks or other plants. Only the tips of the leaves poke above the surface of the soil, the rest remains out of the sun. But leaves need light to be able to make food by photosynthesis. This leaf has a translucent (clear) window in the tip to allow light through the leaf. In times of drought, this species shrinks into the ground.

FRESH DATES
There are many different varieties of dates. Most familiar are the ones that are dried and packed in boxes for export around the world. Dried dates are also part of the staple diet of villagers and desert nomads such as the Bedouin. They are highly nutritious and do not rot.

These varied-patterned agaves have been specially bred

CENTURY PLANTS *above left*
It takes 20 to 50 years for the century plant to produce flowers on a stem up to 30 ft (9 m) tall which grows out of the center of the plant. The flowers are pollinated by nectar-seeking bats. After flowering and producing seeds the plant dies. The century plant belongs to the agave family, members of which are a source of sweet sap for drinks, and fibers for ropes and other products.

FIRE THORN BRANCH
Also called the ocotillo, or coachwhip plant, the fire thorn grows in the deserts of the Southwest. In dry times, it sheds its leaves to conserve moisture. After rains, new leaves grow among the spines; if the ground is wet enough the fire thorn flowers.

WELWITSCHIA
This bizarre plant has only two frayed, straplike leaves, and a huge tap root which may be up to 3 ft (1 m) wide at the top. It grows on the gravel plains in the Namib Desert. Welwitschia is actually a dwarf tree, and may live for a thousand years or more.

Welwitschia leaves usually split into many strips

Leaf absorbs dew

When spread out, each leaf reaches up to 6.5 ft (2 m) long

INSIDE A CACTUS
Cut open a cactus and inside is a mass of water-storing tissue. The vascular or transport tissue, called xylem, not only transports water from the roots but also helps to support the plant. The surface of the cactus is covered with a thick waxy layer which helps prevent loss of water and protects the tissue from the burning effects of the sun.

BARREL CACTUS
A cactus is well adapted to make the most of any water available (p. 326, p. 342) their shallow roots spread out around the plant to absorb moisture from rain or dew. Desert cacti open their stomata (pores) at night to exchange gases for respiration and photosynthesis (the manufacture of food from carbon dioxide and water using sunlight). This reduces the amount of water lost through the stomata. Carbon dioxide is stored in another chemical form until it is ready to be used during daylight.

LIFE-GIVING DEW
Dew from a coastal fog has settled on a salt bush in the Namib Dew from a coastal fog has settled on a salt bush in the Namib shrubs are coated with salt; this is thought to help the plant take in more moisture from the fog.

LIVING STONES
Stone plants are often hard to spot as they are so well camouflaged; this saves them from plant-eating animals. Stone plants are succulents – they store water in their leaves. They grow with all but the tips of their leaves in the ground, and the surrounding soil and stones protect them from intense sunlight. To allow light to reach the underground part of the leaf, the surface of the leaf tips have translucent (clear) windows. After rains, stone plants bloom, producing a single large flower between the leaf pair They grow in southern Africa.

NOT FAIR
This spike of flowers in the Jordanian desert belongs to the leafless cistanche plant. It does not need green leaves for photosynthesis (the manufacture of food from carbon dioxide and water using sunlight) because it taps the roots of other plants for food. Living organisms that steal food and harm their hosts are called parasites.

Continued on next page

Cacti and other succulents

Succulents are plants that survive dry conditions
by storing water in their fleshy stems or leaves.
Cacti are the best-known succulents, with their
bizarre-shaped stems varying from globes growing
close to the ground to tall skyward-pointing
branched forms. They are mainly found growing
wild in the Americas but are not restricted to
deserts. Other desert succulents show a great
variety of forms, including some which look
remarkably like cacti.

*Yellow flowers are followed
by smooth green fruits, which
are eaten by birds; they then
disperse the seeds*

AGAVE CACTUS
A cactus plant that looks
much like an agave (p. 324),
the agave cactus is found
in the dry regions and
grasslands of Mexico.
This cactus grows to
28 in (70 cm), and it
has a tap root which
grows to 12 in (30 cm)
to reach water.

*Cultivated forms
are often grafted onto other
cacti, to make them grow better*

KOKERBOOM TREE
This tree aloe, which grows in drylands of
southwest Africa, can survive several years of
drought, during which time its leaves
shrink, having lost most of their sap.
The kokerboom tree grows several
yards high. Its wood was once used
by the San to make arrows.

Kokerboom
tree in the wild

DESERT ROSE
A succulent which
grows among rocks
in the drylands of Africa
through to the Arabian
Peninsula, the desert
rose has a poisonous
milky sap to deter
animals from eating it.
In good conditions, the
desert rose grows over
6.5 ft (2 m) high. It can
flower in the dry season
even when it has
no leaves.

SILVER DOLLAR
The silver dollar, one of the most
beautiful cacti, is under threat of
extinction, as are many desert
plants, due to people stealing
them from the wild even though
some are cultivated for sale in
nurseries. The silver dollar
grows in the southern U.S. and
northern Mexico among rocks,
sand, and bushes.

LIVING ROCK
Looking like a rock may help
this spineless cactus avoid being
eaten by some animals, but it is
devoured by goats. It grows
among rocks in the southern
U.S. and northern Mexico.

CACTUS DRUG
The mescal or peyote cactus contains the drug mescaline. Since the times of the Aztecs (the ancient Mexicans), this cactus has been gathered from the wild and eaten raw, dried, or consumed as a drink for its hallucinogenic properties. Only the top of the cactus is collected, leaving the large roots in the ground so the cactus regrows. Collection in the U.S. and Mexico is now banned.

This cactus is sometimes called fishhook cactus because of its spines

The saguaro reaches over 40 ft (12 m) in height

The giant saguaro has shallow roots for gathering water, and deeper roots to anchor it in the ground

PRICKLY PEAR
One of the better-known kinds of cactus, prickly pears have been introduced to many parts of the world. This Texas prickly pear is a popular garden plant in the South. Prickly pears position their leaflike lobes (pads) in such a way as to cut down on exposure to the sun. This helps them keep cool.

GIANT HOME
A giant saguaro from the desert of the Southwest and Mexico provides a home for a variety of animals, much like a skyscraper. Like many permanent desert plants it grows slowly: it can take over 40 years for the saguaro to put out a branch. The side of the plant facing the strongest sun has a thicker wax layer to protect it from being burned. It may hold several tons of water in its swollen stems.

CANDY CACTUS *left*
The white inner tissue of this barrel cactus was once cut into cubes to make candy. The cubes were boiled in water first to get rid of any bitter taste, then boiled in syrup before being rolled in sugar and left to dry in the sun. Collection in the wild is banned.

Top view of hedgehog cactus

WHISKER CACTUS
When this plant starts to mature, the spines at the tip of the stems become long and curly, and look like whiskers. This is when the pink flowers appear, and they are followed by red berries. The flowers open at night, so that insects, such as moths, can feed on the nectar.

HEDGEHOG CACTUS
Hedgehog cacti are named for their prickly set of spines. This one is found in North American deserts, from the Great Basin Desert in the north to the Chihuahuan Desert in the south. It grows about 6 in (15 cm) high on rocky slopes, and produces brightly colored flowers after rain.

NOT A CACTUS
This cactus-like euphorbia comes from the fringes of the Arabian Desert. Many euphorbias living in dry regions look like cacti, though they are not related to them. Both cacti and these euphorbias have evolved similar ways to cope with drought by not having leaves, and storing water in their fleshy stems.

Insects

INSECTS HAVE ADAPTED to almost every environment in the world, so it is not surprising to find them living in deserts. Like other desert animals, insects face the problem of finding enough food and water. Some plant-eating insects, such as the caterpillar stage of butterflies, feed on the fresh green plants that spring up after rain. They survive the dry times either as eggs or as pupae (the stage in which the caterpillar turns into a butterfly). Seed-eaters, such as harvester ants, store seeds to last them through the drought; honeypot ants store sugary substances within the bodies of some of their nest mates. Hunting insects get some moisture from their prey. Dew is an important source of water for many insects, and some beetles even have special ways to collect it. To avoid the drying effects of the sun, many desert insects only come out at night.

Like all insects, the jewel wasp has a pair of antennae on its head

Ant lion adult

JEWEL WASP
A jewel wasp takes a drink. Jewel wasps are one of the solitary wasps that live on their own instead of in colonies. The adults feed on nectar from flowers, but their young devour cockroaches caught for them by the adult female. She hunts down the cockroach, stings it to paralyze it, and then drags it into a hole where she lays an egg on it. When the young hatches from the egg it feeds on the paralyzed but live cockroach.

HARVESTER ANTS
These industrious ants collect seeds to store in granaries in their nests. When a scout ant finds a rich supply of seeds, it trails a special odor from the tip of its abdomen all the way back to the nest. Nest mates then follow the trail out to the seeds to collect them for the nest. The ants eat most of the seeds, but they do reject or drop a few, and therefore help plants by dispersing the seeds.

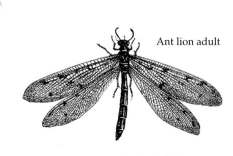

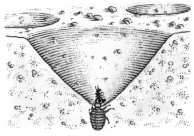

ANT LION
The larva (young) of this winged insect is called an ant lion. As soon as it hatches, it digs a pit in the sand and hides at the bottom with only its jaws exposed, waiting for an insect, perhaps an ant, to come into the pit. When an insect does, the ant lion flicks sand at it so that it loses its footing and slides down to be snapped up by the deadly jaws.

Jointed legs end
in claws for
gripping surfaces

Abdomen points
upwards so that dew
runs into mouth

Shiny outer skeleton
gives the jewel wasp
its name

Two pairs
of wings

BEETLE IN A HEADSTAND
Moisture in the early morning fog in
the Namib Desert has condensed on this
darkling beetle's back; the dew then runs
down into its mouth. This is the only way
this beetle gets a drink. It spends the night
buried in sand, but should there be a
nighttime fog, it will come to the surface.
Dew-collecting beetles also live in other
deserts, such as the Wahiba Sands in the
southern Arabian Peninsula, where there
is coastal fog and high dew fall. Some
darkling beetles make little furrows
in the sand or small hummocks
to collect dew.

Darkling beetle
straightens its
legs to run along
on hot sand

The hard wing cases
are stuck together, so
this beetle cannot fly

White spots are a warning that
the domino beetle is armed and
does not taste good

DARKLING BEETLE
This beetle lives in the Namib Desert, where it feeds on
windblown plant debris and seeds on the surface of
the sand dunes. It is an unusual kind of darkling
beetle in that it has all-white wing cases. These
may reflect the heat and allow the beetle to
stay out in the sun finding food for
longer than black beetles.

DOMINO BEETLE
The white spots on domino beetles'
backs are a warning that these
beetles are armed with chemical
weapons. When threatened, they
squirt a jet of acid at an attacker.
After this, the attacker will be unlikely to
try to eat a beetle with white spots again.
During the day, domino beetles lurk under
rocks and holes made by other animals.
They come out at night to hunt insects and
other small prey. This domino beetle lives
in the drylands of northern Africa
through to the Middle East.

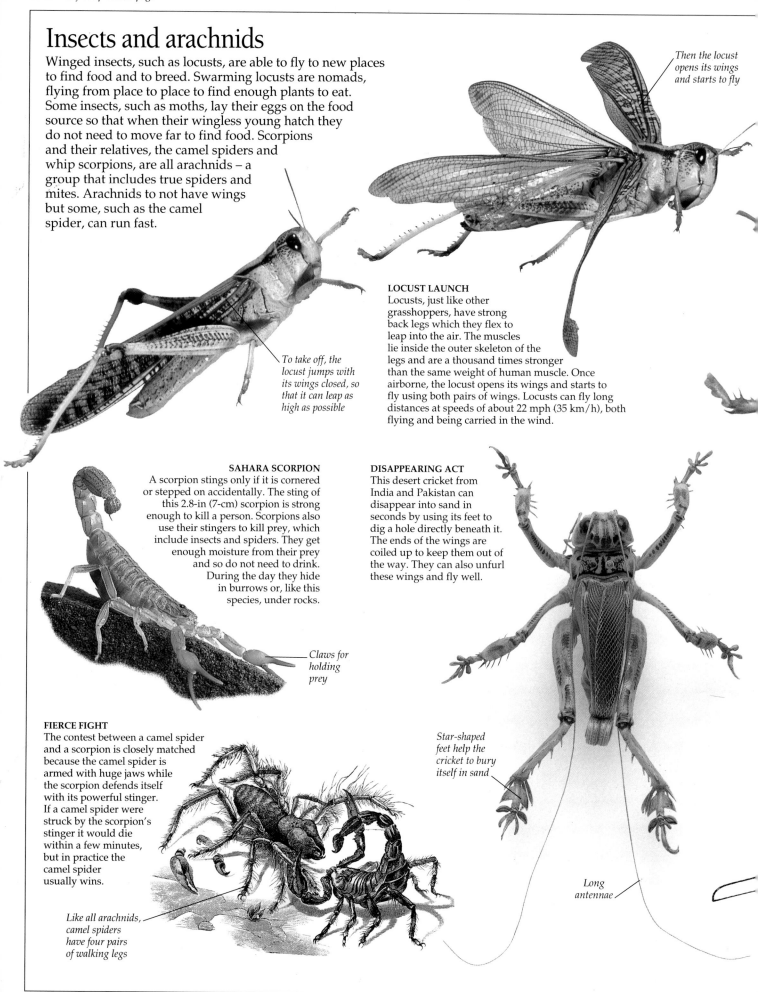

Insects and arachnids

Winged insects, such as locusts, are able to fly to new places
to find food and to breed. Swarming locusts are nomads,
flying from place to place to find enough plants to eat.
Some insects, such as moths, lay their eggs on the food
source so that when their wingless young hatch they
do not need to move far to find food. Scorpions
and their relatives, the camel spiders and
whip scorpions, are all arachnids – a
group that includes true spiders and
mites. Arachnids to not have wings
but some, such as the camel
spider, can run fast.

*Then the locust
opens its wings
and starts to fly*

*To take off, the
locust jumps with
its wings closed, so
that it can leap as
high as possible*

LOCUST LAUNCH
Locusts, just like other
grasshoppers, have strong
back legs which they flex to
leap into the air. The muscles
lie inside the outer skeleton of the
legs and are a thousand times stronger
than the same weight of human muscle. Once
airborne, the locust opens its wings and starts to
fly using both pairs of wings. Locusts can fly long
distances at speeds of about 22 mph (35 km/h), both
flying and being carried in the wind.

SAHARA SCORPION
A scorpion stings only if it is cornered
or stepped on accidentally. The sting of
this 2.8-in (7-cm) scorpion is strong
enough to kill a person. Scorpions also
use their stingers to kill prey, which
include insects and spiders. They get
enough moisture from their prey
and so do not need to drink.
During the day they hide
in burrows or, like this
species, under rocks.

*Claws for
holding
prey*

DISAPPEARING ACT
This desert cricket from
India and Pakistan can
disappear into sand in
seconds by using its feet to
dig a hole directly beneath it.
The ends of the wings are
coiled up to keep them out of
the way. They can also unfurl
these wings and fly well.

FIERCE FIGHT
The contest between a camel spider
and a scorpion is closely matched
because the camel spider is
armed with huge jaws while
the scorpion defends itself
with its powerful stinger.
If a camel spider were
struck by the scorpion's
stinger it would die
within a few minutes,
but in practice the
camel spider
usually wins.

*Like all arachnids,
camel spiders
have four pairs
of walking legs*

*Star-shaped
feet help the
cricket to bury
itself in sand*

*Long
antennae*

330

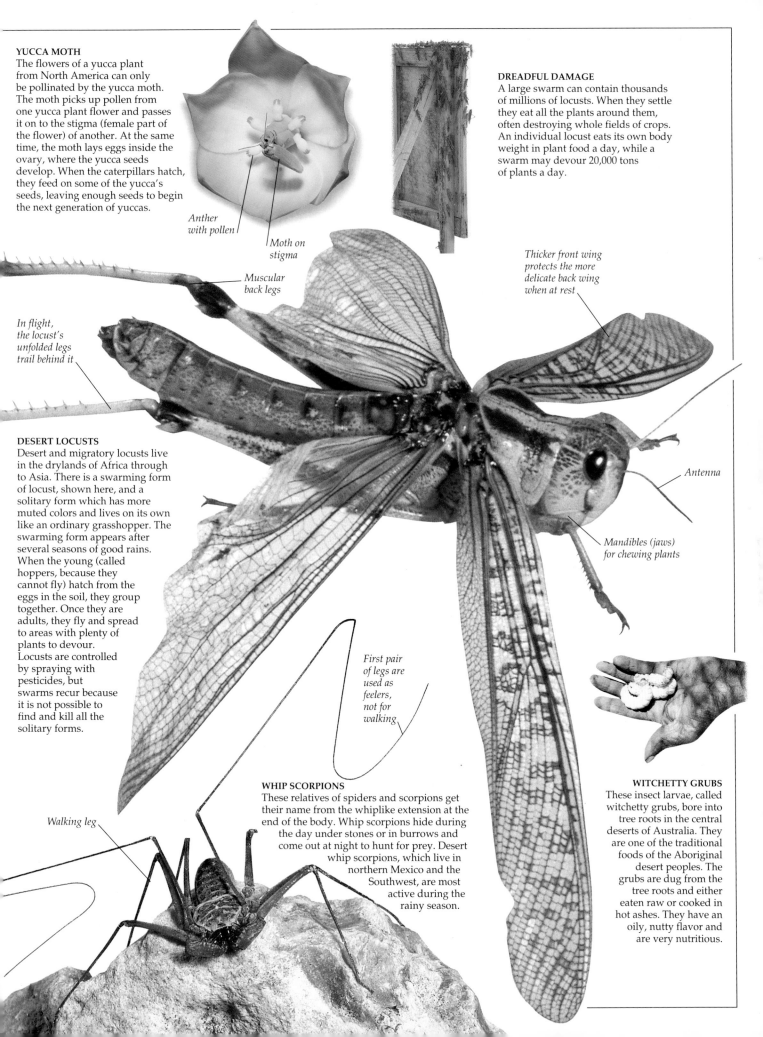

YUCCA MOTH
The flowers of a yucca plant from North America can only be pollinated by the yucca moth. The moth picks up pollen from one yucca plant flower and passes it on to the stigma (female part of the flower) of another. At the same time, the moth lays eggs inside the ovary, where the yucca seeds develop. When the caterpillars hatch, they feed on some of the yucca's seeds, leaving enough seeds to begin the next generation of yuccas.

Anther with pollen

Moth on stigma

DREADFUL DAMAGE
A large swarm can contain thousands of millions of locusts. When they settle they eat all the plants around them, often destroying whole fields of crops. An individual locust eats its own body weight in plant food a day, while a swarm may devour 20,000 tons of plants a day.

Thicker front wing protects the more delicate back wing when at rest

Muscular back legs

In flight, the locust's unfolded legs trail behind it

Antenna

Mandibles (jaws) for chewing plants

DESERT LOCUSTS
Desert and migratory locusts live in the drylands of Africa through to Asia. There is a swarming form of locust, shown here, and a solitary form which has more muted colors and lives on its own like an ordinary grasshopper. The swarming form appears after several seasons of good rains. When the young (called hoppers, because they cannot fly) hatch from the eggs in the soil, they group together. Once they are adults, they fly and spread to areas with plenty of plants to devour. Locusts are controlled by spraying with pesticides, but swarms recur because it is not possible to find and kill all the solitary forms.

First pair of legs are used as feelers, not for walking

Walking leg

WHIP SCORPIONS
These relatives of spiders and scorpions get their name from the whiplike extension at the end of the body. Whip scorpions hide during the day under stones or in burrows and come out at night to hunt for prey. Desert whip scorpions, which live in northern Mexico and the Southwest, are most active during the rainy season.

WITCHETTY GRUBS
These insect larvae, called witchetty grubs, bore into tree roots in the central deserts of Australia. They are one of the traditional foods of the Aboriginal desert peoples. The grubs are dug from the tree roots and either eaten raw or cooked in hot ashes. They have an oily, nutty flavor and are very nutritious.

Reptiles

REPTILES, such as snakes, lizards, and tortoises, do well in deserts because they control their body temperature by gaining or losing heat from their surroundings. This means that reptiles need not expend as much energy as birds and mammals, which use lots of energy to generate heat within their bodies. So reptiles need less food, a scarce commodity in deserts. Using less energy also means that reptiles do not breathe as frequently as birds and mammals do, and this helps them to conserve moisture. Compared to amphibians, such as toads, with their permeable skins, reptiles are better suited to the desert because they have scaly skin to help them conserve moisture.

TORTOISE BAG
A bag made from a tortoise shell that was used to carry scented ointment by Herero women from Namibia. Tortoises are slow breeders, and if too many are killed they will be threatened with extinction.

Black band marks the position of the hood, which is only extended when the cobra feels threatened or curious

TONGUE OUT
Like all snakes, the diadem snake uses its tongue to pick up scents from the air and the ground. The scents are transferred to a sensory organ in the roof of the mouth which detects chemicals. The snake does this to find out what is going on around it.

SPITTING COBRA
The red spitting cobra spreads its hood before spitting venom to defend itself. When attacking its prey, mainly small reptiles and mammals, the cobra bites to inject venom. Like many desert snakes, it hunts at night to avoid the heat of the day.

BRIGHT EYES
The gray banded kingsnake has big eyes which help it hunt for prey at night. It feeds mainly on lizards but also eats other snakes and small mammals. Like all snakes, it seems to stare because it does not have proper eyelids and does not blink: a transparent scale protects its eyes. This snake lives in desert scrub from south Texas to Mexico.

TAKE IT EASY
The desert tortoise from the southern U.S. and Mexican deserts avoids the heat of the day by staying in its burrow. It comes out during the early morning and late afternoon to feed on plants and is partial to red and orange flowers. The desert tortoise takes 15 years or more to reach maturity.

Under severe heat stress in hot sun, the desert tortoise will empty its bladder over its back legs to cool down, while saliva froths over its head and neck

LEAVE ME ALONE
Rattlesnakes warn enemies off by rattling the hollow segments of skin at the tip of their tails. This does not use up water as hissing does. If provoked further, they may strike. Rattlesnakes such as this western diamondback have front fangs that swing forward to inject venom.

BLACK RATTLER
Western rattlesnakes (from the western U.S.) come in a number of different colors. This black version lives in the more mountainous areas of desert in Arizona. Western rattlesnakes living in these areas and the Great Basin Desert group together in a communal den during the cold winter.

SNAKE HEADS
The desert kingsnake has a characteristic black mask covering its head. Reaching 5 ft (1.5 m) long, it can kill rattlesnakes two-thirds of its own length. Kingsnakes kill their prey by constriction, wrapping their body around the victim. The lyre snake restrains its prey by constriction, and injects weak venom from fangs at the back of its jaw. Its eyes have slit-shaped pupils which open up at night, just like a cat's, to help it see in the dark to hunt lizards, mice, and bats in their roosts. The milksnake's bright colors may mimic the colors of the highly venomous coral snakes. Wary of these colors, animals will leave the harmless milksnake alone.

Desert kingsnake from the southern U.S. and northern Mexico

Lyre snake from the coastal desert of Southern California and northern Baja California, Mexico

Red spitting cobra from desert and oases in eastern Africa

HOGNOSE
These snakes are named for their snouts. This one lives in deserts and prairies in the U.S. and Mexico. It feeds on small mammals, and reptiles and their eggs. When threatened, a hognose snake hisses loudly and flattens its head and neck. If the attacker persists, the snake rolls over with its tongue out and pretends to be dead, hoping that it will be left alone.

Sinaloan milksnake from desert fringes and other habitats in western Mexico

Bright colors may confuse or startle potential predators

Overlapping belly scales allow for rapid and agile movement

Continued on next page

Lizards

Lizards are more numerous in deserts than snakes, and they are easier to spot because they are often active during the day, whereas many snakes are secretive and only active at night. Many lizards like to bask in the sun in the early morning to warm up their muscles after a cold desert night. In the heat of the day, they retreat into the shade of rocks or plants, down cool burrows, or even clamber into bushes. Most desert lizards change color to blend in with their backgrounds and avoid being seen by predators. Spiny skins make some desert lizards more unappetizing. When threatened, some lizards put on intimidating displays with gaping jaws. Biting an attacker is always an option but many lizards prefer to run away.

FRINGE-TOED LIZARD
This fast-moving lizard can run across the sand dunes in the Sahara, where it lives. It has a fringe of scales on its feet which act like snow shoes to spread its weight so that it does not sink into the sand. To stay cooler on hot sand, it holds its head and body clear of the surface. The nostrils have valves which close to prevent sand from getting into its air passages.

Fringe of scales on toe

In places, the scales form spines

It is the layer of skin under the scales that changes color

Bearded dragons are darker in the morning to absorb the heat of the sun; they get paler as the day wears on

BEARDED DRAGON
A formidable-looking lizard, the bearded dragon from the dry interior of Australia has spiny skin to protect itself from predators. The beard under the chin expands to make the dragon look even more scary. Bearded dragons feed on a variety of food including insects, bird eggs, newborn small mammals, and some dew-soaked plants. Bearded dragons are active in the early morning and late afternoon. During the heat of the day, they often climb into shrubs where it is cooler.

HORNED TOAD
Despite its name, this is a lizard, not a toad, and it lives in North American deserts. It often sits in the open eating ants, as its pale colors help it blend in with its desert background, making it difficult to spot. Horned toads also lower their bodies close to the ground to get rid of any tell-tale shadows. The spiny skin is another line of defense. If attacked, horned toads can squirt blood from their eyes to put off an attacker.

Colors warn this animal is poisonous

As in the spiny-tailed lizard, the tail is also a fat store

Chameleons are excellent climbers, using their tails and opposing toes to grip plants

GILA MONSTER
The Gila monster is one of only two lizards in the world with a venomous bite. The bite is seldom fatal to humans but causes immense pain. The Gila monster lives in scrub in the Mojave and Sonoran Deserts. Gila monsters are mainly active at night, feeding on small mammals, snakes, and other lizards.

HEADS OR TAILS?
The shingleback from the Australian deserts has a fat, head-shaped tail which makes it hard for a predator to know which end to attack. If a predator attacks its tail instead of the vulnerable head, the shingleback turns around and bites its attacker. Shinglebacks eat a wide variety of food, including insects, snails, and fruit.

CHAMELEON
A chameleon sits on the stem of a welwitschia plant growing in the Namib Desert. Chameleons and other lizards are attracted to the plant because insects like to shelter under the shade of its leaves. Chameleons catch the insects by shooting out their long, sticky-tipped tongues.

Tail also serves as a fat reserve

LIZARD EGGS
These eggs belong to the eyed lizard from northern Africa. Up to 20 eggs are laid in sandy soil and they hatch two to three months later. Eyed lizards reach over 2 ft (60 cm) long. These large lizards feed on insects. small mammals, and other reptiles.

SPINY-TAILED OR DAB LIZARD
One of the hardiest desert lizards from the Sahara, the African spiny-tailed lizard tolerates high temperatures and survives on small amounts of water from dew and on the plants and few insects that it eats. This lizard is active in the day but avoids the midday heat by staying in its deep burrow. If pursued, the lizard runs into a rocky crevice and blocks the exit with its spiny tail. The energy reserve in its fat tail also helps the lizard to endure drought when plants are scarce.

THORNY DEVIL
A spiny body helps to protect this lizard from being attacked. It lives in deserts in Australia, and has a similar ant-eating lifestyle to horned toads. Thorny devils collect rain or dew on their backs, which finds its way down tiny channels into their mouths. These lizards are also known as molochs.

FIERCE FRILLS
The frilled lizard from the Australian desert spreads out the frill around its neck to make itself look larger to scare away enemies. The frill is supported by rods (like an umbrella's) which are attached to a bone at the base of the tongue. When the lizard is angry, it opens its jaws wide, and this automatically spreads the frill. If the pursuer does not retreat, the lizard will charge and bite.

The collared lizard can inflict a nasty bite with its sharp teeth

COLLARED LIZARD
In a defensive pose, the collared lizard opens its mouth in a wide gape. If molested, the lizard will bite. In preference to biting an attacker it will leap away over the rocks where it lives in the deserts of the southern U.S. The collared lizard is an active predator. It hunts during the day for insects, smaller lizards, and small snakes and mice. Highly agile, it can even leap into the air to catch flying insects.

Sharp claws for gripping rocks

Birds

A VARIETY OF BIRDS live in deserts. Some, such as the tiny elf owl, are permanent residents; others, such as the galah, are visitors in search of food. Flesh-eating birds, such as falcons, get enough moisture from eating their prey, and so do not need to drink additional water. Seed-eating birds, such as sandgrouse, have such a dry diet that they need to drink daily. Because there is so little vegetation, desert birds are restricted in the number of places they can nest. Many birds, such as ostriches, nest on the ground, but their young are vulnerable to attack. Others, such as roadrunners, nest in low bushes, and woodpeckers nest in holes in cacti. Where possible, birds seek out patches of shade. For some, flying at high altitudes means escape from the desert heat. Birds have a higher body temperature than mammals, which means that they can tolerate higher temperatures. They do not sweat; instead they pant or flutter their throats so that water evaporates from their air passages to help them cool down.

FINE FEATHERED FALCON

With its wing feathers spread, the lanner falcon is poised to strike. Lanner falcons in the Sahara Desert hunt around water holes for sandgrouse. They spot their prey from a great height and then swoop down to catch birds in mid-air or on the ground. The falcons' sharp talons grip the prey while their hooked beaks rip the flesh. Lanner falcons also catch lizards and feed on swarming locusts on the ground. Because of their superb hunting skills, they are popular birds to train for falconry. Lanner falcons lay three to four eggs on the rocky ledges of desert cliffs.

GALAH

The galah is a cockatoo from Australia. Galahs pair for life, returning to the same nest hole in a tree every year. They regulate their breeding according to conditions, laying as many as five eggs in good years and only one, two, or none in drought years. When the chicks hatch they are helpless and are fed regurgitated seeds. After the breeding season, galahs disperse to wherever they can find seeds, bulbs, and fruit. They have strong beaks for crushing their food. Galahs are good fliers: large flocks of 100 or more birds can travel over 60 miles (100 km) in a day.

ROADRUNNER

As its name suggests, this bird prefers to run rather than fly. It lives in the desert scrub in the Mojave, Sonoran, and Chihuahuan deserts. In the early morning, roadrunners bask in the sunshine to warm up after the cool desert night, but as the sun gets hotter, they move to bushes where it is cooler than on the ground.

LIKE A SPONGE

Male sandgrouse have specially absorbent belly feathers which soak up water like a sponge. In this way they carry water from an oasis or water hole back to their chicks, who peck at their father's feathers to take a drink. Both parents lead the chicks to solid food.

Young ostriches are dull brown and speckled to help them blend with the colors of the desert floor

TOUGH BABIES

Ostrich chicks are able to run around soon after hatching, and they may travel long distances in the desert to find water and food. Chicks from several nests often band together, led by one or two adults. They grow as tall as adults (8 ft/2.5 m) after one year. Ostriches are the largest of all birds.

Male sandgrouse belly feathers trap water between tiny barbules (branches) coming off the barbs (main feather branches)

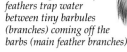

336

MAKING A HOME
A Gila woodpecker visits its nest in a giant saguaro cactus. To make the nest hole, the woodpecker hammers out the soft inner pulp of the cactus. The hole is a cool and secure place to raise the Gila young, which hatch out blind, naked, and helpless. Another kind of woodpecker, the gilded flicker, also makes nest holes in saguaro cacti.

AT HOME
An elf owl peers out from a nest hole in a giant saguaro cactus. The hole was originally made by a woodpecker. Elf owls are one of the smallest owls in the world, reaching about 6 in (15 cm) long. They are found only in deserts in the Southwest and northern Mexico where there are saguaro cacti.

Wing feathers are moved in such a way that the bird has perfect control over its flight

Tail feathers are used to steer in flight and are spread before landing

Deadly talons to catch sandgrouse and other prey

A hooked beak and sharp talons show this is a bird of prey

HARRIS'S HAWK
Like many birds of prey, the Harris's hawk lives in a wide range of habitats, from deserts to grassland and open woodlands in the Southwest and South America. Unlike most birds of prey, female Harris's hawks mate with several males. Nests composed of a platform of twigs are made above ground, such as in cacti or mesquite bushes. Harris's hawks feed on a variety of animals including rabbits, lizards, flickers, and round-tailed ground squirrels.

Mammals

SMALL DESERT MAMMALS escape the extreme climate of deserts by living in burrows. Temperatures within a burrow do not fluctuate as much as those on the surface. The deeper the burrow the better the insulation, so some desert mammals, such as jerboas in northern Africa, dig deeper burrows in summer to escape the heat. During cold desert nights, and in the winter, a burrow is warmer than the surface air. Burrows are also used to store food, such as seeds, for when food is scarce. Many small mammals in hot deserts come out only at night or at dawn and dusk to avoid the heat of the day as well as day-active predators. If they do come out in the day or on moonlit nights, their fur color helps them hide by blending in with their backgrounds. Some small mammals escape predators by leaping out of reach or running away.

PALLID GERBIL
A pallid gerbil can leap about 1.6 ft (0.5 m), pushing off with its strong back legs and landing on its front feet. It can also run fast. Pallid gerbils live in large burrows in the dry sandy part of northwest Egypt. They come out at night to find food, such as seeds. Gerbils have large bony projections in the skull that surround the interior of the ear. These pick up low-frequency sounds, so the gerbils can detect predators in the dark.

Long tail for balance while leaping and running

DWARF HAMSTER
This hamster is only about 3.3 in (8.4 cm) long. It comes from the deserts and grasslands of Mongolia, Siberia, and China, where the winters are bitterly cold. The hamster's thick fur helps to keep it warm. In the most northerly part of their range, dwarf hamsters turn white in winter so that they are camouflaged against the snow if they come out of their burrows. Like all hamsters, dwarf hamsters have big cheek pouches that they can fill with food, such as seeds, to carry back to their burrows.

SHAW'S JIRD
Jirds are related to gerbils and together they are the largest group of small mammals living in the dry regions of Africa and Asia. This large jird, with a body up to 8 in (20 cm) long, comes from Morocco, Algeria, Tunisia, and Egypt.

Tail used to help the jird balance on its hind legs

HOPPING ALONG
Kangaroos have strong back legs so they can hop along at great speed. Some small desert mammals, such as kangaroo rats from North America and jerboas from Africa and Asia, are like miniature kangaroos because they hop on their back legs. For small mammals, hopping helps them to make a quick getaway, and may also confuse the predator.

Red kangaroos live in the Australian deserts

CHINESE HAMSTER
Sitting up on its haunches helps this curious Chinese hamster see what is going on around it. Sitting up also frees its front paws to handle food, such as seeds. Chinese hamsters have longer tails than most hamsters. These hamsters are found along desert fringes and grasslands in Siberia, Mongolia, and Korea, as well as in China.

SPINY MICE

Spiny mice have stiff spine-like hairs mixed with their fur. The stiff hairs make them a little less edible, and they can erect these hairs to make themselves look larger. But their ability to shed their tails may be a greater defense: a predator grabbing a spiny mouse by its tail will be left with the tail in its mouth while the mouse gets away. Spiny mice are active in the early mornings and late evenings as well as at night. They live in rocky areas.

Spiny mice living amongst dark rocks are often a darker color, which makes them harder to see

Egyptian spiny mouse

Rodents have continually growing front teeth

TAKING A SNOOZE

A desert kangaroo rat sleeps in its burrow in the Mojave desert of California. Kangaroo rats are solitary except in the breeding season. They seal their burrows during the day so that the moisture in the air they breathe out is trapped in the burrow. This keeps the burrow humid, so less moisture is lost from the body by evaporation from the nose and mouth.

Arabian spiny mouse

KANGAROO RAT

Kangaroo rats come out of their burrows at night, hopping along on their long back legs. They move from bush to bush searching for seeds. Even on their dry diet, kangaroo rats get by without needing to drink water. They conserve moisture by producing only a small amount of urine and dry droppings. Like all rodents, they do not sweat. In an emergency, they can cool down by licking the fur on their necks.

Big ears to pick up sounds of approaching predators

Eyes positioned to give wide field of view

Strong back legs for jumping

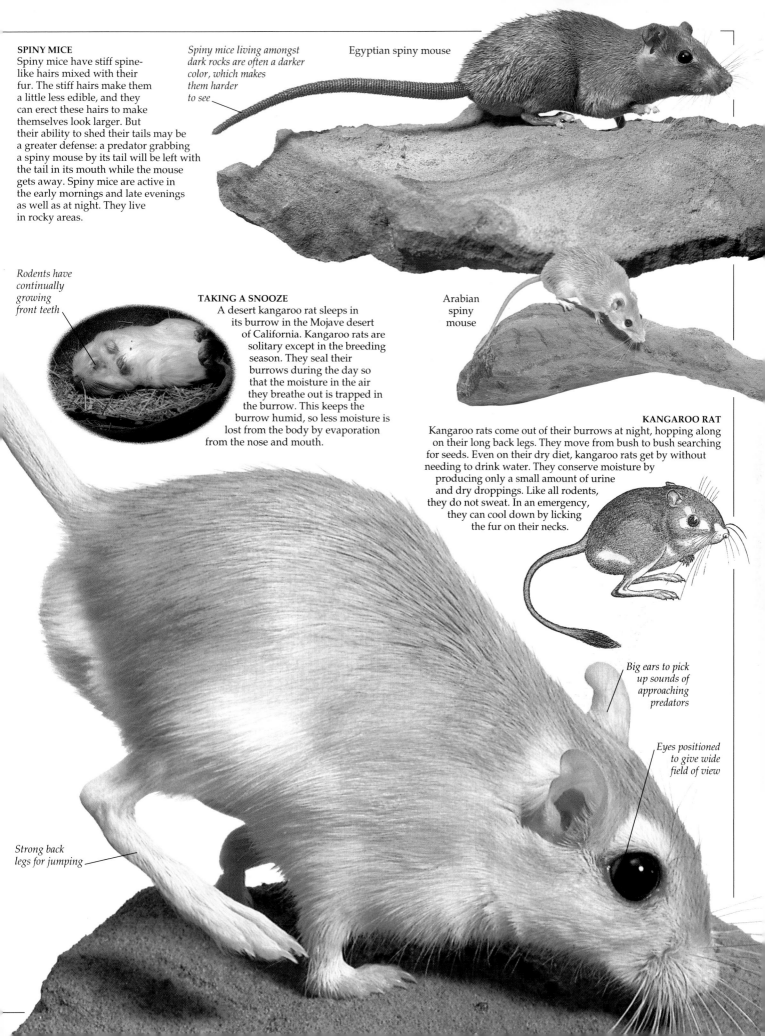

Lions disappeared from the Sahara due to hunting and increasing dryness

Larger mammals

Many of the larger desert mammals, such as desert hedgehogs and foxes, spend the heat of the day in burrows, coming out at night to search for food. Even the dorcas gazelle is known to take refuge in other animals' burrows during exceptionally hot weather. Members of the cat family living in deserts often hunt at night, sheltering in rocky lairs or in any available shade during the day. Whatever the weather, meerkats are active during the day but dive into their burrows when predators approach.

BIG CATS

Lions are still found in the deserts of southern Africa, where they can survive the dry season on moisture from the blood of their prey. In the past lions were more widespread, and even lived in the Sahara. Cheetahs still live in the Sahara but they are exceptionally rare. Cheetahs in the Kalahari often hunt during the cool of the night, instead of during the day.

SPINY ANTEATER

This strange egg-laying mammal is also called a short-beaked echidna. Only three mammals, both species of echidna and the duck-billed platypus, lay eggs; all other mammals give birth to live young. The short-beaked echidna is found in a wide range of habitats in Australia, including the central deserts and Tasmania, as well as in New Guinea. It has a long sticky tongue for slurping up termites and ants.

DORCAS GAZELLE

These gazelles live in herds of up to 50 animals where there is plenty of grazing. They are found from northern Africa through the Middle East to Pakistan and India. Breeding males have small harems of up to seven females. When a female is ready to give birth she leaves the herd to find a secluded place. Gazelles often give birth to twins, which are vulnerable to being eaten by eagles, caracals, and hyenas.

WILD ASS

This wild ass, called a kulan, lives in the deserts of Turkmenistan (the Kara Kum and the Kyzyl Kum), in central Asia. In winter the kulan grows a rich thick coat to keep out the cold. A close relative of the kulan, called a khur, lives in the hot Thar desert of India. Herds of asses are also found in some parts of the Sahara, but these may be domesticated asses which have escaped back to the wild.

Large ears help to detect prey and to lose excess heat

Distinctive ear tufts like those of a lynx

CARACAL

This cat lives in a wide range of habitats including the deserts of Africa and Asia. Caracals are well known for their ability to catch birds, and can even leap into the air to swat a bird in flight. They also hunt reptiles, small mammals, and mammals as large as gazelles. Caracals sleep in caves, rocky crevices, and abandoned burrows.

SAND FOX

Ruppell's foxes live in dens in sandy and rocky deserts in northern Africa to the Arabian Peninsula. They can be active during the day but often come out at night to hunt for small animals. Their feet have furry soles to help them walk on sand.

Large ears radiate heat to keep the animal cool

Good sense of smell to find food

DESERT HEDGEHOG
This hedgehog comes from the dry regions of northern Africa, the Arabian Peninsula, and Iraq. When threatened it rolls up to expose the spines of its coat while protecting its soft underparts. Desert hedgehogs dig burrows which they live in during the day by themselves. In the breeding season, the female looks after the young in the burrow, suckling them for two months. Adult hedgehogs eat birds, eggs, scorpions, and other small animals.

JACKALS
Black-backed jackals live in the grasslands and deserts of eastern and southern Africa. In the Kalahari Desert they feed on a wide range of food including small animals, birds, berries, and wild melons, which are an important source of water in times of drought. Jackals are good at sneaking bits of meat from kills made by other animals including brown hyenas and even lions.

RARE HORSE
Przewalski horses once roamed the dry lands of Mongolia. Since the 1960s they have been extinct in the wild. Fortunately, there are still herds in captivity which are being bred for re-introduction to the wild.

MEERKAT
Meerkats live in groups in the Kalahari and Namib deserts, and in dry open country in other parts of southern Africa. They all work together: a meerkat with its head down looking for food in the wide open desert is an easy target for a bird of prey, so one member of each group scans the horizon from a bush or tree. If a predator is spotted, the guard barks in alarm and the group races to the safety of a burrow. Meerkats also have nannies in the group, which take turns looking after the babies while the mother is out feeding with the rest of the group.

Adapting to desert life

THE DESERT IS A HARSH place in which to live, yet a variety of different kinds of animals thrive there. Their bodies and behavior are adapted to allow them to cope with extreme temperatures, lack of water, and scarcity of food. The same adaptations can be found in different animals; for example, both fennec foxes and desert hedgehogs have big ears to help get rid of excess heat. Some animals with different origins, such as the marsupial mole from Australia and the golden mole from Africa, look similar because they both burrow in sand, but they are unrelated. Humans too, can live in deserts as they are able to modify their surroundings to a much greater extent than animals.

UNDER WRAPS
People in their natural state are not well suited to the desert. But they can build dwellings and wear clothes to protect themselves against the extreme heat and cold of the desert. They also have many ways to get food and drink.

CACTUS
Plants also have to adapt to live in the desert (pp. 324-327). To reduce the loss of water from evaporation, cacti do not have leaves. Spines protect cacti from being eaten, and help prevent heat from reaching the plant.

SANDFISH
Not a fish but a reptile, this skink (a kind of lizard) dives headfirst into the sand when alarmed. The sandfish's snout is shovel-shaped, with the lower jaw slung underneath so that it can dig into the sand. It moves its body in S-shaped curves to shuffle farther down; when under the sand, it holds its legs against the sides of its body. The sandfish spends the night in a burrow and comes out in the early morning and late afternoon to search for insects and other small prey. The fringe-like scales on its feet help it walk across the sand surface.

Smooth scales to help the sandfish slip through sand

WALKING ON SAND
The feet of this gecko from the Namib Desert are webbed to spread its weight and keep it from sinking into the sand. The gecko lives in a burrow in the sand during the day and comes out at night to search for food, such as insects.

Big eyes with slit pupils, which open wide in the dark

SINKING INTO SAND
The sand viper from the northern African and Middle Eastern deserts avoids the hottest part of the day by burying itself in the sand. By wriggling its body it disappears, leaving only its eyes and nostrils peeping out so that it can detect its prey (such as lizards), or approaching danger. The sand viper comes out of its hiding place at night, moving along the surface of the sand by side-winding (moving sideways). It is almost identical in appearance and behavior to the sidewinder rattlesnake of North American deserts.

Sand viper makes body into S-shape

BURROWING IN SAND
The marsupial mole from the central deserts of Australia comes to the surface to eat a gecko. The big flat claws on its front legs are for scooping away sand and the tip of its snout is covered with skin for pushing into it. The mole is blind and has no external ear parts, giving it a smooth head. Like other marsupials, the mole rears its young in a pouch. Its pouch opens toward the tail so that it does not fill with sand as the the mole burrows along.

Waves pass down the body from the tail end

As the viper sinks deeper, sand covers its back

CAMELS
The single-humped dromedary and two-humped Bactrian are well suited to desert conditions (see next page). The embryo (an early stage of development) growing inside a pregnant dromedary has two humps, one of which is lost as the baby develops.

Tail held over head

SHADY TAIL
These ground squirrels live in the deserts of southern Africa. Ground squirrels are usually out and about in the early morning and late afternoon. They use their fluffy tails like parasols to keep off the sun while they look for food, eating seeds, grass, fruit, roots, insects, eggs, and small reptiles. On cool mornings they sunbathe to warm up.

White coat helps to reflect strong sun

ARABIAN ORYX
An exceptionally hardy antelope, the oryx is superbly adapted to the desert. It is small, reaching only 3 ft (1 m) tall at the shoulder, so it can shelter under shrubby trees and needs less food to keep strong. The oryx can walk long distances to find new grazing and is also able to dig up bulbs and roots by pawing at the ground. It does not need to find drinking water, as it gets enough from the dew on plants. Due to overhunting, the Arabian oryx disappeared from the wild in 1979, but an international conservation effort has successfully re-introduced the oryx to part of its former range in the Arabian Peninsula.

FENNEC FOXES
These fluffy foxes are the smallest of the fox family, reaching only 16 in (40 cm) long from the tip of the nose to the base of the tail. Their big ears act like radiators, helping them to lose heat. Fennec foxes spend the hottest part of the day in their burrows, coming out at night to hunt for small animals such as insects, lizards, and jerboas (right). Fennec foxes are found in the Sahara Desert and have also been seen in the Arabian Peninsula.

KEEPING WARM
Dwarf hamsters live in the cold deserts and grasslands of central Asia. Like all small animals, they have a large surface area compared to their volume, which means they lose or gain heat from their surroundings more readily than larger animals. They need thick fur to keep warm.

Fluffing up their fur traps a layer of air between the hairs, which helps them keep warm

Soles of the feet are hairy

Ship of the desert

**Warning!
Camels on the road**

CAMELS CARRY PEOPLE AND GOODS through the driest of deserts, under the burning sun and through swirling sandstorms. They can go for days without water: they have few sweat glands and conserve moisture because their body temperature can rise many degrees before they start to sweat. They also produce concentrated urine and dry dung. Camels eat tough desert plants, and survive for long periods by using the fat stores in their humps. There are two kinds of camel: the dromedary, with one hump, and the Bactrian camel, with two humps. Both kinds have been domesticated, but only the Bactrian camel continues to live in the wild.

**KEEPING
THE SAND OUT**
Camels have long eyelashes
to keep sand out of their eyes. In
a sandstorm, camels keep their eyes
closed and can see well enough
through their thin eyelids to keep
moving. Camels can also close their
nostrils to stop sand getting into
their air passages.

BEASTS OF BURDEN
Camels are excellent pack
animals, and when properly
loaded can carry as much as
600 lb (270 kg). Before cars and
trucks, camels were used to
transport goods vast distances
across North Africa and Asia.
The camels, often 50 or more in
number, were tied together in
single file. These caravans, as
they were called, sometimes
stopped overnight in inns with
large courtyards known as
caravanserais.

ONE HUMP
Camels do not store water in
their humps. Instead, they store fat, which is
gradually used up if they do not eat enough. As
the fat is depleted, the hump shrinks. Dromedaries
can tolerate fluctuations in their body temperature of
11°F (6°C) and they can lose up to one third of their
body fluid, a loss that would be fatal to humans. To
replace it, a dromedary can drink about 18 gal (70 liters)
of water at one time.

*Long legs keep
the dromedary's
body high off the
ground, where the
air can be as much
as 18°F (10°C)
cooler than the
air around
its feet*

TAME CAMEL
The dromedary was domesticated in
Arabia 4,000 years ago and was taken to
North Africa, India, Pakistan, and Australia.

CAMELS FOR SALE
Traders sometimes travel many miles to sell their camels, as they have to this camel market in Egypt. Some of the camels are hobbled by tying one leg up; this is to keep them from moving away from their owners and to stop bull camels from fighting. The price of a camel depends on its breed and condition. Some camels are used for their milk and meat, some are kept as pack animals, and others are bred for riding and racing. Camel hair and skins are also used, and even camel dung is collected for fuel.

GETTING UP
A camel rests on the ground with its legs tucked under its body. It has callosities (thick patches of hard skin) on its legs and chest where the pressure is greatest. To get up, a camel first gets into a kneeling position. Then it pushes up its strong back legs before finally straightening its front legs. Riders mount a camel when it is sitting down and have to hold on tight as the camel rises, see-sawing forward and backward. To sit again, the camel kneels down on its front legs before lowering its back legs to the ground.

Fur in camels' ears prevents sand from getting in

Like the dromedary, the Bactrian camel's two humps are stores of fat, but unlike the dromedary's hump, they flop over when the fat is depleted

RIDING ALONG
Riding camels can cover over 100 mi (160 km) in a day. Racing camels can reach average speeds of 20 mph (33 km/h) during 6-mile (10-km) races.

FLAT FEET
Dromedaries living in sandy deserts have broad, flat foot pads which help them walk on soft sand without sinking. Mountain dromedaries have narrower foot pads to help them walk over rocky ground. Camels do not have hooves; instead their two toes end in claws. The tough soles of their feet can withstand the heat of the sand.

TWO HUMPS
Bactrian camels have two humps, and thick fur to keep them warm during the bitter cold central Asian winters. They molt (shed their thick fur) in the spring. Domesticated Bactrian camels are found in central Asia; fewer than a thousand wild Bactrian camels still survive in the Gobi Desert.

Bactrian camels have long shaggy fur which covers the upper surface of the foot

Camel regalia

THE VAST MAJORITY of the world's camels are domesticated dromedaries. Some people think of them as obnoxious, smelly beasts, but desert nomads have a high regard for their camels, and dress them in magnificent finery. Almost every part of the camel may be dressed, with pieces that are embroidered and decorated with shells, beads, mirrors, and tassels. This highly decorative regalia is brought out for special occasions such as weddings and religious festivals. Because the camel's finery is so beautiful, some of it is also used to decorate people's homes. Among most desert peoples, women generally do the weaving and embroidery, and men make the saddles and harnesses.

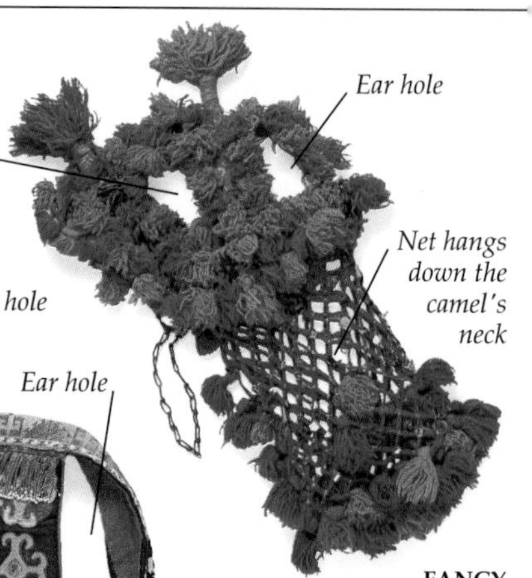

Eye hole

Ear hole

Net hangs down the camel's neck

Eye hole

Ear hole

FANCY HEADGEAR
Camel headdresses are made using a variety of fabrics: the one above, from Iran, is made of sheep's wool; the finely embroidered headdress (left) with beaded tassels is made of silk and comes from Uzbekistan. They are fixed by a chain or tie under the camel's chin.

CAMEL NECKLACES
Necklaces decorate a camel's neck and shoulders. The one below comes from the Sind province in Pakistan. It is made of heavy cotton decorated with shells which are a symbol of wealth. Nowadays, white glass or plastic buttons are used instead of shells.

Loop to hang around the saddle's pommel

Wool necklace made by Baluchi nomads

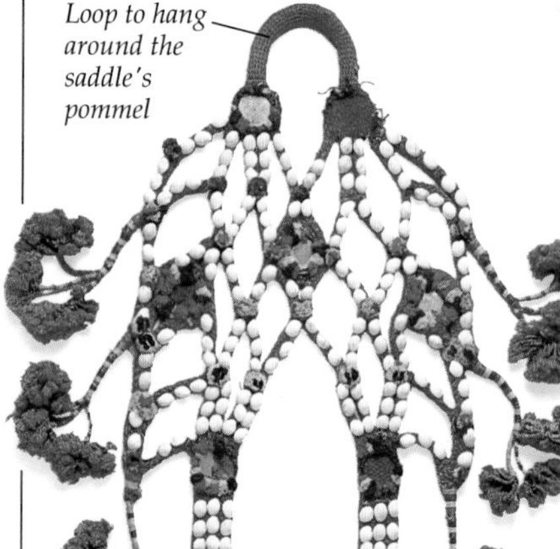

POM-POMS AND TASSELS
Extra pom-poms and tassels are hung from the camel's head and neck. The ones shown above are made from wool by Baluchi nomads who live around the borders of Iran.

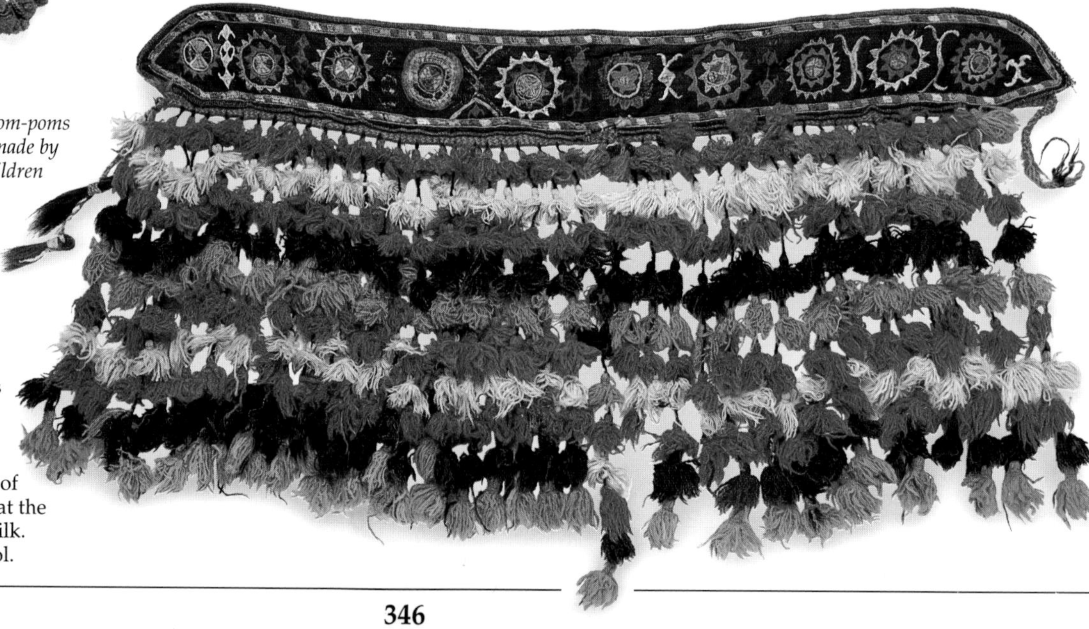

The pom-poms are made by children

CHEST BAND
This chest band comes from Rajasthan in India, where camels are used by peoples in the Thar desert. When not on a camel, this beautiful handcrafted piece would be draped over the doors of homes for decoration. The band at the top is cotton embroidered with silk. The long tassels are made of wool.

The back of the saddle gives the rider some support on long journeys

SADDLE
The beautifully worked wood and leather of this saddle show that it belonged to a wealthy Tuareg; it dates from the beginning of this century. The long straps are fixed under the camel's belly to keep the saddle in place.

DRAPES
Many different-sized drapes can be hung from the camel's shoulders. They are also sometimes hung inside a tent as decorations. The skill and precious materials that have gone into their making show that they were for special occasions or for rich families.

The white beads and complicated knots, called Turk's head knots, are characteristic of work from Uzbekistan

Wooden pommels project through the saddle cover

FANNY PACK
A crupper is for decorating a camel's hindquarters. This one is embroidered in a style typical of the Sind. In the center of each yellow daisy is a mirror that sparkles in the sunlight as the camel walks. The background is filled in with buttons.

The cotton kneeband comes from the Sind

The black tassels are made of goat's hair, and the colored parts are made of sheep's wool

READY TO GO
Outfits such as this one made by the Bedouin are often passed from generation to generation. The harness on the head can be fitted with reins. The saddle is a simple wooden frame which rests on a canvas saddle blanket to protect the camel. Sheepskin makes a comfortable seat for the rider. Saddlebags fringed with tassels hang down each flank of the camel; they can be used for transporting goods or personal possessions. The rider sits with the left leg hooked around the front pommel, with the right leg over the left ankle.

KNEE COVERS
Knee covers, a fun addition to a set of regalia, are not very common. The woollen ones above must have belonged to a magnificent set as they are very finely woven. They were made by Baluchi nomads.

Domesticated animals

PEOPLE HAVE DOMESTICATED animals to use them for their own purposes for thousands of years. Special breeds cope with desert conditions, but livestock is still wiped out in severe drought. Even camels cannot survive the summer months without people to lead them to water and fresh grazing. Although horses are less suited to the desert, the swift-footed Arabian horse is much valued. Dogs are used for their hunting skills. Sheep, goats, and cattle give milk and meat. But the fringes of many deserts have suffered overgrazing by livestock, especially where new bore wells have encouraged people to keep more animals.

OSTRICH
Since ancient times ostrich feathers have been a popular form of adornment. Ostrich eggshells are also used to make jewelry (p. 363). In southern Africa ostriches are farmed for their feathers, and the skin is turned into tough leather for shoes.

A rattle made from hooves from the Southwest

The horse's headpiece matches the royal saddle

Saddle sits on a matching saddle cloth

Arabs carry their tails high

SADDLE FOR A KING
This fabulous horse's saddle is used for the Arabian horses of the kings of Morocco. It is embroidered with a mass of gold thread. The kings use this saddle on state occasions. Such finery is also presented to other heads of state.

SHEEP FROM THE GOATS
Both sheep and goats are kept on the fringes of deserts where there are wells for water. Goats graze on tough vegetation, and they are more tolerant of dry conditions – some breeds only need water every two days. Sheep, however, need to be watered every day. Both sheep and goats provide their owners with milk, meat, and wool. Keeping too many animals destroys desert vegetation because plants are trampled and eaten down to the ground.

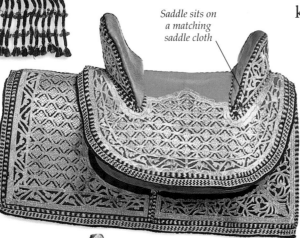

Slender legs

ARABIAN HORSE
Horses were highly valued by the Bedouin for their speed and maneuverability in battle, and they are still much admired today. The Arabian horse is the oldest breed of horse. It originated in the Arabian Peninsula over 4,500 years ago. Often dubbed the desert horse, the Arabian has great stamina and powers of endurance. From the 7th century onward, the Arabian horse was taken to north Africa and to what is now Spain and Portugal as land was conquered for the Islamic faith.

STRANGE BEAST
Bactrian camels were domesticated 4,500 years ago, mainly for use as beasts of burden. When people ride a Bactrian camel, they sit between the two humps.

LAST LIONS
Hunting lions from horseback required good riding skills and well-trained horses, as this 19th-century painting of an Algerian lion hunt shows. The saddle and stirrups helped give the rider a more secure seat. Lions were still common in some parts of the Sahara in the 1850s, but the last one was shot in 1932.

ZEBU
Zebu cattle are more tolerant of heat than other breeds; their fat is concentrated in a hump over the shoulders instead of in an even layer over the body. This works in the same way as a camel's hump, helping heat to escape from the rest of the body more easily. The same principle applies to fat-tailed sheep, which store fat in their tails.

"Dished" face characteristic of the Arab horse: large, bright eyes, flared nostrils and a tapering muzzle

GUANACO
The guanaco has the characteristic long, curved neck of members of the camel family. It lives wild in the Patagonian desert of South America. Llamas and alpacas are also members of the camel family and are considered by some to be the descendants of the guanaco. Llamas are kept for use as pack animals, and alpacas are kept for their wool.

SALUKIS
The Bedouin use these dogs to hunt hares and gazelles, and also when hunting with falcons. With their long legs and back, salukis are superb runners, reaching 40 mph (64 km/h). Females are preferred as hunting dogs because they can run for longer and cope with the heat better. Salukis are one of the most ancient breeds of dog: they originally came from the Arabian Peninsula thousands of years ago.

Dwellings

DESERT PEOPLES NEED SHELTER to protect them from the harsh climate. In some desert regions, people live in permanent homes such as the mud houses of some Native Americans of the Southwest. Nomads, however, need portable homes which they can dismantle and take with them as they move their livestock from place to place. Whether portable or permanent, all desert homes need to be well insulated for protection against the extreme heat and cold. Airy tents of densely woven goat's hair and thick-walled homes are both suitable for desert climates. Desert dwellings also need to be waterproof, for rain is often torrential.

SAN HUT
Traditionally, the San (also called Bushmen) of the Kalahari Desert made shelters using branches thatched with dry grasses. Some only built these shelters in the wet season to keep the rain off. In the dry season simple wind-breaks would provide shelter; warmth at night came from an open fire.

YURTS
Mongolian nomads live in felt tents called yurts. The felt is made of sheep's wool. Sheets of felt are spread over a wooden frame leaving a hole in the top for smoke from a fire to escape.

BEDOUINS AT HOME
Among the Bedouin people of the Middle East and the Sahara, it is the men who receive guests in one side of the tent. The women's quarters are shielded by a woven curtain. The nomadic Bedouin have few possessions to weigh them down as they journey from place to place. Swords, guns, and coffee-making equipment, as seen in this tent, are among their prized possessions.

BIG DISH
This Bedouin dish is large enough to hold a whole cooked sheep. Slaughtering a sheep or goat only happens on a special occasion, such as a religious festival or a visit by an important person. The men sit on the ground, and all eat from the same dish with their fingers. Women and children eat their meal in their own quarters.

Inside the tent there is little furniture apart from floor covers and cushions

It is dark and therefore cool inside the tent

The tent is made of long strips of goat's hair often woven by the women who live in the tent

The sides and back can be lifted up to let a cooling breeze flow through the tent

DOOR SCREEN

This 1930s patchwork camel saddle cover from Uzbekistan was also used as a doorway screen to give a bit of privacy and shade. It is made of silks and cottons, and is embroidered with cross stitch.

Native American pueblo

These underground homes in Matmata (Tunisia) have been in use for more than 2,000 years

STAYING PUT

Not all desert people are nomads. The Native Americans of the Southwest built pueblos (villages) out of mud and wood as well as stone. The people of Matmata, Tunisia, live in cool, cave-like homes dug into the desert ground. Desert housing needs to be well insulated to keep out the heat during the day and to keep rooms from becoming too cold at night. Houses are built with thick walls and small windows for insulation. Living underground provides better insulation against both heat and cold.

BEDOUIN TENT

The tent is made of goat's-hair cloth which keeps the sun off and the worst of the water off during the rare rains. The side walls are fixed to the roof and can be tied down to keep out the wind, sand, or sometimes the cold night air. After a man gets married, the size of his tent increases. A wealthy man with a big family may have several extra sections.

MOBILE HOMES

Nomads carry their homes with them, rather like snails.

If it rains, the fibers absorb water and expand to make the tent waterproof

The tent is supported by poles and tied to the ground with guy ropes. Women usually put the tent up

The women's quarters include their living area as well as places to sleep and cook

Modern Bedouins use lightweight plastics instead of the old wood and metal

Food and drink

SOME DESERT PEOPLES, such as the Aboriginals from central Australia and the San from the Kalahari, once survived entirely by hunting game and gathering food from the wild. Because they traveled from place to place on foot, they carried only a few hunting tools and containers for food. Nomads who have camels, such as the Bedouin from Arabia and northern Africa, can carry more possessions. Domesticated livestock also provide milk and meat. But hunting game means precious livestock need not be slaughtered. While the lifestyles of many desert peoples have changed, some old traditions continue today.

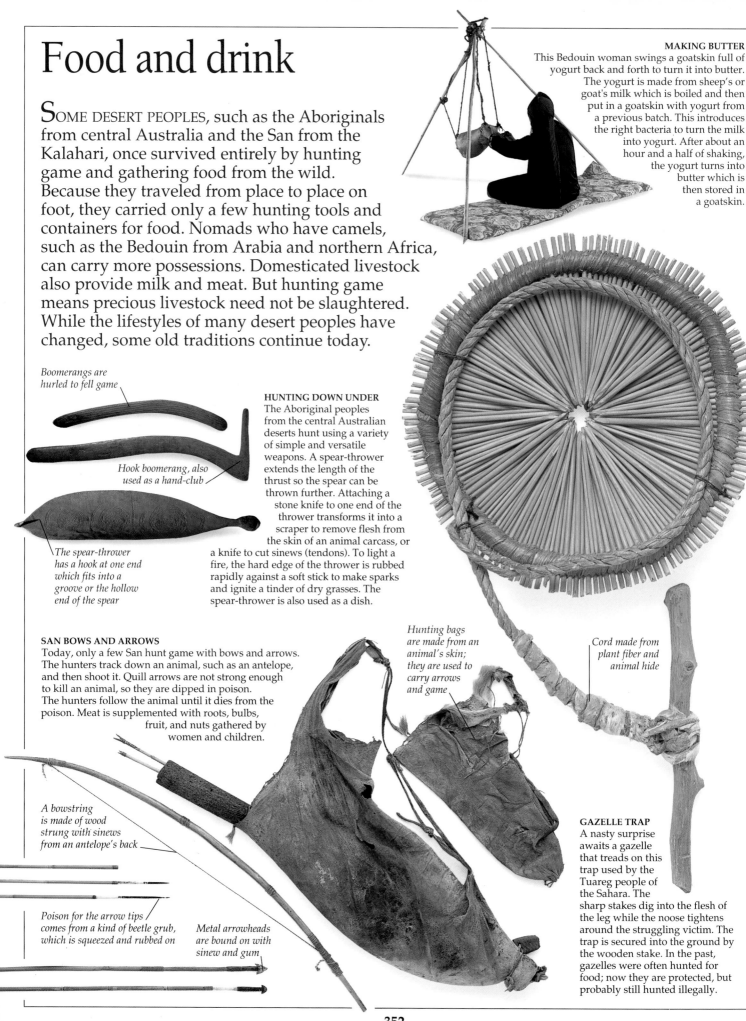

MAKING BUTTER
This Bedouin woman swings a goatskin full of yogurt back and forth to turn it into butter. The yogurt is made from sheep's or goat's milk which is boiled and then put in a goatskin with yogurt from a previous batch. This introduces the right bacteria to turn the milk into yogurt. After about an hour and a half of shaking, the yogurt turns into butter which is then stored in a goatskin.

Boomerangs are hurled to fell game

Hook boomerang, also used as a hand-club

The spear-thrower has a hook at one end which fits into a groove or the hollow end of the spear

HUNTING DOWN UNDER
The Aboriginal peoples from the central Australian deserts hunt using a variety of simple and versatile weapons. A spear-thrower extends the length of the thrust so the spear can be thrown further. Attaching a stone knife to one end of the thrower transforms it into a scraper to remove flesh from the skin of an animal carcass, or a knife to cut sinews (tendons). To light a fire, the hard edge of the thrower is rubbed rapidly against a soft stick to make sparks and ignite a tinder of dry grasses. The spear-thrower is also used as a dish.

SAN BOWS AND ARROWS
Today, only a few San hunt game with bows and arrows. The hunters track down an animal, such as an antelope, and then shoot it. Quill arrows are not strong enough to kill an animal, so they are dipped in poison. The hunters follow the animal until it dies from the poison. Meat is supplemented with roots, bulbs, fruit, and nuts gathered by women and children.

Hunting bags are made from an animal's skin; they are used to carry arrows and game

Cord made from plant fiber and animal hide

A bowstring is made of wood strung with sinews from an antelope's back

Poison for the arrow tips comes from a kind of beetle grub, which is squeezed and rubbed on

Metal arrowheads are bound on with sinew and gum

GAZELLE TRAP
A nasty surprise awaits a gazelle that treads on this trap used by the Tuareg people of the Sahara. The sharp stakes dig into the flesh of the leg while the noose tightens around the struggling victim. The trap is secured into the ground by the wooden stake. In the past, gazelles were often hunted for food; now they are protected, but probably still hunted illegally.

The long woolen tie secures the neck of the bag so not a drop of precious water is spilled

WATER BAG
A goatskin bag is traditionally used by the Bedouin to carry water. In the old days, the Bedouin relied on water from wells in the desert. They planned their routes through the desert by knowing how far their water supply would last between wells. Today, Bedouin often drive into the desert with water-tankers to provide water for themselves and their livestock.

Winnowing basket

This old bowl is well-worn and has metal patches underneath to hold it together

TUAREG COOKING UTENSILS
Nomadic Tuaregs buy grain such as millet by trading rock salt which they carry through the desert on camel caravans, selling surplus milk-products, or earning money from tourism and other jobs. After threshing the grain, it is tossed in a winnowing basket to separate the edible seeds from the chaff (light husks). Millet is pounded and then cooked in pots to make a porridge, which is eaten with a wooden spoon.

Cooking pot

Wooden spoon

This calabash has been repaired with strong stitches of grass and leather

BREAD BOWL
Bedouin women use this wooden bowl to knead dough for bread. Pieces of dough are rotated between the hands to make large flat shapes, which are cooked on a metal tray over a fire. The dough has no yeast to make it rise, so the bread is "unleavened" and flat.

Fine pottery bowls, such as this made by Zunis, are not practical for nomads. The Zunis live in pueblos (p. 351) so can keep such fragile items. This finely decorated 19th-century bowl was used to hold food. The calabash is made from a gourd (the hard fruit of a vine). Calabashes like this are treasured by the Fulani, the semi-nomadic people from the fringes of the Sahara.

Mortar and pestle

MAKING COFFEE
A visitor to a Bedouin tent is treated to coffee, prepared by the master of the tent. Once the visitors have drunk the coffee, they are under the protection of their host. To make the coffee, beans are roasted over the fire and cooled in a wooden dish. After being pounded in a mortar with a pestle, the coffee is added to boiling water with cardamom. The pounding is done to a particular rhythm, which announces to others that there are guests. The coffee is drunk from small cups, and polite guests have three cupfuls, after which they shake their cup and hand it back to their host.

Cooling dish

The coffee is strained with a twig in the spout

The beans are roasted in this pan and turned over with the spoon

The coffee is boiled in the large pot and served from the small pot, which has cardamom added to it

This silk coffee bag must have belonged to a well-to-do Bedouin

The large bag is used to hold coffee beans and the small bag is used for cardamom seeds; both bags are made of leather, and are hung on a tent post

Men's costume

IN THE EXTREME HEAT AND COLD of the desert climate, the traditional costumes of desert peoples such as the Bedouin (from the Middle East and North Africa) and the Tuareg (from the Sahara) are well designed to help them survive. Long, flowing robes shield the skin from the sun and the heat, and allow air to circulate around the body. Loose-fitting clothes also prevent sweat evaporating immediately, which means that the body does not dehydrate so quickly in the very dry air. Headgear shields the head from the sun; veils protect the face and help keep windblown sand out of the mouth. Clothes are also important to keep desert dwellers warm on cold desert nights, and in the winter months, especially in cold deserts. Clothes can also be highly decorative and symbols of wealth and status.

MAKE-UP FOR MEN
Young Wodaabe men wear elaborate face paint when they dance to attract young women. The Wodaabe are nomads of the Fulani race who travel with their livestock between the fringes of the Sahara and the grasslands farther south.

SUN HAT
Hats like this are worn by Fulani men to keep the sun off their faces as they herd cattle. The Fulani people live on the fringes of the Sahara in West Africa, and move with their cattle along fixed routes to new pastures. The hat is made of fiber woven by the men, and the leather decorations are made by the women. This particularly fine hat, with its intricately woven pattern and fancy leatherwork, will have taken at least a week to make; more ordinary hats take about half a day to make.

The leather is stained red with sorghum and black with millet stalks

TROUSER TIES
These magnificent trouser ties were once worn by nomads from Uzbekistan. One of a matching pair was tied around the leg just below the knee between the end of the short baggy trouser-leg and the hosiery (socks and stockings). An Uzbek horseman would seldom be seen without such finery. The ties are made of silk embroidered with chain stitch.

Decorative tassels hang down on one side

Old and new decorations show that this hat has been passed down from generation to generation

HET LEVEN IN DE SAHARA.
3. DE OORSPRONKELIJKE BEVOLKING.
LIEBIG PRODUKTEN : Nuttig en praktisch.
Nadruk verboden.
Uitleg op keerzijde.

TUAREG DRESS
Tuareg men wear veils to conceal their faces while the women's veils are draped over their heads. The men consider it shameful to uncover their mouths.

CEREMONIAL HAT
Such a splendid hat would only be worn for special occasions, such as a boy's passage to manhood. The hat is embroidered with fine cross stitch, and decorated with beads and buttons. The white beading identifies the hat with Uzbekistan, but this hat actually came from neighboring Afghanistan.

ZUNI COSTUME
A striped blanket used to be worn by Zuni Native Americans to keep out the winter cold. Traditional head ties and necklaces are still worn today.

ARAB DRESS
Traditional Bedouin costume includes the long white tunic, sleeveless cloak, and distinctive head cloth. The head cloth is kept on by two heavy black wool coils. The ends of the cloth can be wrapped around the face and neck to protect them from cold (above left). On windy days the ends can be swept back and tucked into the coils (above right). The cloak can be made of camel hair, wool, or cooler cotton. Today a modern-style jacket is often worn instead of the cloak.

SHEPHERD BOY
Nomadic Mongolian herders need warm clothes to survive the bitterly cold winters of the Gobi Desert. Horses have always been important for traveling from one camp to the next. Nowadays motorbikes are also used, but horses are more reliable when fuel is scarce.

On a hunt, San men would carry their arrows in a wooden quiver slung from the shoulder

SAN HUNTER
Some desert people opt to wear very little clothing in a hot climate. The San of the Kalahari Desert traditionally wore very little. Men wore loincloths and women wore short skirts. They also had cloaks which helped them to keep warm during the cold desert night. Today most San dress in modern clothes. Few live in the old simple way of hunting and gathering food from the bush.

UNDER WRAPS
Tuareg men call themselves "the people of the veil." The veil is wound around the head to form a turban which sits low on the forehead, and the remaining folds cover the face and neck. For these once war-like people, disguising their faces had advantages on raids. When a boy reaches puberty he will wear the veil and rarely go without, even when asleep.

Continued on next page

Men's kit

Weapons are not only for fighting: they are status symbols, showing a man's wealth and his position. Some desert nomads, such as the Tuareg and the Bedouin, were well known for their fighting spirit, and a man carried his weapons at all times. Now the more decorative weapons are worn only on ceremonial occasions. Other men of the desert wear different decorative items, and even paint their bodies.

This strap is slung over one shoulder, so that the sword hangs at the back

TREASURED SWORDS
The Bedouin often presented swords with elaborate inscriptions as gifts to visiting dignitaries. The Tuareg sword above would have had the handle, scabbard, and even the blade renewed as it was passed down through the generations. The blade of the sword is double-edged, making it a fearsome weapon.

This Bedouin sword has a blade that is three generations old, but the scabbard is new

Beaded cord to tie cow tail around upper left arm

GOOD LUCK
Among cattle herders in Africa, tails from hoofed animals are sometimes considered to have magical properties. Tails can also be used to whisk away flies in the same way a cow uses its tail. This cow's tail is a good-luck charm worn on the upper arm by African tribal people from Sudan.

BEDOUIN DAGGERS
Daggers were once used in skirmishes and fights, but now they are used to slaughter livestock and on ceremonial occasions. Bedouin men wear them tucked into their belts. The sheaths of these daggers are made of wood covered with silver. Dagger blades are made of steel, and the handles are made of bone, wood, ivory, horn, or plastic, and can, like these, be covered with silver.

HANDY POUCH
Tuareg men wear pouches like this around their necks to carry money and personal possessions as their robes have no pockets. This highly decorated pouch is made of embossed leather; the central green square is embroidered.

FANCY SILVER
The sheath and hilt of this 19th-century Bedouin dagger is decorated with niello. It is made by melting a special powder into dents made in the surface of the silver.

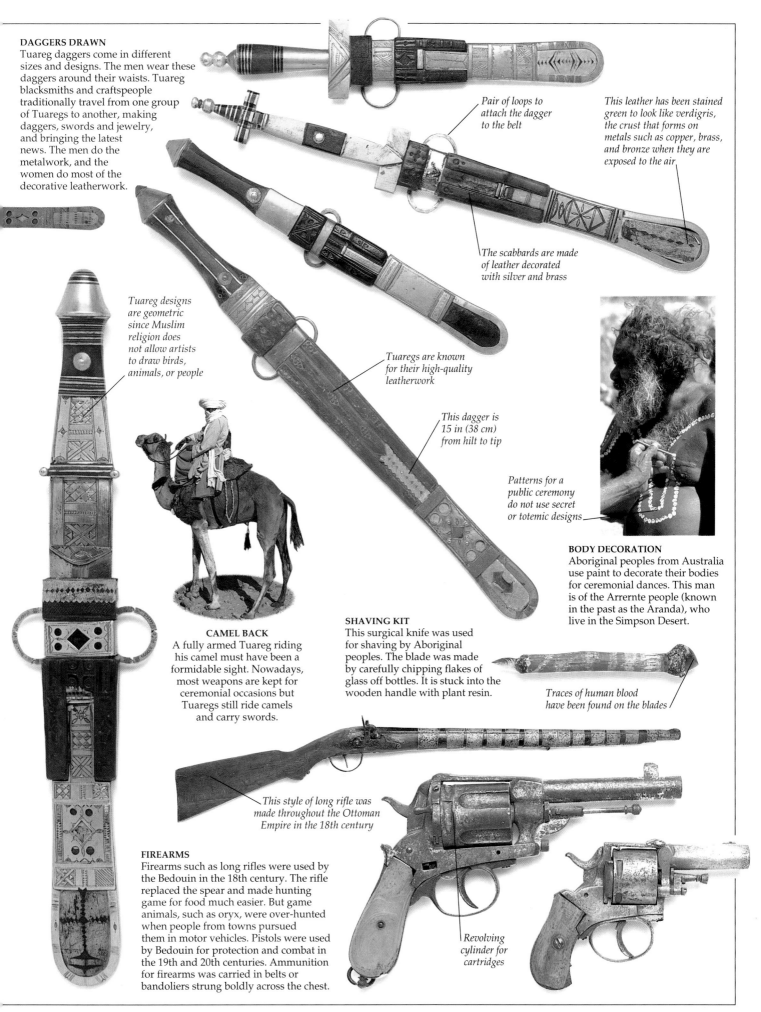

DAGGERS DRAWN

Tuareg daggers come in different sizes and designs. The men wear these daggers around their waists. Tuareg blacksmiths and craftspeople traditionally travel from one group of Tuaregs to another, making daggers, swords and jewelry, and bringing the latest news. The men do the metalwork, and the women do most of the decorative leatherwork.

Tuareg designs are geometric since Muslim religion does not allow artists to draw birds, animals, or people

Pair of loops to attach the dagger to the belt

This leather has been stained green to look like verdigris, the crust that forms on metals such as copper, brass, and bronze when they are exposed to the air

The scabbards are made of leather decorated with silver and brass

Tuaregs are known for their high-quality leatherwork

This dagger is 15 in (38 cm) from hilt to tip

Patterns for a public ceremony do not use secret or totemic designs

CAMEL BACK

A fully armed Tuareg riding his camel must have been a formidable sight. Nowadays, most weapons are kept for ceremonial occasions but Tuaregs still ride camels and carry swords.

SHAVING KIT

This surgical knife was used for shaving by Aboriginal peoples. The blade was made by carefully chipping flakes of glass off bottles. It is stuck into the wooden handle with plant resin.

BODY DECORATION

Aboriginal peoples from Australia use paint to decorate their bodies for ceremonial dances. This man is of the Arrernte people (known in the past as the Aranda), who live in the Simpson Desert.

Traces of human blood have been found on the blades

This style of long rifle was made throughout the Ottoman Empire in the 18th century

FIREARMS

Firearms such as long rifles were used by the Bedouin in the 18th century. The rifle replaced the spear and made hunting game for food much easier. But game animals, such as oryx, were over-hunted when people from towns pursued them in motor vehicles. Pistols were used by Bedouin for protection and combat in the 19th and 20th centuries. Ammunition for firearms was carried in belts or bandoliers strung boldly across the chest.

Revolving cylinder for cartridges

Women's costume

Tʀᴀᴅɪᴛɪᴏɴᴀʟ ᴡᴏᴍᴇɴ's ᴄᴏsᴛᴜᴍᴇs, such as these from Jordan, are well suited to the harsh desert climate. Head coverings, long flowing robes, and layers of material provide insulation from the extreme desert temperatures and protection from the hot sun. Middle Eastern costumes in particular are modest, concealing the shape of the body and covering the arms, legs, and head. In some countries a veil, head cloth, and cloak may also be worn over the clothes when outside the home. More elaborate costumes are a sign of wealth and are only worn for special occasions. Jewelry is also worn as a sign of wealth and for its beauty; some pieces are amulets, worn to ward off evil or injury.

The bands of color are satin stitch and buttonhole stitch

Cucumber amulet

BACK AND SIDES
The back and side views of the Jordanian costume show the elaborate headdress. A simple black scarf covers the woman's head and neck. The silver coins that decorate her forehead are Russian and Ottoman; the coins on the strip hanging down the back are known as Maria Theresa dollars. They were originally from the Austrian Hapsburg Empire, but were still minted long after it fell.

These coins were popular for their high silver content. They were even melted down to make jewelry

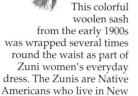

ZUNI BELT
This colorful woolen sash from the early 1900s was wrapped several times round the waist as part of Zuni women's everyday dress. The Zunis are Native Americans who live in New Mexico and Arizona.

BASIC BLACK
Traditionally, desert dresses were made of natural fabrics, particularly cotton, like this one from the 1950s. Now they are made of synthetic fabrics as well, although these are not as cool as the cotton ones. The long amulet is called a cucumber amulet, and it contains a piece of paper with writings from the Koran (the Islamic holy book). It is decorated with crescents, the symbol of Islam. The woman is carrying a Bedouin water jug.

The headband made of silver coins is given upon marriage as part of the dowry (p. 360)

The coral is from the Red Sea or the Mediterranean Sea

A matching cloak is held over one shoulder; it can also be used as a head cover

Instead of being printed on, the pattern in the fabric is created by dying the threads different colors before the fabric is woven

Straw baskets are now more often made of nylon, since modern harvesting methods destroy the straw

COVER YOUR HEAD

Hats are useful for protecting the head from the desert glare. This hat is skillfully embroidered with a complex design from Uzbekistan. The bottom edge is rimmed with one half of a zipper. This is a child's hat.

This dress is made of sateen, which is cotton woven to look like shiny satin

SUMPTUOUS SATEEN

Plenty of material was used to make this beautiful Jordanian costume from the 1930s. Using lots of fabric in this way is a sign of wealth. The woolen belt holds the extra length of the dress up so that the hem clears the ground. The right sleeve of the dress is much longer than the left, so it is rolled and pinned to the shoulder. This was simply a fashion statement of the time. The necklace is made of precious coral and silver, and the cylindrical amulet case contains writing from the Koran.

The wooden stick is for applying kohl to the inner rim of the eyelids

Blue beads ward off the evil eye

MAKE-UP BAG

This padded silk bag was made by a Bedouin woman. It contains a small glass bottle of black eye make-up called kohl, which is made of a mineral ground to a fine powder. Kohl makes the eyes look bigger and is popular with many Muslims and Indian women. It is also believed to protect the eyes from disease and to improve the sight. Kohl is often used on babies and children too.

CAMEL BAG
This beautifully embroidered dowry bag from India would be draped over a camel carrying the bride. The complex design on the strap was drawn by men and then embroidered by women using threads colored with vegetable dyes.

Mirrors decorate the pocket of the bag

Pockets for the dowry

Desert brides

WEDDINGS THE WORLD OVER are a time for celebrations, and great attention is paid to the bride's dress. In Jordan, the bride wears several different wedding dresses. They are then kept to be worn for special occasions thereafter. Both nomad and village brides receive silver or gold jewelry upon marriage, which becomes their personal property. They also receive gifts of money and other traditional gifts of food, such as sugar or rice. The groom and his family go to collect the bride from her family's house in a caravan of cars, with the men shooting off rifles and the women singing on the way. The wedding celebrations last for three days, sometimes longer, with the men in one tent and the women in another. Most weddings happen on a Thursday or a Friday, which is the Muslim holy day.

The pattern is hammered on

The desert veil is very heavy, so it is only worn outside the home

The headdress is a separate square of cloth, embroidered to match the dress

The black design was created in niello

One of a pair of silver head decorations from the Sinai desert, worn over the ears

A bracelet made in Egypt

DESERT VEIL
The designs on this 1940s bridal dress are entirely embroidered, so a great deal of care and time went into its making. The hand-woven belt is decorated with cowrie shells for luck. The band of coins over the face is known as the desert veil, and it is hooked onto the headdress with strings of beads and chains on each side. The outfit is from the Sinai (in Egypt) and southern Palestine.

ALL THAT GLITTERS
A Bedouin woman is given jewelry when she gets married, and it is bought for her by the bridegroom's family or her father. A married woman's jewelry is her own property and gives her some security for the future. She can later buy more when times are good. Early this century, niello (p. 356) became popular because it can be done only on metal with a high silver content. So the purchaser knows that the silver he or she is buying is high grade. Today gold is more popular than the heavy traditional silver pieces.

As well as being decorative, the silk scarf holds the headdress in place

AND THE BRIDE WORE BLACK

Not all cultures have special wedding colors such as the traditional white. This Jordanian bride wears a black dress from the 1950s. She also wears amulets, which are worn to bring the wearer good luck, or as a good omen. The fish is a fertility symbol and is therefore particularly appropriate for a bride. It is a popular Middle Eastern design.

The colorful stripes are sewn in satin stitch, while the rest is done in wave stitch

A silver amulet case which can be opened to insert writings from the Koran

SILK HEADDRESS

A black silk crepe tube is fitted over the bride's head and covers her neck. The silk scarf around her head is Syrian silk woven with gold thread. She is carrying an old brass coffee pot.

A new handle has been put on to replace the old worn one

CAMEL BAG

This interwoven woolen dowry bag would be hung on the camel that carried the bride to her new home. It is from Afghanistan.

DOWRY BAG

This purse comes from Rajasthan in India, and was used by a bride to carry her dowry from her father's home to her husband's. This dowry bag is made from a beautifully embroidered square with three corners sewn together at the center. The fourth corner is the opening flap to the purse. It is decorated with mirrors, a technique called shisha work that is common in western Asian handicrafts.

White cloth is laid over the basic fabric to offset the black and the colors

Jewelry

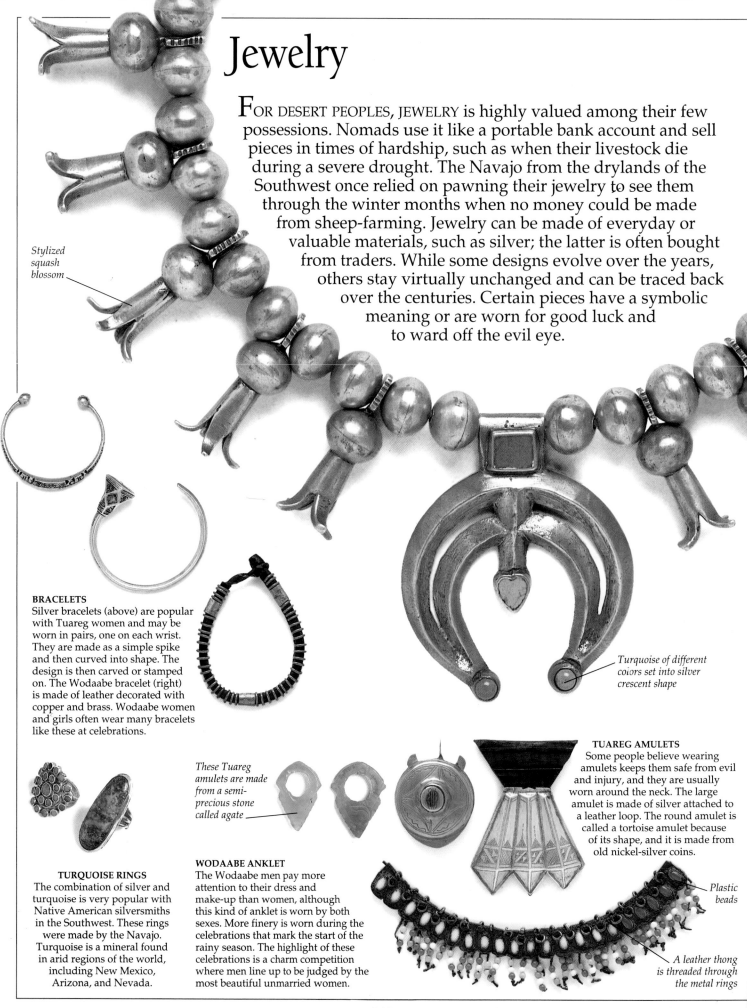

FOR DESERT PEOPLES, JEWELRY is highly valued among their few possessions. Nomads use it like a portable bank account and sell pieces in times of hardship, such as when their livestock die during a severe drought. The Navajo from the drylands of the Southwest once relied on pawning their jewelry to see them through the winter months when no money could be made from sheep-farming. Jewelry can be made of everyday or valuable materials, such as silver; the latter is often bought from traders. While some designs evolve over the years, others stay virtually unchanged and can be traced back over the centuries. Certain pieces have a symbolic meaning or are worn for good luck and to ward off the evil eye.

Stylized squash blossom

Turquoise of different colors set into silver crescent shape

BRACELETS
Silver bracelets (above) are popular with Tuareg women and may be worn in pairs, one on each wrist. They are made as a simple spike and then curved into shape. The design is then carved or stamped on. The Wodaabe bracelet (right) is made of leather decorated with copper and brass. Wodaabe women and girls often wear many bracelets like these at celebrations.

These Tuareg amulets are made from a semi-precious stone called agate

TUAREG AMULETS
Some people believe wearing amulets keeps them safe from evil and injury, and they are usually worn around the neck. The large amulet is made of silver attached to a leather loop. The round amulet is called a tortoise amulet because of its shape, and it is made from old nickel-silver coins.

Plastic beads

TURQUOISE RINGS
The combination of silver and turquoise is very popular with Native American silversmiths in the Southwest. These rings were made by the Navajo. Turquoise is a mineral found in arid regions of the world, including New Mexico, Arizona, and Nevada.

WODAABE ANKLET
The Wodaabe men pay more attention to their dress and make-up than women, although this kind of anklet is worn by both sexes. More finery is worn during the celebrations that mark the start of the rainy season. The highlight of these celebrations is a charm competition where men line up to be judged by the most beautiful unmarried women.

A leather thong is threaded through the metal rings

SQUASH BLOSSOM
This necklace was made by Navajos. The silver squash blossom originally came from a pomegranate fruit design worn by the Spanish who colonized the Americas in the 16th century. The crescent shape also came from the Spanish, who adopted it from the Moors, who were Muslims. Navajos only started to work in silver in the mid-1800s, at first getting silver by melting coins and then as slugs or sheets bought from traders.

Agate necklace from the Sudan

Glass Fulani necklace

Scented necklace from the Sind

SWEET NECKLACES
Almost any material can be made into a necklace provided it can be strung around the neck. Teeth, clay, glass, silk, and stones can all be used. The necklace from the Sind province is strung with cloves as well as silk and glass beads, and the cloves still smell sweet even though the necklace is more than 50 years old. The Fulani necklace dates from early this century and was worn by young girls and men.

Aboriginal necklace, from central Australia, made of kangaroo teeth and painted gum

HAIRPIN
Decorative items can be used to adorn all parts of the body. This golden pin from the Sudan would enhance any hairdo.

Ostrich shell disks

BEADS AND BAUBLES
The yellowy beads on these necklaces from the Sahel (south of the Sahara) are made from a fossil resin called copal, which is a young form of amber. It is highly prized all over North Africa. The copal in these necklaces was mined in Chad, but the necklaces themselves were strung in Niger by Tuaregs. The outer necklace also has bone, silver, glass, and ostrich shell beads.

NOT QUITE A CROSS
Some of these Tuareg crosses resemble the ancient Egyptian ankh (symbol of life). The Tuaregs are Muslims but their silversmiths are influenced by many cultures. There are about 21 different Tuareg crosses, and men wear them to show that they belong to a particular clan. Inventive Tuareg silversmiths sometimes use recycled materials in their jewelry: the silver often comes from melted-down silver coins, and the red part from cars.

Part of the red taillight from the back of a car

Black design burned onto bone beads

Copal resin is aromatic when rubbed

363

Spinning and weaving

ONE WAY DESERT NOMADS express themselves artistically is in weaving. Woven material can be decorative and still have a practical purpose. Wool for weaving comes from the nomads' own livestock or is bought in towns. First the wool is spun to make yarn; then it may be dyed before being woven. Heavy weaving machinery is not practical for a nomadic lifestyle, so looms tend to be light and simple. Bedouin women are highly skilled weavers, making long strips of tent cloth, tent curtains, cushion covers, saddlebags, and regalia for their camels and horses.

SPINNING A YARN

Bedouin women use cleaned sheep's wool bought in bulk, or wool sheared (by the men) from their own goats or sheep. The purpose of spinning is to line the threads up and twist them to make a strong yarn. A Bedouin woman's first job is to tease the wool apart to make it more even. Then she spins and winds the yarn on the spindle. The whole process is repeated until the spindle is full. The thread is then unwound from the spindle and looped back and forth to make a loose skein of wool.

Metal hook on top of spindle

Cross on the end of the spindle holds the wool in place

TEASING OUT
The spinner pulls out the wool and loops it around the hook on top of the spindle.

SPINNING
After quickly rolling the spindle on her thigh, she holds it up and lets it hang to spin.

WINDING
She then winds the yarn around the handle of the spindle.

Camel symbols are used as Islam does not allow pictures of animals

The ties are used to secure the band

CAMEL BAGS
A handy way to take goods on a camel is to pack them into bags which are attached to the saddle. Camel bags are used to carry trade goods on caravans or personal possessions when a group of nomads moves from one place to another. Abstract designs are usually woven in as the bag is made, and tassels are a popular decorative addition.

CHILD'S WORK
The weaving and pattern on this camel chest band from Uzbekistan are rather uneven, which means that it was made by a girl of about ten years of age with wool left over from her mother's work. Girls are taught to weave in traditional styles by their mothers.

Synthetic dyes used here give much brighter colors than the more subtle natural dyes

WARP THREADS
The warp threads are stretched between the metal poles. The two sets of warp threads are held apart by a wooden blade; the shuttle is passed between warp threads to weave a weft thread.

The shuttle is simply a stick with wool wound around it

WEFT THREADS
After the weft thread is passed through the first set of warp threads, the second set must be pulled up; the weaver does this by hand. Now she can pass the shuttle back through to make another weft thread.

The Bedouin ground loom is a set of poles, pegs, and blocks, so it is easy to set up and transport

Peg to keep the tension of the warp threads, which is extremely important for even weaving

RAINBOW COLORS
Once Bedouin women only used natural dyes to color wool from their sheep. Now a wide range of synthetic dyes is used. Wool is dyed in skeins and then hung out to dry. The skeins have to be wound into balls before weaving. Although traditionally nomadic Bedouins used a ground loom, modern Bedouins who live in towns have upright looms, which are easier to use.

USING THE BLADE
Each time the shuttle is passed through, the weaver jerks the edge of the blade back against the last weft thread to pack the thread in.

This woman has traditional Jordanian Bedouin tattoos on her face

USING THE HOOK
After a few rows, the weaver packs the weft threads down with a metal hook. The more packing or beating she does, the denser the material becomes. By tightly packing the weft threads, only the warp threads will show in the completed work.

The simplest and most easily available materials are used

Sheep's wool is softer and easier to spin and weave than goat's wool.

WEAVING A RUG
A loom can be as long as 13 yd (12 m). The widest cloth is about 3.25 yd (3 m) and needs two women to work the loom. A rug such as this one, about 4.3 yd (4 m) long, would take two or three days to make. Traditionally the Bedouin celebrated the beginning of the weaving period.

Goat's wool is reserved for tent cloth; sheep's wool is used for rugs and other furnishings

Arts and crafts

IT IS A STRUGGLE TO SURVIVE in the desert, but nomads and villagers still find time to brighten their lives with beautiful things. Some crafts have a practical use while others are made for ceremonial purposes or for pure enjoyment. These crafts are not just treasured by their creators but are often bought by tourists, and some items, such as certain Native American pottery, are highly valued by art collectors. Craft materials, such as clay and wood, can be found in the desert; other materials are a by-product of livestock. Modern materials are also used to enhance old designs.

BEAUTIFUL BEADS
Some San women and girls wear beads woven into their hair. They thread their own bracelets, anklets, necklaces, and headwear. Today they buy the beads, but they used to make them from ostrich eggshells.

SADDLE CUSHION
A cushion makes the saddle more comfortable so that the rider can endure long journeys through the desert. This leather cushion is used by the Tuareg on the camel saddle. The fringeless part sits behind the front pommel (p. 347).

Single string and bow string made of horse hair

These designs are typical of Tuareg work

The frame is made of wood with goatskin stretched over it

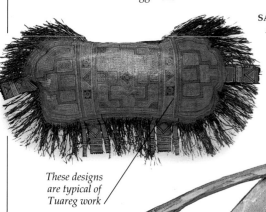

BEDOUIN FIDDLE
To some ears, the Bedouin fiddle makes a rather mournful sound. Men, having learnt how to play the fiddle as children, play it around the camp fire for their guests. The Bedouin are well known for their hospitality and, as part of their way of life, will give food and shelter to strangers in the desert.

ROCK ART
The inscriptions on this rock from the desert in Jordan date back at least 2,500 years. It shows a herd of healthy camels (with fat humps) and their youngsters. Rock art is found in many deserts and gives clues as to what these places were like in the past and who lived there.

This photograph dates from the turn of the century

HOPI DOLL
Native American Hopis are dryland farmers from Arizona. They make dolls, called kachinas, to teach their children about their beliefs in spirits of plants, animals, ancestors, and even places. *Kachina* is also the name given to the spirits themselves and to masked dancers who represent the spirits at ceremonies, some of which are to bring rain. The dolls are carved from the roots of the cottonwood tree and then coated in white clay before being painted.

Modern kachinas are painted with poster paints

SILVER AND GLASS
Tuareg silversmiths used to make their wares for the Tuareg nobles, but many now stay in towns where they work for the tourist trade. They make Tuareg crosses using a process called the lost wax method: the form is carved in wax and a mold is built around it. The wax is then melted and poured away. Melted silver is poured into the empty mold, and when it is solid, the mold is pulled apart to reveal the cross. Finally, the surface is worked to create the patterns.

The inscription, in classical Arabic, is a verse from the Koran. It is worn to give protection to the wearer.

This design represents feathers

PERFECT POTTERY
Pottery has been made by Native Americans in the Southwest for at least 1,600 years. Pots are made for cooking, storing foods, and for ceremonies. These unusual black pots were created by the famous potter Maria Martinez from San Ildefonso in New Mexico. She invented the distinctive color by using special clay and sand from the desert, and adding cow manure to the fire; the pots had to be fired at exactly the right temperature. She used the traditional open kilns, which are difficult to use since a gust of wind can easily ruin the whole firing.

The design is burned and stained into the wood

DIDGERIDOO
Although didgeridoos are not traditional desert instruments they are now widely used by many Aboriginal peoples. Originally, they were made from branches that had been hollowed out by termites. A suitable branch was found by walking through the bush tapping on trees listening for a hollow sound.

MADE FOR TWO
This camel saddle frame, made for a dromedary, can hold two people. It is used by nomads trading between the Sind province in Pakistan and Afghanistan. Such a fine saddle would belong to a tribal chief. The wood is overlaid and inlaid with brass for decoration and strength.

Exploring the desert

DESERTS ARE AWESOME PLACES, where those unaccustomed to their harshness risk dying of thirst and starvation. For centuries, explorers have been lured into the desert, seeking fame and fortune. Explorers often used established trade routes such as the Silk Road to the Far East, or helped to develop new routes, like Burke and Wills, who crossed the central deserts of Australia. Explorers often relied on local people to help them find their way: desert dwellers such as Aboriginal peoples could find their way through the desert without compasses or maps. Desert inhabitants also knew how to find food and water in the desert, while many explorers had to go laden with supplies. Today, the deserts have all been mapped but the dangers still exist, and with new ways to travel, there are still adventures to be had.

WILFRED THESIGER
Thesiger was one of the first Europeans to explore the world's most infamous desert, the Empty Quarter (Rub 'al-Khali) of the Arabian Peninsula. The desert gets its name from being so inhospitable; no one lives there except in the winter months, when the Bedouin visit it to graze their camels on plants that have sprung up after rain. Thesiger made several journeys on camelback through the Empty Quarter and Oman with his Bedouin companions, covering thousands of miles between 1945 and 1950.

ON THE WAY TO TIMBUKTU
The German explorer Heinrich Barth crossed the Sahara in 1850 and spent several years in the fabled city. Timbuktu began as a Tuareg settlement in the 12th century, and it developed into an important trading point for gold, salt, and slaves, and a center of Islamic scholarship. The first European to reach the legendary city was the Scottish explorer Gordon Laing, in 1826. The French explorer René Caillié also made it to Timbuktu in 1828, but few believed he had actually been there until his account of the city was confirmed by Heinrich Barth.

COMPASS
A compass has a needle that turns to align itself with the magnetic north and south poles. Ever since the compass was invented, probably in Europe and China in the 12th century, this instrument has helped people find their way.

SAHARA BY BIKE
Modern bicycles are so tough and lightweight they can be ridden long distances across difficult terrain. For anyone exploring the desert, clothing to protect the skin from sunburn is essential. A bicycle repair kit and adequate supplies of food and water are also vital.

Head covering to prevent sunburn and overheating

Water bottle

Baggage evenly distributed over the bicycle

DEATH AT COOPER'S CREEK
The first European crossing of Australia was from south to north, starting at Melbourne. Robert Burke and William Wills led the expedition, leaving a group at Cooper's Creek on the way. The crossing was difficult; many died from starvation and exhaustion. Burke died at Cooper's Creek (above) on his return southward in 1861. Only one of the final team survived, with the help of Aboriginals.

The wing is stretched over a frame supported by wires

One person sits behind the other

The person in front grips this bar

Propeller

Engine

SAHARA BY MICROLIGHT
Christina Dodwell is a modern British explorer who likes to use unusual modes of transportation on her journeys. For her 7,000-mile (11,265-km) journey across Africa via the Sahara, she chose a microlight. With her co-pilot, she flew this tiny aircraft across the astounding landscape of the Sahara. Here, they have stopped off in Mali.

MARVELOUS MICROLIGHT
Because they fly so slowly, microlights are able to fly much closer to the ground than other light aircraft, so the passenger and pilot can see much more of what is happening beneath them. They can also travel as high as airliners, to avoid a bumpy ride through low layers of turbulent air. A microlight can land in 75 yd (69 m) on any reasonably flat piece of ground. Weighing only 330 lb (150 kg), the machine can be packed into the back of a truck.

SILK ROAD
Silk was one of the most valuable goods to be exported from China. The Chinese domesticated the silkworm thousands of years ago, getting from each cocoon a silk thread up to 3,000 ft (900 m) long. Silk was traded overland along a route called the Silk Road. This covered 4,300 miles (7,000 km) from China in the east via the mountains and deserts of Central Asia to Europe in the west. Silk and spices went west, in return for wool, gold, silver, and horses.

MARCO POLO GOES EAST
In 1271 Marco Polo set off for the Far East with his father and uncle, both Venetian merchants. They followed the Silk Road through Mesopotamia (Iraq), Persia (Iran), Afghanistan, and across central Asia and the Gobi Desert to China. Marco Polo was employed by the Mongol leader Kublai Khan and traveled on missions throughout his great Mongol empire. The Polos eventually returned to Venice in 1295. Marco's published account of his travels gave the Europeans an astonishing account of the Far East.

TRADE BEADS
These glass beads were made in the 18th century for trade with Africans, especially those living in West Africa. They could be exchanged in Africa for food, precious stones, metals, and artwork.

Index

Acknowledgments

Dorling Kindersley would like to thank:

EARTH

Henry Buckley, Andrew Clarke, Alan Hart and Chris Jones at the Natural History Museum; Professor Ken McClay, Sun Professor of Structural Geology at Royal Holloway University of London; John Catt at Rothamsted Experimental Station; the staff at the Institute of Oceanographic Sciences Deacon Laboratories; the staff at the British Antarctic Survey; Brian Taylor and Fergus McTaggart at the British Geological Survey; Frances Halpin for assistance with the chemistry experiments; The Old Southern Forge for the iron on page 29. **Project editor:** Charyn Jones; **Art editor**: Jane Bull; **Design assistant:** Helen Diplock; **Production:** Adrian Gathercole; **Special photography:** Clive Streeter; **Picture research:** Caroline Brooke; **Managing editor:** Josephine Buchanan; **Managing art editor:** Lynne Browne; **Editorial Consultant:** Dr John Cope, University of Wales College of Cardiff, Wales; **US editor:** Charles A Wills; **US consultant:** Professor Warren Yasso, Teachers College, Columbia University; **Illustrations:** Stephen Bull; **Photography:** Andy Crawford, Mike Dunning, Neil Fletcher, Steve Gorton, Colin Keates, Dave King, James Stephenson, Harry Taylor, Peter York; **Index:** Jane Parker

OCEAN

For their invaluable assistance during photography: The University Marine Biological Station, Scotland, especially Professor John Davenport, David Murden, Bobbie Wilkie, Donald Patrick, Phil Lonsdale, Ken Cameron, Dr. Jason Hall-Spencer, Simon Thurston, Steve Parker, Geordie Campbell, and Helen Thirlwall. Sea Life Centres (UK), especially Robin James, David Copp, Patrick van der Merwe, and Ian Shaw (Weymouth); and Marcus Goodsir (Portsmouth), Colin Pelton, Peter Hunter, Dr. Brian Bett, and Mike Conquer of the Institute of Oceanographic Sciences. Tim Parmenter, Simon Caslaw, and Paul Ruddock of the Natural History Museum, London. Margaret Bidmead of the Royal Navy Submarine Museum, Gosport IFREMER for their kind permission to photograph the model of Nautile David Fowler of Deep Sea Adventure. Mark Graham, Andrew and Richard Pierson of Otterferry Salmon Ltd. Bob Donaldson of Angus Modelmakers. Sally Rose for additional research, Kathy

Lockley for providing props, Helena Spiteri, Djinn von Noorden, Susan St. Louis, Ivan Finnegan, Joe Hoyle, Mark Haygarth, and David Pickering for editorial and design assistance. **Project editor:** Marion Dent; **Art editor:** Jane Tetzlaff: **Managing editor:** Gillian Denton; **Managing art editor:** Julia Harris; **Research:** Celine Cerez; **Picture research:** Kathy Lockley; **Production:** Catherine Semark; Special thanks to the University Marine Station (Scotland) and Sea Life Centres (UK); **Extra photography:** Ray Möller, Steve Gorton; **Model Makers:** Peter Griffiths and David Donkin; **Artwork:** John Woodcock and Simone End; **Index:** Hilary Bird

SEASHORE

Dr Geoff Potts and the Marine Biological Association of the United Kingdom; The Booth Museum of Natural History, Brighton, for supplying the specimens on pages 178–181; Trevor Smith's Animal World; Collins and Chambers; Wallace Heaton; Jane Williams; Jonathan Buckley; Barney Kindersley; Dr David George, Dr Paul Cornelius, Dr Bob Symes, David Moore, Ian Tittley, Arthur Chater, Dr Ray Ingle, Gordon Patterson, Dr John Taylor, Solene Morris, Susannah van Rose, Alwyne Wheeler, Chris Owen, and Colin Keates of the Natural History Museum. **Project editor:** Elizabeth Eyres; **Art editor:** Miranda Kennedy; **Senior editor:** Sophie Mitchell; **Managing editor:** Sue Unstead; **Managing art editor:** Roger Priddy; **Illustrations:** John Woodcock; **Special photography:** Dave King. Richard Czapnik for help with design. Ella Skene for the index. Victoria Sorzano for typing. Fred Ford of Radius Graphics for artwork.

POND AND RIVER

The Booth Museum of Natural History, Brighton; Ed Wade, and Respectable Reptiles, Hampton, for help with the amphibians and reptiles; Richard Harrison and Robert Hughes, Upwey Trout Hatchery, for help with the trout eggs; Jane Parker for the index; Fred Ford and Mike Pilley of Radius Graphics, and Ray Owen for artwork; Anne-Marie Bulat for her work on the initial stages of the book; Carole Ash, Neville Graham and Martyn Foote for design assistance; Kim Taylor for special photography on page 213; Dave King for special photography on pages 214–215, 222–223, 238–239 and 248–249.

The author would like to thank: Don Bentley for loan of equipment;

Mike Birch of Mickfield Fish Centre; Max Bond and Tim Watts of Framlingham Fisheries; CEL Trout Farm, Woodbridge; Keith Chell and Chris Riley of Slapton Ley Field Centre; Wendy and David Edwards; Ellen and Chris Nall, Jacqui and Tony Storer for allowing their ponds to be sampled; David "Biggles" Gooderham and Jane Parker for help with collecting; Andrea Hanks and staff at Thornham Magna Field Centre; Alastair MacEwan for technical advice; Ashley Morsely for fish care; Richard Weaving of Dawlish Warren Nature Reserve; John Wortley, Andy Wood and colleagues at Anglian Water Authority. **Illustrations:** Coral Mula 220bl; 222ml, bl, br; 221tl, ml; 224ml, m: 225mt; **Picture research:** Millie Trowbridge; **Project editor:** Sophie Mitchell; **Art editor:** Pamela Harrington; **Managing art editor:** Jane Owen; **Special photography:** Philip Dowell

JUNGLE

Mark Alcock; the staff of the Royal Botanic Gardens, Kew, in particular Jenny Evans, Doris Francis, Sandra Bell, Phil Brewster, Dave Cooke, John Lonsdale, Mike Marsh, and John Norris; David Field and Sue Brodie of ECOS, the Royal Botanic Gardens, Kew; Mark O'Shea, herpetologist, and Nik Brown and Pete Montague of the West Midland Safari Park; the staff and keepers of Twycross Zoo, in particular Molly Badham, Donna Chester, and John Ray; Robert Opie, Jim Hamill, Jane Beamish, and Mike Row, British Museum, Museum of Mankind; Martin Brendell of the Natural History Museum; Janet Boston of the Liverpool Museum; Helena Spiteri for editorial help; Susan St Louis, Isaac Zamora, Ivan Finnegan, and Sarah Cowley for design help. **Project editor:** Miranda Smith; **Art editors:** Andrew Nash and Sharon Spencer; **Managing editor:** Simon Adams; **Managing art editor:** Julia Harris; **Production:** Catherine Semark; **Picture research:** Kathy Lockley; **Researcher:** Celine Carez; **Maps:** John Woodcock; **Additional photography:** Peter Anderson (284-285); Geoff Brightling (279tr); Jane Burton/Kim Taylor (263cl and cr, 279cl); Peter Chadwick (262cr); Frank Greenaway (258tl, 269tr and br, 274tl and bl, 275tl, 281cl, 283r, 298b, 299b, 300c, 301b, 302cr); Colin Keates (253cr, 300tl); Dave King (304b); Cyril Laubscher (253tr); Karl Shone (278-279, 308bl); Kim Taylor (286tr, 296-297); Jerry Young (262cl, 263b, 269br, 275bl, 277tr, 281tl, 299tr, 309b); **Index:** Hilary Bird

DESERT

In Jordan, for their generous, unstinting help: K.D. Politis; Hiyam Khateeb and Sami Ajarma of the Ministry of Tourism and Antiquities; Hammad Hamdan; Tony Howard, Di Taylor; Suleiman Hamdan; Jamal As'hab; Abdellah Mohammad; Mazieb Atieeq; Mahmoud; Sabhah; Aryouf Ajaleen; Um-Magab; Widad Kamel Kawar and her daughter and friends; Imman Alqdah at the Folklore Musuem, Amman; Dr Jonathan Tubb and colleagues; For kindly providing props and help: Moira and Margaret Broadbent; B & T World Seeds; Joliba; London Zoo; Mark O'Shea; Pitt Rivers Museum, University of Oxford; Debbie Platt; David Gainsborough Roberts; Peter Rodway; Twycross Zoo (Vera Richards, Michael Darling, John Campbell, Janet Hall, James Bayley, Denise Cox, Alan Bates, Sonia Chapman, John Voce, John Ray); Dr David H. Thomas at the School of Biology, University of Wales at Cardiff; David Ward, Dr Jeremy Young. For design help: Manisha Patel and Sharon Spencer; for editorial help: Helena Spiteri Map pages 312–313: Sallie Alane Reason; Artworks page 327al, page 327cl: Andrew Nash; page 350: Ts Davaahuu; Kachina doll, page 367: William Lomayaktewa; **Project editor:** Caroline Beattie; **Art editor:** Jill Plank; **Managing editor:** Julia Harris; **Researcher:** Celine Carez; **Picture research:** Cynthia Hole; **Production:** Catherine Semark; **Additional photography:** Andy Crawford; **Editorial consultant:** Professor John Cloudsley-Thompson; **Index:** Ann Barrett

PICTURE CREDITS:

(t=top, b=bottom, c=center, l=left, r=right)

EARTH

B & C Alexander 65b. Biofotos/Heather Angel 17tl. Bodleian Library, Oxford 15br; 15tr. Bridgeman/Royal Geographical Society 14tl. /Louvre, Paris 58tl. Oriental Section, Bristol Museums and Art Gallery 15b. British Antarctic Society 12br; 25tr; 38bl; /E.Wolff 25br; /R.Mulvaney 25bc; /NOAA 45br. British Geological Survey 12tr; 27br; 67tl. Bruce Coleman Picture Library /Jules Cowan 23clb; /M.P.L.Fogden 26cl. James Davis Photography 56-57b. Joe Cornish 61l. John Catt 58r; 58bc. Mary Evans Picture Library 28cr; 30tl; 36bl; 36bc; 40cr; 46tl; 66tl; /Explorer Biblioteca Reale, Torino 12bl. ffotograff/Charles Aithie 56cl; 58bl; 62tr; /Jill Ranford 57tc. Greepeace/Loor 24bl. Gwynedd Archive Service 34cb. Robert Harding Picture Library 43tr; 43bl; 45cla; 50clb; 53cr; 69cr; /Y. Arthus Betrand Explorer 62cr; /Margaret Collier 62cl; /Ian Griffiths 56tr. Hulton Deutsch 37tl. Image Bank/Joanna MacCarthy 46cr; /H.Wendler 59tr. Institute of Oceanographic Sciences: Deacon Laboratory 44tr; /MIAS 39tr. Impact/Martin Black 15bl. Japanese Archive 48tl. Mansell Collection 14cr; 14br; 24tl; 40tr; 52tl; 66tr; 68tr. NASA 12tl; 16tl; 17tr; 17c; 18bc; 40br; 55tl; 55c; 63tl. National Archives of Canada 47tl; 68clb. National Maritime Museum Publications 36br. National Oceanic and Atmospheric Administration/National Geophysical Data Center 42bl; 42tl; 43c; 43tcl; 43br. Natural History Museum Picture Library 19cbr. Image Select/Ann Ronan 28tl. Clive Oppenheimer 31l. Oxford Scientific Films/John Downer 55tr; /Mills Tandy 61br; /Konrad Wothe 52cr. Planet Earth Picture Agency/Peter Atkinson 16cr; /Peter David 38tl; Ivor Edmonds 65tr; /David George 30c. Princeton University: Department of Geological and Geophysical Sciences 44tl. Science Photo Library/ Dr Gene Feldman/ NASA GSFC 38c; /Mark Bond 32tl; /Tony Craddock 54c; /John Downer 43bv; /European Space Agency 7c; /Douglas Faulkner 44cl; /James King-Holmes 67cr; 67crb; /G. Muller, Struers MBH 35tc; /NASA 43tl; 51cla; 64cr; /Peter Ryan Scripps 44tr; /Soames Summerhays 51b; /U.S.

OCEAN

American Museum of Natural History: 77tl (no. 419(2)); Heather Angel 104bc. Ardea /Val Taylor 128tl. Tracey Bowden /Pedro Borrell: 121tc.
Bridgeman Art Library /Prado, Madrid 75tr; /Uffizi Gallery, Florence 82tr. British Museum 120tr. Cable & Wireless Archive 110tr. Bruce Coleman Ltd /Carl Roessler 88c; Frieder Sauer 92tr; Charles & Sandra Hood 93tc; Jeff Foott 94tr, 122tr; Jane Burton 104bl; Michael Roggo 123tl; Orion service & Trading Co. 124br; Atlantide SDF 130tr; Nancy Sefton 129br. Steven J. Cooling 127tr. Mary Evans Picture Library 77tr, 78tr, 85tl, 86tl, 94tl, 99tr, 100tr, 106cl, 111tr, 114tr, 115tl, 116bk, 118tr, 120c, 126tl. Ronald Grant Archive 108cl, 121bl. Robert Harding Picture Library 91tl, 98tr, 98bc, 105br, 123tr, 129tl. Institute of Oceanographic Sciences 112lc. © Japanese Meteorological Agency / Meteorological Office 78l. Frank Lane Photo Agency /M. Newman 77bc. Simon Conway Morris 72tr. N.H.P.A. /Agence Natur 110c. Oxford Scientific Films /Toi de Roy 95t; Fred Bavendam 109tl. Planet Earth Pictures/Peter Scoones 75tl.; Norbert Wu 76-77c, 86cl, 106tr, 106tl, 107tl, 108tr; Gary Bell 89br, 121tr; Mark Conlin 91c, 102br; Menuhin 95tc; Ken Lucas 96tl; Neville Coleman 99cr; Steve Bloom 103c; Andrew Mounter 104br; Larry Madin 109br; Ken Vaughan 117cr; Georgette Doowma 129cr. Science Photo Library /Dr. G. Feldman 92; Ron Church 119cr; Simon Fraser 56bl. Frank Spooner Pictures 113tr, 113cc, 120br, 120bl, 126tr, 126cr. Tony Stone Images, Jeff Rotman 119lc. Stolt Comex Seaway Ltd 127l. Town Docks Museum, Hull 129tr. ZEFA 102cl, 122ct.

SEASHORE

Heather Angel 138br, 149ml, 156tr, 168tl & b, 175br. Ardea: 180bl. Mark Boulton /Bruce Coleman Ltd: 134tl. Professor George Branch: 138b. Jane Burton/Bruce Coleman Ltd: 171tl. Bob & Clara Calhoun/Bruce Coleman Ltd: 163m, 169m. N.Callow/NHPA: 157. G.J.Cambridge/NHPA: 141m. Laurie Campbell/NHPA: 150t. James Carmichael Jr/NHPA: 175bl. C.Carvalho/Frank Lane: 149mr. Eric Crichton/Bruce Coleman Ltd: 146tl. Nicholas Devore 137l/Bruce Coleman Ltd: 135m. Adrian Evans/Hutchison Library: 136m. Mary Evans Picture Library: 134m, 140tl, 144 & 145b, 146b, 149tr, 152tr, 153, 156tl, 162, 164tl, 175tr, 181tl, 183tl, 184tr & m, 186bl, 187tr. Kenneth W. Fink/Ardea: 182bl. Jeff Foott/Bruce Coleman Ltd: 150b, 156ml, 157bl. Neville Fox-Davies/Bruce Coleman Ltd: 151m. J.Frazier/NHPA: 176tr. Pavel German/NHPA: 177m. Jeff Goodman/NHPA: 166mr & br. Ian Griffiths/Robert Harding Picture Library: 135b, 137bl. Michael Holford/Victoria and Albert Museum: 152br. Scott Johnson/NHPA: 157br, 174m. Tony Jones/Robert Harding 137tr. M.P.Kahl/Bruce Coleman Ltd: 134bl. Frans Lanting/Bruce Coleman Ltd: 138tl. Richard Matthews/Seaphoto Ltd: Planet Earth Pictures: 181m. Marine Biological Association of the United Kingdom: 188tr. M.Nimmo/Frank Lane: 134tr. Fritz Polking GDT/Frank Lane: 170m. Dr Geoff Potts: 156b. Niall Rankin/Eric Hosking: 180br. Ann Ronan Picture Library: 134br. John Taylor/Bruce Coleman Ltd: 169br. Kim Taylor/Bruce Coleman Ltd: 165tr. Roger Tidman/Frank Lane: 136tr. Bill Wood/NHPA: 166ml. Gunter Ziesler/Bruce Coleman Ltd: 155b.

POND AND RIVER

Heather Angel: 229tr; 231br; 239br. G.I.Bernard/Oxford Scientific Films: 237ml. B.Borrell/Frank Lane Picture Agency: 225m. Bridgeman Art Library: 220tr. British Museum/Natural History: 234tl. B.B.Casals/Frank Lane Picture Agency: 225t. John Clegg 233tl. G.Dore/Bruce Coleman Ltd: 234mr; 246tr. Fotomas Index: 225ml. C.B. and D.W.Frith/Bruce Coleman Ltd: 227br. Tom and Pam Gardener/Frank Lane Picture Agency: 224br. D.T.Grewcock/Frank Lane Picture Agency: 248br. Mark Hamblin/Frank Lane Picture Agency: 225bm. David Hosking/Eric and David Hosking: 213m; 223ml. Mansell Collection: 199m, tr & ml; 221ml; 235br. L.C.Marigo/Bruce Coleman Ltd: 228bl. Mary Evans Picture Library: 208tl; 209tr; 216bl; 226tr. Dr Morley Reed/Science Photo Library: 225bl. Jany Sauvanet/Natural History Photographic Agency: 226ml. Richard Vaughan/Ardea: 244mr. Roger Wilmshurst/Frank Lane Picture Agency: 215t

JUNGLE

Bridgeman Art Library/Royal Botanic Gardens, Kew: 264bl, 281c; /Leiden, Rijksmuseum voor Volkenkunde: 284bc; /British Museum: 285tr; /Royal Geographical Society: 306br; /Bonhams: 308bc Bruce Coleman Ltd: 255tl; /M.P.L.Fogden: 258tr; /G.B.Frith: 261tl; /Konrad Wothe: 262c; /Jane Burton: 273tl; /D.Houston: 274br; /WWF/H.Jungins: 279tl; /Dieter and Mary Plage: 282bl; /Peter Ward: 283bl; /Dieter and Mary Plage: 292tr Mary Evans Picture Library: 292tl Michael & Patricia Fogden: 252bc, 259br, 259bl, 260c, 260tr, 281tr, 297bl, 309tr Robert Harding Picture Library: 276lc, 280tr, 285tl, 308tl, 309tc Hutchison Library /Isabella Tree: 285br; /Dr Nigel Smith: 288br Frank Lane Picture Agency /E.& D. Hosking: 257tl; /Silvestris: 277bl Mansell Collection: 306tr Natural History Museum, London: 305 N.H.P.A. /Morten Strange: 254tl; /Otto Rogge: 261r; /Stephen Dalton: 270cr, 279cr; /Kevin Schafer: 289tl; /G.I.Bernard: 296cr; /Stephen Kraseman: 296tr; Planet Earth Pictures /Andre Bartschi: 254bl; /Peter Scoones: 255tr; /Andrew Mounter: 267tl; /John Lythgoe: 268bl; /Anup Shah: 293br; /David Maitland: 302tr; /Mary Clay: 303bc Premaphotos Wildlife /K.G.Preston-Mafham: 295br,
302c, 303br Raleigh International Picture Library /Chris Rainier: 307br Harry Smith/Polunin Collection: 256tr Still Pictures/Edward Parker: 252tl; /Norbert Wu: 275tr, 298tr Survival Anglia /Frances Furlong: 286bc; /M.Kavanagh: 294tr Syndication International: 304tl; /Natural History Museum: 306tr c.Alan Watson/Forest Light: 254cr M.I.Walker/Microworld Services: 264bc

DESERT

Ardea, London Ltd/Ian Beames: 329c; /Kenneth W. Fink: 328c; /Mike W. Gillam: 348bc; /Clem Haagner: 346ar, 349ac; /Peter Steyn: 332bl; /Alan Weaving: 324–325b, 329br. British Museum: 326a. Caroline Cartwright: 330al, 331br. Lester Cheeseman: 351al. Bruce Coleman Ltd/Jen and Des Bartlett: 337ac; /M.P.L.Fogden: 331acl; /Jeff Foott: 312cl, 328bc, 340acl; /Carol Hughes: 312cl; /Steve Kaufman: 343ar; /Rod Williams: 341al. Compix/E.Terry: 350al Philip Dowell: 344–345c. e.t.archive: 370bc. Mary Evans Picture Library: 313bc, 317acr, 350cr, 351ar, 355acr, 369c. Robert Harding Picture Library/Elisabeth Weiland: 350ar. Hutchison Library/Christina Dodwell: 370cr; /André Singer: 357cr; /Leslie Woodhead: 354ar; /J.Wright: 350br. Image Bank/Ted Janocinski: 317ar. Impact Photos/Ian Cook: 350–351b; /Penny Tweedie: 331br. Mike Linley: 323ac, 324bcl, 331acr, 332bl, 333al, 335ar, 336cr, 340cr, 369b. MacQuitty International Photograph Collection: 315bcr, 320acr, 351cr. MountainCamera/Chris Bradley: 227bc, 363c; /John Cleare: 368br; /Matt Dickinson: 368bl. Peter Newark's Pictures: 367ac. N.H.P.A. /A.N.T: 318al, 322bl; / Anthony Bannister; 324acl, 325cr, 330cr, 342bcl, 366al; /Peter Johnson: 334bl, 355bl. Christine Osborne/Middle East Pictures: 348cl. Oxford Scientific Films/B.G.Murray Jr, Earth Scenes: 314al; /Owen Newman; 317al. Axel Poignant Archive: 352cl. Premaphotos Wildlife/K.G.Preston-Mafham: 322cr. Trevor Springett: 321ar. © Wilfred Thesiger. Reproduced by permission of Curtis Brown. Photo – Royal Geographical Society, London: 368al; Vernet's The Lion Hunt reproduced by permission of the Trustees of the Wallace Collection: 350al. Tony Waltham: 321br; 348b. Jerry Young: 334bcl, 334bc, 334br, 340ar, 340–341b, 341bc

Every effort has been made to trace the copyright holders and we apologise in advance for any unintentional omissions. We would be pleased to insert the appropriate acknowledgment in any subsequent edition of this publication.